Looking Back
Reaching Forward

Reflections on the Truth and Reconciliation Commission of South Africa

Charles Villa-Vicencio
and
Wilhelm Verwoerd

UCT
PRESS

University of Cape Town Press
CAPE TOWN

Zed Books Ltd
LONDON

LOOKING BACK REACHING FORWARD
Reflections on the Truth and Reconciliation Commission of South Africa

First published in South Africa by
University of Cape Town Press
PO Box 14373
Kenwyn 7790
Cape Town
South Africa

ISBN 1-919713-49-2

Published outside South Africa by Zed Books Ltd, 7 Cynthia Street, London N1 9JF
and Room 400, 175 Fifth Avenue, New York, NY 10010

Distributed in the USA exclusively by St Martin's Press Inc
175 Fifth Avenue, New York, NY 10010, USA

A catalogue record for this book is available from the British Library
US CIP has been applied for

ISBN 1 85649 819 0 Hb
ISBN 1 85649 820 4 Pb

Cover design: Luke Younge
Front cover image: William Kentridge, *Ubu and the Truth Commission, UCT Press, 1998*
DTP by RHT desktop publishing cc, Durbanville 7550, Cape Town
Set in 11 points AGaramond

Contents

SECTION 1
The historical context and origins of the Commission

SECTION 2
The philosophical framework of the Commission

Acknowledgements

We acknowledge, with gratitude, the many persons who made this book possible. These include the contributors, as well as Judge Richard Goldstone, who kindly wrote the Foreword. Professor Ariel Dorfman and Dr Barney Pityana read and recommended the book to readers. The Ecumenical Foundation of Southern Africa provided funding. We are grateful to Dr Renier Koegelenberg for arranging this. Ms Kelly Hicks assisted with the secretarial and compilation process. Gail Jennings applied her editorial skills to a manuscript that included the styles and idiosyncracies of the different contributors. Rose Meny-Gibert and Glenda Younge, of UCT Press, managed the editorial and publication process in a gracious and professional manner. We are grateful to all concerned.

All proceeds from the sale of this book will go to the President's Fund for those found to be victims by the TRC.

List of contributors

Kader Asmal Minister of Education, Republic of South Africa

Louise Asmal Human rights activist and former Hon. Secretary of the Irish Anti-Apartheid Movement

Rajeev Bhargava Director, Centre for Political Studies, Jawaharlal Nehru University, New Delhi

Nkosinathi Biko Graduate of the University of Cape Town and media consultant

Mary Burton Former Commissioner, Truth and Reconciliation Commission

Janet Cherry Lecturer, Department of Sociology, University of Port Elizabeth and former Researcher at the Truth and Reconciliation Commission.

Hugh Corder Dean of the Law Faculty, University of Cape Town

Johnny de Lange ANC Member of Parliament, Republic of South Africa

Willie Esterhuyse Professor of Business Ethics, Business School, University of Stellenbosch

Don Foster Professor of Psychology, University of Cape Town

Ginn Fourie Senior lecturer in the Department of Physiotherapy, University of Cape Town

Jakes Gerwel Former Director-General in the Office of the State President

Richard Goldstone Justice of the South African Constitutional Court

Priscilla Hayner New York-based researcher on truth commissions

Yazir Henry Participant in the Truth and Reconciliation Commission process and part-time researcher

Richard Lyster Former Commissioner, Truth and Reconciliation Commission

Mxolisi Mgxashe Freelance journalist

Piet Meiring Professor of Theology, University of Pretoria

Ebrahim Moosa Visiting scholar, Stanford University, California

Njongonkulu Ndungane Archbishop of Cape Town, Church of the Province Southern Africa

Dumisa Ntsebeza Former Commissioner, Truth and Reconciliation Commission

Wendy Orr Former Commissioner, Truth and Reconciliation Commission

Ronald Suresh Roberts Author and Johannesburg-based lawyer

Colleen Scott Freelance writer and researcher on international human rights issues, based in Amsterdam

Ronald Slye Assistant Professor of Law, University of Seattle, Washington

Sampie Terreblanche Retired Professor of Economics, University of Stellenbosch

Paul van Zyl Former Executive Secretary of the Truth and Reconciliation Commission

Wilhelm Verwoerd Lecturer, Department of Philosophy, University of Stellenbosch and former researcher, Truth and Reconciliation Commission

Charles Villa-Vicencio Former Director of Research, Truth and Reconciliation Commission

Nomfundo Walaza Director, Trauma Centre for Survivors of Violence and Torture, Cape Town

Foreword

JUDGE RICHARD GOLDSTONE

To its eternal shame in one case, and to its enduring credit in another, South Africa has made two important and lasting contributions to international law. The first is the crime of apartheid, which was born with the first National Party government in 1948. It has become a new species of international crime and is included in the definition of 'war crimes' in the 1998 Treaty on an International Criminal Court, which was approved by 120 nations in Rome in July 1998. The second is the Truth and Reconciliation Commission (TRC); it succeeded in establishing an unusual form of truth commission that used the granting of amnesties in order to expose the truth. This second experience, I would suggest, will positively influence the form of any future truth commissions in the 21st century.

Prior to the Second World War, consideration was seldom given to prosecution of war criminals or to leaders of nations who were party to serious violations of the human rights of their citizens. It is for that reason that the Nuremberg Trials were considered groundbreaking. That such trials have never been repeated is not for the want of wars or the commissions on war crimes during the intervening 54 years. There are two primary reasons to explain that phenomenon. The first is that Nuremberg was 'victors' justice'. It was the exercise of power by four victorious nations over the leaders of the conquered enemy their people had grown to hate and over whose territory they had absolute control. That situation has not occurred again since the Second World War. The second reason is that until 1993, there has been a complete absence of a system of international criminal justice, and so long as criminal leaders were immune from prosecution before their own national courts, they had nothing to fear from the international community. While the judgment at Nuremberg has fired the imagination of all people who protest egregious human rights violations, the promise held out by it that such atrocities would never again be allowed to occur has not been realised.

The question of having to deal nationally with past human rights viola-tions is one that has only become relevant during the past three decades or so. It has arisen in the context of nations that moved from repressive regimes to forms of democratic government. A substantial number of newly elected democratic governments in countries in Central Europe, Latin America and Africa have been faced with this kind of dilemma.

The catalyst for political change in those countries has varied. After the Second World War it was the defeat of Nazi Germany. In Latin America, it was the inability of military dictatorships to resist popular demands for freedom and democracy. In Central Europe, it was the fall of the Berlin Wall and the dismemberment of the Soviet Union. In South Africa it was the victory of the national and international anti-apartheid movement.

The common problem faced by those societies was how to deal with their own recent pasts. They had to find a way of building new democratic institu-tions while not ignoring the cries for justice and acknowledgement from the victims. In most cases it was recognised that in a perfect society all victims of serious human rights abuses would be entitled to full justice: trial and, if guilty, punishment. But those countries had anything but perfect societies. Many of them had fragile, infant democratic governments in place. In the Latin American cases, in particular, some of the new governments were in place only by the grace of the previous military leadership which had the choice, if they considered it necessary to protect their own interests, to resume power. In any event, the number of human rights violations and the number of perpetrators made it impossible to prosecute a meaningful number of the offenders. Alternative forms of justice were sought.

At the cost of over-simplification, there were three options open to those societies:

- to forget the past and grant blanket amnesties to the perpetrators;
- to prosecute the perpetrators or at least the leaders;
- to establish truth commissions before which the victims would be given the opportunity of publicly testifying about their experiences.

There were variations of these solutions and sometimes there was an overlap between them. In South Africa, for example, the Truth and Reconciliation Commission was able to offer amnesties to the perpetrators in return for full public confessions of guilt. Concurrent criminal trials were also held. Where alleged perpetrators applied for amnesty, prosecutions were invariably sus-pended pending the outcome of the amnesty application.

The first option, of granting a blanket amnesty to the perpetrators of these massive crimes, need not detain us. It is unacceptable and should be rejected by any decent people who have any feeling for justice or empathy for the victims. Forgiveness by the criminals themselves of their own crimes is a certain recipe for future hate and violence. Such impunity is an unambiguous message to all would-be war criminals, that they could go about their own dirty work secure in the knowledge that they will not be called to account.

The other two options, in my opinion, are both forms of justice. While criminal prosecution is the most common form of justice, it is not the only one. The public and official exposure of the truth, especially if the perpetrator is a part of that process, is itself an important form of justice. Thus truth commissions or public inquiries share with criminal prosecutions the ability to bring significant solace to victims. Common to all forms of justice is public acknowledgement for the victims. I have witnessed time and again in South Africa, Bosnia and Rwanda the importance of that acknowledgement to victims. It is frequently the beginning of their healing process. Common to all forms of justice is also the punishment of the perpetrators. Without punishment the calls of the victims for justice will be converted into hate and the desire for revenge. Criminal prosecutions provide both the elements of acknowledgement and punishment. So too do some forms of truth commissions. Again, the South African Truth and Reconciliation Commission is an illustration of this. The victims received full public acknowledgement – wide reporting in the electronic and print media and, in the final report of the Commission, a permanent record of the evidence. On the other side, the perpetrators suffered a very real punishment – the public confession of the worst atrocities with the permanent stigma and prejudice that it carries with it.

I turn to consider the public interest in exposing and recording the truth about past human rights abuses. I would suggest that there are four advantages:

- the prevention or curbing of denials and revisionism;
- the prevention of a recurrence;
- the removal of the perpetrators from public office;
- individualising the guilt of the perpetrators and thereby averting collective guilt being ascribed to groups.

I will consider each in the context of criminal trials and truth commissions.

Without the Nuremberg Trials and the meticulous presentation by the prosecutors of the evidence of the Nazi crimes, the work of Holocaust deniers would have been substantially more successful than it has been. The evidence of the persecution of Jews, gypsies and homosexuals was proved beyond reasonable doubt and most of it through the Nazis' own documents. Their meticulous records included the names and number of most of those murdered, raped and tortured.

In South Africa, the denials had begun well before the end of apartheid. The numerous allegations of the victims had been described by the perpetrators of the crimes of apartheid as the dishonest propaganda of the liberation movements. Many white South Africans believed the security policemen that political activists detained by them had committed suicide. Many believed that Steve Biko had died in consequence of injuries inflicted on him by innocent policemen, who acted in self-defence when he attacked them. The fact that those responsible for his murder and those of other victims have testified before the Truth and Reconciliation Commission has made it difficult, if not impossible, for those denials to have any currency. In this context it must be taken into account that more than 20 000 victims told their story to the Commission and more than 7 000 perpetrators applied for amnesty. The cumulative effect of this mass of evidence is a powerful record of the history of the human rights abuses committed during the apartheid era. It will become part of the common history of future generations of South Africans.

This experience of South Africa highlights what is probably the greatest advantage that a truth commission has over prosecutions – national or international. Truth commissions, by definition and by the structure of their functioning, have a much wider focus than prosecutions. They are able to investigate human rights abuses spanning a much wider time frame. They are also able to look much further for the causes of these abuses. This they do in a relatively shorter period than could be expected of prosecutions. In this way, truth commissions are concerned largely with establishing the broader picture within which individual prosecutions can or may be located.

International criminal courts, in many situations, can have a greater impact than the process of national prosecutions. The fact that an international tribunal is concerning itself with the victimisation of people who have suffered because of the crimes of their own leaders can have a significant impact. That has already been the impact for some people of the work of the two United Nations ad hoc International Criminal Tribunals.

The work of the International Criminal Tribunal for the former Yugoslavia has on occasion dramatically refuted false denials. Within days of the Bosnian Serb army invading Srebrenica, in July 1995, there were allegations of the mass murder by that army of thousands of innocent men and boys. Most of the victims were civilians who had sought sanctuary in what the Security Council had declared to be a United Nations 'safe haven'. Needless to say, the Bosnian Serb government and army denied those stories as yet another malicious and false allegation made against them by the Muslims. When the Tribunal announced that it was to exhume a mass grave in the area, a spokesperson of the Bosnian Serb army denied the existence of such a grave in the area. If it did exist, he stated, it could only contain the bodies of people slain on the battlefield. The many bodies that were exhumed were those of men and boys killed by a single bullet wound to the head. Their hands had been bound behind them with wire. The estimated date of their death, according to the forensic evidence, coincided with the fall of Srebrenica. That evidence has effectively stopped those denials.

Whether the truth can prevent the recurrence of these kinds of human rights violation, it is too early to say. However, what is impressive is that some of the democracies that have been built on the ashes of the victims of repression have a constitutional foundation that is calculated to prevent their repetition. They are being governed with an openness and a transparency that will certainly retard a slide back to repression. Free political activity, freedom of expression and an independent judiciary are a bulwark against the kinds of criminal activities that were the features of military and communist dictatorships and apartheid South Africa.

Whether international justice can act as a deterrent in respect of the commission of war crimes and other human rights abuses in other countries or regions, it is also too early to state with any certainty. However, if one can extrapolate from national experiences, there is room for cautious optimism. There is only one way to curb criminal conduct and that is through good policing and an efficient criminal justice system. In any country there is a direct relationship between the effectiveness of policing and the crime rate. If would-be criminals believe that there is a good prospect of their apprehension and punishment, they will think twice before embarking upon a course of criminal conduct. I cannot believe that it would be different in respect of the international crime rate. Until very recently international criminals have had nothing to fear from the international community in respect of even the most egregious criminal acts committed at home. This is because international criminal law has not been enforced. This is changing dramatically, as evidenced by the establishment of international criminal tribunals and by the recognition of international jurisdiction in a case such as Spain's extradition application in the English courts against General Pinochet.

In those countries where there have been criminal prosecutions and truth commissions in which perpetrators have been named, the removal of criminals from public office has usually followed. Exposing the nature and extent of human rights violations frequently reveals a systematic and institutional pattern of gross human rights violations. That undoubtedly assists in the identification and dismantling of those institutions and that might well have the effect of deterring similar occurrences in the future.

Without the public recording of the truth there will always be a tendency to ascribe guilt not to individual criminals but to ethnic, religious or other groups, or even whole peoples. Again, I refer to the South African experience. The 17 commissioners who served on the Truth and Reconciliation Commission came from all sectors of South African society – black, white, English and Afrikaans; so, too, the victims. It becomes difficult in that situation to cast the blame for all the human rights abuses on all whites or all Afrikaners. But for the work of the Truth and Reconciliation Commission, ascribing collective guilt to such groups would have been inevitable.

During my visits to the former Yugoslavia, and particularly Belgrade, I was astounded by the manner in which the Serbs I met were consumed by their historical hatred of Croats and Muslims. Most meetings I attended began with a history lesson. If I was lucky the lesson began in the 14th century with the Battle of Kosovo. It would certainly include the unspeakable treatment of Serbs by the Ustasha collaborators with the Nazis during the Second World War. It was no different in Zagreb or Sarajevo, where collective guilt was ascribed to Serbs or Muslims, as the case may be. In the Balkans, violence has been erupting periodically over a span of 600 years. Very seldom have the perpetrators of that violence been brought to account, and so their victims were denied justice.

I have no doubt that the official and public exposure of past serious human rights violations can have an important beneficial effect on a society embarking upon the difficult journey to democratic rule and reconciling people who were, in the recent past, at war with each other.

The chapters in this volume focus on many important but less obvious problems that were associated with the South African Truth and Reconciliation Commission. Many of them emerge from the experiences of 'insiders', so to speak. They are written by commissioners, senior staff members and others closely associated with the Commission. They demonstrate a candour that is refreshing and an objectivity that is unusual and commendable so soon after the event.

One reads with fascination the tension that grew between the Truth and Reconciliation Commission and the ordinary courts, especially with regard to the requirement of fairness to the witnesses and also the perpetrators who came before it; in the United States this is understood as 'due process'. One reads, also, of the frustration relating to the work of the Truth and Reconciliation Commission given the lack of any resources with which to make really meaningful reparations to the victims of apartheid. I have found these chapters both interesting and thought provoking.

I have no doubt that they will be an important guide and reference for all people interested in societies emerging from oppression to freedom.

Introduction

CHARLES VILLA-VICENCIO AND
WILHELM VERWOERD

Archbishop Desmond Tutu, in his Foreword to the *Report of the South African Truth and Reconciliation Commission*, suggests that the five volume report 'provides a perspective on the truth about a past that is more extensive and more complex than any one commission could, in two and a half years, have hoped to capture'. He argues that 'others will inevitably critique this perspective – as indeed they must. We hope many South Africans and friends of South Africa will become engaged in the process of helping our nation to come to terms with this past and, in so doing, reach out to a new future.'[1]

As an important step in this process, we need to come to terms with the incomplete and, in some ways, controversial contribution of the Truth and Reconciliation Commission (TRC) to transitional politics in South Africa. This means engaging in vigorous, open and critical debate on the work, and more specifically, the Report of the Commission. This anthology is designed to promote this kind of debate. It does not include the voices of those who reject the Commission in principle. As such, it is a book of 'internal' critique and reflection. Different voices from within this broad category are included – voices from within South Africa and from international observers, from those who worked within the TRC and those who participated in its hearings, from commissioners and survivors, from men and women across racial and age divisions. Passionate personal reflections are placed alongside academic analyses in an attempt to capture different perspectives in the TRC debate.

Despite the huge attention attracted by the uniquely public TRC process, both locally and overseas, many questions remain unanswered or tend to be neglected – not least concerning the historic origins of the Commission, its place within international human rights debate and the principles underlying the work of the Commission. The Commission's findings, in particular, have generated both criticism and support, while little serious attempt has been made to grapple with the underlying mandate of the Commission that gave rise to the findings. This anthology is intended to help fill some of these gaps. It is intended to deepen debate on the contested TRC process.

It is indeed only to the extent that there is broad-based public debate and that divisive issues are sincerely wrestled with by opinion makers that the work undertaken by the Commission can contribute positively to the South African transitional process. No *ex cathedra* statement by the Commission, any politician, academic or ideological group should be allowed to foreclose this process. A careful and honest reading of the nuanced positions, adopted by the Commission as well as its fiercest critics, is essential to ensure that the limited though vital potential of the TRC process be fulfilled.

It is only through democratic encounter of this kind that the nation-building exercise can be fully appropriated and internalised by the broad population. National coexistence and the ultimate goal of national reconciliation rather than individual reconciliation (as important as this may be) can only happen as we get to know one another through engaging in debate. The actual journey in this regard is itself part of the reconciliation process.

Debate must continue. Judgment time is not yet. Only history can deliver the final word on the South African transition. This judgment is likely to be made on the basis of whether the victims and survivors of past atrocities truly enjoy the dignity of being acknowledged as human beings. This will presumably include the ability to share in resolving the major issues facing the nation. Above all it will involve all South Africans enjoying a material standard of living that makes this possible.

Political settlements rarely occur with textbook clarity, and the South African transition has been an untidy one. The multiple objectives thrust upon the nation are nowhere better captured than in the words of Chief Justice Ismail Mahomed. He was Deputy President of the Constitutional Court when the Azanian Peoples' Organisation (AZAPO) and others brought an application concerning the validity of the Promotion of National Unity and Reconciliation Act to the Court in 1996 (Case No. CCT 17/96). Drawing on the 'postamble' to the Interim Constitution, he reminded us that the TRC was but one initiative in a bridge-building exercise. It was designed to take the country from a deeply divided past, characterised by strife, conflict, suffering and injustice, to a future founded on the recognition of human rights, democracy and peaceful coexistence. Chief Justice Mahomed spoke of the agonising balancing act between the need to provide for justice to victims and the need for national reconciliation.

The chapters that follow are grouped in order to identify the key areas of debate – as part of the above-mentioned bridge-building exercise. They highlight the need for:

- A narrow and a broad reading of the Commission's Report. A detailed analysis of specific aspects of the Report needs to be undertaken in relation to a reading of the Report through a wide-angle lens.
- Further exploration of the consensus that emerges in the chapters around a number of important issues.
- Consideration to be given to key tensions and unresolved issues that emerge from a reading of the chapters.

A narrow and broad reading

There is a need for a focused and in-depth reading of specific concerns pertaining to the work of the Commission. This focus needs to take place within the context of a broader reading of the entire Report. The particular must be seen in relation to the whole.

An in-depth reading

In his Foreword, Judge Richard Goldstone notes that the chapters in this volume 'focus on many important but less obvious problems' associated with the TRC. The need to look beyond the obvious should also be applied to an overall assessment of the Report. Judge Goldstone reminds us that we should be careful about jumping too quickly to conclusions about this multi-dimensional process, which, inevitably and necessarily, has been filtered and simplified through the eyes of the mass media. The high-profile court actions launched against the TRC illustrate the point.

Supporters of the Commission lamented the negative impact that this had on the work of the Commission. The Commission's detractors, in turn, delighted in what was often seen as the underlying weaknesses of the Commission. Hugh Corder, in his contribution to this volume, looks deeper, placing this aspect of the TRC process in historical perspective. In so doing he draws attention to the more positive side of the court challenges:

> *No one familiar with South Africa's history or with the ill-fated demise of many less ambitious attempts to install constitutional democracies on infertile ground in other circumstances would be foolish enough to argue that the rule of law is forever secure as the organising principle of government in South Africa. There seems little doubt to me, however, that the challenging litigants' choice of law as the means of asserting their concerns and the resilience of the TRC in reply represent small but triumphant steps on the way to securing a constitutional democracy.*

Nkosinathi Biko, in turn, defends the right of those who challenged the constitutionality of the amnesty process as a basis for grappling with meaningful transition. It constitutes what he defines as a 'democratic engagement with an aspect of the Constitution'. Constitutional democracy is indeed working.

The similar in-depth and analytical reading is needed regarding the Report as a whole. Essential sections in this Report have, unfortunately, not received this kind of attention. This applies above all to the Mandate chapter, which is the key to the unlocking of the principles that underlie difficult decisions and the Commission's findings.[2] Debate around this issue is discussed in the chapters by Kader Asmal, Louise Asmal and Ronald Suresh Roberts on the one hand and in Mary Burton's on the other. Their contributions are discussed later in this Introduction. The Commission has also often been criticised for failing to address a particular concern (whether 'forced removals', 'Bantu education' or 'racial capitalism'), whereas the Commission has judged it to have fallen outside its mandate. An important question is whether this mandate was adequately interpreted by the Commission or, for that matter, adequately conceived by the drafters of the TRC legislation. Careful, in-depth reading is required in this regard. This can only result in debate that will continue for some time to come. Many of the chapters that follow impinge directly and indirectly on this issue.

Reading with a wide-angle lens

The Report was handed to the President in October 1998. The amnesty process remains incomplete. Proximity to a complex, unfinished process, in turn, makes it difficult for those involved in the work of the Commission as well as those who, for various reasons, are most critical of its work to assess the work as carefully and objectively as is required. South Africans do not, however, have the luxury of allowing time to create the necessary distance. This makes vigorous and critical debate of the Commission's work important – even if time will ultimately alter or even strengthen the critique. It is at the same time important that specific critiques be weighed against the overall objectives of the Report.

A wide-angle approach is also important for two additional reasons:

■ The mandate of the Commission required that in providing 'as complete a picture as possible' of the events under its mandate, it should at the same time reflect the 'motives and perspectives' of all concerned. Indeed, to the extent that the 'motives and perspectives' of the worst offenders are analysed and an attempt is made to understand them, to that extent is a nation better equipped to work towards ensuring that similar atrocities do not occur in the future.

■ The work of the Commission must be understood in relation to a broader international debate on human rights. Dumisa Ntsebeza's reflection on the history of the international quest for human rights, from the time of the United Nations Declaration of Human Rights to the present, is important in this regard. The work of the Commission should also be understood in relation to other truth commissions. The chapter by Priscilla Hayner makes an important contribution in this regard. Ron Slye considers the South African amnesty process in relation to the global amnesty debate. Paul van Zyl, in turn, reflects on the South African transitional process in relation to international tribunals and the International Criminal Court.

Points of consensus

Breaking the conspiracy of silence and denial

The importance and complexity of seeking to overcome silence and denial is reflected on in a number of ways and from different perspectives: Yazir Henry writes as a person who has suffered deeply and given testimony before the Commission. Ginn Fourie, who lost her daughter in an attack on the Heidelberg Tavern in Cape Town, tells her story. Don Foster seeks to uncover the psychological and social forces that contribute to the making of perpetrators. Wilhelm Verwoerd compares the silence that marked the aftermath of the Anglo-Boer War with that of disclosure that comes in the wake of the apartheid years. Nomfundo Walaza writes critically from her perspective as a clinical psychologist and director of the Cape Town-based Trauma Centre, while Wendy Orr explains the Commission's attempt to facilitate healing through its reparation and rehabilitation policy.

Truth

Several authors address the complexity of the nature of truth. Janet Cherry grapples with the nature of historical truth by reflecting, *inter alia*, on a number of amnesty applications. Willie Esterhuyse addresses the importance of moral truth and the need to practice truth. Colleen Scott, in turn, provides a thoughtful piece on different notions of reality, drawing on insights gained from legal and other challenges to Commission.

Reconciliation

Several authors emphasise the fact that the process of reconciliation has only just begun. Nkosinathi Biko speaks from the perspective of his family in the amnesty process. Jakes Gerwel reflects on the institutional changes that make for national reconciliation. Archbishop Njongonkulu Ndungane and Sampie Terreblanche speak of the need for structural economic change.

Mxolisi Mgxashe, as an experienced journalist, reflects on the work of the Commission in seeking to promote reconciliation. Charles Villa-Vicencio raises several questions concerning that nature of political coexistence and reconciliation, while considering different levels of 'getting on with life'. Ebrahim Moosa and Piet Meiring, from Muslim and Christian perspectives respectively, raise a number of religious questions that impinge on the work of the Commission and the process of reconciliation.

Unresolved issues
The nature of the Commission

The Commission was never required to glorify heroes or praise noble people. Its task was the identification of gross violations of human rights and those responsible for them – as a basis for ensuring that similar violations are not repeated in the future. It is equally important to recognise, however, that the need to identify perpetrators cannot be allowed to continue indefinitely – if there is a national commitment to closure on the past. The implications are extensive. They impinge on trials that emerge as a result of failed amnesty applications and the failure of some to apply for amnesty – a position reiterated by the present administration. Former President Mandela stated his government's opposition to a general amnesty. What will be the implications of pending trials on senior government officials and those outside of government? The debate has only started. Chapters in this volume by Nkosinathi Biko, Ron Slye, Richard Lyster and several others provide important comment to be considered in this regard.

The narrowness of the mandate

Directly related to the nature of the Commission is, of course, the perceived narrowness of the Commission's mandate. This too has been raised and questioned by some of the contributors to this volume. Nomfundo Walaza challenged the Commission for not doing enough to facilitate the healing of individual victims and survivors, as well as for concentrating too narrowly on the 'promotion of national unity and reconciliation'. Kader and Louise Asmal and Ronald Suresh Roberts in their chapter suggest that the failure of the Commission to stretch the mandate has resulted in an inadequate reflection of the suffering that apartheid produced. Sampie Terreblanche suggests that insufficient attention was given by the Commission to the structural nature of the evil – while he suggests that the institutional hearings undertaken by the Commission provided a basis for this to happen. Several others, Archbishop Ndungane among them, suggest the mandate was too narrow to bring adequate levels of healing. Johnny de Lange presents the thinking behind the focused mandate in the deliberations of those responsible for drafting the legislation.

Justice

Huge debate continues in relation to the nature of justice. If justice be no more than an eye for an eye, a tooth for a tooth and a pint of blood for a pint of blood, the TRC was indeed devoid of justice. The Commission is founded, however, on the basis of there being more to justice than that. Rajeev Bhargava suggests the a truth commission necessarily has a limited objective – aimed at helping to establish a 'minimally decent society' within which there are minimal standards of justice. Paul van Zyl reflects on the place of 'transitional justice' in the journey from a society moving away from oppressive rule to the affirmation of democracy and human rights. Hugh Corder's chapter on the legal challenges that confronted the Commission also raises important questions on the nature of justice, as does Johnny de Lange's piece on the origins of the Commission. Charles Villa-Vicencio writes on the nature of restorative justice as an underlying principle of the Commission – a principle, he argues, that should underlie all dimensions of justice. The debate needs to be viewed in the context of Dumisa Ntsebeza's survey of the history of the quest for human rights extending from the UN Declaration of Human Rights to the founding of the International Criminal Court. Priscilla Hayner's chapter on the South African Commission in relation to other truth commissions needs also to be considered in defining the nature and possibility of justice in transitional societies.

International law

One of the more vexing problems underlying the *TRC Report* is the issue of international law. Mary Burton's chapter addresses this matter in some detail. The chapter by the Asmals and Roberts raises a host of important questions regarding the Just War theory. It suggests that the separation of the distinction between just cause and means is outdated and ought to be re-examined. They accept that this 'does not allow individual war criminals to escape responsibility' for their actions. Yet they maintain that the fine distinction regarding cause and means put forward by the Commission looks untenable. This, they suggest, results in the Commission failing to provide guidance in such matters for the future. The question is whether the distinctions between cause and means made by the Commission are indeed outdated.

Carlos Nino, the late Argentinean human rights lawyer, has warned against what he calls 'epistemic moral elitism', which gives moral primacy to a particular moral perspective – whether that of a ruling party, an individual or a state commission. The Asmals and Roberts will need to convince a large number of human rights scholars and activists that the TRC was not justified in finding that certain actions, undertaken by the ANC in the course of fighting what the TRC accepts was a just war, were gross violations of human rights. Particular cases need to be debated in order to promote a better understanding of different perspectives on the past. It is another matter to suggest or imply that because a particular cause is a just one, the actions that follow should be considered as being beyond moral or legal enquiry.

Whose reading of the international conventions is correct? Has the Commission indeed treated both sides equally? What does one make of the primary finding by the TRC that the predominant portion of the gross violations of human rights was committed by the apartheid state and its security forces?[3] The TRC has further emphasised that those fighting against apartheid and those fighting to defend it cannot be equated?[4] Is it legitimate to argue that the engagement in a just war by the liberation movements requires that actions undertaken in pursuit of that war be judged by different criteria to actions undertaken in the pursuit of unjust wars? Does this not create a dangerous loophole that will allow innocent civilians to be harmed with impunity? Is this not, *inter alia*, what the Geneva Conventions are seeking to prevent? These are issues that deserve the most careful consideration.

Debate is important

Endless debate is not enough to heal a nation, entrench democracy and promote national reconciliation. It is, however, an important part of it. 'Tomorrow is Another Country.' 'The Past is a Foreign Country.' The metaphor is differently employed. The journey from the past to the future can only be successfully pursued to the extent that the issues that continue to divide the nation are addressed. These include deeply entrenched economic divisions; most authors have made the point, either directly or indirectly. Perceptions, values and an understanding of the past need also to be addressed. This is what makes ongoing debate so very important. Mary Burton has put it thus:

> *If reconciliation and national unity are to be achieved in South Africa, a clear understanding of the past conflict will be indispensable. The fact is that lines are often blurred, that truth is hard to find, and common perceptions difficult to reach. The Commission has been as open as it can to scrutiny of how it reached its findings, so that South Africans can better learn to put the past behind them and together set standards for the future. The final word has not been spoken. Again, careful, rational discussion must continue.[5]*

Section 1

The historical context and origins of the Commission

The struggle for human rights: from the UN Declaration of Human Rights to the present

DUMISA NTSEBEZA

In the history and evolution of International Human Rights Law and International Humanitarian Law, 1998 was arguably a watershed year.

Almost 50 years ago, the United Nations General Assembly proclaimed the Universal Declaration of Human Rights, against the backdrop of a war that had been fought, from 1939 to 1945, with a savagery that shocked the world. It had been a war characterised by the most incomprehensible acts of man's inhumanity to man. Human life, at the hands of fascist and Nazi dictatorships – the regimes of Italy's Mussolini, Japan's fascist warlords and Germany's Hitler – had meant very little. Millions of Jews, gypsies, homosexuals, and races held to be inferior and subhuman by these fascist regimes, were sent to their demise without the slightest compunction. Countless accounts of torture, maiming, severe ill-treatment and the elimination of people using all kinds of grotesque methods have been told so often that one would have expected such deeds would never happen again. Indeed, the Universal Declaration of Human Rights, in its preamble and in the articles comprising the document, recognised that 'disregard and contempt of human rights had resulted in barbarous acts that have outraged the conscience of mankind'.[1] It reaffirmed the Nations of the World's faith in fundamental human rights, in the dignity and worth of people, and in the equal rights of men and women.

2

The declaration was proclaimed 'as a common standard against which all would strive, by teaching and education, to promote respect for the inalienable rights and freedom of humans the world over'.[2]

Thus, discrimination was shown up as a violation, as was slavery or servitude, torture and cruel, inhuman or degrading treatment or punishment. Arbitrary arrest and detention were prohibited. In short, the declaration dealt with a whole range of freedoms and rights, the observation and practice of which, it was hoped, would guarantee that nothing as abhorrent as what had happened during the Second World War would ever occur again.

Fifty years since the declaration

In 1998, the 50th anniversary of the Declaration was celebrated throughout the world. In France, for example, from 7 to 12 December, Paris was host to a week-long programme of celebrations and reflections.

Yet, even as these celebrations were being held, the international scene was stained with the blood of those who, in the 50 years since the Declaration, had been tortured, maimed and murdered in genocides, wars and conflicts that took place with no regard for the declaration. The heroic struggles of the people of South East Asia ended in the genocidal excesses of, for example, Pol Pot of the Khmer Rouge regime. His authoritarian rule left millions of people dead. The Eastern European regimes, hailed at the end of the war as beacons of hope for a brave new world of socialism, were shown to have been hell-holes of the grossest forms of oppression and violations of basic human rights.

In Latin America, savage dictatorships enjoyed the tacit approval and support of the Western world. In Africa, apartheid was born in the very year of the Declaration and it became an example of the worst form of repression and oppression masquerading as a legitimate 'democracy'. The genocides in Rwanda and Burundi had become household names, frightening nightmares that defy any attempt to find logical explanations. Even as Paris examined the 50 years since the Declaration, killings of genocidal proportions were taking place at Kosovo. This was arguably the final chapters in the madness, operating under the name of 'ethnic cleansing' that left Yugoslavia unrecognisable from its former self. So clearly 1998 was a year in which the nations of the world were forced to take stock – it was about time too. The picture was grim.

Processes at play since 1948

Numerous attempts were made by various communities to deal with their pasts, in an attempt to inculcate a culture that observed human rights. Latin American societies that had experienced savage conflagrations, despite the Declaration, had begun to seek ways and means of dealing with their horrendous pasts. One such method – practised in Chile, Argentina and Uruguay, among others – was the route of commissions, similar to our Truth and Reconciliation Commission, that sought to expose the truth of what had happened in order to find a basis for the reconciliation of those aggrieved communities.

Other communities, however, opted for the criminal justice system. The former Yugoslavia and Rwanda, it was felt, could be dealt with only by prosecuting the perpetrators of what the international community saw as extremely serious crimes against humanity. Thus the International Criminal Tribunals for the former Yugoslavia were born in 1993 and for Rwanda in 1994.

Indeed, there was a persistent cry calling for the establishment of an International Criminal Court. At the end of 1998, it became a reality. In July that year, the Statute for an International Criminal Court was adopted by the United Nations Diplomatic Conference of Plenipotentiaries in Rome, and some United Nations member states, including South Africa, signed the Statute.

The International Criminal Court is the subject of a more thorough discussion elsewhere in this book. It should suffice to say that in taking stock of what had happened in the 50 years since the Declaration of Human Rights in 1948, the Rome Statute, in its preamble:

- reaffirmed the common bonds that bind humanity, but expressed concern that the delicate mosaic of a common world culture and shared heritage may be shattered at any time;
- stated that during this century, millions of children, women and men became victims of unimaginable atrocities that shock the conscience of humanity;
- recognised that such crimes threaten the peace, security and wellbeing of the world;
- affirmed that such serious crimes should not go unpunished and that prosecution at national level must be assisted by international cooperation;
- signified the determination of the world to put an end to impunity for perpetrators and thus contribute to the prevention of such crimes.[3]

1998 watershed

By 1998 the world was showing an increasing intolerance towards those who were, with impunity, perpetrating gross violations of human rights. The Rome Statute provided the jurisprudential, philosophical and legislative basis for the punishment of those who violate international human rights and humanitarian law.

The clearest indication that the world mood was changing, and that the perpetrators of violations of human rights could no longer strut the world with impunity (even if they had made their own arrangements domestically), was the arrest, in the United Kingdom, of General Pinochet at the insistence of the Spanish government. The issue to be decided, on an application by Spain for General Pinochet's extradition to Spain to stand trial there, was whether he was protected by the diplomatic immunity attached to him as former head of state and current senator in Chile, where alleged atrocities were perpetrated under his rule. The question was whether acts of torture and hostage-taking were done in the exercise of his functions as head of state.

The majority in the House of Lords [Lord Nicholls, with Lords Hoffman and Steyn concurring] found in favour of the Spanish government![4]

The speech by Lord Nicholls in the first decision is most informative and is echoed in most of the other opinion. He stated, among others, that 'torture of his own subjects, or of aliens, would not be regarded by international law as a function of a head of state. All states disavow the use of torture as abhorrent, although from time to time some still resort to it. International law has made plain that certain types of conduct, including torture and hostage-taking, are not acceptable conduct on the part of anyone. This applies to heads of state, or even more so to them than it does to everyone else; the contrary conclusion would make a mockery of international law.'

He concluded by referring to a judgment of the Nuremberg International Military Tribunal (of 8 August 1945), which contained the following passage:

'The principle of international law, which, under certain circumstance, protects representatives of a state, cannot be applied to acts condemned as criminal by international law. The authors of these acts cannot shelter themselves behind their official position to be freed from punishment.'[5]

From Nuremberg (in 1945) to the House of Lords (1998), it appears we have turned full circle. And yet, in that same year, the South African Truth and Reconciliation Commission, in the most unexpected and dramatic way, submitted its report to the president.

South Africa, for reasons that are also canvassed elsewhere in this work, never opted for the Nuremberg-type approach. The TRC's Report claims that the process sought to heal the South African nation, to promote national unity, to grant amnesty to perpetrators, to give victims an opportunity to tell their stories and, hopefully, promote not only reconciliation, but also the observation of a human rights culture in South Africa, where violations of human rights would never take place again.

It is a further purpose of this chaper to look at the processes and actions of the South African Truth and Reconciliation Commission, its actions and the findings procedures that sought to verify the findings and look at the extent to which they could be relied on. It is intended too, by way of concluding remarks, to look at the position of South African perpetrators and their vulnerability or otherwise, firstly, *vis-à-vis* extraditions from South Africa to stand trial elsewhere, and secondly, *vis-à-vis* their ability to travel elsewhere.

The TRC process

The Commission's mandate was carried out by the actions of, in the main, three committees, namely The Amnesty Committee, The Human Rights Violations (HRV) Committee and The Reparations and Rehabilitations Committee. There was also an Investigative Unit, established in terms of the Act, working in collaboration with the Research Department, which conducted investigative enquiries. By far the most comprehensive investigative process was conducted under the auspices of the HRV Committee. This is the process that not only led to a findings process that determined whether a person was or was not a victim, but one that led to the identification of perpetrators.

The findings process that identified victims of gross violation of human rights took place largely through the work of the HRV Committee. It is not my intention to give a detailed account of the various steps that were taken to identify a victim. It is an extremely elaborate process. The HRV Committee received statements from about 21 000 victims. The process that led to a finding of whether an applicant qualifies for victim status began with statement-taking and involved, among other processes, registration of statements, data processing, data capturing, verification and corroboration, an information management process that led to pre-findings on a regional basis, to pre-findings and eventually findings on a national level.

It was a tedious, but essential process, one that included the work of regional and national investigative units, the management of information gathered and evaluations and technical analyses of this information, relying on modern technology for speed of cross-referencing and verification.

For example, if a person alleged that in May 1987 he was one of a group of protesters that marched to Pollsmoor to demand the release of Nelson Mandela, that during this march they were tear-gassed and assaulted and fired at by the police, that his brother died in the incident and so on, the verification process would involve what came to be known as low-level corroboration. This would be done by the Investigative Unit. It would involve enquiries made at police stations, libraries, hospitals and mortuaries around the dates in question to establish if, in fact, there had been such an incident, if there were death certificates and/or post-mortem results relevant to the death mentioned. Details would be checked and double-checked to establish if they are verifiable. If more investigation were necessary, there would be referrals to investigators until a findings process was possible.

Certain investigations, especially those that showed a high level of authorisation and/or involvement of certain institutions and/or a certain pattern of abuse and/or reflected national or international dimensions (eg cross border raids, the murder of individuals across South African borders), usually involved special investigations. They were almost exclusively pro-active investigations initiated by the Investigative Unit itself. They seldom arose from statements received from victims. However, some statements from victims did lead to more intensive investigations. In all investigations, whether on the basis of statements or on the basis of initiatives by the Investigative Unit, had to be authenticated. It has always been crucial that any finding be based on verifiable or authenticated evidence.

Some statements formed the basis of public hearings. Right from the beginning, the question of whether perpetrators could be named by victims in public hearings became a very controversial issue and one that took the TRC to the Supreme Court of Appeal, the highest court in the country. A well-known case was the one where two police officers, Du Preez and Van Rensburg,[6] interdicted the TRC from publicly hearing evidence from victims in circumstances where they were not given prior notice.

Their argument, essentially, was that S 30(2) sub-sections (a) and (b) of the TRC Act (No. 34 of 1995) had to be read disjunctively and that, on that basis, they were entitled to a prior notice and a right to be heard beforehand on a matter that might be to their detriment. Thus, if we were to hear disclosures from Mrs Mthimkhulu, as we were preparing to, about their involvement in the torture, poisoning and disappearance of Mrs Mthimkhulu's son, Siphiwo Mthimkhulu, we had to provide them with an opportunity to make representations. We had to give the two officers not only prior notice that they were to be mentioned in a public hearing, but also provide them with information on the basis of which such a hearing was to be conducted. If we refused to do so, they had a legal basis to prevent us from holding such a hearing.

The TRC's argument was that they were not entitled to such information or notice for purposes of a hearing; that they would be entitled to such notice and information only if and when the TRC was contemplating making a finding to their detriment – in a sense, an argument calling for a conjunctive reading of (a) and (b) of S 30 (2). To appreciate the various arguments, which, admittedly, are very simplistically stated, I quote S 30 (2) (a) and (b) here in full:

(2) If during any investigation by or any hearing before the Commission (a) any person is implicated in a manner that may be to his or her detriment; (Para (a) substituted by S 15(a) of Act No 87 of 1995); '(b) the Commission

contemplates making a decision that may be to the detriment of a person who has been so implicated. The Commission shall, if such person is available, afford him or her an opportunity to submit representations to the Commission within a specified time with regard to the matter under consideration or to give evidence at a hearing of the Commission (Para (b) substituted by S 15 (b) of Act No 87 of 1995).

The Cape High Court agreed with the TRC and, on that basis, the TRC was able to hold hearings, naming perpetrators without necessarily having to give them reams of information and notices before a hearing. This was, however, reversed by the Supreme Court, a major drawback that had to be dealt with for virtually the whole of 1997 onwards, but one the TRC had anticipated. Even during the period during which it was not obliged, as a matter of law, to give notices for purposes of a hearing, the TRC erred on the side of providing perpetrators, who might be named by victims to their detriment, as much documentation as possible. The TRC usually gave them 21 days' notice. This was particularly applicable when the TRC served them with subpoenas in terms of S 29, whether these subpoenas were for them to appear in a public hearing (like for the so-called Trojan Horse incident) or in a private hearing, the so-called in camera investigative inquiries for gathering information from implicated persons. The contents of these in camera investigations would remain confidential until the Commission decided to release such contents.

Thus, the legal position, although it changed after the Supreme Court ruling, did not really cause a disruption of the Commission's work. It only added the number of times the S 30 notices (and accompanying documentation) would be sent to the would-be perpetrators.

It was also apparent from the provisions of S 30 that before a finding could be made to a perpetrator's detriment – and it is now common cause that such detriment or prejudice would come if alleged perpetrators were named publicly, like, for example, in the report the Commission handed over to the president – such a perpetrator was entitled to a notice considered in S 30.

In its report, the Commission made several findings against individuals, organisations and institutions. These findings, made on the basis of the Commission's satisfaction that allegations relevant thereto had been investigated, checked and authenticated by verifiable evidence, and that they meet the Commission's standard of proof – namely, proof on a balance of probabilities – have been communicated to the implicated persons, office bearers of implicated institutions or organisations right across the political spectrum.

The response, not unexpectedly, has been swift and sure – and threatening. What happened in the run-up to the handing in of the Report is now a matter of historical record. Former President FW de Klerk, in an 11th hour litigation, sought to prevent the Commission from publishing its Report on the basis that certain findings made against him were not justifiable. The compromise was that the case would be fought and argued at a later date, but that the Report would be published with the offending finding blotted out in black – a picture that reverberated throughout the world when it was published in that form.[7]

The ANC, also along similar lines, made its own ill-advised attempt to prevent publication. Their endeavour was less successful, if more spectacular on the day.[8]

Currently, an action is underway, by the former National Intelligence Service (NIS) chief, Dr Neil Barnard, in which he seeks to challenge virtually each and every letter of the published report. He is demanding, as he believes he is entitled to, the disclosure of all the documents that may have informed the commissioners of the work of the NIS. It sounds nightmarish, but it is true.[9]

Since the De Klerk and Barnard cases are still *sub judice*, I shall say no more about them, save to mention that the process, despite its aim to promote national unity and reconciliation, is already being seen by others as having failed to achieve that objective; the litigations by De Klerk and Barnard are already cited as examples that militate against the whole notion of goodwill, nation-building and reconciliation.

My brief comment would be that it is too early for anyone to judge whether the process has or has not achieved its objective to promote reconciliation.

Amnesty

This process is for those making a full disclosure of all the circumstances relevant to the offences applicable to them. Since they 'confess' to their past misdemeanours, they obviously implicate themselves. Where gross violations of human rights, as defined by the Act, occurred and amnesty is granted, amnesty applicants must appear in public and are subjected to cross-examination by lawyers appointed for the victims.

Thus, this process, insofar as public naming of people to their detriment is concerned, is subjected to less procedural fairness procedures than that which the HRV process demands. The only occasion where procedural fairness must be complied with is when others are implicated. The process provides implicated persons with an opportunity to be heard.

The amnesty applications are investigated to ensure that there is full disclosure. In some cases, this has taken the form of confronting perpetrators with facts in-camera, investigative enquiries held in terms of S 29 or using perpetrators' own statements and checking them for corroboration, and against other known facts from other information in the TRC process. There have been cases where, after realising that the Commission knows more than they were prepared to reveal in their statements, perpetrators have provided 'further particulars' in contemplation of a hearing so that they can fully comply with the requirement to make a full disclosure. The 'further particulars' so provided are again subjected to further scrutiny. Consequently, although there is now no Investigative Unit as such, the amnesty process has been vested with an investigative capacity by transferring all investigators, who were largely involved with HRV-related cases, to the Amnesty Committee to investigate and 'beef-up' amnesty applications. The amnesty process was also able to identify victims who had not applied for that status or were not identified as such during the HRV process.

An example is where a few persons are known to have applied for victim status with regard to the Boipatong Massacre. It is quite conceivable that during the amnesty hearing, names of victims who were not mentioned before, might come to the fore. The Amnesty Committee is competent to confer victim status on such people if it is satisfied that they have been correctly identified as such.

Conclusion

It is clear that the Commission has gone out of its way to provide corroborated evidence through a number of processes and activities. This has sometimes been done at great cost. When the TRC decided to hold a public hearing on the Chemical and Biological Warfare (CBW) programme, not only were investigators working around the clock to interrogate witnesses and negotiate deals with the office of the Attorneys General, who feared a public hearing might prejudice their prosecutions, but they also had to provide investigative material for both the panel and the implicated perpetrators. After the hearing, they were closely involved in the findings process and once again advised the relevant persons, who were given an opportunity to make representations before the TRC findings were published in the final Report.

The Investigative Unit has also been involved in an exhumations process. In some cases, it was evidence given by the perpetrators that led to exhumations, in other cases it was through tenacious processes of investigations. The methodology is quite complex, so I will not go into it here. Suffice to say that whatever information led to exhumations was often backed by independent corroborative evidence. In one classical case, the TRC was given photographs by a victim's brother of himself and his slain brother. He gave these to the Commission before the exhumations began. In the photograph, his brother, Barney Molokoane, was wearing boots he had bought for him before he went on that ill-fated mission. As the Commission went to the grave identified by the investigative process to be Barney Molokoane's, they came across the boots and were able to match them with the ones in the photograph.

The Investigative Unit needed no more proof that the remains they were exhuming were those of Barney Molokoane's. In this case, where there were no amnesty applications to lead investigators to his grave, this was proof beyond a reasonable doubt. The Commission only requires proof on a balance of probabilities. In conclusion, let me recall one of many stories of the TRC.

I read the following account in a newspaper,[10] under the headline 'Policeman Recalls Ambush Incident'. It was about an amnesty application by Walter Tanda, capturing the testimony of someone called Meyer.

Meyer, an inspector at the Bellville police station, was testifying at the hearing of APLA operative Walter Tanda, who is seeking amnesty for his role in an attack on a Claremont restaurant in 1992, and several attacks on the police. Tanda, now in training in the SA Air Force, told the hearing earlier this week that the attacks on the police were attempts to acquire arms and ammunition for APLA cadres.

Meyer testified that he and an assistant constable, named Mkhwanazi, were driving in Guguletu on the night of 12 January 1993 when they came under fire. Mkhwanazi ducked and Meyer felt as if a brick had struck his shoulder. 'I was shot through the left side of my chest. I could feel a hole there, directly over my heart.' Unable to reach for his weapon, he saw through the window that the gunman was about to shoot again. 'I called Jesus' name, called on him to help me. I felt the shots as they passed me ... they struck everywhere around me, but I was not shot.' He restarted the van, and heard bullets striking the canvas blinds at the back as he accelerated away.

Mkhwanazi had been hit in the head and another bullet ripped through his intestines. He died later. Meyer said he was rushed to hospital by a police reaction unit. One of his lungs collapsed on the way. At the hospital it was established that there was no damage to bone or nerves, but that the bullet had punched a huge exit wound in his back, narrowly missing his heart as it went through.

He said at one point during his recuperation that he had been unable to speak and was told that this was a symptom of shock. He also received psychological treatment and sleeping pills 'because in the nights I got night-mares that people were shooting at me'. He had recovered physically, but still had sleep problems, including occasional nightmares.

Meyer told the hearing that he had, however, reconciled with Tanda and shaken his hand, and that Tanda had offered to meet his family, who had also suffered stress as a result of the shooting. He said in an interview afterwards that the TRC was a good thing, as it enabled people to deal with their fears. Sapa.

Postscript

At the beginning I suggested that the international community was showing signs of being increasingly tired of the impunity of perpetrators of gross violations of human rights. Even though, at this stage, it appears that perpetrators can 'get away with it' if they have been granted amnesty in their domestic jurisdictions, that luxury is threatened by the contents of the legislation for the establishment of the International Criminal Court – certainly for future crimes against humanity. What the Pinochet saga has shown, however, is that even those South Africans who have applied for, and have received amnesty, are very vulnerable when they travel abroad. Their consolation lies in the fact that in terms of South African extradition laws as they currently stand, they would not be extradited for crimes for which the South African TRC process has granted them amnesty.

Not so those who either did not apply for amnesty, but should have done, or those whose amnesty applications have failed. They are extraditable, for example, to Angola, Botswana or the UK, and could stand trial there for serious crimes in those jurisdictions. They would also travel outside South Africa at their own risk.

With regard to perpetrators who are seized outside our borders after they have been granted amnesty, it appears that, while they may not successfully raise the granting of amnesty by our TRC as a valid defence, the fact that they were granted amnesty would be a mitigating factor. This would be so, because the TRC has, by and large, received worldwide support. In particular, its amnesty process, to the extent that it calls for public accountability from each perpetrator, has been received very positively, the view being held that the public confessions go some way to dissuading a culture of impunity – something aimed at by the International Criminal Court.

By any account, however, it seems clear that the message of the Pinochet drama is that perpetrators of crimes against humanity must, in expiation of the atrocities connected to them, further atone for their misdemeanours by staying at home.

Grounding, after all, is a recognised modern form of punishment for delinquents. It may be no more than an irritation to the offender, but it serves as a reminder to the offender that rules are there to be observed.

International rules and principles aimed at protecting human rights need more attention than most. It is only in the observation of those rules and the protective mechanisms that the International Criminal Court and the TRC put in place that the world will again be fully conscious of human rights, as it was 50 years ago when the Universal Declaration of Human Rights was proclaimed.

The historical context, legal origins and philosophical foundation of the South African Truth and Reconciliation Commission

JOHNNY DE LANGE

South Africa enters the new millennium having achieved formal political liberation, with the smooth change-over of government in 1994 being one of the most outstanding liberation achievements of this century. It marks an appreciation by both black and white South Africans of the fact that they share a common destiny, and that no one would benefit from mutually debilitating conflict. This was made possible and re-enforced by a policy of reconciliation and reconstruction that seeks to narrow the gap for those forces that might have had plans to subvert the transition by violent and other means.

In 1995, the South African parliament, through a unique, democratically verifiable process – after a prolonged, consultative process – established the South African Truth and Reconciliation Commission (TRC), by passing the Promotion of National Unity and Reconciliation Act (No 34 of 1995) (referred to in this chapter as the Act). Although the establishment of truth commissions had become a widely used tool in the recent past – by countries involved in a transition from dictatorship to democracy – the TRC marked a unique moment in world history. It was the first time that a nation had created a truth commission through a public and participatory process, by way of an Act of parliament. The TRC also featured unique and historic characteristics, discussed by Priscilla Hayner in the next chapter.

International context

The last decade-and-a-half has witnessed the demise of a whole range of certainties, which have irrevocably altered and shifted the world order as we knew it. The balance of world forces has undergone profound changes with the unravelling of the socialist world system. The East/West dichotomy has given way to a unipolar world order, dominated by the United States of America. This period of flux has witnessed an explosive change towards democracy, as a number of countries have become involved in a political transition from a form of dictatorship to democracy. This unique period of history caused by, or coinciding with, the end of the Cold War, has provided a window of opportunity for an accelerated emergence of many democratic or semi-democratic governments, mainly in Second and Third World countries, where all protagonists in the conflict can participate and find their place.

These transitional processes unleash new problems in society and create new possibilities and solutions. The type of transition is crucial for future solutions, because it defines and even limits future options. For nations in transition, emerging from a period of political turmoil, particularly if it has been associated with violations of human rights (referred to from here on as violations), the greatest challenge to the transformation process is the question of how to deal with the (recent) past and its legacy. This legacy invariably encompasses each aspect of that society – for example, the political, social, economic, cultural, ideological and ethical or moral spheres. For the purposes of this chapter, I am interested mainly in one aspect: how to deal with the problem of justice in the process of transition to democracy.[1]

South Africa is still in such a period of transition – the last decade has witnessed a gradual shift from an illegitimate, minority dictatorship to a more humane, democratic society.

Taking into account the enormous differences that exist between transitional processes, national traditions, material circumstances and the freedom of political and legal options, two somewhat imprecisely defined and mostly opposing models have been developed in international jurisprudence for dealing with violations in transitional situations. In the last two decades, the most defining characteristic of these models has been the many variants that have mutated from the basic approaches contained in either model, to suit the specific circumstances of the transition in question. In an attempt to simplify matters, I shall refer to these as the 'justice model', which deals with the question of prosecution and punishment (the elements of retribution), justice and accountability forming the central tenets of this approach; and the 'reconciliation model', (with the elements of truth and reconciliation forming its central tenets) of which the so-called truth commission is the most often used example in recent times, with the Chilean example being the most successful of the completed commissions.

For reasons that shall emerge, South Africa may, at least, have created a new variant of either model or, at best and for the first time, created a unique model containing essential elements of both, as a mechanism suited to its transition, to deal with its legacy of violations.

The historical context of the South African TRC

For almost 350 years the majority of South Africans were excluded from participating in the political and economic life of the nation. Successive con-stitutions – in 1910, 1961 and 1983 – were used as instruments to consoli-date white hegemony, excluding the vast majority of the population in terms of the colour of their skin.

This system of apartheid, declared a crime against humanity by the interna-tional community, consisted of millions of acts and omissions performed daily, consciously and unconsciously, that were woven into a system, which not only ensured privilege for a few, but also attempted to criminalise, from the cradle to the grave, those excluded from such privilege. Therefore, the very essence of apartheid permeates each aspect of our individual and collective lives, and is interwoven into the very fabric of society. The moral fabric of our society has through all the abuse and mismanagement been torn asunder. South Africa is thus a country in the midst of a complex and painful transition from a pariah, white-minority dictatorship to a democratic, constitutional state; a country divided into two distinct nations – one rich, privileged and mainly white; one poor, marginalised and mainly black; from a stagnating economy into a world player holding its own among developing countries.

The government has called for a comprehensive and integrated approach to deal with the legacy of the past. This approach is best captured in the strategic objective – during this transitional period – that amounts to the social transformation of our society into a united, democratic and prosperous society. Transformation is seen as a holistic project to change the attitudes, consciousness and material conditions of our people, and in a meaningful way to reflect the values that we struggled for and are now embodied in our constitution and in the human rights culture we strive for.

The main content of this programme is the transformation of the political, economic, social, ideological and moral aspects of the apartheid dispensation. This is achieved by building a single nation that acknowledges the diversity of its people; instilling a new sense of patriotism; healing the wounds of a shameful past; liberating black people from political and economic bondage;

eradicating gender inequalities and women's oppression in particular; improving the equality of life for all through the eradication of poverty and the attainment of the basic needs of the majority; and creating a culture of democracy and human rights.

Flowing from the above, three elements of this programme, namely reconciliation, reconstruction and development, have been identified as forming the kernel of our social transformation project during the transition. Arising from this approach is the attainment of the twin goals of socio-economic justice (economic reconstruction) and the restoration of moral order in our country (moral reconstruction). They have crystallised as the two issues that have to be vigorously pursued to achieve social justice as a means of dealing with South Africa's legacy of its past. I concentrate mainly on the latter in this chapter.

One of the ways to start the healing process in South Africa is an honest assessment of the illness within our society, in an attempt to give people, both perpetrators and victims, an opportunity to face the past and its consequences and to start afresh. The creation of a truth commission offered the opportunity to deal with the past without dwelling on it and to establish the moral foundation from which to build a truly new South Africa. Hence, the genesis of the TRC.

While the TRC is a product of our country's unique history and the nature of our particular transition, we share many similarities with other transitions, especially in South America and Eastern Europe, which necessitated compromises that placed certain limitations on the final scope of our TRC. I mention but a few such issues:

- a stalemate was reached (an equilibrium in the balance of forces) with neither side an outright victor;
- a negotiated settlement ensued – not a revolutionary take-over;
- a gradual shift from a dictatorship (a minority illegitimate government) to democratic majority rule;
- a fragile democracy and a precarious national unity;
- the capacity of the outgoing regime, including the military and security forces (which commanded huge resources) to delay or derail the process or, at the very least, support and promote resistance to change;
- a legacy of oppression and serious human rights violations;
- a commitment to the attainment of a culture of democracy and human rights, and respect for the rule of law;
- a determination to avoid a recurrence of human rights violations;
- the establishment of a constitutional state (Rechtstaat), marking a shift from parliamentary sovereignty to constitutional sovereignty;

- a constitutional commitment to reconciliation and nation-building;
- a constitutional obligation placed on the new democratic parliament to provide for a process of amnesty for acts committed with a political motive, arising from the conflicts of the past.

Legal origins of the TRC

We had no option but to create the TRC. Many reasons may be cited, of which I mention but a few.

- Our call for a truth commission did not come from the constitution, or any law, but from our morality as people who want to heal our nation, and restore the faith of those in our country and the international community in our common future.
- The international community expected us to deal with our past in a way that derives its legitimacy and morality from the international human rights practice and the conventions we have agreed to adopt.
- A truth commission enables us to deal with this unfortunate part of our past in a structured and manageable way, in contrast to the alternatives of people taking the law into their own hands or Nuremberg-type trials.
- South Africans needed to create a common memory that can be recognised or acknowledged.
- The establishment of the TRC was an honourable conclusion to our shameful past. It did not take place in a vacuum. The idea – not the detail – germinated in the crucible of struggle and was born in the engine room of political negotiation. The manner in which our transition unfolded through the process of political negotiation made the establishment of a truth commission possible. I would even venture to say that the final settlement of the negotiation process, codified in the interim constitution, contained the seeds of the TRC. (The issue of a truth commission for South Africa did not come up for discussion in the negotiations process, although it did form part of public discourse at the time.)[2]

Genesis of the TRC Act

I turn to a brief analysis of a few events that form the bedrock of the historical and legal origins of the TRC, as encapsulated in the Act.

Although justice is essential for any emerging democracy, international law does not unconditionally demand the prosecution, in all instances, of violations of human rights;[3] it also permits the discussion of amnesty, in fact, in some international conventions it is not only allowed but encouraged.[4]

During most recent transitions, especially those involving a move away from a (military) dictatorship, a common scenario would be that prior to the establishment of a truth commission, the government would declare a general amnesty for those involved in all crimes during the prescribed troubled period, thus creating a situation of impunity. This removes any incentive for perpetrators to confess to violations of human rights, perpetuating a conspiracy of silence.[5] In my view, the existence of such a general amnesty has been the main reason for the hegemony of the military, security and other government forces, involved in violations, remaining virtually intact during such transitions. This enabled the military to remain outside the reconciliation processes of these countries, especially in the activities of truth commissions. The lack of acceptance of blame has meant that the issue of moral reconstruction has largely failed.

Since our transition entailed a gradual, though marked shift from one legal order to another, it necessitated the acceptance of legal continuity. In constitutional, legal and practical terms this meant that the apartheid legal order remain the law of the land, even if unconstitutional, until amended by the democratic parliament, or declared unconstitutional by the Constitutional Court. The preconditions for negotiations and subsequent negotiations thus took place within the existing legal framework of the apartheid regime. This favoured the old regime and agents of the apartheid state who would be protected from culpability if they had acted within the parameters of the apartheid legal order, such as the Police and Defence Acts. Equally, it doubly disadvantaged the liberation movements in legal terms. Not only did they not have the same (legal) protections, but the fact that apartheid laws remained intact actually criminalised some of their individual actions.

Let me illustrate this legal vulnerability with an example. Assume that before February 1990 a unit from the South African Defence Force (SADF) and Umkhonto we Sizwe (MK) were engaged in a shoot-out inside the borders of the country; one soldier from either side is killed. The SADF soldier who killed the MK soldier would have acted legally within the confines of the Defence Act, without any consequences; the MK soldier, for the same act, would be guilty of murder, could be prosecuted and should apply for amnesty. Entirely different consequences for exactly the same actions. It is only if apartheid operatives act outside of apartheid law that consequences arise and they have to apply for amnesty.

This example highlights one of the factors contributing to the hegemony of the security forces remaining intact – with nefarious activities of the past being cloaked in silence – during the period of preconditions for negotiations and the negotiations process itself. This hegemony was only broken through the TRC process, especially in respect of the police.

This compromise, involving the acceptance of the legal framework of apartheid, was made despite the fact that the liberation movements always regarded the apartheid regime and its 'legal order' as illegitimate. This compromise – without which the negotiations process would never had got off the ground – kept arising in various ways throughout the negotiations, as well as during the TRC process. The last occasion arose with the publication of the TRC report.

In 1993, the African National Congress (ANC) established a commission of enquiry (the Motsuenyane Commission) to investigate allegations of human rights violations in some of its camps that operated in exile and to determine the extent of responsibility for transgressions against its code of conduct. This commission found that human rights violations had, in fact, occurred in some instances and named the perpetrators.[6]

The National Executive Council (NEC) of the ANC recognised that violations had occurred, representing a breakdown in the chain of command that can, but should not, occur under difficult 'siege' conditions under which it operated. On behalf of the organisation, it accepted collective moral responsibility and expressed a profound sense of regret for each and every transgression, to all who suffered as a result of breaches of its norms. The report was made public and its recommendations accepted. In September 1993, the NEC took a policy decision calling for the establishment of a truth commission to investigate all the violations of human rights – killings, disappearances, torture and ill-treatment. Its role would be to identify all abuses of human rights and their perpetrators, to propose a future code of conduct for all public servants, to ensure appropriate compensation for the victims and to work out the best basis for reconciliation. In addition, it would provide a moral basis for justice and for preventing any repetition of abuses in future. The ANC emphasised that it would not be a Nuremberg tribunal. Perpetrators in its own ranks should be dealt with, together with other transgressors, within the framework of such a commission.

The establishment of the Motsuenyane Commission has been recognised internationally as an historic event, insofar as it marked the first time that a liberation movement had engaged an independent commission to investigate its own past of human rights abuses. The commission's report and the response of the ANC must thus be seen as part of the process of dealing with our past. This historic decision marked a watershed, striking a blow in favour of accountability, against the climate of impunity. Seven months before the first democratic elections, the ANC, as the government-in-waiting, had not only established a precedent, it had bound itself to dealing in the future with past violations and to do so by way of its preferred option: a truth commission.

The adoption of the interim constitution was a revolutionary break with the past. It is the legal foundation upon which all legality rests. It is a decisive break with Westminster-type parliamentary sovereignty, ushering in a constitutional state (Rechtstaat), where the constitution is supreme and committed to observing human rights and the rule of law.

It has been said by many that the interim constitution (Act No 200 of 1993) is, in fact, a peace pact reached between the minority, apartheid forces and the disenfranchised, marginalised majority lead by the ANC, in a situation where neither was defeated, yet neither was victor. As a peace pact, it is obviously an instrument of political compromise. This peace pact is most clearly captured in the unique epilogue, with the heading 'National Unity and Reconciliation', which states:

> *The constitution provides a historic bridge between the past of a deeply divided society, characterised by strife, conflict, untold suffering and injustice, and a future founded on the recognition of human rights, democracy, peaceful co-existence and development opportunities for all South Africans, irrespective of colour, race, class, creed or sex.*
>
> *The pursuit of national unity, the wellbeing of all South African citizens and peace require reconciliation between the people of South Africa and the reconstruction of society. The adoption of this constitution lays the foundation for the people of South Africa to transcend the divisions and strife of the past, which generated gross violations of human rights, the transgression of humanitarian principles in violent conflicts and a legacy of hatred, fear, guilt and revenge.*
>
> *These can now be addressed on the basis that there is a need for understanding, but not for vengeance, a need for reparation, but not for retaliation, a need for ubuntu but not for victimisation.*
>
> *In order to advance such reconciliation and reconstruction, amnesty shall be granted in respect of acts, omissions and offences associated with political objectives and committed in the course of the conflicts of the past. To this end, parliament under this constitution shall adopt a law determining a cut-off date, which shall be a date after 8 October 1990 and before 6 December 1993, and providing for the mechanisms, criteria and procedures, including tribunals, if any, through which such amnesty shall be dealt with at any time after the law has been passed.*
>
> *With this constitution and these commitments we, the people of South Africa, open a new chapter in the history of our country...*
>
> *[the Epilogue] shall not... have lesser status than any other provision of this constitution... and such provision shall for all purposes be deemed to form part of the substance of the constitution...'*

The adoption of the epilogue, on 5 December 1993, was both historic and dramatic. It was the last clause to be finalised and adopted, and marked a breakthrough on the vexed question of amnesty. The issue of amnesty became bitterly contested in the negotiation process. The call from the former government, led by FW de Klerk and the National Party, as well as the security forces, led by the generals, and supported by some in the international community, local media and business circles, was for a blanket amnesty for all protagonists in the conflicts of the past. Many prominent jurists and human rights organisations were totally opposed to any form of amnesty. This arose from a climate of impunity created by the many cases of general amnesty that have been granted in countries that are changing from dictatorship to democracy. The former government's position was totally unacceptable to the ANC, to the point that it was prepared to stall the process.

The final compromise was agreed to at the 11th hour to persuade the security forces and the extreme right wing to participate in the elections. The amnesty clause was combined with somewhat of a misnomer, the so-called 'sunset clause', which guaranteed job security for civil servants, including the police and army, for the next five years. To put it bluntly, these compromises were accepted to avoid stalling the process. It is a widely held view, by serious commentators, that without this specific compromise, there would have been no settlement, no interim constitution, no elections, no democracy and a possible continuation of the conflicts of the past.

It can be argued that the compromises, obvious or implicit, in the epilogue may form the basis of the lack of distinction between the roles of the main protagonists in the conflicts of the past. Much later, in the negotiation process, in the TRC process and when the TRC issued its 'final' Report, the interpretation of the legal consequences of these political compromises often became a bone of contention.

The South African way

The interim constitution and the historical and legal factors analysed above reflect some of the political constraints and objectives, as well as the legal parameters that our founding fathers and mothers agreed to place on us, as we forged ahead in creating a new dispensation.

The objective of the TRC was to address the legacy of the past by promoting national unity and reconciliation, to contribute to the healing of our nation. It had to do so, firstly, by developing as complete a picture as possible of the causes, nature and extent of the gross violations of human rights committed from 1 March 1960 to 10 May 1994. Secondly, it had to facilitate the granting of amnesty to persons who would make a full disclosure of all the facts relating to acts associated with a political objective. Thirdly, the TRC was required to establish and make known the whereabouts of victims, restore the human and civil dignity of survivors by giving them an opportunity to relate their own accounts of the violations they suffered, and recommend reparation measures. Fourthly, the commission was obliged to compile a report detailing its activities and findings, and recommend measures to prevent future abuses.

I now analyse firstly, the broad philosophical framework forming the foundation of the Act and the TRC and, secondly, each of three essential components.

Foundation of restorative justice

After the formal acceptance of the interim constitution at the end of 1993, we were immediately faced with the awesome responsibility of giving meaning to the constitutional commitment to genuine reconciliation and reconstruction in pursuit of national unity.

We were faced with a very critical question: was South Africa going down the road of (retributive) justice or was it seeking reconciliation as it addressed its apartheid legacy? These options at the time were presented as being mutually exclusive. The debate appeared to be centred in two camps: on the one hand, on the victims of violations seeking that alleged crimes be accounted for (avenged) by means of retributive measures; on the other hand, perpetrators seeking impunity by way of a general amnesty.

This approach was not compatible with the manner in which our transition had unfolded. We had to find a formula rooted in the need to achieve a balance between dealing with our past and finding a way forward that was in the best interests of the country as a whole. A win-win situation was called for. To secure a decent future, we had to subvert narrow, party-political, sectarian or even personal interests to a higher, nobler goal for our divided country as a whole to emerge from a shameful past as the winner. The road to the promotion of reconciliation and the pursuit of national unity had to tread a delicate balance along the precarious precipices between reconciliation and retributive justice. The challenge was how to achieve both justice and reconciliation – not just one or the other. To achieve this we had to promote a process of genuine reconciliation in our country within the context of attaining social justice through transforming our country into a united, nonracial, nonsexist, prosperous democracy, based on a human rights culture.

In our country, therefore, reconciliation is pivotal to the process of bringing justice to all, but not justice in its narrowest sense, the kind that demands trial and punishment. Rather, there has to be justice, but justice in its broadest sense – collective justice, social justice, a restorative justice that seeks to address and deliver to the collective – that is aimed at nation-building and reconciliation. It is a justice that focuses on the future, rather than the past; on understanding, rather than vengeance; on reparation, rather than retaliation; on *ubuntu*, rather than victimisation. To do this we had to avoid the constraints of retributive justice. We had to broaden our perception of justice beyond punishment. We had to look at the fate of victims and the whole political and social framework in which the violations took place. We had to balance justice and reconciliation.

The secret to unlocking this South African model lies, to a large measure, in the approach adopted in the handling of the amnesty issue. It is very important, therefore, to understand the distinction between the component of the TRC that investigates human rights violations and the component dealing with the amnesty process. Although they are to some extent inter-dependent, the amnesty component derives its authority from the constitution, whereas the human rights component claims its authority from our morality, our humanity. The latter is victim-driven, the former perpetrator-driven.

The process of granting amnesty to perpetrators of violations is perpetrator-driven and could have the effect of once again marginalising the suffering of countless victims – a win-lose scenario. Therefore, the granting of amnesty, without dealing with the wounds of the past and our duty to victims, and without addressing our international obligations, will undermine the process of reconciliation. It would be imperative, then, that we deal with the legacy of our brutal past, together with the question of amnesty, on a morally acceptable basis. While the constitutional requirement must be met, the issue of restoring the dignity of victims must also be addressed – a win-win scenario.

The answer will ultimately be found in accommodating amnesty in a delicate manner, within a truth commission that has a victim-centred approach. Individual victims and our society as a whole could not continue to carry the burden of atrocities without acknowledgement. Amnesty would have to address the plight of victims and survivors, but this too had to be addressed in a broader context, for the sake of political imperatives. The wounds inflicted by apartheid would continue to fester for generations to come, if there was no acknowledgement or exposure and coming to terms with the pain and suffering caused by apartheid. We had to provide for an individualised amnesty process that would acknowledge and respect the victim. It had to be a balanced amnesty process that retained, at least, a minimum threshold of accountability of past violators, acknowledgement of the victims, and public sanction and opprobrium. Between the requirement for amnesty and the need to find a victim-centred approach lay the balance. To put it bluntly, we could never build a nation and promote national unity without some form of acknowledgement from perpetrators, which would lead to reconciliation.

Restorative justice is essentially a forward-looking and inclusive process. It allows for the building of reconciliation through the joint process of satisfying the interim constitution by granting amnesty, where appropriate and after full disclosure, while allowing the people who have carried the terrible burden of suffering and grief to come forward and speak to the nation. As the then Deputy President of the Constitutional Court, Justice Mohamed, so poignantly captured this despair and hope:

> *The Act seeks to address this massive problem by encouraging survivors, and the dependants of the tortured and the wounded, the maimed and the dead, to unburden their grief publicly, to receive the recognition that they were wronged and, crucially, to help them discover what did in truth happen to their loved ones, where and under what circumstances it happened, and who was responsible ... With (the amnesty) incentive, what might unfold are objectives fundamental to the ethos of a new constitutional order.*[7]

In the process we have done something quite unique. As the former Minister of Transport, Mac Maharaj, eloquently puts it:

> *We have taken the concept of justice in its broadest sense and found a formulation that meets the specific requirements of our country – a formulation that contains a strong element of restorative justice, while limiting retribution to public exposure and shame to be faced by the perpetrators, whose names and deeds are becoming known.*[8]

Twin goals are achieved: providing victims with a soft place to deal with hard issues and providing perpetrators with a hard place to receive soft(er) results. For the perpetrator, it may be 'softer' justice, but they would remain between a rock and a hard place with the need for full public acknowledgement. In the process, justice is not only being done – it is seen to be done. It is restorative justice in its essence, but also contains essential elements of retributive justice in that the truth is told, lies are exposed and the perpetrators are becoming known. It may not be perfect justice – justice does not exist in its perfect state and compromises have to be made for the greater collective good.

Although the final formula arrived at was uniquely South African, it was the product of an extensive examination and application of solutions to our peculiar transition. The final formula, at best, has created a unique model that has charted a possible middle road between the reconciliation versus the justice model dichotomy or, at least, a unique variant of either model. For want of a better phrase, it is a restorative justice model or a social justice model, being an innovative hybrid of all those essential elements of both the reconciliation and justice models. In the process, South Africa has developed a new model for dealing with state criminality, choosing a path between the extremes of full-scale prosecutions and general amnesty.

I will now analyse the threefold combination of (a) the 'amnesty carrot': the perpetrator-driven incentive of amnesty in return for full and truthful public acknowledgement of politically motivated violations; and (b) the 'TRC (investigations of human rights violations) stick': the victim-driven possibility of being named publicly as an alleged perpetrator and investigated under wide investigative powers; and (c) the 'judicial sledgehammer': the justice-driven possibility of ongoing prosecutions until amnesty is granted. These components formed a potent triad designed as a creative multi-pronged approach for attainment of truth, by flushing out violators of human rights who adopted a 'wait-and-see' approach and to break the usual hegemony and conspiracy of silence, which is endemic in security forces operating under authoritarian rule.

Amnesty component

The South African formulation is an entirely new creation, which has no parallel in other societies in transition and contains various unique features. Amnesty comes into question only when a crime is established in an individual case, on personal application and with the cooperation of the perpetrator. It is a two-stage process before the Amnesty Committee: in the first stage, criminal liability is established and, in the second, when appropriate, amnesty is granted if there has been full disclosure and the criteria in the Act (based on the Norgaard principles – see Endnotes 17.19, p299) have been met. Victims have certain statutory protected rights in respect of the amnesty process. In accordance with a constitutional right to remain silent, the Act provides a criminal-procedural protection for the amnesty applicant under which evidence that may incriminate is later made inadmissible in court.

Another unique feature is that the Amnesty Committee has the sole discretion to decide whether the statutory requirements have been met. There is no possibility of appeal, only the possibility of review by a court of law, from cases decided by it.

In this process the relationship between truth and reconciliation is sensitively balanced: the perpetrators must personally apply in the prescribed form within a certain time limit; appear at a public hearing; make a full, public confession; comply with the (Norgaard) criteria for amnesty; recognise the wrongfulness of the deed, in public; and acknowledge the truth. The crime is condemned legally and publicly, the report is published and the parties named. The full disclosure of a violation by the criminal replaces the need for punishment, if it is found that all the requirements have been met. In the context of a system in transition this connection between amnesty and disclosure is innovative. One commentator has observed that it is a solution that is 'both politically intelligent and legally workable'.

There is a further important reason for dealing with the amnesty question within this broader framework. It is necessary for restoring the moral order, particularly in respect of the legal issue and the institutions administering justice. It is necessary after the apartheid depravity to re-establish the primacy of the rule of law and the principle of accountability. This precondition is central to the credibility, legitimacy and efficacy of the justice system, as well as the success of the criminal justice system, the fight against crime and corruption, and to put an end to the prevailing sense of impunity.[9]

The investigation of human rights violations component

This component (to be referred to as the HRVC) focused on the victims of gross human rights violations, as defined in the Act, namely killing, kidnapping, severe ill-treatment and torture. Therefore, it was not intended to deal with the many wrongs of the past, but only the above-mentioned physical human rights violations, during a specified time period.

The HRVC in its composition, functioning and *modus operandi* should be focused on all the victims in our country and create a safe place where they can come in a dignified manner to deal with very hard issues – like their own personal pain. Therefore, the HVRC had to allow victims to tell their stories in the language of their choice, the aim being to record not only the truth of our disturbing past, but, more importantly, to restore the human and civil dignity of those victims. In turn, once we have examined the extent and the circumstances of the victims, a regulatory framework must be established by parliament through which we can address reparations and the rehabilitation of victims, where the emphasis is not on compensation.

Another unique feature of our TRC is the extensive powers of subpoena, and search and seizure vested in it, allowing it to act in a proactive way. If perpetrators adopt a 'wait and see' attitude regarding the 'amnesty carrot', then the TRC may use its 'TRC stick' of search, seizure or subpoena to flush out perpetrators or obtain information pertaining to violations.

The (restorative and retributive) justice component

What then of justice? The instinctive response of most people is that crime deserves punishment. In an ideal world, those responsible for repression and violations should be prosecuted, brought to trial before a court of law and, if convicted, serve the punishment. But let us for a moment contemplate the unimaginable. What would have happened if in 1994 we followed the route of Nuremberg-type trials; or the Argentina-type selective prosecutions of prominent apartheid politicians (such as PW Botha or FW de Klerk), or senior generals in the army, police or intelligence services (such as Constand Viljoen, Johan van der Merwe or Neil Barnard); or we had sought solutions through the conventional courts? In the light of my above analysis, any of these variants of the justice model would not only have been most inappropriate to follow but in some instances would have been dangerously irresponsible. I list but a few further reasons.

■ The legal system and the Commission were meant to be complementary and work in tandem, with the latter compensating for the limitations of the former. In the reconciliation versus justice debate, a fundamental aspect that is often forgotten is an analysis of the 'hidden' effects of the positioning of the Commission between the triad (*trias politicas*) of the justice system, the legislature and the executive. The Commission has an ambivalent relationship to the legal order: it is not a legal institution in that it is not constituted as a court of law; it does not determine individual criminal liability or order criminal sanctions. On the one hand, the Commission can bypass the legal process, in clearly defined legal situations, by naming perpetrators before they have been convicted and by granting amnesty before a perpetrator has been through the trial process and convicted. On the other hand, despite the existence of the Commission, the role of our courts and the prosecuting authority within the criminal justice system remains firmly in place.

The TRC, particularly in the incentive of individualised amnesty, must be seen as a one-off window of opportunity in a magnanimous gesture by the nation when perpetrators can voluntarily come forward and confess all. The message is clear: if you do not use this opportunity, do not expect further sympathy from the nation.

Some commentators seem to miss the point that the justice system remained intact and unaffected before, during and after this opportunity; criminal and civil jurisdiction are only ousted once amnesty has been granted. Until that point, it is the duty of the police to investigate and pursue each past violation of human rights; it is the duty of the prosecuting authority to continue prosecutions; and it is the duty of the courts to complete trials. At the same time, prosecutions during the life of the Commission – as illustrated with the trials of De Kock, Niewoudt, Coetzee, Basson and others – fed directly into the TRC process by convincing many wavering perpetrators that they were on their own and that it would be in their best interests to testify, in the hope of gaining amnesty.

- The Nuremberg tribunal was an exceptional case in history: a transitional situation marked by total military victory or defeat, depending from which perspective one looks at it. It is important to note, however, that this model has never been repeated since 1946. In any case, even if feasible, the political consequences of Nuremberg-type trials could have had calamitous consequences for peace in our country.[10]

- There was a high degree of continuity in state institutions in its structures and organisations, especially with regard to personnel. This problem manifests itself in two ways. In the first place, a lingering 'apartheid memory' continues to restrict the development of trust and allegiance in the new political dispensation and its institutions. The day after the election, the same persons who served the apartheid regime became the implementers of our new human rights culture. If we had followed this route, it would have meant that we would have handed the investigation of apartheid atrocities – in the case of the police and the security forces – back to the same people who now admit publicly that they were responsible for vile deeds. If they could not solve these cases before the elections, because they were deeply implicated, why would they be able to do so afterwards? In the second place, the whole legal order, especially the criminal justice system, suffers from a serious crisis of credibility, legitimacy and efficacy. This was as a result of the apartheid law and the persons whose task it was to uphold and implement it. Because of this, perceptions of the previously disenfranchised, mostly black communities regarding the judiciary and magistracy have been adversely affected.

   What chance would we have had of competent, honest, professional investigations, prosecutions and trials in such an environment? How much truth would we have uncovered with perpetrators conducting the investigations? How many convictions would we have seen? The unsuccessful trial of the former Minister of Defence, Magnus Malan, who refused to apply for amnesty and whose defence was paid for by the state, is an apt reminder of the frustration that such a process entails.

- Even a healthy, professional criminal justice system would simply not have the capacity to cope with the sheer volume of unresolved human rights violations committed over a period of 34 years.

- Ordinary criminal and civil courts, inquests and commissions of enquiry do not necessarily discover the truth. Civil and criminal processes are prohibitively expensive, slow, limited in scope and even predictable. The ordinary rules of evidence in a court of law often serve to exclude, rather than admit, information. The mere threat of a civil claim or criminal prosecution often produces an impenetrable screen of lawyer-driven obfuscation.

The justice system, therefore, often inhibits the achievements of many of the benefits of truthfulness. Yet, the most important human factor is the hurt and humiliation that many have suffered, and the inability of courts or inquests to bring some relief to that hurt or humiliation.

- The indisputable facts remain that although in the recent past there were signs, internationally, that the number of prosecutions for past violations of human rights in transition situations are slightly on the rise, it is more the exception than the rule to prosecute and punish those responsible for abuses. Furthermore, in most instances where persons have been prosecuted, they have benefited from amnesty deals, pardons, early release from prison or, at least, suspension of further prosecutions. In most instances where prosecutions do occur, a minority of perpetrators are brought to trial; trials end inconclusively due to inadequate evidence; only the 'foot soldiers' are usually put on trial, not the top echelons of the dictatorship; and the number of persons involved in abuses is far too great to bring to trial.

Conclusion

While the focus of the TRC was on seeking the truth in order to restore the moral order, serious delays in the improvement of the quality of life threaten any attempts at reconciliation. If we do not deliver on economic justice, then no matter how reconciliatory we are or whether we know the complete truth about our past or not, the whole South African liberation project could be put in jeopardy, with social and political upheaval. Revealing the complete truth of our shameful past, without achieving economic justice or, conversely, attaining economic justice without revealing the complete truth spell failure and even disaster. This is anathema for transformation.

The TRC is but one mechanism we have pursued to enable us to address moral issues of our past and, in particular, various forms of physical violence we unleashed on each other. It is important to stress that reconciliation, reconstruction and development are a process. The TRC is not meant to equal reconciliation. The TRC cannot bring reconciliation *per se* – it can only create a space to facilitate the process. The TRC's importance is that it came at the beginning of the process. It was the first time that a South African government – the democratic one – through the creation of the TRC acknowledged that terrible wrongs had been done to its people, mainly by the old government, and provided them with a state-instituted mechanism, independently managed and controlled by civil society.

Same species, different animal: how South Africa compares to truth commissions worldwide

PRISCILLA HAYNER

In late 1996, Yasmin Sooka, a member of the South African Truth and Reconciliation Commission (TRC), travelled to Guatemala to speak about the first year of the Commission's experience. The Guatemalan government and armed opposition had agreed to set up a truth commission when their civil war came to an end and they thought they might learn from the South African experience. To be called the 'Historical Clarification Commission', the Guatemalan commission was instructed to look into hundreds of massacres and an estimated 150 000 to 200 000 killings or disappearances during the country's 36-year war.[1] But the powers, investigative methodology and the truth-seeking process expected of the Guatemalan commission was so vastly different from what was being played out in South Africa, that Yasmin Sooka had a difficult task in trying to describe the South African commission.

Guatemalans had, of course, heard about the South African truth commission, as it received news coverage worldwide, but its powers and practices were radically different to the Guatemalan experience. Hundreds of public and televised hearings, where victims and perpetrators took the stand to describe past atrocities? Survivors directly questioning their former perpetrators, in public, even about the exact details of torture and other abuses? An individualised application process for perpetrators to receive amnesty? The power of the Commission to subpoena any individual to give testimony, and to search premises and seize evidence as necessary? None of these elements were included in the Guatemalan truth commission's mandate, nor were they even considered when the terms of the commission were negotiated.

In general terms, the Guatemalan commission shared much with other Latin American truth commissions: it was mandated to collect testimony from victims and witnesses, in private, over six to 12 months (it eventually extended to 18 months), and to prepare a final report summarising its findings. As was true of earlier truth commissions, such as those in El Salvador, Chile and Argentina, the commission was given no subpoena or search and seizure powers, held no formal connection to any amnesty arrangement, and could hope to obtain perpetrators' stories only through the voluntary cooperation and good will of individuals invited to give testimony. But Guatemalan human rights and victims organisations were disappointed about other limitations that were written into the commission's mandate, which seemed to weaken it even further, especially the fact that the commission was forbidden to 'individualise responsibility' and that its work was not to have any 'judicial aim or effect'.[2]

Because the South African commission has received so much international attention, other countries considering truth commissions have been turning to South Africa as their model. When the Prime Minister of Cambodia, Hun Sen, first expressed interest in a truth commission in early 1999, he referred to the South African TRC and announced that he intended inviting Desmond Tutu to Phnom Penh for a visit. Likewise, when various organisations and political actors in Sierra Leone, Nigeria, Lesotho and Indonesia proposed creating a truth commission in their respective countries, in 1998 and 1999, they have often described their interest in setting up a 'South African-like truth commission'. In part, South Africa is the main reference point for new truth commissions, because it is by far the best known of such commissions to date. Its extraordinary public hearings, revelations and political reverberations were covered in the news in virtually every country in the world, and captured the imagination and admiration of many transitional, political and civil society leaders worldwide. But those who refer to that commission as their model probably have several aspects of the commission in mind, which reached beyond most other commissions: a public process of disclosure by perpetrators and public hearings for victims; an amnesty process that reviewed individual applications and avoided any blanket amnesty; and a process that was intensely focused on national healing and reconciliation, with the intent of moving a country from its repressive past to a peaceful future, where former opponents could work side by side.

Each of these three aspects of the South African commission – the hearings, the amnesty process and the emphasis on healing and reconciliation – could be criticised for falling short of their original aims, in part due to political constraints and the limitations of any short-lived process, and in part due to decisions taken by the Commission itself. Victims in South Africa have been disappointed that the Commission did not fully investigate every case, did not accommodate everyone who wanted to appear in a public hearing, and granted amnesty to unrepentant perpetrators, while failing to attract some key actors to apply for amnesty. But those observing the Commission from outside the country were less aware of these frustrations or limitations, and the revelations in South Africa certainly looked quite attractive, compared to the fear, silence, lies and impunity of many countries coming out of a repressive past. Despite the attraction, the South African truth commission may not be the appropriate model for many other states – in fact, the mandate and operation of the Guatemalan commission was much closer to the norm and may have more elements that are more appropriate to other countries. But regardless of whether a South African-like truth commission process can be repeated elsewhere, or whether elements might be borrowed for other national circumstances, there are many unique qualities of the South African Commission that should be recognised.

An increasing interest in truth commissions worldwide

Truth commissions have been multiplying rapidly around the world and gaining increasing attention in recent years.[3] Although there have been 20 such bodies in the past 25-odd years, many have received very little international attention – such as those in Chad, Sri Lanka, Uganda and the Philippines – despite considerable attention from the press and public at the national level. Others, such as the United Nations-sponsored Commission on the Truth in El Salvador, which finished in 1993; the Chilean National Commission on Truth and Reconciliation, completed in 1991; and the Commission on the Disappeared in Argentina, which published its report in 1984, have received much international attention and helped to shape new commissions elsewhere.

The increased interest in truth commissions is, in part, a reflection of the limited success in judicial approaches to accountability, and the obvious need for other measures to recognise past wrongs and confront, punish or reform those persons and institutions that were responsible for violations. Successful prosecutions of perpetrators of massive atrocities have been few, as under-resourced and often politically compromised judicial systems struggle to confront such politically contentious crimes. With an eye on building a human rights culture for the future, many new governments have turned to mechanisms outside the judicial system to confront, as well as learn from the horrific crimes of the past.

Transitional truth-seeking bodies have become much more common in the 1990s. Only in the last few years have these bodies been studied comparatively and, with the conclusion of the El Salvador Commission on the Truth in 1993, referred to generically as 'truth commissions'. As officially sanctioned commissions, these bodies investigate and document a pattern of abuses in the past, leaving recommendations for the prevention of such abuses in the future. While they go by many different names, these bodies share certain common elements and are created for similar purposes. By 'truth commission', a fairly specific kind of investigatory commission is inferred. I point to four identifying characteristics. Firstly, a truth commission is focused on the past. Secondly, it does not investigate a singular event, but the record of abuses over a period of time (often highlighting a few cases to demonstrate and describe patterns or large numbers of abuses). Thirdly, a truth commission is a temporary body, generally concluding with the submission of a report. And finally, a truth commission is somehow officially sanctioned by the government (and/or by the opposition, where relevant) to investigate the past. This official sanction gives the commission more power, as well as access to information, protection to undertake investigations, with a greater likelihood that its conclusions and recommendations will be given serious consideration. Truth commissions can thus be distinguished from other human rights inquiries, such as those undertaken by national or international nongovernmental organisations (NGOs) or special inquiries into a specific event.

We should expect differences between commissions, as each country must shape a process out of its own historical, political and cultural context. Unlike courts, which generally stand as permanent bodies, and about which there are many international norms regarding their appropriate structure, powers, and the minimal standards under which their proceedings should be undertaken, there are many aspects of truth commissions that will vary from country to country.

Of course, those preparing the groundwork for the truth commission in South Africa were aware of many of the previous truth commissions, as well as other transitional mechanisms (such as lustration in Eastern Europe) that had been put in place around the world. South Africa very consciously reached out to persons, who had played pivotal roles in Chile, El Salvador, Argentina, Germany and elsewhere, bringing a number of central actors to Cape Town in 1994 for two international conferences to discuss transitional justice options. These conferences contributed to some of the ideas that eventually helped shape the South African Truth and Reconciliation Commission.

How South Africa stands apart

The South African Truth and Reconciliation Commission can be distinguished from other truth commissions in a number of ways, especially in the powers vested in the Commission, including its amnesty-granting power; the quality of public hearings; the manner in which the terms of the commission were crafted; and the overriding focus on reconciliation as a primary goal of its work.

Powers

The most striking difference between the South African Commission and other truth commissions is found in one of the most prominent and controversial aspects of its work: its power to grant amnesty to individual perpetrators. No other country has combined this quasi-judicial power with the investigative tasks of an administrative truth-seeking body. While this amnesty-granting power has been controversial, and a disappointment to many victims, it is a far greater improvement over the unconditional blanket amnesties that have been put in place in many other countries, especially in Latin America. Such blanket amnesties require no individual identification of crimes or perpetrators, usually preventing any judicial action on all human rights abuses that took place prior to the date the amnesty was granted. The South African process, in contrast, turned the amnesty application process into a tool to uncover details of past crimes, making South Africa the first country in the world to hear detailed testimony about crimes directly from the perpetrators themselves.[4]

Because other commissions have not had the power to grant amnesty to perpetrators, there has been few incentives for perpetrators to come forward with their stories. The detailed accounts that have emerged directly from perpetrators in South Africa contrast sharply with elsewhere, where commissions have received very little cooperation from those responsible for past abuses or those affiliated with institutions implicated in abuses. In Argentina and Chile, for example, only a few perpetrators came forward to provide information, and then only under a shield of confidentiality. In addition, South Africa joins just three or four other truth commissions that have chosen to publish in their final report the names of those found to be responsible for abuses.

In addition to its amnesty component, the TRC held other powers that were much stronger than those of other truth commissions to date: its subpoena power, and broad search and seizure powers have not been seen elsewhere, for example. Only a few other commissions have held the power of subpoena (such as Sri Lanka and Uganda); most commissions have had considerable difficulty obtaining information they knew was in the hands of the government or armed forces.

The TRC's investigative powers were also strengthened by a fairly sophisticated witness protection programme, a first among truth commissions, which allowed fearful witnesses to come forward with information that might put them at risk. Finally, the staff size and budget of the TRC set it apart from other such commissions, as its budget was several times larger than any other truth commissions before it.

The TRC was also the first truth commission to have its powers or operations challenged in court. The TRC has been challenged in court a number of times, resulting, for example, in a Constitutional Court approval of the amnesty provision, in one case, and a court-directed requirement to provide sufficient advance notification to those who were to be accused in public of committing abuses, in another. The Commission itself also took the stand against PW Botha when he was charged for refusing to abide by a subpoena to appear before the Commission.

Process

The very public process of the South African Commission also stands out from most other commissions to date. A few truth commissions have held public hearings for victims to give testimony, but in far fewer numbers. In Uganda, for example, the commission heard all testimony in public, although it heard from only a few hundred witnesses in total. In the first years of that commission's work, its hearings were broadcast live on the radio and earned a wide following and enthusiastic public response. But as the commission's work wore on for a number of years, it lost the intense interest of the public.

In Sri Lanka, a commission on persons who had disappeared began to hold hearings in public, and received considerable press coverage, but decided to close its doors after deponents received threats after providing testimony. In contrast, most other truth commissions have taken testimony only in private. In those cases, information from the commissions' investigations emerged only with the release of the final commission report. These confidential processes of collecting testimony thus cannot engage the public in a process of reflection over the course of its work, depending entirely on the effect of the final report to attract attention and public review. In this sense, the TRC in South Africa was much more focused on the process of gathering the truth and engaging the public in confronting the hard facts about the past, where other commissions have focused almost exclusively on producing a final report, providing almost no window into the truth-seeking process itself, except for those who have chosen to give testimony.

The Commission in South Africa included other aspects of inquiry not seen elsewhere, such as the sectoral and institution-focused hearings on churches, the medical establishment, the press, the business sector and other areas. These hearings opened the Commission to direct input from NGOs, policy advocates and other observers, who have monitored patterns of abuses in the past or who had proposals for policy improvements for the future. The heavy involvement of NGOs in advocating improved Commission policies and practices, and helping to introduce the Commission to local communities, was a great strength of South Africa, even while the Commission itself resisted some of NGO criticism, and did not make full use of NGO offers of assistance. The transparent working style of the Commission, together with the public hearings, allowed NGOs to monitor the Commission's work closely. In comparison, other commissions have typically held very few press conferences during the course of their work, if any at all, and gave no information to the public about what investigations were to be undertaken. While NGOs in other countries have often submitted cases from their files to increase the testimony received directly by the commissions, and sometimes have been consulted as the commission designed its recommendations, they have usually been much less involved in the ongoing work of the commission. In no other country, for example, has a truth commission accepted victim statements collected by NGOs as primary information for its database of violations.

Crafting of terms

The final shape of the South African TRC resulted from the year or so that was spent drafting its terms, including releasing drafts of the legislation for comment, holding hundreds of hours of public hearings in parliament on the proposed terms, and incorporating some of the key comments of the many national NGOs that pushed for strong terms. Without this process, the mandate of the Commission would surely have been much weaker, as would have been the political and public support for the Commission. Despite the more than one year delay in starting work, the South African Commission benefited greatly from this process of inviting input. Likewise, the open selection process of commissioners, where candidates were interviewed in public sessions, is strikingly different from other countries, where most commissioners have been appointed by the president or legislature with no opportunity for public nomination or review.

Most truth commissions to date have been created without the opportunity for public debate on their terms. Many have been established through presidential decree, with an incoming president appointing the commissioners and dictating the commission's mandate without much consultation, outside of his or her own close advisors. While presidentially appointed commissions have the advantage of being established quickly and avoiding the political infighting that may result from a weak or split legislature, they usually do not begin their work with broad public or political backing, or even a full understanding of the public for their mission. In Argentina and Chile, for example, the new civilian presidents decided that passing national legislation in Congress would either take too long or require too many compromises. Both countries independently created their commissions as one of their first official acts, taking advantage of the initial wave of public support for the civilian government and, especially in Argentina, the reduced power of the armed forces. The commissions in Haiti, Sri Lanka, Chad and Uganda were also put in place through presidential action with little public debate on terms.

A few truth commissions in the past have also been created through national legislation, as in South Africa. In addition, there are now two examples of truth commissions created through a negotiated peace accord – in El Salvador and Guatemala. In El Salvador, the peace negotiations worked out terms to the mandate, and gained the support and signatures of the parties to the talks, before most outsiders even knew it was being discussed. In contrast, those at the Guatemalan peace talks were under intense pressure from human rights and victims groups, which organised far in advance to push for a strong truth commission.[5]

Reconciliation

The degree of emphasis on reconciliation as a goal of truth-seeking has varied greatly between commissions. Not all truth commissions have framed their work around this goal, neither have they presumed that reconciliation would naturally result. Those that have – including South Africa's TRC and the National Commission on Truth and Reconciliation in Chile – have found it to be a very difficult mission.

A distinction, of course, should be made between individual reconciliation and national or political reconciliation. The strength of a truth commission is usually in advancing reconciliation on a national or political level. By speaking openly and publicly about past, silenced events, and by allowing an independent commission to clear up high-profile cases, a commission can ease some of the strains that may otherwise be present in national, legislative or other political bodies. An official accounting and conclusion of the facts can allow opposing parties to debate and govern together without there being latent conflict and bitterness over past lies. This is not to suggest that the knowledge or memory of past practices should not influence current politics, but if basic issues continue to be a source of bitterness, political relationships may be strained. In a negotiated transition out of civil war, these latent tensions may be of special concern, as opponents can move quickly from the battlefield to the floor of congress.

On an individual level, however, reconciliation is much more complex and difficult to achieve by means of a national commission. There certainly are examples of a truth commission process leading directly to individual healing and forgiveness for some individuals, but knowing the global truth, or even the specific truth about one's own case, will not necessarily lead to a victim's reconciliation with his or her perpetrators. Forgiveness, healing and reconciliation are deeply personal processes, and each person's needs and reactions to peacemaking and truth-telling may be radically different.

But from even before its inception, South Africa's TRC was presented as a way to reconcile a fractured nation and heal the wounds of its troubled soul. The message from the Commission was clear, setting the public's expectation on the hope that reconciliation would actually be reached in the course of the Commission's two-and-a-half years of operation – even while the meaning of the term was never clearly defined. By implication, victims and survivors understood the message to be directed at them, as asking them to reconcile with their perpetrators, which led to frustration, even anger, from those who would not or could not forgive quite so easily, or who first requested a sincere apology and perhaps symbolic reparation from the wrongdoer. As might be expected, with such an emphasis on reconciliation, the commission's success was judged in part on whether and how much 'reconciliation' was perceived to have resulted from its work, and in its last months, especially, was criticised for its lack of success.

In contrast to South Africa and Chile, some truth commissions in the past have not assumed that reconciliation would be achieved in the course of their work. For example, in Argentina the term is almost never used, and most people have firmly rejected the idea of 'reconciling' with those responsible for widescale torture, disappearance and terror. In fact, the only person to talk of reconciliation in Argentina was President Carlos Menem, who in 1990 cited it as the reason for awarding pardon to the military leaders then serving time in jail for their crimes under the military regime.[6] Likewise, the commissions on forced removals and disappearances in Sri Lanka did not suggest that reconciliation or forgiveness would result from their work – they saw their task more simply as documenting who had disappeared and recommending reparations to their families. To suggest individual reconciliation in Sri Lanka would have been unreasonable, rights advocates said, since not one perpetrator in Sri Lanka had stepped forward to express regret or even acknowledge responsibility. Instead of asking for forgiveness, the Sri Lankan commissions called for justice in the courts and presented the names of the accused to prosecutors for further action.

Part of the reconciliation focus that was so prominent in South Africa resulted from the religious overtone to its work. Archbishop Desmond Tutu's personal perspective, priorities, personality and moral authority created an emphasis on reconciliation heavily influenced by Christian values, an impression perhaps strengthened by the religious background of the Deputy Chair, Alex Boraine, and made explicit in the various church services that welcomed the Commission around the country. Perhaps the ramifications of this approach, and the positive, as well as limiting influence of this religious tone, have not yet been fully appreciated. However, it is a striking difference when the TRC is compared to other commissions that have generally been regarded more as legal, technical or historical investigations, with very little suggestion of a process rooted in religious convictions.

Conclusion

With such fundamental differences between the South African Truth Commission and those elsewhere, the TRC begins to look like a very different kind of process. But despite the great differences, the South African Commission shared many similarities with other truth commissions, and was created with similar motivations in mind. The experience around the world shows that a legacy of past abuse does not fade quickly from memory. Official measures to address these abuses can at least begin to remove the pain and anger emerging from the past, and truth commissions, if done well, can help to remove the silence and denial about these unspeakable crimes, and put in place measures to prevent their ever happening again.

As important and powerful as a truth-seeking process can be, however, South Africa has learnt first-hand what was already evident elsewhere: that knowing the truth is never enough. South Africa's past is as present as it was before the Commission began. But recognising the importance and permanence of this legacy is yet another manner of honouring those who suffered from illegitimate violence, and recognising the importance of building safeguards for the future. In the end, finding and knowing the truth should be seen as just one step towards a long-term goal of learning from history and keeping memory alive.

Justice without punishment: guaranteeing human rights in transitional societies

PAUL VAN ZYL

As the millennium approaches, societies across the world are reviewing past human rights abuses with renewed vigour. The agreement to establish an International Criminal Court (ICC) is indicative of the world's determination to deal justly with the past. It is a cause for celebration that the majority of nations resolved to create a court to pursue criminal accountability for gross violations of human rights. But there is a hidden danger too. Prosecution and punishment, however important, should not be viewed as the only, or even the most important, means to end impunity. If we confine to courts the struggle to guarantee human rights, we ignore many other important initiatives designed to assist victims, rebuild societies and defend democracies.

In this chapter I hope to offer an approach to dealing with the past that is not concerned solely with prosecutions. I do so for a number of reasons. Firstly, the debate in international law regarding state obligations in the wake of mass violations has tended to focus too much on the 'duty to prosecute',[1] with the unfortunate consequence of neglecting the exploration of other strategies. Secondly, the ICC at some stage will have to rule on the permissibility of amnesties or other mechanisms that fall short of ensuring full accountability for past crimes. My view is that it should not focus solely on prosecutions, but should rather take cognisance of the full spectrum of state initiatives designed to end impunity. Thirdly, because transitional societies invariably confront political and practical difficulties in attempting to prosecute perpetrators, the law cannot ignore this reality and must seek to encourage credible alternatives, rather than simply condemn, when punishment is realistically not possible. Otherwise, the law will be increasingly ignored and cease to encourage appropriate state conduct. Under 'Legitimate grounds for failing to prosecute' I outline two reasons why a society may legitimately decide not to prosecute those responsible for human rights abuse. Under 'Dealing with the past – state obligations under international law' I present an overview of a state's international obligations in dealing with a legacy of human rights abuse. In this section I also discuss the conditions under which it may be possible to derogate from these obligations. Under 'Transitional justice – a framework for judicial review' I suggest a framework for judicial review of state violations in the wake of gross violations of human rights.

Legitimate grounds for failing to prosecute

There are two legitimate reasons why a successor government may be unable to prosecute those responsible for human rights abuses during the tenure of a prior regime. The first reason is that the security forces[2] under the control of the previous regime may be so powerful that any attempt to prosecute them or their political allies could lead to one or more of the following:

- a refusal to allow a transition to democracy;
- a return to military rule or a *coup d'etat*;
- an outbreak or resumption of hostilities;
- the killing of civilians or political opponents;
- significant damage to the country's economy and infrastructure.

In assessing the legitimacy of this reason, it is important to realise that a successor regime may decide not to prosecute for a number of illegitimate reasons, which include excessive timidity, an interest in preserving the power and prerequisites associated with political office, a desire to conceal its own involvement in human rights abuses, and a willingness to pander to political or economic elites.

Nevertheless, in many circumstances militaries do present substantial and genuine threats to established democratic governments and to society as a whole. It would be irresponsible to demand the prosecution of perpetrators if this would lead to the loss of hundreds of lives or result in significant damage to a country's economy or infrastructure. In such cases, successor governments may, for principled reasons, elect not to prosecute so as to avoid a widespread loss of life or massive social and economic disruption.

A second legitimate reason a state may choose not to prosecute is that insuperable practical difficulties may make it impossible to punish more than a small percentage of those responsible for human rights violations. A combination of the scale and nature of past crimes, an absence of evidence and a dysfunctional criminal justice system may prevent a state from punishing. These practical realities, when they are realities, must be acknowledged by bodies, including the International Criminal Court, because too often successor regimes are held to have violated their 'obligation' to punish in circumstances where it was impossible to do so. Specifically, newly established regimes often confront the following practical difficulties when attempting to prosecute.

They often inherit criminal justice systems that are practically inoperative. This may be because perpetrators have deliberately murdered personnel, such as judges and prosecutors, to prevent future accountability.[3] In certain countries, criminal justice systems were created in a climate of oppression and human rights abuses. Law enforcement personnel were trained and authorised to employ methods of evidence-gathering, prosecuting and adjudicating that would be impermissible in a constitutional democracy.[4] It may be necessary to re-train virtually the entire police force before it can play an effective role in dealing with crime under a democratic dispensation.[5]

Furthermore, in some cases those who staff the criminal justice systems retain a strong institutional loyalty to the old regime and, therefore, cannot be relied upon to prosecute its operatives. In some cases the very individuals charged with investigating political crimes were involved in, or complicit with, the commission of such crimes. It may take many years before sufficient numbers of new recruits are trained to undertake this task.

Transitions from repressive rule are regularly accompanied by enormous social, economic and political change. These changes may result in significant social upheaval and dislocation and in many instances lead to a dramatic increase in crime.[6] Successor regimes are often unable to cope with current crime and may run the risk of being overwhelmed by lawlessness if they divert significant resources to attempt to solve political crimes, many of which occurred up to 15 years earlier.[7]

In many transitional societies there are insufficient skills and resources to solve ordinary crime committed by common criminals. It is, therefore, almost impossible to solve crimes committed by highly trained security force operatives skilled in covert operations and expert in concealing evidence. It is equally hard to prosecute political leaders, who provided general authorisation for such crimes. In many cases the leadership of repressive regimes issued ambiguous orders to the security forces, thereby enabling them to 'plausibly deny' that they authorised or condoned human rights abuse.[8]

Most post-transition societies are in economic crisis or face significant economic challenges. Difficult choices need to be made about the appropriate allocation of scarce resources. They must choose whether to prioritise the building of houses, schools, jails, hospitals or courts. They must also decide whether to hire more teachers, doctors, police officers or judges. When a high percentage of the population is homeless or unemployed and unable to access basic services, it is often impossible for a government to justify a sufficient allocation of resources to the criminal justice system to make prosecutions a viable prospect.[9]

Transitional governments often cannot afford the cost of hundreds or even thousands of trials that would have to be held in order to prosecute those responsible for human rights abuses. The accused in many of these trials are former state employees (generally members of the security forces), and in some cases governments are then obliged to pay for the costs of their legal defence.[10] Even in cases where governments do not pay for defence costs, they are still required to use large teams of investigators, prosecutors and witnesses for prolonged periods of time if they hope to secure convictions. Often the only way to ensure the safety of witnesses is to place them on expensive witness protection programs within the country or abroad. The prosecution of thousands of perpetrators is an expensive endeavour that may divert resources from pressing societal needs.[11]

Human rights trials often require an enormous amount of time to prepare and conduct. This is particularly so when the perpetrators are important, wealthy or supported by powerful domestic or international constituencies. Such perpetrators can afford excellent defence lawyers and the high-profile nature of their trials often results in delays caused either by extremely thorough preparation by the prosecution or by diplomatic or political interference. The extradition proceedings regarding General Augusto Pinochet are an excellent example of this. It took almost six months from the date of his arrest for the United Kingdom's highest court to make a final determination on a narrow jurisdictional question. If Pinochet ever stands trial for the crimes he is alleged to have committed, it will take years before his guilt or innocence is finally established. The financial cost of prosecuting Pinochet will also be enormous, with certain estimates putting the price as high as $48 million.[12] The trial of former South African State President PW Botha, for the relatively minor offence of failing to comply with a subpoena issued by the Truth and Reconciliation Commission (TRC), took almost nine months from the date charges were laid until his conviction and sentencing. A trial on more substantive charges, such as murder,[13] would last considerably longer. It is not only the trials of high-profile perpetrators that can be drawn-out and time consuming. Attempting to prosecute low-level perpetrators, the so-called 'trigger-pullers', can also be lengthy. Two hit-squad trials in South Africa (the 'Malan Trial' and the 'De Kock Trial') lasted a combined period of almost two-and-a-half years and secured only one conviction.

Transitional societies are often left with a legacy in which thousands (sometimes hundreds of thousands) of people are victims of gross violations of human rights. Criminal justice systems are designed to maintain order in societies where violation of law is the exception. These systems simply cannot cope when, either as a result of state-sanctioned human rights abuses or internal conflict or war, violations of law become the rule. This is because, in order for criminal justice systems to serve as a check on the arbitrary exercise of power and private acts of vengeance, information must be gathered and presented in accordance with accepted evidentiary rules. Furthermore, trials must be conducted in a fair and impartial manner. As detailed above, the time and resource implications are enormous. It is not simply due to an absence of will or insufficient power that thousands of perpetrators in Argentina, South Africa, Ethiopia, Rwanda and postwar Germany, Belgium, Holland and France have remained unpunished.[14] Germany made the most comprehensive attempt yet to punish the tens of thousands of perpetrators responsible for mass crimes during the Second World War. Postwar Germany faced minimal political resistance to prosecutions and inherited a relatively efficient and functional criminal justice system, but only managed to secure fewer than 7 000 convictions from a total of 85 882 cases brought to trial.[15]

Furthermore, a majority of those convicted received relatively mild punishment and served only a small percentage of their sentences. Even those who argue strenuously that states have a 'duty to punish' those responsible for gross violations of human rights concede this duty is impossible to fulfil when these violations have occurred on a massive scale.[16]

All the difficulties referred to above apply to domestic trials, but many of the same problems occur before international courts and tribunals. In addition, international courts and tribunals must overcome their own sets of problems. Firstly, they must obtain jurisdiction over those they seek to punish. Serbia's failure to cooperate with the International Criminal Tribunal for the former Yugoslavia has effectively prevented the tribunal from beginning with the trials of a large percentage of indictees. Secondly, although the current international tribunals are comparatively well resourced,[17] they will never have the resources to allow them to prosecute more than a relatively small number of perpetrators. International criminal tribunals and courts will, therefore, have to make difficult decisions in setting priorities. Although there is some debate about how these choices should be made,[18] there is consensus that they should try to prosecute high-level perpetrators responsible for authorising, organising or committing heinous crimes. While this may be a sensible allocation of scarce resources, it means that those selected for prosecution are, in most cases, precisely those individuals an international body is least likely to be able to place in custody. If the success rate[19] of the international tribunals is any indication of the eventual performance of the ICC, then, notwithstanding the important contribution international prosecutions make towards ending impunity, we should not rely too heavily on this approach to promote human rights.

Dealing with the past – state obligations under international law

It is important to recognise that prosecutions are only one of the obligations that international law imposes on successor regimes. To appreciate this aspect of international law it is instructive to focus on decisions of the Inter-American Commission on Human Rights (the 'Commission') and the Inter-American Court of Human Rights (the 'Court'), which are consistent with relevant international law. Moreover, both the Court and the Commission have had to review amnesty laws and human rights initiatives in several Central and Latin American countries in the wake of gross violations of human rights. Their decisions are, therefore, influenced by the abstract requirements of the law, as well as the objective circumstances in the countries under scrutiny.[20]

In its 1985/86 annual report, the Inter-American Commission seemed to endorse amnesty laws provided they were passed by democratic institutions and some effort was made to discover the truth about past human rights abuse. The report states:

> *The Commission considers that only the appropriate democratic institutions – usually the legislature ... are the only ones called upon to determine whether or not to decree an amnesty or the scope thereof, while amnesties decreed previously by those responsible for the violations have no juridical validity ... Every society has the inalienable right to know the truth about past events, as well as the motives and circumstances in which aberrant crimes came to be committed, in order to prevent a repetition of such acts in the future. Moreover, family members of the victims are entitled to information as to what happened to their relatives. Such access to the truth presupposes freedom of speech, which of course should be exercised responsibly; the establishment of investigating committees whose membership and authority must be determined in accordance with the internal legislation of each*

country, or the provision of the necessary resources so that the judiciary itself may undertake whatever investigations may be necessary.[21]

Three years after this report, the Inter-American Court of Human Rights handed down a groundbreaking decision. In the Velásquez Rodriguez case,[22] the family of an activist who had disappeared in Honduras, challenged the terms of the Honduran amnesty, which made it *de facto* impossible to discover the truth about his disappearance or to receive some form of compensation for his death. The Court held that a state had:

*a legal duty to take reasonable steps to prevent human rights violations and to use the means at its disposal to carry out a serious investigation of violations committed within its jurisdiction, to identify those responsible, to impose **appropriate punishment** and to ensure the victim adequate compensation* (emphasis added).[23]

The Court did not define what it considered to be 'appropriate punishment', but it did refrain from calling for the criminal prosecution of those responsible for disappearances, despite the fact that legal representatives for the victims called on it to issue such an order.[24] The only sanction imposed by the court against the Honduran government was monetary compensation. Furthermore, the court declined to order the payment of punitive damages, stipulating that the term 'fair compensation' used in article 61(1) of the Court, should be interpreted as compensatory and not punitive.[25] The Velasquez Rodriguez judgment indicates that in 1988 the Inter-American Court placed greater emphasis on discovering the truth and ensuring prevention and redress than on an unconditional obligation to prosecute.

Four years after the Velásquez Rodriguez case, the Inter-American Commission on Human Rights handed down three decisions on amnesties adopted by the governments of Argentina,[26] Uruguay[27] and El Salvador.[28] In each case the Commission concluded that the amnesty violated a state's obligations to investigate gross violations of human rights, to identify those responsible, to provide victims with adequate compensation and to prosecute and punish perpetrators. However, as in the Velásquez Rodriguez case, the Commission failed to recommend to either the Argentinean[29] or Uruguayan[30] governments that perpetrators of human rights violations be prosecuted or punished. Only in the Salvadoran case did the Commission explicitly recommend:

an exhaustive, rapid and impartial investigation concerning the event complained of, in order to identify all the victims and those responsible, and submit the latter to justice in order to establish their responsibility, so that they can receive the sanctions demanded by such serious actions (emphasis added).[31]

In 1997, the Inter-American Commission clarified its attitude towards amnesties. In two decisions regarding the self-amnesty that the Chilean military granted to itself in 1978, the Commission recommended that the Chilean government conduct investigations for the purpose of:

identifying the guilty parties, establishing their responsibilities and effectively prosecuting, thereby guaranteeing to the victims and their families the rights to that justice that pertains to them (emphasis added).[32]

The Chilean amnesty decisions confirm that the Commission now views prosecution and punishment as an important component of a state's obligations in dealing with a legacy of human rights abuse.[33] In a similar finding the Commission recommended that the Peruvian government repeal its amnesty law and punish those responsible for the disappearances of a number of individuals.[34]

The above rulings show that by 1998 the Commission had held that a state must fulfil five obligations in confronting gross violations of human rights committed by a previous regime: investigate the identity, fate and whereabouts of victims; investigate the identity of perpetrators; provide reparation or compensation to victims; take affirmative steps to ensure that human rights abuse does not recur; and prosecute and punish those guilty of human rights abuse.

Plainly, the jurisprudence of the Court and Commission has evolved. In the mid-1980s, they granted successor states a wide discretion in developing a response to human rights abuse. By the late 1990s they set out a number of specific obligations a state must fulfil. It is no coincidence that the Commission and Court have, over the past 10 years, adopted more stringent standards. As democratisation has deepened in Latin and Central America, and militaries have loosened their grip on power, these bodies made recommendations that governments are more capable of fulfilling than they were a decade ago. This illustrates an important point about the nature of international obligations. It is futile and perhaps even counter-productive to impose obligations on states, that they cannot fulfil or can fulfil only at great cost. A prudent approach must carefully consider whether a state is actually able to discharge its duties. Our review of the rulings of the Inter-American Commission reveals that in most cases it recommended punishment only when it was reasonably confident that a state could fulfil this obligation. For example, at the time the Commission published its 1985/6 report,[35] which adopted a permissive attitude towards amnesties, Pinochet presided over a powerful military government in Chile. The prosecution of those responsible for torture and 'disappearances' in Chile was, therefore, impossible. However, by 1997, when the Commission handed down the Chanfeau Orayce[36] opinion, which mandated prosecutions, the military had loosened its grip on power and Chile was ruled by a civilian government. The Commission's decision was informed by this shift in the balance of power, which made prosecutions at least possible.[37]

The Commission's approach to accountability is responsible and pragmatic, but its reasoning is flawed. Courts should not respond to the reality that a party might not be able to fulfil an obligation under law by ruling that no obligation exists. Rather it should affirm the general obligation and then articulate the circumstances under which a party may legitimately fail to comply. In the context of transitional justice, a judicial body should not fail to recommend prosecutions because of a well-founded belief that this may be impossible. Instead it should assert that a state must investigate human rights abuses, identify perpetrators, pay reparation, transform state institutions and punish perpetrators, unless it is able to demonstrate that there are legitimate grounds to derogate from these duties. Only by requiring a state to carry the burden of proof in justifying its non-compliance will the normative commands of human rights law be adequately protected and entrenched. This is also appropriate from an evidentiary standpoint because a state will ordinarily possess the relevant facts.

Derogation

Once the requirements of international law have been established, it is important to consider under what circumstances, if any, a state can derogate from its obligations. Of the obligations listed above, the duty to prosecute is likely to prove most difficult for transitional regimes. This is not to suggest that successful investigations or the payment of reparation are easily achieved. Nor does it imply that the transformation of state institutions to prevent the recurrence of human rights is a simple endeavour. However, for the reasons outlined above[38] I believe that the prosecution of perpetrators presents special problems that would be irresponsible and impractical to ignore.

Without exploring the complexities of the derogation doctrine,[39] it is sufficient to note that a state is entitled to derogate from its duty to punish in the following two circumstances: the existence of a grave threat to the life of the nation and impossibility of performance.

The existence of a grave threat to the life of the nation

A state may derogate from an international obligation if 'an exceptional situation of crisis or emergency [exists] which affects the whole population and constitutes a threat to the organised life of the community.'[40] In order for derogation on this basis to be permissible, a state must comply with the following conditions:

- it must provide reasons to justify its failure to punish;
- it must outline the exceptional nature of the threat, which prevents punishment;[41]
- it must demonstrate that the measures taken (for example, an amnesty) are proportional to the threat posed;
- it must apply its decision not to punish (or grant amnesty) in a non-discriminatory manner;
- while it may be permissible, under certain exceptional circumstances, not to punish, it is never permissible to derogate from certain inalienable rights (such as the right to life and the right not to be subjected to torture).[42]

Impossiblity of performance

A state may derogate from its duty to punish if, owing to the state of its criminal justice system or the scale and nature of the crimes committed, it is objectively unable to prosecute those responsible for human rights violations.[43] It is a well-established rule of international law that treaties should not be interpreted to impose impossible obligations on states.[44]

Transitional justice – a framework for judicial review

In this chapter I have sought to articulate a successor state's obligations under international law to deal with a legacy of human rights abuse. As explained earlier, in certain instances there may be serious obstacles to fulfilling the obligation to punish, the two most important of which are the threat posed by powerful security forces and the difficulties entailed in prosecuting those responsible for mass or systematic violations of human rights. In these circumstances international law permits a state to derogate from its obligation to prosecute and punish perpetrators. This derogation should be conditional on a state fulfilling a range of other obligations. I now set out four requirements that judges[45] and other entities should consider when assessing whether a state that fails to prosecute has, nevertheless, fulfilled its obligations under international law.

Requirement one

A state must present detailed and convincing evidence to demonstrate it was unable to prosecute those responsible for human rights abuse. A failure to punish is permissible only if a transition from undemocratic or repressive rule would not have occurred and the country would have suffered severe consequences without some form of amnesty agreement. Severe consequences include the death or injury of significant numbers of people, serious long-term economic damage or prolonged and serious conflict or war.

A failure to punish is also permissible only if the state is unable to prosecute more than a very small percentage of those responsible for human rights abuse. The state must list the reasons[46] why it is unable to prosecute and why some form of amnesty arrangement will achieve the other obligations imposed by international law.[47]

A state must also show that the costs of allocating sufficient resources to make it possible to prosecute perpetrators are prohibitive and that there are other pressing social needs (such as housing and health care) to which the state intends to allocate its scarce resources. A court should carefully scrutinise the state's assertion that it is unable to punish on the grounds set out in the paragraph above. A state must present a convincing case as to why the granting of amnesty or pardon is preferable to simply doing nothing and waiting until it has the evidence or resources to bring prosecutions. For example, a state may choose to offer a limited and conditional amnesty if this provides perpetrators with an incentive to make full disclosure, thereby achieving some measure of truth, acknowledgement and accountability that would not otherwise be obtainable through the criminal justice system. Furthermore, a state may seek to justify a conditional amnesty offer to provide for the orderly release of suspects who have been incarcerated for lengthy periods and for whom there is no reasonable prospect of achieving convictions, especially if they are held in unacceptable conditions.[48]

Requirement two

The second requirement for states that fail to prosecute, yet fulfil other obligations, is for a majority of citizens to freely endorse the transitional justice policy that the state has adopted.[49] In some cases, this may be evidenced by legislation passed by a democratically elected parliament. In other cases, the policy may be ratified by popular vote in a referendum or plebiscite. A self-amnesty granted by a repressive regime can never satisfy this requirement and may be regarded by a court as void *ab initio*.

Requirement three

A state that fails to prosecute perpetrators for the reasons outlined above must make a good faith effort to comply with all other obligations under international law.[50]

A state must endeavour to discover the truth about victims. This should include investigations to discover the identity, fate and whereabouts of victims, as well as an official acknowledgement of their suffering.[51]

A state must also aim to discover the identity of perpetrators. Where possible, individual responsibility should be attributed for authorising and perpetrating human rights abuse. A state must, furthermore, take meaningful steps to ensure that human rights abuse does not recur and endeavour to abolish or transform state institutions directly or indirectly responsible for human rights abuse. It should also attempt to promote a culture of human rights among its citizens. This may entail a number of measures, such as exerting civilian control over the security forces, retraining and restructuring the security forces, providing human rights education for all state employees and including human rights awareness in educational curricula.

A state must provide victims of human rights abuses with adequate reparation. This may take a number of forms, including the payment of state pensions, free access to health care, educational institutions or state housing, and the provision of appropriate mental health care. The state should also consider providing some form of symbolic reparation by establishing permanent monuments or memorials to remember and honour victims or by establishing a national day of remembrance. It may not be possible for a state to identify every victim, name every person responsible for human rights abuse, pay full compensation to all victims or instantly transform every institution responsible for human rights abuse. A state must, however, demonstrate that it has made, and continues to make, a *bona fide* effort to achieve all these objectives.

Requirement four

A state that fails to punish must actively minimise the extent to which this impedes the fulfilment of its other international law obligations. For example, a state may not pass a blanket amnesty, because this serves to conceal the truth about the fate of victims and the identity of perpetrators. A corollary of this requirement is that any amnesty law should be structured so as to assist in the fulfilment of a state's remaining international law obligations. For example, the granting of amnesty should be conditional on disclosure of the truth regarding the crime for which amnesty is sought and the victim of that crime. Furthermore, victims of crimes in respect of which amnesty is granted should automatically be entitled to reparation. In addition, a state should consider disqualifying persons to whom amnesty is granted from holding public office as a means to facilitate the transformation of state institutions.

If a state is able to show that it has satisfied all four of these requirements, a domestic or foreign court applying international law or an international judicial body should hold that the failure to prosecute perpetrators is a legitimate derogation of the duty to punish. Accordingly, judicial bodies should not overturn domestic amnesties or subject perpetrators to criminal penalties.

There are two exceptions and one qualification to this approach. No court should be required to uphold amnesties for crimes against humanity or genocide, nor should a third state be required to apply this approach in instances where its own citizens have been victims of human rights abuse.[52] Furthermore, nothing in this approach should preclude individuals from bringing civil claims against perpetrators in the courts of third countries.[53]

Changed circumstances: a post-hoc dilemma

Presume that a state legitimately grants amnesty, because there is a substantial threat to the life of a nation or that it is practically impossible to prosecute.[54] Several years pass, resulting in a significant change to either or both of these circumstances. That is, there may be a significant decrease in the threat presented by the security forces or the criminal justice system receives sufficient resources and evidence to prosecute significant numbers of perpetrators. Should a domestic, foreign or international court take the new context into account when considering the validity of an amnesty law?

The law is constantly required to develop rules to deal with changed circumstances. In the criminal law of most countries, convictions may be set aside on the basis that exonerating evidence emerges after a trial. Similarly, when amendments are made to criminal law, the difficult problem of dealing equitably with persons convicted and for acts that are no longer crimes, or which carry lesser sentences, must be confronted. Unfortunately, the principles applied in these cases are of little use when considering whether to uphold amnesties under changed circumstances. When used properly, amnesties are mechanisms designed to facilitate a transition from undemocratic and repressive rule to representative government in which human rights are protected. An obvious dilemma is presented when one seeks to overturn the mechanism that permitted a transition, because circumstances now exist, that no longer necessitate the granting of an amnesty. There is no easy solution to this problem. A domestic court should probably not use the decrease in the power of the military as a basis for invalidating an amnesty, provided that the amnesty initially complied with the requirements listed above. If domestic judiciaries rescind amnesties as soon as militaries are no longer a threat to society, then militaries will seldom, if ever, agree to a transition to democratic rule. This may cause a country to suffer the type of irreparable harm, in the form of widespread loss of life or severe economic damage, which this chapter seeks to avoid. Alternatively, if militaries do agree to transitions, they will structure the hand-over so as to entrench their power and will actively resist any reform efforts that may erode their grip on government and render them liable to prosecution. In this scenario, the military will present a constant threat to democracy and it will retain a perpetual veto over democratic decision-making. This may forever impede the transition to genuine democracy, thereby creating the basis for continued conflict and human rights abuse.

Furthermore, a domestic court should not overturn an amnesty procedure that was established in order to cope with severe resource and evidentiary problems.[55] If thousands of perpetrators, from whom there is no reasonable prospect of obtaining convictions, are granted amnesty after they have satisfied appropriate conditions,[56] it would be unfair to undo this amnesty when the resource and evidentiary constraints that first motivated the amnesty no longer apply. Perpetrators who make full disclosure of their crimes in exchange for amnesty may plausibly claim that their rights have been violated if they are later prosecuted for disclosed crimes. On the other hand, if a government facing resource problems chooses not to grant amnesty, but rather to wait until its criminal justice system is sufficiently equipped to undertake large-scale prosecutions, perpetrators have not been prejudiced, because they cannot rely on a deal that was not made.

If domestic courts should uphold certain amnesties, notwithstanding a change in circumstances, what attitude should foreign or international courts take if the initial concerns that motivated the amnesty no longer apply? The same dangers exist. Militaries may be more reluctant to relinquish power even with guarantees, such as amnesties, if they know these can be overturned by foreign and international courts. However, if militaries are offered a measure of security at home, they are less likely to resist a transition or continue to pose a threat to democratic rule solely because an international court may not uphold an amnesty. It is unlikely that the threat of international prosecutions will prove decisive in a military's decision whether to allow a transfer of power, particularly if it is provided with an assurance against extradition. If a member of the military foolishly places himself under the jurisdiction of a foreign or international court, that court should be entitled to overturn an amnesty in the state of the military officer. However, it should do so only if it can be demonstrated that military forces no longer pose a substantial threat to the nation. An international court should be entitled to consider whether the prosecution would pose a substantial threat and decide not to prosecute if this, together with the other requirements listed above, are satisfied.[57]

Implementation

Whether a state has complied with its international obligations in the wake of gross violations of human rights is not an issue solely for domestic courts. Other entities are responsible for applying these principles too.

The International Criminal Court, international tribunals and foreign courts

These judicial bodies must decide whether a state has complied with its obligations under international law. For example, a court may rule that a blanket amnesty is invalid and that an alleged perpetrator may be prosecuted. It may also rule that an amnesty is invalid, because victims have been provided with inadequate reparation, that a state has failed to discharge its responsibility to name specific perpetrators or that there has been a failure to take sufficient steps to transform institutions responsible for human rights abuse.

Foreign governments

In the formulation of foreign policy and the structuring of international relations, foreign governments should also assess whether a successor state has complied with the requirements articulated in this chapter. A failure to comply may jeopardise the provision of foreign aid, the expansion of trade and investment, the entry into international organisations or international cooperation on a range of issues. Conversely, a demonstration that a state has made a good faith effort to comply with its obligations may result in greater cooperation and assistance.

International organisations

International organisations such as the United Nations, the World Bank and the International Monetary Fund should assess whether a successor state has complied with these requirements in deciding on the nature and extent of the assistance they provide. They may also stipulate that certain forms of assistance are conditional on a government complying with these requirements.

International mediators and negotiators

They too should use these requirements as a basis for determining what terms and conditions are acceptable and unacceptable in the brokering of peace agreements and other conflict resolution initiatives.[58] For example, they should inform parties that blanket amnesties are not an option under international law and that any settlement must include measures designed to provide assistance to victims of human rights abuse.

Transitional governments

They should apply this framework in formulating their policies designed to deal with the past. If they have the power and resources to prosecute perpetrators, they are obliged to do so. However, they need not become fixated with punishment if they can find *bona fide* reasons why they are unable to prosecute. In these circumstances they should allocate the time, energy and resources they would have committed to prosecutions to fulfilling their other international law obligations.

Conclusion

Building a human rights culture and entrenching the rule of law in the wake of mass violence is a complex and difficult task. Transitional societies face considerable political, social and economic challenges. New governments often have a precarious grip on power and struggle to maintain peace and stability. They cannot always rely on efficient and loyal state institutions to defend their mandate or implement their policies. In this context, it is not always possible or prudent to demand prosecutions. International law cannot turn a blind eye to these realities. Punishment for past wrongs is a very important, but not indispensable, strategy in dealing with the past. And finally, an inflexible approach to punishment should not divert resources or distract the international community from formulating and implementing other initiatives designed to promote and protect human rights.

Section 2

The philosophical framework of the Commission

Can truth commissions be justified?

Making moral judgements

Moral expectations and legal challenges

Religious and moral perspectives

The moral justification of truth commissions

RAJEEV BHARGAVA

This chapter consists of three claims that together offer a tentative moral justification for the very idea of a truth commission. I begin my argument by introducing a distinction crucial to understanding the point underlying truth commissions – that point between what I call a minimally decent and a barbaric society. A *minimally decent* society is governed by minimally moral rules. A complete breakdown of such rules characterises a *barbaric society*. In this context, what makes these rules moral is their capacity to prevent excessive wrongdoing or evil and not their ability to promote a particular conception of the good life, including a substantive conception of justice. Such moral rules include negative injunctions against killing, maiming or ill-treating others, and also what the philosopher Stuart Hampshire calls *basic procedural justice*. This is a term that connotes fair procedures of negotiation that form the basis for untidy compromises between incompatible visions of a better life, made possible due to acceptable restraints on unmeasured ambition and limitless self-assertion.[1]

Towards a minimally decent society

My *first* claim then is that truth commissions help societies transfer from a barbaric to a minimally decent condition, primarily by the confidence they build in norms of procedural justice.

The phrase 'minimally decent' implies that the best available ethical standards in a society are unrealised. A minimally decent society is not free of exploitation, injustice or demeaning behaviour. It may not even embody political equality. Yet, it is a social order in which almost every voice is heard, some visibility for everyone is ensured in the political domain, and even the most marginalised and exploited are part of negotiation, howsoever unequal the conditions under which it takes place. On the other hand, in a barbaric society, where basic procedural justice is dismembered, the entire mechanism of negotiation and arbitration does not exist.

Usually, the violation of norms of procedural justice begins with the politically motivated deployment of excessive force. In the early stages of regression into barbarism, gross violations of basic rights, namely physical intimidation, torture, murder, even massacres, occur on a fairly large scale. Active deliberation and opposition are brutally terminated. This initial use of massive force may eventually make physical coercion more or less redundant, as indifference and submissiveness are routinely generated in a depoliticised environment. The noteworthy point here is that in either case, the demise of basic procedural justice is a political evil that creates political victims.

A person who is robbed on the highway or systematically exploited on agricultural land or in the factory is a victim, but not a *political* victim. A political victim is one who is threatened, coerced or killed, because of his or her attempt to determine what their own society is or what it will become in the future. When political victims suffer violence, they are not merely harmed physically, however. The act of violence transmits an unambiguous message – that their views on the common good do not count, that their side of the argument has no worth and will not be heard, that they will not be recognised as participants in any debate and, finally, that to negotiate is worthless. In effect, it signals their disappearance from the public domain. When excluded from the political domain, such persons may be described as politically dead, as was the case with the law-abiding, but politically silenced subjects of former communist states.[2] If the collapse of basic procedural justice brings political death, then clearly its restoration marks the political rebirth of members of a society. This is why, by making the restoration of basic procedural justice their primary objective, truth commissions focus on the rehabilitation of political victims.

Before I mention how truth commissions facilitate the transition of a barbaric society to one that is minimally decent, it is necessary to emphasise again that such societies are beginning their ascent from hell; they are taking the first, faltering steps away from a situation of gross injustice on a massive scale, probably brought about by people with profoundly deadened moral sensitivities. When it comes to a society standing precariously on the threshold of moral restoration, it is important that we look at it bottom-up rather than top-down. I mean that we must remain firmly anchored in low-level ground realities and begin our search for relevant moral principles from here. We must not first reach out for high, near-perfect ethical standards only to subsequently judge ground realities with their help. And, in the ground reality of such societies, the only reasonably certain thing is a diffuse agreement that enough evil has been wrought and that relief from it is urgently required.

It is important to understand fully the significance of this. It does not mean that enmity or estrangement has ceased between victims and perpetrators or between conflicting groups. Nor that they have begun to view each other with equal respect. Such attitudes may not even be on the distant horizon of a society surfacing from an evil past. However, it does mean that a space has opened up for a new order on terms not entirely unfavourable to all political actors, that a temporary reprieve from civil war or tyranny exists, as well as the hope that this can be prevented in future. It also means that force has begun to give way to negotiation and, although relative advantage still accrues to one group, no one has a sense of *complete* victory or defeat.

Normally, such transitional moments emerge out of a settlement in which former oppressors refuse to share power unless guaranteed that they will escape the criminal justice system characteristic of a minimally decent society. Or it typically arises because former victims do not fully control the new order they have set up and lack the power to implement their own concept of justice. However, such transitional moments can also come about by other routes. It is entirely possible that former oppressors are comprehensively vanquished, but current victors, victims of the previously existing barbaric society refuse on moral grounds to avenge themselves, or fully implement the conventional criminal justice system. In short, former victims refuse on moral grounds to don the mantle of victors, something someone like Gandhi might well have done.

What I am trying to get at is that at issue here are transitional situations of extreme complexity, replete with moral possibilities, including grave moral danger. The danger is obvious: victims may forever remain victims and their society may never cease to be barbaric. But what is often missed is that seeds of moral progress are also present herein, because former victims are saved the awesome responsibility of wielding absolute power and, therefore, may escape the devastating consequences of being corrupted by its use. As a result, the possibility is foreclosed that past wrongs will be annulled only by fresh acts of equally excessive wrongdoing. (I have in mind events in the former Soviet Union.) Instead, we are presented with the possibility of confronting past wrongs by means other than the use of force or the wilful manipulation of the criminal justice system. So, what may begin as mere political constraint opens up moral possibilities and it is *these* possibilities that lend moral weight to mechanisms like the Truth and Reconciliation Commission (TRC).

How then does a truth commission facilitate the transition from a barbaric to a minimally decent society? How does it stabilise basic procedural justice? For this to happen, the entire society, and particularly the victims of barbarism must begin to believe that conditions of civil war, tyranny or gross injustice have receded, and that from now on decisions are likely to be made by negotiation rather than by brute force. This is made possible only when grave injustices of the past are publicly acknowledged as grave injustice, as an evil, when perpetrators of this evil take full responsibility for their wrongful acts and victims move from passive disengagement with the world to active engagement with it.

This engagement is effected by the fulfilment of two characteristic obligations. Firstly, there is the obligation to oneself, to learn to live one's life again and rebuild relations with fellow citizens, friends and family. Secondly, there is an obligation to others, particularly to the memory of loved ones who have been killed. Victims and survivors need to tell stories of their victimisation, relate their version of events, point out the aggressor and amplify his aggression. In doing so, victims express retributive emotions of deep resentment and a cry for justice. Because physical injury also leaves them mentally scarred and without any self-respect, they need to reclaim their self-esteem. A truth commission helps to achieve all this and is an instrument to get a collective acknowledgement of gross injustices. In fact, just as a coronation creates a king, just so a truth commission gives birth to a new moral order by announcing that basic procedural justice is firmly installed. This is an important symbolic function of truth commissions and by no-means an optional extra. When a truth commission successfully performs these functions, it restores the public health of a traumatised society and helps mend the deeply fractured intimacy among victims of barbarism. The argument to let bygones be bygones and get on with building a common future fails to address the needs of victims. In such transitional societies, a policy of forgetting is quite simply a morally inadequate response.

A delicate balance

My *second* claim revolves around a distinction between symmetric and asymmetric barbarism. Let me explain these terms, with which I am not entirely comfortable. A barbaric society, in my view, bifurcates into two sorts of situations. One, where the generation of evil is causally connected to actions of a particular group that usually controls the main levers of political power and which, by its violation of minimally moral rules, bears primary responsibility for evil. Other groups in this situation, normally the victims, have no such responsibility and indeed continue to hold on to a distinctively moral viewpoint. This is an asymmetrically barbaric society. In the second, social and political evil are collectively generated by practically everyone in society. This is a society altogether beyond the pale of morality. All hell has broken loose, there is a general madness in the society, and the distinction between perpetrators and victims has collapsed. I call this situation a *symmetrically barbaric society*. This point needs restatement. Norms of basic procedural justice can come apart if all relevant parties withdraw their consent to them or even if only one of them does so. When no party abides by norms of basic procedural justice, then we descend into a *symmetrically barbaric society*. When only one violates these norms and others are keen to enforce them, and particularly when the violating group is politically dominant, then we inhabit an *asymmetrically barbaric society*.

On the basis of this distinction, my claim is the following: when a society moves away from symmetric barbarism, then some mechanism to deal with gross injustices of the past, something like the South African truth commission is necessary and sufficient for achieving minimal decency. But options are somewhat limited when a society moves towards minimal decency from asymmetric barbarism. In these circumstances, it is more or less imperative to have a truth commission like the South African model, although it will not be sufficient. Indeed its success in achieving a minimally decent society depends on the performance of complementary institutions and agencies, many of which must take into account the substantive conception of injustices meted out to former victims.

In my view, a failure to maintain this distinction is disastrous. It is not enough, therefore, to have minimal decency as one's objective. One must be equally sensitive to the kind of barbarism from which one is extricating oneself. If in transiting from situations of asymmetric barbarism, we behave as though we are getting away from symmetric barbarism or vice versa, then despite our best intentions, we may regress further. Let me explain. Consider the period of the partition of India. The fear and radical uncertainty generated by new borders drawn on the basis of religion forced people out of their homes in the hope of living securely with people of their own ilk – more than 10 million people crossed borders. It is an understatement to say that this 'transfer of populations' was violent. Nearly a million were slaughtered, and almost a 100 000 women were abducted and raped by marauders belonging to a religion other than their own. Responsibility for this savagery cannot be laid at the door of any single religious group, however. It makes no sense in such situations to revive the distinction between victim and perpetrator or to make the 'victim's status as victim the constitutive pillar of a new political order'.[3] The restoration of the moral order, and in particular the consolidation of basic procedural justice, is the primary need in such situations, and a truth commission or some equivalent mechanism is sufficient for this purpose.

Consider, alternatively, South Africa today. It occupies a delicate, unstable ground and, unless fully alert, its members can easily walk into two explosive moral land-mines. If former victims don the mantle of victors and seek comprehensive retributive justice in either its no-nonsense, revolutionary form or its liberal, democratic form, then they may instantly transform former perpetrators and beneficiaries into current victims. And, if the distinction between victim and perpetrator is obliterated, South Africa may tragically degenerate into a situation faced by the former Yugoslavia or parts of India during its partition. This would be a disaster, because South Africa has so far been characterised by asymmetrical not symmetrical barbarism. The deep irony in South Africa is that at the very moment it begins to consolidate a system of basic procedural justice and perhaps move beyond it, it faces the greatest danger of hurtling into a symmetrically barbaric society. In one fell swoop, this has also created a deep moral dilemma for the oppressed group. A false move on its part can send the whole country spiraling from a clearly recognisable moral situation into a condition of complete moral 'normlessness'. The very special situation in South Africa must, therefore, be kept in mind before an appropriate response to it is worked out. This is why, in opposition to critics who denounce it, I believe a South African truth commission has been desperately needed.

It is important that former victims do not turn into perpetrators, that symmetrical barbarism is not generated in South Africa. It is equally a mistake to commit the opposite error, to turn a blind eye to its asymmetrical barbarism and to believe that South Africa is dominated by features of a symmetrically barbaric society. If victims (usually blacks) and their oppressors (usually whites) are treated identically or if the deep humiliation of the 'non-political' victims of apartheid is not properly addressed, we may yet discover that the road to a minimally decent society inevitably goes via a symmetrically barbaric society. Against blind defenders of the South African Truth and Reconciliation Commission, who believe it to be a remedy for all the troubles of a beleaguered nation, I am compelled to take the view that a truth commission is necessary, but *not* sufficient for the creation of even a minimally decent society in South Africa.

Collective responsibility

My *third*, entirely negative claim is that a truth commission must not aim to bring about reconciliation, but try only to accomplish a minimally decent society – this in itself is no mean feat. By reconciliation, I mean an end to enmity through forgiveness, achievable only when perpetrators and beneficiaries of past injustice acknowledge collective responsibility for wrongdoing, shed their prejudice and victims regain their self-respect through the same process. The view that truth commissions should work towards reconciliation is usually criticised for two reasons with which I disagree. The first challenges the coherence of collective responsibility and, therefore, finds the very issue of collective forgiveness redundant. The second argument criticises the idea of forgiveness as being morally inappropriate. I do not find the notion of collective responsibility incoherent or the idea of forgiveness morally unworthy.

For me, a victimised group can forgive former perpetrators if they take collective responsibility for wrongdoing and repent. Allow me to elaborate this point. In my use of the term, 'responsibility' does not amount to a legal liability for an act. It is linked rather to what men and women decide to do. I believe that most of our acts and decisions are irreducibly social and, therefore, responsibility for them is social too.[4] Three things follow, if this is true. Firstly, the domain of moral responsibility spills over beyond what is directly caused by an individual. Secondly, an entire collective group can be held responsible for harm to others.[5] Thirdly, guilt and blame must be seen to be part of a continuum that also contains shame and remorse. In short, groups may be held morally responsible for wrongs and individuals can partake in that responsibility, be guilty or feel tainted.

Allow me to move from the perpetrator to the victim. Why should the victim forgive? Forgiveness implies foreswearing resentment towards the person who inflicted moral injury.[6] It is hard to take the view that the foreswearing of resentment is always morally appropriate. After all, there is nothing intrinsically wrong in resenting perpetrators of evil. Indeed, since such emotions are woven into one's sense of self-respect, a person who does not resent wrong done to him or her very often lacks self-respect. Under what conditions then is it morally justified to forgive? Clearly, only when the self-respect of victims is enhanced by forgiveness, or at least is not undermined by it. This in turn happens when former perpetrators admit their wrongdoing, distance themselves from the wrongful act and join the victims in condemning the act, as well as their own past. Only under these conditions can the self-respect of victims be restored and enhanced. Is it possible to achieve this within the functional parameters of the TRC?

Truth commissions cannot *aim* to bring about reconciliation through this process of collective acknowledgement of grave wrongs-cum-forgiveness, because reconciliation requires a profound change in people – a deep and drawn-out process. The process of shedding prejudice and taking responsibility for wrong done to others begins with the wrongdoer admitting the absence of a good reason for the act. This must turn into an acknowledgement that the reason for the action springs from the deepest recesses of the person's being. Since a genuine confrontation of this fact takes place not just in the mind, but at the level of gut and feeling, acknowledging that you have been one of the 'bad guys' will be extremely painful. We might say of such a person that at that point the very soul is punished. This punishment of the soul must necessarily involve a profound change of identity, which must be witnessed by the victim if he or she is to be convinced that forgiveness is appropriate. Truth commissions, which need to operate within certain time constraints, in the immediate after-math of confronting evil, are simply not equipped to bear the burden of effect-ing this fundamental transformation. Truth commissions like the South African one can, of course, contribute towards creating conditions for reconcil-iation in the future. But such reconciliation, if and when it happens, can be only a fortunate by-product of the whole TRC process, and not intentionally brought about by it.

Restorative justice: dealing with the past differently

CHARLES VILLA-VICENCIO

Jose Zalaquett[1] defines the two overall objectives of a truth commission as the *prevention of the recurrence of human rights abuses* and, to the extent that it is possible, *the reparation of the damage caused*. Reaching beyond the confines of judicial punishment as an end in itself, truth commissions are essentially instruments of *restorative* justice. Restoration is aimed at victims, perpetrators and communities in a situation of political transition from undemocratic rule to the first phases of democracy and the affirmation of human rights.

The question is whether the non-prosecutorial values of truth commissions are capable of delivering the objectives defined by Zalaquett. Some argue that the promotion of the rule of law, which encapsulates the ideals of a truth commission, depends on a 'duty to prosecute'. Aryeh Neier puts it this way:

> *In a given situation, such as an aeroplane hijacking, submitting to terrorist demands may save lives. But a consensus has developed worldwide that giving in to the demands of terrorists only inspires more terrorism. The way to stop terrorists is to ensure that they derive no profit from their acts.*[2]

Does restorative justice, as manifest in the South African Truth and Reconciliation Commission (which includes qualified amnesty), offer a *via media* that enables the transitional state not to fall prey to either *too much* or *too little* justice? The former holds the danger of precipitating a backlash from perpetrators capable of undermining the democratic process in its earliest and most vulnerable days. The latter could militate against the ability of victims and survivors to come to terms with the past – a matter that, in the long term, could come back to haunt the nation.

Rather than providing an alternative to the goals of the established justice system, restorative justice seeks to recover certain neglected dimensions that make for a more complete understanding of justice. It has to do with the stance that Martha Minow locates between vengeance and forgiveness.[3] Tony Marshall's working definition of restorative justice provides the broad parameters of its goals: 'Restorative justice is a process whereby all the parties with a stake in a particular offence come together to resolve collectively how to deal with the aftermath of the offence and its implications for the future.'[4] At a political level it involves former adversaries seeking to deal with the past as a basis for creating a better future for all involved. It includes the restoration of the moral worth and equal dignity of all people, while striving for the establishment of some measure of social equality between all sectors of society.[5]

The debate between Lon Fuller and HLA Hart on legal positivism in the 1950s is poignant to the debate on restorative justice.[6] Fuller asked what it is that gives legitimacy to 'a constitution for a country that has just emerged from a period of violence and disorder in which any thread of legal continuity with previous governments has broken'.[7] He offers a twofold response that embraces *ethical idealism* and *political reality*. It involves, he argues, 'certain moral qualities' and 'acceptance by the majority of the people concerned' of the proposed way forward. It has to do with what Ronald Dworkin, speaking in a different context, refers to when he speaks of the 'law beyond law' that inspires us to discern 'the best route to a better a future'. Effectively, it concerns 'the people we want to be and the community we aim to have'.[8] In the words of the postscript of the South African Interim Constitution (Act No 200 of 1993), it involves the promotion of a:

> ... *secure foundation for the people of South Africa to transcend the divisions and strife of the past, which generated gross violations of human rights, the transgression of humanitarian principles in violent conflicts and the legacy of hatred, fear, guilt and revenge. These can now be addressed on the basis that there is a need for understanding, not vengeance, a need for reparation, not for retaliation, a need for ubuntu, not victimisation.*

Restorative justice 'seeks to redefine crime: it shifts the primary focus of crime from the breaking of laws or offences against a faceless state to a perception of crime as violations against human beings ... It encourages victims, offenders and the community to be directly involved in resolving conflicts.'[9] This need is neglected, if not frequently ignored, by conventional forms of justice.

In pursuit of justice

Dirk van Zyl Smit reminds us that prison was traditionally 'regarded as a place for detention of people and not for their punishment'.[10] Customary law in pre-colonial South Africa similarly made no allowance for imprisonment as a form of punishment.[11] It seems, then, that an unintentional side effect of prosecution and detention has become an end in itself. A result is a failure to enquire with sufficient vigour into what transforming purposes are served by punitive forms of justice that fail directly to promote the restoration of both victims and perpetrators.

Recidivism rates indicate that criminal justice that focuses primarily on punishment has not been an adequate means of deterrence.[12] In politically driven conflicts, whether national or international, it seems even less likely that the threat of punishment is sufficient to curtail human rights abuses. Historically fixed mind-sets, entrenched prejudice and the kind of ideological bloody-mindedness that drives militant perpetrators of political crime, are forces simply too powerful to be prevented by the possibility of future prosecution. To argue that the threat of punishment will deter those who violate human rights and international conventions is indeed a bit like arguing that the threat of capital punishment deters crime. If this were the case (and there is little evidence to support it), those who support the deterrence argument need to ask whether the threat of prosecutions would not make authoritarian regimes more reluctant to seek a political settlement with those who want to end their rule. Trials are often necessary, but frequently insufficient to deal effectively with crime – whether politically or otherwise motivated. *More is required.*

This chapter seeks to focus on the neglected dimensions of a holistic theory of justice. It involves the restoration of relationships as a basis for the prevention of the reoccurrence of human rights abuses and the reparation of damage to the personal dignity and material wellbeing of victims.

As democracy necessarily includes more than universal franchise, so it is wrong to reduce justice to a functioning judicial system. It has to do with a nation committed to a set of moral values that provides the basis of what Lon Fuller refers to as a 'relatively stable reciprocity of expectations between law-giver and subject'.[13] This involves holding in creative tension a number of important ideals that sometimes appear to contradict each other – ideals that extend beyond the capacity of any single judicial procedure to deliver. Restorative justice is, as such, a theory of justice that needs to pervade all of society, rather than a specific act in and of itself. In a situation of political transition it must include the following eight concerns.

- An organised system of justice based on international standards of human rights. This includes the entrenchment of the right of all persons to a legal defence and access to courts that administer the law in an even-handed and efficient manner – even in the face of the most hideous gross violations of human rights and ruthless manifestations of crime.

- The administration of justice to the benefit of all involved. In a situation of political conflict, the ending of hostility and the institution of peace are as important as the right to legal redress. Punishment should not be seen as an end in itself.

- The promotion of moral values that make for a shared commitment to the creation of a society governed by the rule of law. It involves citizen participation in public debate and the creation of social structures that generate sufficient trust to enable peaceful transition to happen.

- The need to hold accountable all those responsible for the gross violations of human rights, focusing on those directly involved in these violations, as well as those who condoned past deeds, or who simply allowed them to happen, or who chose to look the other way.

- The issue of collective *criminal* guilt. Karl Jaspers, in his celebrated essay written shortly after the institution of the Nuremberg Trials, rejected this concept of collective criminal guilt, while arguing that all Germans needed to share *political* responsibility for the past. He spoke of a 'new world waiting to be built'. He warned that 'unless a break is made in the evil chain, the fate that overtook us will overtake the victors – and all mankind with them'.[14] This, he argued, is the responsibility of all, not only those who appeared before the judges of Nuremberg.

- The acknowledgement of the importance of memory. Luc Huyse suggests that memory is the ultimate form of justice. It needs, however, to be a rich and inclusive memory (sometimes called 'thick memory') that captures the gradations of responsibility for the past. 'Truth,' Huyse suggests, 'is both retribution and deterrence, and it undermines the mental foundation of future human rights abuses.'[15] It is this that justifies the focus on victim testimony as witnessed in our TRC. It, in turn, accentuates the importance of more story-telling – not one story but many. It is only through 'the widest possible compilation of people's perceptions, stories, myths and experiences ... [that we] can restore to memory and foster a new humanity,' writes Antjie Krog. This wide truth, she suggests, is 'perhaps justice in its deepest sense.'[16] The genre of memory must be allowed to flow where it will, giving expression to bitterness and anger as well as life and hope. It is at the same time important to recognise that the 'politics of memory' can be abused by politicians to fuel the fires of hatred, as seen in the case of the Anglo-Boer South African War, Northern Ireland and the situation in the former Yugoslavia. It is important to include stories that embrace and affirm restoration in the nation's repertoire of story-telling. Memory as *justice* and, not least, as *healing* is at the same time often about victims working *through* their anger and hatred as a means of rising above their suffering – of getting on with life with dignity.

- The need for punishment, where necessary. To put aside debilitating hatred and anger (where this is possible) is not necessarily a substitute for punishment. It does not mean that the 'impersonal processes of a justice system, the inherent operations of a theory of desert' be ignored.[17] Punishment within the confines of the rule of law needs, however, in situations of political transition to be aimed, where possible, at the reintegration into society of perpetrators as a basis for contributing to the restoration of society as a whole.

- The rehabilitation of victims. This is dealt with elsewhere in this book. It is an immensely complex matter. The Act governing the work of the TRC does not require perpetrators to take responsibility for contributing to the reparation of the lives of their victims. The response of the state to the recommendations of the Commission, in turn, threatens to redefine the ambit of reparations. There is also limited evidence that moral persuasion is sufficient to convince either perpetrators or benefactors of apartheid to play a role in this regard. This raises important questions about the responsibility of the state regarding material reparations.

The theory of restorative justice that follows seeks to hold the ideals identified above in a creative tension. The point has already been made. It seeks to restore relationships between victims and perpetrators as a basis for preventing the re-occurrence of human rights abuses and making reparation where possible for past damage, dimensions often neglected in conventional systems of criminal justice.

Restorative justice

The priority within transitional societies, where the emphasis is on former enemies who need to learn to live together, makes the difficult quest for alternative forms of justice important. The acid test of restorative justice is whether it will succeed where punishment has failed – to reduce the repetition of human rights abuses and facilitate the emergence of a more just social order. As such it must restore the human dignity and the material wellbeing of victims and survivors, while enabling perpetrators to become re-integrated into society. Chief Justice Ismail Mahomed (writing as deputy president of the Constitutional Court at the time) has stressed the need to enable perpetrators, through the amnesty process, not only to escape a jail sentence, but 'to become active, full and creative members of the new order'. Victims and perpetrators need to cross the 'historic bridge' (referred to in the preamble of the interim constitution). Mahomed suggests that this should not be 'with heavy, dragged steps delaying and impeding a rapid and enthusiastic transition to the new society at the end of the bridge'.[18]

The complexity of pursuing justice in a transitional society is immense. It requires a political-legal initiative that is flexible enough to meet the different needs associated with nation-building – all of which have the capacity to derail the fragile initiative for peaceful coexistence and national reconciliation between former enemies.

There is a place, in this milieu, for retributive justice that affirms the place of *lex talionis* ('an eye for an eye, a tooth for a tooth') as an alternative to unbridled revenge.

Deterrent justice has a place in seeking to limit atrocities in the future.

Rehabilitative justice addresses the needs of the perpetrator – no nation can afford unrehabilitated torturers and killers.

Compensatory justice, which requires beneficiaries of the old order to share in programmes of restitution, needs to be explored.

Justice as the affirmation of human dignity recognises the equal dignity of all people.

Justice as exoneration affirms the need for the records to be put straight where persons have been falsely accused by the state and/or within their own communities.

The application of these imperatives needs to be explored in relation to what can be defined as three important phases in a viable theory of restorative justice: *acknowledgement*, *reparation* and *reconciliation*. The aim of restorative justice is, in the words of Joy Liddicott, to 'make things right' between adversaries.[19] It is, to again employ Dworkin's phrase, to find 'the best route to a better future'. Inherent to this approach is both political and judicial flexibility. The magnitudes of its demands make restorative justice, almost by definition, a somewhat ambitious ideal, or what John Braithwaite calls 'an immodest theory'.[20] It constitutes a set of optimal ideals in the difficult pursuit of peace. It involves commitment to transformation that extends beyond any one judicial procedure or political initiative.

Acknowledgement

Aryeh Neier's harsh words for both FW de Klerk and Thabo Mbeki are instructive.[21] When De Klerk appeared before the TRC, he insisted that he had not directly or indirectly ever suggested, ordered or authorised any previous gross violations of human rights. The Commission found that he 'displayed a lack of candour' in this regard. His apology was qualified. This persuaded Judge Richard Goldstone to argue:

To apologise meaningfully for apartheid, President de Klerk would have had to admit that there was no justification at all for the policy he had helped implement. He would have had to admit that it was a morally offensive policy. He did neither of those things. I do not believe I would be doing him an injustice by suggesting that his apology sprang from his perception that apartheid was a mistake, not because it was morally offensive, but because it failed and that it was well meant'.[22]

Thabo Mbeki, then deputy president, was clearly more forthcoming than De Klerk. The Commission acknowledged this and accepted his testimony with appreciation. Neier's concern is that Mbeki coupled his apology with the assertion that 'it would be morally wrong and legally incorrect to equate apartheid with the resistance against it'. This too was accepted by the Commission.[23] Whether intentional or not, however, in so doing, Mbeki was seen by some to be ameliorating the actions of his organisation, which included the execution of 34 people in ANC detention camps. Archbishop Desmond Tutu, chairperson of the Commission, criticised Mbeki for what he saw as Mbeki's qualified apology. Nicholas Tavuchis' definition of a meaningful apology is instructive: 'To apologise is to declare voluntarily that one has *no* excuse, defence, justification or explanation for an action (or inaction).'[24] A newspaper headline at the time captured the difficulty with which politicians responded to the gross violation of human rights by their followers: 'Ag, we're sort of sorry', it read.

Politicians were not the only ones reluctant to accept responsibility for the past. The focus of the TRC was on certain gross violations of human rights, rather than on the more mundane, but traumatising dimensions of apartheid from which all white South Africans benefited. Eugene de Kock, the Vlakplaas commander, was labelled by the media as 'prime evil'. Jeffrey Benzien, a Western Cape Security Branch policeman, who demonstrated his notorious 'wet bag' method of torture before the amnesty committee, was seen on television screens and captured on the front page of most newspapers in the country. Such killers and torturers have been represented as psychopaths, aberrations and misfits. De Klerk singled them out as the 'rotten eggs' among the other disciplined, professional security force members. This tended to result in 'ordinary' white South Africans not taking responsibility for the past. In crypto-biblical style, many silently observe: 'I thank you, God, that I am not a murderer, a torturer or an assassin – that I am not like Eugene de Kock or Jeffrey Benzien.'

For all the failures of the TRC to engender a sense of shared responsibility among white South Africans as a basis for creating a more vigilant society in the future, political trials provide an even less viable option. The duty of the court is to prosecute against a charge sheet. Tina Rosenberg contends: 'Trials that seek to do justice on a grand scale risk doing injustice on a small scale; their goal must not be Justice but justice bit by bit by bit. Trials, in the end, are ill-suited to deal with subtleties of facing the past.'[25] The bigger picture is essentially ignored and lesser players in the drama remain largely untouched. This persuades Minow to argue for truth commissions not as 'a second best alternative to prosecutions', but instead a form better suited to meet the many goals pertinent to a situation of transitional politics.[26]

The TRC has done no more than invite South Africans to take responsibility for their role in the past. The resources of the nation's artists, storytellers, journalists, teachers, religious communities, NGOs and opinion-makers need to be harnessed to ensure that the honest ownership of the past is acknowledged. In a word, acknowledgement is incomplete.

Reparation

The TRC Act limited, from the beginning, the activities of the Commission regarding victims. It could *grant* amnesty to perpetrators. It could do no more than *recommend* reparation to victims. The matter is discussed elsewhere in this book. Suffice it to say, four broad areas (as identified by the *TRC Report*), which were beyond the capacity of the TRC to engage, wait to be addressed.

One is the counselling and healing of victims, addressed by trauma clinics and similar initiatives. This invaluable work needs to be extended to make facilities available to traumatised people across the nation.

The second is the healing and rehabilitation of perpetrators. The focus of the TRC on victim testimony has been a major strength. Interestingly, the peace initiatives in Northern Ireland have been criticised for being focused on perpetrators in its prisoner release programme. Those supportive of the Northern Ireland initiative defend their perpetrator focus, arguing that it is ultimately in the interests of victims that perpetrators be re-integrated into society.

Another area that needs to be addressed is the issue of narrowing the gap between the rich and the poor. Archbishop Njongonkulu Ndungane and Professor Sampie Terreblanche deal with this matter in the final section of this book. The public silence around the TRC's report on the business and labour hearings and their recommendations still needs to be addressed.

Lastly, there is the promotion of human rights and democracy. The participation of traumatised people in their own healing and in finding solutions to the nation's problems is a key ingredient to social transformation. The affirmation of socio-economic rights in the Bill of Rights and recommendations on reparation by the TRC are insufficient in themselves. The participation of those victimised by the past in claiming these rights is crucial. This requires a society within which free speech, the right to organise and open, critical, debate is guaranteed.

Reconciliation

Political wisdom in transitional politics has to do with steering the ship between impunity and unrestricted punishment (what Odysseus would have seen as the *only* passage between Scylla and Charybdis). The long and fragile journey to reconciliation with a measure of justice is the focus of several chapters in this book. Restorative justice is a tall order. Its demands extend beyond prosecution and the courtroom. It includes punitive justice where necessary, while ultimately addressing the covenant the nation has made with itself concerning the values captured in the postscript to the interim constitution.

Howard Zehr suggests that from a restorative justice perspective the South African TRC 'is flawed, opportunities have been missed, but the importance of this understanding [of justice] – not only in South Africa, but for the world – must not be underestimated. It is a bold step on an uncharted path.'[27] It has been suggested in this chapter that restorative justice by definition extends beyond any particular political initiative or judicial procedure. It has to do with what President Mandela in his final address to the opening of Parliament in February 1999 called the 'RDP of the soul'. It involves what Shimon Perez, speaking in a different context, calls 'not a dogma, [but] a civilisation, a set of attitudes to peace, justice and equality'.[28]

George Bizos argues that South Africa had a choice between 'the silence of perpetrators without justice being done, and learning the truth without perfect justice having been done'. The choice of the latter involves amnesty. In this situation, he concludes that if justice and amnesty 'are not sisters, they are at least first cousins'.[29] No model of justice covers all the stops. Restorative justice, not least in a situation of political transition, is about not neglecting those 'stops' that prepare the way for victims and perpetrators, their respective families, their communities and the nation as a whole to learn to live together after years of enmity. This is never an instant affair. It takes time. It involves *ubuntu*, which is a new experience for many people.

A strong case is to be made for allowing the people in each particular transitional situation to decide for themselves with what set of problems they can best afford to live. The battle between those supporting the International Criminal Court and those in favour of truth commissions has only just started. This battle is, in fact, indirectly waged in a number of essays in this anthology. It is directly addressed in the chapter by Paul van Zyl.

Making moral judgements

MARY BURTON

Any structure like the South African Truth and Reconciliation Commission (TRC), created after a period of conflict as one of the mechanisms for sustaining peaceful coexistence between past adversaries, must necessarily base its findings on moral principles. Although such commissions are necessarily constrained by the circumstances prevailing in the new, and sometimes transitional, governing systems, their decisions should stand the test of international scrutiny and also of widespread and lasting national acceptance. The South African Commission sought to meet international standards, but its work and its report evoked a measure of controversy – not least in government circles. Its lasting acceptance will depend on increasing understanding of its principles and of its criteria for making judgements. It will also depend on the way in which its recommendations are carried out.

During the parliamentary debate on the report of the TRC, Thabo Mbeki, then deputy president, referred to the positive contribution made by the Commission to the discovery and exposure of the truth, the cultivation of a spirit of remorse, and the encouragement of reconciliation between perpetrators and victims. However, he took issue with the Commission on specific judgments it had made, speaking of its 'erroneous logic … including the general implication that any and all military activity that results in the loss of civilian lives constitutes a gross violation of human rights'. He suggested that the Commission's findings were 'contrary even to the Geneva Conventions and Protocols governing the conduct of warfare'. This is a clear misperception of the Commission's conclusions, which were, in fact, based on careful study of the Geneva Conventions and Protocols, and gave careful consideration to how gross violations of human rights should be defined in the context of a war situation or a state of internal conflict. The early meetings of the Commission devoted considerable attention to the delicate dividing lines between the different categories of acts carried out during the 34-year period it was to review. Indeed, no chapter in the report received more attention than the Mandate Chapter, which deals with these matters. It was debated over a seven-month period and ultimately enjoyed the broad support of all Commissioners. It deserves careful reading.[1]

The mandate given to the Commission by the provisions of the Promotion of National Unity and Reconciliation Act served to assist with this process of definition. However, the legislation also created constraints that were to cause the Commission considerable difficulties. Among the particular issues to be faced were the criteria for the granting of amnesty, the definition of 'gross violations of human rights', the requirement of even-handedness, the notion of the responsibility of leaders for the actions of their followers, and the need to measure the rights of persons accused of violations against the rights of the victims.

Amnesty

The provision for the granting of amnesty to people who applied and who fulfilled the criteria had to be accepted as the result of the political negotiations that had permitted the transfer of power to a democratically elected government. It was an aspect of the Commission's work that was hotly contested at the public meetings and workshops organised to inform the public, and one about which Commissioners were closely questioned during media interviews. Many of the Commissioners themselves found it difficult to be reconciled to the idea that perpetrators of abuses should escape punishment. Even towards the end of the Commission's life, there were public protests against specific decisions of the Amnesty Committee. Public opinion continued to be divided about the benefits of amnesty, and the families of many victims continued to press for justice.

Nevertheless, the Commission as a whole was obliged to come to terms with its prescribed duty, and assume its power for the granting of specific amnesty where the conditions were fulfilled. But even within the bounds of the legislation, there was scope for debate about what were politically motivated offences, or what would be construed as full disclosure. Ideally, all the members of the Amnesty Committee should have been involved in discussing these issues. The considerable autonomy bestowed on the Committee by the legislation, in retrospect, is a significant weakness in the legislation. The fact that the majority of its members were not Commissioners meant that they were not exposed to the often intense debates on these matters that took place in the Commission. Although the legislators may have intended the autonomy of the Amnesty Committee to ensure the impartiality of the Amnesty Committee, this separation created some difficulties and confusion that might otherwise have been avoided. It could be argued, for instance, that the Amnesty Committee's initial granting of amnesty to a number of African National Congress leaders, which was challenged in court by the Commission itself and was sent back for review, need never have happened if there had been close consultation between the committees (not in order to influence decisions by the Amnesty Committee, but to create a shared awareness of the task of the Commission as a whole).

The amnesty application from the ANC leaders could be regarded as a symbolic action intended to demonstrate their acceptance of collective responsibility for actions taken by others, which they might not have authorised or approved, or might not have known the details, but which they recognised as having been carried out in support of their cause. Since the legislation did not provide for amnesty for such unspecified actions, it might have been best to refuse the amnesty, but welcome the gesture. Indeed such a response might have encouraged other leaders to take similar steps to acknowledge political, moral or what Karl Jaspers called 'metaphysical guilt'.[2] Such acknowledgement of responsibility from all political sectors could also have helped victims to come to terms with the amnesty process. It would have lifted some of the burden of guilt from amnesty applicants, or at least set their actions in a political context. The only acceptable reason to choose the path of amnesty, instead of trials, was in order to promote peace and reconciliation. It was important for those who had to make decisions about granting amnesty to keep this aspect in mind as they weighed up the other requirements set down in the legislation.

A further constraint created by the legislation lay in the differentiation between the 'gross violations of human rights' that were to be investigated by the Committee on Human Rights Violations, and the 'politically motivated offences' that would qualify for amnesty. This resulted in a dissonance between persons who were found by the Commission to have been victims of gross violations of human rights, and those found by the Amnesty Committee to have been victims of politically motivated offences. This had particular implications for the task of formally finding a person to be a 'victim' and, thus, eligible for reparations.

Defining 'gross violations of human rights'

The Commission's Report deals extensively with this definition in its Mandate Chapter.[3] Even this detailed discussion cannot convey the often tormented deliberations that took place in the Commission before final decisions were taken. Decisions had to be made not only on moral grounds, but also on practical grounds.

In the first place, the Commission was strongly challenged by submissions brought before it arguing that apartheid legislation had created a series of gross violations of human rights: the denial of the franchise, the unequal allocation of land and mineral wealth, residential segregation, as well as discriminatory practices in education, social services and work opportunities. The Commission freely accepted that the long history of racially based injustice formed the foundation on which the society had been based, but the Promotion of National Unity and Reconciliation Act had clearly delineated the specific kinds of gross violations that had to be examined. It would have been impossible for the Commission to cover the whole range of apartheid policies and practice – some of the matters raised were addressed through other government initiatives, such as the Land Claims Court and reforms in education and social services.

Nevertheless, the Commission clearly stated in its Report that issues based on racism created the context within which the specific violations had taken place. The Final Report would expressly place the particular incidents within the broader context. It is worth noting that whereas supporters of apartheid were wont to say that it was not an unjust system *per se*, but rather that it had not worked according to plan, there are few voices now raised to articulate this view. Ex-president De Klerk, in his submission to the Commission as leader of the National Party, made an apology for the pain and suffering caused by apartheid practices. Marthinus van Schalkwyk, leader of the New National Party, went further in parliament during the debate on the *TRC Report*, stating that apartheid was 'immoral' and 'unjust'. This remarkable change of attitude can be at least partly attributed to the success of the Commission in revealing the extent of the damage done.

The Commission concurred with the internationally accepted view that the apartheid system was a crime against humanity. The discussion within the Commission was not so much about the injustice and inhumanity of the system, which was not contested. It centred more on the question of whether the use of the words, 'crime against humanity', were so emotionally loaded as to hinder rather than foster the process of reconciliation. For a particular sector of South Africans, a 'crime against humanity' was equated with genocide, and was not accepted as a description of apartheid. The international documentation and definitions were carefully studied and a detailed appendix to the Mandate chapter laid out the arguments, including the distinction between genocide and a crime against humanity. Forced removals of groups of people, for example, are generally acknowledged as a crime against humanity, and these did indeed form part of the apartheid policy.

The legislation referred to 'killing, abduction, torture and severe ill-treatment'. Most of the statements made to the Commission fell into the last category, and the Commission interpreted them broadly rather than narrowly, in keeping with general international practice.[4] The result was that the members of the Committee on Human Rights Violations devoted considerable time and attention to findings concerning victims of severe ill-treatment. It could be argued that this energy would have been better spent investigating and debating such major violations as killings and torture, particularly since evidence in these matters was often difficult to obtain. This might have allowed the Commission to undertake fewer, but more detailed enquiries, and to provide the families of such victims with the kind of information they generally sought and expected. On the other hand, the fact that the legislation specified severe ill-treatment, without giving it a more precise definition, suggested that the legislators intended to create scope for investigation of a wide range of offences. The extensive record of incidents of severe ill-treatment, experienced throughout the country over the 34-year period under scrutiny, has created the richest possible picture of the suffering experienced by thousands of people. This is part of the legacy that needs to be used to ensure that such atrocities never happen again. It may well be that international attention should be given to the categorisation of violations of human rights. Some areas are absolutely straightforward: there can be no doubt that rape, solitary confinement, mutilation and poisoning constitute severe ill-treatment.

What of detention without trial? The Commission considered setting a minimum period beyond which such detention should be regarded a gross violation, and examined the provisions made in a number of countries. Suggestions varied from three to 14 days. Yet evidence generally suggested that when aggressive interrogation and torture took place they usually did so within the first three days, or even the first 24 hours. The Commission eventually agreed that detention without trial itself constituted severe ill-treatment, leaving the specific period open and assessing the individual cases on their particular circumstances.

What of the frequent use in South Africa of bannings and banishments? The Commission agreed these constituted severe ill-treatment and were, therefore, gross violations in terms of the Act.

Many of the statements referred to the destruction of a person's house through arson or other attacks, and these had indeed formed part of the political conflict in many areas. After lengthy consideration, the Commission agreed that the loss of a person's dwelling under such circumstances did constitute severe ill-treatment, since it involved not only material loss, but also emotional and mental suffering. The destruction of other property, such as a vehicle or business premises, was not considered a gross violation. This raised an interesting problem in that a number of people were granted amnesty for the destruction of such property (businesses or vehicles), and the Amnesty Committee identified the owners of such property as victims, referring their names to the Reparations Committee. This can be justified as legally appropriate, since the granting of amnesty effectively deprived such victims of their right to bring a claim for damages. However, it typifies the difficulty of having different committees of the same Commission operating according to different criteria.

The principles established by the Commission for making all these decisions are spelt out in the Report. It cannot convey the tension experienced by the committee members in wrestling with the difficulty of responding to a deponent that his or her experience was not sufficiently severe as to constitute a gross violation of human rights. Where could the line be drawn in each case? An elderly priest, obliged to jump from the window of his church when tear-gas was fired into it, and suffering considerable and lasting damage to his knees? A woman running in a crowd from volleys of rubber bullets, falling and being trampled on? A person in a bar when a bomb exploded, who still suffers psychological trauma, even though he was not physically injured?

'Just war' and 'just means'

The violations that were considered by the Commission had to be 'politically motivated' and deriving from the conflicts of the past. This clearly included all such actions taken with the intention of bringing about political change and actions carried out to resist such change. It brought the Commission face to face with the concept of a just war. The Report lays out its views on the concept of a just war, and points out the particular difficulty of applying the relevant international principles and criteria to 'unconventional wars' – internal rebellion, civil war and guerrilla warfare. While recognising that many supporters of the South African government regarded military and police activities to combat unrest as legitimate action to protect the country from a communist-inspired onslaught, the Commission concluded that 'those who fought against the system of apartheid were clearly fighting for a just cause, and those who sought to uphold and sustain apartheid cannot be morally equated with those who sought to remove and oppose it'.[5]

The processes of the Commission engendered considerable public debate in South Africa about whether any actions carried out by a liberation movement could be considered illegitimate. There may well be a large sector of the population that believes all such actions to be justified. It would also appear that many people who supported the government's forces were sympathetic to the old adage that 'all's fair in love and war'. The concept of *jus in bello* – justice in war, or what is known as just means – the principle that even in war there are rules of justice that prevail in all circumstances, has until recently not been widely known. The political leadership of all parties, however, clearly recognised the principle. Spokespersons for the government of the time and for the liberation movements spoke of steps that had been taken to prevent or limit actions that would contravene it. Leaders took responsibility for legitimate actions carried out under orders, but often refused to acknowledge accountability for the actions of people they defined as rogue elements or rotten apples. Amnesty applicants, on the other hand, generally spoke of their understanding that they were acting under orders, however unspecific, and that they had a free hand to use whatever means were necessary.

It is important for the future of South Africa that ongoing attention be given to this discussion. While it is understandable that political leaders should pay tribute to the courage and determination of those who waged a liberation struggle, or to soldiers whose duty it was to obey orders, it is necessary to acknowledge that some acts were, and remain, indefensible. Internationally, there is a need for continued examination of what can be expected of participants in unconventional warfare. In particular, the proper treatment of prisoners of war and of suspected traitors and spies needs to be further specified in international codes of conduct.

The African National Congress (ANC) is in a strong position to make a valuable contribution to such a debate. The fact that it established commissions of inquiry to look into allegations of detention, interrogation, torture and executions in its own camps, that it accepted their findings and that it made frank admissions to the TRC, stands to its credit. ANC spokespersons at various hearings acknowledged responsibility, although in some cases this was accompanied by explanations, excuses and rationalisations. The last-minute legal challenge to the TRC's Report was a disappointment to the Commission, as were statements by some ANC spokespersons rejecting its findings.

It is essential that the organisation participates in discussions on these issues. Clearly further debate is needed to ensure that a firm foundation is established on which future conduct in and out of war can be based. It is not enough for the former Deputy President simply to state that the Commission's findings contradicted the Geneva Conventions and Protocols. The deliberations of the Commission in this regard are there to be read and debated – and challenged, if necessary, against chapter and verse of these declarations.

The ANC had first-hand experience of the difficulties of identifying informers and spies, of sifting evidence and weighing allegations, and of conducting trials in extremely adverse circumstances. It would bring to a theoretical discussion a realistic perception of what could be expected: what would be the minimum requirements for protection of the rights of the accused in such circumstances? South Africa's newly integrated police and military forces could also make a useful contribution to an international study of acceptable mechanisms for maintaining peaceful conditions in troubled transitional societies. The international community could be well served by a grounded analysis of the Geneva Conventions and Protocols in the light of unconventional war.

Combatants

As the flow of statements increased, the Committee for Human Rights was confronted with the question of the status of combatants. Members of armed formations, whether they served the state or the liberation movements, were clearly identified as combatants and, thus, defined neither as perpetrators nor victims of gross violations of human rights, except where 'grave breaches' of conduct occurred as spelt out in international agreements. (These are documented in the Report and include torture, extra judicial executions, and cruel, humiliating and degrading treatment.)[6]

Every combatant taking up arms or participating in other ways in the armed struggle had done so consciously (even if unwillingly, as many conscripts testified). Soldiers in MK and APLA, as well as members of the SADF, who were killed or injured could not be classed as victims. It would have been contrary to international principles, and also to the understanding of the military forces themselves. In spite of this, the Commission recognised that the loss of every single life in South Africa's political conflict and the suffering of every combatant was a personal and human tragedy. The experience of the conflict, and the pain and losses incurred, were obstacles to the reconciliation and unification of the country. This is an aspect that must not be overlooked when steps are taken towards rehabilitation and reconciliation: those combatants who were not victims of gross violations in terms of the Act (and therefore not eligible for reparations through the TRC process) should qualify for military pensions or other provision.

Although it was relatively straightforward for the Commission to identify combatants when they were soldiers in specific armed formations, it was much more difficult when the combat was waged by unofficial or semi-official groups. A member of a self-defence unit, for example, would clearly define himself or herself as a combatant in the struggle, but could scarcely fit the international criterion of being part of an organised force under a command responsible for the conflict.[7] A member of the police force, in a situation when the police were called upon to control resistance, could be considered a combatant, yet if the same police personnel were attacked (or committed a gross violation) when not on duty, they could be victims or perpetrators. These uncertain areas in which the Commission was obliged to make findings based on the circumstances of each case indicate a need for further international clarification of the criteria to be used.

The list of victims

The five-volume report presented to President Mandela at the end of October 1998 contained a partial list of victims – those whose statements had been dealt with at the time of publication. The final list of names is to be published in a supplementary volume, yet it must be emphasised that even this can never be regarded as a complete list of those who suffered death or injury. There are other records available – registers compiled by other organisations, official lists of casualties, and other documentation. There were violations that took place outside the 34-year mandate of the TRC, or which took place outside South Africa's borders and could not be investigated. There are also many deeds that have gone unrecorded and many people who have chosen not to speak, either about abuses they committed or experiences they suffered. The list compiled by the Commission, therefore, is like so much of its work: symbolic, as well as factual. It is an actual list of people who suffered gross violations of human rights and were named in statements made to the TRC, or who were revealed through the process of amnesty.

Understanding as a means toward reconciliation

If reconciliation and national unity are to be achieved in South Africa, a clear understanding of the past conflict will be indispensable. The fact is that lines are often blurred, that truth is hard to find, and common perceptions difficult to reach. The Commission has been as open as it can to scrutiny of how it reached its findings, so that South Africans can better learn to put the past behind them and together set standards for the future. The final word has not, however, been spoken. Again, careful, rational discussion must continue.

When the assassin cries foul: the modern Just War doctrine

KADER ASMAL, LOUISE ASMAL AND RONALD SURESH ROBERTS

In our book, *Reconciliation through truth: a reckoning of apartheid's criminal governance* (1997), we emphasised that the Truth and Reconciliation Commission (TRC) was set up to stir debate, not to announce incontrovertible truths:

> *Our state-sponsored Commission has no monopoly on processes of historical rectification. It is not the sole forum of the voices of the South African people, nor will it provide the only resource for the subsequent interpretative efforts of an unbounded range of historians, intellectuals or schools of thought. This is not to say that it can avoid making judgments of its own. It must judge. But also it will be judged.*[1]

That judgment time has now come. Overall, the Commission completed an enormous task with great humanity and strength, and produced a considerable record of undoubted value. The Commissioners listened with sympathy to heart-rending testimony from hundreds of victims and survivors of the apartheid years, and gave a voice to those who had been silenced for so long. It criticised unsparingly the former regime's violence towards neighbouring states, revealed or confirmed considerable detail about mysterious deaths and disappearances, and gave an eye-opening account of the apartheid chemical and biological warfare programme that had for so many years been successfully covered up.

And yet, the Commission, at least in one respect, failed to come to terms with the heart of its mandate, and failed in a manner that bears on the usefulness of its Report as a whole. On the one hand, it declared firmly that apartheid was indeed a crime against humanity. On the other, it failed to draw some of the necessary conclusions from this finding. The whole apartheid system could rightly be labelled a gross violation of human rights, yet the Commission failed to review the terms of its mandate and so was unable to suggest a coherent concept of the 'gross violations of human rights', which were the subject of its investigation. It condemned human rights violations that were central to apartheid, causing apartheid to be condemned as a crime against humanity, in particular its racial divisions and its social engineering of the country into racially segregated enclaves. Nevertheless, the Commission concluded that these violations may not have been 'gross' as defined by the Promotion of National Unity and Reconciliation Act of 1995 (referred to in this chapter as the 'Act'), which gave birth to the Commission.

Thus, in construing an act that deliberately gave them much scope to exercise moral judgment in the interpretation of their mandate, the Commissioners treated a narrow definition of gross human rights abuse as though it were definitively settled by the relatively broad language of the Act, language that both permits and requires that the Commissioners embark on moral and political evaluation in construing their mandate.[2] The term 'gross violation of human rights' is broadly defined in the Act to include 'any violation through killing, abduction, torture or severe ill-treatment of any person' or 'any attempt, conspiracy, incitement, instigation, command or procurement' to commit the foregoing.[3] The Commission's sporadic doubts about whether – or to what extent – apartheid social policies constituted gross human rights abuses cannot be blamed on the Act, which was amply phrased so as to permit a different answer, one that the Commissioners chose not to embrace.

Quite apart from the ample terms of the Act, the words 'gross violations of human rights' and their application to apartheid in particular have long histories within the United Nations (UN) and other international bodies. There is no doubt that the terms used in the Act derive from international usage, and in particular from the United Nations Commission on Human Rights. This usage referred to the atrocity of apartheid, and not to the individual acts of abuse to which the enforcement and defence of apartheid gave rise. Thus, for example, when this UN Commission resolved, in its Resolution 8 (XXXIII), to examine information relevant to gross violations of human rights and fundamental freedoms, 'as exemplified by the policy of apartheid practised in the Republic of South Africa,' it was not referring to individual acts of abuse but to the inherent injustice of and suffering caused by the apartheid laws.

This interpretation can be found in many UN documents and resolutions. To cite but one further example: the UN Sub-Commission on Prevention of

Discrimination and Protection of Minorities in its resolution 1 (XXIV) of 13 August 1971 specifically stated that it would accept communications as admissible only if they 'reveal a consistent pattern of gross and reliably attested violations of human rights and fundamental freedoms, including policies of racial discrimination, segregation and of apartheid ...'.

This is not to deny that 'gross violations of human rights' also include the individual acts of abuse, torture and murder on which the Commission largely concentrated. But the Commission's failure to put individual acts in their due moral, political and international legal contexts has subverted the underlying intention of the Act, and has certainly given rise to skewed press coverage in South Africa. To some extent, the press found justification for its reportage in the introduction to the Commission's Report by its chairperson, Archbishop Desmond Tutu, and in his remarks at the press conference introducing the Report.

'Our country is soaked in the blood of her children, of all races and political persuasions,' Archbishop Tutu states in his foreword. In a perhaps laudable, but certainly mistaken attempt to be even-handed, Tutu in his foreword takes examples from all sides of the conflict, giving the impression that the apartheid police were no more guilty of murder than were the members of Umkhonto we Sizwe, the African National Congress's armed wing. Of course, the statistics in the body of the Report prove this impression false, but the initial wrong impression is difficult to erase. The points made by the Archbishop, in the first few paragraphs of the Report, refer to individual cases of abuse, and thus reinforce the emphasis on the criminality of individual actions, rather than on the criminality of the apartheid system, which gave rise to the actions.

In any case, it is simply not true that South Africa is 'soaked in the blood of her children of all races', even if the Archbishop did not mean 'children' to be taken literally. Very few civilian supporters of the apartheid regime died. Indeed, by comparison with other countries in the world, few people of whatever political persuasion died in the course of actual conflict. This is in contrast to the thousands who died or disappeared in some of the Latin American countries that have also set up truth commissions. Guatemala's truth commission, for example, documented the killings of more than 200 000 people in the civil conflict, and the massacre of over 600. African children died in South Africa mainly due to apartheid policies that banished them to unhealthy environments. Only second to that did they die because of military violence. Yet the Commission did not unambiguously pronounce this 'a gross violation of human rights'.

Conversely, the Commission states that the term 'severe ill-treatment' (a sub-category of the Act's gross human rights definition) does include 'the destruction of a person's house through arson or other attacks, which made it impossible for the person to live there again'. So rendering a house uninhabitable was a gross human rights abuse, but forced removals were not. The Commission thus failed to generate a defensible concept of 'gross violations of human rights', which were, according to the governing legislation, the principal subject matter of its investigations. Instead, the Commission defined human rights abuse as wrongs inflicted by one person on another, rather than inflicted by a state on groups that it racially defined and then violently disfavoured.

The root of this failing, we now argue, is the Commission's inability to resolve the central moral, political and legal issue: the significance of the Just War doctrine in the apartheid conflict. The Commission has not given enough weight to the impact that apartheid has had on international law and morality in the postwar era. The long-term existence of a pariah regime – an outlaw government – among nations has changed the law of nations itself. Particular moral and legal concepts emerged to deal with this unprecedented situation, one analogous to, yet different from the situation of national liberation movements generally. The key question (can an unjust regime participate in and benefit from the rules governing the just conduct of law?) arose with particular force and with jurisprudentially innovative results in the case of apartheid.

Ultimately, apartheid comprised, in international law, a breach of the laws of war. And as such it required a new approach, to which the Commission could have contributed, but has not, in dealing with the norms that bind those who resist the infliction of illegal military force upon them.[4] The liberation movement possessed a particular moral and legal claim, arising from this predicament that has been crudely summarised as the Just War doctrine. But, in fact it is much more than that. To show this, we look at the Just War doctrine itself and then go on to demonstrate the related, yet quite different moral and legal claim possessed by the anti-apartheid movement and neglected by the Commission, to the detriment of its Report.

From the Just War doctrine to *jus ad bellum* and *jus in bello*

The Just War doctrine can be traced back to ancient Rome and through St Augustine and St Thomas Aquinas to the early days of international law when, as might be expected, most of the powerful, colonising states relied on that interpretations of the doctrine, which suited their expansionist ambitions.

One reason for the early 20th century disrepute into which the Just War doctrine fell was the argument – admittedly, not a logical corollary of the Just War doctrine, but one frequently used – that once the cause was just, the conduct of the war need not acknowledge restraint. At heart this is a debate, fundamental to international law, over whether war is justiciable (whether it is capable of being regulated by legal constraints) or whether that aspiration is merely a hopeless vanity of lawyers.

Those who maintained that the conduct of war could be meaningfully influenced by legal notions were understandably opposed to the idea that the justice of the cause of war (*jus ad bellum*) might settle the separate question of the justice of the manner in which the war was conducted (*jus in bello*). The Just War doctrine, which sometimes seemed to conflate and settle these two questions as though they were one, consequently fell into disrepute among many sections of enlightened international legal opinion. But the conflicts of the 20th century – not least the battle against apartheid itself – have caused many jurists to re-examine these ideas.

Legitimacy, state sovereignty and the Just War doctrine

In the classic positivist Just War model, the merits of the conflict between opponents and supporters of apartheid is irrelevant, and only the actual conduct of the parties demands scrutiny. Certain commentators on the work of the TRC have adopted this view, which proceeds as though international law and morality stopped evolving in the 1920s.[5]

In fact, had this been so, the question of just conduct in the execution of war could not even arise, because a liberation movement, conducting a war of national liberation, would have been denied legal status in international law, since it lacked the status of a state.[6] But since then, and in particular in the light of the atrocities committed by states and resisted by non-state 'partisans' and governments in exile in the Second World War, international law's subservience to the power of states has declined. Before the Second World War, a war of national liberation, in which citizens rose up against a colonial power, would have been treated as an internal rebellion, in which the sovereign state had discretion to suppress as it saw fit. Since 1945, in particular after Article 1(4) of the 1977 Geneva Protocol I, national liberation movements may have access to the benefits of the status of combatant, imposing on illegitimate colonial states the constraints of war-making, which would classically have been reserved for interstate conflicts only. This modification was made after express consideration of the South African struggle, among others.[7] Self-determination was recognised as a right, and the United Nations General Assembly passed a number of resolutions affirming the right of the liberation movements to conduct their struggle 'by all available means, including armed struggle'. If, as the Commission states, the 'ANC is morally and politically accountable for creating a climate in which supporters believed their actions to be legitimate', then international bodies, such as the UN, must also share in the Commission's opprobrium.

The fact that the nature of the struggle was taken as relevant to the status of those involved led certain commentators to object that Just War doctrine was exerting 'a curious recrudescence'[8] both because third party states were permitted and exhorted to attack illegitimate colonial states and also because the positivist criteria (eg substantial control of contested territory) that have previously governed access to the benefits of the laws of war were being waived in favour of liberation movements. They were granted the benefits of combatant status, even if they manifestly fell short of the objective attributes of statehood or near-statehood.[9]

In short, the horrors of the mid-century and the subsequent horrors of apartheid made international lawyers unwilling to overlook the pariah nature of certain illegitimate states, those whose illegitimacy violates the very core, the *jus cogens*, of international law. Equally, post-1945 international law was unwilling to overlook the justness of the cause of the opponents of such states. States in general, and the apartheid state in particular, could lose their right to defend themselves[10], while liberation movements, such as the ANC, could acquire protected status as combatants in international law, even though they were not states.[11]

In the end – and here we approach the heart of the present analysis – these developments dismantle the otherwise tidy distinction between the justice of the cause of war (*jus ad bellum*) and justice in the execution of war (*jus in bello*). An utterly illegitimate state, whose everyday acts are illegal under international law, simply lacks any capacity to act justly in the execution of war. Its ordinary acts of governance inflicted on its own citizens, let alone its acts of war inflicted on other states, are illegitimate and inherently foul of the requirements of justice.

This fact is evident in international law. Article 85 of Protocol I (1977) to the Geneva Conventions, governing the conduct of war, stipulates that certain heinous actions shall constitute 'grave breaches' of the laws governing the conduct of war. States are required to make such acts punishable under their own domestic criminal laws and to prosecute offenders vigorously. These 'grave breaches' in the conduct of war, as listed in Article 85(3) of Protocol I, include familiar offences, such as indiscriminate attacks on civilians. But of enormous significance for the present analysis is the new grave breach of the laws of war listed in Article 85(4), deriving from 'practices of apartheid and other inhuman and degrading practices, involving outrages upon personal dignity, based on racial discrimination'.

Apartheid, which came to be considered a just cause of war (*jus ad bellum*) is here, in the explicit terms of Protocol I, acknowledged to constitute, in and of itself, an unjust means of war. Article 85(4)(c) confirms that apartheid violates, in and of itself, the requirements of *jus in bello*, a development that indeed we can see prefigured in the original Geneva conventions themselves. Article 3, common to all four Geneva Conventions, provides that all persons not involved in the conflict, including combatants who have laid down their arms, 'shall in all circumstances be treated humanely, without any adverse distinction founded on race, colour, religion or faith, sex, birth or wealth, or any similar criteria'. Yet apartheid imposed adverse distinctions on all blacks, combatant or otherwise, in prison or otherwise, who fell under its sway.

In philosophical terms the laws of war are 'convention-dependent'. That is, they are forms of reciprocal obligations that set out to minimise unnecessary harm to all concerned. In this context 'what one's opponent does ... are facts of great moral importance. Such facts help one to determine what convention, if any, is operating, and thus they help one to discover what his moral duties are.'[12]

The comforting symmetry that has thus far dominated the Just War debate needs, therefore, to be questioned. Commentators, some of them well meaning, have conceded that the liberation movement had just cause (*jus ad bellum*) and that the apartheid regime did not. But they have unjustifiably insisted that the significance of this first concession falls away as one addresses the second question, just conduct of war (*jus in bello*). Given the convention-dependent nature of the morality of war, and apartheid's wholesale breach of those conventions, the question of *jus ad bellum* cannot be arbitrarily separated from the latter question of justice in the conduct of the cause, *jus in bello*. The effect of doing this would be to reduce an important debate over the justice of the collective initiation and conduct of the anti-apartheid struggle to a debate over individual criminal or quasi-criminal liability.

Those commentators who treat the laws of war as absolute (rather than convention-dependent) rules of conduct advance their arguments by explicit reference to analogies with criminal conduct.[13] The analogy is misleading, since 'warfare, unlike ordinary criminal activity, is not an activity in which individuals engage as individuals or as members of voluntary associations. They enter into war as members of nations. It is more proper to say that the nation is at war than that its soldiers are at war.'[14]

It is important to be as clear about what this argument proves as about what it does not. It does not allow individual war criminals to escape responsibility under the claim that 'they were only following orders'. Nor does it excuse individuals from moral responsibility for their actions.[15] Nor does it license uninhibited attacks on white civilians in response to apartheid's wholesale onslaught against black ones. The liberation movement remained bound by requirements of proportionality. And, in fact, it observed these requirements, a fact that the Commission nowhere sufficiently credits and which must affect the status of civilian deaths as gross human rights violations.

Constand Viljoen conceded, in his just war testimony before the Commission, that apartheid's methods 'brought war closer to politicians and also brought soldiers closer to politics', circumstances under which 'certain political officials can be regarded as combatants'.[16] Similarly, given the militarism of society under apartheid, the drafting into military functions of farmers in border areas, the Key Points Act that militarised suburban civilian sites, such as factories, the compulsory conscription laws that systematically converted civilians into militarists, and the electorate's sustained support, over decades, of apartheid's criminal governance, the easy application of an absolute rule against harming civilians is unsustainable. Nevertheless, the ANC never invoked these arguments as an unrestrained mandate to attack civilians. Exercising restraint, for which it has not been sufficiently credited by the Commission, the ANC did all in its power to minimise civilian casualties. The civilian casualties of apartheid number thousands of dead, and millions of forcibly removed people, including infants, who could not survive in areas where there was no water. Conversely, estimates of the civilians who fell at the hand of the resistance movement vary between 68 and 2 000, depending on which source one consults.

There is simply no proportionality between the two sides of the struggle, a fact that is lost in the Commission's decision to individualise its definition of gross human rights abuse. The Commission's implicit resort to criminal or quasi-criminal notions of responsibility in defining what counts as a gross human rights abuse treats like and unlike the same way. And this is a failure deriving from a lack of political and ethical understanding. A regrettable loss of human life in the course of a proportional response to apartheid's wholesale criminality cannot be assessed in the same way as the violence of apartheid itself.

The convergence of human rights law and the laws of war

Since apartheid is *ipso facto* a grave breach of the laws of war, any state practising apartheid is required, by Article 85 of 1977 Protocol I, to enact domestic laws, making apartheid itself criminal and punishing its practitioners. The fact that the apartheid regime refused to acknowledge this does not lessen the validity of international norms, since the dissent of the perpetrator itself cannot alleviate international law liability in respect of a violation of the *jus cogens*, the settled core of international law.

The most important point for present purposes is this: the old, seemingly simple distinction between fighting the good fight, the just cause (*jus ad bello*), versus justice in the conduct of that battle (*jus in bello*) is no longer so simple. This is recognised by commentators of various political stripes, including academic opponents of the new developments. One such observed: 'the precise nexus between armed conflicts and practices of apartheid is not clear, but the confusion between the 'cause' for which the conflict is being waged and the conduct of the conflict is clear'.[17]

Modern international law in relation to apartheid and the resistance to it denies, or at least severely curtails the scope of a conventional distinction between the just cause (*jus ad bello*) and the just conduct of the war (*jus in bello*). The apartheid regime was denied any resort to the notion that it was conducting its war against the liberation movement in a just fashion, because apartheid itself constituted a grave breach of the laws of war. This again is a point that has not been credited in the Commission's analysis to date. The separation of the laws of war (which some call international humanitarian law) from international human rights law (governing the basic international requirements of humane governance) is outdated.

> *Traditionally, these two branches of international law have addressed separate sets of issues: international humanitarian law has been concerned with the treatment of combatants and non-combatants by their opponents in wartime, while international human rights law has been concerned with the relationship between states and their own nationals on peacetime. Yet, even in earlier times they shared a fundamental concern: a commitment to human dignity and welfare, irrespective of the status of the individual (combatant or non-combatant) and of the circumstances under which his rights and responsibilities are to be exercised (peacetime or wartime).*[18]

The relatively recent Rwandan and Yugoslavian events, no less than apartheid before them, throw into question the inherited distinctions between civilian and military spheres, combatants and non-combatants. But in the case of apartheid, the system itself was viewed by Article 85 of 1977 Geneva Protocol I as a breach of the laws of war. An apartheid regime can neither initiate nor conduct a just war, and its wholesale disregard of conventions of societal and military justice creates moral and political leeway in the strategies adopted by those who oppose it. Otherwise, the indiscriminate hardship of economic sanctions, which did not distinguish between combatants and non-combatants, must be equated with the systematic, economic criminality of the apartheid system – an argument unlikely to appeal to the Commission's chairperson, who was among the most prominent advocates of anti-apartheid economic sanctions.

It is, therefore, wrong to analyse the conduct of the apartheid regime in terms that would apply to a legitimate state at war. The notions of proportionality and the prohibition against specific conduct that are the essence of the Geneva Convention and the Protocols are irrelevant in relation to the conduct of the apartheid regime, which was inherently a grave breach of the laws of war. It could never plead proportionality.

And what of the converse? What are the implications of all this for assessing the conduct of the liberation movement? How should one judge the conduct of those who continue to be victims of ongoing and systematic grave breaches of the laws of war? The Commission does seem to acknowledge that the two sides to the conflict were not equivalent, in terms of 'forces deployed, members or justice' (Vol 5, p 276), but it becomes strangely tentative when it states that 'the violence of the powerful, the South African state, was not necessarily equal to the violence of the powerless'. The Commission has not pursued this reasoning and so does not seem to have grasped the full extent of apartheid's illegitimacy under international law, and its status as a continuing grave breach of the laws of war. In this essay we have suggested a possible way to address this question, an approach founded in the recognition of the convention-dependent nature of the laws of war, applicable to apartheid's wholesale violation of those conventions. This late in the day, months after the publication of the Commission's Report, this debate is, alas, yet to begin in earnest.

Conclusion

Instead of coming to terms with the collective nature of apartheid's atrocities, the Commission has adopted a definition of gross human rights violations that individualises the conduct of persons on each side of the conflict, and then measures them against the same moral yardstick. This disregards the fundamentally different international law fabric of the contending sides.

Even if it were possible to identify 'identical acts' of individual atrocities committed by adversaries on each side of the conflict, this disparate moral, political and international legal fabric would remain. A stone thrown by a township dweller was not the same legal and moral act as a stone thrown by a soldier.[19] But already the notion of 'identical acts' dissolves into nonsense, because the soldier would not need to throw a stone, where hand grenades and Casspirs stand ready – where the resources of a state are at hand.

But let us assume, momentarily for the sake of argument, that one could identify a series of identical acts. The point would then become: is the moral, political and legal quality of the act identical, even if the physical action is the same? Here we approach the outer edge of international law. This is not a settled area of law, a place of clear precedent. There is no blanket of conventional wisdom to comfort us here. This fact is in itself significant: there is little settled law in this area, in part because those resisting criminal governments – for example, the anti-Nazi partisans in Second World War Europe – were never in the unseemly position of being placed on trial. However, the negotiated nature of the South African transition has produced a new set of circumstances that compel us to consider the issues afresh.

At Nuremberg, Goering attempted to defend Nazi atrocities by complaining that the Nazi occupiers were faced with an emergency situation 'caused by conduct violating international law, that is, by the unleashing of guerrilla warfare' by the partisans. This fact, he claimed, 'justified the army commanders to take general measures to remove these conditions brought about illegally'.[20]

General Taylor, for the prosecution, successfully rebuffed this argument, urging that the people of the occupied countries 'had every right to rise and defend themselves by armed force, because the Germans themselves so flagrantly violated the laws of war ... If the occupying forces inaugurate a systematic programme of criminal terror, they cannot thereafter call the inhabitants to account for taking measures in self-defence. This nowhere appears in so many words in the Hague Convention, but it is in entire harmony with the purposes of the articles, and I think no one will be heard to deny that this is the only conclusion that is possible in accordance with 'the principles of the law of nations, as they result from the usages established among civilised peoples, from the laws of humanity, and the dictates of the public conscience.'[21] This conclusion must be particularly apposite in the South African case, where apartheid's civil and political institutions and policies – let alone its military forays – constituted an ongoing severe breach of the wars of law.

Similarly, in the *Einsatzgruppen*[22] case, where the German defendants sought to escape liability for the execution of thousands of Jews, the Germans invoked the argument that their actions were legitimate reprisals against a civilian population that was failing in its alleged international law obligations of quiescence towards an occupying army. In order to invoke the doctrine of retaliation, the tribunal said that the Germans would first have to establish that the occupied Russian population behaved illegally. In order to establish the illegality of particular acts of resistance in Russia, the tribunal continued, 'it would still have to be shown that these acts were not in legitimate defence against wrongs perpetrated upon them by the invader. Under international law, as in domestic law, there can be no reprisal against reprisal. The assassin who is being repulsed by his intended victim may not slay him and then, in turn, plead self-defence.'[23]

How far is the doctrine of legitimate reprisals relevant to the conduct of a just war by a liberation movement that was subjected, over four decades, to a system which, in its everyday emanation, was a continuing 'grave breach' of the laws of war? How does the absolute bar, in the 1949 Geneva Conventions, against reprisals directed at civilians operate in a situation where civilian actions (the bureaucratic implementation of apartheid) themselves constitute a 'grave breach' of the laws of war? Was it right for the Commission to have dubbed as gross violations those civilian casualties that were not the deliberate result of anti-apartheid reprisals, but the collateral result of morally calibrated resistance efforts, aimed at military and police targets? How does Michael Walzer's much-debated concept of 'supreme emergency', which authorises, *in extremis*, otherwise unacceptable military strategies, apply to strategies taken up by a population that for decades suffered the continuing and severe infliction of war crime?[24]

These are important debates that the TRC never adequately considered. The Commission, for instance, distinguishes between the liberation movement's killing of military personnel, which it says was not a gross violation of human rights, and the killing of police force members, which the Commission considers could amount to a gross violation of human rights. This distinction, between hard and soft targets within the apartheid security forces, is questionable even from a narrow military perspective. The police force was a principal instrument of enforcing the apartheid laws, more feared in the townships than the military. In the light of the intrinsic criminality of apartheid itself, the Commission's fine distinctions look untenable.

The Just War doctrine has certainly outgrown its positivist and 'classical' baggage, but its post-Second World War evolution is all too frequently overlooked in South African debates. Rules that began, classically, as guides for the conduct of sovereign states and that were, therefore, symmetrical in their application, have been extended to the legitimate struggles of national liberation movements, where such symmetry is often a nonsense. The applicability of justice in the conduct of struggle action (*jus in bello*) to the case of legitimate movements for national liberation is an area that was institutionalised only in 1977, with the Geneva Protocols of that year. Thus in this, as in so many other respects, South Africa and its TRC were a new departure, both for South Africa and the rest of the world. The Commission had extraordinary success in many of the aims it was mandated to fulfil, but it failed in its moral judgment of the issues pertaining to the Just War doctrine. In this significant aspect of its work, on which we in this chapter have concentrated, the Commission was thus unable to contribute to the advancement of that doctrine beyond the level of outdated obeisance to the status of national states.

As the then Deputy President Thabo Mbeki said in his speech to the joint sitting of the Houses of Parliament on 25 February 1999:

Each one of us has a right and a duty to rebel against tyranny ... The great masses who engaged in a superhuman effort to rid themselves of tyrannical rule, their heroes and heroines, who gave up everything for freedom, remain unsung.

The Commission had an unenviable task of investigating innumerable complaints of human rights violations and sifting through the mass of testimonies within the time limits it set for itself. If it failed satisfactorily to sort through the wilderness of data presented to it, and itself to provide a morally defensible guide in future conflicts, it did provide a wealth of material on which such judgment can be made. Its work has shone a light into the dark recesses of apartheid which will illuminate our future debates and provide a rich source of material for the study of the infamy of apartheid. It is against this background that the heroism of those who struggled against apartheid must be judged.

The law and struggle: the same, but different

HUGH CORDER

Those in South Africa who have been involved over the decades with social justice have reacted in different ways to the role that law and the legal process can play in achieving an acceptable measure of that happy condition. Traditionalists argued for the maintenance of 'law and order' at all costs, denying the necessity to pursue the fight against the government's injustice through extra-legal means: thus the 'rule-by-law' lobby.[1] Liberal democrats pleaded persistently for the return to the 'rule of law', that socio-legal construct rooted in the Victorian ideology of empire and 'fair play', which is such an unspoken fundamental in the Westminster system. Over time, however, the most perceptive in this group recognised the futility of many of such arguments in the face of the unremitting pursuit of apartheid evil through all means, often unlawful. They began to argue for a vigorous pursuit of the small measure of justice, which they believed to be immanent in any ordered system of law, no matter how impoverished, through the exploitation of judicial choice in the interpretation of the ambiguities of the language of the law. They sought support for their stance in the 'coloured vote' and other cases of the 1950s, in which the Appellate Division in particular resisted the infamy of some early apartheid measures.[2]

The context

By the late 1970s, however, a deep-seated disillusionment about the potential of the law as a means to contain statutory evil and to achieve justice had set in on all sides,[3] especially post-Soweto. Some, of course, had long since reached this point, electing armed struggle as the last resort in the early 1960s, and going into exile to plan and train for such a strategy. Into this despondent atmosphere came the reports of the Wiehahn Commission into Labour Legislation in 1979-1980, which promised some improvements to the position in law of black workers and their representative organisations, and provided for such bodies to register with the Department of Labour/ Manpower. In other words, such benefits as the system allowed were available only to those who were prepared to play the game according to the rules laid down by law.

This initiative of the apartheid government unleashed a sometimes angry debate within the independent trade union movement and in the pages of the *South African Labour Bulletin*.[4] The crux of the opposing views was that participation in 'the system' would lead, on the one hand, to a bridgehead from which the whole edifice of capitalism/apartheid in the economy could be undermined, and, on the other, to co-option such that the opposition to that system would be neutralised and the end of apartheid postponed for years. Those who argued for strategic and vigorous engagement generally won the day, and it was fairly convincingly argued by the end of the 1980s that real gains, rather than meek co-option, had been the result.[5] In many ways, however, this argument was replicated in different spheres throughout that decade, and the outcome was mostly the election of the second strategy: thus the boycott of the tricameral parliament and the system for local government of urban blacks, as well as the bantustan-independence route, which largely dried up after 1982.

These disputes inevitably impacted on law and its potential as a tool for combating evil and achieving social justice. At certain law faculties, a minority of staff and students pursued these issues inside and out of the lecture halls, and there was similar debate within the practising profession, albeit within an extremely small, but vocal group.[6] A range of organisations sprung to life in this climate, the most noteworthy being the Legal Resources Centre, Lawyers for Human Rights, the National Association of Democratic Lawyers, the Black Lawyers' Association and the Centre for Applied Legal Studies. Advice offices sprang up in many rural towns and all the main cities, pushing the limits of the law as an agent of social change.

Perhaps the most celebrated 'sub-debate' that took place during these years was one that centred on the necessity for a bill of entrenched rights as part of any democratic legal order in a future South Africa. Once more, there were those who argued passionately that such an instrument was counter-majoritarian and would serve merely to preserve unjustly achieved wealth and power, while others proposed a more nuanced vision of democracy that was predicated on the inalienable basic rights of all. The eventual outcome of this difference of opinion was signalled by the adoption of the Constitutional Guidelines by the African National Congress (ANC) in exile in 1988, a document that itself included a bill of rights as one of its foundation stones.[7]

What has all of this to do with the Truth and Reconciliation Commission (TRC)? It is my argument in this brief piece that the TRC process represents vividly the outcome of this last point of debate, in essence the triumph of the idea of governmental power regulated and thus limited by law. The seal was set on this contractual compromise by the interim constitution, of which the TRC was the direct result, and reaffirmed in the final constitution of 1996. There are inevitable and often unjustified casualties and beneficiaries of any such election of a system of government, especially at a time of social transition.

It is in this context that the legal challenges to the TRC should be examined and evaluated. In sum, it seems that, once the rule of law/domination of the legal process/supremacy of the constitution enforced by judicial review had become established and accepted by the major political players as the 'lowest common denominator' or arena within which the hand-over of formal power and transformation of the substance of social relations was to take place, the game had to be played according to the agreed rules, and there could be no deviation from the cardinal features of the deal. The TRC process was one of the most important elements in that constitutional compact, which explains the highly contested passage of the enabling legislation, the Promotion of National Unity and Reconciliation Act,[8] as well as the continuing challenges through the courts.

The challenges

The legal disputes in which the TRC became embroiled are clearly described in the Commission's Report,[9] several of which also appear in the law reports. It is convenient for the purposes of this chapter to set out the main features of what I see as three categories of legal questions raised against the Commission.

Contesting the fundamentals

The first and perhaps most critical challenge that the TRC faced in court threatened to derail the whole undertaking. The Azanian People's Organisation (AZAPO) and the Biko, Mxenge and Ribeiro families (each of which had lost members in the apartheid struggle) questioned one of the key provisions of the Promotion of National Unity and Reconciliation Act – that which excluded the civil or criminal liability of those who had been granted amnesty by the TRC for gross human rights violations, as well as the vicarious liability of any body that could have been ordinarily held so responsible. The applicants argued that this amounted to an unjustifiable limitation of their constitutional right of access to court. Their success in this application would have struck at the heart of the entire truth and reconciliation process, but they failed before the Cape Supreme Court[10] and the matter went to the Constitutional Court.

For this court, its then Deputy President, Justice Mahomed, crafted a typically elegant series of reasons why the appeal could not succeed.[11] While he acknowledged the righteous indignation of those who had suffered most grievously under apartheid, Justice Mahomed built his judgment on the sentiments contained in the 'postscript' to the interim constitution, among which was that full amnesty of this type was an indispensable part of the entire negotiated settlement. He further argued that although individualised and direct civil liability was not allowed, the state could nevertheless be expected to make possible some other form of reparations for the surviving victims of apartheid. The court showed a keen sensitivity for the politics behind the arguments by finding that reaching the truth was much more improbable without encouraging its telling by the prospect of amnesty.

Thus was the constitutional compact preserved, and the TRC could proceed with its work. But a second, individual and localised challenge was more enduring and at one stage threatened to undermine the Commission's authority. In December 1997, after a long series of skirmishes in 1996 and 1997, the Commission finally ordered former State President PW Botha to appear before it to answer questions regarding his role as chair of the State Security Council. Botha belligerently neglected to comply and was prosecuted for this act of defiance in early June 1998. In late August he was found guilty of this offence, and sentenced to a large fine and a suspended term of imprisonment.[12] It seems clear that Botha's actions were intended to mobilise the former regime's supporters against everything the TRC stood for, but he failed in this attempt, not least because of his remarkably intransigent and hectoring manner.

Thus the Commission survived challenges in court from both sides of the political spectrum, either of which would have undermined the causes of truth and reconciliation, had it succeeded.

Questioning the Commission's procedures

One of the most difficult questions that faces any commission of enquiry, such as the TRC, is the extent to which it should adhere in its processes to the strict standards of impartiality and procedural fairness demanded of a court of law determining guilt or innocence. On the one hand, the Commission was an administrative body set up to enquire into a period of political history, to write a record and make recommendations, and two of its three committees – the Human Rights Violations (HRV) Committee and the Reparation and Rehabilitation (R and R) Committee – were generally composed of non-lawyers. On the other hand, the Amnesty Committee consisted entirely of lawyers (including several judges) and functioned almost as a court of law with the power to make legally binding decisions. The avowed purpose of all the activities of the Commission was to arrive at the 'truth', further indicating its formally legalistic nature, and the services of lawyers were retained by potentially 'guilty' parties from the outset.

The enabling act recognised this problem in Section 30, which required the Commission to follow prescribed procedure or to determine its own such procedure. It stipulated, furthermore, that 'during any investigation by or any hearing before the Commission', it had to give 'any person ... implicated ... to his detriment' or in respect of whom the Commission contemplated making a decision that might be to that person's detriment an opportunity to submit representations or give evidence about the matter 'within a specified time'. It can be seen that this provision required (rather imprecisely) a degree of procedural fairness to be observed, and it would have been advisable for the Commission to have determined a process in advance, in order to create a framework and some certainty, but this never happened. According to the Commission's own report,[13] its East London office 'ran into problems' in ensuring compliance with its legal obligations.

As a result, a number of legal actions involving former high-ranking police officers in the Eastern Cape were brought against the Commission,[14] all relying essentially on the argument that, if they were to be named as alleged violators of human rights by witnesses before the HRV Committee, Section 30 demanded that they be given proper and sufficient advance notice of the allegations against them, the substance of such allegations and reasonable opportunity for rebuttal. The Commission's difficulty was that although statements were taken from such potential witnesses in advance, their oral evidence did not have to be confined to such statements, and it argued that in any event hearings before the HRV Committee amounted to an administrative enquiry and that those named could address the allegations subsequently.

The court decision that most seriously impacted on the work of the TRC in this regard was that of the Appellate Division in Du Preez and Van Rensburg v TRC, delivered early in 1997.[15] The court held that any administrative authority (such as the Commission) was under a 'general duty to act fairly' in all circumstances, and that the notice given to the appellants had been deficient both in time and detail. An alleged perpetrator ought to be enabled by the notice to be present to hear the evidence, to see the demeanour of witnesses and to be provided with an opportunity to rebut the evidence.

This decision, although it was to be welcomed in the general context of South Africa's administrative law, marking a significant advance on previous practice in regard to the demands of fairness, had a substantial retarding effect on the work of the Commission. For example, the Commission had to employ extra staff to deal with the administrative burden of sending notices containing the substance of all allegations a full three weeks before any hearing. This legal finding also impacted negatively on the TRC's capacity to provide a sensitive and supportive atmosphere for victims, who thenceforth ran the risk of immediate cross-examination and confrontation with those whom they had alleged to be the perpetrators. The notice-giving obligation was furthermore present once the Commission reached the stage of writing its report, having to alert those whom it intended to 'name' as violators of human rights.[16]

This case (and there were other similar ones) demonstrates clearly how the formal requirements of the law can benefit even those who are alleged to have treated them with contempt in the past, and how easily a legalistic approach can take root. This trend is clear in the last group of legal challenges to be reviewed.

Party politics and obfuscation

The Commission also became embroiled in disputes with political parties across the spectrum. The National Party questioned its impartiality in court, while the Inkatha Freedom Party complained about the same issue to the Public Protector. The attempt by the leadership of the ANC to obtain amnesty jointly initially succeeded before the Amnesty Committee, but this action was then taken on review by both the National Party and the TRC itself. Hundreds of former defence force senior officers also alleged bias in a complaint to the Public Protector. Except for the review of the joint amnesty granted to the ANC leadership, which was set aside by the Cape Court and referred back to the Amnesty Committee, all of the above matters made media headlines, but ended inconclusively.

Several other challenges to the refusal of the Amnesty Committee to grant amnesty were taken on review to the Supreme Court without success. On the other hand, an accused on trial for acts committed in the cause of the apartheid regime succeeded in claiming the transcript of some evidence given to the Commission by a former accomplice.[17] Finally, there were several dramatic legal challenges in the last days of hearings held by the HRV Committee into the chemical and biological warfare programme of the former government in June 1998. Several witnesses sought rulings from the

Commission on points of law relating to their evidence, and one of them, Dr Wouter Basson, pursued with his challenge before the Cape High Court. He was, however, ordered to appear before the HRV Committee, and answer questions lawfully put to him.

This last category of legal challenges shows the ease and frequency with which legal process was resorted to by those dissatisfied with the TRC enterprise generally. This account is not complete, but certainly gives a good representation of the legal context in which the Commission operated. What does this tell us about the TRC, the law and politics post-apartheid?

The lessons

It was almost inevitable that the TRC would become embroiled in legal disputes when one considers what was expected of it against the horrendous background of apartheid. The idea of 'truth' and 'reconciliation' in many ways clash with each other, and the Commission was to some extent a noble but flawed product of intense political bargaining and compromise. Thus it was bound not to satisfy many in South Africa, but particularly those who, on the one hand, urged radical change and retribution and on the other hand wanted 'bygones to be bygones'. Better planning by the Commission on its procedures might have saved it a little embarrassment and limited delays in its hearings, but it should not come at all as a surprise that its work was subject to litigious scrutiny.

Perhaps of greater significance is the fact that opponents of the TRC's work resorted not to violent protest, but sought their day in court. Furthermore, such persons generally, albeit grudgingly, were prepared to abide by the decisions of the courts. For a country where state action had been accurately classified as 'lawlessness' only a decade previously, such a shift in strategy was extraordinary – especially because transformation of the judicial bench has proceeded slowly, and many of the judgments involving the TRC were handed down by judges appointed under apartheid.

What does this tell us about future governance in South Africa? Some might argue that the dominance of law is a temporary phase, induced by the wealth of possible remedies that are suddenly available and a weariness of the violence that has been the stuff of political activity for so long. I would prefer to point to the ready commitment to the principle of constitutionalism that has characterised so much of government action since 1994, and which is remarkably apparent in the reactions of former President Mandela to court orders adverse to the state.[18]

No one familiar with South Africa's history, nor with the ill-fated demise of many less ambitious attempts to install constitutional democracies on infertile ground, would be foolish enough to argue that the rule of law is forever secure as the organising principle of government in South Africa. There seems little doubt to me, however, that the challenging litigants' choice of law as the means of asserting their concerns and the resilience of the TRC in reply represent small but significant steps on the way to securing a constitutional democracy.

The choice, appointment and ultimate survival of the TRC provided a complex and deeply contested test case for the democratic ideals enshrined in the constitutions. It is my contention that the Commission generally acquitted itself well in the democracy-enhancing aspect of its impossible mandate, and that the legal challenges served to demonstrate this aspect of its work clearly. It must be acknowledged, nevertheless, that some of the cases outlined above show that the disjuncture, which is often present between 'law' and 'justice', can perhaps be explained by the pursuit of some greater goal. In other words, while it is accepted that there is often no good reason for rules of law not to further justice, sometimes it may be that a noble goal, such as successful political transformation and compromise or the value of adherence to a relatively predictable and fair legal process, might justify such discrepancies and apparent injustice to some. Thus, instead of arguing that 'an injury to one is an injury to all', perhaps it would be justified to acknowledge that 'an injustice to one leads to greater justice for all'. Whether these sacrifices will have been worth the cost remains to be seen.

Combating myth and building reality

COLLEEN SCOTT

Facts versus reality

In March 1968 an Aer Lingus flight inexplicably went into a spin and crashed into the Irish Sea. There was not a single survivor. More than 60 people died, but only 14 bodies were recovered. Bonnie Gangelhoff lost both her parents in this crash. In her article to mark the 31st anniversary of the continuing uncertainty surrounding the largest aviation disaster in Irish history, she writes: 'For 30 years many of us have known the disquietude that comes when family members vanish for no reason and there are no bodies to put in the ground, no way to say the proper prayer or final good bye.'

The Irish Ministry of Transport and Power released a sketchy official report in 1970, which raised more questions than it answered. Neither the Irish nor the British will release key documents about the crash, and there are disturbing suggestions that many documents may have been shredded.

Gangelhoff wrote of the gathering for those who had lost family and friends in this tragedy: 'We found out that there were still plenty of us who wanted to know the truth about what happened to our mothers, fathers, sisters and brothers. And we are not going away.'[1]

Every single person who lost someone on that flight knows that they are really dead. How much more difficult is it to rebuild a life on the other side of a loved one's disappearance if you do not know – really know – whether or not that person is dead? How much of any individual human being's future is the price of such hope?

The South African Truth and Reconciliation Commission

Twenty-eight years later, in April 1996, the South African Truth and Reconciliation Commission (TRC) opened the first of 76 human rights violations (HRV) hearings in East London. National and international media flooded the four-day hearing. They were witness to and reported the first stories of torture, murder, injury, detention and disappearance in such a way that the perceptions of millions of people were challenged. And slowly, as the deluge of stories neither faltered nor slackened, old, comfortable assumptions were painfully changed. A little less than a year-and-a-half later, the HRV hearings were closed. But the TRC's Amnesty Committee hearings had already begun, and were generating a new flow of excruciatingly powerful information about crimes that had been committed during apartheid.

There is a question of reality. There is a question of need. These questions are immutably linked. And there is another, related question: to what degree can any judicial process, or the definition of justice as it is most frequently assumed, answer either of these prerequisites?

The truth that came out of these TRC hearings is about delivering justice, but not as in 'justice equals punishment of those proven guilty in a court of law'. For the TRC, justice is about uncovering what really happened: it is about establishing the reality of the past. This essential form of the truth would not have been found were it not for the amnesty process.

Yet truth is also a matter of the victims and survivors being able to tell their stories, to tell the truth of their experiences and to make this truth public. There will always be a gap between the factual truth and the reality, which includes both factual truth and emotional truth. To recreate the reality that existed before, the TRC clearly demonstrated that the factual truth must be present and accounted for. But it has also shown the absolute requirement of making room for the emotional truth of the victims, the survivors and the perpetrators. All of these people must tell their stories: if the intention is to foster peaceful coexistence and reconciliation, all of these people must be heard.

To say that the TRC was controversial would be a radical understatement. Thanks to the transparency of the entire process, it even generated controversy outside the country. Several of the South African political parties declined to accept the TRC officially. Still, many individual members of those parties offered testimony to the HRV and many of them did apply for amnesty: the sum of all these parts was infinitely greater than the whole.

To provide just one example of how this worked, in July 1997 the Inkatha Freedom Party (IFP) officially withdrew support from the Commission. But seven IFP members applied for amnesty for their part in 56 incidents of violence in the KwaZulu-Natal region in the early 1990s. A little less than a year later, when their amnesty application was heard, these IFP members admitted that they carried out a reign of terror in an effort to eliminate the ANC from the area.

When the hearing began, only a handful of spectators were present. A week later, more than 1 000 people were attending and plans were announced to bring in more busloads of area residents, including IFP supporters.[2]

The TRC created a direct link between amnesty-granting and truth-telling: amnesty for truth. If perpetrators had not come forward a lot of truth and a lot of reality of that time would have been lost. Paper trails and evidence regarding perpetrators of gross violations of human rights do exist. But not a lot of it.[3] And also not enough to successfully prosecute all perpetrators of gross violations of human rights during apartheid.

The agonising cascade of information coming out of the TRC hearings was challenged many times, particularly in courts of law. And although only a few of these challenges had the specific intent of silencing the torrent of raw information pouring from the TRC, the effect of most of them would have been just that: muzzling the flow. In two-and-a-half years the TRC faced a barrage of litigation from perpetrators who did not wish to be named in HRV hearings, from survivors who did not require more information out of amnesty proceedings because they knew what had happened to their loved ones and wanted to see perpetrators punished, and from political parties that had constitutional and bias problems with the process.

Legal challenges

In his chapter in this book, Hugh Corder examines some of the legal challenges to the TRC. I must also note the first legal challenge to the TRC's work, filed by AZAPO (the Azanian People's Organization), Ms NM Biko, Mr CH Mxenge and Mr C Ribeiro.[4]

The Constitutional Court upheld the constitutionality of the section of the Promotion of National Unity and Reconciliation Act of 1995, which allowed amnesty to be granted when applicants were found to have fulfilled all the requirements of the Act. In its decision, the court recognised that the desire to see perpetrators of human rights violations prosecuted and then punished for their inhuman conduct was legitimate. But Justice Mahomed also noted that 'much of what transpired in this shameful period [of apartheid] is shrouded in secrecy and not easily capable of objective demonstration and proof. Loved ones have disappeared, sometimes mysteriously, and most of them no longer survive to tell their tales ...'. He noted further:

The Act seeks to address this massive problem by encouraging these survivors and dependants of the tortured and the wounded, the maimed and the dead to unburden their grief publicly ... and, crucially, to help them to discover what did in truth happen to their loved ones, where and under what circumstances it did happen, and who was responsible. That truth, which the victims of repression seek so desperately to know is, in the circumstances, much more likely to be forthcoming if those responsible for such monstrous misdeeds are encouraged to disclose the whole truth with the incentive that they will not receive the punishment, which they undoubtedly deserve if they do. Without that incentive, there is nothing to encourage [perpetrators] to make the disclosures and to reveal the truth.

The court noted that the alternative to granting amnesty to perpetrators was to keep intact the abstract right for survivors to pursue civil or criminal prosecution of perpetrators. But the right to do this held much less than even an abstract possibility of success. In 98 cases out of 100, it would prove to be impossible to dig up information through adversarial court proceedings: the necessary evidence to convict or to win a civil judgment simply does not exist.

By its very nature and purpose, the focus in a courtroom must be on the accused in an attempt to prove guilt. In its goal to establish as much reality as possible, the essential nature of the TRC – and of many other truth commissions – demands that the focus must be of at least equal intensity on the experience of victims and survivors, as it is on perpetrators. This is also justice.

It is a safe bet that the people who filed this challenge to the amnesty provision had neither the wish nor the intention to choke off the stream of information pouring out through the TRC hearings. The fact remains: if they had won this suit, a cloud of appalling silence would have been the final consequence. If the TRC amnesty committee had lost the power to grant amnesty to perpetrators who made a full confession not only of what they had done but also of why they had done it, the ability of the TRC to recreate the reality of life under apartheid would have been crippled beyond repair.

Establishing the reality

This leaves a question with regard to an expectation of fairness, as when individuals seek some form of retributive justice rather than the restitutive justice the TRC worked to deliver. Leaving aside the central proposition of reconciliation and the central reality of a negotiated settlement that lead to South Africa's first democratic election, there is one overriding fact to be dealt with. On what basis can indictments – never mind convictions – be sought?

During a press conference in Rome in June 1997, the then President Nelson Mandela admitted that South Africa's drive to investigate human rights abuses during apartheid may leave some 'big shots' untouched. He said,

'You can't act against someone unless there's clear evidence ... There's very little evidence to convict the [top leaders] who actually authorised actions.'[5]

In October 1997 the HRV committee convened an institutional hearing of the Legal Community. Although hundreds of pages of written submissions came in, all members of the judiciary declined to appear at the hearing itself. The clearest argument submitted in support of this failure to be present was that it 'would somehow negatively affect their independence and would, therefore, harm the institution of the judiciary in its current rule in South Africa's constitutional democracy'.[6]

However one cares to interpret this non-cooperation, it is particularly interesting to note the submission offered by Cape Judge President, Justice Gerald Friedman. In his submission, Justice Friedman wrote that the apartheid era courts were faced with the dilemma of weighting testimony from a detainee about how he was assaulted, against the denials of the police and the security forces, who were backed by a district surgeon. 'Despite cross-examination, it was very often impossible to find that their testimony was untruthful, since the court has in each case to make its findings on the evidence that is placed before it. If the police were prepared to lie under oath, as it now transpires they were, there was little the judicial officer could do. Findings of culpability have to be based on evidence; suspicion is not enough.'[7]

The South African TRC was – and is – about peeling away deceit and exposing reality. Jose Zalaquett, a Chilean activist and lawyer who served on his country's Commission on Truth and Reconciliation, wrote, 'Memory is identity. Identities consisting of false or half-memories easily commit atrocities.'[8] The TRC's work has made many false or half memories extremely difficult to sustain.

The information which flowed out of the TRC hearings, and the reality the TRC painted with it, was desperately needed by all the citizens of South Africa: people had to know what their government had really been doing. Now they do, and they know in ways that cannot be realistically challenged.

Of course this does not mean that some people will not dispute or deny the full reality – and its implications – as made clear by the TRC and in the Final Report. But those who attempt to denounce the reality of the past will have a much tougher time gaining adherents to any mythology they may care to concoct in relationship either to the apartheid government or to the conduct of South Africa's civil war.

As noted in Professor Corder's chapter, the TRC was ordered to give due notification to alleged perpetrators who would be named in any public fashion. Accordingly, in September 1998 the TRC sent out notices to over 400 people and organisations across the political spectrum who had not applied for amnesty, but who would be mentioned in the final Report.[9] FW de Klerk received one of these notices and by threatening legal action that could have stopped the public presentation of the report, succeeded in having the findings, which followed his citation, blacked out in the published Report. This matter remains unresolved at the time of going to press.

The report also cited liberation forces, including the ANC, for moral and political responsibility for some gross violations of human rights. The ANC responded with the statement that the TRC was 'casting the same shadow between freedom fighters and apartheid masters'.[10] An ANC spokesperson later said, 'Whatever the efforts to besmirch our struggle by denouncing it as a gross violation of human rights, the ANC, Umkhonto we Sizwe and the millions of people who were part of this struggle will always be proud of what they did to ensure that, in the process of destruction of a vile system, they did not themselves resort to vile methods of struggle on the basis that the means justified the end.'[11]

The day before the final Report was to be submitted to former President Mandela, the ANC announced the intention to take legal action to block publication. That challenge was heard just hours before the long-awaited Report was to be made public.[12] It failed, and the final Report was released. (It is important to note that Mandela backed the TRC's finding that the ANC was guilty of gross human rights violations in the fight against apartheid.)[13]

The only way to say 'never again' and have some plausible hope of seeing the intent of that statement fulfilled is to really understand what happened before and, over time, to develop increased comprehension of why it happened in the first place. The answers to these questions are never simple: finding them requires an understanding of reality that embraces both the factual and the emotional truth of the past. Accomplishing this is not within the competence of a court of law; it is neither the function nor the purpose of a court of law. As Judge Richard Goldstone has pointed out, 'in many ways, a truth commission can be far more inclusive.'[14]

Each bit of information brought forth was another facet of the truth added to the picture of the reality the TRC has laboured to build. This information was of vital importance for many victims and survivors, and it is the only thing that will make future mythologies about what happened in the past impossible to sustain. It is a tragic fact that some survivors still do not know what happened to those they loved, or even the reasons behind their own detention, torture or injury. But given the limited amount of time the TRC has had to function (and the number of challenges to what they were doing), what has been made plain in the course of the Commission's work has been nothing less than awe-inspiring.

Truth and reconciliation as performance: spectres of Eucharistic redemption

EBRAHIM MOOSA

In March 1999, Public Broadcasting Services (PBS) television in the United States aired a 90-minute documentary on the Truth and Reconciliation Commission (TRC) entitled 'Facing the Truth with Bill Moyers'. It was a moving and soul-stirring documentary. It brought home to millions of viewers some of the more discreditable features of South Africa's past. The producers tried to bring across the complexity of discovering the truth in South Africa. The documentary also showed how reconciliation was the intended outcome of the TRC, but at the same time indicated how elusive that objective was.

Ethics and morality in public life

Einstein used to say that there are questions that only children can ask. But once asked, these questions shed new light on our perplexities. For those concerned with the role of ethics and morality in public life, the foremost question is how to make sense of the historic role that the TRC played in South Africa. The more important question is whither morality, truth, justice and reconciliation in the next few decades. These are important issues as the country tries to retrieve its moral compass and give content to the ideals of emancipation after the dark days of apartheid and centuries of colonialism. Anyone who thinks that these are easy questions with equally simple answers needs to correct such misapprehensions. Surely the unique constitution of

South Africa contains the elements of emancipation, but can take form only in the material conditions that affect the lives of millions. While this vision will remain as long as the country and people are committed to democracy and freedom, as we know it, people do not live by visions alone.

The *TRC Report* was released and its findings made public. In terms of the constitution, that formal process of discovering the truth, or at least part of it, had come to an end. But while the constitution brought to life and terminated the TRC as a formal process, several of its provisions suggest that the purposes and goals of the TRC need to be realised beyond the life of a formal process, especially the goal of national reconciliation. As a formal quasi-judicial mechanism, the TRC was only one element of the process of national reconciliation, after a long history of alienation and discord. In this respect it fulfils only the legal requirements of the political compromise that brought about the new South Africa. More importantly, it played a cathartic role for most of the time in the life of the newborn nation. In this respect it must be viewed as an 'event' that prefigures other momentous events. Any event of this magnitude is actually a performance. A performance is when the actors have already configured the purpose of the play and there is a hope that other participants and viewers will also understand its message. World history, especially sacred history, has a long record of narratives of performance: the genesis story, Abraham's sacrifice of his son and the crucifixion of Jesus. It is as performance that the TRC event has greater value as symbol, myth and spectacle. This brings us to the language of the TRC or, more precisely, it makes us ask: what are the language categories of the TRC event?

Western legal thought has for centuries grown and developed its sensibilities of justice and truth from the language of obligation. John Caputo, a scholar of philosophical ethics, argues that the language of obligation traces its roots back to Abraham,[1] with the preparedness of the Patriarch to respond to God's command and to act instinctively: bind the legs and get ready to slaughter his son. This symbolic act of obedience epitomises the language of obligation, particularly in the Abrahamic tradition, Judaism, Christianity and Islam. With this trace or spectre, the law humbles us with the majesty of its unconditional command that will not compromise. This is the language of transcendence, where our conscience is shocked by a voice from without. It provides us with an understanding that the standard of judgment between truth and falsehood emanates from a locus outside and beyond us. Obligation disrupts and creates discord by a call that comes from without. This is the law that makes Abraham love the law more than God.

In Western philosophy, which is mainly Greek in its origins, this sense of obligation that creates discord and subjection will not do. In ethics, or more precisely philosophical ethics, truth is something that the subject already has, already owns or is herself. 'I, Plato, am the truth.' The Muslim mystic Mansur al-Hallaj, who never recovered from his state of ecstasy and utter immersion into the spirit of the divine, said: 'I am the (t)Truth!' If Abraham is dependent on a master or a teacher for instruction, then the philosopher or the mystic is autonomous. The voice of ethics is from within, not from without, on the level of immanence and not transcendence. The voice of ethics is entirely in 'the spirit of Greek beauty and autonomy, of *harmonia* and reconciliation, and the Christian spirit of love'.[2] In order to understand the moral language of the TRC event, it would therefore be instructive to get a sense of the moral language that prevailed in South Africa prior to this event.

In the 1970s and 1980s in particular, religion increasingly played a pivotal role in mobilising sections of the public against apartheid rule. The churches in particular, with high profile clergymen and theologians, followed by leaders from smaller religious groups, such as Jews, Muslims, Hindus and Buddhists, also played a significant role in this respect. One has to bear in mind too that certain independent churches and African traditional religious representatives played a less visible political role, but one whose influence in the anti-apartheid struggle has as yet not been satisfactorily accounted. Generally, the language employed by the religious sector can be characterised as one of moral indignation against the horrors of racism and state violence. This dramatically manifested itself in the emergence of a South African liberation theology among Christians and Muslims, as well as black theology. Liberation theologians, in particular, emphasised the language of obligation. It held the architects and supporters of apartheid accountable for their lack of obligation to the standards of justice and fairness set out by the transcendental Creator.

Christians, Jews and Muslims reminded their compatriots of the Hebraic justice of the God of Moses that awaited all tyrants, in the same way that He dealt with the Pharaohs of old. The message was clear: victory against the oppressors would be assured and decisive; justice for past wrongs would be swift and exacting. God's preferential option, indeed His obligation, was to be on the side of the oppressed and downtrodden. Many a verse of the Bible or the Qur'an was interpreted to speak of an emancipation and liberation that spoke the language of transcendence: obligation.

Miracles and compromises

No one expected that the miracle would come from 'within': that the prisoner and jailer, the oppressor and oppressed, the lion and the lamb would have to drink from the same stream. Many observers believed the South African conflict to be a fight between ruling whites and dispossessed blacks. The political compromise defied both the prevalent political and moral-theological logic that had been orchestrated for several decades. Once the compromise had been struck it became apparent that the discourses of liberation on which were based the dreams of future utopias and expectations of vengeance and justice would have to be modified, amended or, at times, abandoned. Throughout the negotiating phase, the politicians knew well this would inevitably happen, but in order to lend some credibility to the process of negotiation they had to retain at least some semblance of the language of obligation. In the end, the language of ethics triumphed: Greek beauty, the Spirit, reconciliation and love. In short, the truth was not something that came from 'without' but from 'within'. It came from memoranda, conferences and smoke-filled rooms. The truth was what the 'party' (parties) said it was. The truth was not measured, but manufactured. To be charitable, we can say that the truth was negotiated. It was this truth that rescued South Africa from a revolutionary abyss. It is also the very same truth that will hover as a spectral figure over the country's uncertain future.

Yet, no one is prepared to say that we have changed course from Jerusalem to Athens. It is clear that South Africa has abandoned the language of obligation (Abraham and his descendants) and embraced the language of *harmonia* (Athens) and the modern commentators of the Greek philosophers, people like Frenchman Jacques Derrida. Whether the TRC moved South Africa's ethics from Jerusalem to Athens or to a halfway point between them can be gauged from a poignant moment in Moyers' documentary. Thandi, a survivor of apartheid's horrors, tells of the unbearable torture that she had to endure at the hands of the police. She narrates how she was tortured and raped by four policemen. Her technique of survival, she says, was to remove her soul from her body during those horrific hours of torture. The only way she could survive and retain her sanity to this very day was to disembody herself. She left her body to the police vultures and retreated with her soul into the corner of the interrogating room. Then she looked at her body from afar. She witnessed with her soul how the masculinity of the apartheid police devoured her flesh. How she will reconcile herself with her tormentors was not very clear in the documentary. She seemed to have grasped the truth, like many of those who participated in the TRC hearings. Her most insightful reply was that she would be reconciled only if she could retrieve her soul from the corner of the torture chamber, where she had left it several years ago.

Thandi's words bespeak the symbolism and the aesthetics of reconciliation of so many other survivors. Many who appeared before the TRC, in fact expressed a need for symbols: the need to get a death certificate, to visit the mass graves of victims, to identify a burial site or to know the time and place of death. The stories of both supporters of apartheid and those who opposed it were placed in the same ethical register. It was like looking at a Grecian urn against a black backdrop and then a black profile against white background. Which one is the true image? Both and neither. Such is the ambiguity and the complexity of our time.

In most instances during the TRC hearings, victims, but sometimes aggressors, were subjected to the same process: a disturbance, a rupture of their senses, an outpouring of their being. It was an awesome experience, one that made people truly tremble. Yet this happened even while there was no judge and no threat of sanctions. If there was an explanation, then it should be attributed to an outpouring of the human conscience. The TRC is what linguists would describe as a 'performative' event. By means of this performance it enacted the theories, principles and agreements concluded by once hostile foes: the forces of apartheid and the forces of liberation. Yet it also played another role. A particular kind of work or function was performed by the TRC. Can one say that the TRC fulfilled the role of 'as if' (that is, as if it were some kind of court of justice). 'As if' it performed the function of Nuremberg. As if reconciliation between antagonistic racial groups had occurred. As if the truth were disclosed. The motif that repeatedly comes to mind is that of 'as if': a simulacrum? The TRC played the role as if it were taking confession and offering redemption.

Those who witnessed the life of the TRC and its various representations in the media and public life cannot avoid the conclusion about the performative nature of the TRC. From the very inception of the legislation that brought the TRC to life, the result of historic and epoch-making political com-promises in modern times, it was marked by three paradoxical elements: determinism – a verdict (already known), a mystery and the grotesque. These elements permeated this secular Eucharist. It was indeed a process determined, because the multitude of perpetrators, even if they confessed, would not be subjected to the justice of obligation experienced at Nuremberg. Despite the determinism, it was mysterious. It fed the need to know and uncover the mystery of the past. This in itself only made the past more mysterious and compounded the mystification. It was grotesque, only if one reclaimed transcendence, Abraham and obligation. If one suspended the Abrahamic criterion to hear the Law and act, it was indeed grotesque. If we followed the ethics of the Greeks, then the TRC is one great celebration of the beauty of *harmonia* and reconciliation.

In short, the TRC defied all our accepted conceptions of justice, law, order and fairness. It requires a faith in the *mysterium* of the event, a faith in the rite of reconciliation, a belief in the rituals of confession, rather than an expectation in the outcome of the process. The key to understanding this version of truth and reconciliation lies locked into the drama and performance of the TRC itself. Justice in the post-apartheid South Africa, at least as configured in the TRC legislation, no longer places the emphasis on transcendent criteria of values. Justice is now celebrated by means of immanence, the here and the now. Implicit is the suggestion that justice and injustice are part of the same, there is no distance, there is no space and there is no distinction between body and spirit. They are both identical. The metaphors of morality to which we had become accustomed previously have been radically changed, by an event.

The path to redemption

Let me explain my use of the metaphor of Eucharistic redemption. During antiquity, the Eucharist in Christianity was essentially about reconciliation. The general doctrine was that you could share the meal in the body of Christ only if you acknowledged unholiness. So when one acknowledges wrongdoing by confession, only then does the embrace of reconciliation between two human beings become a possibility. It is then that the kiss of peace between two enemies can become meaningful. But the language of the Eucharist goes along two vectors: the language of reason and the language of mystery. It is born within a paradox; a body which is simultaneously also the spirit; absent and present; the eternal coexistence of antinomies. What reason cannot grasp has to be relegated to faith. Implicit in the Eucharist is that what human beings cannot forgive among themselves is relegated to the realm of God. There will always be the residual absence of true peace. Yet it is the transforming ability of the word that Eucharistic theology represents, that also serves as the saving grace of humanity.

In a somewhat analogous manner 'the word' (the Report) of the TRC as the bureaucratic 'body' of modern South Africa is endowed with powers to confer grace/salvation and pardon those sinners who confessed to their wrong. The TRC represents the miracle of the event of negotiation. It is only within the body of the TRC that this redemption can be attained. Outside this body one cannot be saved for the deeds committed in defence of apartheid or those wrongs committed in dismantling apartheid. Now that the legal and material life of the TRC has come to an end, truth and reconciliation may or may not pursue its trajectory. From now on we may foster truth and reconciliation by invoking the memory of the TRC. The redemptive memory and spirit of the TRC will mark the post-TRC period. All actions will be projected to the spirit of the Report. We will draw our healing power from the spirit of the Report that will have to remain within

South Africa as long as the memory of pain, alienation and the incision of the past remains. The question remains, whether this will be possible and at what cost.

Surely it is difficult to suppress the Christocentric features of the TRC. The performance of the TRC event resonates a redemption of the sins of apartheid. The suffering and oppression experienced by the disenfranchised was dramatised or performed twice in the lives of many people. The first was at the instance of the injury itself – whether it is that of the victims or the trauma of their dependants. The second dramatisation was in the theatre of the TRC event itself, where these sins were replayed to the benefit of a variety of hosts: Commissioners, the media, observers, the aggrieved, the archivists, the psychologists and the politicians, to mention but a few. In what way did the TRC turn the suffering of the heroes of liberation into a gift of sacrifice for the new South Africa? Is this gift and its seismic after effects not the *tremendum mysterium* that makes us tremble at our very human nature? It brings home the realisation that such a gift of sacrifice can be made only once, and never again. In some way, this sacrifice can be justified as a necessity. Without this sacrifice, as well as considering the impossibility of justice that prefigured it, the discourse of reconciliation may not have been possible. At the same time one must bear in mind that total and absolute reconciliation cannot be realised. For this reason reconciliation was the most viable solution in a context that was riddled with incompleteness, incoherence and the co-existence of opposites.

It was exactly this paradox: the inevitability that both victims and aggressors would have to share the same symbolic and political space in the new society. One would recall that it was the apartheid parliament that legitimated the process for recognition of the interim constitution. An illegitimate institution or at best a quasi-legitimate body, such as the National Assembly – after the cessation of hostilities between the apartheid state and its opponents – gave birth to the legitimate order. Surely, the linearity of the Abrahamic logic of justice would have insisted on clear boundaries, identifiable guilt and commensurate punishment. This is what the family of Steve Biko demanded. A call for the logic of the law, a call for Nuremberg. The law applied at Nuremberg is not necessarily justice: it is the law applied to deal with crimes against humanity. But it is a kind of law that was very much in keeping with the response of Abraham to the divine command. The Greek heritage to our understanding of justice is less concrete, compared to the Semitic sensibilities of law and justice. Jacques Derrida argues that the law must constantly be critiqued, in his words, 'deconstructed'. His reflections on justice deserve to be quoted at some length:

But justice is not the law. Justice is what gives us the impulse, the drive, or the movement to improve the law, that is to deconstruct the law. Without a call for justice we would not have any interest in deconstructing the law ... Justice is not reducible to the law, to a given system of legal structures. That means that justice is always unequal to itself. It is not coincidental with itself ... I tried to show that justice again implied non-gathering, dissociation, heterogeneity, non-identity with itself, endless inadequation, infinite transcendence. That is why the call for justice is never fully answered. That is why no one can say: 'I am just.' If someone tells you 'I am just,' you can be sure that he or she is wrong, because being just is not a matter of theoretical determination. I cannot know I am just. I can know that I am right. I can see that I act in agreement with norms, with the law. I stop at the red light ... To speak of justice is not a matter of knowledge, of theoretical judgment. That's why it's not a matter of calculation. You can calculate what is right. You can judge; you can say that, according to the code, such and such a misdeed deserves 10 years of imprisonment. That may be a matter of calculation. But the fact that it is rightly calculated does not mean it is just.

A judge, if he wants to be just, cannot content himself with applying the law. He has to reinvent the law each time. If he wants to be responsible, to make a decision, he has not simply to apply the law, as a coded programme, to a given case, but to reinvent in a singular situation a new, just relationship; that means that justice cannot be reduced to a calculation of sanctions, punishments or rewards. That may be right or in agreement with the law, but that is not justice. Justice, if it has to do with the other, with the infinite distance of the other, is always unequal to the other, is always incalculable. You cannot calculate justice. Levinas says somewhere that the definition of justice – which is very minimal, but which I love and which I think is very rigorous – is that justice is the relation to the other.[3]

Derrida's reflections challenge the ontological boundaries to which we have become accustomed. Justice as an inherited concept was always measured by sanctions. Now he urges us to think of the impossibility of justice. The closest we can come to justice is to relate to the 'other'. If the TRC event destabilises our sensibilities, then it is due to the fact that it introduces us to a postmodern understanding of justice. Of course, the TRC event is an exceptional and extraordinary event. It will remain a miracle and a mystery, side by side – the normal justice system continues to function and responds with its array of sanctions; not with a call for reconciliation with the 'other'. This should bring home the point that the making of the new South Africa was a post-modern event. A modern society manufactured by post-modern means, at the end of the 20th century. South Africa became a country not by revolutionary means, but by a 'desire' to be a country. It occurs by the dictum of 'as if': as if a nation were born; as if the state is unconditionally sovereign; as if peace had returned; as if violence had ended; as if reconciliation had taken place; and as if Abrahamic justice had occurred.

There is thus a gap between what was expected and what has happened. The questions that arise are the following: does the TRC occlude, naturalise and saturate the events of the past? To what extent does South Africa ground itself in an ethics of responsibility? Between an ethics of responsibility and the proclivity to domesticate the past, in that space, the incompleteness and lack of totality of reconciliation, truth and justice abides. It is the void that cannot be filled. It will remain the testament and patrimony for future generations.

Postscript

In October 1998 Archbishop Desmond Tutu, chairperson of the TRC, handed over the book of confessions, the *TRC Report*, to President Nelson Mandela and with that act ended his official mandate. The mood at the handing-over ceremony was sombre and tense. A few hours before the ceremony there was an attempt by the ruling party, the African National Congress (ANC), to block the publication of the Report by means of a court interdict. The report had some critical things to say about the party of liberation. The eleventh-hour events clearly were an attempt to unveil the mystery and scuttle the miracle itself: the ANC wanted to subject the Report to the logic of Abrahamic justice and delete its name from the book of deeds. We are innocent, they cried. To South Africa's credit the court action failed and the Report stood as it was written. Scholars of religious texts and scripture have some idea how crucial segments of texts, messages and reports can become garbled, confused and how they can disappear. The ANC wanted just that: pages to disappear and some volumes (or chapters in volumes) to be subjected to rigorous editing. Such is the stuff of which great myths and legends are made. However, they were prevented from demystifying the mystery, by the law itself.

South Africa's final act of decolonisation in April 1994 and its accession to majority rule and democracy occurred at the same conjuncture when world market capitalism was also triumphant. It is a capitalism that can make people feel 'as if' they are part of the globe through electronic media, advertisement and cyberspace communication. It brings the 'desire' to own the benefits of capitalism to everyone, from the squatter communities of Crossroads and Alexandria township to their counterparts in Buenos Aires and Jakarta without providing the means to attain it. The epitome of this market capitalism is that its product is the intense desire to own consumer goods in the form of Nike and Reebok sports shoes, Coca Cola and MacDonald's fast foods, without them ever being able to legally own these with their limited means. The paradoxical conditions that prevail make it possible for vigilantes to act as revolutionaries and pretend to be agents of emancipation; it enables law and order to foment disorder and subversion; and it permits those in custody government to pay lip service to democracy without acting democratically. In a society in which magic and charisma are celebrated as a virtue, it is difficult to see how the reality principle can replace the principle of simulation.

Events such as the TRC not only introduce us to a performance, but also to a simulation of reality. Transgression and violence are much less serious since they contest only what is real. Simulated conditions, in turn, are much more dangerous, since they interfere with the very principle of reality. It is infinitely more dangerous, because it suggests that law and order and everything we take for real are nothing more than simulation. These are the pessimistic conditions under which both 'truth' and 'reconciliation' have to take place in the future. In order for that to occur, one way out would be to bracket the memory of the TRC event as a special event, but never hold it up as a model for reconciliation and for the discovery of truth. In other words, the memory of the TRC event itself may have to be repressed if South Africa wishes to break out of its cycle of surreal existence in so many spheres of life.

The *baruti* versus the lawyers: the role of religion in the TRC process

PIET MEIRING

'No! This is not the way to do it.'

Archbishop Desmond Tutu, who was to chair the first Johannesburg hearing of the Truth and Reconciliation Commission (TRC), looked his audience straight in the eye. Earlier in the morning, in the vestry of the Central Methodist Church where the hearing was scheduled to take place, Dr Fazel Randera, chief of the Johannesburg office of the TRC, discussed the proceedings of the coming days with the Archbishop. Nothing was left to chance. This hearing (from 29 April to 3 May 1996) would set the pattern for many to follow. The world media would be present and most of the diplomatic corps accepted invitations to attend. Politicians and senior government officials indicated that they also would attend. Former President Nelson Mandela was to make an appearance.

Fazel Randera, together with a number of colleagues, voiced their concern. The previous hearing, in East London, as well as numerous TRC ceremonies of the previous weeks, were far too 'religious' for their taste. The many prayers, the hymn-singing before and during the hearings and the religious wrappings of the process were out of place. The TRC process was a legal process and should be conducted in a juridical style. That Desmond Tutu arrived at most hearings wearing his archbishop's vestment, complete with clerical collar and crucifix, they had to accept. But, surely, it was a juridical hearing in Johannesburg, and not a Sunday service in the St George's

Cathedral in Cape Town, that was to take place today as well as in the days to follow. 'Of course we need a solemn and dignified opening,' Fazel explained, 'but why not follow the example of Parliament these days. Let us have a moment of silence – of quiet meditation for those who felt like it – and get on with the programme.'[1]

Tutu gamely accepted Fazel's suggestion: 'It is the Johannesburg office's hearing. I will do as you say.' At the stroke of 9 a.m., the TRC procession moved into the hall. One after the other, Tutu and his colleagues shook hands with the victims in the first three rows. He proceeded to the stage to address the audience. 'We will observe half a minute's silence,' he said, 'before we commence with our programme.' The first witness was announced and asked to take the oath. The stage was set.

But Tutu was patently uncomfortable. He was unable to start with the proceedings. He shifted the papers on the table in front of him. He cleared his throat. When he spoke to the audience, he said: 'No! This is not the way to do it. We cannot start without having prayed. Close your eyes!' In his inimitable way, the Archbishop placed the hearing of the day in the Lord's hands, asking that Jesus Christ, who himself is the Truth, guide us in our quest for truth, that the Holy Spirit of God grant us the wisdom and grace we need. After a resounding 'Amen', he announced with a disarming smile: 'So! Now we are ready to start the day's work…' Fazel and his colleagues equally gamely accepted the Archbishop's instinct and ruling. From that day onwards all TRC hearings were to start – and be closed – in a proper fashion.

The *baruti* versus the lawyers

This does not mean that the debate on the role that religion had to play during the process, on the religious trappings of the TRC, had been resolved. Right to the end of the life of the TRC, voices within and without the TRC made themselves heard on the subject. The four *baruti* (the pastors) among the TRC Commissioners and committee members, together with a number of colleagues, most of them staunch church goers, strongly identified with the Archbishop's sentiments in this regard. Others – the lawyers, the politicians and some of the academics serving on the TRC – sympathised with Fazel Randera. It was a friendly debate, each allowing the other their views on the matter, but it did raise a number of issues that were difficult to answer.

From outside the ranks of the TRC the debate carried on, with equal verve. Heated arguments were presented by a number of NGOs, by political group-ings and by the public at large. One of the sharpest comments was from Cosmas Desmond, a former Catholic priest, who campaigned during the last election as a member of the PAC. He was concerned about the fact that besides Desmond Tutu (obviously appointed to the TRC 'to be John the Baptist to Mandela's messiah'), four other churchmen – together with activists, who in the past had close connections with ecumenical bodies – were appointed to the TRC. The churches were over-represented on the Commission, Cosmas Desmond retorted, and this did not bode well for the work of the TRC.

> *Such is that over-representation that the question arises as to whether the TRC is an arm of the state or the church. Most church leaders, including Archbishop Tutu, agreed that the new South Africa would be a secular state. Yet the first meeting of the Commission's Reparations Committee was opened not only with prayer but with an exclusive Christian one. And it appears to be assumed that all decisions of the Commission will be informed by Christian values. This would not be bad – though it would still be unacceptable to some – if the norms or values were indeed Christian. But the word 'Christian' is all too often simply a synonym for 'Western'. This is clearly illustrated in the Commission's individualistic understanding of human rights and their violation, rather than a more African (and, I would contend, more Christian) approach.[2]*

The TRC 'liturgy'

Looking at the situation from the outside, the strong emphasis on the religious aspects of the TRC process should have been expected. The South African community is by and large a religious community. The vast majority of South Africans belong to one of the Christian denominations or to the Muslim, Hindu, Buddhist, Bahai, Jewish or African traditionalist communities. Although many serious questions may be raised about the commitment of many of the adherents – the percentage of purely nominal membership is steadily climbing – the influence of the churches and other faith communities is still a force to be reckoned with. From the onset, the faith communities were involved in discussing the possibility of a truth commission and eventually in the drafting of the TRC Act. Workshops and conferences to further the aims of the TRC and to identify the churches' and other communities' role in the process were the order of the day. And when the TRC hearings started, the local churches were the staunch co-workers of the Commission, helping to disseminate news, to encourage victims and perpetrators to approach the TRC and to act as facilitators and spiritual guides throughout the life of the Commission.

Early in the life of the TRC, a TRC 'liturgy' spontaneously developed, which very soon set the pattern for most of the Truth Commission hearings throughout the country. At the Service of Dedication and Blessing of Commissioners of the Truth and Reconciliation Commission in St George's Cathedral in Cape Town (on 13 February 1996), a beautiful liturgy was introduced: the singing of hymns, prayers (inter-denominational and inter-faith), readings in many languages, the lighting of candles and the presenting of olive branches. These elements were repeated at most hearings in many parts of the country. Archbishop Tutu, with his sense of occasion as well as his intuitive understanding of the spiritual needs of the victims and the audience, made ample use of the hymns and prayers not only to open and close the meetings but to guide the process through difficult, sometimes traumatic, moments.

At the TRC's first victims' hearing (East London, 19 April 1996), Mrs Nomonde Calata, widow of Fort Calata (one of the 'Cradock Four'), was momentarily overcome with grief, while relating the story of her husband's abduction and murder. Her anguished wails filled the hall. The audience and the Commissioners at the table were shocked into silence. When Tutu, after allowing a few minutes for Mrs Calata to compose herself, needed to start the session again, he intoned in his own voice the Xhosa hymn *Senzeni na* ('What have we done?') Everyone, even the journalists and security personnel, joined in the singing. Tears flowed. But the atmosphere was set for the rest of the day. The lesson was properly learnt and at many future meetings, in a particularly difficult situation, the singing of a hymn or a prayer saved the day.

Spiritual wells

The role played by the faith communities went far beyond mere reflection on the TRC process and the provision of local infrastructures and services, even of providing a 'liturgy' for the hearings. In the quest for truth and reconciliation – for the eventual healing of the nation – the spiritual contributions of the different faith communities were of extreme importance. 'Religion is central to this process of healing,' wrote Tutu six months into the life of the TRC. 'We need to reach deep into the spiritual wells of our different religious traditions practised in this country in order to draw strength and grace with which to address the challenges of healing and of nation building.'[3] He added – providing an answer for Cosmas Desmond's objections – 'Those of us who stand within the Christian tradition have, perhaps, a special responsibility in this regard, because this nation has through the years employed Christian theological resources to promote apartheid – a system that is today accepted by people throughout the world as a crime against humanity.' At the 'faith communities' hearing in East London (in November 1997), representatives of the 'other' communities – the Jewish, Muslim, Hindu and African traditionalist –

were able to table a number of religious and ethical principles that could be of extreme value to the process of truth and reconciliation in the country.

I would like to touch on three issues in this regard: the process of remembering, the quest for truth and the costliness of reconciliation.

Remembering

A Catholic colleague once remarked that South Africans, after 1994, leap-frogged from a time of pain and struggle right across to a time of jubilation and celebration – forgetting that in-between the two poles we owe ourselves a time of remembrance, a time of mourning. To neglect this 'middle time', the season of remembering and mourning, means not only to impoverish our national life misses, but the opportunity to deal with the ghosts of the past, which surely will return, to continue to haunt us for decades to come. 'Of course we need to close the books on the past,' the Chairperson of the TRC often told audiences, 'but we can close the books only after they have been properly opened.' Bettelheim has commented: 'What cannot be talked about, cannot be put to rest, and if it is not, the wounds will continue to fester from generation to generation.'[4]

The religious beliefs and experiences of many South Africans facilitated this process. Father Michael Lapsley, himself a victim of the struggle, who was severely and permanently injured by a letter bomb and who was instrumental in conducting a series of 'healing of memories' workshops throughout the country, wrote: 'For Christians, we need to remind ourselves that we belong to a remembering religion. "Remember when you were slaves in Egypt" is a constant refrain of the Old Testament ... The words of Jesus – "Do this in memory of me" – are said at every Eucharist.'[5]

Christians should be willing to remember, and eventually to forgive, Lapsley contended. We should not allow our memories to destroy us. Forgiveness is always the Christian calling, 'but no one should suggest that forgiveness is glib, cheap or easy. What does it mean to forgive those who have not confessed, those who have not changed their lives, those who have no interest in making it up to the relatives of victims and the survivors of their crimes? If you forgive a murderer, does that mean that there should be no justice?'

Remembering means that victims should be provided the opportunity to tell their stories and that others – perpetrators, bystanders, the general public and the nation as a whole – are willing to sit down and listen. We need one another's stories. Stories become the glasses through which we look at one another's lives, the heart-throb by which we experience each other's anguish and pain, as well as our triumphs and our peace. Not to listen is the final insult. Eli Wiesel, who spent his life documenting Nazi atrocities, once remarked:

At the risk of offending, it must be emphasised that the victim suffered more profoundly from the indifference of the onlookers than from the brutality of the executioner. The cruelty of the enemy would have been incapable of breaking the prisoner; it was the silence of those he believed to be his friends – cruelty more cowardly, more subtle – which broke his heart.[6]

During the TRC hearings, the Commissioners presiding at the table often called upon the victims and their relatives to allow their deep-seated religious beliefs, as well as the support they were receiving from their faith communities, to sustain them through this process of mourning and remembering. According to the testimony of many, it often happened that a painful, traumatic appearance before the TRC was transformed into a cathartic experience. The tears, regularly seen on television newscasts at night, were mostly tears of healing. On the other hand, the many instances when believers – especially from the white community – failed to be present at the hearings, when they chose to ignore the stories, failed to 'sit where they sit' (Ezekiel, 3:15), indicate a missed opportunity but also serve as an accusation with which they will have to live for decades to come.

Truth

Central to the mandate of the TRC was to try and establish the truth about the past – in the words of the then Minister of Justice Dullah Omar, when he introduced the TRC legislation to Parliament, to 'join in the search for truth without which there can be no genuine reconciliation'. I still remember the long discussions we had in the TRC office in Johannesburg: how does one establish the truth? Modesty, it seemed, becomes everyone in their search for truth. We took some courage from the often quoted words of Michael Ignatief that although we will never be able to present a perfect picture, to establish the final truth, what the TRC indeed should be able to do was 'to curtail the number of lies that up to now had free reign in society'.[7]

But the quest for truth had a deeper side to it. Searching for the truth, in the tradition of all religions, is a spiritual exercise. Finding the truth goes well beyond establishing historical and legal facts. It has to do with understanding, accepting accountability, justice, restoring and maintaining the fragile relationships between human beings, as well as with the quest to find the Ultimate Truth, God Himself. Leading the nation on this road indeed posed a huge challenge to the faith communities in the country. The search for truth needed to be handled with the greatest sensitivity. Would that not be the case, the nation could bleed to death. But if we succeeded, it would lead to a national catharsis, peace and reconciliation, to the point where the truth in all reality sets one free.

I have seen this happen. When a perpetrator, after much anguish and embarrassment, eventually unburdened himself to the amnesty committee, when he made a full submission of all the relevant facts, after the questioning and cross-examination had come to an end, it was as if a cloud was lifted. On the last day of his appearance before the TRC, when he had to testify to his role in the Khotso House bombing, ex-Minister of Police Adrian Vlok told me: 'When the final question was asked and when the legal team of the South African Council of Churches indicated its satisfaction – that the team was willing not to oppose my amnesty application – my heart sang. I got a lump in my throat and I thanked God for his grace and mercy to me.'[8]

Victims experienced the same; the truth did indeed set them free. After a particularly difficult testimony at an East London hearing, when an aged Xhosa woman described the terrible tortures inflicted on her 14-year-old son – a story that had most of the audience struggling with their emotions – the women remarked on the blessing of being given the opportunity to place the truth – her truth – on the table. 'Oh yes, Sir, it was worth the trouble [to testify]. I think that I, for the first time in 16 years, will fall asleep immediately tonight. Perhaps tonight I will be able to sleep without nightmares.'[9]

Reconciliation

More difficult even than the quest for truth is the quest for reconciliation. The rather naïve expectation – at the onset of the TRC's work – that once we have welcomed truth in at the front door of our house, reconciliation would slip in by the back door, proved to be wrong. There were instances of reconciliation among perpetrators and victims. 'Sometimes the Lord knocked your feet out from underneath you when, at the most unexpected times and places, things started to happen,' Tutu remarked. 'The mercy, forgiveness and generosity He planted in people's hearts! Our God is truly a God of surprises!'[10]

One of the major difficulties we had to face was that of definition. What does reconciliation really mean? What does it entail? Lengthy discussions were held at TRC meetings. On the one hand, there were lawyers, jurists and politicians who, with feet planted firmly on the ground, warned that we should not be too starry-eyed when we speak about reconciliation. When the dust settles in the streets, when the shooting stops, when people let go of one another's throats, be grateful. That is enough! That is, in our context, as far as reconciliation goes. Archbishop Tutu and the *baruti*, on the other hand, favoured a far more lofty definition. When they spoke about reconciliation they clothed it in religious terminology. Referring to Paul's Second Letter to the Corinthians, it was often said that only because God had reconciled us to him by sacrificing his Son Jesus Christ on the cross, true and lasting reconciliation between humans became possible. Trying to define reconciliation, references were often made to the Shalom, the peace that God alone could provide (see Psalm 85). In similar fashion, spokespersons for the other faith communities used deeply religious terminology, referring to the deepest sources of their beliefs, when they joined in the debate.

On one issue there was total agreement. Reconciliation was a costly and very fragile exercise. Also that it would be impossible to refer to reconciliation without also taking into account the issues of justice, accountability and restitution. And to help this process to succeed, each of the faith communities carried an inescapable responsibility.

Faith communities' hearing

How big a responsibility the churches and the other faith communities had became evident at the special hearing in East London in November 1997. Representatives of 41 groups were invited to comment on their most fervent beliefs on the above-mentioned issues and give an account of their conduct during the apartheid years. It proved a humbling experience for all groups – not only for the Afrikaans churches that were traditionally at the side of the previous government (even to the point of providing a theological argument for apartheid) but also the churches and communities on the 'other side', who traditionally opposed apartheid. Not one community remained untouched and uncontaminated by the past. There was a lot to confess to one another, and much to be forgiven.

But there were also dreams to share and commitments to make. My lasting impression of the East London hearing was that of a community of believers – Christians, Muslims, Hindus, Jews, Buddhists and African traditionalists – who took hands to move into the future together, devoted to the process of truth and reconciliation. As to affirm their resolve, a number of far-reaching proposals to the faith communities in South Africa, emanating from the hearing, were incorporated in the TRC's final Report to the nation.[11]

'It seems to have worked'

What, then, should be said of the religious component of the TRC, of the ongoing debate between the *baruti* and the lawyers? I would like to leave the last word to Jorge Heine, the Chilean ambassador to South Africa, who with the experience of the Chilean truth commission behind him was invited to contribute an article to a Sunday newspaper. The TRC had already closed its doors and the final Report was being prepared when Jorge Heine observed:

> *The powers and resources (of the South African TRC) are much more significant than those of the Chilean commission ... Yet, ironically for a body with such strong statutory powers, the South African Commission stands out for the relative absence of lawyers (except the amnesty committee) and an extraordinary religious component. Sitting at the hearings held at the Central Methodist Church in downtown Johannesburg some time ago, watching Archbishop Desmond Tutu say a prayer and Alex Boraine call on some of the witnesses, I could not help but reflect that this would have been unthinkable in many countries where the separation of church and state is taken seriously.*
>
> *Yet it seems to have worked in South Africa, where there is a great religious diversity but where the strongly Christian subtext of repentance and forgiveness that pervades the Commission's proceedings conveys both the right message as to what reconciliation is all about. It manages to put at ease humble, profoundly decent South Africans who have been offered, often for the first time, the opportunity to state their case...* [12]

In the end, it seems that both the *baruti* and the lawyers had a role to play.

Section 3

What the Commission sought to achieve

The Truth

A space for victims to speak and the right of perpetrators to be heard

Amnesty

Coexistence, healing and reconciliation

Understanding perpetrators

Reparation and the healing of victims

Historical truth: something to fight for

JANET CHERRY

Acts of injustice done
Between the setting and the rising sun
in history lie like bones
each one

The Ascent of F6, WH Auden & Christopher Isherwood

If only discovering and setting down the truth was like the discovery by an archaeologist of the bleached bones of some ancestor of the human race. The bones may be fragile, but when put together the pieces of the skeleton can offer a semblance of scientific truth; unfortunately, the uncovering of the truth of human acts is rather more complex.

As Auden writes, the violations of human rights that occurred in our collective history do not disappear or disintegrate: they lie for decades, for centuries even, until acknowledged by society.

This was the role of the Truth and Reconciliation Commission (TRC): to uncover and acknowledge that truth, so our society could at last be free and move forward. The first listed objective of the TRC was to:

> *... establish as complete a picture as possible of the causes, nature and extent of the gross violations of human rights which were committed during the period from 1 March 1960 to the cut-off date, including the antecedents, circumstances, factors and context of such violations, as well as the perspectives of the victims and the motives and perspectives of the persons responsible for the commission of the violations.*[1]

134

The third objective was to establish and make known the fate or whereabouts of victims. In some respects, and at the most obvious level, these objectives were achieved: the exhumations undertaken by the TRC, for example, dug up the skeletons of those who had been secretly assassinated and restored the grisly remains to their families for proper burial. Together with the burial went a more-or-less accurate version of what happened and the public acknowledgement of how they died and who killed them. Along with the pain came 'closure' of a kind.

'Straightforward' cases

The case of Phila Portia Ndwandwe is one of the most striking and significant examples of this process and what it achieved. A young woman who superficially led a 'normal life' (as normal as life could be for a black woman under apartheid in KwaZulu-Natal in the 1980s), she was the acting commander of an underground network of Umkhonto we Sizwe (MK), the military wing of the ANC. She was abducted and interrogated by the South African security police in August 1986. In their applications for amnesty, the policemen responsible claimed that they interrogated her and tried to recruit her as an informer. She was by all accounts a remarkably tough and courageous person; she refused to cooperate and was executed with a blow to the head, which rendered her unconscious, and a bullet through her skull. Her clothes were removed – 'to prevent identification'. Her pelvis was clothed in a plastic bag, fashioned into a pair of panties indicating an attempt to protect her modesty. Her body was buried in a secret grave on a remote farm used by the police for such purposes.[2]

It can be argued that had the Truth Commission not set in motion the process that uncovered her bones, she would still be believed by some to have been a traitor. MK operatives who disappeared without trace were sometimes believed to have become askaris, members of the liberation movements who were 'turned' to work for the police or military against their former comrades. In this extraordinary case, the TRC process not only resulted in the truth about her loyalty, her heroism, her death and the whereabouts of her remains being disclosed; it also resulted in a more lasting form of dealing with the past – her child, a baby at the time of her death, was reunited with her parents. Her parents had not only found out what had happened to their daughter – they found a grandchild, a continuation of her existence, of whom they were unaware.

This case seems to illustrate without question the value of the TRC process for a country such as South Africa. In such cases, the possibility of amnesty being granted for human rights violations committed with a political motive was successful in persuading members of the security forces to come forward with previously undisclosed information.

Many of the mysteries of the apartheid era were revealed in this way: who killed Matthew Goniwe or Tennyson Makiwane; and what happened to those who disappeared, such as Siphiwe Mthimkhulu or Timothy Seremane. These were not always straightforward killings by the security police, either: some were killings by the liberation movements of their enemies, and some were killings where both sides bore some responsibility, as in cases where security force agents infiltrated liberation movements and made false accusations.

Less 'straightforward' cases

A good example of such a complex case is that of Ben Langa. Langa, a student and community activist, was killed by two MK members in June 1984. Both MK members, Lucky Payi and Sipho Xulu, were sentenced to death and executed for the murder on 7 September 1986. They claimed that they had been given orders by the ANC to kill Langa, as he was believed to be a police informer. The ANC apologised to the Langa family for its 'error'. The truth came out in the TRC process: another MK member, George Martins, applied for amnesty for Langa's death, saying that he gave information to the ANC about Langa's movements, which led to his assassination. Moreover, Payi and Xulu were ordered by another MK member with the codename of 'Fear' to kill Langa. The ANC believed that 'Fear' was a highly placed security police agent, whose handlers had told him to make the allegation about Langa and carry out the execution – in order to cause 'serious disruption of underground and mass democratic structures in the area and intense distress to the Langa family'.[3]

'Fear' was subsequently arrested by the ANC's security apparatus in exile and died while under interrogation. The ANC report on his death claims that he poisoned himself. The fact that he was in the custody of the ANC forces suggests that he may have died as a result of torture. He was found to be a victim of human rights violations – despite that fact that the ANC claimed that he was a state agent being 'handled' by Major Stadler of the security police headquarters, as claimed by the ANC.

Even in complex cases such as this, where there is a chain of causality, where perpetrators of human rights violations are also victims and where both security forces and liberation movements bear the responsibility for the deaths of innocent people, the Commission sometimes managed to 'put things right' (if only to the extent that the truth became known and publicly acknowledged).[4]

Yet for every case that was 'solved', where bones were dug up, where names were revealed, where torture was described, where people's actions were exonerated, there are the cases where the truth remains elusive.

There are two particular areas where this is the case: the one concerns contradictory evidence and the 'sanitising' of events; the other concerns the dilemma around informers and betrayal. These pose uncomfortable questions. The information that follows is neither easy to read nor fully comprehend; it has all emerged in public through TRC hearings, but has not been much talked or written about, presumably because of the discomfort it causes.

The security police (to their credit) have not been prepared to reveal the names of the myriad informers who assisted them in their 'dirty work'. Where they have acknowledged responsibility for specific acts, they have implicated only one another. Presumably by prior arrangement they agreed to apply for amnesty for some acts and all give roughly the same version of what happened. As a result, in most cases killings are presented as having been 'clean' and 'humane', and torture is usually denied. They spoke of sleeping potions being given, or victims rendered unconscious, before being executed with a single shot to the head. Whether true of not, it could be argued that it is better for the families of victims that the full horror of what may have occurred is not told. It is also easier for perpetrators to face their own families on the basis of this evidence. The problem comes where the perpetrators do not agree on the exact sequence of events. In such cases, the victims or their families are left with a sense of unease – whose version to believe?

There are two cases of human rights violation in Port Elizabeth that illustrate these dilemmas clearly. One is the case of the abduction and murder of the so-called PEBCO Three;[5] the other is the assassination of the Motherwell Four.[6]

The details of these cases are well known to many who have followed South African politics or the TRC over its three-year life span.

The PEBCO Three were leaders of the Port Elizabeth Black Civic Organisation who disappeared in May 1985. They had been telephoned and asked to go to the airport to meet someone from the British embassy. They never returned from the airport, and security police applied for amnesty for their abduction and killing.[7]

This case, at least as it is publicly and superficially known, is like Phila Ndwandwe's case: straightforward and successfully resolved. Yet if the surface is scratched, the ugliness and confusion of recording such events becomes apparent.

There is still the uncertainty about what did actually happen. The dead tell no tales, so the public has to rely on the truth being told by those who killed them. In this case, however, the perpetrators told three versions. There were three groups of perpetrators involved: the white security policemen from Port Elizabeth; the white security policemen from Vlakplaas, the coordinators of illegal operations; and the black policemen and askaris assigned to assist in the operation. According to Port Elizabeth security policeman Gideon Nieuwoudt, the PEBCO Three were taken to a remote Karoo farm where they were interrogated but not tortured, and drugged before being shot. Their bodies were then burnt, to destroy the evidence, and the ashes thrown into the Fish River.

According to one of the black policemen, however, they were assaulted during interrogation; at the amnesty hearing a policeman asked the families of the dead men for forgiveness, expressing his shame at what he had been required to do. According to askari Joe Mamasela, the three men were brutally tortured during interrogation, and killed one by one in each other's presence. Mamasela, too, expressed his contrition to the families of the deceased.

What are these families, and indeed, what is the amnesty committee to make of these conflicting versions of the truth? While the amnesty committee can decide to refuse amnesty on the grounds that some applicants are not making a full disclosure, it does not assist the families for whom both versions are difficult to bear. Should they believe the white security police, who have an interest in 'sanitising' the truth, as that truth is more palatable? Or should they believe the black policemen who have expressed remorse, who tell of how their loved ones were tortured to death?

The appalling account is made worse by another, even more disturbing aspect of Mamasela's version. He claims that after severe torture, and after watching his comrades being killed, one of the PEBCO Three confessed to being an agent of the National Intelligence Service (NIS). The security police then kept him alive overnight, and called in a senior member of this government service to verify the information. The NIS officer verified the information, but according to Mamasela, he 'gave the go-ahead' for the activist to be murdered, on the grounds that his information had not been of great use to them.

The implications of this information are enormous. If indeed one of these activists was a paid informer of the state, then the security police not only erred in identifying him as a target for assassination, but when confronted with their error, cynically proceeded to carry out their orders.

In fact, this 'error' would seem to tally with allegations that the three were not all originally identified as the targets for this 'hit' – they were killed just because they happened to be the three who responded to the invitation to go to the airport. Even more cynical was the NIS's complicity with this decision, if Mamasela's version is to be believed. Moreover, another important arm of the previous government's intelligence apparatus is directly implicated in gross human rights violations – something they have categorically denied. Yet the amnesty committee of the TRC had no means of verifying the information, denied by other members of the security police; it also has no investigative capacity to take the matter further. Mamasela's version is easily discredited, as he is not considered a 'reliable witness' and is prone to exaggeration; yet what would his interest have been in creating such an extraordinary tale?

The Motherwell Four case is, if possible, even more bizarre. A group of (white) security policemen (again from Port Elizabeth and Vlakplaas) applied for amnesty for blowing up three of their (black) colleagues and an askari with a car bomb.[8] Gideon Nieuwoudt, who pressed the button to detonate the bomb, said it was not an easy thing to do, as the victims were his colleagues. He was convicted for their murder. Again there were different versions – not concerning how the act was committed but of the motive for killing these men.

The first motive, presented in the court case, was that these men had been involved in fraud. Yet few believe that even notorious security police officers would kill their colleagues for minor acts of dishonesty. The second motive, which is the one most widely believed, is that the black policemen had threatened to disclose information about the murder of the Cradock Four and thus had to be eliminated to prevent these dark secrets from emerging. The third motive, presented to the TRC amnesty committee by the security police, was that the men had 'changed sides'; they had not only passed on information to the ANC but had actually been recruited by the ANC in Lesotho. The man who was alleged to have recruited them is conveniently dead; the ANC could not confirm to the TRC that they had been recruited – or indeed, any aspect of the story.

Again, amnesty aside, the question remains: where does this leave the families of the dead men? Did they die as villains, as hated security policemen, distrusted not only by their community but by their white colleagues too? Or were they really unacknowledged heroes, prepared to risk their lives in order to assist the liberation movement at a crucial time? Perhaps the truth lies somewhere in-between, in a messy place where their loyalties were not clear – neither to themselves nor anyone else.

While amnesty decisions on these two cases are still outstanding, it is unlikely that they are going to provide clarity concerning the above versions of what happened. If there are three different versions of an event, then someone must be telling lies, but this does not bring them any closer to determining which version is true. And where does this leave the perpetrators, not to mention the families of the deceased? The perpetrators may feel that they have bared their souls, risked everything in applying for amnesty, been portrayed as brutal killers, and yet their motives and their understanding of events have not been believed. The families of their victims, the black community in general – and probably the amnesty committee – do not know what to believe. All versions hold bitter options – and the truth remains elusive.

The issue of betrayal

Even in the most clear-cut cases, such as that of Phila Ndwandwe, there is the unresolved question of her betrayal. One of her relatives asked, in anguish, the question that goes to the heart of the problem of recording 'historical truth' – not 'who killed her' but 'who betrayed her?'

The issue of betrayal is probably the most difficult of all to confront, and this is the reason why truth commissions have trodden carefully around it rather than forced communities and individuals to face the truth.

Timothy Garton Ash has dealt with this issue in his reflections on the East German secret police and their myriad informers. He looked at the 'routine, bureaucratic forms of infiltration, intimidation and collaboration that characterised the German communist dictatorship'[9] and comes to the conclusion that his quest for the truth would, in some cases, have been better left unwritten. In South Africa, the liberation movements were also extensively infiltrated, but this was not a manifestation of the 'quieter corruption of mature totalitarianism' as Ash puts it. It was the brutal, desperate attempt by the apartheid state to gain information that would enable it to retain control in an increasingly anarchic situation. Informers and collaborators were bought, bribed or blackmailed into providing information; the rewards were low, and the cost of discovery high. It is probably true to say that it was the very effectiveness with which the security police managed to infiltrate the liberation movements that made the 'struggle' such an awful, secretive, intolerant, distrustful affair. Suspected 'casual' informers were burned alive in some cases by the 'comrades' in black communities; those working as security police agents infiltrating the liberation movements in exile were tortured and executed if discovered. It is still very hard for people to acknowledge the past, and the hardest thing of all to forgive is betrayal. An enemy, met on equal terms, can be forgiven for the killing of a loved one or a comrade. One of your own side, whose betrayal led to such a death, cannot be so easily forgiven.

All liberation struggles have their saints, their martyrs and their heroes – and the corresponding villains. It has been said that history is always written by the victors. Yet the writing of history such as it emerged in the TRC hearings can sometimes destroy this hagiography: the valiant youth who defied the police becomes merely a drunken thug; the brave freedom fighter is revealed as a traitor. The villain can even be revealed as a 'decent man' who had little room in which to move.

This is not confronting the question of the culpability of the 'big fish' of the security forces – those who gave the orders or who carried out the torture and assassination of activists. It is a history that includes the 'small fry' – those black policemen, for example, who shot and killed or injured so many of the township youth. Why did they do such terrible things – 'killing their own people', as it is often put in racially minded South Africa? How does the TRC portray this history? The 'banality of evil' and the complexity of guilt is represented well by two little-known cases that were heard at the Human Rights Violation hearings in Grahamstown in the Eastern Cape. These cases did not involve senior white security policemen or senior black leaders in the liberation movement, and thus did not receive much attention, yet they illustrate something about the nature of such acts that poses a fundamental challenge to the accepted history of the anti-apartheid struggle.

This accepted history presents defenceless, unarmed black youth pitted against merciless, well-armed white policemen. When the youth show defiance – shouting slogans, singing freedom songs and perhaps even throwing a stone or two – they are gunned down in cold blood. These two cases show another reality.

In every South African township overseen by a Black Local Authority (BLA), most residents saw the Authority as a form of control by the apartheid state, and only 'sellouts' or 'Uncle Toms' accepted the power and influence of the councillors. Many councillors were forced to resign by the 'comrades' of the liberation struggle, many had their homes destroyed, and some were killed. Some councillors, in turn, armed themselves and killed the young people who threatened to kill them. The community knew only that they had been shot by a councillor – and they came to be seen as heroes of the struggle. Their families approached the TRC and made statements to this effect – they testified at the public hearings that their sons were victims of gross human rights violations. In one case, the mother of a young student activist, Mntunyane Kuhlane, testified that Councillor Ntsikelelo Botha shot her son dead in a house in Port Alfred during May 1986 'for no apparent reason'.

The man who had been named as the perpetrator appeared in person and explained his version of the incident. He was visiting relatives in another town, he said, and not acting as a BLA official at the time, when the house was invaded by an angry mob. They attacked him, and he was stabbed repeatedly with screwdrivers and struck on the back of the head with an axe. The crowd would surely have stabbed or bludgeoned him to death if he had not retaliated. He took out a small firearm and fired blindly – into the air, into the crowd – in desperation. He then lost consciousness in this tiny township house, in this room full of fighting people. He did not aim to kill anyone, he explained – he was under attack; his life was threatened. He was sorry about what had happened, and about the deaths of the boys, but he did not feel that he had had any choice.

Clearly there are cases where councillors, municipal policemen and other black policemen acted in an unreasonably and disproportionately violent manner, but there are also cases like the above, where the township youth seem to have been the aggressors. The youth were often not passive victims. They had chosen to be involved in a certain manner – the consequences of which could be death. They can be portrayed as heroes or soldiers on one side of an unequal war – certainly they were angry victims of oppression – but they cannot, with historical accuracy, be seen as passive victims of human rights violations by a brutal state machinery.

None of the above is intended to exonerate those who perpetrated human rights violations on behalf of the apartheid state; nor is it intended to establish a position of absolute moral neutrality in the struggle between the apartheid state and its opponents. What it is necessary to demonstrate is the complexity of establishing the truth, the nuances of particular cases, and the difficulty that many people on both sides of that struggle have in accepting this more nuanced truth.

Journalist Svetlana Aleksiyevich illustrates this point graphically:

The mothers of (Soviet) soldiers killed in Afghanistan would come to the courtroom with their photographs and medals. They would weep and cry: 'See how young and beautiful they were. Our sons.' And there I am reporting that they killed, out there. And to me they'd say: 'We don't need your kind of truth. We have our own truth.'[10]

Similarly, the mothers of the boys who attacked the councillor do not want to believe that their children were aggressors. The wives of the PEBCO Three do not want to contemplate that one of their husbands may have been a traitor. And on the other side, those who tortured and killed cannot make sense of their actions outside the philosophical framework in which they committed them. Michael Ignatieff puts it this way:

Peoples who believe themselves to be victims of aggression have an under-standable incapacity to believe that they also committed atrocities. Myths of innocence and victimhood are a powerful obstacle in the way of confronting unwelcome facts.[11]

Has the truth been found?

Has the South African Truth and Reconciliation Commission established the truth? Has it established, at least, a truth, a version that may be accepted by most people? Archbishop Tutu, in the foreword to the *TRC Report*, asserts that 'We believe we have provided enough of the truth about our past for there to be a consensus about it… We should accept that truth has emerged even though it has initially alienated people from one another. The truth can be, and often is, divisive.' The *TRC Report* quotes Ignatieff's claim that 'all that a truth commission can achieve is to reduce the number of lies that can be circulated unchallenged in public discourse.'[12]

My fear is that in the attempt to establish a consensus on 'the truth', many of the complexities and nuances of the truth are lost. It seems that we have to acknowledge that the truth that the TRC has uncovered is, at best, only a partial truth. And while half a loaf is definitely better than no bread at all, it may be more valuable to see historical truth as a continually unfolding process – not something that is past but something that is still part of the present, still contested and still under construction.

I am not quite as cynical as Michael Ignatieff, though, who asserts:

For what seems apparent in the former Yugoslavia, in Rwanda and in South Africa is that the past continues to torment because it is not past. These places are not living in a serial order of time, but in a simultaneous one, in which the past and the present are a continuous, agglutinated mass of fantasies, distortions, myths and lies.[13]

As a historian, I hold that there is one reality, and that truth is not relative; it can be known. This does not make it easy to find, nor does it mean that all will agree with the way it is interpreted or written by a particular individual. Yet there was only one sequence of events leading to the death of the PEBCO Three – despite the different testimonies of those present. Not all versions of history are equally valid, for example that of someone who does not remember the truth, or chooses not to tell the truth. It is inevitable that historical truth – especially that arising out of bitter and violent conflicts – is contested, but this does not give equal validity to all versions. It does, however, make the work of the historian more difficult and more interesting.

I thus prefer the quote of Albert Camus, who said that 'Truth is as mysterious as it is inaccessible, and it must be fought for eternally'.

Truth as a trigger for transformation: from apartheid injustice to transformational justice

WILLIE ESTERHUYSE

The Truth and Reconciliation (TRC) Report states clearly that the Promotion of National Unity and Reconciliation Act required the Commission to 'look back to the past and forward to the future'.

In this sense, the TRC was required to establish a truth that would 'contribute to the reparation of the damage inflicted in the past and to the prevention of the recurrence of serious abuses in the future'. The Report went on to clarify this vital point: 'It was not enough simply to determine what happened. Truth as factual, objective information [cannot] be separated from the purposes it is required to serve'. The Truth Commission was not only about uncovering facts about past gross human rights violations – it was about placing those terrible truths on public, national record. It was about the full and public acknowledgement of factual truth.

This acknowledgement, this 'healing and restorative truth', is indeed 'central to the restoration of the dignity of victims'.[1] But acknowledgement is not enough. The 'emerging truth' must unleash 'a social dynamic that includes redressing the suffering of victims'.[2]

'Reconciliation,' as the concluding sentence of the Report puts it, 'requires a commitment, especially by those who have benefited and continue to benefit from past discrimination, to the transformation of unjust inequalities and dehumanising poverty'.[3]

This chapter further develops the links, alluded to in the *TRC Report*, between truth and transformation in post-apartheid South Africa. It is based on the firm belief that the painful truths uncovered and acknowledged by the TRC demand urgent and far-reaching action. These truths should become a trigger for transformation.

What is transformation?

But what does 'transformation' mean? It has become one of the most commonly used words in post-1994 South Africa. To the vast majority of South Africans it signifies the dramatic changes that have taken place in the country's traditional relations of power and privilege, changes that are destined to continue for at least the next 10 to 15 years.

Admittedly, a clear and nationally mobilising understanding of transformation is still lacking in South Africa. To some, transformation 'smells of revolution' – as stated by a teacher during a private discussion – and of a deliberate attempt by the new political elite to marginalise the previously advantaged class.

Others use the word 'transformation' as a mobilising battle-cry in their attempt to get hold of the levers of power, or to gain access by whatever means to the resources and riches of the country. To many it is simply the key to positions of power and privilege.

Transformation is nevertheless a crucial concept in South Africa's new language of transition and democratisation. It is not just a concept with cognitive aspects waiting to be analysed. It also represents a vision of a thoroughly changed South Africa – a vision inspiring policy-making, strategic thinking, project planning and a variety of other functions and activities.

Transformation, as a vision, constituted one of the main driving forces for the establishment of the TRC in order to facilitate, direct and give flesh and blood to this vision. It is only within the context of a clearly understood and effectively executed vision that it becomes possible to transform the urge for retribution into a search for true reconciliation. In fact, the process of reconciliation – and it is a process, not a once-off event or happening – is part of a much deeper and bigger process: the process of transformation.

In order to understand something of the complex and hazardous journey from apartheid injustice to transformational justice, it is necessary to deal very briefly with apartheid. I will then develop an argument in favour of 'transformational justice' – or a future that differs significantly from the past.

As so aptly stated by the negotiators of the Interim Constitution (Section 232:4), 'South Africa has arrived at a point where she faces the challenge of building a bridge between the past (a deeply divided society characterised by strife, conflict and untold suffering and injustice) and the future (founded on the recognition of human rights, democracy and peaceful coexistence).'

The bridge metaphor, of course, does not imply continuity or evolutionary change. It is a definitive break, a leaving behind.

This break, nevertheless, has to go through a transitional phase, a phase of breaking down as well as reconstituting and developing justifiable structures and patterns of coexistence.

The TRC and the truth about apartheid injustice

Whatever criticism may be voiced against the TRC, its procedures, its findings and even its members, it cannot detract from or cancel a basic truth brought to the fore by this institution: the ideology, system and policies of apartheid institutionalised and internalised strife, conflict, suffering and injustice. Apartheid allowed for legally sanctioned and ideologically justified injustices, making possible human rights atrocities of an extreme form.

The stories told to the TRC by victims and perpetrators were so horrifying that they could not remain untold in a South Africa in need of a bridge between the past and the future.[4]

Listening to these stories one can be informed by one of two (or both) distinct sets of assumptions. Firstly, it is possible to hear the stories as events that have befallen some fellow South Africans – personal and individualised histories of people who had the bad fortune to cross the path of an adversary. This treatment of the stories is not out of bounds. Hearing personal and individualised histories of suffering, or listening to the motivations, experiences and emotions of perpetrators, is part of a person-centred ethic and the generation of attitudes imbued with forgiveness, compassion and empathy.

But are the events these stories relate of a purely coincidental nature? Should they remain personal and individual histories? Or should they be treated as part of a more comprehensive story-line – the one concerning an ideology and its power and privilege relations; the story of systemic injustice and structurally generated human rights atrocities? Are these stories really only isolated events or do they constitute the hermeneutic trigger-points of a much bigger text: the history of apartheid?

These questions explore a second set of assumptions. Personal and individual histories of suffering or evil-doing are usually intrinsically related to systemic conditions. Provision should therefore be made for a comprehensive socio-ethical approach when dealing with the past.

It is an assumption of this chapter that apartheid is one of the most dehumanising and totalitarian ideologies to have become embodied in political hegemonies of the 20th century. That is why the question as to whether apartheid might not also have produced something of value is as futile as asking whether Nazism brought about some good things. The system and policies developed on the basis of the ideology of apartheid were inherently immoral with regard to its core values – establishing the conditions and space for the violation of fundamental human rights.

This assumption and socio-ethical approach with regard to apartheid find clear expression in the *TRC Report*:

> *Building on an inherited social practice [of segregation], apartheid imposed a legal form of oppression with devastating effects on the majority of South Africans ... over almost half a century, apartheid became the warp and weft of the experience of all who lived in South Africa, defining their privilege and their disadvantage, their poverty and wealth, their public and private lives and their very identity.*[5]

> *[It] needs constantly to be borne in mind that, while the state and other operatives were committing the violations documented in this report, a much larger pattern was unfolding. These may not have been 'gross' as defined by the Act, but they were, nonetheless, an assault on the rights and dignity of millions of South Africans ... Thus, while only some 21 300 persons filed gross human rights violations petitions with the Commission, apartheid was a grim daily reality for every black South African...*[6]

It is this systemic and all-pervading character that provides the background to the present investigation. During the apartheid years, people did many evil things. Some of these are the gross violations of human rights with which this Commission had to deal. But it can never be forgotten that the system itself was evil, inhumane and degrading for the many millions who became its second- and third-class citizens.[7]

The painful truth – especially for many people who supported the previous government – is that the immoralities that attended apartheid were not accidental or epiphenomenal. They were inherent to apartheid. That is why apartheid was not a mere political policy or a set of reasonably coherent and consistent policy measures with which acceptable political objectives were being pursued. On the contrary, apartheid was in its policy means and policy objectives morally unacceptable. In fact, characteristic of the system of apartheid was the intertwined nature of its means and ends. Thence apartheid acquired for most of its adherents the character of a closed worldview and restricted outlook on life, one that had the status of an article of faith. The sanction given to apartheid by the Afrikaans churches, among other institutions, reinforced this character.[8] Ultimately, apartheid functioned as an end in itself.

Apartheid left its marks on three fundamental dimensions of the South African political system: its value system, its structure and its political culture. The wide-ranging legacy of apartheid also extends beyond the political system. This truth has been powerfully illustrated by the series of institutional/sectoral hearings held by the TRC.[9] This means that apartheid could not just be 'abolished'. Still less could it be done away with merely by getting rid of the masters of apartheid and replacing them with others. It could only be abolished by transforming the structure, culture and values it produced in such a way that a new dispensation with a new structure, culture and values could receive institutional embodiment.

South Africa is still busy with this process. It can be a long and difficult process. It is therefore necessary to discuss the issues of transformation and transformational justice in order to understand something of the post-apartheid era we are building.

Transformation

For a number of reasons the term 'transformation', important though it may be in any discussion of change, has become a potentially bewitching and misleading one in South Africa. This illustrates what philosophers Friedrich Nietzsche and Ludwig Wittgenstein once described as the dangerous and even tyrannical dimension of language, where metaphors – the tools of language – become stale gatekeepers to the world of created meanings while ensnaring the users thereof in dogmatic and one-sided interpretations. Hence the need for conceptual clarity, for resisting the temptation 'to misrepresent to ourselves the way in which we really use words'.[10]

In an attempt to liberate the meaningful usage of the term from its bewitchments, it is necessary to bear in mind that although we talk 'change' when we talk 'transformation', we do not talk about any particular kind of change.

In the human, cultural world – the world of politics, economics, social interaction, organisations, institutions and created structures – the word 'change' generally functions as an umbrella term for two distinct processes triggered by human interventions. They differ in terms of the nature of the interventions, the objectives of the interventions and the outcomes of the interventions.

In *Strategies for cultural change*, Bate[11] refers to these interventions as strategies for order and continuity (conforming strategies) and strategies for change and discontinuity (transforming strategies). The processes have been referred to as *first-order change* and *second-order change*.

With first-order change, the system itself, including its structure, culture and defining values, does not change. The change process takes place within the confines of the system itself and in terms of the basic principles and values of the system. The main purpose of the intervention is to preserve the fundamentals and the existing order of things by changing the non-fundamentals.

This category of change is more usually known as adaptation, renovation, adjustment, incremental change or piece-meal engineering. The objective is to change behaviour within a prevailing system without affecting the culture, structure and defining values of the system. Change is, moreover, regarded as an evolutionary process.

Second-order change is of a more radical nature. Its primary objective is not to intervene in the operations of an institution but to transform its structure, culture, defining values and overall form. Martel[12] quite rightly refers to this prototype of change as structural change, emphasising that a fundamental transformation of an institution's total make-up is on the agenda.

Bate[13] coins the phrase 'form- or frame-breaking' to underline the decisive nature of second-order change. Strategies aimed at transformation inevitably break the evolutionary chain of development, creating discontinuity and variance of form. Put differently, transformation means a new institution, a new culture and a new direction.

The concepts of *structure, culture* and *defining values* clearly refer to key elements of second-order change; they form a family relationship and cannot be discussed as separate 'entities' (this methodological mistake is often made). It is impossible to change the structure of an institution without also changing its culture and defining values.

Second-order change, or transformation, affects the patterns and values in terms of which people behave, turning traditional habits and routine responses upside down. For this reason transformation inevitably creates conflict and uncertainties.

A decisive aspect of transformation is that it goes hand in hand with a *paradigm shift* or mind-set change. We act and think in terms of frames of reference or paradigms, as is illustrated by the very commonly used justification: 'This is the way I have always done it.'

Mind-sets, frames of reference or paradigms reflect our prejudices, our values, our beliefs and our social conditioning. They can be 'hard' or dogmatic, in the sense of conditioning us to cling to them for better or for worse. They can also be 'soft', displaying our willingness to change and explore new possibilities.

Accepting a new paradigm requires a period of transition. Kuhn[14], writing about paradigm shifts in science, makes the valid point that a paradigm shift 'is seldom completed by a single man and never overnight'.

Whatever the case may be, paradigms 'mould' the way we look at things or experience the world and each other. They usually restrict our vision and understanding, limiting our capacity to come up with creative solutions. Transformers and paradigm shifters are therefore usually 'highly opinionated, action-oriented types whose speciality is rocking the corporate boat'[15]. They are innovators, creators and inventors rather than imitators, copiers or improvisers[16].

The need for transformation

In South Africa the need for transformation is linked to some environment-specific considerations. The most important of these are moral and strategic.

The moral perspective should be obvious: how to transform a racially based organisational and economic pattern, a legacy of the past, into a commonly shared, open and non-racial, non-sexist pattern? The main objective of structural change inspired by a moral perspective is to establish legitimacy and moral acceptability. Without legitimacy no institution can survive.

This is no easy task, given that discriminatory patterns and practices in South Africa are not of a mere coincidental nature but stem from structural conditions. These conditions have created vested interests as well as 'entrenched' mindsets or paradigms on both sides of the racial divide.

One of the issues on the agenda is equitable access to scarce resources, opportunities and skills. Another important issue is the need to establish cross-cultural and cross-racial economic alliances in order to stabilise the country politically and socially. At present, affirmative action and black economic empowerment are the procedures used to address these issues, but it should be noted that they do not constitute the full scope of transformational or structural change. In the South African context, in particular, they represent specific aspects of transformation, albeit important moral and political aspects. Transformation, however, entails much more than affirmative action or black economic empowerment.

This becomes clear when one analyses the strategic perspective of transformation within the South African context, with its socio-economic inequalities and extreme levels of poverty. Democratising South Africa and setting up viable structures embodying the vision of a non-racial and non-sexist democracy are laudable strategic objectives, but should be underpinned by strategies aimed at alleviating the plight of the poor, effectively addressing socio-economic inequalities and establishing a thriving economic environment. In a strategic nutshell: a stable and viable democracy in South Africa is dependent on vigorous (people) development and economic growth. To this end the structural transformation of South Africa is inevitable.

Much progress has been made in this regard. The policy document on 'Growth, Employment and Redistribution' (GEAR), combining economic growth strategies and reconstruction and development strategies, was a major achievement. The outcome of the implementation of these policies and strategies will have a decisive impact on South Africa's future political and social stability.

The important point here is that the concept 'transformation', strategically applied to the South African context, does not refer to the domain of politics only. In fact, it would amount to a strategic blunder if the transformation of South Africa were viewed solely from a restrictive political perspective. A holistic perspective is best suited when talking about South Africa's transformation.

In this regard it should also be emphasised that transformation includes much more than the establishment of legitimacy for institutions and organisations. Transformative interventions also have to enhance performance, productivity, efficiency and competitiveness. Transformation is about an improved order of things.

These and other strategic challenges necessitate a view of transformation that surpasses the narrow political definition. It is therefore in the strategic interest of all South Africans, rich and poor, white and black, that a well-planned and thoroughly executed vision of transformation should succeed, thereby making South Africa a winning country.

Transformational justice

The concept 'transformational justice' refers to the notions of justice that drive and also legitimise the process of transition and transformation. Transformation, as it is understood in this chapter, inevitably implies a vision – a dream of what the country could or should become; a picture of the kind of future desired. A vision, of course, is always value-laden, expressive of what we believe in. The values inherent to the vision constitute the normative dimension of transformational processes and strategies. Put differently, the values express the notions of justice inspiring and guiding the process and strategy.

It is necessary to functionally distinguish between two sets of notions of justice in order to gain some understanding of what transformational justice entails. The distinction is not meant to imply that these notions can be divorced or isolated from one another. But from a functional point of view the making of the distinction is possible, for the simple reason that notions of justice within a context of transformation and transition are never available in a ready-made or securely packaged form. They arise from the awareness and realisation that the past – and the present that emerged from it – is something to be liberated from.

The first set of notions of justice could be termed 'converting values', ie those values that convert us to break with the past and its legacy because of the unjust systemic nature thereof. They impel us to declare 'Never again'.

This brings us back to the value of the TRC process and the Report. Converting values go hand in hand with our 'moments of truth', as they are commonly called. In these moments of truth the past and present are seen in a completely different light. A new moral awareness arises, more often than not accompanied by guilt and shame.

On many occasions, the hearing of personal stories of suffering, and the understanding of these stories as stories of suffering and systemic injustice, triggers moments of truth. It is during these moments that human beings are motivated to genuinely utter the phrase 'It was wrong' and begin to understand what justice signifies in view of the evil-doings of the past.

An example accompanying the TRC process will illustrate this point. After having acquainted himself with some of the stories told before the TRC, a conservative Afrikaner phoned and, in a voice conveying his anguish, uttered one sentence only: '*Ek skaam my tot in my boude*' [I am deeply ashamed]. Over the past few years many Afrikaners have expressed similar feelings in private conversations, and even in the letters pages of Afrikaans newspapers. A number have commented on the powerful impact of Antjie Krog's book on the TRC, *Country of my skull*. Her extensive use of testimonies from TRC victim hearings and her honest existential struggle, as an Afrikaner, to respond to the many, many victims who had Afrikaner surnames on their lips while testifying about their violations at the hands of the security police have moved many people deeply. These responses illustrate the converting potential of the TRC process.[17]

For many the testimonies before the TRC – from victims and perpetrators, such as Benzien, Cronje, Hechter, Mentz, Van Vuuren and De Kock – provided much more than cold objective and factual information. These testimonies encouraged moments of truth, where people were converted to an understanding of what injustice is, while at the same time becoming aware of a new notion of justice. Confronted by the stories, the face of evil became visible to these people, giving birth to a feeling of shame and to a notion of justice. The latter is of particular importance, for through this feeling of shame, a moral responsibility for what went wrong in the past may also be acknowledged. In other words, in the confrontation with the past a dialectical tension often develops. Within the context of this tension we begin to see things in a different light and experience a new moral consciousness.

But converting values remain blind without legitimising values – without positive notions of justice that create new commitments and motivate us to constructively intervene in the legacy of the past. The values connected with this position legitimise the process of transformation.

Our constitution is imbued with legitimising values such as 'democracy', 'non-racial' and 'non-sexist'. In fact, the constitutionally entrenched Bill of Rights should be read as the legitimising values and conception of justice underpinning the processes of transition and transformation.

But how to get those who have profited from the past to realise that an *awareness* of the injustice is but one side of the coin, and that the other side demands deliberate *interventions* in order to transform South African society. This is one of the most serious ethical, political and strategic challenges facing our country. What is needed in particular is a national consensus on and commitment to a set of legitimising values underpinning the process of transformation.

Moreover, it needs to be emphasised that this will remain an idealistic dream without decisive leadership. Conger articulates the significance of leadership during times of transition and transformation extremely well when he writes: 'While we have learned a great deal about the necessity of strategic vision and effective leadership, we have overlooked the critical link between vision and the leader's ability to communicate its essence. In the future, leaders will not only have to be effective strategists but rhetoricians who can energise through the words they choose.'[18]

After everything has been said and done about transformation, it has to be emphasised that without vision and value-driven leadership, transformation will remain blind. And a discussion of transformation without a discussion of leadership – and what transformational leadership entails – is empty. While it has to be accepted that transformation, for strategic and moral reasons, is South Africa's bridge to the future, it unfortunately also has to be accepted that too little attention is being devoted to the question of what kind of leadership is needed to effect the required change.

No transformation without moments of truth, no reconciliation without transformation

This discussion of transformation and the limited though vital potential of the TRC process to support the transition from apartheid injustices to a transformed society proceeds from this fundamental presupposition: there is something like a 'legacy of apartheid'. The repeal of key laws that legally sanctioned apartheid did not mean the revocation of this legacy. It is a legacy that will be with us for a considerable time.

Accordingly, the debate about apartheid and about transformation will not come to an end very soon.

Although the full nature and extent of the legacy could not be investigated here, there is one point that should be stressed: there can be no enduring reconciliation in this country without the transformation of that which apartheid left in its wake. In fact, the values entrenched in the constitution of the country – the development of a non-racial, non-sexist democracy on the basis of reconciled relationships – are not possible without such a far-reaching transformation.

That is why reconciliation within the context of a country like South Africa is not based simply on confession of guilt and the asking of forgiveness. Acts such as these, painful as they may be for some, are but the first steps on the road to reconciliation.

Reconciliation that can lead to a culture of trust and freedom also requires that structural and other reparations and adjustments take place. Put differently, reconciliation must become flesh and blood through concrete deeds, through making sacrifices, through transformation. Reconciliation can therefore never be a cheap word. It is a costly word that was bought with blood.

Reconciliation necessarily has as its converse side the fundamental change of relationships as well as of conditions within which distorted relationships previously existed. Apartheid was, after all, not just an article of faith or attitude of people. It was a structure, supported by a value system and culture. It was not just something in the heads and hearts of people. It was also a practice that affected people's humanity and dignity and which led to appalling forms of inequality.

The moral and strategic aim of transformation and of the leadership it implies is not to continue the status quo but to change it in such a way that the policy and practice that led to structural and other forms of injustice will be eradicated. Therewith is added not just a deed to the words of reconciliation; but space is created for the continuation of the reconciliation process.

Towards the recognition of our past injustices

WILHELM VERWOERD

We, the people of South Africa,
Recognise the injustices of our past;
Honour those who suffered for justice and freedom in our land ...
We therefore, through our freely elected representatives, adopt this
Constitution as the supreme law of the Republic so as to –
Heal the divisions of the past and establish a society based on democratic
values, social justice and fundamental human rights;
Lay the foundations for a democratic and open society in which
government is based on the will of the people and every citizen is equally
protected by the law...

Preamble to the Constitution of South Africa 1996

The Truth and Reconciliation Commission (TRC), on behalf of 'the people of South Africa', gave flesh to our constitutional commitment to 'recognise the injustices of our past'. The TRC helped current and future generations of South Africans to put a face, a human face, to many of 'those' who suffered and often continue to suffer. The TRC, more effectively than any previous truth commission, also made it possible for some of those responsible for the suffering to speak and to be seen. The TRC thus fulfilled the vital task of placing on public record the painful price of 'justice and freedom in our land'.

The TRC process also proved to be a humbling experience. The many controversies, confusions and imperfections accompanying this incomplete process of public, official acknowledgement highlight how difficult it is and will be to implement the vision contained in the Preamble of our new Constitution.

For example, the TRC was mandated to focus on a relatively narrow category of politically motivated gross human rights violations, which clearly represent just the tip of the truth about the large-scale socio-economic injustices and other human rights violations under the system of apartheid. For some critics the high-profile TRC attention given to some injustices obscured the truth about other, more widespread injustices.[1] Thus the acknowledgement of some injustices appear to have undermined the recognition of many other injustices. Apart from questions surrounding the scope of the TRC's mandate with regard to past injustices, the nature of adequate 'recognition' was/is also the source of criticism. Many victims whose suffering was morally, symbolically acknowledged at TRC human rights violation hearings now expect more tangible, material recognition, such as the individual monetary reparation grants recommended by the TRC. The TRC process furthermore brought to the fore some tensions between the twin constitutional goals of 'recognising the injustices of our past' and 'honouring those who suffered for justice'. Some critics feel that the TRC's concentration on the suffering of all 'victims' of (some) injustices has neglected and even dishonoured the memory of the heroes who struggled for justice and liberation from apartheid.

With the benefit of hindsight it is clear that some of these criticisms could have been avoided by institutional redesign. The TRC could have been given more power to implement tangible reparation and resources for therapeutic support, for example, or more resources to explain the complex workings and limitations of the TRC to the general public; there could also have been a separate committee on reconciliation. Other problems accompanying the TRC process, on the other hand, such as the unrealistic reparation expectations of victims appearing before the TRC and the handling of particular amnesty decisions and findings procedures, should be placed before the Commission's own door.

I believe that much of the criticism and confusion surrounding the TRC process is a sign of a deeper problem though – a lack of consensus about what can and what cannot reasonably be expected from this bold experiment in responding to (some of) the wrongs of our past. We are still groping for the language to adequately assess the significance of the TRC.[2] We do not have enough clarity about where the TRC process fits into the bigger picture painted by the Preamble of the Constitution, so we struggle to distinguish the process from and link it to other means of recognising past injustices and 'laying the foundations for a democratic and open society', such as the Reconstruction and Development Programme, the Land Claims court and certain cases handled by the criminal justice system (eg the trials of Eugene de Kock and Ferdie Barnard). Archbishop Tutu formulated this point in his own inimitable fashion:

> One of the first lessons we learned in dealing with Biblical literature was asking 'what is its literary type or genre?' Because once you knew the answer to that question we would not pose inappropriate questions of the literary piece, expecting it to provide information it was never designed to furnish. So, for instance, if when reading Wordsworth's poem The Daffodils and encountering the lines 'And all at once I saw a crowd, a host, of golden daffodils… dancing in the breeze', you were to ask, 'by the way, which band was playing?' or 'who were the dancing partners?' you would have missed the bus quite comprehensively.

He went on to claim that 'many people have been making much the same sort of mistake about the TRC', for example expecting the TRC to follow the same procedures as a court of law.

'They accused the TRC of allowing wild allegations to stand untested and unchallenged. They did not seem to understand when we said, especially of the victim hearings, that the primary purpose was to give people who have been silenced so long the opportunity of telling their story in a sympathetic setting which was victim-friendly, as required by the Act'.[3]

I agree with the Archbishop that the standards of procedural justice to protect the rights of the accused within a temporary, investigative institution such as the TRC should not be judged by those applicable to the criminal justice system.[4] I would add that the limited potential healing of victims appearing at a single, public hearing should not be evaluated with an intimate, long-term therapeutic relationship in mind; nor should the promotion of 'national unity and reconciliation' be measured by the yard-stick of interpersonal reconciliation between particular victims and perpetrators.[5]

To address the underlying and often neglected challenge of clarifying the genre of the TRC process, I believe it is necessary to take a step (or three) backwards. After all, how are we to focus clearly on the central meanings of a complex, contested, unfinished process when we are still standing so close to it? So instead of directly discussing specific points about the rights of perpetrators and the imperfect recognition of the violated, I suggest we take a more indirect route. This route involves contrasting the TRC with two highly tempting but deeply problematic ways of dealing with past injustices: forgetting and selective remembering.

Forgetting and denial versus remembrance and recognition

Let us 'forget' for a moment the TRC with all its imperfections and visit the Arena Chapel in Padua, Italy. There, in the centre of a series of paintings depicting vices such as anger, envy and pride, we will find Giotto's 'Inguistizia'. His portrait shows us how injustice looks to victims. The face of Injustice has a male profile that looks to the right. Small, fang-like teeth at the sides of the mouth and the chin thrust forward speak of coldness and cruelty. In his right hand is a nasty pruning hook, not a sceptre; his left hand holds a long sword, pointing downwards; he wears a ruler's or a judge's cap, but it is turned backward. Around him is a gate in ruin; the trees surrounding him are rooted in soil where there is a theft, a rape and a murder. The scene is watched by two soldiers, but they do nothing, and nor does the ruler.[6]

Let us briefly remember how contemporary societies have responded to the injustices in their pasts. Think of the continuing Turkish suppression of the terrible truth about the 1915 Armenian genocide.[7] Or the limited recognition by the Japanese of their wartime atrocities, for example the 1937 Rape of Nanking (where more than 300 000 Chinese were slaughtered by Japanese soldiers);[8] or the belated, reluctant attempts by Germans to truly face their Nazi past;[9] or the complex ways in which the partial recognition of the consequences of slavery continues to poison race relations in the United States. Tragically, Giotto's 'Inguistizia' remains an all too familiar face, haunting victims, challenging perpetrators, bystanders and beneficiaries.[10]

Looking at this face of injustice makes me see our TRC process with different eyes. Noticing the insult that indifference adds to the injuries of victims, the 'second wound of silence'[11] caused by 'Inguistizia's fang-like teeth, I become more and more appreciative of Archbishop Tutu's tear-filled eyes. Surely there is huge difference between the TRC's attempt at remembering and recognition of victims and the more typical, morally indifferent alternative of 'let's forget and move on'. Indeed, the TRC process placed on record the dangers of this kind of moral insensitivity. As the then Deputy President Thabo Mbeki put it, during an address in February 1998:

> *And because some decided neither to see nor to hear, we can, today, hear the stories told at the Truth and Reconciliation Commission that speak of a level and extent of human depravity that could never have heard the meaning or been moved by the poetry of the words,* umntu, ngumntu ngabantu! *[people are people through other people].*[12]

Mbeki went on to link the work of the TRC with a call for us to recover our soul as a nation:

The political order that tore our country apart is now no more. Yet it gave us a bitter heritage, which we must strive to overcome. Above all else we must create the situation in which the soul can sing and louder sing to restore a social morality that says the pursuit of material gain at all costs is not and cannot be what distinguishes us as South Africans; [we must create] a patriotism that is imbued by love and respect for the fellow citizen, regardless of race, colour, gender or age, and a recognition of our common humanity.[13]

His call to enable our national soul 'to sing and louder sing' was an extension of the following beautiful imagery in WB Yeats' *Sailing to Byzantium*:

An old man is but a paltry thing
A tattered coat upon a stick
Unless soul clap hands and sing
And louder sing
For every tatter in its mortal dress.[14]

Perhaps Yeats' imagery may be even further extended to throw light on the fragile deeper meanings of the TRC process: the public victim hearings provided spaces for singing – where we could sing sad songs for some of the biggest tears in our 'mortal dress', where we could lament some of the scars in our body politic. The TRC process gave us opportunities to clap hands, softly, for those who have survived... But it also was a place to refrain from singing. To listen, respectfully, in silence[15]. A place to cover our faces in shame for our moral blindness and deafness to the suffering of fellow South Africans, in the past and in the present. In the words of the then President Nelson Mandela:

All of us, as a nation that has newly found itself, share in the shame at the capacity of human beings of any race or language group to be inhumane to other human beings. We should all share in the commitment to a South Africa in which that will never happen again.[16]

This intimate connection between a nation with a healthy 'soul' and facing past injustices with open eyes and ears highlights the importance of the remembrance and recognition facilitated by the TRC. For the simple truth is that 'by remembering and telling, we ... prevent forgetfulness from killing the victims twice'.[17] Thus 'memory is not only a victory over time, it is also a triumph over injustice'.[18]

But what about the wide range of past injustices not directly recognised by the TRC?[19] I think Sydney Kentridge is essentially correct. At a recent seminar in Sussex, Kentridge emphasised that the TRC's main responsibility was not to focus on the more visible, well-documented legacy of systematic racial discrimination but to expose as much truth as possible about those violations that tend to be cloaked in denials and would otherwise, in all likelihood, have remained obscured from the public eye. This applies in particular to the covert torture, killings and abductions by agents of the former state. The point is that in post-apartheid South Africa, especially as far as white South Africans are concerned, the potential for forgetfulness has been very high. It is difficult for 'outsiders' to appreciate the extent to which apartheid – seen by many Christian nationalist Afrikaners as anti-communist 'separate development' – was indeed 'darkness masquerading as light'. Through the public testimonies of so many victims and the more or less full disclosures by those responsible for gross violations of human rights at amnesty hearings, the powerful 'conspiracy of silence',[20] the temptation to forget, or to continue denying these past injustices, has been seriously challenged. Much of what transpired in this shameful period is no longer 'shrouded in secrecy', nor hidden in 'crevices of obscurity'.[21] As a 1998 editorial in the mainstream Afrikaans magazine *Insig* put it:

> *[But] the anger, shock and disillusionment experienced by the ordinary person upon hearing about deeds for years covered up and denied cannot be wished away by party political interest groups. It happened, this is the reality, it was necessary that the truth be exposed, even though the process was not always perfect.[22]*

For most South Africans the face of the apartheid state was, of course, not only the face of Giotto's 'Inguistizia' – a ruler and his soldiers ignoring the plight of victims. The state itself was the main violater of its citizens, through bureaucrats enforcing dehumanising laws, but also – as the TRC has proven – using the Benziens, De Kocks and Mamaselas to torture and kill those who dared to challenge those laws. Without the TRC process our new democratic state would have resembled Giotto's unjust ruler. The morally deaf and blind face of this soulless ruler helps us not to forget the immense symbolic significance of the TRC process. This significance is epitomised by TRC Commissioners, appointed by the legislative arm of the state, sympathetically listening to painful stories and acknowledging victims' sense of injustice. Our new state could not have prevented the victims' first death or torture or severe ill-treatment, but the TRC is visible proof of the commitment to prevent the 'second wound' inflicted by denial and forgetting. As someone said at a TRC public meeting I attended, 'At last we have a state with a human face!'

Selective remembering versus inclusive recognition

To fully appreciate the central meaning of the TRC process it is not enough to place it in an international context. For me perhaps the best mirror is right before our eyes, in our own history. As we begin to evaluate the TRC process, preparations are under way to commemorate the 100th anniversary of the outbreak of the Anglo-Boer South African War, a war that saw 26 000 Afrikaner women and children (amongst others) die in British concentration camps. It is highly illuminating to reflect on the selective, 'ethnic' remembrance of this suffering by Afrikaner nationalists, in contrast to the TRC process. So let us look back beyond the current TRC to the limitations and sad fate of what has been termed the 'first Truth and Reconciliation Commission'[23] on South African soil.

Many people in South Africa remember Emily Hobhouse for her passionate condemnation of the British government for abuses committed against Boer women during the Anglo-Boer South African War (1899-1902). She is widely respected for the selfless relief work she undertook in the concentration camps. It is a less well-known fact that after this war she organised food, clothing and ploughing and harvesting equipment for the Boer families returning to their farms, which had been devastated by Kitchener's scorched earth policy. Johan Snyman, in 'Interpretation and the Politics of Memory', describes how she went further than these concrete reparation measures and 'on her own started the first Truth and Reconciliation Commission in South Africa. She collected sworn statements by survivors, and had them published, first in *The Brunt of the War and Where It Fell* in 1902, and then again in *War Without Glamour*, or *Women's War Experiences Written by Themselves, 1899–1902* in 1924. Her aim was to impress upon the British public the need for some form of requital or at least some compensation for the survivors and a public condemnation of the colonial officials and military officers who were responsible for these transgressions'.[24]

The vital point highlighted by Snyman is that for Hobhouse the human suffering of these Boer women had a universal significance beyond narrow ethnic borders. Her speech at the 1913 inauguration ceremony of the Women's Memorial in Bloemfontein contained these words:

Your visible monument will serve to this great end – becoming an inspiration to all South Africans and to the women in particular ... For remember, these dead women were not great as the world count greatness; some of them were quite poor women who had laboured much. Yet they have become a moral force in your land ... And their influence will travel further. They have shown the world that never again can it be said that women deserve no rights as citizens because she takes no part in war. This statue stands as a denial of that assertion.[25]

For Hobhouse the suffering of these Boer women formed part of a worldwide struggle for recognition; their sacrifices contributed 'towards a greater solidarity of humankind against the indifference to suffering'. It is this message – speaking across the political divides between Boer and British and between white and black – that gave the suffering of the Boer women and children such 'moral force'. It was this message that was censored in subsequent decades as Afrikaner nationalists increasingly monopolised the meaning of the suffering of the 'Boer war' for themselves. This is vividly illustrated by the following omissions from Hobhouse's prophetic speech in later commemorative issues (censored passages emphasised):

*In your hands and those of your children lie the power and freedom won; you must not merely maintain but increase the sacred gift. Be merciful towards the weak, the downtrodden, the stranger. Do not open your gates to the worst foes of freedom – tyranny and selfishness. **Are not these the withholding from others in your control, the very liberties and rights which you have valued and won for yourselves?...***

__We in England are ourselves still but dunces in the great world-school, our leaders still struggling with the unlearned lesson, that liberty is the equal right and heritage of man, without distinction of race, class or sex. A community that lacks the courage to found its citizenship on this broad base becomes a 'city divided against itself, which cannot stand'...__

...__Does not justice bid us remember today how many thousands of the dark race perished also in the Concentration Camps in a quarrel which was not theirs? Did they not thus redeem the past? Was it not an instance of that community of interest, which binding all in one, roots out all animosity?__[26]

It was, of course, not only Emily Hobhouse's speech that was censored. None of the many Afrikaans books on the war I read as a child nor any of my school history books contained any reference to the 13 315 Africans that, according to official figures, also died in concentration camps[27]. Never did I learn about atrocities committed by the Boers themselves. I grew up with a perception of myself as a member of a minority 'victimised' by 'British imperialism'. I was only reminded of the horror done to the people I saw as 'my people'. Infused with this narrow, exclusive kind of remembrance it became more difficult to see the many horrors done by 'my people' – during the what is better known as the South African War (1899-1902), but especially during the apartheid years.

That is why the current TRC process is so significant. This institution was the outcome of an extensive, democratic process, receiving its mandate from the legislative arm of the new state, representing in a real sense the people of South Africa. This highly public and transparent TRC was not the lonely effort of a single woman, struggling to get her government's attention. Furthermore, given the remarkable inclusivity of this TRC process, it has a much better chance of getting the kind of message across that was advocated long ago by Emily Hobhouse. Anyone who attended a victim hearing or read transcripts of these hearings, or read the Report, will attest to the fact that victims from all sides of the conflicts of the past were included in the process. Similarly, the amnesty process has succeeded in drawing out perpetrators from all parties. The series of special and sector hearings allowed the Commission to throw its net wider than any previous truth commission in other parts of the world. Of course, there is much to be criticised about these aspects of the TRC process and the relative inclusivity is no guarantee that the temptation to/existence of selective remembering has been overcome or will be avoided in future. The point is that this TRC has been a vast improvement on the 'first TRC' nearly 100 years ago. It should now and in future be much more difficult for certain groups to monopolise the meaning of past suffering to the detriment of all the people in South Africa. The TRC process showed that we, the people of South Africa, are serious about our Constitutional commitment to recognise the 'injustices of our past'.

Remembering the victims and rescuing the horrible from forgetfulness

Why do we remember past injustices? 'This answer is simple and transparent,' says philosopher Paul Ricoeur. '[W]e must remember because remembering is a *moral duty*. We owe a *debt* to the victims. And the tiniest way of paying our debt is to tell and retell what happened [to them] ... We have learned from the Greek story-tellers and historians that the admirable deeds of the heroes needed to be remembered and thus called for narration. We learn from a Jewish story-teller like [Elie] Wiesel that the horrible – the inverted image of the admirable – needs to be rescued still more from forgetfulness by the means of memory and narration.'[28]

This perhaps too simple answer helps me focus on the strengths and inherent limitations of the TRC process. It broadly defines the genre of this process. One might say that the TRC was required to act mostly like a Jewish story-teller and not a Greek one. In other words, the partial fulfilment of our moral duty to remember the victims and to rescue the horrible from forget-fulness should be the primary lenses through which we should read this complex process. In the words of Antjie Krog: 'For me the Truth Commission microphone with its little red light was the ultimate symbol of the whole process: here the marginalised voice speaks to the public ear, the unspeakable is spoken – and translated – the personal story brought from the innermost of the individual binds us anew to the collective.'[29]

She is referring to the so-called 'victim hearings' where the trauma of survivors of specified categories of gross human rights violations were given centre stage. But her description can to some extent also be applied to the public hearings of the Amnesty Committee, where the little red light is still flickering, perhaps more loudly; where often 'the unspeakable is spoken', translated and recorded, *so that these horrors will never be forgotten.*

Some of the facts and the findings emerging from these victim and perpetrator hearings will be challenged by lawyers and historians. Given the higher standards of evidence they should work with (under fewer time and resource constraints), I would expect some of these criticisms to help us move closer to more reliable factual and historical truth about particular aspects of the period covered by the TRC mandate. But the limitations of the TRC's search for factual truth should not obscure the vital moral truths gathered by this process. Truths about moral evils, past injustices and gross human rights violations. In other words, the genre of the TRC story is pri-marily a 'morality of the depths', specifying 'the line beneath which no one is allowed to sink',[30] concentrating on minimum protections for human dignity, emphasising minimum standards of decency.[31] Its focus on what happens if human rights are not respected is of great potential significance, especially for our children and their children, for this painful process gave us some of the tools to build probably the most effective bulwark against future violations.[32] Its window on some grievous wrongs of the past provides us with invaluable raw material for nurturing a culture of human rights, for 'recovering' the soul of our nation.[33]

This significance might be undermined, however, by too little consensus on the genre of the TRC process. For example, appearing under the heading 'Tutu's Report tells the truth but not the whole truth',[34] Jeremy Cronin's review criticises the report for focusing too much on 'the little perpetrator' inside each of us. He is concerned that not enough room was given to celebrate the struggle, the 'little freedom fighter, the collective self-emancipator that we all could be'. He asks: 'What about the humanist, *ubuntu*-filled ways of cross-ing the bridge instead of only recognising the potential for evil in each one of us?' Cronin, a prominent leader in the South African Communist Party, is of course not the only one asking these kind of questions. My sense is that these questions are pointing to very important dimensions of our constitutional commitment to 'honour those who suffered for justice and liberation', but they miss the bus as far as the TRC process is concerned. I believe this *Mail & Guardian* editorial is closer to the truth:

> *The Final Report could be described as the founding document of the new South Africa... The term 'founding document' is more commonly used to describe a country's Constitution. And there are grounds for pride in the South African Constitution ... But, for all that, the Constitution is a theoretical exercise, in large part the product of intellectual effort in the ivory towers of academia. The Final Report, in a very real and immediate way, defines us. With all its horrors, it is the earthly product of the blood and tears attendant on a difficult birth. It is a testament to the equality of man, if more in the disregard for the tenets of humanity than the observance of them. In a sense it bestows the legitimacy of experience on the Constitution, which might otherwise seem remote to our society.*[35]

Conclusion

As we begin to look back on the TRC, criticism is certainly important and often justified. Yet so much attention is given to the dirty bath water that we run the risk of throwing out the fragile baby as well. I believe this 'baby' is above all the limited but deeply meaningful process of official, public, inclusive remembrance and recognition of key past injustices. This understanding implies that we need other forums to remember and to honour the admirable deeds of the heroes. We need to continue the process of allowing the many, many more victims of other past injustices to tell their stories and be recognised. We need to move beyond this 'tiny' way of repaying our debt, if we are truly committed to establishing *'a society based on democratic values, social justice and fundamental human rights'*.

Where healing begins

YAZIR HENRY

Despite the faults and problems associated with the Truth and Reconciliation Commission (TRC), it provided a space for some people to speak, to reach out, to express their pain and to face themselves. It also helped them to face the nation. Some of us had difficulties with its construction and process. This aside, it contains important lessons and it sends serious messages and warnings to human beings in South Africa and around the world.

I share what I have gained after coming into contact with this process – offering a personal account of my experience through the TRC. I hope that what I write will be a reminder to South Africans and people elsewhere that the will to live together in peace can be far stronger than individual wills that may give expression to other emotions.

I endeavour to set aside my many moral and conceptual problems with the TRC, especially to the extent that it trivialised the lived experience of oppression and exploitation. Committed as it was to national reconciliation, it too often played down the full extent of human suffering. This carries the danger of undermining the culture of socio-economic human rights and the need for justice that grew out of and through resistance to apartheid's socio-economic exploitation and its military-political domination.

I also listened to my psychotherapist's advice that the TRC could be my only hope of surviving the physical and psychological deterioration I was undergoing because of my experiences at the hands of the state.

My testimony?

I have been called many names, had my story located within the context of other stories and had several different histories imposed on me since testifying before the Human Rights Violations Committee of the TRC. The most hurtful of these 'identities' is one that places me as the agonised confessor or the betrayer that should be pitied.

In Antjie Krog's book *Country of my skull* there is a chapter entitled 'The narrative of betrayal has to be reinvented every time'; here she uses a version of my testimony, duly edited to fit the narrative. Other pieces concerning me have appeared under titles such as 'Betrayal was the price of my family's lives', 'Agonised confession moves listeners to applause' and 'Former MK member collapses after admitting betrayal'. I do not only question the intentions of these authors. I also draw attention to the context within which my story has been told – and the serious personal consequences this has had for me.

The following article is an example of the manner in which my testimony has been appropriated, interpreted, retold and sold:

The pain was overwhelming, the tension almost unbearable. As Yazir Henry struggled for nearly an hour to tell his harrowing tale to the TRC's Human Rights Committee, a gamut of emotions played across his pale face. At times his fine-boned features, framed by his dark hair and eyebrows, were cold and disdainful, and he gazed at the audience – or perhaps a few individuals in the audience – with undisguised anger.

Several times he drew his lips back in anguish, baring his teeth in a way that turned his face almost skeletal. Occasionally he leaned his head right back on to his shoulders, trying to relieve the appalling pain that seemed to concentrate his neck muscles. His voice, interspersed with sobs, sighs and coughs, fell and rose with his emotions, his clear tone ringing through [the University of Western Cape's] Great Hall.

With other phrases his voice cracked and shattered – especially when he referred to his comrade-in-arms, whom he had betrayed to the security police just as someone else had done to him. 'I was 19, I don't think anyone in the world should have been given such a choice,' he said of his decision to lead security police to Anton Fransch as a quid pro quo for them not killing his mother and four-year-old nephew. 'The brutality and the tenacity with which they questioned me, and my knowledge of what they had done to others … made their threat to kill my family very real.'

He later told journalists, 'I am extremely tired, I have so little energy left. I just want to be judged for who I am, that's all. I just want to be given a chance to start life again – I've been living in a nightmare.'

It was a nightmare of concentrated pain that etched itself into the consciousness of all who heard it, prompting Archbishop Tutu to tell him that he had listened with deep reverence as many in the audience rose to their feet.
(*Cape Argus*, 7 August 1996)

This is the reported story with which I am obliged to live, although in reality my story is more nuanced and more complex.

My space?

The TRC process was intended to provide a space within which people were able to speak and to tell their stories of abuse and violation. For varying reasons this did not and does not exist elsewhere in our society. For me this was the most positive aspect of the TRC.

Although the actual hearings formed only a part of the complex procedural, ideological and political processes of the Commission, the hearings were the only contact most people had with the Commission. Most people were unaware of the complex maze that constituted the basis for this artificial space controlled by the TRC Act and the personnel and procedures within the institutional framework of the TRC.

At the time of my hearing in August 1996, the TRC provided a space into which I could reach out in desperation. In many ways, for me, it was 'the rolling of the dice'. Up until then I had been denied an opportunity to tell my truth as I knew it and had to live and survive within a context of pain and silence imposed by several truths and untruths. This was a context in which I had neither the space nor the ability to contest perceptions about me or the process of which I was a part.

So like the vast majority of witnesses, albeit for reasons of my own, I sat in the witness box awaiting my chance to face South Africa and to tell the world what had happened to me. I was asking for the opportunity to be judged only for who I was, in the context of what happened to me. For me there was nothing further to lose, nothing worse could happen to me. In the weeks, months and years that followed my few hours in that space, I came to realise how the complexity of this maze would colour and re-colour my experience, and how its limitations and positive aspects are bounded by a complex gamut of contradiction that needs to be learnt from and carefully communicated in a sensitive manner to society as a whole.

Some limitations

The TRC created an expectation within the hearts and minds of those who came before it that it would be able to provide a form of immediate reparation. This happened at different stages and levels but was compounded by the statement-takers and the Commissioners; at the end of individual statements and testimonies they asked witnesses what they wanted the Commission to do to alleviate their personal and family situations.

For a year and a half after my testimony, during which I had broken down physically, I had almost no contact with the Commission. I remember reading an email written by one of the Commissioners almost two years later, where she said that 'in her medical opinion I was on the verge of a psychotic breakdown'. The lack of sensitivity with which my story was treated once it left the confines of that space and became part of the public domain was immediately apparent – my face and the story of my life were flashed across the country, on television, in newspapers, magazines and books, and often out of context. It was out of my control and done without my permission.

Although my family and I made some efforts to stop this, it became clear that the TRC had neither the time nor the logistical capacity to honour or protect the space it gave me in which to bear my soul and tell my story. The TRC had already moved to its next space, to its next set of witnesses. My life had changed completely from the point at which I sat in the witness box to the time that I had to be carried from the stage into a debriefing room.

In the two and a half years since occupying that space, I have survived one attempt on my life and I have been accosted and humiliated several times in public for reasons relating to my entering the space provided by the TRC. At the same time I am realising dreams that would never have been possible had I not entered it. In spite of all the limitations and difficulties, what was important about this space was that it provided, even if only briefly, the opportunity to face not only myself but also everyone else – from Commissioners to the people listening in the hallways and elsewhere. It was an opportunity for me to face my past and at the same time interface with the present, in ways that have enabled me to begin a journey of healing.

What good came out of it?

After my testimony I could not interact with anybody other than the members of my immediate family. It felt as if I had spent everything that was inside me and that the slightest bit of external pressure would finally and completely crush me. In the weeks that followed my relationships with everything and almost everybody began to redefine themselves. This transformation was so extreme that even the air that I breathed felt different. I could never have imagined what availing myself to the space – of breaking my silence – would do to my life. It seemed to take all the courage and strength that I had from me.

There were people who were unable to believe or relate to what I said. Despite the denials by individuals who were directly or indirectly responsible for what had happened to me, the human response to my willingness (driven by my instinct for survival) to face my past in a painful, open and truthful way was huge. Although I received negative responses from some quarters, I received overwhelmingly positive responses. Most people who spoke with me directly or indirectly conveyed to me a message that suggested that we are all fallible and human – whether we wish to admit that or not. I realised that I had survived and needed to get on with the rest of my life.

This has enabled me to come to terms with my past and take a firm grip on my present, and with continued pain view the future with renewed hope. This process allows me to remember but also believe that we as humans are all interdependent, that we can only exist through our common humanity.

This experience has convinced me that it is possible to create a space where we are able to face each other as human beings. It has persuaded me that we must face our history in order to realise that our future is one that we share. If we fail to do this it will be impossible to progress toward a future in which we coexist peacefully. The TRC initiated a process within which coexistence and eventual reconciliation may be achieved. It is up to all of us to make this possibility a reality.

Accountability

The negotiated settlement in South Africa has left our society with an inevitable degree of continuity between the old and the new. It has been argued that this is in the interest of national reconciliation and that it will safeguard the nation against civil war. This has limited the framework of the TRC and hampered our efforts to obtain a truth that acknowledges the extent to which apartheid bedevilled society. It undermines an attempt to show the extent to which imposed separation and exploitation resulted in the alienation, estrangement and ultimately the militarisation of almost all the sectors of our society. It gave rise to a reality in which the security forces largely enjoyed impunity – and were supported by the ideological, political, economic, legal and psycho-social framework of apartheid.

The violent disruption of protest marches that occurred in the Western Cape in mid-1999 raises a number of concerns in this regard. The manner in which the South African National Defence Force and the South African Police Service have chosen to deal with conflict poses the question why the new order is so similar to the old. It makes one wonder whether the lessons of our recent past have been integrated into post-apartheid reality. This, in turn, raises the question of the extent to which the TRC and the new South African state has held the former institutions of the apartheid state, especially those of the armed forces, accountable for past abuses.

Our new government, regardless of its arguments of political realism, must in the interests of truth and justice deal with the tyranny of our past in a more direct manner. The indiscriminate failure to punish certain individuals, without exposing the institutional framework that bred and nurtured these

individuals to public scrutiny, can only leave open a window for the continuation of past violations. Only in this way will the call 'never again' reverberate
through the nation with more than a hollow sound.

Currently there has still been very little acknowledgement by the overwhelming majority of whites who supported and benefited from the system
of apartheid. There is, in fact, no conducive public space available for whites
in which to admit that they benefited from apartheid and were caught up in a
vicious system that also deprived and traumatised them. This failure makes it
almost impossible for whites and others who supported the former regime to
take responsibility for the past as a basis for creating a better society.

Reconciliation

Despite the rules governing amnesty, in the opinion of many who suffered at
his hands, the decision, for example, to grant amnesty to Warrant Officer
Jeffrey Benzien has not promoted reconciliation. It will remain unpopular
and continue to be contested and widely regarded as illegitimate – not least
because Tony Yengeni and Ashley Forbes, who were tortured by him, publicly
opposed his amnesty application.

There is a perception in the community that he did not make full
disclosure and his actions were disproportionate to his political motivation.
He also showed very little remorse and in some ways, because of his attitude,
continued to torture Yengeni and Forbes and others in his appearance before
the Commission. He asked Yengeni to remember how he gave up not only his
arms but also his comrade Bongani Jonas without the security police having
to lay a finger on him. He asked Forbes to tell the audience that he (Benzien)
had not only brought him ice-cream and books but also broke bread with
him and played with him in the snow during his detention.

I remember asking myself how a process that was supposed to be holding
him accountable for his brutal and systematic torture of people could go so
horribly wrong. I struggled with my anger and resolved not to participate in
any further amnesty proceedings – even though I knew that the people
responsible for torturing and nearly killing me would apply for amnesty. I
realised that the amnesty process was hampering my own efforts to deal with
the trauma of capture, detention and the obligation to watch a comrade and
friend die in front of me as a result of the police opening fire with guns and
hand grenades.

The TRC's inability to provide a precedent for deciding who is to be held
accountable and how sends an unclear message to the South African
population. How are we, as South Africans, to create, build and consolidate a
democratic human rights culture on the basis of an official culture that

continues to tolerate extreme violence in the enforcement of legislation that was itself illegitimate?

Reparation

Closely linked to the amnesty process is reparation. Central to the understanding of reparation policies as forwarded by the TRC is the realisation that reparation is necessary to the extent that it is possible. Only in this way can progress be made towards peaceful coexistence – as a basis for the promotion of a human rights culture.

It has generally been accepted and openly stated in the TRC Act that survivors and their families should be compensated as a basis to counterbalance the generous and comprehensive amnesty process available to perpetrators. It has also been accepted both on moral and legal grounds that this be the responsibility of the present state.

It is not clear whether the government is ready to own this responsibility. The release of the TRC's final Report, with its recommendations on both interim and more extensive reparation, has been ambiguously responded to by government. Its response has been confusing, inadequate and disconcerting.

Financial compensation alone is clearly inadequate and unacceptable – if this is intended to provide a quick-fix solution that hastily seeks to close the book on the atrocities of the past. The group of persons benefiting from such grants is limited. It excludes those who did not make statements and those who were victims of human rights abuses who do not fall within the ambit of the TRC's conceptualisation of victimhood. The administration of Urgent Interim Reparation policies have proven seriously problematic, as these reparations have been completely disconnected from the human trauma that surrounded the space provided by the TRC. This has I feel reduced the symbolic sense of the reparation of trauma, led to a re-experience of past trauma and created new traumas. These are matters discussed more extensively elsewhere in this anthology.

Clearly there is a place for individual compensation. There is consensus on this among survivors. But more needs to be done. It is my experience that the acceptance of a small amount of money as reparation has in no way alleviated the depression, pain and frustration that typifies an unfinished process of healing. And yet the precarious socio-economic conditions we face force us to accept the limited financial aid. It is the responsibility of government to face this reality. It is not enough to protest that there are no funds available.

Conclusion

It is important that my criticisms are viewed in a constructive manner. It is my hope, as a person who has experienced war and who to a certain extent continues to live in its shadow, that we in South Africa avoid yet another period of conflict.

Despite all its problems, the TRC provided a space where people could face, however painfully, the atrocities and abuse of their past. Crucially, the space set up and controlled by the TRC was an important one that must be extended to other sectors of our society. South Africa remains a deeply divided society. It needs safe spaces in which people can continue to tell their stories and where dialogue can continue – or begin to take place.

It is my contention that we in South Africa, ranging from top government officials to ordinary people in the street, must stop and take an introspective look at ourselves. This can be a beginning to the healing process. We need to realise that although a lot rests on the shoulders of government, every South African has a responsibility to ensure that the lessons of pain and suffering that penetrate our daily lives are acknowledged and addressed. The price paid by those witnesses who testified before the TRC is only the beginning of a process that must be carried forward by every one of us. The TRC has initiated a process. It has not healed the nation. It could never do this.

I have been part of a large group of combatants that since the 1990s experienced military demobilisation, maladaptation to a postwar society, the consequences of a loss of prior educational opportunities, serious postwar trauma and chronic unemployment. Although I have known a sense of social and personal disintegration, I have come to realise that healing must take place within and through each and everyone living in South Africa. I have discovered that the pain of facing the past is both bearable and possible within a context of caring and wrestling with the truth of past injustices. Painful as it is, the truth should not be suppressed. Apartheid affected everybody. Everyone has a story to tell. People need to be given the opportunity to tell these stories, since there are different perceptions of truth. These different perceptions need to be addressed. I have tried to tell my story and share my truth. I am also still trying to make sense of my story for myself and to discover what is my truth.

Justice and amnesty

RONALD SLYE

Decision 1: A group of youths enter a church firing machine guns and throwing hand grenades, resulting in 11 deaths and dozens of others wounded among the peacefully assembled congregation. The operation was ordered by other members of a political organisation to which the attackers belonged. The killers are granted amnesty in part because the organisation to which they belonged had identified all members of a particular race as enemies, making this attack consistent with that ideological position and a legitimate act with a political objective.[1]

Decision 2: Members of a political organisation attack a bus in apparent retaliation for a racially motivated killing committed by members of the same organisation that attacked the church in Decision 1. The bus is chosen because of the racial composition of its passengers. Seven passengers are killed. Two of the three applicants are granted amnesty because they were following the orders of their superior, the third applicant. The third applicant was denied amnesty, as there is no evidence that his organisational superiors ever approved of this specific attack, although the attack is consistent with the ideological principles of the organisation.[2]

Decision 3: Members of a political organisation attack and kill a woman based on her race. There is no evidence that the attack was specifically ordered by other members of the organisation, although it was consistent with the general ideological principles of the organisation. All the attackers are granted amnesty.[3]

Decision 4: Four men kill three individuals in an attempt to acquire resources for their political organisation. The killing of two of the victims is justified in part by their race, and the ideological principle of the amnesty applicants that members of the victims' race are inferior and a threat to their existence. This ideological principle is generally supported by established political organisations to which they do not formally belong, but which they have adopted as their own guiding principle. They are denied amnesty.[4]

174

Decision 5: A man orders his subordinates to kill all the members of a house in which some are suspected of involvement in seditious political and military activity. The wrong house is chosen, and 11 unintended individuals are killed. The man who gave the order is granted amnesty.[5]

Decision 6: An individual is instructed by another member of his political organisation to plant a bomb at a shopping mall frequented by members of a particular religious and ethnic group to which the organisation is opposed. It is a motion-sensitive bomb, so it will explode when a person comes near it. The bomb kills the policeman who discovered it. The individual is granted amnesty.[6]

These are descriptions of just six of the more than 100 amnesty decisions concerning gross violations of human rights that have been made in the last two years. As very brief summaries they do not include some of the subtleties involved in each case, but are, I think, still fairly accurate narratives. I have not chosen them as representative of the decisions already made, but to highlight some of the troubling issues presented by the decision to include amnesty as part of the truth and reconciliation process, and to illustrate the difficult task of defending the moral and legal legitimacy of that decision.

How does one reconcile the above decisions? Is there a common logic, a set of general principles, that we can discern from this pattern of decisions that makes us comfortable in accepting them as legitimate and just? In other words, does the South African amnesty provide justice? And what is it that we mean by 'justice' when we ask if the amnesty provides it?

I suggest that we look at the amnesty's relationship to two conceptions of justice: justice as reflected in the principles of international law (what I will call justice as legal legitimacy) and justice as reflected in our beliefs about what is right and wrong (what I will call justice as moral legitimacy).

The question of the justice of amnesty can be broken down into two related questions. First, is the general decision by the South African government to grant amnesty legitimate? Second, are the specific decisions of the amnesty committee to grant or deny amnesty in a particular case – its implementation of the amnesty provisions – legitimate? The first question is indifferent to the decisions summarised above. The second focuses directly on the substance of those decisions.

Amnesty and the principles of international law

The legitimacy of granting amnesty to individuals responsible for gross violations of human rights is an issue that has preoccupied international lawyers, diplomats, advocates, politicians and scholars at the end of the 20th century. Despite the growing use of amnesties by states undergoing fundamental social transformations, and the concurrent increase in the use of international tribunals to hold individuals responsible for violations of international criminal law, there is surprisingly little international law that directly addresses the legitimacy of amnesties. There is a fair amount of state practice, but little evidence of an international consensus among states, of the law that does, or should, apply. There are a handful of decisions by some state courts, and even fewer by international tribunals. Every international tribunal that has addressed the issue has held that amnesties for gross violations of human rights violate fundamental principles of international human rights law; with a few exceptions, state courts that have evaluated those same amnesties have reached the opposite conclusion and upheld their legality. In every case in which a state court has evaluated its own country's amnesty for human rights violations, it has upheld the amnesty;[7] in every case in which a state court has evaluated another state's amnesty for human rights violations, it has refused to give the amnesty any legal effect.[8]

Although there is scant international jurisprudence concerning amnesties, critics of amnesties for violations of human rights point to various principles of international law and policy to argue for the moral and legal illegitimacy of amnesties. They make three basic criticisms.

First, they argue that amnesties violate well-established principles of international law that obligate a state to prosecute individuals responsible for certain gross violations of human rights. International conventions against torture, genocide, war crimes and terrorism explicitly state or strongly imply such an obligation. A weaker version of this criticism is that while a state may not be obligated to prosecute in every individual case (thus recognising the legitimacy of some form of prosecutorial discretion), a state does not have the power to protect an individual from future accountability through a grant of amnesty. This is a claim concerning the content of state obligations under international law.

Second, they argue that while amnesties may contribute to short-term social stability, in the long-term they undercut efforts to establish a stable democracy that honours human rights and the rule of law. The criticism is that such amnesties send a signal to would-be violators that if they are powerful enough to create enough uncertainty or instability they may escape accountability. Aryeh Neier voices this critique when he argues eloquently against 'giving in' to amnesties, noting that they create a culture of impunity that only encourages further human rights violations.[9] This is a claim concerning social stability, and in particular the importance and content of the rule of law.

Third, they argue that amnesties violate a victim's fundamental rights under international law. International tribunals that have addressed the legitimacy of amnesties have pointed to four principles that amnesties violate: the right to a fair trial; the right to judicial protection; the right to justice; and the right to a remedy. This is a claim concerning individual rights, and in particular the rights of victims.

Each of the above criticisms taken alone might be sufficient to suggest that amnesties for gross violations of human rights should be prohibited or discouraged. Taken together these three claims provide a formidable attack against those who would use amnesties to protect human rights violators, and thus a formidable challenge to the South African amnesty.[10]

How does the South African amnesty address these three criticisms? In other words, what is the amnesty's claim to justice? Those who claim that the amnesty increases justice offer the following three basic responses to the above criticisms:

- the amnesty reflects the sovereign will of the people in balancing individual accountability for past violations with the political realities of a successful transition to democracy;
- the amnesty increases justice by increasing our knowledge about the past ('truth'), and that this increased knowledge provides some justice, however incomplete, to victims and society;
- the amnesty increases justice by holding individual perpetrators accountable for their actions.

The first response is an assertion of state sovereignty. It says that, given the lack of consistent international practice and law in the area, a state is entitled to a fair amount of deference concerning the manner in which it addresses accountability for past human rights abuses. The legitimacy of this assertion depends on how much the decision truly reflects the will of the South African people. The South African amnesty is the only amnesty, with the possible exception of the Uruguayan amnesty, that can claim to reflect the sovereign will of its citizens.[11] The legislation that determined the form amnesty would take in South Africa was the subject of a prolonged and robust parliamentary process during which individual victims, their representatives and a large cross-section of civil society participated.[12] As a result of this public process, significant changes were made to the amnesty legislation, most notably the addition of provisions requiring that amnesty hearings be conducted in public rather than in camera as originally proposed. The South African amnesty thus has a strong claim to democratic legitimacy insofar as it reflects the sovereign will of the people concerning the appropriate balance between past accountability and present stability.[13]

The second response concerns the interpretation of the individual rights of victims and the minimum requirement for ensuring and respecting those rights. It asserts that revealing the truth about past violations and providing some form of official acknowledgement to victims of the wrong they suffered contributes to justice.[14] There is no question that the amnesty contributes to 'truth', or knowledge about past events, more substantially than any previous amnesty. The South African amnesty is uniquely structured to encourage inquiry and revelation concerning past human rights violations. While other amnesties have allowed investigations to proceed concerning amnestied acts,[15] none before the South African amnesty has been structured in a way to force applicants themselves to reveal information about their own activities and responsibility. While there may be some question about the quality of the information produced by the South African amnesty,[16] there is no doubt that we now know more about certain violations than we would have done without it.

The third response focuses on the perpetrators and their acknowledgement and accountability. It brings us back to the decisions I briefly summarised at the beginning of this chapter, and is the focus of my remaining remarks.

Accountability

Accountability describes a wide variety of mechanisms for identifying individual and group responsibility. To hold someone to account is to identify an individual's responsibility for an act, and to impose some cost or benefit upon that individual as a sign of approval or disapproval. The theory of democratic accountability is based on the belief that subjecting elected officials to periodic elections holds them accountable for their policies and official acts. Accountability should not be confused with punishment. Punishment describes one possible consequence of finding an individual responsible for a particular act or series of acts.

There is no doubt that the South African amnesty holds applicants to account for their actions. It requires applicants to make full disclosure of their involvement in human rights violations, and subjects their application to a discretionary decision-making process. The relevant question then is not whether the South African amnesty holds individuals accountable for their actions but *how* it holds them accountable, and whether such accountability is sufficient to constitute justice.

There are two ways that the amnesty holds individuals accountable: through a mandatory process and through substantive decisions.

The process-oriented aspect of the amnesty's accountability is accomplished through the following requirements: amnesty applicants must publicly associate themselves with a specific violation; and applicants must disclose and acknowledge their specific involvement. If the act for which they are applying is severe enough, applicants must testify publicly concerning their involvement and must publicly answer questions from the state, victims and representatives of the individuals and communities they harmed. Substantive accountability is found in the decisions of the amnesty committee concerning who should be granted amnesty – decisions like the six summarised at the beginning of the chapter. Individuals who are not granted amnesty are vulnerable to further measures of accountability, including the possibility of punishment, through the civil and criminal justice system.

The substantive decision whether to grant amnesty is based primarily on two requirements: did the applicant make 'full disclosure' of his involvement and was the act 'associated with a political objective'.[17] The full disclosure requirement furthers the truth and acknowledgement function of the process-oriented form of accountability. While the ability of the committee to determine if an applicant has in fact made full disclosure is dependent on the quality of other sources of information available to the committee (including information provided by the investigations unit of the Truth and Reconciliation Commission), such testimonies generally do increase the amount of truth and acknowledgement, and thus contribute to justice.

While some applications for amnesty have been denied, based on the failure to meet the full disclosure requirement,[18] the more interesting and controversial decisions are based on the political objective requirement. It is these latter decisions, including their reasoning, which may have the most profound impact on the amnesty's long-term legitimacy.

The 'political objective' requirement for amnesty

The requirement that an act for which amnesty is sought be associated with a political objective is based on extradition law.[19] Under well-accepted principles of extradition law, a state may refuse to extradite an individual to another state if the individual in question is being sought for an act that qualifies as a 'political offence'. While all states accept in principle the legitimacy of the political offence exception, there is no consensus on the definition, interpretation and application of the exception. The South African amnesty defines an act as political, and thus eligible for amnesty, if it is committed under the orders of, or in furtherance of the goals of, a well-established political organisation. While the legislation directs the amnesty committee to look at other factors in determining whether an act is political or not,[20] in practice the committee has mostly looked to whether an authorised superior in a recognised political organisation ordered the act, or whether the act was closely related to an explicit programmatic statement of an established political organisation. Thus the act for which amnesty was granted in Decision 1 was found to be political since it was ordered by an organisational superior. The same is true for the granting of amnesty to the two subordinates in Decision 2, and the granting of amnesty in Decision 6.

The effect of the amnesty's interpretation of 'political' is to place a fair amount of power with the state, political parties and other political organisations in decisions concerning amnesty. Whether an individual is granted amnesty or not may depend on whether the state or a political organisation admits to having ordered the action in question, or whether the action is considered consistent with the political and programmatic goals of the organisation as expressed by its governing bodies (if any) or leaders. In theory, this should result in ultimate responsibility and accountability resting with such governing bodies and leaders. This principle is reflected in the denial of amnesty to the third applicant, the man who ordered the attack, in Decision 2. In practice, however, few political superiors have taken explicit responsibility for ordering such atrocities, and have therefore not been held accountable. In some cases where the individual responsible for the orders was involved, amnesty has been granted, as reflected in Decision 5. In cases where an act is considered political if it is consistent with the general ideological principles of an organisation, the lines of responsibility are less clear. In Decision 3, for example, it is not clear which individual superiors should or could be held responsible for this implementation of a general ideological principle.

'Following orders'

There are two aspects of its definition of 'political' that weaken the amnesty's claim to legitimacy. The first affects the amnesty's legal legitimacy, the second its moral legitimacy. Although the restriction of amnesty to acts associated with a political objective may have as its inspiration a well-established principle of extradition law, the codification of this political requirement in the amnesty legislation, and its interpretation by the amnesty committee, is in conflict with a basic tenet of international human rights law established by the international tribunal at Nuremberg after the Second World War. One of the fundamental principles established at Nuremberg, and generally followed ever since,[21] is the illegitimacy of 'following orders' as an absolute defence to the commission of an international crime. Nuremberg shifted the claim of 'following orders' from an absolute defence to liability for a crime to a mitigating factor in determining the appropriate punishment. The removal of 'following orders' as an absolute defence established the moral and legal responsibility of each individual for his acts, and asserts that individuals, including military personnel, are moral beings who not only can, but also must, discern right from wrong and act accordingly.

The South African amnesty weakens the principle that an individual is morally and legally responsible for the consequences of his or her own acts. While an amnesty applicant who was following orders is still subject to the process-oriented accountability discussed above, he or she is exonerated under the substantive provisions of accountability. One interpretation of this result is that following orders becomes, through the granting of amnesty, an absolute defence for responsibility for a criminal act. This is especially troubling in those cases where the act violates another individual's fundamental human rights and constitutes a crime under international law.

The amnesty decisions that turn on whether the perpetrator was following orders are less of a threat to the legal legitimacy of the amnesty if we believe that justice is achieved through the process-oriented accountability discussed earlier. If the amnesty's process-oriented accountability meets the minimal requirements of justice as reflected in international law, then the substantive decisions that provide amnesty to individuals who were 'only following orders' may be more appropriately interpreted as reaffirming the principle that following orders is a mitigating factor rather than an absolute defence.

Privileging political violence

The threat to the moral legitimacy of the amnesty process is based on a more fundamental criticism of the privilege afforded political violence over non-political violence within national and international law. Under the South African amnesty process, an individual who killed or tortured in the name of a political ideology is preferred over an individual who committed similar or lesser acts for 'non-political' reasons. Thus two private security guards who tortured and killed an individual suspected of the common crime of robbery were denied amnesty,[22] while individuals who committed similar acts against political opponents were granted amnesty.[23] This distinction can be justified by the argument that individuals who commit acts of violence in the name of a political ideology are more easily rehabilitated and less of a societal threat, especially in the context of a society that has undergone or is undergoing fundamental political change.

The assumption is that such individuals are driven to commit violent acts because of their political ideology and sense of justice (or injustice), and that now that the reason for their decision to commit violent acts is gone they will revert to being productive and respectful members of society. The fact that an individual committed an act of violence in the name of a political ideology, however, certainly does not mean that such an individual will not commit further acts of violence; he may have always been, or now may have become, comfortable with violence as a means of social interaction. In fact there is ample evidence in South Africa that political organisations used individuals who had committed non-political crimes in the past to further their political struggle;[24] that individuals who committed acts for political purposes were also involved in acts that could not be considered in furtherance of any political ideology or goal;[25] and that some individuals who committed acts of violence in the context of a political struggle continued to commit such violent acts after the conflict ended.[26]

More fundamentally, the privilege afforded political violence under the amnesty process sets a dangerous precedent for future political advocacy, and a dangerous signal to a society that is trying to establish popular legitimacy based on the rule of law.[27]

A personal anecdote illustrates the danger of privileging political violence. A person working with gang members in the Cape Flats approached me at a conference and suggested that many of the individuals involved in gang violence would gladly put down their weapons and talk if they received amnesty. 'Why,' this person asked me, 'should individuals who participated in some of the most gruesome forms of torture, who deliberately targeted women and children for extermination, be eligible for amnesty? If they could receive amnesty for such acts, why couldn't gang members receive amnesty for acts that were certainly no worse, in return for their willingness to make full disclosure?'[28] In other words, 'If them, why not me?'

Conclusion

The South African amnesty is clearly the most innovative amnesty yet attempted. It is also an amnesty that has a stronger claim to moral and legal legitimacy than do any of its predecessors. Its contribution to truth and acknowledgement, and its procedural and substantive accountability, contribute to justice for victims of human rights violations committed during the apartheid years.

Yet the focus on politically motivated violence – and in particular the specific interpretation of political acts adopted by the amnesty legislation and interpreted and applied by the amnesty committee – weaken the legal and moral legitimacy of the South African amnesty. While the amnesty adequately addresses many of the criticisms aimed at its foreign predecessors, it still raises troubling questions concerning its relationship to justice and accountability.

Whether history will conclude that the amnesty's accomplishments outweigh its more troubling features is not clear. Part of the reason for this lack of clarity is attributed to the fact that at the time of writing the amnesty process continues – it is thus hard to reach firm conclusions concerning the accomplishments and failures of an ongoing process. But our uncertainty concerning the amnesty's relationship to justice is also attributable to a lack of consensus concerning what justice demands in the face of such widespread and systematic violations, and what justice demands during periods of fundamental political change.

While a strong argument can be made that the South African amnesty violates fundamental principles of international human rights law, the more interesting question is whether an acceptance or tolerance of the South African amnesty may result in a change in what we as the international community believe international law should, and maybe do, require in such circumstances.

If the South African amnesty continues to be considered a success in navigating the heretofore competing claims of accountability and peaceful transitions, then it may act as a positive model for other countries undergoing similar fundamental changes, and may provide insights into what international justice should demand in such circumstances. For South Africa the question is whether the amount of accountability provided is sufficient to satisfy the demands of justice so that social energies and resources can be devoted to building a truly non-racial democracy. For the rest of the world, and in particular for the international human rights community, the question is whether the amount of accountability provided will be strong enough to act as a deterrent against future human rights violations, and yet not so onerous that future repressive regimes will hesitate to give up power.

If the answer to both these questions is yes, then the South African amnesty will have a substantial impact on the development of an increasingly important area of international law.

If the answer is no, then the South African amnesty will be viewed by future observers as another illegitimate attempt to subordinate the rights of individual victims in the name of social stability, and to privilege the private interests of the powerful at the expense of the public interest of human rights and the rule of law.

Amnesty: the burden of victims

RICHARD LYSTER

Commissioners of the Truth and Reconciliation Commission (TRC) spent a disproportionate amount of their time explaining, justifying and defending to observers, journalists and ordinary victims the vexed question of amnesty. No other aspect of the Commission's work has generated so much controversy, anger, misgiving and, to a lesser extent, litigation. The scenarios of grey-suited security policemen admitting to the secret murder of icons of the liberation struggle generated frustration and anger – in the families who sat disbelievingly in the public galleries of the Amnesty Committee as well as in the millions of newspaper readers and television watchers throughout South Africa.

In his foreword to the *TRC Report*, Chairperson Archbishop Desmond Tutu devoted three-and-a-half pages to the question of amnesty, skilfully ameliorating its harshness and reminding us of the fragile transitional context within which amnesty must be understood:

> *We could not make the journey from a past marked by conflict, injustice, oppression and exploitation to a new and democratic dispensation characterised by a culture of respect for human rights without coming face to face with our recent history. No one has disputed that. The differences of opinion have been about how we should deal with that past; how we should go about coming to terms with it.*

There were those who believed that we should follow the post Second World War example of putting those guilty of gross violations of human rights on trial as the Allies did at Nuremberg. In South Africa, where we had a military stalemate, that was clearly an impossible option. Neither side in the struggle (the state nor the liberation movements) had defeated the other and hence nobody was in a position to enforce so-called victor's justice.

However, there were even more compelling reasons for avoiding the Nuremberg option. There is no doubt that members of the security establishment would have scuppered the negotiated settlement had they thought they were going to run the gauntlet of trials for their involvement in past violations. It is certain that we would not, in such circumstances, have experienced a reasonably peaceful transition from repression to democracy. We need to bear this in mind when we criticise the amnesty provisions in the Commission's founding Act. We have the luxury of being able to complain because we are now reaping the benefits of a stable and democratic dispensation. Had the miracle of the negotiated settlement not occurred, we would have been overwhelmed by the bloodbath that virtually everyone predicted as the inevitable ending for South Africa.[1]

The Archbishop also reminded us that in Chilean playwright Ariel Dorfman's celebrated work *Death and the Maiden*, it is only when the bound perpetrator admits to his former victim that he did indeed rape and torture her that she agrees to let him free. His admission restores her dignity, and her experience is confirmed as real and not illusory.[2]

And yet it never was – and should never have become – the duty of Commissioners or Commission staff to defend and explain the concept of amnesty to a demanding and restive public. Similarly, public criticism of the Commission over the existence of amnesty – and there was plenty of it, nationally and abroad – was misguided, as the entire question of whether apartheid's assassins and torturers would be prosecuted or given amnesty was signed and sealed as part of the *realpolitik* of the pre-election talks in 1994, between the De Klerk government and the ANC.[3]

Much of this criticism is probably because the details of the negotiated amnesty agreement took a number of years to finalise – and then it still had to be implemented. The TRC was given this unenviable task. Thus the South African TRC became the first truth commission to be given the power to grant amnesty to individual perpetrators. No other state had combined this quasi-judicial power with the investigative tasks of a body established primarily to uncover the truth. In other commissions, where amnesty was introduced to protect perpetrators from being prosecuted for the crimes of the past, the provision was broad and unconditional, with no requirement for individual application or confession of particular crimes. The South African format had the advantage that it elicited detailed accounts from perpetrators and institutions, unlike commissions elsewhere that received very little co-operation from those responsible for past abuses.

These advantages of the South African amnesty process, however, have been overshadowed by the criticism that the TRC denied justice to the victims of gross human rights violations. Some say that the TRC was a political as well as a moral compromise, which irrevocably undermined the position of victims.[4]

Why amnesty?

Why then did the government take this far-reaching and radical step of allowing the perpetrators of gross human rights violations to escape prosecution and those who had already been convicted and imprisoned to walk free?

- The difficulty of securing successful prosecutions was a primary factor in opting for the amnesty option. The War Crimes Tribunal in The Hague is evidence of this difficulty – after many years and many millions of dollars, it has made little headway in its work.
- The lengthy delays and the high cost of litigation were also important factors.
- There is little evidence that retributive criminal justice – the imprisonment of perpetrators – achieves anything more than a short-term need for revenge. The failure of the Nuremberg Trials in Germany to deal adequately with Germany's past suggests that even if such trials were possible in South Africa, they would not have served the national reconciliation process. Do capital punishment and retributive prison sentences contribute to respect for human dignity, or do they vindicate those who promote revenge and violence as the answer to human conflict?
- Furthermore, the long-term imprisonment of political criminals often elevates them to heroic status, which does not serve the reconciliation process. As Jorge Correa said in his writings on Chile, ideological fanaticism cannot be ameliorated or countered through a prison sentence. If anything, it motivates the person involved to pursue his or her aims on release from prison.[5]
- The nature of political trials is that they deliver a narrow form of truth. They reveal details about a specific case, but are seldom able to outline a broader pattern of events over a period of time; they certainly cannot analyse institutional responsibility, general state practices or the root causes of conflict, all of which are usually the focus of a truth commission.[6]
- Retributive justice also places a financial burden on the state with its need to rehabilitate and restore perpetrators, for example, but these and other issues fall outside the scope of this chapter.[7]

It is in this context that the policy and legislation makers argued for amnesty on the basis of full and public disclosure. This would be of maximum benefit to a large number of victims and their relatives, whose most fundamental need was to know who was responsible for the death, torture or disappearance of their relatives and why they did it. It would also provide an enduring acknowledgement that what happened to them and their loved ones was wrong.

The amnesty process is a vigorous legal process. Those people seeking amnesty had a limited opportunity to apply for amnesty, and people who did not take that opportunity now face at least the possibility of prosecution. Those who did apply were subject to investigation, public enquiry and cross-examination. They were obliged to make a full disclosure of what they did, their motives and under whose orders they were acting.[8]

Amnesty and victims?

Many policy-makers, clerics, academics, Commissioners, political and social analysts and observers agree about the benefits and pragmatic advantages of the amnesty process within the context of a truth commission. Why, then, does the amnesty process still continue to undermine the moral tone of the work of the TRC? The test is not whether the Chairperson of the Commission finds the amnesty process morally acceptable, or whether the politicians who negotiated the 'historic compromise' in 1993 found it politically expedient; the more important question – and the answer to which will have long-term consequences and repercussions – for the process of reconciliation is the following: how is the granting of amnesty viewed by victims, their families and the communities in which they live?

The problem is that the amnesty process disrupts the conventional criminal justice process. The absence of trials and punishment creates a vacuum that can easily be filled with potentially explosive emotions of anger, bitterness and resentment, with detrimental effects for both victims and society at large. Impunity for criminals tends to conflict with a basic sense of justice, with a deep need for retribution.[9] How did the TRC process deal with these deep emotions?

Many – probably most – of the victims who found themselves on public platforms at hearings of the Human Rights Violations' Committee expressed views on reconciliation that were to some extent influenced by the public imperative of the TRC: forgiveness was the proper thing to do, and amnesty for the perpetrators should necessarily follow. But often very different views were expressed privately by victims, to friends, family members, social workers, psychologists and journalists, and it is clear that a pervasive duality exists among victims who see conventional punishment as a powerful emotional and symbolic resolution to their personal suffering.

Perhaps the best response is to accept the common definition of criminal justice and to acknowledge openly that amnesty is unjust. This acknowledgement should also involve a recognition of the reality and legitimacy of the anger and frustration. It can then be made clear that the Truth Commission was not trying to achieve justice, and that guaranteeing amnesty is the painful price that the country has to pay for peace, for the negotiated settlement in 1994 that led to the country's first democratic elections.[10]

Yet one can go a step further and emphasise that justice does not only operate at the level of the individual; it also operates at the level of the social order, to describe the transition from an unjust apartheid system to a democratic system of government. This means that although individual justice is limited, some measure of social justice is achieved through the TRC process.

This view was also expressed by the former Minister of Justice, Dullah Omar:

> *We have a nation of victims, and if we are unable to provide complete justice on an individual basis … it is possible for us to ensure that there is historical and collective justice for the people of our country. If we achieve that, if we achieve social justice … then those who feel aggrieved that individual justice has not been done will at least be able to say that our society has achieved what the victims fought for during their lifetimes, and that at that level … justice has been done.*[11]

Proportionality?

It has been widely accepted that the position of victims would be ameliorated in a number of ways, which include the implementation of the principles of proportionality in the execution of the amnesty process, individual reparations and reparations at a symbolic and community level.

The Norgaard principles (drawn up by Carl Norgaard, former president of the European Human Rights Commission – see endnote 17.19, p299), which relate to proportionality, are enshrined in the Promotion of National Unity and Reconciliation Act as factors to be taken into account when deciding whether an act has a political objective:

- the motive of the person who committed the act, omission or offence;
- the context of the act;
- the legal and factual nature of the act, as well as *the gravity of the act*;
- the object or objective of the act;
- whether the act was executed in response to an order or on behalf of or with the approval of a political organisation or the state;

- the relationship between the act and the political objective pursued, and in particular the *directness and proximity of the relationship and the proportionality of the act to the objective pursued.*[12] (emphases added)

There is no space here for a review of the decisions of the Amnesty Committee. It is also perhaps premature to comment too critically on the Committee's methodology and approach, bearing in mind that its work is not complete and its final report has not been published – this will appear as a codicil to the Report of the Commission during 2000. Yet most commentators of the amnesty process would agree that the principle of proportionality as defined in section 20(3) of the Act has not been ignored by the Amnesty Committee. The principles are complementary and should be applied collectively when looking at a particular set of factual circumstances in the context of an amnesty application.

How then, within these legislative parameters, can one explain the granting of amnesty to a group of men who beat and stabbed to death a young woman because she was white? And if the principles were applied, on what basis was amnesty granted to men who killed people praying in a church?

In both the Amy Biehl murder and the St James church massacre, the only discernible principle that was applied was that of the following of orders from above. Both cases were politically charged affairs, at the time of the conviction of the accused in the criminal case and even more so at the time of the amnesty hearing.

The perpetrators in both cases were members of the Pan African Congress (PAC), which has been relentlessly critical of the entire Truth Commission process, and particularly of its failure to grant amnesty to some PAC members who had carried out killings and robberies, allegedly with a political motive.

In the Biehl case, the parents of the victim had stated publicly that they would not oppose amnesty for the perpetrators. At worst, then, one cannot rule out the possibility that extraneous factors influenced the Committee in its decision. At best, one must accept that section 20(3)(e) of the Act (acting in response to an order of a political party) was the pre-eminent and overriding criterion considered. Any other factors then that might militate against the granting of amnesty, such as extreme and unwarranted brutality against wholly defenceless people, necessarily fall away.

Reparations

The issue of individual reparations for victims was used throughout the TRC process to appease victims' anger over the amnesty process and the 'instant justice' for amnesty applicants, who walked away from long prison sentences with increasing regularity.

During the course of the Commission's hearings, victims were asked what they would like the Commission to do for them. Many said that they wished the Commission to find the bodies of their husbands or children, or to erect a memorial for the members of their communities who had died in the struggle against apartheid.

Large numbers of people also asked the Commission to compensate them financially for their losses. The Commission felt that this was appropriate and that, in accordance with the principles of national and international law and practice, financial compensation should be granted to people that the Commission found to be victims of gross human rights violations. The right of victims of human rights abuse to fair and adequate compensation is well established in international law.

In the past three years, South Africa has signed a number of important international instruments, which place it under an obligation to provide victims of human rights abuse with fair and adequate compensation. The provisions of these instruments, together with the rulings of those bodies established to ensure compliance with them, indicate that it is not sufficient to award 'token' or nominal compensation to victims. The amount of reparation awarded must be enough to make a meaningful and substantial impact on their lives. In terms of United Nations Conventions, there is well-established right of victims of human rights abuse to compensation for their losses and suffering.[13] The Commission made it clear in its report that it was important that the reparation policy adopted by the government should be in accordance with South Africa's international obligations, and that the award to victims must be significant.

Thus again was the harshness of the amnesty process ameliorated for victims. The Reparations and Rehabilitation Committee spent considerable energy and time debating the issue of reparation, and refining a formula that in its final form would see victims paid an amount of R26 000 over a six-year period.[14]

Most recent signals from government indicate, however, that it does not see itself as liable or responsible for the wrongs of its predecessor. The message seems to be that the country cannot afford an individual reparations policy and that if any reparations are to be paid they will benefit communities, not individuals.

In spite of the deep sense of betrayal that victims will justifiably and undoubtedly feel, there is much to be said for community reparation. Andrew Feinstein and Melanie Verwoerd have argued that while the majority of South

Africans still live with the consequences of apartheid, whites enjoy the fruits of decades of racially determined selective state expenditure. Whites should therefore accept the need for fundamental structural transformation, be it subsidisation of impoverished local authorities, a more equitable balance in the distribution of health facilities, the need for greater state resources to flow to schools and libraries in black areas and the need for water provision, transport and telecommunication infrastructure to those areas neglected for so long.[15]

This is undoubtedly correct, but this sort of macro-societal reconstruction is hugely problematic and notoriously difficult to implement; it raises enormous expectations and has no end point. The failure of the Reconstruction and Development Programme (RDP) should have been ample warning to those seeking to embark on a similar programme. The most likely scenario is that any attempts to establish what amounts to another RDP will be abandoned as too impractical and too expensive.

Whether or not victims' aspirations will be met by purely symbolic reparation is a moot point.

Blanket amnesty?

Finally, on top of this rather bleak scenario from a victim's perspective, is the real possibility of a general amnesty for political criminals who did not apply for or who were refused amnesty by the TRC. Despite assurances from people like President Mbeki that a general amnesty is not being contemplated, indications are that there are powerful forces, particularly in KwaZulu-Natal, that are likely to move the government in that direction. Those most likely to be prosecuted by the office of the Director of Public Prosecutions for apartheid-era crimes belong to a group of powerful and highly placed office bearers of the Inkatha Freedom Party. With the political rapprochement at the time of the 1999 election between that party and the ANC government, a scenario in which members of the national and provincial parliaments are charged for murder and conspiracy to murder is not one that could be easily contemplated.

Detailed proposals of such a general amnesty scheme have already been discussed and, not surprisingly, they contemplate the opposite of the fairly rigorous amnesty provisions listed above – no full or public disclosure necessary. Proponents of the call for a general and, in effect, blanket amnesty say that indemnifying political criminals will somehow foster a climate of political tolerance.

It is difficult to understand this view. As political commentator and editor of the *Sowetan* newspaper Mike Siluma said: 'One wonders if such a step might not send out the wrong message to KwaZulu-Natal's warlords – that murders, as long as they are political, need not be followed by prosecution. In the absence of at least the threat of prosecution, what is to stop them from using violence again to gain electoral advantage for their political masters?'

Siluma went on to say:

> *And what of the victims, those whose families and loved ones were killed and maimed, often in the most brutal fashion? Are they expected to simply forget the whole thing, as if nothing had happened? How is this supposed to aid the nation-building and reconciliation of which everyone has suddenly become a champion?*[16]

Whether or not a general amnesty is granted, the victims of South Africa's apartheid years will remain at the lowest end of the social and political order. Ironically, the Preamble to the South African Constitution states that in order to advance reconciliation and reconstruction, amnesty shall be granted in respect of acts, omissions and offences associated with a political objective, and committed in the course of the conflicts of the past. The passage of amnesty over the past three years questions the assumptions on which this portion of our Constitution is based.

Amnesty and denial

NKOSINATHI BIKO

South Africa's challenge is to prepare a firm foundation for a new order, and to do this it has to reckon with history. One of the mechanisms adopted to ensure this new order is the Promotion of National Unity Act (the Act), which led to the establishment of the Truth and Reconciliation Commission (TRC).

It is perhaps too soon to judge the success of the Commission; future generations will be better able to determine the full impact of transitional politics in South Africa. It is evident, though, that this process has not been without flaws, and in this chapter I consider the amnesty process of the TRC as but one aspect of this transition.

The granting of amnesty to perpetrators of a crime against humanity is inherently contentious. It is a radical departure from the core principle underlying the struggle – that apartheid was a crime against humanity. The families of Bantu Steve Biko, Griffith and Victoria Mxenge and Dr and Mrs Rebeiro were the first public voices to challenge the amnesty clause of the Act. Even before the basis of the challenge was disclosed, the media published an accusation toward these families by a senior member of the TRC that 'certain people think the TRC is a cash cow'. The accusation misconstrued our intentions, and it was also blatantly insensitive toward what we had been through. It was evident that some within the Commission were far removed from the experience of many who were in different ways struggling to make sense of political transition. Tempting though it was to respond to these kinds of remarks, we took a painful and principled decision not to respond to them and to focus on our objectives. For the media, of course, the battle-lines had been drawn between the TRC and the three families. Our opposition was not, in fact, to the TRC *per se*. It constituted a democratic engagement with an aspect of the Constitution. Well, the dust is beginning to settle around this matter and perhaps it is time to revisit the purpose of our intervention.

Amnesty

According to the Act, there are essentially four overriding requirements upon which amnesty may be granted:

- The act of commission or omission for which amnesty is sought must amount to a gross violation of human rights as defined in the TRC Act.
- The applicant must be able to prove that the act or omission was motivated by political factors.
- In testifying before the Commission, the applicant must make full disclosure.
- The applicant must be able to demonstrate proportionality between the act/omission for which amnesty is sought and the desired outcome.[1]

Why did we challenge the Constitution? It involved the age-old problem of how far the state can be empowered to act on behalf of its citizens. We noted that some South Africans were content with the granting of amnesty to those who maimed or killed their family members, but we also knew there were a significant number who were adamant that they would like to have their day in court in order to confront the perpetrators of evil deeds.

We, the families who turned to the Constitutional Court, believe that there are two rights in the Constitution that do not blend well. One is consistent with progressive constitutions worldwide, it involves the right to seek recourse in a court of law if and when a citizen is wronged. The other, covered in the Postamble of the Interim Constitution, gives the TRC the right, through its Amnesty Committee, to grant amnesty if the applicant is seen to have met the criteria already identified. This means that those who want to exercise their constitutional right to settle matters through the judicial system are not able to do so. In the Biko, Mxenge and Rebeiro court application we challenged the constitutionality of this consequence.

The Constitutional Court decision was not in our favour – the question remains to what extent its decision was above political influence. The dismissal of our application was unfortunate, but there did remain the opportunity to pursue our objective on a case by case basis.

In this example from the Steve Biko case, it is clear the extent to which those (at least in this instance) who pursued amnesty did so without the slightest intention of meeting the necessary requirements for amnesty.

Based on their written submission to the TRC, we were convinced that Warrant Officer Beneke, Warrant Officer Marx, Sergeant Niewoudt, Major

Snyman and Captain Siebert, the five applicants in the Biko case, were nowhere near meeting the conditions for amnesty. Consistent with their evidence at the inquest in 1977, they adhered to the theory that Biko was injured in a 'scuffle', provoked by his 'sitting down without permission during an interrogation session' – a theory presented at the inquest that prevented the appropriation of blame to any one individual. Although they applied for amnesty against prosecution for murder, none of them admitted to engaging Biko in a manner that resulted in his death.

Our family was curious about how they would argue a case of political motive that was consistent with the 'scuffle' theory. What party political principles were being pursued by insisting that Biko stand rather than sit? How proportional were their actions to their desired outcome? Regarding full disclosure, counsel for the family, Adv George Bizos, had to painfully extract details of that fateful incident from people who were less than forthcoming.[2] There were also huge discrepancies between their collective evidence and the forensic findings. It is also interesting to note that the applicants had timed the application to fall within the prescription period in the event that their application was unsuccessful. This meant that if the TRC decided against amnesty, they could rely on the fact that it was 20 years since the incident. This, they assumed, meant they could not be prosecuted – whatever the outcome of the amnesty application. All this placed the matter well outside the bounds of reconciliation.

Months later the Amnesty Committee dismissed the application for amnesty for the killers of Biko. The intention of the perpetrators to challenge the amnesty decision simply adds salt to the wound that we as a family suffer. The five who acknowledge their involvement in Biko's death have now been deprived of the protective vale of amnesty, and the Attorney General of the Eastern Cape as well as the family are considering prosecution.

This decision would have been celebrated, save for the fact that the day following the announcement, the killers of the Rebeiros were granted amnesty. Earlier in the process the killers of Mxenge were also judged to have met the conditions for amnesty. I am not conversant with the facts of the other two cases, but I am uncertain how the killers of Florence Rebeiro, a mother and housewife, could have got around the political motive require-ment. I am equally uncertain how the killers of Mxenge, whose brutal murder is surpassed by few others, met the proportionality requirement.

Since these events we have had the opportunity to observe the TRC process – noting with regret the increasing concessions made by victims in order to accommodate perpetrators.

Many people have received vital information from the TRC concerning the whereabouts of the remains of their relatives or the identity of those responsible for their death. Yet there is much to suggest that the process has only scraped the surface in a growing phase of a lack of acknowledgement, if not denial, on the part of those who orchestrated, implemented or benefited from our shameful past. It is this that ultimately stands in the way of national reconciliation.

There are two main categories of perpetrators: those who participated actively in apartheid structures and those who benefited from the system. The first category comprises people such as the police and the army; some gave orders, some obeyed orders, and many, confident of the protection they would enjoy, took matters in their own hands in pursuing their evil deeds. The second category is made up of these enfranchised persons who had the capacity to vote injustice out of power. Some chose not to exercise their right, or in a token manner voted against the government while enjoying the benefits of its policy. Many voted an unjust government into power on repeated occasions. Bluntly put, white South Africa, by virtue of acts of commission or omission, prolonged the existence of discrimination in general and apartheid in particular. In this context, the single most painful aspect concerning transition has been the obvious disinterest of many white South Africans in TRC hearings. Apart from those applying for amnesty, few chose to attend the hearings. For many whites the victim hearings were a non-event. Under apartheid some possibly 'did not know', but when the occasion presented itself for the nation to face the truth in order to effect reconciliation, few were prepared to do so. The question is whether the process was about truth and reconciliation at all. For some it was about amnesty – as a basis for ensuring that those directly implicated in the atrocities of the past were able to join the ranks of the indifferent.

The suffering of victims

There is nothing that can be done to make amends to those who have suffered the loss of a loved one. Many victims have been broken. Others have been able to contexualise their experience and transcend it, drawing solace from the fact that it was the consequence of a sacrifice for the good of many and a struggle that had a moral foundation. Young men and women dedicated their youth, knowing they were fighting to remove an unjust order, judged by the world to be a crime against humanity. For many others, the decision to join the security forces was forced upon them by the brutality of the system – through detention without trial, torture and murder. All of this is well documented by the TRC.

The transitional process often seems to ask of victims that they be blind to the very source of their comfort – which is the clear moral distinction between the two sides involved in the war. While the *TRC Report* makes a distinction at the level of 'just cause', many white South Africans see both apartheid agents and freedom fighters as simply acting in pursuit of political objectives. They fail to recognise the criminal nature of the apartheid cause. There were, of course, some actions in the freedom movement that resulted in unacceptable actions. People pursued personal agendas in the name of the struggle and there were those who were the victims of political intolerance.

The victims of apartheid have shown huge tolerance regarding those responsible for their suffering. Yet, while the National Party has changed its name to the New National Party, FW de Klerk still cannot remember for what he needed to apologise. PW Botha also did not think it necessary to apologise. In response, the Chairperson of the Commission chose to pay him a personal visit. The message to victims is that the Commission, at least when it came to PW Botha, was willing to bend over backwards to accommodate perpetrators of the former regime.

Reparation and suffering

There is a growing gap between the expectations of the people and the likely political deliverables, which is why I am reluctant to discuss reparation and suffering in the same sentence.

There is, at the same time, little doubt about the need for reparation, particularly for the many families who lost breadwinners. Despite the promises of reparation that have raised the expectations of many desperate families, the State says it is not in a financial position to compensate. Yet some perpetrators continue to be employed by the State or are beneficiaries of state pensions.

The transition lacks sensitivity to the psychological needs of victims both in terms of reparation and support. Many victims have found that the Commission failed to treat the amnesty decisions with the sensitivity they deserve. For example, the family of Ashley Kriel came to hear of the decision to grant amnesty to his killers through the media. The need for a viable support programme is rather obvious, considering the fact that for most of the victims this was the first time they spoke openly about their suffering. In addition, the victims came face to face with people who were the embodiment of their suffering. It was obvious that the experience was traumatic for many victims, yet few were given adequate access to psychological services.

How have the TRC and other government initiatives brought the nation close to reconciliation? The truth is that national reconciliation is a product of changing social and economic conditions that continue to be a daily challenge, particularly for the bulk of South Africans. For this reason, reconciliation is as much an exercise in economics as it is in spirituality or personal attitudes.

Those who have suffered have acted generously. Yet the privileged classes in South Africa lack the wisdom to acknowledge the shamefulness of our past and their part in it. Yet mere words are not enough; there must be a willingness to ensure that those at the bottom of the pit are high on the national agenda. Until this willingness takes place, national reconciliation (including the Reconstruction and Development Programme, employment equity and economic empowerment) will be crushed under the weight of 'the huge denial'.

The full impact of amnesty has not yet been seen or assessed. There is no indication, however, with a few notable exceptions, that it has persuaded many perpetrators or beneficiaries of apartheid to move radically beyond the denial of *their* involvement in the tragedy of the past. The nation would do well to bring its resources to bear on the need for this to happen.

Getting on with life: a move towards reconciliation

CHARLES VILLA-VICENCIO

The Truth and Reconciliation Commission (TRC) was doomed to failure before it began, if it was ever thought that it could reconcile the nation in the face of all the entrenched problems associated with centuries of colonial and racial oppression. Whatever the excessive expectations of some concerning the reconciling potential of the TRC, the Commission from the outset defined itself as simply contributing towards the laying of a foundation on which national unity and reconciliation could be built. The TRC Act quite literally speaks of the *promotion* of national unity and reconciliation. Such initiatives within the Commission that have facilitated individual reconciliation constituted important instances of what *can* happen between former enemies, without being the primary objective of the Commission.

This chapter identifies the limited contribution of the TRC to a foundation for national reconciliation – recognising that the entire body politic cannot be cleansed in a single initiative. It identifies certain further minimal steps that are required to strengthen this foundation. It emphasises the importance of reconciliation as a *political* goal.

The dangers involved are not insignificant. A state-sanctioned programme on national reconciliation can lead to a new brand of nationalism – which plays down a focus on justice and basic human rights. It has been suggested that a nation so committed is almost invariably tempted to overlook the demands of the individual for justice.[1] This warning must be heeded. It is at the same time important to recognise that the TRC was required, by the legislation governing its work, to name the gross violations of human rights committed by the major political groupings in South Africa. In so doing it evoked the anger of the ruling African National Congress (ANC), the National Party (NP) and the Inkatha Freedom Party (IFP). It was, among other things, accused by the ANC in KwaZulu-Natal of damaging ANC/IFP relations in the province by drawing attention to past gross violations of human rights. Rapprochement initiatives between political parties may, in the name of political expediency and national reconciliation, overlook the demands of justice. It will not, however, be possible to accuse the TRC of not having sought to identify those responsible for human rights abuses.[2] Whether it has done enough in this regard will need to be weighed in the light of the national compromise regarding justice and the need for national reconciliation enshrined in the Interim Constitution and the Promotion of National Unity and Reconciliation Act, No 34 of 1995. Whether is has gone too far in exposing the past is open to debate.

Laying a foundation for reconciliation

Whatever the designs of the ruling elite and those most intimately involved in the TRC process, most victims and survivors experience deep resentment towards those responsible for their misery. Their primary objective is *rarely* reconciliation. They are (understandably) preoccupied with their own trauma and/or fired by the belief that revenge will bring relief. They want the perpetrator to be identified and, usually, punished. Yet there are people like Cynthia Nomveyu Ngewu, whose son, Christopher Piet, was one of the Gugulethu Seven shot by the police in March 1986. Asked for her response to the position of those who supported the imprisonment of perpetrators, she replied:

> *I do not agree with this view. We do not want to see people suffer in the same way that we did suffer, and we did not want our families to have suffered. We do not want to return the suffering that was imposed upon us. So, I do not agree with that view at all. We would like to see peace in this country ... I think that all South Africans should be committed to the idea of re-accepting these people back into the community. We do not want to return the evil that perpetrators committed to the nation. We want to demonstrate humaneness towards them, so that they in turn may restore their own humanity.*[3]

The warning of Jose Zalaquett, who served on the Chilean National Truth and Reconciliation Commission, cannot be ignored. 'Leaders should never forget that the lack of political pressure to put these issues on the agenda does not mean they are not boiling underground, waiting to erupt.'[4] The demand by many Chileans, almost 10 years after the establishment of the Chilean Commission, that General Augusto Pinochet stand trial following his arrest in the United Kingdom underlines Zalaquett's point.

The legislation governing the TRC at the same time challenges the nation as a whole (victims, survivors, perpetrators, beneficiaries and bystanders) to transcend resentment, retribution, fear and indifference, as a basis for the creation of a new future. In the words of the Interim Constitution, South African society should be driven by 'a need for understanding but not for vengeance, a need for reparation but not for retaliation, a need for *ubuntu* but not for victimisation'. In pursuit of these ideals, the victim is asked to give priority to his or her obligations as a *citizen* rather than a *violated person* in the creation of a new and different kind of society – within which the bigger picture of national unity and reconciliation is promoted. Donald Shriver suggests that 'vengeance (however understandable from the perspective of the victim) ultimately kills politics, if by politics we mean negotiations between groups that permit people to realise their mutual interests without destroying those very interests in acts of violence.'[5] GH Mead suggests that in a democratic order, a responsible citizen is required, in stepping into the voting booth, to vote for someone else's interest in addition to his or her own.[6] Rajeev Bhargava notes that if former victims don the mantle of victors and seek comprehensive retributive justice in either its no-nonsense revolutionary or its liberal democratic form, they may instantly turn all former perpetrators and beneficiaries into victims. If the distinction between victims and perpetrators is obliterated, South Africa is likely to be in the same state as former Yugoslavia or like India during its partition. '*This would be a disaster.*'[7] Kole Omotoso suggests that 'the question that all victims must answer [is] at which point do we become what we are fighting against?'[8]

But what about the aggrieved individual? Wilhelm Verwoerd, in an article in the *Sunday Independent* (6 December 1998), records his conversation with a young woman named Kalu: 'What really makes me angry about the TRC and Tutu is that they are putting pressure on me to forgive … I don't know if I will ever be able to forgive. I carry this ball of anger within me and I don't know where to begin dealing with it. The oppression was bad, but what is much worse, what makes me even angrier, is that they are trying to dictate my forgiveness.' Her words capture the pathos involved in the long and fragile journey towards reconciliation. No one has the right to prevail on Kalu to forgive. The question is whether victims and survivors can be enabled *to get on with the rest of their lives* in the sense of not allowing anger or self-pity to be the all-consuming dimension of their existence. It is a tall order. It involves taking responsibility for their own lives as well as the future direction of the nation. It involves becoming a *citizen* in the fullest sense of the word. Verwoerd quotes Ashley Forbes, a torture victim of the notorious Jeffrey Benzien. Although critical of the decision to grant Benzien amnesty, arguing that he failed to make full disclosure, he observed: 'I forgive him and feel sorry for him. And now that the TRC has showed what happened, I can get on with the rest of my life.' It is not important that every victim deal with his or her past in this manner. It is important, *for their own sake*, that those who suffered most are enabled to get on with life. This does *not* mean forgetting the ghastly deed. This is usually not possible and probably not helpful. It does *not* mean necessarily becoming friends with the person responsible for one's suffering. Very few accomplish this. It *does* mean dealing with the 'ball of anger' that prevents one from getting on with life. Dan Stein, in a thoughtful article, suggests that the ultimate 'revenge of those who survived the Holocaust was not the Nuremberg trials, but rather going forward and succeeding with life.'[9] Put differently, they were able to rise above their suffering to the extent of regaining their human dignity and participating in the reconstruction of society. In so doing they reached an important milestone within restorative justice – without ever suggesting that the past can even be fully overcome. It lingers on in numerous different ways.

The TRC has provided a context within which victims and survivors can begin to deal with the past:

- It exposed a great deal of *truth about the past*. Never again will South Africans be able to say 'we did not know'. Many South Africans would not have been forced to think about the past. More important, it provided vital information for victims and survivors. Information about the past is not always enough to start the healing process, although it constituted a turning point in this regard for Ashley Forbes and some others. Babu Ayindo, writing on the International Criminal Tribunal for Rwanda, suggests that truth telling is at the heart of most 'African traditional justice systems' that aim to reintegrate both the offender and the victim back into society.[10]

There are questions to which the victim clearly needs answers, in the absence of which he will conjure up his own. For instance, the witness/victim needs to know why particularly his wife, father, daughter, for example, were maimed or killed. Ayindo fears that 'at the end of the day, the success of the tribunal will be determined not by how much healing has taken place in the Central African nation but by how fast cases would have gone through the international criminal court.'

- It provided *catharsis for some victims and survivors*. Cathartic models of counseling emphasise the importance of verbalising past trauma, recognising the importance of doing so in a safe space with an empathetic audience. Suffice it to say some anecdotal evidence suggests that testimony before the Commission has assisted some individuals and their families, without suggesting that all those who come before the Commission benefit from the experience.[11] Dan Stein suggests that 'arguably social structures can theoretically exert a more important influence on post-traumatic reactions than individual psychotherapy interventions.'[12] It assists the victims and survivors to feel exonerated in situations where they have been falsely accused (criminalised) or belittled in the community, providing them with what Dumisa Ntsebeza, the head of the TRC's Investigative Unit, calls 'a public opportunity to salvage what is left of their human dignity'. It provides a basis for what Martha Minow calls the necessary *taming, balancing and recasting* of anger and desire for revenge as a first step in the process of reinterpreting one's life and future options for living in a morally ambiguous and socially complex society.[13]

- The TRC initiated a process of exploration into the process of trying to explain *why* perpetrators committed the dreadful deeds they did. To suggest that a society (above all victims and survivors) still so close to the reality of the past can (or even want to) *understand* perpetrators is to expect too much. To put pressure on those who suffered to do so is indeed almost obscene. The aphorism 'to understand all is to forgive all' does not explain the complexity of estranged relations. George Bizos argues that 'to be understood is a form of forgiveness'.[14] He is probably too hopeful. For those perpetrators who seek to bare their souls and come clean, however, it is important (for them) to feel that they have been 'heard' and that an attempt has been made to understand them. This *can* become a turning point in their reintegration into society as responsible citizens. For the victim this, in turn, can constitute a first step towards healing and towards reconciliation.

- The TRC has reminded us of *the capacity of apparently decent people to sink to such a level where they can commit the most atrocious evil*. It reminded us too that the complexity of perpetration extends beyond those who send the signal or pull the trigger. We should never lose sight of what Hannah Arendt calls the 'banality of evil'. Michel Foucault speaks in a similar manner of 'fascism within' that is potentially within humanity itself. It is a form of fascism, he suggests, which 'causes us to love power; to desire the very thing that dominates and exploits us'.[15] Leon Jaworski, chief prosecutor in the earliest European war crimes trials after the Second World War, asks himself how it is that apparently decent people, by their silence and acquiescence, allow the murder of others so systematically? The question haunted him all his life and in 1960 he published a book entitled *After Fifteen Years* in which he effectively said: 'Watch out. It can happen to you.'[16] The TRC made a clear distinction between those who killed in pursuit of liberation (which it saw as a just goal – while recognising that the means employed by those so engaged were not always just) and those who resorted to gross violations of human rights to uphold apartheid. In making these distinctions it initiated a process of identifying the social forces that nurture perpetration. Society needs to take responsibility for those it spawns and nurtures if it is to redress the forces that contribute to the violation of fundamental human rights. The chapter on motives and perspectives of the perpetrators in the *TRC Report* has been singled out in a *Sunday Independent* review as perhaps *the* most important chapter in the entire Report. Don Foster, who facilitated the drafting of that chapter, contributes an important chapter on the same subject in this volume.

■ The testimony of amnesty applicants shows the extent to which *many of the nation's worst perpetrators were themselves victims of a political system and cultural milieu* that promoted violence. Jacques Pauw's encounter with Paul van Vuuren is interesting in this regard. His defence as an amnesty applicant was essentially that he had sinned in darkness.[17] At least Paul van Vuuren was straight and honest, suggests Pauw. Van Vuuren's father was a policeman at Sharpeville in March 1960. He tells us that 'there was always talk of war and communism and the *swart gevaar* (black danger) ... I didn't really listen, but it made an impression on me.' Reluctant at first to kill, eventually he would do it with a sense of abandon. 'Yes, I enjoyed what I was doing, because I thought it was the right thing to do. It was the enemy I was killing. I felt I was busy with big and important things.' The French philosopher Victor Hugo once wrote: 'If a man sins because of darkness, the guilty one is not he who sins but he who causes the darkness.'[18] Bizos writes of the huge pressure that General Joffel van der Westhuizen experienced to get the security situation under control in the Eastern Cape in the 1980s. General Magnus Malan, the Minister of Defence, visited the area, demanding an end to the unrest. Van der Westhuizen, anxious to satisfy the demands of Malan, responded by ordering Colonel Lourens du Plessis to send the signal that ultimately led to the assassination of the Cradock Four (Matthew Goniwe, Sparrow Mkhonto, Fort Calata and Sicelo Mhlauli).[19]

There are, of course, heroic stories of individuals who withstood the forces to which Van Vuuren and Van der Westhuizen apparently succumbed. They often paid a high price for this resistance. Those who succumb to evil are, in turn, required to face the legal consequences of law. It is perhaps one of the few ways of fostering political and ethical responsibility in the tough world that makes for brutality, genocide and terror. To attempt to understand the nature of the pressures that gave rise to the corrupt sense of morality and natural justice is not to condone it. It can, in fact, be a basis for the identification of an early-warning system for the prevention of similar atrocities in the future.

■ However inadequately implemented, the TRC *has placed on record the need for reparation for victims and survivors* and signalled the need for economic restitution. Its Report recognises that political exploitation and imposed deprivation, in the absence of all other means of relief, necessarily provide fertile ground for the resort to armed rebellion. Just War theory and the position of the TRC regarding apartheid as a crime against humanity is, in turn, carefully articulated in the final Report of the Commission and further debated in two chapters in this volume, written by Mary Burton and Kader and Louise Asmal and Ronald Suresh Roberts. The Report further, notably in a chapter on the institutional hearing on business and labour and in its recommendations, emphasised the need for the bridging of the yawning gap between and the rich and poor.

The mandate of the TRC was a narrow one, focusing on specific gross violations of human rights, defined as killing, torture, abduction and severe ill-treatment. While the *political* dimensions of the context within which these violations occurred (either with a view to upholding or overthrowing the status quo) have been partially addressed through democratic elections, many of the *material* causes of the conflict continue to provoke anger. Through the TRC the nation may have bought space and time within which these causes can be addressed, although a deep sense of social injustice continues to prevail among the nation's poor. The Commission has signaled an urgent need for brewing discontent to be addressed.

To the extent that a truth commission contributes towards the laying of the above foundation, it can potentially assist victims and survivors in a limited way to begin to deal with the suffering associated with the past. But more is needed.

Extending the foundation

Changing circumstances make changing demands. There are, however, certain demands which are likely to persist: these constitute essential ingredients to a social contract that regulates racial, economic and democratic transformation – which lays the foundation on which national reconciliation can be promoted.

- Testimony of victims before the TRC constitutes the initial public step in the process of South Africans getting to know one another after generations of isolation, exploitation, estrangement and mutual suspicion. It is a process that needs to be extended – and to the extent that various sectors of society have regarded the Commission as pursuing a witch-hunt of one kind or another, alternative means of sharing life's stories need to be found. The genre of stories that grapple with the past and expose the present – not in order to fuel ideological divisions or to preach moralisms but to sensitise and to heal – is only beginning to be born. Poets, dramatists, musicians, song-writers, painters, sculptors and story-tellers are needed to help heal the nation.
- This story-telling process will inevitably underline the economic disparity which characterises the country. For this to be redressed it will involve a willingness of both the wealthy and the ordinary middle classes who struggle to pay the bills to have less in order that others may have a little more. The yawning gap between rich and poor in South Africa simply must be bridged. The United Nations Development Programme figures show that the standard of living of white South Africans is comparable to the 24th most wealthy nation in the world, Spain. The standard of living of black South Africans is 124th in the world, after the Democratic Republic of the Congo. Judge Richard Goldstone suggests that this maldistribution can be redressed in one of two ways – 'by bloody revolution that would bury the wonderful advances we have experienced in the past few years' or 'by the use of the law, and that requires the cooperation of the whole body politic'.[20]
- For this to happen it is essential that the *democratic process in all its dimensions be entrenched* to ensure free access to information, the freedom of expression and complete transparency in public debate. Bluntly put, the needs of the poor will not be addressed because of a set of socio-economic clauses in the Constitution or the moral conviction of leaders alone – it will take political organisation, public pressure and (probably) a measure of militancy by the poor themselves. If there are no viable democratic structures in place for this to happen peacefully, the eruption is likely to take place in another way.

The proposed broadening of the foundation is perhaps best addressed though the debate generated by the then Deputy President Thabo Mbeki's 'I am an African' speech in May 1996. The philosophical dimensions of the discussion surrounding it aside, the crucial (although at times tedious) question concerning *who is an African* has huge political and reconciliatory dimensions. Robert Sobukwe, the late PAC leader, argued that the only criteria in determining an answer to this question is whether a person regards Africa as his or her home. The ANC's Freedom Charter, in turn, states: Africa belongs to all who live within it, black and white. Two observations are in order:

- To make Africa home means caring about its problems – poverty, underdevelopment and alienation. 'Yesterday's colonisers', whites, need to take on this responsibility. It is also in their self-interest to do so.
- Those whites and people of other ethnic origins who choose to be African need, in their present vulnerability, to be assured that their vigorous participation in the African family is to be welcomed rather than tolerated by indigenous black Africans. Cultural inclusively – a sense of South Africa being *one nation* within which difference is celebrated rather than tolerated – still waits to be born. This kind of inclusively ultimately involves more than negotiation and arbitration. It involves the more subtle reality of shared commitment, recognising that reconciliation is made that much more difficult in the absence of a serious commitment to redress the vestiges of a past which is still with us. The testimony of a participant in the TRC youth hearings in Athlone deserves reflection:

Reconciliation is only in the vocabulary of those who can afford it. It is nonexistent to a person whose self-respect has been stripped away and poverty is a festering wound that consumes his soul.[21]

The prerequisites for reconciliation to become a possibility are frequently changing. It is, at the same time, never the right of the state, any state body or any individual to demand that any victim forgive or be reconciled to a person responsible for his or her wrongs. It *is* the task of those responsible for the crafting of an integrated and viable state and who are committed to good governance to ensure that the essential ingredients that make for national unity and reconciliation are being addressed. In the words of the TRC's Report, there is a need to restore and affirm the dignity of *all* South Africans. 'In the process, the sons and daughters of South Africa [will] begin to feel at home.'[22]

Reconciliation as a political imperative

Albie Sachs suggests that 'the greatest reparation that can be given to the most traumatised of our people is to guarantee them full, equal citizenship, and to assure them the dignity of being acknowledged as human beings'. He continues that 'rights relate to how we see ourselves and how we connect up with others'.[23] It is the *connecting up with others* that this chapter is about. It is *politically* important that it happen. It is at the same time not something that we can leave to the politicians and state bureaucrats, the Constitution or a state commission to deliver. It involves the participation of people at every level of society.

It is helpful, perhaps, to distinguish between two different levels of connecting up. The one is captured in what the TRC Act calls 'peaceful coexistence'. The other concerns the higher notion of 'reconciliation'.

At the lowest level, *coexistence* could imply no more than a willingness not to kill one another – a case of walking by on the other side of the street. At a higher level it involves working together as a basis for putting in place those things that make for coexistence – an appropriate legislative structure, a civil service, legitimate policing and the like. It involves arguing with one's political adversaries late into the night, accepting that the next day it will be necessary to live and work together at a number of different levels. As such it requires the first step (often reluctantly) towards honoring one's political commitments – if only out of self-interest. It involves ways of identifying and responding to the fears and aspirations of those on the extremes of the political spectrum, with a view to incorporating as many as possible within these groups into the bigger national agenda. It involves refusing to allow past wrongdoing and resentment towards others to undermine the political process. Jakes Gerwel, elsewhere in this volume, suggests the nation has done remarkable well in this regard.

Reconciliation involves more. It implies the restoration and sometimes the establishment of a hitherto non-existent relationship of trust. This takes time. It involves hard work and persistence. It is likely to include compromises. It requires an understanding of the other person's fears and aspirations. It necessitates the building of trust and respect for the rights and legitimacy of political opposition groupings. It does not necessarily imply forgiveness.

Forgiveness involves more than reconciliation. It usually comes, if at all, at the end of a process of cooperation and reconciliation. It is deeply personal. Jeffrie Murphy, in a helpful essay on forgiveness, argues that 'we do all need and desire forgiveness and would not want to live in a world where forgiveness was not regarded as a healing and restoring value.'[24] It is more than the Christian imposition some have suggested it is.

These different levels of *connecting up* tend to nest inside each other – a bit like Chinese boxes or Russian dolls. Different groups within society find themselves at different levels of interaction and no one group or individual within society is perhaps ever fully at home in either one or other category of engagement.

A powerful dialogue between the Polish dissident Adam Michnik and the then Czechoslovakian President Vaclav Havel, in November 1993, captures the tension inherent to a nation seeking to redeem itself. Michnik tells that when he was in prison he resolved never to seek revenge. Yet he kept repeating to himself a fragment of Zbigniew Herbert's poem: 'And do not forgive, as it is not within your power to forgive on behalf of those betrayed at dawn.' We can forgive harm done *to us*. It is not in our power to forgive harm done *to others*. 'We can try to convince people to forgive, but if they want justice, they are entitled to demand it.'[25] Think, however, of the impact that forgiveness could have on the nation.

It is essential that South Africans agree to coexist. National reconciliation is necessary for South Africans to become dedicated citizens of one nation. Forgiveness involves more. It is a coveted ideal to be gently pursued. It cannot be imposed.

Reconciliation: a call to action

MXOLISI MGXASHE

Archbishop Desmond Tutu's foreword to the Final Report of the Truth and Reconciliation Commission (TRC) serves as the most appropriate introduction to the theme of this essay. His foreword captures, in typical Desmond Tutu fashion, the real essence of the mandate of the TRC – a mandate that was meant to rebuild, rehabilitate and reconcile souls that had been split apart and damaged by almost three-and-a-half centuries of colonialism, slavery and apartheid. Tutu makes these apt observations in tracing the history of the factors that gave birth in December 1995 to the Truth and Reconciliation Commission.

All South Africans know that our recent history is littered with some horrendous occurrences – the Sharpeville and Langa killings, the Soweto uprising, the Church Street bombing, Magoo's Bar, the Amanzimtoti Wimpy Bar bombing, the St. James Church killings, Boipatong and Sebokeng. We also knew about the deaths in detention of people such as Steve Biko, Neil Aggett and others; necklacings and the so-called 'black-on-black' violence on the East Rand and in KwaZulu-Natal which arose from the rivalries between the Inkatha Freedom Party (IFP) and United Democratic Front (UDF), and then the IFP and later the African National Congress (ANC). Our country is soaked in the blood of her children of all races and of all political persuasions ... [1]

Talking of the transitional options South Africans had to choose from, in their quest for peace, healing, coexistence, reconciliation and reconstruction of their lives, Tutu observed:

We could not make the journey from a past marked by conflict, injustice, oppression and exploitation to a new and democratic dispensation charac-terised by a culture of respect for human rights without coming face to face with our recent history. No one has disputed that. The differences of opinion have been about how we should deal with the past; how we should go about coming to terms with it. There were those who believed that we should follow the post Second World War example of putting those guilty of gross violations of human rights on trial as the allies did at Nuremberg. In South Africa, where we had a military stalemate, that was clearly an impossible option. Neither side in the struggle (the state nor the liberation movements) had defeated the other and hence nobody was in a position to enforce so-called victor's justice... [2]

The TRC was formally established in December 1995 with a mandate from the Promotion of National Unity and Reconciliation Act (No 34 of 1995) to:
- establish as complete a picture as possible of the causes, nature and extent of the gross violations of human rights committed from 1 March 1960 to 10 May 1994, by conducting investigations and holding hearings;
- facilitate the granting of amnesty to persons who make full disclosure of all the relevant facts relating to acts associated with a political objective;
- establish and make known the fate or whereabouts of victims;
- restore the human and civil dignity of such victims by granting them an opportunity to relate their own accounts of the violations;
- recommend reparation measures in respect of those violations.

In its final Report handed to President Nelson Mandela in Pretoria on 29 October 1998 (in five volumes), violations of human rights are categorised to include those committed by the apartheid state outside South Africa; by the apartheid state inside South Africa; and by the liberation movements and the homeland governments.

The Report made this observation about the consequences of gross human rights violations on people's lives:

The apartheid system was maintained through repressive means, depriving the majority of South Africans of the most basic human rights, including civil, political, social and economic rights. Its legacy is a society in which vast numbers of people suffer from pervasive poverty and lack of opportunities...

The psychological effects are multiple and are amplified by the other stresses of living in a deprived society. Hence, lingering physical, psychological, economic and social effects are felt in all corners of South Africa. The implications of this extend beyond the individual – to the family, the community and the nation...

South Africa's history of repression and exploitation severely affected the mental wellbeing of the majority of its citizens. South Africans have had to deal with a psychological stress which has arisen as a result of deprivation and dire economic conditions, coupled with the cumulative trauma arising from violent state repression and intra-community conflicts...[3]

On the former liberation movements' part in the gross violations, the ANC, for instance, was found morally and politically accountable for violations committed in the context of its 'people's war' and others committed in exile in its camps. The PAC was similarly found morally and politically accountable for acts perpetrated by its militant wings, Poqo and APLA, in the course of its armed struggle and in its own camps in exile.[4]

The Commission's Report acknowledged that for its recommendations on reconciliation and unity to become a reality in the country, the energy and commitment of all South Africans would be required, as well as proactive steps from all institutions, organisations and individuals. 'One of the essential goals of the Commission was to ensure that there would be no repetition of the past. For reconciliation to have any chance of success, it is imperative that a strong human rights culture be developed...'[5]

Criticism on all fronts

Throughout its existence, the TRC had been pressurised and severely criticised by almost all sides of the ideological spectrum. The former functionaries of the apartheid state and its apologists, who had called for blanket general amnesty, were critical because the concept was turned down. Most of the letters and opinions expressed in the white press said that the TRC would be an expensive exercise and that the resources could be better spent on building houses for poor people – a charitable thought that is reminiscent of the story in the Bible about Judas Iscariot's attempts to dissuade Maria from using some expensive oils on Jesus Christ because they could have been sold and the money used to feed the poor.

Other critical voices said that the TRC was not going to contribute anything towards healing and reconciliation, but would instead open wounds that had almost healed. Activists from some segments of the liberation movement voiced their strong objections against what they felt was the

Commission's leniency towards the apartheid perpetrators. They had no confidence, for instance, in the principle of 'restorative justice' that the TRC preferred to 'retributive justice', which sought Nuremberg-type trials. Ironically, the man who presided over the most repressive era of the apartheid state, PW Botha, and former Apla Director of Operations, Letlapa Mphahlele, concurred on one thing – that the TRC was 'a big circus'.

Yet South Africa's history would never have been enriched as it has been by the information the TRC was able to dig out on the apartheid state, its various organs of repression and the methods of torture it used (perfected at the notorious Vlakplaas station), as well as details and explanation of what happened in exile in the camps of the liberation movement. This information will be stored in the archives as rich reference and healing reading work for generations after generations of South Africans, international scholars and others who may want to know what happened.

What came out of the TRC process shocked even the former liberation movement, which did not always know exactly to what extent its own cadres were brutalised. Some relatives whose kin had been tortured and killed were only too happy to know what had happened to them; they were further healed by the series of exhumations that gave the victims a more dignified burial in recognition of their contribution towards the new dispensation.

The findings of the final Report brought about some dramatic scenes, with the ANC and the former President FW de Klerk taking the Commission to the Cape High Court. De Klerk applied for an interdict – which was granted – that set aside the finding that he had condoned the bombing of South African Council of Churches headquarters, Khotso House, in Johannesburg in 1986. The ANC, in turn, could not accept the findings that it was 'morally and politically accountable' for gross abuses of human rights, and this, in its view, 'demonised' the liberation movement's Just War and struggle to overthrow a system that had been condemned as a 'crime against humanity' by the United Nations. The ANC's case was thrown out on legal grounds.

The PAC, which was also found morally and politically accountable for gross abuses, also registered its protests against what it saw as an equation of the just cause of the former liberation movement with the 'criminal acts' of the apartheid state.

The Azanian People's Organisation (Azapo), which had not cooperated with the TRC from day one, sniped at the ANC for 'attempting to muzzle the TRC'. The Inkatha Freedom Party (IFP), the New National Party (NNP) and the Freedom Front (FF), which had similar findings against them, boycotted the handing-over ceremony.

More questions than answers

Was there any validity in the claims made about the TRC by both its white and black antagonists? Was the TRC able to provide the healing that formed part of its mission and mandate? Was the TRC able to contribute effectively towards reconciling the victims and the perpetrators? And if so, to what extent has it created a climate in which whites and blacks could now be said to be ready to bury the hatchet and reconcile in the spirit described in the Postamble of the Interim Constitution on how the pursuit of national unity, the wellbeing of all South African citizens and peace required reconciliation between the people of South Africa and the reconstruction of society. These are likely to be the most commonly asked questions by anyone who followed the work of the TRC since its inception. How far are South Africans ready to coexist and forget the differences fostered by racial and colour divisions of the past, so that in the words of the SABC motto, they become one (*Simunye*).

The fallacy of the rainbow nation

One thing that is certain is that South Africa no longer has a legislation and a state – with its army, police, prisons and other tools of repression – that fosters racial discrimination and hatred. The new Constitution not only abhors this culture – it goes further to pronounce against discrimination based on people's sexual preferences. The irony is that those who continue to live in the past have a constitutional right to take to court anyone who calls them 'racists'. In their own private parties they probably abuse the 'kaffir' Mandela, and tell their black employees who complain of low wages to go and tell that to Mandela. Yet this same Mandela has often been criticised for having gone too much out of his way to be extra nice to white people. A great deal of the TRC healing and reconciliation dose will have to be injected into some of the schools that exploit the flag of a 'rainbow nation', yet go on prac-ticing the same racism that was prevalent during apartheid.

In his contribution to the six-hour debate in Parliament on 25 February 1999 on the *TRC Report,* the then Deputy President Thabo Mbeki observed that 'South Africa is still an apartheid society'. He showed its historical connections with Kirstenbosch's Botanical Gardens, 'the remains of a 340-year-old almond and thorn-bush hedge planted by Jan van Riebeeck to ensure the safety of the newly arrived white European settlers by keeping the menac-ing black African hordes of pagan primitives at bay.' He said black and white had to be kept apart, circumscribed by an equation that described each as the enemy of the other, and each the antithesis of the other. 'At first it was thought that the thorns of the almond and thornbush hedge would suffice as the ramparts to protect the enclave of 'European civilisation' perched precariously at the Cape of Good Hope to advance the purposes of the then temporary sojourners...'

The fallacy of the 'rainbow nation' in South Africa today is loudly proclaimed by the huge gaps that still exist between the affluence of the average white person living in the suburbs and the poverty of black South Africans living in the townships. So when one talks of coexistence among South Africans, one is also implying coexistence between poverty and affluence, because these are the worlds that will for a very long time continue to exist in the country unless something drastic is done to find and create the resources to improve things – such as reparations from those business concerns that made a kill from apartheid.

The TRC was not mandated to attempt to correct this situation because it was beyond its capacity and resources. But it conducted public hearings on the collaboration of the business community with apartheid. The following was part of its findings on the matter: 'Business was central in the economy that sustained the South African state during the apartheid years. Certain businesses, especially the mining industry, were involved in helping to design and implement apartheid policies; the white agriculture industry benefited from its privileged access to land. Other businesses benefited from cooperating with the security structures of the former state. Most businesses benefited from operating in a racially structured context...'[6]

The results of the first national census to be conducted in the post-apartheid era (held in 1996) were published in October 1998. The raised the issue of unequal distribution of resources very strongly. The following is extracted from a story in the *Cape Times* written by Melanie Gosling entitled 'The Real Rainbow Nation emerges':

The long-awaited Census '96 results released yesterday [19 October] paint a picture of a South Africa sharply divided between the rich and poor, in which quality of life is still linked to race. The vast discrepancies revealed on nearly every level of life prompted President Nelson Mandela to call on South Africans to rededicate themselves to transforming society by wiping out the poverty and imbalances of the past.

The census indicated that one in five South African adults had received no formal education at all, and that a mere six percent had any tertiary education in a population of 40,5-million people. The highest level of education for a quarter of the population is 'some' primary school, and fewer than one in five South Africans had completed matric. A third of the population was unemployed, and of those who had jobs, more than a quarter earned less than R500 a month. African women were identified as having been the hardest hit on most levels and comprised the highest proportion of the unemployed and formed the biggest group of unskilled workers. In contrast, observed the *Cape Times*, half of the country's small group of white males were employed in the country's top managerial, professional and technical posts.

Fifty-five percent of the population lived in formal houses while 16% had to make do with shacks; many still lived in 'traditional houses' in the rural areas. Running water and flush lavatories in the home were a luxury for most South Africans. There were huge differences between income groups, with 62% of South Africans earning less than R1 501 a month and only 11% earning over R4 500 month. About five percent of the working population were managers and only 11% were professionals and 30% were unskilled.

While whites occupied the bulk of the managerial positions, 73% of blacks worked in unskilled or artisan jobs. Only 11% of blacks were managers or legislators. About 45% of blacks and 42% of Indians were not economically active, compared with 35% of coloureds and 33% of whites. The lack of education reflected the apartheid past, with nearly a quarter of all blacks having received no education at all, compared with 10% of coloureds, 7% of Indians and only 1% of whites. Twenty-four percent of whites have post-school qualifications, compared with 10% of Indians, 4,5% of coloureds and 3% of blacks.[7]

According to Mandela, 'it will take time to absorb the full detail of this intricate picture of our complex society. But the broad outlines should act as a clarion call to rededicate ourselves, in every sector of the our society, to the historic mission of a generation charged with transforming South African society in order to eradicate the poverty and imbalances that derive from our past.'[8]

It is not just the statistics that give us a big picture of what really needs to be done in South Africa to realise the much-needed peace, stability, healing, reconciliation and coexistence. The thinking of large numbers of South Africans about their plight and specially about the efforts of the TRC were revealed in nation-wide interviews conducted by the *Cape Times* Special Assignments Team of Roger Friedman and Benny Gool. The interviews, called 'True Colours', were published in the *Cape Times* on 24 April 1998. I have selected some samples from the interviews.[9]

Things are just getting worse and worse. Look at all the violence, the murders. It was never like this in the past. The Truth and Reconciliation Commission is a good thing. I watch it on the news, though most of the news is in Bantu language and I cannot understand. I think when the National Party ran the country things were different.

Louise Arendse, coloured factory worker from Malmesbury.

Those times were definitely worse than now. But work is very scarce. When I go to the white people and ask for work they say I must ask Mandela. My one wish is that water is made available to all. I was getting water from a tap on the side of the hill, but then the white man came and switched it off.

Victor Ntsokolo (means hard times) Mane, unemployed black man from Malmesbury.

The boere here are just the same as they always were. They pay you as little as they always did, and we still stay in squalor, exposed to tuberculosis. I've heard of the TRC, but it was never here. I will vote for the ANC again because it is more important than the NP for the quality of our lives.

Jan Martins, coloured pensioner from Piketberg.

I believe people are moving further and further away. Racism is still a huge problem. We were accused of it and now they are practising it. The TRC should have been a good thing, but it's only about one race. White people's feelings don't matter anymore...'

Peet Myburg, white police officer from Piketberg.

I don't think things have improved in the new South Africa, life is getting harder and money scarcer. I sometimes hear about the TRC on the radio, but I don't attach much importance to it because it is not always true. You cannot believe what you see or hear in the media. I will vote for the same party next year as I did last time, but its identity is my secret. I can tell you that since the ANC came into power it's as if the devil has been let loose in the country.

Dina Zumri, coloured cleaner from Clanwilliuam.

South Africa is busy going down the drain. It used to be whites on top, then coloureds, and then blacks, I would like to say Kaffirs. Now the swargat is on top, the white man is second and the coloured is sitting in the shit. Last week we were at the beach. We went to Monwabisi. Then this kaffir started fighting with us. This native called my daughter a terrible thing, I asked him: 'How can you call my daughter a prostitute? Did you lie on her breasts?' You should have seen how rude he was. I hit him lekker. I don't let people play with me even if I am a woman. If anyone touches my children I become a tiger. I think the TRC is a lot of rubbish, the past is gone and the kaffirs are still killing people on the farms. We are NP supporters here. All the years we were with them. You should have a look in the garage, we have a lovely large poster of De Klerk.

Margaret Walker, coloured factory worker from Cape Town.

I cannot say things are coming right. They treat us like dogs here. White people just don't like us, they take us blacks and coloureds and have no peace for us. I know about the TRC, they tell the truth there. Old men like President Mandela and Archbishop Tutu tell the truth and shame the devil. That's all I know.

James Bisholo, unemployed black man from Middleberg.

A call to action

In his input in the special debate on the TRC in Parliament on 25 February 1999, the greatest inspirer of this whole reconciliation movement in South Africa, Nelson Mandela, said the debate on reconciliation could not be exhausted in just three hours and needed much more time and the broadest possible forum. 'But above all,' he said, 'the *TRC Report* is a call to action.' He continued:

And as we put together our thoughts on the challenges ahead, we need to remind ourselves that the quest for reconciliation was the fundamental objective of the people's struggle, to set up a government based on the will of the people, and build a South Africa which indeed belongs to all. The quest for reconciliation was the spur that gave life to our difficult negotiations process and the agreements that emerged from it. The search for a nation at peace with itself is the primary motivation for our Reconstruction and Development Programme to build a better life for all.

I would like once again to record our appreciation of the Commission, Archbishop Desmond Tutu, his fellow Commissioners and their staff and field workers for the service they have rendered to the country and for the continuing work of the Amnesty Committee. Their dedication to a difficult painful task has helped us through a historic stage in our journey towards a better society. The TRC issues a call, which we strongly endorse, for a recommitment in both public and private sectors, with renewed vigour, to the transformation of our structures and corporations through a combination of affirmative action, employment equity together with the strengthening of a culture of hard work, efficiency and honesty…

What makes a perpetrator?
An attempt to understand

DON FOSTER

As one part of its multi-sided brief, the Truth and Reconciliation Commission (TRC) was required to report on 'the causes, motives and perspectives' of persons responsible for perpetrating gross human rights violations. The *TRC Report* of the Commission did so in Chapter 7 of Volume 5. The aim of this chapter is to provide a summary of the key findings of the TRC in respect of perpetrators and to interrogate those findings in the light of possible limitations, inadequacies and unresolved issues. I do not intend to come to definitive conclusions; I propose rather to facilitate on-going debate in some of the key areas that are as yet imperfectly understood.

To what extent did the *TRC Report* provide an adequate understanding of these 'causes, motives and perspectives'? Has it advanced our knowledge of this field? Is it a partial and incomplete set of findings? What could have been done differently, or better? Where do we go from here?

Lest the TRC be misunderstood and falsely accused of grandiosity, the chapter entitled 'Causes, motives and perspectives of perpetrators' begins with a set of disclaimers arguing that findings are 'incomplete' and 'premature' since the amnesty hearings are still under way. Furthermore, not all categories of perpetrators were adequately represented, as some failed to apply for amnesty. The *TRC Report* admits to unavoidable partiality in so far as certain groups failed to cooperate fully with the Commission. Such groups included the Inkatha Freedom Party (IFP) and its supporters, some township 'vigilante groups' and 'necklace' killers, state-employed torturers and some ANC-aligned self-defence units. Documentary evidence from all categories of perpetrators was not necessarily available to the TRC; the complete tale is yet to be told, and may never be complete. More than 50 years after the Holocaust, new tales and perspectives are still being presented.[1] The *TRC Report* does not make foolhardy claims for completion; it is an 'agenda for future research rather than a closed book'.[2]

From any reasonable perspective it is quite clear that the conflict in South Africa was not equal, whether seen in terms of resources, military forces, goals and ends or in terms of a Just War perspective. Despite some claims to the contrary, the *TRC Report* was quite clear in recognising the inequality of this struggle: 'violence of the powerful, the South African state, was not necessarily equal with violence of the powerless, the disenfranchised, oppressed and relatively voiceless black majority'.[3] Noting that perpetrators came from all sides of the struggle, the TRC nevertheless stated unequivocally that this non-equivalence means that protagonists in the 30-year conflict were motivated by quite different political perspectives.[4] Given the context of a non-equivalent struggle, the TRC also recognised that 'an unhappy characteristic of oppression is that violence is often committed by the powerless against other oppressed groups'[5] and that such so-called black-on-black violence 'was expressed in many forms in South Africa', chiefly but not exclusively in the zonal antagonisms in KwaZulu-Natal. However, to depict violence among the oppressed as black-on-black violence is both unfortunate and potentially racist, since such a label 'masks the role of the state in orchestrating or steering such divisions'.[6] Again this underlines the non-equivalence of the sources of atrocities: the former South African white regime must be seen as the primary source of racist oppression and economic exploitation which constituted the grounds and motives for violent struggle.

The TRC position on perpetrators

An analysis of the vast set of TRC materials reveals some similarities in the accounts given by perpetrators on all sides of the struggle:

Similarities: shared accounts of the motives of perpetrators

Acts constituting gross violations of human rights varied considerably and included killings, bombings, abductions, torture, parcel-bombings, necklace-murders, cross-border raids, military-type actions and many other forms. Clearly such acts range from calculated and intentional actions to unplanned and accidental incidents that took place because things 'went wrong'. In accounting for such a range of acts, four sets of discourses were discernible in perpetrator explanations:

- *'We were at war'*
  All sides employed this account to explain intentional actions.
- *Denial*
  Parties from all sides denied that they knew fully what was happening or denied specific orders for atrocities even while supporters made claims to have acted under senior authorisation.
- *'We made mistakes'*
  To varying degrees, all parties admitted to unintended consequences, grey areas, aberrations from claimed policy and plain errors.
- *Lack of restraint and discipline*
  This was most clearly articulated in a United Democratic Front (UDF) submission. Other parties also conceded, to varying degrees, that they failed to exercise enough restraint upon their zealous followers, either because of insufficient communication channels or because of a lack of will to discipline 'their own' (which may have run the risk of alienating political supporters). Some statements expressed covert pride regarding violent actions of 'their own'. At times security police were even decorated for such actions.

The problem of perspectives

The *TRC Report* lists a number of problems regarding perspectives, such as a difference in perspective between the powerful (the state and its agents) and the powerless. Perpetrators such as military conscripts could also be regarded as victims, and there is the problem of the 'askaris' – victims turned perpetrators.

And, of course, there is the difficulty inherent in the position the TRC was required to take – that of a disinterested, objective, third-party perspective of highly politicised and emotive events.

This section of the Report, drawing on Baumeister's[7] recent psychological thinking on the nature of evil, describes a fundamental difference in perspective and experience of events between perpetrators and victims – that of the importance of the act or event. Discrepancies may exist on a number of fronts, not least in respect of the question of motive: why did the act or event occur.

Victims tend to see the act as maliciously intentional or find it difficult to comprehend altogether. Perpetrators provide comprehensible reasons for their actions – as in the examples given above – and seldom claim a malicious motive. If there is merit in such claims of a psychological 'magnitude gap' between perspectives of victims and perpetrators, it bodes ill for a mutually comprehensible understanding of the past. These are tough nettles to tackle: the *TRC Report* deserves credit for placing such issues firmly on the agenda rather than glossing over them.

Explanations of motives and causes

The *TRC Report* sets out three primary political contexts for a political understanding of perpetrators:

- the Cold War, including the role of the superpowers and the virulent strand of anti-communism that took root in white South Africa from the 1950s onwards;
- anti-colonial struggles across the African continent, which escalated rapidly after the Second World War;
- apartheid and the liberation struggle, which turned to armed struggle in 1960 following the banning of the ANC and PAC.

These contexts do not, however, provide a complete explanation for motives and causes. The *TRC Report* also debates a range of further potential causes, and sets out some non-acceptable versions. It is clearly opposed to reductionist explanations such as those that claim atrocities are due to biological, atavistic or essentialist aspects of 'human nature' (eg it is inevitable that humans will be aggressive or destructively violent) or pathology or psychological dysfunction. Neither of these accounts are warranted if atrocities occur only in particular and limited historical periods, nor if violence is committed mostly by men.

Furthermore, violence was too widespread and systematic in patterning to allow for understanding in terms of psychological dysfunction. While not denying that sadistic personality types (those who are purported to take pleasure in hurting others) may self-selectively find a home in militaristic organisations, the Report suggests that such types are few and that sadism is not innate but is acquired over time. The Report further suggests that although it is premature to draw final conclusions, it is likely that 'severe psychological dysfunction is not a primary cause' of gross violations of human rights.

If the TRC rejects explanations rooted in sweeping claims about 'human nature' or psychopathology, then what does it propose? The Report sets out an explanation in terms of four sets of interrelated factors – authoritarianism, social identities, particular situations and ideological language – and proposes two additional but traditionally neglected factors: special organisational forms and secrecy and silence.

Authoritarianism

Authoritarianism is understood as a cluster of social beliefs and a tendency to be drawn uncritically into a conservative grouping. It manifests primarily in behavioural tendencies that show submission to strong in-group leadership along with hostility towards members of stigmatised (eg racialised) and less powerful groups. There certainly is psychological evidence that authoritarianism manifested unusually among white South Africans, particularly Afrikaans-speakers,[8] expressed primarily in terms of intolerance and hostility towards black people, people on the left and civil liberties in general. This tendency may not be a direct cause of violence, but may instead operate as a selective device, in which particular organisations attract those keen to submit to authority, obey orders uncritically and attack resistance groups (which in South Africa meant blacks, liberals and leftists).

Social identities

Collective or group identities rather than personal identities or personality types constitute the pre-conditions for violence. In situations of intergroup conflict, people act primarily in terms of their social identities (ethnic, racialised, national) rather than their individual personality attributes.

Which social identities played a significant role?

Racism and racialised identities constituted a central dynamic, interlocking with ethnic identities such as Afrikaner-nationalism. Political identification in terms of allegiance to political party, for example the National Party, also would have been salient. In explanations of atrocities, one particular form of social identity – masculinity – has frequently been ignored. The key claim in this section of the Report is that various forms of social identities combine or intertwine to produce persons able to commit atrocities.

Situations as triggers of violence

Research over decades has argued persuasively that violence manifests as a result of particular situational influences rather than the character, morality or personalities of protagonists. The Report outlines two clusters of situational factors: those that bind people into groups, rendering them susceptible in particular to obey authority figures and group norms, and those that distance perpetrators from victims.

'Binding in' processes turn on the degrees of hierarchy, surveillance and legitimacy of authorities, along with identification of group norms and values. When authorities encourage or tacitly approve of violence, even if formal orders are not given, and 'binding in' processes are powerful, then violence is likely to be the outcome – and this is more so if situations are organised as routine and repetitive: the impulse to obey orders becomes unquestioned. Even under such circumstances, however, mass atrocities are unlikely, unless accompanied by the second set of factors: distancing from the victim.

This distancing also involves a multiple set of processes, including stereotyping, prejudice, stigmatisation and dehumanisation; these all work together to render victims as 'other', inferior and as 'creatures to whom normal morality does not apply'.[9]

Dehumanisation may further be exacerbated by a factor not mentioned in the *TRC Report* – that of conspiracy thinking.[10] This is a social process in which a purported secretive, hidden agent is vilified as the source of all wrong. In South Africa, shrouded communists were targets of such conspiracy imaginings. This is a particularly dangerous process as it promotes political paranoia, and conspiratorially constructed enemies are frequently deemed worthy of assassination; the murders of Ruth First and Chris Hani are examples in the South African struggle.

Time sequencing is touched on in the Report as a further characteristic of noxious situations. Small first steps bind people into a situation, which enables further, more dreadful deeds. Sequencing of events, such as 'tit for tat' revenge operations, were frequently witnessed in South Africa. Events spiral in escalating sequences in circumstances akin to 'dialogues of violence'.[11]

Language and ideology

A novel contribution of the *TRC Report* is the claim that ideological language is a major factor in gross violations of human rights. Informed by the social constructionist movement, the claim is that language does things: it gives orders, creates conspiracies, manufactures enemies and motivates people for action. Apart from the ideological role in manufacturing racism and conspiracy thinking, language is more directly implicated in the 'triggers' of murder, illustrated by extensive TRC investigation into the meaning of the words and phrases 'eliminate', 'take out', 'neutralise', 'make a plan' and 'had to be removed'.

Those in authority denied the sinister interpretation, but those in more junior positions maintained little doubt as to the deadly meaning of such orders. Language and ideological processes also operate in terms of sequences, spirals and accelerations. As Du Preez[12] suggested in his study of genocide: 'The sequence consists of acts of increasing violent contempt for outsiders. It may start with words and uniforms and end in killing'.[13] This emphasis on ideological language seems a useful addition to the more usual list of factors.

Two neglected factors

Two further factors, which we can only briefly touch on, are the role and place of special organisations and the contribution of secrecies and silences in enabling atrocities.

Clearly, on all sides, only a handful of people were actively involved as perpetrators, chiefly those in various special organisations and often specifically recruited and trained for the task. In the South African case most of these organisations, ranging from the Broederbond to Vlakplaas, were secretive and shrouded in silence. On the other hand it was the relative silence on the part of the media, the state, the general populace and even many religious organisations that condoned the continuation of tortures, disappearances and other atrocities. Such silences were not entirely broken by the TRC process – many stories remain untold. Drawing attention to these aspects seems both sensible and justified.

The *TRC Report* closes with two specific case examples, of torturers and of 'mob' killings, then offers some concluding remarks on the future prevention of atrocities.

Limitations and future issues

Assessed against its brief, the TRC appears to have done a more than adequate job – under less than optimal circumstances and within a tight time-frame – in throwing some light on the 'causes, motives and perspectives' of perpetrators. The chapter provided extensive samples of quotations from leading politicians, from special hearings and from ordinary perpetrators, to illustrate and support the claims.

In a rare media assessment of the full *TRC Report*, Jeremy Gordin[14] in *The Sunday Independent* gave his opinion on the chapter on causes, motives and perspectives:

> *[It is] a fascinating and wide-ranging analysis that may yet prove to be a seminal summary of the subject. That particular chapter could be said to sum up the entire Report. For the Report, though its central subject is unspeakable horror, is passionate, moving and full of hope in that it attempts to move beyond mere blame. It is also closely argued – and yet it is written lucidly and is accessible.*

It is, however, not the complete story. More remains to be done. By its own admission the TRC awaits further information, in particular the completion of the amnesty hearings and judgements, which should be concluded by the end of 1999. Reports of the amnesty process will undoubtedly provide rich sources of further information, but even this may be insufficient to probe deeper understandings of perpetrators.

For one, it still appears likely that certain categories of acts (such as necklace murders, tortures, actions by the far-right wing and revenge killings in KwaZulu-Natal) will remain under-represented in amnesty cases. What will be revealed in the instance of amnesty applications of 37 top ANC leaders (currently refused due to their collective representation) remains uncertain. The numerous incidents of train-killings in Gauteng in the early 1990s remain something of a mystery. Key senior officers of both defence and police forces have not applied for amnesty. The case involving chemical warfare and the secretive Roodeplaat Research Laboratory will be heard as a criminal case rather than as an amnesty hearing; the full tale may not be told by the time the TRC amnesty proceedings close their doors.

Furthermore, the amnesty process itself may be flawed as a procedure geared to understand perpetrators' actions. Its goals are different. The key criteria for an amnesty judgement turn on three matters: full disclosure; evidence of a political motive; and proportionality of the deed in its context. These may well serve as adequate tools for the amnesty decision process but may not necessarily serve to facilitate psychological and political understandings of atrocities.

An ideal-state scenario

What could have been done if the TRC had aimed for a full understanding of perpetrators – assuming sufficient funding and time? The question is one of an ideal-state scenario, but here is a sketch.

All perpetrators could have been put through a comprehensive battery of psychological assessments, in part to provide a more complete answer to the questions of psychopathology and personality-type than were provided above. I confess to being no great believer in the efficiency of such tests, but if they had been done, they would have satisfied at least some (positivists) that the issues had thoroughly been probed.

Similarly, assessments could have been effected on constructs such as authoritarianism and adherence to particular group ideologies.

More important, and most neglected, detailed case histories should have been taken, canvassing not only personal biographies but descriptions on the *modus operandi* of special organisations – recruitment, training, operations, morale and links to higher authorities. Work of this sort, systematically conducted with each perpetrator appearing before the amnesty process, would have allowed for more probing psychological profiles of perpetrators and their motives. The current quasi-legalistic amnesty procedures have failed to back such materials.

Personal case studies of perpetrators are sorely lacking. The recent book by Eugene de Kock[15] makes a start in this direction and contains some useful pointers, but is too thin on biographical matters. De Kock expressly denies that his childhood or family influences played much part, but there is little analysis of the ideological influences of Afrikaner nationalism within his family and school backgrounds. Pumla Gobodo-Madikizela[16] has embarked upon important case-study work of De Kock and a group convicted in the 1980s of a crowd killing: this work is awaited with keen anticipation.

Gender, entitlement and emotions

Given the history of atrocities during the 20th century, the neglect of gender issues and the question of male violence is simply astonishing.

The *TRC Report* to its credit points to the neglect of the study of masculinity and violence. It is abundantly clear that the overwhelming majority of perpetrators of ghastly deeds both in South Africa and elsewhere have been male. It is, of course, only in the past decade or so that masculinity has become a topic of widespread research attention, and while male violence against women has come under the spotlight, most studies of genocide and mass violence fail even to note that perpetrators are chiefly male. What is it about masculinity that under certain circumstances renders such an identity form so noxious? What are the circumstances? All of this awaits research.

The TRC chapter on women,[17] also to its credit, touched on the issue of women perpetrators, but the evidence was anecdotal, and stories were told from the angle of victims, not perpetrators themselves. This section amounted to a few pages only. This matter requires research focus. How many perpetrators in the South African struggle were women? From which sides were they? Were they involved in killings? (We know of some ANC women who planted bombs, but as far as anecdotal evidence goes, it seems as though such actions did not result in deaths.)

Two other psychologically orientated topics warrant investigation: entitlement and emotions. Sharon Lamb,[18] in a recent study of both victims and perpetrators in matters of sexual abuse, raises the question of entitlement as a possible line of explanation. Entitlement raises interesting questions of the relation between particular ideologies, construction of social identities (eg whiteness, masculinity) and individual psychology. Closely related is the issue of egotism raised by Baumeister[19] in respect of revenge as a possible motive. While both entitlement and egotism are linked to the notion of perpetration with a sense of moral righteousness, the two constructs are not identical and need some teasing apart. There is ample evidence in the files of the TRC that some people were able to kill and torture, if not necessarily with pleasure, then certainly with a sense of pride and ego-involvement.

Since the thesis of the 'banality of evil' has come to dominate explanation, so has the issue of emotion become neglected. Common-sense understandings would readily accept that strong emotions should be linked to heinous deeds, but intellectual accounts have too frequently dealt poorly with emotions. In this regard the recent work of Thomas Scheff[20] is important in opening new lines of inquiry. His claim is that unacknowledged shame leads to cycles of interminable conflict and aggressive tendencies. Whereas pride produces social bonding and solidarity, unrecognised shame driven down by embarrassment is likely to lead to alienation, rage and a drive for power and destructive violence. In this view, acknowledgement of shame accompanied with genuine apology may facilitate reconciliation.

Four more minor issues may require further attention. First is the question of biological understandings, particularly of male violence. Dan Stein[21] has taken up this question in South Africa, and it will at least be interesting to follow proceedings.

Second is the rather odd attempt of some psychologists and psychiatrists to link perpetrators' actions to post-traumatic stress disorder (PTSD). I believe these claims are both wrong and morally reprehensible, and agree with Nicholas,[22] who has vehemently rejected such hypotheses.

Third is the further understanding of crowd killings; we still need some insiders' accounts of such issues to throw more light on the subjective experience of collective violence.

Lastly is the question of historicity of atrocities. As collective phenomena, why do they suddenly escalate, in many different parts of a country at particular times only? There are many speculative accounts, but these need to be backed by more detailed historical case analysis.

Reconciliation

Finally, we should raise the larger questions of reconciliation and the further prevention of atrocities – two not necessarily related aspects. If perpetrators' actions are primarily political (not biological or psychological) in governance, then prevention will necessitate political solutions – chiefly a fully participative, open, accountable democratic form.

Then what about reconciliation? All are agreed that the process of reconciliation, if indeed fully achievable, is something far larger than the life of the Truth and Reconciliation Commission and will take far longer.

Does understanding perpetrator actions facilitate reconciliation? Reconciliation among whom? If directly between perpetrator and victim, the psychological 'magnitude gap' between these two categories, as outlined by Baumeister,[23] suggests it may be a gulf too great to bridge, as neither can really see, hear or grasp the perspective of the other.

If reconciliation depends upon mutual understandings, we should not be optimistic.

But forgiveness, even without full mutual understanding, is another motive – and points to many years of searching, investigating, yearning and hoping. People may be able to forgive, even if they cannot forget or fully understand.

And if we hope for a better system of relations among us, perhaps that feeling should be our touchstone.

A personal encounter
with perpetrators

GINN FOURIE

In order to contextualise my experience with the perpetrators of our daughter's death at the Heidelberg Tavern, Cape Town, on 31 December 1993, I offer cameos of a tortuous journey from then to the time of writing in early 1999. My sense of grief and loss are indescribable and ongoing, and I shall not attempt to elaborate on this.

31 December 1993 – Death

My husband, Johann Fourie, arrived home with no forewarning of the news, to find a car belonging to friends parked in our driveway; they told us the unbelievable news of what became known as the Heidelberg Massacre, and that it was possible that our daughter Lyndi was a victim. One of the friends took us to the morgue while others answered our telephone, which by this time was ringing incessantly. The shock and sense of unreality was shattered by seeing her beautiful body on a cold gray slab ... too pale, too quiet, too still, and we were not allowed to touch her. Never to hear that melodious laugh and experience that gentle humour again. No more her arms around me, relaxed and free to be together... it was all too much to absorb... we had the days and weeks and months and years ahead to do this.

3 January 1994 – The funeral

The funeral service was conducted by my brother Ian Hartley. He had coun-selled us to participate in the service in any way that we felt comfortable; he said that it would be appropriate to cry if we needed to and that we were not to feel bad about it. I prayed without a tear, although reading the prayer now brings a flood:

Gracious Father
You gave your only Son
to bring healing for every soul on earth.

Thank you for our only daughter
May healing come through her death
to each person she touched – especially those who murdered her.

Mary, Mother of God, our children died at the hands of evil men
Lyndi had no choice, no time
But your son said it for her:
'Father forgive them, they do not know what they do'.

We gave her bed and board and some love
You gave her forgiveness and a love that was:
honest,
pure,
selfless,
colour and gender free.

Dear God, she taught me well of you
able to listen,
able to hear,
That was her life that you gave her
Her death was swift and painless, thank goodness
My heart is broken
The hole is bottomless
It will not end
But you know all about it.

Thank you for the arms,
the lips,
the heartbeats
of family and friends to carry us.

I trust you with my precious Lyndi
This planet is a dangerous place to live
I know that you will come soon to fetch us
I wish it were today
But I will wait for your time.

We suspected that the Pan African Congress (PAC) was responsible for this act because of its similarity to the earlier St James Church Massacre, also in Cape Town on 25 July 1993. There were no names or faces attached to the killers, only a sense that God could forgive them. In the service Ian said that the most appropriate Christian response to violence is to absorb it, as Lyndi's soft body had done on that fateful day. My admiration of Mahatma Gandhi and Martin Luther King's stance on firm resistance without violence was well established. Yet the full impact of 'absorbing violence' would only become real to me later, after putting names and faces to the killers.

November 1994 – The criminal trial

Three young men had been detained within a week of the Heidelberg Massacre and were now standing trial. I sat in the Supreme Court in Cape Town, looking at them in the dock: Humphrey Gqomfa, Vuyisile Madasi and Zola Mabala. I was confronted by my own feelings of anger and sadness, and wondered how I could possibly respond appropriately. Somehow I could engender no hate, in spite of the grim reminders presented by a video and the close-up colour photographs of Lyndi and three others lying dead in the tavern. The prisoners' faces were expressionless and they demonstrated clear resistance to the process of the law. I felt an unexplainable sense of empathy and sadness for them – it was quite a predicament for them to be in. Now, there was no support for them from the organisation that had inspired their 'freedom fight'. Each one was represented by a separate advocate.

I sent a message to them via the interpreter for the court, in which I said that if they were guilty or felt guilty, I forgave them. Maybe I was beginning to absorb the violence?

During a pause in proceedings, before the judge entered the court, they beckoned to me to come to the dock. Two of the prisoners shook my hand and said: 'Thank you, but we do not know why we are here!' I responded that the judge was waiting to hear from them and that if they didn't know why they were on trial they should enter the witness stand, which they had refused to do up until then. Their stoicism immediately returned and they moved away. I interpreted this gesture to mean cognitive dissonance or conflict about the possibility of exposing their commanders. They were convicted of murder and sent to prison for an average of 25 years each.

The words used by the judge were that they were mere puppets who had enacted a violent crime against humanity, a crime that had been strategised by more cunning and intelligent people than they were.

As a final act of defiance the three refused to be present in the courtroom for the passing of sentence, and they were forcibly brought into the dock.

October 1997 – the TRC hearing

The Heidelberg Three, as they had become known, said that they were sorry for the crimes they had committed. There was no indication of that sorrow. The expressionless faces, impatient with the cross-questioning, and their joyful descriptions of how they had sung slogans on the way to the Heidelberg that night did not convince us of the sincerity of their professed sorrow for the survivors. They were treated as heroes by their supporters in the audience.

The survivors and the family members of the dead were given the opportunity to address the hearing:

Ginn Fourie: Molweni Amadoda *(Good day gentlemen).*
Applicants: Molo Mama *(Good day mother).*
Ginn Fourie: I am very sorry that I can't express my thoughts and feelings in Xhosa. I think you remember me. At the criminal trial, I asked the translator to tell you that I had forgiven you. Do you remember that?
Applicants: Yes, we remember.
Ginn Fourie: I shook your hands. Mr Gqomfa was unwilling and he looked the other way, but I certainly shook Mr Mabala and Mr Madasi's hands. Nothing has changed. I still feel exactly the same way and I do forgive you because my high command demonstrated to me how to do that by forgiving his killers.

I want to tell you who Lyndi was. Her Xhosa friends knew her as Lindiwe. Lyndi was a true child of Africa. She was happiest hiking in the mountains, riding horseback with her dog out in the countryside. She was just finishing a Bachelor of Science in Civil Engineering and had spent a lot of time designing and thinking about how it would be possible to improve the infrastructure in places like Khayelitsha, so that running water and waterborne sewerage would be available to the homes of people who had suffered oppression and discrimination.

She spent her vacations with one of the large engineering companies in the Western Cape. During lunch times the black men would tell her about their lives. She would come home in the evenings and tell me the tragic stories of hopelessness and despair which they felt as labourers, with no opportunity for improvement. She understood and wept to know that this was happening in her country.

She helped me to understand how subtle my own prejudice and racial discrimination was, nothing blatant, but it was in the very fibre of my being. She was totally willing to treat everyone as an equal and she did that openly and freely. Her black friends were as close to her as her white friends. Lindiwe could have been your friend. You did your own cause immeasurable harm by killing her. She was totally opposed to violence. She was a gentle person who cared for not only the people, not only the little people, but the animals and the flowers, the ecology of our land and the world.

Shortly after our daughter's death, as a medical person, I had to go straight back to the wards of Groote Schuur Hospital and treat others who had been shot. I needed to do that without showing any bitterness or resentment. God gave me that grace. I think that the reason for my being here this week and particularly today, which is very important to me, is to tell you that on that day you ripped my heart out. Lyndi was one of the most precious people that this country could have produced (I confess that I am biased).

I resent being called a victim. I have a choice in the matter – I am a survivor. Lyndi was a victim – she had no choice. Also I have just had major surgery which I trace partly to the result of the stress and trauma of her violent death. There is a strong correlation between colon cancer and major stress. So first you ripped my heart out, and now half of my gut.

I am happy that you are well. I hope that emotionally and psychologically you can be well because you have been programmed killers though you repeatedly said that you were acting under orders from your high command. You could not tell us how you felt while killing innocent people, which indicated to me that you may have been trained to 'not feel' and I recognise how important that would be in a killing machine – to be unable to feel, but just to carry out orders indiscriminately. I have no objection to the granting of amnesty for you, but there are enough indiscriminate killers on our streets and in our countryside. My fear is that we may have three more.

I wish that the violence could end, and perhaps with time and counselling this can be so. I trust that counselling will be made available to you as it has been made to us as survivors. Lindiwe would have wanted to hear the stories of your lives. I am interested as a woman who has experienced the pain and frustration of oppression to hear about your experiences.

We came here hoping to hear the truth about who the people in 'High Command' were who organised this whole atrocious and cowardly opera-

tion. I am not convinced that the truth has been revealed, and until such a time, I am not happy for you to disappear into the woodwork.

I know that it must be terribly frightening to reveal who the 'High Command' is because your lives may be in jeopardy if you do get amnesty. But I thank you for being able to look me in the eye and for hearing my story.

January 1998 – final day of the TRC hearing

The Heidelberg Three asked to speak to me – the message came through the PAC parliamentarian Patricia de Lille, who asked to be present. Their legal advisor, Advocate Arendse, asked to be there too. I agreed to meet them after lunch, which was a mistake because the warders had no time to spare and were anxious to get the prisoners back to distant prisons.

Gqomfa spoke on behalf of the group. He had led the cadres in the attack on the Heidelberg Tavern. He said that they wanted to thank me for my forgiveness; they would take that message of peace and hope to their communities and to their graves, whether or not they were given amnesty. Gqomfa said that if someone were to kill his child he didn't think he could forgive them. I was profoundly moved by their acceptance of my gift of forgiveness; I recognise, in retrospect, that this was another step in the healing process. I asked them to tell me why they hated white people enough to indiscriminately kill them.

Madasi said that his father had been killed by a white man. (Madasi has a sister called Lindiwe, he said, so had connected with Lyndi's Xhosa name.) Mabala explained that his family was killed by white security force members in a riot near East London – he was lucky to escape.

I reiterated to them the importance of counselling in order to deal with their hurt, hate and military socialisation. Gqomfa responded: 'We would welcome counselling, and rather with the survivors so that true reconciliation can take place.' The insight of such a statement was staggering. I had not thought of having counselling together.

The warders insisted that the meeting adjourn – a hug for each indicated the depth of community we had entered into in this short while. The amnesty applicants then shackled themselves, which symbolised to me the enormous responsibility that accompanies freedom of choice and the sad outcome of making poor choices. Tears came to my eyes. Humphrey Gqomfa turned to the interpreter and said, 'Please take Mrs Fourie home'. Once more I was amazed by the sensitivity and leadership potential of this man – this same man who was a perpetrator of 'gross human rights violations' against my own daughter.

Stages of healing

As I reflect on my journey from tragedy to healing, I can discern the following stages:

- Owning the feelings of excruciating pain, grief and loss of Lyndi.
- Accepting the graciousness of God's forgiveness and love in my own life.
- Somehow absorbing the violence of Lyndi's death, which I sense as a miracle.
- Feeling empathy for the prisoners in their fear and confusion at the criminal trial.
- Offering forgiveness to Lyndi's killers, whom I regarded as evil men.
- Episodes of direct communication with the perpetrators, where I tried to be honest about my pain and fears and listened to reasons for their hurt and hate.
- The perpetrators acceptance of responsibility for the hideous crimes which they had committed and their apologies.
- The perpetrators gracious act of accepting my forgiveness and the healing for us all, symbolised by embracing.
- Lastly a vision for reconciliation on a larger, national scale.

Provision of counselling for 'perpetrators'

In early February 1998 I met Archbishop Tutu to ask about counselling for 'perpetrators of political violence' – those for whom the TRC process had been established. I found that although provision had been made for the counselling of survivors, none had been made available to assist the perpetrators face their own demons and then integrate into a society where there are mixed feelings about perpetrators of violence being granted amnesty.

Jacques Ellul,[1] a French theologian and sociologist, formulated five laws of violence; he proposes that 'violence creates violence, begets and procreates violence. The violence of the colonialists creates the violence of the anti-colonialists, which in turn exceeds that of the colonialists. Nor does victory bring any kind of freedom. Always, the victorious side splits up into clans that perpetuate violence'. In Ellul's Law of Sameness, he suggests that it is impossible to distinguish between justified and unjustified violence, between the violence that liberates and the violence that enslaves. The violence that liberated Eastern Europe from Nazism enslaved it to Communism. 'All who draw the sword will die by the sword' (Matthew 26:52). There is no qualifier for the 'all'. Even those who draw the sword with good intent expose themselves to the consequences of violence. This is not a decree of God – it is a statement of fact. The person who carries a violent weapon thinks differently to the one who does not. This violent thinking results in actions that often cause more violence.

In her book on urban violence and health, Gilbert[2] states that South Africa is a particularly violent society. She suggests a link between the social context of urban violence and the mental health of that community. This is a likely clue to the occurrence of continuing violence where counselling is often unknown and/or unaffordable – and add to this the racial and cultural tensions that have never been dealt with in any significant way.

Lisak *et al* [3] report on the relationship between a history of abuse and perpetration of violence. In their study of 126 perpetrators, 70% were abused in childhood. Perpetrators who were both sexually and physically abused manifested significantly more gender rigidity and emotional constriction than abused non-perpetrators. Furthermore, De Ridder[4] shared with me her findings at the Trauma Centre: clients who had been referred as victims of violence but who had also been perpetrators were more anxious to work through their distress as perpetrators than as victims.

The cycle appears to be one of experiencing abuse to becoming a perpetrator, then consequently being on the receiving end of the law (which sometimes even involves police brutality – an ongoing problem that needs serious attention). There have been encounters between 'survivors' and 'perpetrators' and their descendants in other countries in recent times, particularly in Germany. Bar-On[5] writes of four encounters between descendants of survivors and descendants of perpetrators of the Holocaust. These encounters are seen as an attempt to build social bonds out of the silence and pain of the past. Kaslow[6] describes the importance of these meetings where in some cases second-, third- and fourth-generation descendants have sought out activities that would bring them together, to interact and move toward some rapprochement in the here and now and for the future. Kaslow cites two conferences, one in Budapest in 1994 and a follow-up in Guadalajara, Mexico, in October 1995:

The interchanges about their memories and deeply entrenched feelings were heated, emotional and profound. All involved indicated they had experienced great anguish about coming, and in being present, and that during the session they felt some relief and gained some understanding of the 'other'. They urged continuation of this dialogue process.

South Africa has a history of racial and cultural tensions, which impact on every member of society. From the diary of my great, great maternal grandfather (fifth generation), who was an 1820 Settler and farmed along the Fish River, comes a vivid description of the so-called 'Kaffir Wars' in the 1830s. He writes about how he mistrusted the Xhosa people after raids and killings by them. Says his biographer, J Collet:

While the underlying cause of conflict was possession of the land, the stock that grazed it were the sharp point of conflict. For the settler, cattle meant milk, meat, transport and wealth; for the tribesmen cattle were not only these but the basis of their culture; without cattle no man could even get a wife.[7]

At the turn of the century the Anglo-Boer South African War brought further rifts between all the language and race groupings in the country. And one cannot ignore the impact of the violence of the First and Second World Wars, experienced by soldiers of all races from South Africa. This was followed within a few years by the freedom struggle against apartheid. Can we afford to wait any longer for an attempt at reconciliation?

Politics is a system of organising control of power. Our political parties have inspired, instigated and provided the backing, infrastructure and weapons for violence. As a society we must face this ongoing violence and deal with it today, as it has been presented in the TRC hearings. The old issues remain 'land and cattle' (possession and redistribution of wealth), only now in more subtle, sophisticated and complex forms (including the ballot box).

I would like to suggest that all the political parties be given the opportunity, following the TRC hearings and granting of amnesty, to demonstrate their accountability by:

- providing funding for the debriefing of their members who have received amnesty;
- ensuring that all their members who have been perpetrators are notified and encouraged to attend counselling.

There are existing counselling services offered by health centres and NGOs; these could be extended, but they would need additional funding.

Once the debriefing groundwork has been done, perhaps our dream – Humphrey Gqomfa's and now my own – of having co-counselling at nationwide conferences for survivors and perpetrators could be realised. We cannot afford to wait for the second-, third- and fourth-generation descendants of this traumatic and ongoing violence. We must take the initiative in attempting to understand the 'other' and so start the process of reconciliation and healing in our broken land.

Reparation delayed is healing retarded

WENDY ORR

The Promotion of National Unity and Reconciliation Act, No. 34 of 1995 (the Act) mandates the Truth and Reconciliation Commission (TRC) to 'promote national unity and reconciliation ... by ... restoring the human and civil dignity of ... victims ... by recommending reparation measures in respect of them;'[1] Reparation is defined as including 'any form of compensation, *ex gratia* payment, restitution, rehabilitation or recognition;'[2] The functions of the Commission pertaining to reparation are to 'make recommendations to the President with regard to:

- the policy that should be followed or measures which should be taken with regard to the granting of reparation to victims or the taking of other measures aimed at rehabilitating and restoring the human and civil dignity of victims;
- measures that should be taken to grant urgent interim reparation to victims.'[3]

Of note is that the Act does not at any stage refer to the 'healing' of victims. The drafters chose instead to use the term 'restoration of human and civil dignity' and the rather odd 'rehabilitation'. The TRC Committee responsible for drafting the policy of reparation was *not* called the 'Reparation and

Healing Committee' but the Reparation and Rehabilitation Committee (RRC). Conventionally, rehabilitation is used to refer to recovery or restoration of normal functioning (or as close to normal as possible) after a physical injury, or when referring to the behavioural 'rehabilitation' of, for example, substance abusers or criminals. (Perhaps it would have been more appropriate to use the word 'rehabilitation' in association with perpetrators? One may also ask why the healing and/or rehabilitation of perpetrators has been completely ignored in the Act and hardly addressed by the TRC.)

The concept of healing

Healing is a much more encompassing term than rehabilitation; it can be interpreted within a number of paradigms – physical, spiritual and psychological. Yet the aim of reparation, according to the Act, is *not* to achieve healing but to restore dignity. These are not synonymous.

How, then, has the concept of healing come to be so closely identified with the work of the TRC? Without a doubt, TRC members developed their own discourse and language, which was not strictly dictated by the legalistic parameters of the Act, and the concept of healing was part of this discourse. Nevertheless, healing was interpreted within different approaches and models.

Probably the best known of these is the spiritual or religious paradigm espoused by the Chairperson, Archbishop Tutu. Is spiritual healing a function of reparation? Surely not?

The most obvious interpretation of healing is according to a medical model – you are injured, you are healed; you have a wound that heals. Not many victims required this type of healing. Injuries sustained as a result of violation had 'healed' years ago. Certainly there were ongoing physical consequences, but these required rehabilitation or treatment; they could not be 'healed' in the strictly organic sense. It is probably within this strictly medical model that the Act's objective of reparation as rehabilitation can be most easily fitted. The concept of psychological healing became deeply entrenched in the work of the TRC and it also became one of our defined objectives of reparation.

We also understood healing as a process rather than an event. Various interventions facilitated by the TRC, such as hearings, truth revelation, concrete reparation, counselling and letters of thanks and acknowledgement could be part of that process, but no one intervention can achieve healing. The TRC could not deliver 'healing', just as it could not deliver 'reconciliation'. Reparation should facilitate healing, but except perhaps for healing according to a strictly physiological or medical model, reparation alone cannot heal. The fact that the TRC was placed in the context of other restorative measures, such as the Land Commission, social reforms and changes in health-care provisions, emphasises the fact that our reparation measures should be seen as part of a much broader healing process.

Shaping our understanding of reparation

Faced with these various paradigms and differing discourses, one of the first tasks of the RRC was to attempt to clarify how the major role players, particularly government, victims and the RRC itself, understood and interpreted reparation. This, predictably, presented us with one of our first major dilemmas – the huge gap between the expectations of victims and the understanding of reparation by Government and its capacity (and even willingness) to deliver. Attempting to clarify how Government and/or Parliament understood reparation was not easy. Obviously, no one wanted to commit to anything beyond what was already in the Act. Ultimately, the RRC had to fall back on its own working definition and use that as the starting point for negotiation of the policy with Government.

To define and shape our own understanding of reparation, the RRC turned to international literature and experience and undertook a national consultative process. Our initial working definition of reparation was dubbed 'the five Rs': redress, restitution, rehabilitation, restoration of dignity and reassurance of non-recurrence.

Internationally, reparation has been implemented on a fairly limited scale in various situations – following the Chilean Truth Commission, for the Second World War Japanese-American internees and for the Japanese 'comfort women' imprisoned by the Imperial Army – and has been primarily in the form of monetary 'compensation'.

This has initiated much debate, interestingly more from observers and commentators than from victims themselves. Those who are not victims seem to have more trouble accepting money as a form of reparation than the victims do. Does this speak to some need within ourselves to make atonement beyond the seemingly impersonal payment? Symbolic reparation is essential, whether it be an apology, a monument, a day of remembrance or some other culturally appropriate intervention, but the importance of symbolism does not minimise the need for concrete and financial reparation measures.

Much has been made, both in South Africa and internationally, of the apparently modest requests for reparation made by testifiers at TRC public hearings. This has been overstated. Analysis of TRC data shows that when deponents are making a statement in private, they most commonly ask for money or compensation. This is not to say that their requests are extravagant or unreasonable, but it does point to the fact that, at a public hearing, witnesses perhaps feel embarrassed to ask for money or are intimidated by being in the spotlight. The fact that very modest requests for largely symbolic measures were made in public should not mask the reality that impoverished victims also asked for and need money. It is impossible to meet the mandate of restoring human and civil dignity when dignity is undermined by the daily struggle to survive.

Canvassing the opinion and expectations of victims proved to be a risky, but unavoidable, enterprise. We simply could not formulate a policy without asking victims what they needed. But by asking deponents, in an open-ended fashion, what their needs were, we allowed expectations to run riot, without realistic containment. Nevertheless, the analysis of victims' requests, as recorded in the 'Victim Statement', was immensely useful to the RRC in preparing policy recommendations. The most common requests were for money and/or compensation. In addition, many victims asked for services that money can purchase, such as housing, education and health care. The second most common request, however, was for 'investigation' of the violation – in other words, a request for the truth.

The RRC as an implementer, not a proposer

The TRC's daily interaction with victims soon made us acutely aware of the limitations that the Act placed on us in terms of the provision of reparation. We had no authority, infrastructure or resources to assist victims in any way. Our strictly defined mandate was to draft policy recommendations to be presented to the President. We were not implementors – we were proposers. But victims found it (understandably) difficult to make this differentiation. To victims, the TRC was the organisation taking statements, inviting victims to hearings, investigating violations. They thus assumed that the TRC should, could and would provide the requested assistance or intervention.

Our lack of capacity to provide assistance became increasingly difficult to explain. Delays in the process of policy adoption and implementation meant that victims saw no tangible sign of – or even government commitment to – reparation for months or even years after an individual had made a statement or testified at a hearing. The final insult was the fact that perpetrators granted amnesty walked free as soon as the favourable finding was made by the Amnesty Committee – literally free if they had been imprisoned and figuratively free from criminal and civil prosecution if they had not. This apparent disparity in the treatment afforded perpetrators and victims was extremely damaging and was completely contrary to the stated aim of 'restoring human and civil dignity' of victims. This delay in delivery of reparation, particularly contrasted with the 'immediate delivery' of amnesty, was perhaps the most distressing issue for victims and organisations representing victims. It was as distressing for the RRC and our staff. One of our staff members said in despair: 'I've run out of stories to tell victims about why they have not received reparation – I don't know what to tell them anymore.' Our reparation policy proposals, imperfect as they were, would probably have been an acceptable compromise if victims had experienced the benefit of reparation with as little delay as possible.

Unable to do anything to address these constraints, although we did dream of amendments to the Act, the RRC felt compelled to deliver policy recommendations to the TRC, for adoption and presentation to the President, as quickly as possible. We believed – naïvely, it has transpired – that the sooner we presented policy proposals, the sooner some sort of reparation would be delivered. The Reparation and Rehabilitation Policy, as contained in the TRC's Report, does little to reflect the tough debate, conflicting opinions, occasional sense of despair and constant compromise experienced in and by the Committee.

The 'closed list' approach

We had to confront the unavoidable fact that only a very small percentage of the 'victims of apartheid' would benefit from individual reparation. The Act's definition of a victim immediately excluded millions of South Africans who, while they may not have suffered a gross violation of human rights in terms of the Act, nevertheless suffered the daily violation of living under apartheid. Our first painful step was thus to limit reparation recipients to those who had been found to have suffered a gross violation of human rights, as defined in the Act. The next logical, but difficult, step was to recommend a 'closed list' approach. This meant that anyone whose name had not been mentioned in a Victim Statement by the time the Human Rights Violations Committee closed the statement-taking process on 15 December 1997, would not be eligible for consideration as a victim, and thus would not receive reparation. This further limited the pool of recipients and meant that thousands of people who might indeed have met the stipulations of the Act would not be able to access reparation because they had not accessed the TRC.

This last matter was the subject of ongoing debate within the RRC and the TRC. We all knew that, practically, we could not present Government with an open-ended list of victims and thus a limitless reparation bill. However, we agonised over whether the TRC had indeed made every conceivable effort to reach as many victims as possible to enable them to make statements. The 'closed list' recommendation was finally and reluctantly accepted, many months after it had first been tabled. This issue illustrates the difficult role that the RRC had to play of being intermediary between victims and Government. We had to 'package' victims', needs and expectations in a way that was practically implementable by and acceptable to government, but our role was primarily to be victim advocates. The two roles were often in conflict.

Money versus services

This was another area of ongoing debate. Should reparation take the form of a 'service package' tailored to the expressed needs of the recipient, such as a particular combination of health care, tertiary education and counselling, or housing, schooling and a new wheelchair? This seemed attractive. Government, supposedly, already provided these services and reparation recipients could simply be slotted in where appropriate. This would surely be more appealing to Government than being presented with a huge bill of x rand per victim. Money also seemed a terribly impersonal way of acknowledging a violation; would victims want to be so crassly 'bought off'? Finally, there is no ready formula for establishing the monetary value of suffering.

Closer inspection revealed massive problems with the service approach. Services are not without cost, and we could not expect Government to approve free or low-cost services to victims without an estimate as to what the actual cost would be. Some sort of financial limit would have to be put on the cost of the package per recipient, which would, inevitably, mean that many (if not most) recipients would not receive everything that they felt they needed. There are huge disparities in the provision of services between rural and urban areas and from one province to another. Reparation recipients in poorly resourced areas would thus be prejudiced and would not receive equal reparation to those, for example, in a large urban area. The mere process of needs' assessment costs money. How would the practical process of preparing a suitable 'package' for each and every victim (and his/her dependents) be operationalised? Needs change. A recipient who wants assistance with funding of tertiary education today may receive a bursary from another source tomorrow and may then see counselling as a significant need.

How to determine 'need'?

These confounding factors in the implementation of a service approach to individual reparation finally convinced us that we had to investigate a straightforward financial approach, or what came to be called 'the individual reparation grant'. After consultation with an economist, we proposed that each individual who had been found by the HRVC to be a victim be given an annual cash grant for six years.

This became the topic of sometimes acrimonious debate within the TRC. Objections voiced included, for example, that victims might not spend their money responsibly. What about the danger of people wasting their money on luxuries? How could we ensure that the money would be used appropriately (that is, how *we* thought it should be spent)? Unfortunately, the patronising tone of the debate tended to feed into pre-existing racial tensions. What seemed to be happening was that white 'beneficiaries' of apartheid were resisting financial reparation for black 'victims' of apartheid. The stance of the RRC was that, while we obviously hoped that the money would be used to access services, it was ultimately the choice of the individual to use the money as he/she saw fit. Not everyone agreed with us.

Another issue around monetary reparation was whether the amount given should be differentiated according to 'severity/extent of need' and/or 'present financial status'. In other words, if someone had suffered/was suffering more as a result of the violation, should they not receive more money, and should 'poor' people receive the same amount as 'wealthy' people'? Of course, one's immediate response is that the money should go to those who need it most. But how does one determine need?

A true story will illustrate. At the HRV hearing held in Athlone, Cape Town, we heard testimony from two young men. They were almost the same age (late twenties) and came from similar socio-economic circumstances. They had both been shot by police (in different incidents) when they were in their late teens. One (let's call him Mandla) had been shot in the eye and had lost his eye as a result, but the remaining eye had reasonably good vision. The other (alias Thabo) had been shot in the head; the part of his brain responsible for vision had been damaged and he was completely blind. On the basis of these facts and the impartial evidence of the severity of the injury and the consequences thereof, it would seem obvious that Thabo had been more severely injured, had suffered more serious consequences and should receive more money. But a closer examination of the situation revealed that an assessment of need based simply on type of and consequence of injury can be grossly misleading.

Thabo was upbeat, confident and self-sufficient. He had a job with Telkom, could support himself, had a girlfriend (who came to the hearing with him) and could not identify any real needs for himself. Mandla was depressed and weepy, he had no job, depended on his mother, lamented the fact that he could no longer play soccer and that women were not interested in him because of his disability. Thus, on a closer examination of the situation, Mandla should get more money. Does this mean, however, that we penalise Thabo for coping – that we encourage dependency? In addition, while it was possible in the cases of Thabo and Mandla, because they came to a hearing, to do an (admittedly still superficial) assessment of needs and circumstances beyond simply accepting the bland facts of the nature of the injuries, how could this be done for more than 20 000 victims?

Thus, for practical and moral reasons, we recommended that victims receive the same amount of money, regardless of 'degree of suffering' (whatever that might mean). Again, this was the subject of debate within the Commission. It was interesting that many Commissioners perceived physical disability resulting from the violation as more 'deserving' of reparation than emotional and psychological dysfunction. Their stance was, for instance, that someone who had lost a leg should receive more money than someone unable to work because of Post Traumatic Stress Disorder. That old prejudices and misconceptions about psychological disability were still so entrenched was disappointing, but perhaps not surprising.

Practical and moral arguments also swayed our opinion about the second proposed basis for differentiation. Should 'poor' people receive more money? Morally, we felt that, if reparation was an acknowledgement of the fact of the violation, anyone who had been violated should receive the same amount. From a practical point of view, discussions with those involved in means testing in other environments – such as hospitals and universities – convinced us that means testing was difficult to design, costly to implement and tedious to monitor. Most of the people who came to the TRC are poor. Implementing a method of excluding those few who were not poor would not be cost effective. Finally, the fact that reparation would only be given on application meant that the conspicuously well-off could exclude themselves by not applying.

We proposed that the amount of money given should constitute an amount to acknowledge the suffering caused by the violation, an amount to enable access to services and an amount to subsidise daily living costs. The only differentiation recommended was that people living in rural areas should receive a greater amount to enable access to services, and that family size would influence the amount given to subsidise living costs. The amount we recommended was based on the median annual income household income for a family of five in South Africa in 1997.

In retrospect

The way in which we approached these issues has been outlined in some detail, because the RRC has been criticised (even from within the Commission) for its failure to differentiate according to income or degree of suffering, for not deciding on the service package route and for apparently arbitrary decisions about amounts.

The final policy document does not reflect the debates and the basis for many of our decisions. One of the reasons that the final policy was so long in formulation was precisely because we felt compelled to explore all these options and to take policy decisions that were as fully informed and widely consulted as possible. It is important to note that, in addition to the individual reparation grant, we did make a number of recommendations relevant to service provision, community reparation and broader symbolic reparation.

Looking at the process in retrospect, my sense is that one of our failures was our inability to deliver some form of reparation or supportive intervention almost immediately. The fact that perpetrators felt the benefit of a positive amnesty decision at once, while victims have had to wait years for the token amount allowed by the urgent reparation regulations (and will have to wait even longer for whatever final reparation is actually delivered) has not facilitated healing. I feel very strongly that the TRC (rather than Government) should have had the capacity to implement urgent interim reparation much more expeditiously. Provision should have been made for the preparation of an approach to urgent reparation before the first victim statements were taken. The concept of urgent reparation became a complete farce when its delivery only started shortly before the end of the TRC in October 1998.

Statements made by President Mandela at the opening of Parliament in 1999 indicated that individual, financial reparation was unlikely and that the focus would be on symbolic reparation. This caused an outcry of anger and disappointment from victims. In the parliamentary debate on the TRC Report on 25 February 1999, statements were more ambiguous. President Mandela said that the TRC's reparation recommendations were 'broadly acceptable' and that 'to the extent that resources allow' individual reparation grants should continue to be made to identified surviving families and victims. He also said, however, that reparation cannot be 'proportional' – only symbolic. It seems that, what the one hand is conceding, the other is denying.

The then Deputy President, Thabo Mbeki, said that reparation should be in the form of redistribution, reconstruction and development, but also stated that individual reparation in the form of cash and services should be considered. He emphasised, as did the then Minister of Justice, Dullah Omar, that 'no fighter for liberation ever engaged in the struggle for personal gain' – and that the 'only reward' sought was 'freedom'. Minister Omar went further to say that Government must address the plight of victims 'without diminishing the struggle by ascribing monetary value to it'. He suggested consideration of a special pension rather than 'large' monetary grants.

A few final points

These are all important considerations, but a number of points should be made in response.

Firstly, not all victims were conscious 'freedom fighters'; some victims were not involved in any way with the liberation struggle. I would even go so far as to say that the majority of victims had not decided consciously that they were willing to risk life and limb for the struggle. Many were bystanders, caught in the crossfire or the bomb explosions; civilians trapped by township violence; some families were not even aware that children or spouses were active in the struggle; many who were detained and tortured, for example, were politically active and involved, but not willingly 'fighters'. It is not unreasonable to suppose that many who did die may not have wanted financial reward for themselves, but would have wanted their families to be taken care of.

Secondly, by providing special pensions for members of the liberation armies, Government has already taken the step of 'rewarding' or recompensing those who fought for freedom. The implementation of the special pensions bill was a significant factor influencing the RRC's decision to recommend individual financial reparation. We believed that Government had set a precedent with this legislation, but one that excluded thousands of people who may not have been formal members of a liberation movement or who were excluded by the stipulations of the bill, for example that a recipient had to be 35 or older in 1996.

Thirdly, the fact that individual reparation will only be provided on application means that those who do not want a financial reward for being part of the struggle can exclude themselves if they so wish. What is important is that the victim has control over this choice, rather than simply having to accept Government's decision on the matter. In fact, many of those who fought for freedom did not come to the TRC precisely because they chose not to be defined as 'victims' and did not want reparation.

Finally, the RRC did consider very seriously the option of a type of 'special pension', but chose not to go this route because it seemed that it would, ultimately, be more costly than a limited number of payments. A pension implies a regular payment until the death of the recipient. As many victims and survivors are still relatively young, this could amount to decades of payments. We were also discouraged by the fraud and massive administrative problems presently experienced within the pension system. If administrative problems can be overcome and if Government can afford pensions for victims, I doubt there would be much objection to this option, providing, of course, that the pension was a reasonable one.

Will the TRC's Reparation Policy proposals contribute to healing? I believe very strongly that they *can*, but much will depend on whether and how much they are diluted during adoption by Parliament and how speedily reparation is delivered. The TRC can no longer effectively lobby for the adoption and implementation of reparation policy. Pressure will have to come from civil society, nongovernmental organisations and human rights institutions. Reparation delayed will mean healing retarded, and perhaps a deepening perception of justice denied.

Insufficient healing and reparation

NOMFUNDO WALAZA

If we are to accept that at the core of the Truth and Reconciliation Commission's (TRC) formation was a national gain (a political settlement and avoidance of bloodshed), then we have to face the unfortunate reality of a conflict between the interests of victims and survivors on the one hand and those of the nation as a whole on the other.

The post-apartheid government established the TRC to uncover 'gross violations of human rights' committed with political motives between 1 March 1960 and May 1994. The Commission was mandated to promote national unity and reconciliation. This meant establishing as complete a picture of human rights abuses as possible; making known the fate of victims; restoring the dignity of survivors by allowing them to relate their experience of oppression; giving amnesty to those who make full disclosure of their acts; and making reparations.

Archbishop Desmond Tutu, in the many publications issued by the TRC while in operation, repeatedly thanked those who told their stories to ensure that the nation would know what happened in the past, so that wounds might be healed, so that hurts might be forgiven and so that reconciliation would follow. He acknowledged that victims had paid a heavy price for freedom and for the acquisition of a peaceful transition. He never fully explained how these noble ideals of healing, forgiveness and reconciliation could be translated into achievable realities.

There are aspects of the South African Truth Commission that attracted international attention, not least the notion of reconciliation, even though there was no clear mechanism proposed whereby this could be achieved. Knowing some of the problems incurred by the truth commissions that preceded ours, we ought to have better anticipated the problems awaiting us.

Some have argued that reconciliation was made unattainable largely because there were no mechanisms located in communities to facilitate the process. The best attempt to provide such a mechanism was the establishment of the victim-offender mediation process. This process was often undermined by the 'half-truths' given by some perpetrators. Others, including the former State President PW Botha, refused to participate in the process at all. One can neither legislate nor proclaim reconciliation from above.[1]

In hindsight, we know that there were aspects of the TRC that angered, frustrated and harmed victims. The inherently conflicting and sometimes contradictory functions of the TRC process impacted negatively on the achievement of its aims and objectives. It is, of course, important that all of us who participate in this fragile and growing democracy count our gains in the same breath that we acknowledge our losses. In other words, it is important to acknowledge the gains that were made by the TRC process without losing sight of the inherent difficulties that undermine any attempt to realise the objectives of the Commission.

The notion of healing

The process of the TRC was geared towards the promotion of national healing. This process should have started with the healing of individuals. The work of the Trauma Centre for Survivors of Violence and Torture with the deponents of the TRC has taught us that it is important that individuals be assisted with their pain. This can have ripple effects on those around them – their families, communities and the nation as a whole. Helping survivors of violence has also taught us that in order for healing to have lasting effects, most of it has to start within. Part of the healing of an individual entails letting go of anger and resentment; this can be extremely difficult where there is no proper acknowledgement of the pain and suffering by those around them.

In this respect, one cannot over-emphasise the importance of the individual being liberated from the clutches of their perpetrators – and from the arms of the state whose purpose was to destroy them. It is equally important for victims to be freed from the poverty that was part of their oppression. Unfortunately, the TRC failed to set up mechanisms to enable this to happen.

NGOs mainly shouldered the work of sustaining deponents during the time of the Commission with sometimes little or no support from the TRC.

Although there was ample evidence to support the crucial role to be played by mental health professionals and organisations in providing services, proposals made to the Commission at its inception were received with a degree of ambivalence; Commissioners cited a lack of funding, time constraints and lack of resources. Most Commissioners further argued that providing mental health services was not part of the enabling Act and therefore outside their mandate. NGOs were, in turn, simply not able to reach as many deponents as they would have liked, mainly because of lack of skills and financial constraints. During a conference held at the Centre for the Study of Violence and Reconciliation in April of 1998, Professor Mamdani asked how healing could happen without addressing problems of forced removals, pass laws, racialised poverty and racialised wealth.[2] One wonders what would have happened if the Commissioners simply refused to operate within the limitations of the Act that ignored the suffering of many South Africans, whose daily pain fell outside of the Commission's mandate?

Some gains in the healing process

- The TRC has broken the deathly silence, at least in white circles, on the grotesque consequences of the apartheid system. It is hoped that as a result, human rights abuses will never happen again.
- For the first time the pain of victims and survivors was nationally acknowledged. This counteracted the propaganda that had prevailed before. No one will ever again be able to say that the atrocities of the past did not happen. The problem is, of course, that some of the people identified as 'beneficiaries' of the apartheid regime – those who were complicit to its policies and who did not stand up to oppose its machinery – refused to watch as the stories unfolded before their eyes. They claimed that to watch was too painful, perhaps because the process of hearing the truth for the first time threatened their 'comfort zones'.
- The process was designed to assist victims and perpetrators to break with the past. This aided the healing process. Some victims testified that by talking of what happened to them and their loved ones, they could better face the future with a level of dignity.

There are additional gains that could be identified. In time both further losses and gains, not evident at present, will no doubt become evident. Hopefully, at that point the beneficiaries, victims and perpetrators will all with the benefit of distance have a clearer idea of their responsibility. Bluntly stated, one would hope that those who benefited and continue to reap the fruit of the policies of the previous government will assume a greater responsibility in order to help redress the imbalances and thereby further the aims of reconciliation.

In order to truly evaluate the contribution of the TRC, however, it is necessary to ascertain whether truth-telling ostensibly to advance reconciliation is sufficient to redress the plight of individual victims/survivors and their families who suffered. Judith Herman captures the ambiguity of truth-telling:

> Telling the truth about terrible events [is a] prerequisite both for the restoration of social order and for the healing of individuals victims – when the truth is finally recognised, survivors can begin their recovery. But far too often secrecy prevails and the story of the traumatic event surfaces not as a verbal narrative but as symptom.[3]

Thoughtful words. The TRC process failed adequately to address the insights contained in Herman's words. To have separated truth and secrecy could have aided the process of healing for many survivors and victims. In addition, dire social circumstances make it difficult for individuals to deal with traumas on an ongoing basis. Impoverished living conditions and lack of available ways to escape these, of course, further threaten the process of their healing. This is what makes the need for reparation important.

Reparations

The granting of amnesty was an integral part of the work of the TRC. It was largely to the benefit of perpetrators. Reparation and rehabilitation ought to have been viewed as more important – to the extent that they benefit victims. Although the TRC highlighted reparation policy as being central in promoting national unity, there has been minimal delivery in this regard. This slow delivery has resulted in some victims questioning whether it will happen at all. The Commission was, of course, dependent on the government to deliver reparations. This non-delivery could, and indeed should, have been challenged more aggressively by the TRC – whose task it was to facilitate healing.

Of course there are a number of concerns about reparation, which need to be addressed. I mention only a few.

Immediate reparations

Proper implementation of this much-needed policy could have sent a powerful message that the nation cared. Attempting to restore the dignity of victims during the process rather than afterwards could have boosted the morale of the victims and added to the positive gains achieved by the TRC. The

Commission would have done well to have challenged the state to deliver reparations as part of the ongoing TRC process.

Individual financial reparations

Victims were asked to sacrifice justice in return for reparations. The fact that the Government now appears to be turning away from individual reparations in favour of community and symbolic forms of reparations is a betrayal of the promises made to victims.[4] They are being sidelined and unacknowledged by the very process that was designed to help them. Some feel their stories have been 'used' by the TRC to provide 'as complete a picture as possible' of the past, without their essential needs having been met. The Trauma Centre, the Centre for the Study of Violence and Reconciliation, the KwaZulu-Natal Project for Survivors of Violence, Khulumani and other NGOs have lobbied the Government on behalf of victims.[5] The indication so far is that while the Government has not totally ruled out the possibility of individual reparation, financial reasons are likely to be advanced as the reason for no delivery. The TRC's failure to involve NGOs and community groups in the conceptualisation and promotion of individual reparations has clearly weakened its influence in persuading government to respond positively.

Symbolic reparations

Victims have begun to ask about the cost effectiveness of building memorials when they are struggling to put food on the table. Proper consultation with communities is needed in this regard. It is also unlikely that the poor will accept these as an alternative to direct assistance.

Community reparations

Limited resources and the lack of individual skills are likely also to hamper the delivery of community reparations. The Government should make sure that victims and survivor's needs are not subsumed within the wider process of redress. This would undermine the process of recognition that is essential for the healing of victims. The TRC has made some important gains in providing recognition to victims. It would be a pity if this is not reinforced by Government.

Institutionalised reforms

The TRC has recommended institutional and legislative reforms and good governance to ensure accountability and the prevention of abuse. These are urgently needed to assist victims – yet here too they should not be subsumed into general legislative and other forms of reparation. The point has been made – recognition is important.

Conclusions and recommendations

Although many South Africans and the international community have applauded the TRC gains, it needs to be pointed out that healing and adequate reparation can still emerge as its death knell. Many providers of healing viewed the Commission as having leaned towards legalistic rather than therapeutic concerns. This imbalance is likely to have far-reaching implications.

For some of us, the handing over of the *TRC Report* to the President is seen, in addition to all else, as 'passing the buck'. There is unfinished business that the Commission has failed to address. It has not gone unnoticed that many Commissioners 'disappeared into thin air' as soon as the Report was handed to the President – some even before then. The outstanding work can, of course, still be done – through the remaining structures of the Commission and/or through Commissioners working voluntarily with NGOs.

There are also fears that government officials do not feel passionately enough about victims. There are many demands being made on Government. Where do the needs of victims feature in this hierarchy of demands? There is a widespread concern among victims and organisations whose task it is to support them that there could be yet further delays or a failure to deliver on recommendations made by the Commission regarding reparations. It is the task of the whole nation to ensure that this does not happen.

Creative ways need to be found to involve victims, survivors, their families and communities in the implementation of reparation policy – whether at the level of financial payment or symbolic reparation. It is imperative that payments do not polarise those who receive them from those who do not. The involvement of the communities could greatly assist here. The involvement of the community in the provision of services and building of monuments is also important. This could ensure community support and minimise vandalism. It must, however, be stressed that this process must go hand in hand with the alleviation of poverty. 'Unless economic justice is the first item on the agenda with all that this means, unless health, homes, water, electricity and, most importantly, jobs become part of the quest for reconciliation, we will remain the very divided society we are.'[6]

Despite my concerns, I believe that were it not for the hard and painful process of the TRC, South Africa would not be where it is today. I would like my comments to be understood in the context of my role as a therapist/healer. They must be understood as stemming from the pain and suffering I saw in the eyes of the many victims and survivors who took part in the TRC hearings – and who later came to the Trauma Centre for counselling. I also hope that my comments help in implementing reparation policy in a manner that gives dignity to victims.

Section 4

After the Commission

An opportunity for peace

NJONGONKULU NDUNGANE

South Africa has barely emerged from its baptism of fire. The miracle of transformation, which saw a smooth transition from apartheid to democracy, is a cause for great celebration and thanksgiving. It is a basis for hope. It shows how people can rise above their ideologies and personal agendas to seek the common good.

All the necessary instruments for a sustainable democracy, such as a new Constitution, a Constitutional Court, a Commission for Human Rights, a Public Protector and a Commission for Gender Equality, are in place. We are engaged in a process of nation-building that encompasses major demands for reconciliation, reconstruction and development. This nation-building task involves the precarious and difficult task of striving for long-term economic growth as well as addressing the pent-up needs and expectations of people who have already waited too long for their needs to be met – and who have been obliged to make do with far too little for far too long.

The Truth and Reconciliation Commission (TRC) was one instrument charged by the state to initiate a journey away from a horrendous past to a future characterised by national reconciliation. However, its limited mandate and duration did not allow it to dig deep enough to provide a vision that will make for lasting peace. This, by definition, means there are still substantial issues that need to be resolved.

Poverty and inequality

One of the greatest crises facing South Africa is poverty. Apartheid has left an enormous legacy of economic and social distress. Approximately half the population lives in acute poverty. Many people go hungry, are exposed to disease and are illiterate, unemployed and homeless. And yet poverty is not just about income. It is about the loss of human dignity. It is also about human suffering and the denial of opportunities for advancement. This is particularly telling in a world of huge material resources and dramatic technological achievements.

Redressing the legacy of poverty and inequality is South Africa's most important priority and greatest challenge. Eradicating poverty is essential to the consolidation of our new democracy. It is a precondition for social justice, peace and stability in our land.

The new South African Constitution has created an environment and a mechanism for the full enjoyment of human rights. The Bill of Rights makes provision for traditional civil and political rights, such as the right to equality, human dignity, freedom of association and expression. Our Constitution is unique in its further references to the rights of access to housing, health care, food, water and social security, to an environment that is not harmful, to health and wellbeing and to basic education. These are fundamental rights that must never be viewed as secondary. They are an integral part of human rights applicable to everyone.

South Africa is, at the same time, a society of great disparity between the rich and the poor. The socio-economic gulf – as measured by the GINI coefficient – is second only to that of Brazil. Infant mortality in some rural areas ranks with the worst in Africa. Seven million South Africans live in shacks. There are 12-million people without access to safe drinking water and 21-million without adequate sanitation. The rate of unemployment is over 30%. Yet the general standard of living of white South Africans, despite the economic stagnation of the past 25 years, remains among the highest in the world. This is largely a consequence of racially structured economic and political policies designed to benefit the white minority and to disadvantage the majority of South African citizens.

What is clear to all who will see is that white monopoly of both economic and political power was entrenched early on in our history. Sampie Terreblanche directly addressed this matter in his submission to the Commission. It helps to explain why Nelson Mandela insisted, on the day of his release in February 1990, that 'the white monopoly of political power must be ended'. 'We need a fundamental restructuring of our political and economic systems to address the inequality of apartheid and to create a genuine democratic South Africa,' he said.

The reality is that political liberation has been realised. We now face the enormous challenge of restructuring the economy. The point was well made by Francis Wilson in his keynote address at the National Poverty Summit, in June 1998:

> *What happened in 1994 was that the scaffolding of apartheid was destroyed, but not the pillars. The pillars of land distribution remain. The pillars of inequality remain. What we have changed is the scaffolding that we created. We need to knock down those old structures and start recreating.*[1]

In the words of the *TRC Report*:

> *The huge and widening gap between the rich and poor is a disturbing legacy of the past, which has not been reduced by the democratic process. It is morally reprehensible, politically dangerous and economically unsound to allow this to continue. Business has a particularly significant role to play in this regard.*[2]

Drinking from a theological well

St Bernard of Clairvaux, an 11th-century monk, observed that everyone has to drink from his or her own wells. Gustavo Gutierrez uses this axiom to describe the spiritual journey of Latin American Christians: 'From what wells can the poor of Latin America drink?'[3] The subterranean streams that feed into the moral and cultural wells that sustain the hopes and fire the visions of the people of South Africa are many. I offer comment on one such well – that of the Judeo-Christian tradition. It provides spiritual resources that make for hope among many Christians. Perhaps inevitably it is a theological resource that inspires the poor rather than the rich. And yet it has a message for the rich as well. It reminds them of their duty to be stewards of God's resources. Not least, it reminds them of God's special concern for the poor and what it means to be a part of Gods' total scheme for the redemption of the entire earth.

In examining the issue of equity, we recall that the world's major religions, which influence our moral behaviour, constantly remind us of the worth of human beings. Thus, from whichever well we may drink, there is a common recognition that human beings are made in God's image. We are 'God-like' – we have the power to govern the earth, but our power is *derived power*. We are required to exercise it on the basis of ethical and moral stewardship. This involves the need to show care, a willingness to share and a commitment to conservation. The world's major religions, at the same time, hold that God is not only the *creator* – he is also the *author* of life. As *creator* he provides the resources of the earth for the wellbeing of the entire created order, while as *author* he requires that we use these resources in a manner that reflects his generosity and caring. He requires that we fit into his total scheme of things – into his script. It is a script that shows respect for all people. It is one that favours no one person over another. It suggests that to the extent that we honour this mandate, we enhance the possibility of living in peace and harmony with one another. To the extent that we seek to lord it over one another, to that extent do we generate conflict. The briefest reflection on the apartheid years suggests this teaching is not too far off the mark.

The fact that we are all created in God's image and we all have a role to play in his script implies two important moral affirmations:

- Each person is of unique and intrinsic worth and dignity. Speaking in a Christmas broadcast in 1944, during the Second World War, Pope Pius XII reminded the world that 'the dignity of man is the dignity of the image of God.' There is a rabbinical saying that notes: 'Before every human being there walks an angel proclaiming: "Make way, make way for the image of God."' Theologically this means that no one human being can ever discredit or exploit another.

- We are all called to exercise stewardship over the resources of the earth. The scriptures teach: 'Let them have dominion over the fish of the sea and over the birds of the air, and over the cattle and over all the wild animals of the earth' (Gen 1:26). The key word is 'dominion'. It comes from the Latin word *dominium*, which means lordship – yet lordship in the sense of property-ownership. In terms of the culture of the day, the lord had the right to service from his tenants, but he had the duty to see to their wellbeing. Dominion ought to be interpreted as the dominion of God, which is informed by a spirit of love and caring. It implies a duty to protect. The dominion of people over the earth ought never to be understood as a charter for unrestricted exploitation. Our dominion is derived dominion. It is given by God for a specific purpose.

This involves accountability. In the organisation of socio-economic life and the earth's resources, we have a responsibility to promote the welfare of humanity.

The Judeo-Christian religion tells us that 'the world and all that is in it belongs to the Lord; the earth and all who live in it are His' (Ps 24:1).

In the words of UNICEF:

The day will come when the progress of nations will be judged not by their military or economic strength, nor by the splendour of the capital cities and public buildings, but by:

- *the wellbeing of their peoples;*
- *their levels of health, nutrition and education;*

- *their opportunities to earn a fair reward for their labours;*
- *their ability to participate in decisions that affect their lives;*
- *the respect that is shown for their political and civil liberties;*
- *the provision that is made for those who are vulnerable and disadvantaged;*
- *the protection that is afforded to the growing minds and bodies of their children.*

The Jubilee vision

The Jubilee vision is spelt out in Leviticus 25:8ff. Its underlying theme is to bring about a just order in society. 'Consecrate the 50th year and proclaim liberty throughout the land to all its inhabitants. For it is a jubilee and is to be holy for you; eat only what is taken directly from the fields. Do not take advantage of each other, but fear your God.' We see the same strands of wisdom in Deuteronomy, in the first two verses of Chapter 15: 'At the end of every seventh year you are to cancel the debts of those who owe you money. This is how it is to be done. Everyone who has lent money to a fellow Israelite is to cancel the debt; he must not try to collect the money; the Lord himself has declared the debt cancelled.'

The Jubilee vision is one based on the notion that God's gifts to humanity are bountiful and unlimited. The stories of creation in Genesis describe the richness and abundance of life enjoyed by those humans who first peopled the earth. Genesis represents life – in all its splendour and bio-diversity – as the gift of God. It was a land 'flowing with milk and honey'.

While God was glorious in his generosity, he also imposed a law. The law of the Sabbath requires that every seventh day his people had to rest; on that day they had to place limits on their consumption of his gifts and had to stop exploiting the land, their animals and each other. The law of the Sabbath was later extended to include a periodic halt in the exploitation of land – every seven years. These limits were both just and economically and environmentally sound. This teaching (esoteric as it may seem to some) is about how to be human on this fragile earth. God can well be described as the founding member of the Green Party.

The biblical drama goes further: Every seven times seven years (in the 49th year) a different discipline was imposed by the Sabbath law. Again, periodically, in the Jubilee year, the law required creditors to cancel debts; slaves had to be freed by their masters and land that had been taken had to be restored to its rightful owners.

It was this imposition of the Sabbath law, the law of Sabbath economics, which ensured that greed and accumulation did not go too far. It disciplined both lenders and borrowers, instituting a form of economics that restricted the greed of the powerful by placing limits on their power, their riches and their land. It is a form of economics that ensured that the poor were not exploited to the point of destitution and despair. They were periodically given a chance to start again.

The vision of Jubilee – 'the year of the Lord's favour' is a vision that releases the poor from the prison of indebtedness and dependent poverty. But it is also a Jubilee for the powerful. They are given a new vision for the right use of riches. They are required to recognise the true value and dignity of the poor. By being required to recognise the dignity of others they are themselves called to a new level of humanity. This has, of course, to do with a person being a person through other people. The Jubilee message is portrayed in the idiom of the time in which it was written. Its substance has something to offer this 'new' South Africa. It involves *ubuntu* theology.

A time for decision

In his 1999 New Year message, His Holiness Pope John Paul II said that the millennium is a time for decision and a time of hope. He called upon us to become heralds for human dignity. He said that this is the time to put into action mechanisms that would bring about hope to the millions of people who are trapped in the cycle of poverty. As we stand at the cusp of the new millennium we need creative, innovative and imaginative minds to reform the South African economic system so that everyone has everything basic for human life. We need responsible stewardship, linked with equitable sharing of God-given gifts and resources, for the general wellbeing of all. It is a prerequisite for a stable future. We possess the resources and technology. All that is required is the political will and economic commitment. Political liberation must be converted into socio-economic liberation.

As a first step in addressing the plight of the poor we need to:

- build an asset base for the poor, which includes access to land, decent homes and basic human necessities;
- stimulate economic activities through targeted interventions, which include providing subsidies and training programmes for community building;
- design financial safety nets, which include innovative cash transfers to help alleviate need and at the same time stimulate local economic initiatives.

The TRC has made several recommendations regarding the bridging of the gap between the rich and the poor. They deserve careful consideration. There is an equally urgent need to reform macro-economic policy to ensure that it enhances the total quality of human life. Nobel Peace Laureate Professor Amartya Sen has emphasised that the validity of any economic policy should be assessed on the basis of whether it takes into account its impact on people who are on the downside of the economy. He says that it is necessary to bring social deprivation into the domain of public discussion and create systems for social opportunities – such needs cannot be left to market forces.

The market is *not* always right. In many parts of the world, market forces have been shown not to be the panacea that market purists dream of. Time and again, they have caused hardships for the poor. Market forces are unlikely to result in acceptable social outcomes because of their very commitment to promoting the wellbeing of those who already have plenty. Such forces do not have a commitment to overriding even the most despicable political policy or ruling despots. All they do is to exacerbate poverty, exclusion and social conflict. Market forces have no regard for the worth or dignity of people in non-economic, human terms. They proceed, unabated, irrespective of the human condition, often contributing to impoverishment.

Perpetuating the status quo undermines reconciliation, reconstruction and development in the new democratic South Africa. It will make poor people poorer and rich people richer, with the resultant threats to peace, stability and economic growth. We need to create models of hope and trust that will give the poor – who are the vast majority of people in this country – a new chance. We have a responsibility to ensure that all people have the same opportunities to reach their full potential.

This requires a new *kairos*. It is decision time. We stand on the threshold of the next thousand years in the history of humankind. The first Christians stood on the threshold of the first millennium in a state of hopelessness after the crucifixion of Christ. But God raised Christ from the dead. This is the hope that sustains us. The opportunity to start anew is the gracious offer of God. We need to seize the moment to address the economic challenges that face this nation. If we fail to alleviate poverty we will have missed a wonderful opportunity to create peace.

Dealing with systematic economic injustice

SAMPIE TERREBLANCHE

The finding of the Truth and Reconciliation Commission (TRC) that 'business was central to the economy that *sustained* the South African state during the apartheid years'[1] should not be allowed to give the impression that business was *neutral* towards apartheid and sustained the government only indirectly through its 'normal' business activities. The slogan applicable to sport during the apartheid years – 'there can be no normal sport in an abnormal society' – was equally applicable to business. There could not have been 'normal' business while the apartheid system (or racial capitalism) was in place.

Findings on business

The TRC grants the point that 'certain businesses, especially the mining industry, were involved in helping to *design* and implement apartheid policies'.[2] This understates the situation. There can be no doubt that the apartheid system (or, more correctly, the system of racial capitalism) was deliberately constructed in a very close *collaboration* (conspiracy?) between (white) business and (white) politicians to create a (mainly African) labour repressive system on behalf of white business. This was originally mainly in the mining and agricultural sectors.

The TRC acknowledges that 'the mining industry ... benefited from migratory labour and the payment of low wages to black employees'.[3] The gold-mining industry did indeed benefit enormously from migrant labour, the compound system, the extraordinary low wages and the relatively poor safety and health conditions in the gold mines. The wages paid by Anglo-American and the other gold-mining corporations in 1972 were in real terms more or less 15% lower than the level of 1911, in spite of the fact that the gold price increased on several occasions.[4] The agricultural sector – especially the maize farmers – benefited perhaps as much (if not more) from paying extraordinary low wages to farm workers whose mobility (and bargaining power) were seriously constrained by the strict application of the pass laws.

The findings of the Commission that 'business failed in the hearings to take responsibility for its involvement in state-security initiatives specifically designed to sustain apartheid rule [or white supremacy]'[5] touched on a very important matter. This is such a serious matter that it is a great pity – or even deplorable – that the Commission did not explore it in much greater detail. Some of the most respected corporations – under the leadership of a managerial elite with high public esteem – were hand in glove with Armscor during the 1980s, when it was one of the few moving concerns. The corporations that were in collaboration with Armscor were in effect an integral part of the total strategy and they made huge profits by being part of the resistance against the struggle.

The Commission furthermore stated that 'the white agricultural industry benefited from its privileged access to land and that it failed to provide adequate facilities and services for employees and their dependents'.[6] The agricultural sector was – together with the gold-mining industry – the sector that benefited quite substantially from *systemic* exploitation during the first three quarters of the century. While the exploitative activities of the gold-mining industry were supported by the migrant labour and the compound systems, the agricultural sector (again, especially the maize farmers) was supported by the strict application of pass laws and the very generous subsidies paid to farmers. The Commission is in fact mistaken to think that the agricultural sector benefited mainly from its privileged access to land. Although access to land was important, its really privileged position was based on its access to very cheap and bounded black labour. The fact that the South African Agricultural Union was not prepared to testify before the Commission should have been deplored in the strongest terms possible.

The tentative and restrained nature of the findings of the TRC on business must be ascribed to its unwillingness or unpreparedness to accept the argument that business had been (for at least the first three quarters of the

266

century) an *integral* part of the system of racial capitalism, and that it was in this capacity guilty of *systemic exploitation*. I return to this argument.

Recommendations on business

In its recommendations on business, the TRC makes an appeal to business to play a *voluntary* role in compensating black Africans for the disadvantages of apartheid. The TRC says 'that business could and should play an enormously creative role in the development of new reconstruction and development programmes'.[7] From a moral point of view these kind of requests have a positive ring to them. What should be remembered, however, is that the exploitation of blacks did not happen voluntarily. It was compulsory and *systemic*. It was based on an economic and political system embedded in a network of compulsory leg-islation and justified by ideologies that were propagated as self-evident truths. To expect that business will be prepared to compensate the blacks *voluntarily – and to the necessary degree –* for the injustices committed towards the majority of them for almost a century is not only too idealistic but also rather naïve. To give businesses the opportunity to pay off their 'apartheid debt' through 'charity' will boil down to an opportunity to let them off the hook.

The statement of the TRC 'that the huge and widening gap between the rich and poor is a disturbing legacy of the past … [and something that] is morally reprehensible, politically dangerous and economically unsound …'[8] is a statement with which nobody can – and ought – to differ. The problem is that the TRC does not explain the *causative* role played by the *systems* of white political dominance, racial capitalism and/or apartheid over a considerable period of time in bringing about (and in sustaining) white wealth and white privileges, on the one hand, and black poverty, black deprivation and black humiliation on the other.

The TRC proposed that 'considerations be given to the most appropriate ways in which to provide *restitution* for those who have suffered from the effects of apartheid discrimination'.[9]

Unfortunately, the TRC does not indicate which group of people or institutions were the most likely to have benefited from 'apartheid discrim-ination', and should therefore be responsible for carrying the burden of the proposed restitution. Instead of trying to establish a causative link between the main 'beneficiaries' and the 'victims' – those who suffered most from the effect of systemic exploitation – the TRC proposed that the feasibility of five means of empowering the poor (from a wealth tax to a surcharge on golden handshakes) should be considered by the government. The five proposals are a rather strange potpourri. The only thing they have in common is that they are all possible ways of collecting additional government revenue. The wealth or income to be taxed does not necessarily accrue from *systemic exploitation* during the apartheid period.

The TRC regards the perpetuation of the gap between rich and poor as a threat to *peace and stability*. The Commission is quite adamant that the widespread poverty makes meaningful economic growth and national stability impossible. It comes to the conclusion that 'if a wealth tax is not the way forward, then some other measures should be sought and implemented as a matter of urgency'. Few will differ with this argument. The TRC does not, however, motivate its plea for redistributive measures in terms of rectifying the *social injustices* caused by the exploitative systems. If we look at the inequalities and abject poverty – without taking the historical context into account – we can put forward (as the Commission has done) a strong argument for comprehensive redistribution measures. But if we look at the inequalities and poverty in South Africa in their proper *historical context* and take the *structural* and/or *systemic exploitation* of the apartheid system (broadly defined) over a period of at least 100 years into account, then the removal of these extreme inequalities and the abject poverty is not only an issue of *redistribution* (to maintain peace and stability) but it becomes a more pressing matter of *restoration of social justice* through the necessary systemic reform and reconstruction.

In the final paragraph of my presentation before the TRC, I put forward the following argument:

> *Greater knowledge and a better understanding of the systemic injustices – that have been part of the South African system for at least 100 years – are necessary to succeed with a programme of white adult education about the true nature of 20th-century events, something highly needed en route towards a durable reconciliation. Without a clear understanding of the systemic nature of the exploitation that has taken place, it would also not be possible for the beneficiaries (mainly whites) to make the necessary confession, to show the necessary repentance, to experience the necessary conversion and to be prepared to make the needed sacrifices. Confession, repentance, conversion and sacrifices are not only prerequisite for forgiveness (by the victims), but also a precondition for promoting social stability and systemic justice in the long run. Social stability and systemic justice are, in their turn, preconditions for economic growth and job creation.*

It is necessary to consider possible reasons why it was not possible for the Commission to associate itself with understanding and conviction with the systemic approach to South African history. The reasons for this rather strange attitude of the Commission justifies further exploration.

The business-friendly argument versus the systemic exploitation argument

The TRC acknowledges that from among the various perceptions of the relationship between business and apartheid, two dominant positions emerged at the hearings:

One view, which sees apartheid as part of a system of racial-capitalism, held that apartheid was beneficial for (white) business because it was an integral part of a system premised on the exploitation of black workers and the destruction of black entrepreneurial activity. According to this argument, business as a whole benefited from the system, although some sections of the business community (most notably Afrikaner capital, the mining houses and the armaments industry) benefited more than others did.[10]

The other position, argued mainly by business, claims that apartheid raised the costs of doing business, eroded South Africa's skills base and undermined long-term productivity and growth. In this view, the impact of apartheid was to harm the economy.[11]

According to the Commission, these opposing arguments mirrored a long-standing debate over the relationship between apartheid and capitalism. The TRC also granted the point that these opposing arguments were relevant for the task facing the Commission because 'these contrasting accounts imply different notions of accountability'.

If the second view was accepted by the Commission (which it did not), it would have been necessary for it to agree with business that apartheid placed obstacles in the path of skills development and profitability, and that business was a 'victim' and not a partner or collaborator in the apartheid system.

Although it may be true that from the 1960s all kinds of bottlenecks in the supply of especially skilled labour were experienced and that apartheid was since then not always conducive for economic growth, any attempt by the TRC to portray business as a 'victim of apartheid' during the greater part of the 20th century would have resulted in all kinds of absurdities. To explain this view, it is necessary to distinguish between the period before and after 1974. If South Africa had been a 'normal' democratic society before 1974, the government's social spending on people other than white would have been at least seven or eight times higher than was the case before 1974. Both the wages paid by (white) business and taxes on white business and white individuals would have been much higher. Until more or less 1974, South Africa was to a large degree a typical colonial society in which an internal white colonial elite enriched themselves by exploiting the indigenous population. Irrespective of how conducive the system was to promote economic growth, the typical colonial exploitation that took place during this period cannot be denied.

In the 20 years after 1974, however, South Africa experienced a period of creeping poverty. During this period the annual growth rate was only 1,7%, while the real per capita income declined by 0,7% annually. To blame this long period of 'stagflation' on the apartheid system *per se* would not be fair. During this period the National Party (NP) government relaxed several apartheid measures, but to counteract the intensification of the liberation struggle the government implemented its very costly total strategy. The struggle was fought mainly in the economic arena and caused almost irreparable harm to the economy.

When business over-emphasises in its submissions to the Commission the 'cost' of apartheid for the business sector, it is not always clear whether they referred to apartheid *per se* (the intensified system of racial capitalism) or to the disruption caused by the struggle and the resistance to it. In the 20 years from 1974 until 1994 the remnants of racial capitalism were systematically abolished. What was at stake in the struggle and state resistance was the perpetuation of the system of white political dominance. Many of the business representatives who gave testimony before the Commission stated, without the necessary proof, how strongly they opposed apartheid in years gone by. Although it may be true that some of them were against the restrictive discriminatory legislation still applicable on the use of labour, few, if any, were openly against the perpetuation of white rule during the 1970s and 1980s. Business will do well to acknowledge this.

It is indeed a pity that the Commission did not investigate in greater detail whether the 'costs' business blamed on 'apartheid' should in effect be blamed on the struggle and the resistance against it. It should be remembered that most big corporations were in rather close collaboration with the NP government during the 1970s and 1980s and that they were part of the total strategy against the alleged total onslaught.

The Commission did two valuable things in its reaction to the testimony of business.

Firstly, it asked the following important question: If it is true that businesses were the 'victims of apartheid', why did they not do more to hasten the demise of apartheid? Although some of those who testified before the Commission have agreed that they could have done more to fight apartheid, they always tried to qualify their inactivity against apartheid with all kinds of unconvincing excuses.

Secondly, the Commission rejected the arguments of Ann Bernstein that 'corporations are not institutions for moral purposes' and that 'life is not a moral play'. In its rejection of the Bernstein argument, the Commission included the following paragraph and this statement deserves the whole-hearted support of the business community.:

> *The mandate of the Commission requires it to make recommendations to ensure that past violations of human rights do not recur in the future. This requires a conscious commitment to realistic moral behaviour grounded in a culture of international human rights law. It would be a sad day for the nation, faced as it is with the opportunity for renewal, if business were to dismiss social concern, business ethics and moral accountability in labour relations as being of no direct concern to itself.*[12]

In its Report, the Commission provides a good summary of the arguments of the two dominant positions that have emerged between the 'pro-business' and the 'systemic exploitation' school. The really disturbing fact about the Commission's findings and recommendations on business is that while on the one hand it does not accept the 'pro-business' argument that business was a 'victim' of apartheid, on the other it does not accept the 'systemic exploitation' argument unequivocally, but only by implication. Although the TRC tends in its recommendations towards the 'systemic exploitation' argument, it does so without certainty and without conviction.

On the day that Nelson Mandela was released from custody in February 1990, he said:

> *The white monopoly of political power must be ended and we need a fundamental restructuring of our political and economic systems [plural] to address the inequality of apartheid and to create a genuine democratic South Africa' [my emphasis].*

In a *systemic* analysis of South Africa's recent history, it is appropriate to ask *when* and under *which* circumstances the political and economic systems – to which Nelson Mandela referred – were *created* and whose fundamental *restructuring* was, according to him, already long overdue in 1990.

It is clear that when the systems of racial capitalism and white supremacy were created or *institutionalised*, a white monopoly of both *economic* and *political* power was entrenched and that from then on (until 1990–96), the two white elite groups (Afrikaans and English speakers) were empowered to use their respective *economic and political* powers – in close collaboration with each other – to *enrich* themselves and to *impoverish* people other than white. The Commission would have done well to concentrate more explicitly on the reasons for the abject poverty and the extravagant wealth. The central point to grasp is that poverty and wealth are structurally linked. They are two sides of the same coin. South Africa is confronted not only with a poverty problem but also with an equally disturbing wealth problem. This fact must be central in any attempt to solve both.

In my presentation before the TRC, I quoted from an article by Professor Mahmood Mamdani in which he made an important difference between 'perpetrators and victims on the one hand and beneficiaries and victims on the other':

> *In the South African context, perpetrators are a small group, as are those victimised by perpetrators. In contrast, beneficiaries are a large group, and victims defined in relation to beneficiaries are the vast majority in society … Which is more difficult: to live with past perpetrators of an evil [ie apartheid] or its present beneficiaries? If perpetrators and victims have a past to overcome, do not beneficiaries have a present to come to terms with? If reconciliation is to be durable, would it not need to be aimed at society (beneficiaries and victims) and not simply at the fractured elite (perpetrators and victims)? … If evil is thought of [not only in individual and legal terms, but mainly] in social [and/or structural] terms … does not the demand for justice turn mainly, if not wholly, into a demand for systemic reform?*[13]

I commented in my presentation as follows:

> *The questions asked by Mamdani are extremely relevant. We have no choice but to answer positively on all the questions he asks in the quotation above. I am in agreement with Mamdani that social justice demands that those who have been the beneficiaries of the power structures of white political supremacy and racial capitalism have a responsibility to make quite a substantial sacrifice towards those who have been the victims of these power structures.*

In its Report the TRC refers to Mamdani's distinction between 'perpetrators and victims' and 'beneficiaries and victims'. It suggests that his distinction 'deserves careful attention'.[14] To fail to address Mamdani's argument is rather deplorable.

The business sector's inclination towards myth-making

It is necessary to explore, on a deeper level, the TRC's failure to accept the argument of 'systemic exploitation'. Was the Commission intimidated by the 'managerial elite' who gave testimony before it? To what extent was the TRC oversensitive towards the business sector with which the new government has developed such a friendly relationship? Can it be that the TRC was not prepared to make findings and recommendations that would have antagonised business – or the working relationship between government and business?

The business sector was, with a few exceptions, not prepared to acknowledge its participation in the *construction* and *maintenance* of apartheid (or, more correctly, racial capitalism). In their submissions and in the evidence they gave at the business hearings, few members of this sector were prepared to acknowledge that they benefited from the apartheid system. Looking at the restrained findings of the TRC on business, one must come to the conclusion that the TRC was indeed restrained by the recalcitrant attitude the majority of businesses took toward anyone who dared to blame them for being an integral part of racial capitalism, or who suggested that they benefited. It is presently politically very incorrect to acknowledge any association, whatsoever, with the now discredited apartheid system. It is also politically incorrect to be too harsh on business.

The TRC failed to respond adequately to the obvious ploy by business to use the opportunity the TRC afforded them for a 'public relations exercise', in which they tried to whitewash their own involvement with apartheid. According to American economist Kenneth Galbraith, the power of the managerial elite critically depends on its ability to create, by way of ideological propaganda, an attractive *image* of themselves other than what is the true *reality*.[15]

The TRC has failed to address the gap between the *myth* the majority of businesses tried to propagate about themselves and the *reality* of their association with white supremacy, racial capitalism and apartheid during the greater part of the 20th century. Mitigating the recalcitrant attitude displayed by business, one must recognise the fact that the majority of today's managerial elite were not in their present position before 1970 – when racial capitalism and apartheid were in their most exploitative phase. To expect today's managerial elite to be aware of the intentions and business policies of their fathers and grandfathers would require a historical perspective that few are prepared to explore. Business people are not inclined to look backwards – only forwards.

Two of the most blatant examples of corporate attempts at *myth-making* are the submissions and testimonies of the Chamber of Mines and the Anglo-American Corporation. It was rather shocking that neither were prepared to acknowledge that African mineworkers were exploited and degraded to sub-human beings from 1910 until the beginning of the 1970s. It is to the credit of the Commission that it included these rather critical remarks on both the Chamber of Mines and Anglo-American.

The TRC comments as follows on the Chamber of Mines:

> It is regrettable that the Chamber of Mines made no mention in its submission of the active role it played in constructing and managing the migrant labour system. Although the foundations of this system were laid before the 1960s, the Chamber had a significant formative impact on the

apartheid political economy during the period under review by the Commission. There is plenty of evidence to show that, directly due to the monopsonistic power of the Chamber of Mines (which was set up with this purpose explicitly in mind), black wages on the mines were lower – at least until the mid-1970s – than they would almost certainly otherwise have been ... The image of gold-mining magnates accumulating vast wealth at the expense of African mine workers, whose wages stagnated in real terms until the 1970s, is a stain on the mining industry – and one it needs to recognise. For most of the 20th century, the greatest point of contact between African workers and business occurred on the mines. The shameful history of sub-human compound conditions, brutal suppression of striking workers, racist practices and meagre wages is central to understanding the origins and nature of apartheid. The failure of the Chamber of Mines to address this squarely and to grapple with its moral implications is regrettable and not constructive.[16]

Anglo-American is responsible for perhaps the most glaring attempt at myth-making in South African business today. In its submission, it emphasised the sharp increase in black wages from the early 1970s onwards. What is conspicuous for its absence is that not a single word is said in its submission about the extraordinary low wages paid to black migrant labour in the period from 1934 (when the price of gold increased considerably) until 1972. It is conceded that the Commission's mandate was to investigate gross human rights violations from 1960 onwards. One would therefore have expected that Anglo-American, in all fairness, would have acknowledged the low wages and the poor living, health and safety conditions of migrant workers during the 1960s. Its testimony to the TRC is a twisted version of the truth. It included a list in which successive chairmen articulated their opposition to apartheid, while failing to address the character of racial capitalism of which it was a leading force. Anglo-American was, therefore, like many businesses, guilty of a lamentable degree of hypocrisy by stating its opposition to apartheid but continuing (at least until 1972) to profit from apartheid and from super-exploitative wages paid to black workers.

The Commission comments as follows on Anglo-American's submission:

Anglo's submission was also flawed [like the submission of the Chamber of Mines]. Its most glaring feature was to sidestep the African wage issue ... The submission records that black wages ... tripled in the early 1970s. This selective presentation of wages developments is misleading and fails to mention that real African wages on the gold mines were higher in 1915 than they were in 1970.[17]

A time frame too short and a mandate too narrow

Perhaps the main reasons for the Commission's inability to do full justice to an investigation about the *social injustices* inherent in the systems of white political dominance and racial capitalism are, in last resort, to be found in its time frame, which was too short, and in its mandate (or focus), which was too narrow (or too limited). It was apparently not possible for the TRC to make a proper historical analysis of the systemic exploitation that has taken place in South Africa from at least the beginning of the 20th century.

In its chapter on historical context,[18] the Commission acknowledged the shortness of its time frame and the narrowness of its mandate. It is a pity that it did not explicitly make the point in the chapter on business that a comprehensive systemic analysis of the exploitative nature of South Africa's political and economic systems was, therefore, outside its grasp. If the Commission could have granted this point, it would also have been appropriate for it to propose that the government should appoint a Commission for *Justice and Reconciliation* with a long enough time span and a wide enough mandate to make a proper investigation of the systemic exploitation that has been an integral part of South Africa's history since the 17th century.

We are now faced with the problem that it is very difficult and unlikely that labour will be able to reconcile the beneficiaries and the victims of systemic exploitation. The fact that the beneficiaries of systemic exploitation are not exposed or pressurised to make the necessary sacrifices militates against this.

The Commission's governing Act limited its investigation to gross violation of human rights from 1 March 1960 to 10 May 1994. Gross violations of human rights were defined as the 'killing, abduction, torture or severe ill-treatment' and the 'attempt, conspiracy, incitement, instigation, command or procurement to commit' such acts. The Commission's task was restricted largely to individual acts in which human rights were grossly violated. The findings of the Commission were also largely of a legal kind. Given this focus, it was hardly possible for the Commission to concentrate properly on a historic analysis of systemic exploitation and systemic violations of human rights.

In its methodological chapter, the Commission showed willingness to stretch its mandate: 'Institutional Hearings: The purpose of these hearings was to enrich the Commission's analysis of human rights abuses by exploring how various social institutions contributed to the conflicts of the past.'[19]

This sentence begs the question. If the Commission saw the need to investigate the contribution of social institutions to conflict and human rights abuses, why did the Commission not undertake a proper historical analysis of two of the most important and all-embracing social institutions in South

Africa's 20th-century history – the social institutions of white political dominance and of racial capitalism?

Problems arose because the Commission was required to investigate human rights violations committed only in the period 1 March 1960 to 10 May 1994. To understand the formation period, the character and perpetuation of the systems of white political dominance and racial capitalism, it was necessary – if not compulsory – to turn the clock back to at least the mining revolution at the end of the previous century and the beginning of this one.

Apartheid as a crime against humanity

The Commission comes to the important conclusion that 'apartheid, as a system of enforced racial discrimination and separation, was a crime against humanity.'[20] This conclusion has rather important implications for the Commission's findings and recommendations on business.

In addressing the question of business involvement in gross human rights violations, most business submissions and testimonies adopted the view that gross human rights violations involved active, deliberate participation by individual business persons. On the strength of the Commission's original individualistic and legalistic approach on human rights violations, business found a convenient loophole to distance itself from the evil of apartheid and individual responsibility for the 'criminal' results of apartheid.

The Commission's conclusion that apartheid was indeed a crime against humanity because the apartheid system *per se* was immoral and 'criminal' closes the loophole used by business – that it was not directly (individually) guilty of any crime. If it is indeed true that apartheid (and for that matter also racial capitalism) was a criminal system, then those who operated in it for decades and were enriched by it cannot wash their hands of its results and walk away as businesses are inclined to do.

The Commission was unfortunately not vigorous enough in this regard in its findings. If it had made its conclusion (that apartheid as a *system* of enforced racial discrimination and separation was a crime against humanity) applicable to business, it would have had no option but to conclude that the business community had an enforceable (legal) responsibility to rectify the evil consequences of the criminal system. Against this background the proposal for a wealth tax for restitution purposes would certainly have been a very appropriate one. The Commission has suggested that this option, among others, be considered. It has failed to specifically promote it.

National reconciliation: holy grail or secular pact?

JAKES GERWEL

A much contested – though at one time quite influential – notion of the liberation struggle in South Africa was contained in the thesis of a two-stage revolution. This thesis posited as a first phase the attainment of national democracy, to be followed by a quest for the socialisation of the means of production.

An implicit temptation in current discussions of national reconciliation is to assume an analogous two-stage approach, as if national reconciliation is a project subsequent to the conclusion of the struggle for democracy. National reconciliation was, however, concurrently imbedded in the anti-apartheid and democratic struggle. What the attainment of democratic government achieved was to free up institutional and other forms of social energy for the *advancement* and *consolidation* rather than *initiation* of national reconciliation.

The anti-apartheid struggle (used here as a collective to describe the variety of political and social forces internally, in exile and in prison that combined to oppose and seek the overthrow of the white minority-ruled polity and social order) often characterised itself as an exercise in nation-building at the same time as it represented an opposition to a racially based system. Its nation-building character, it would claim, was not only teleologically derived from its end goal of a united South African nation but resided as much in the form, processes and informing ideologies of its conduct.

The concept of non-racialism as espoused by a dominant strand of the anti-apartheid movement emphasised the analytical and strategic value of uniting in struggle, ideally under African leadership, participants from different communities or national groups – thereby advocating the sought-after objective as well as anticipating it and laying its foundations in and through the process.

A more contested but equally influential conceptual tool emanating from a section of the anti-apartheid movement was the typification of the South African social formation as colonialism of a special type. At the heart of this concept was the theoretical and strategic assumption of the (latent) unity of the post-1910 South African nation. South Africa was approached in struggle as a late-colonial society in which coloniser and colonised inhabited and belonged to a shared political and geographical terrain without assuming that the coloniser had a home elsewhere.

The nature of the resistance and liberation struggle as well as the societal goals it posed were fundamentally influenced by the above concepts, which were derived from the particular analytical reading of the nature of the contested social and political space. National reconciliation was a tool or means of struggle as much as a 'reconciled nation' was the goal to be achieved by that struggle.

A latent national unity

This sense of 'positive future trends' already being manifest in the perverted present (though not yet fully realised), always seemed to motivate key aspects of the South African political struggle. This partly explains why even in the fiercest periods of clashes between forces of resistance and suppression the conflict was not typified or ideologically presented as purely or totally racial. The integrated and racially interdependent (though fundamentally unequal) nature of the economy, the history of urbanisation, the political processes following the last wars of colonial dispossession and the social impact of the fundamental shifts in the economy in the decades immediately prior to the establishment of the Union of South Africa, represent some of the material factors that underlie this accentuated (and in many ways typically South African) awareness of a latent national unity.

The 'miracle' of the eventual peaceful transition from racial minority rule to non-racial democracy is significantly demystified by such an acknowledgement of this political history, which also places in a somewhat different perspective some current renderings of the demand or wish for national reconciliation. Such a reading would emphasise that national reconciliation is not a new process waiting to be initiated in a situation of threatening large-scale disintegration; and that the current, more spiritual notion of reconciliation as being primarily acts amongst individual or sets of individual actors can be usefully complemented by an institutional and material approach.[1]

Stark divisions

The Truth and Reconciliation Commission (TRC) process dramatically highlighted in the public consciousness particular stark aspects and dimensions of the divisions of apartheid South Africa. It focused, as mandated by its founding legislation, on gross violations of human rights that were to stand as the most tangibly horrible reminders of that 'past of a deeply divided society characterised by strife, conflict, untold suffering and injustice' of which the Interim Constitution speaks in its postamble enabling the setting up of the TRC.

The mutual commitment to the historic compromise that led to the cessation of political hostilities and a negotiated political settlement (and which, I argue, has long historical antecedents in South African political struggle) would not allow for the criminalisation of all the myriad measures of discrimination, exploitation, oppression and dehumanisation on which minority rule apartheid was founded. Only the specified categories of killings, abduction, torture and severe ill-treatment of persons were defined by the legislation as within its ambit. These limited categories of human rights violations, subsequently heard and publicised by the TRC, had in a sense to symbolically carry the burden of that entire past of division, strife, conflict, suffering and injustice.

The pure horror of those narratives of suffering, degradation and the personal tragedy, of human beings caught up and involved as victims and perpetrators, could not but have focused the national attention and awareness on the deeply personal and emotional levels at which people in this society, given its history, should (also) reconcile with each other and with themselves for their part in that structured brutality. The most important shift at a general conceptual level that the work of the TRC may well have brought about, was the redirecting of public understanding of national reconciliation from the formal statist view, which seemed to dominate during and immediately after the epoch-making negotiation phase, to a more human substantive understanding based in social history and biography.

There had been a long-held criticism, for example from some international solidarity supporters of the South African liberation struggle, against this alleged statism, which in theoretical approach and political strategy was said to place a primacy on the transfer of state power rather than on a more radical transformation of underlying social forces and relations. Whatever the merits of this line of criticism might have been, it alludes once more to the identification of that theoretical and strategic strand in the South African political struggle, that eschewed the simple desire for the destruction of the state or some radical post-colonial alteration of the demographic content of nationhood, and from which stemmed the historical capacity to negotiate a peaceful transfer of political power, with its ensuing remarkable constitutional continuity of state obligations and responsibilities.

Political and constitutional unity

During and immediately after the negotiations and elections and in the early period of the government of national unity, reconciliation was predominantly understood and celebrated as the mutual search among erstwhile political foes for and the formal attainment of the political and constitutional unity of the country. The TRC, its subsequent 'spiritualisation' of the understanding of reconciliation notwithstanding, was itself conceived as a primarily formal measure in that overall political settlement. Subjective factors such as the dominant presence of religious personalities and a general liberal-Christian perspective in the Commission significantly contributed to the subsequent amplified spiritual approach to reconciliation. The genesis of the TRC, though, is to be found in the sober politics of accommodation borne out of a historically conditioned sense of shared South African nationhood.

The TRC process and report represent a mixture of biography, social history, religion and jurisprudence. The untidy though seemingly unworried crossing of genre boundaries in many ways mirrors the nature of the South African process of reconciliation, and serves as a salutary reminder of the essential secularity of the Commission's work. A society perhaps ultimately remembers, and reconciles itself with the painful aspects of that memory, best and most enduringly, through the long process of the work of its writers and artists. It is in the construction of such a lineage of narratives of national remembrance that the TRC may be found to have made its most lasting contribution. As an event of story-telling, confession and forgiving, within a quasi-judicial framework, it represented a unique moment in the country's history – an interstitial pause for a nation to acknowledge its unity and intimate inter-connections also in perversity and suffering.

In its report the TRC acknowledges that it was impossible for it to 'reconcile the nation' because of limitations of time, resources and mandate. The latter is the most relevant and decisive of these limitations, as the Commission was charged not with the initiation or conclusion but the *promotion* of national unity and reconciliation – in other words the advancement or encouragement of a process or result. The interim Constitution envisaging and the legislation establishing the TRC were the products or acts of an already reconciled or at least reconciling political collectivity. The Committee for a Democratic South Africa (CODESA) that proposed such a mechanism through the negotiated interim constitution, the cabinet of the Government of National Unity that sponsored and drafted the founding legislation, and the parliament that passed it into law, represented powerful institutional expressions and manifestations of national unity and reconciliation.

A confidence in national unity

South Africa, notwithstanding the complex of divisions and differences of various sorts, levels and intensities that may exist within it, is decidedly not an unreconciled nation in the sense of being threatened by imminent disintegration and internecine conflict. On the contrary, on the scale of world affairs it serves as a singularly successful example of a country with racial and ethnic diversity, histories of strife and strongly competing interests that had resolved its potentially destructive conflicts consensually and had demonstrated within itself the political will and institutional means to cohere. The absence of external mediators, sponsors or guarantors in the complex and fraught transition process as a considered decision of the political leadership, signified a national confidence based on a particular historical self-definition.

Assertions by two political leaders at the close of the last session of the first democratic parliament inadvertently juxtaposed themselves as complementary references to on the one hand, the history of, and on the other, a confidence in, the future of national unity. The South African President referred to the fact that the people of South Africa finally chose a profoundly legal path to their revolution, while the leader of an opposition party postulated as one certainty, the permanent disappearance of civil war as a danger to the country.

The achievement in South Africa of a constitutional state of this nature and that particular process, is the single most telling statement of national reconciliation. It is of note that the Union of South Africa, which defined the territorial and juridical arena within and over which the modern struggle around the politics of racial domination and subjugation was conducted, came out of a series of highly destructive wars of colonial dispossession and imperial conflict. Modern-day South Africans averted a widely predicted civil war and racial conflagration and produced one of the most acclaimed democratic and diversity accommodating constitutions in the world.

It is important to recognise the 1996 Constitution as not only a founding pact, and hence starting point, but equally importantly as the culmination of a long process of resistance against segregation and apartheid, in defence of the unity of the post-1910 South African nation. This recognition provides a valuable qualification to the approach emphasising the novelty of the nation and its challenges of reconciliation. The constitutionally enshrined multi-party system of democratic government – itself a central institutional agency of reconciliation – requires a certain abandoning of historical perspective – as part of what South Africans have come to regard as an exercise in 'levelling the playing field'. The liberation movement, for example, had to be 'reduced' to equal historical status as all other parties in the democracy in order to avoid a dangerous conceptual and practical erosion of the distinction between movement and nation, party and government, government and state. However, a perspective that also recognises historical specificity – in particular that the major liberation struggle had from inception, and consistently, been a defence of the ideal of the non-racial unity of the South African nation – could serve to fortify the confidence in continuous nationhood. This historical perspective should not, however, automatically be seen to translate today into choices and actions undermining the newly established democracy in South Africa.

We, the people of South Africa

It might be true, as the French philosopher Jacques Derrida suggests, that 'the people' typically invoked in founding declarations of independence and nationhood do not exist prior to such declarations.[2] That is, the signature invents the signer. This 'fabulous retroactivity' is, however, much less applicable in the case of the 1996 South African Constitution. 'We, the people of South Africa', who in the Preamble are said to adopt the Constitution, concretely existed and interacted as such long prior to the adoption, and demonstrated that existence most evocatively in the 1994 elections. Nations, no matter how apparently homogenous, always exist and cohere as so-called imagined communities. There is no 'natural nation' – as is so vividly shown in the case of Somalia, which is among the most ethnically homogenous societies in Africa. This imagining of community, however, takes place through institutions and in material conditions of coexistence and survival. There is, in a sense, a solid history to the materiality of the South African nation.

The basic contention in this chapter is that there tangibly exists a political basis to a united South African nationhood and that the nation as political and juridical entity is not threatened by disintegration or social disruption. Divisions, differences and conflicting interests of various kinds, levels and intensity occur throughout this society and some of these are remnants, even uninterrupted continuations, of defining features of the contradictions of apartheid and colonial South Africa. None of these, however, can be said to threaten the legal, political or constitutional order. South Africans act out their differences within the framework of their constitution.[3] While many individual victims and perpetrators of gross human rights violations are not reconciled, and group-based memories of discrimination will probably remain for a long time, the country has progressed far on the road of political reconciliation.

The constitutional accommodation of two potentially disruptive forces comes to mind: the aspirations to a separate ethnic *volksnasionalisme* on the part of what is referred to as right-wing Afrikaners, and the insistence that a tribally based traditional authority be recognised. It is a gross fallacy, no less excusable by the facileness it is arrived at through extrapolation from the country's past, that the major or generic divide or index of dominant contradiction in South Africa continues to be simply race. These two examples of political tensions that were once of high disruptive potential for the South African polity demonstrate a generic contradiction between pluralistic modernity and ethnic traditionalism. This contradiction cuts across simple racial lines. The South African Constitution, alert to the centrality of diversity in the definition of nationhood, created the space and mechanisms for these tensions to be continuously negotiated.

It is in reconciling these and other expressions of diversity and difference that the defining national project in South Africa faces its challenge. Modern social organisations and formations have become much too complex for the quality and intimacy of informal and primary relations to be the indices – or, in the modern jargon, 'decisive performance indicators' – of the health of those social units. (Even marriage, the smallest of social units and one that, moreover, is based on primary affective considerations, adapts to and continuously negotiates difference and conflict and seeks underpinning in contracts.) It is, put in perhaps over-simplified terms, unrealistic to expect everybody in such a complex organisation as a nation to love one another. Human social reality is intrinsically contradictory, and a late 20th-century society with the history of South Africa no longer seeks for such idealistic denial or obfuscation of contradiction. Institutionalised commitment to consensus-seeking, cultivation of conventions of civility and respect for contracts have become the mechanisms of solidarity in contemporary society, replacing the organic idiom of 'love for neighbour' that might to a greater extent have made older, less complex societies cohere. It is as diversity, difference and inequality that the major contradictions of contemporary South African society are expressed and have to be negotiated in ongoing, dynamic and multi-facetted social processes. The nature of societal discourse and the recurring themes of public conversation shape the outcomes of patterned social behaviour – and it is not clear that the current usage of the concept of national reconciliation does not in fact contribute to a disourse of division. It focuses in a theoretically deficient and empirically unsubstantiated manner on racial groups as the primary subjects of reconciliation and encourages abiding deficiency assumptions in the national self-consciousness. A critically refined elaboration of the notion of national unity may prove more purposeful in defining and practically advancing the major post-apartheid national project.

The South African Constitution and the process through which it was arrived at must – after the necessary deconstruction and debunking of political rhetoric and procedural expedience – be accepted as the signal of something real in the collective national will. The Constitution's recognition and acknowledgement of diversity as unifying and emancipatory can in the reading of national texts not be dismissed as insignificant rhetoric. Indeed, aspects of the institutional political behaviour in recent years tend to affirm the existence of a compelling epistemology of difference accommodation in South Africa. Majoritarian political movements in power, as is the case in South Africa, will tend towards emphasising the levelling dimensions of national unity. There are, however, concrete signs of a broad recognition that the production of difference, rather than its denial, constitutes the medium of a nation's identification. Certainly recent theorising on the subject supports this.[4] Briefly stated, the creation of spaces of difference redirects the nation's authority away from authoritarian constructs of identity.

The rhetorical invitation by the country's political leadership that the Constitution be made 'a living document', needs to be seriously responded to by individual and organised citizens as part of the building and the consolidation of national unity. This applies as much to the Constitution's diversity-accommodating provisions as to any other. One tendency until now has been, on the one hand, to interpret and anticipate, and on the other to articulate and act out significant diversity demands as being primarily ethnic or ethno-cultural. This seems innocently ignorant or deliberately disregarding of the constituent nature of modern theory, which regards social movements as expressions of the fluidity of identity, more so than static definitions of race or ethnicity.

The liberation/democratic movement in government has a particular responsibility for guarding, promoting and strengthening national unity, as the political expression of a 'reconciled nation'. Operating in a multi-party democracy might have meant abandoning claims to historically privileged status, but its history of being the main carrier of the idea of the unity of the South African nation places a special responsibility upon it.

Differently stated, material inequality is a major source of division in

South Africa. As such, the alleviation of poverty must be one of the government's primary responsibilities in seeking to promote reconciliation and national unity. The structures of inequality were historically (and to a large extent continue to be) racially based. The history of the liberation movement at the same time challenges the nation to transform those social patterns. It needs to do so without emphasising and entrenching in the national discourse and consciousness those very indicators of division (racial and other) against which it led the national struggle. The relatively rapid deracialisation of South African capital and changing demographics of property together with a steady provision of basic services and facilities are to be read as indicators of a movement, incomplete as it may be, away from historical divisions.

The regulation of competing interests and the containment of antagonistic contradictions through the development of institutions for consensus-seeking and conventions of civility in public life, are the responsibility of government as well as civil society. It is through these measures, coupled with a respect for contracts as a basic ingredient of decency in a modern society, that makes social coherence posible.

South Africa's social and political history has equipped it with the foundations of quite a sophisticated political-intellectual culture. The roots of these are to be found, *inter alia*, in the strong Enlightenment dimensions of early resistance theory, and the internationalist nature of the subsequent struggle, as well as the indigenisation of what were originally the settler-colonial elements of the society. It is within that culture that reconciliation is to be dealt with as a dynamic and complex set of ongoing processes.

South Africans can only benefit from constantly reminding themselves of the opening lines of the Preamble of their Constitution: 'We ... recognise the injustices of our past; honour those who suffered for justice and freedom in our land; respect those who have worked to build and develop our country; and believe that South Africa belongs to all who live in it, united in our diversity.' We need to take the challenge seriously.

Conclusion

It is wrong to suggest that South Africa is a wholly or predominantly unreconciled society because it contains within it a number of residual and enduring contradictions. Diversity and difference are realities with which nations throughout the world continue to struggle. The good news is that South Africa is grappling to come to terms with these and to grow as a nation in relation to such realities. It is not national policy to seek to eliminate difference through ethnic cleansing or the hitherto destructive policy of apartheid. Social and economic inequality present a more serious strain in the life of the nation. This needs to be addressed with increasing vigour during the next phase in the consolidation of the South African democracy.

Important for the nation-building process is a political quest, which must ensure that tensions within the body politic do not destroy either the gain made or the civility required to redress the nation's most stubborn problems. There are indications of consensus beginning to emerge across political divisions that suggest an emerging agreement on the nature of the nation's most urgent needs, despite sharp disagreement on how to overcome them. Despite conflict, a sense of political coexistence and civility is beginning to emerge in South African politics. This must be both sustained and promoted.

The TRC constituted an important moment in the transitionary process – within which deeply human, subjective forces were allowed to attain precedence over the objective forces of state politics. The extent to which the tensions and inevitable pain associated with remembering the past were accentuated, should not be allowed to distract from the remarkable progress the nation has already made on the journey of political coexistence. The appeal is that we do not pathologise a nation in relatively good health by demanding a perpetual quest for the Holy Grail of reconciliation.

Endnotes

Introduction

1 *TRC Report*, Vol 1, p 2.
2 *TRC Report*, Vol 1, Ch 4; see Appendix to this volume, p 304.
3 *TRC Report*, Vol 5, p 212.
4 *TRC Report*, Vol 1, p 67; see Appendix to this volume, p 304.
5 See Ch 7 in this volume.

SECTION 1
The historical context and origins of the Commission
Chapter 1

1 Preamble to Universal Declaration of Human Rights.
2 *Ibid.*
3 Preamble to the Draft Rome Statute.
4 In an unprecedented move in British legal history, the House of Lords revoked its own decision on a petition from Pinochet's lawyers, who argued that the fact that Hoffman did not disclose that his wife was an activist in Amnesty International, one of the NGOs that had called for his extradition, was fatally defective. The matter has since been argued before seven Lords and judgment, at the time of writing this article, is pending.
5 Regina v Bartle and the Commissioner of Police for the Metropolis and others EX Parte Pinochet (on appeal from a Divisional Court of the Queen's Bench Division). Regina v Evans and Another and the Commissioner of Police for the Metropolis and others EX Parte Pinochet (on appeal from a Divisional Court of the Queen's Bench Division).
6. Du Preez and Another v Truth and Reconciliation Commission 1997 (3) SA 204 (A). See also 1996 (3) SA 1997 (CPD).
7 Frederik Willem de Klerk v The Truth and Reconciliation Commission and Another – Case No 14930/98.
8 African National Congress v The Truth and Reconciliation Commission – Case No 14800/98.
9 Lukas Daniel Barnard and Another v Desmond Mpilo Tutu and Another – Case No 16822/98.
10 *The Sowetan*, 11 September 1998, p 3.

Chapter 2

1 For a comprehensive examination of this subject, see Neil J Kritz (ed), *Transitional Justice* (3 volumes), United States Institute of Peace (1995); 'State Crimes – Punishment or Pardon', The Aspen Institute (1989); D Bronkhorst, 'Truth and Reconciliation – Obstacles and Opportunities for Human Rights', Amnesty International Dutch Section (1995).
2 See Priscilla B Hayner, 'Fifteen Truth Commissions – 1974 to 1994: A Comparative Study', *Human Rights Quarterly*, 16 (1994); and Priscilla B Hayner, 'Commissioning the Truth: Further Research Questions', *Third World Quarterly*, 17(1) (1996).
3 For the international law position on whether there is a duty to prosecute and punish past violations of human rights, see generally the following: 'AZAPO v President of the Republic of South Africa' 1996 (4) SA 562 (CC); John Dugard, 'Is the Truth and Reconciliation Process Compatible with International Law? An Unanswered Question', *SAJHR*, 13(2); Diane F. Orentlicher, 'Settling Accounts: the Duty to Punish Human Rights Violations of a Prior Regime', *Yale Law Journal*, 100 (1991); Carlos S Nino, 'The Duty to Punish Abusers of Human Rights Put into Context: the Case of Argentina', *Yale Law Journal* 100 (1991); Bronkhorst *op cit* 90; Aspen Institute *op cit.*
4 For example, Article 6.5 of the Second Protocol to the Geneva Conventions states that 'at the end of the hostilities, the authorities shall endeavour to grant the broadest possible amnesty'.
5 See J Kollapen, 'Accountability: the Debate in South Africa', *Journal of African Law*, 37 (1993); G Simpson, 'Blanket Amnesty Poses a Threat to Reconciliation', *Business Day*, 22 December 1993.
6 See *Motsuenyane Commission Report* (23 August 1993); 'Response of the NEC of the ANC to the Motsuenyane Commission Report' (28 August 1993).
7 AZAPO, *op cit.* para 17.
8 See Mac Maharaj, 'Justice or Reconciliation:

the Situation in South Africa Today', Address to Justice or Reconciliation Conference, Chicago University (25 April 1997).

9 See generally, Jeremy Sarkin, 'The Trials and Tribulations of South Africa's Truth and Reconciliation Commission', *South African Human Rights Journal* 12 (4) (1996); Ian Liebenberg, 'The Truth and Reconciliation Commission in South Africa: Context, Future and some Imponderables', *SAPR* 11 (1996); George Bizos, SC, *No One to Blame? In Pursuit of Justice in South Africa* (Epilogue), David Philip & Mayibuye Books (1999); Gerhard Werle, 'Without Truth, No Reconciliation: the South Africa Rechtstaat and the Apartheid Past', Inaugural Lecture – University of Humboldt, Berlin (1995).

10 Kader Asmal, MP, *Coping with the Past: A Truth Commission for SA*, Mayibuye (May 1994:27); See generally, K Asmal, MP, 'Victims, Survivors and Citizens: Human Rights, Reparations and Reconciliation', Inaugural Lecture, University of the Western Cape (25 May 1992).

Chapter 3

1 At the conclusion of the commission's work, it was able to state definitive numbers of 160 000 killed and 40 000 disappeared during the course of the conflict, 93 percent of these by forces of the state.

2 Human rights advocates and survivors were also very disappointed with the original six to 12 month deadline for the commission to conclude its work. But the commission quickly gained a reputation for competence, and gained the support of virtually all sectors in Guatemala as it undertook its work; its mandate was thus eventually extended to 18 months, concluding in February 1999. Surprisingly, many concluded that its inability to name perpetrators turned into a positive attribute: its sweeping statements of responsibility at the top levels of government provided sufficient evidence for rights advocates to pursue cases against former heads of state, while the commission itself avoided narrowing its focus to the evidence of responsibility on specific cases, and instead layed out facts to establish strong patterns and policies of abuse.

3 For a more detailed description of truth

commissions since 1974, see the author's forthcoming book on truth commissions (London: Routledge, 1999). See also, Priscilla B Hayner, 'Fifteen Truth Commissions,' *Human Rights Quarterly,* 16 (1994), or Priscilla B Hayner, 'Commissioning the Truth: Further Research Questions,' *Third World Quarterly,* 17 (1996).

4 The fact-finding potential of the South African amnesty process was never used to the full, however. Perhaps due to time pressures or a different set of priorities between different parts of the commission, the Amnesty Committee did not fully explore the questions that could have been asked of amnesty applicants, such as information on the chain of command that authorised certain crimes, for example.

5 While the El Salvador and Guatemalan commissions were administered by a UN office and had members appointed by the UN, they operated independently and were not UN bodies *per se.* In Guatemala, only the chair was appointed by the UN; in El Salvador, the commissioners were appointed by the UN Secretary General after consultation with the Parties to the peace accord.

6 See *Human Rights Watch*, 'Truth and Partial Justice in Argentina: An Update' (New York: *Human Rights Watch*, April 1991, p 69).

Chapter 4

1 See, for example, Diane Orentlicher, 'Settling Accounts: The Duty to Prosecute Human Rights Violations of a Prior Regime', *Yale Law Journal,* 100 (1991).

2 In this chapter, I use the term 'security forces' to refer to the military as well as paramilitary units, the police and other armed formations loyal to, or under the control of, a previous regime responsible for human rights abuse.

3 According to several experts, more than 80 percent of the Rwandan judiciary survived the genocide in that country, despite the fact that they were deliberately targeted. See William Schabas, 'Prosecuting International Crime: Justice, Democracy and Impunity in Postgenocide Rwanda – Searching for Solutions to Impossible Problems', *Crim. LF,* 7, (1996), pp 523-32.

4 This is certainly true of South Africa. Under apartheid, the police regularly extracted 'con-

fessions' through torture, rather than relying on more difficult, but legitimate, evidence-gathering techniques. This left them unprepared to solve crime under a constitutional order.

5   In some cases, it is not appropriate to 'rebuild' criminal justice systems that have been destroyed during past conflict. This is because, prior to their destruction, they were biased, corrupt and did not dispense justice in compliance with international standards. In such cases, criminal justice systems must be reconstructed 'afresh', rather than restored to their previous state. See Schabas, *supra* note 3, p 531.

6   Post-communist Russia and post-apartheid South Africa are perhaps the best examples of this phenomenon.

7   This assertion must be qualified in circumstances where those responsible for past 'political' crimes are currently involved in purely criminal syndicates. In such cases, dealing with past crimes may contribute to reducing current crime. However, in transitional societies there is no necessary correlation between past and present crime.

8   In South Africa, bodies such as the State Security Council (which comprised of key political and security force leadership) issued policy directives that included instructions to 'eliminate' and 'neutralise' anti-apartheid activists. Members of the security forces testified before the Truth and Reconciliation Commission that these directives clearly authorised the killing of political opponents. Politicians disputed this interpretation, claiming that they intended only to authorise legal methods to combat resistance.

9   Schabas, *supra* note 3, p 532, captures the issue succinctly in the Rwandan context: 'Realising judicial guarantees ... depends on resources, these rights cannot be guaranteed in the same way in a poor country as in a rich country, despite the admonition in relevant international instruments to the contrary. They are positive rights, not negative rights, in that they require a state to act, not to abstain from acting. Consequently, a state, such as Rwanda, must make hard choices between investing in its judicial and correctional system in order to meet the norms set out in the ICCPR or to invest in education, health care

and environmental protection, so as to respect the claims of the ICESR ...'

10 In just two 'hit-squad' trials in South Africa, the government was required to pay over R17 million ($2.1 million) to defence attorneys.

11 For a more detailed discussion of the costs of political trials in South Africa, see Paul van Zyl, 'Dilemmas of Transitional Justice: The Case of South Africa's Truth and Reconciliation Commission,' *Journal of International Affairs*, 52 (1999), p 647.

12 According to reports by Spanish news agency EFE (1/15/1999).

13 The TRC found PW Botha guilty of, *inter alia*, deliberately planning gross violations of human rights, including the killing of political opponents. See the *TRC Report*, Vol 5, Ch 6.

14 'It should be kept in mind that no judicial system, anywhere in the world, has been designed to cope with the requirements of prosecuting crimes committed by tens of thousands, directed against hundreds of thousands. In Europe, following the Second World War, it is doubtful whether 87 000 people [the number of people awaiting trial in Rwanda after the genocide – this number has since risen to almost 110 000 in 1999] were judged by all of the courts of the most highly developed legal systems. Even a prosperous country, with a sophisticated judicial system, would be required to seek special and innovative solutions to criminal law prosecutions on such a scale.' See Schabas, *supra* note 3, p 534.

15 Tina Rosenberg, *The Haunted Land: Facing Europe's Ghosts After Communism* (New York: Vintage Books, 1995, p 312).

16 Orentlicher, *supra* note 1, p 2596, concedes on this point: 'In a country like Argentina, where some 9 000 persons are estimated to have disappeared during the military junta's "dirty war against subversion", a requirement that the government attempt to prosecute everyone who may be criminally liable, could place impossible demands on the judiciary. Even a well-functioning judicial system would be incapable of discharging such a burden, much less can this be expected following the wholesale collapse of the judicial process.'

17 Exact figures are difficult to obtain and calculate, but interviews by the author have ascertained that the current budget for the International Criminal Tribunal for the

former Yugoslavia is approximately $100 million per annum.

18 Madeline Morris, 'The Trials of Concurrent Jurisdiction: The Case of Rwanda', *Duke J Comp. & Int'l L.* 7 (Spring 1997), p 349.

19 Measured by the number of convictions obtained per dollar spent or per year that each tribunal has been in existence.

20 Other international judicial bodies that have ruled on this issue include, *inter alia*, the European Commission and Court of Human Rights, the Human Rights Committee established pursuant to the International Covenant on Civil and Political Rights and the Committee against Torture.

21 Annual Report of the Inter-American Commission on Human Rights, 1985-1986, pp 192, 205.

22 Velásquez Rodríguez Case, Inter-Am. Centre for Human Rights (ser. C) (4) (1988).

23 *Ibid.* para 174.

24 N. Roht-Arriaza, 'State Responsibility to Investigate and Prosecute Grave Human Rights Violations in International Law' *Calif. LR,* 78 (1990), p 473.

25 For a fuller discussion of this issue, see T van Boven, 'Study Concerning the Right to Restitution, Compensation and Rehabilitation for Victims of Gross Violations of Human Rights and Fundamental Freedoms', United Nations Economic and Social Council, E/CN.4/Sub.2/1993/8 (1993), p 38).

26 See Inter-American Commission on Human Rights, Report No 28/92 (2 October 1992).

27 See Inter-American Commission on Human Rights, Report No 29/92 (2 October 1992).

28 Las Hojas Massacre Case, Case No 10.287, 1992-3 (1993).

29 The government of Argentina was urged to 'pay the petitioners just compensation for the violations referred to in the preceding paragraph [and] adopt the measures necessary to clarify the facts and identity of those responsible for the human rights violations that occurred during the past military dictatorship'. Inter-American Commission on Human Rights, Report No 28/92 (2 October, 1992) para 52.

30 The commission only recommended to the government of Uruguay that 'it give the applicant victims or their rightful claimants just compensation [and that] it adopt the

measures necessary to clarify the facts and identity of those responsible for the human rights violations during the de facto period'. *Ibid.* para 54.

31 *Ibid.*; see note 28 above.

32 Chanfeau Orayce v Chile (1997) at 512.

33 The commission held that 'amnesties constitute a violation [of Article 1.1 of the Inter-American Convention on Human Rights] and they eliminate the most effective measure for the exercise of those rights – the trial and punishment of the responsible individuals'. *Ibid.* p 526.

34 In Ruiz Davila v Peru, 1997 (1997) at 742, the commission recommended that 'the Peruvian state carry out a serious, impartial and effective investigation of the facts by means of the competent organs to establish the whereabouts of Estiles Ruiz Davila and to identify those responsible for his detention-disappearance, and *by means of appropriate criminal proceedings to punish those responsible for such grave acts in accordance with the law'* (emphasis added).

35 See note 21 *supra.*

36 See note 32 *supra.*

37 The Chilean government still confronts legal obstacles to prosecutions, in the form of the self-amnesty passed by the military. Furthermore, while the military generally supports democratic rule, it is not clear how it would respond to the widespread prosecution of its leaders.

38 See 'Legitimate grounds for failing to prosecute', above.

39 For a more detailed discussion on derogation see F. Aolain, 'Legal Developments: The Fortification of an Emergency Regime', *Alb. L Rev,* 59, pp 1366-7; Shestack, 'Human Rights in Crisis: The International System for Protecting Human Rights During States of Emergency', *A.J.I.L.*, 90, pp 171; Gardeniers, Hannum and Krugey, 'The 1981 Session of the UN Sub-Commission on Prevention of Discrimination and Protection of Minorities', 76 *A.J.I.L.,* 76, pp 409-10; R Quinn, 'Will the Rule of Law End? Challenging Grants of Amnesty for Human Rights Violations of a Prior Regime: Chile's New Model', 62 *Fordham L Rev,* 62, pp 945–6; R Macdonald, 'Derogations Under Article 15 of the European Convention on Human Rights', *J Colum*

Transnat'l L., 36, p 225; F Aolain, 'The Emergence of Diversity: Differences in Human Rights Jurisprudence', *Fordham Int'l LJ*, 19, p 101.

40 Lawless v Ireland, Ser. A, No 3, 1 Eur. HR Rep 15, (1961), pp 31-2.

41 Even Orentlicher observes that 'international law does not, of course, require states to take action that poses a serious threat to vital national interests'. See note 1 *supra*, p 2596.

42 Certain scholars, such as Roht-Arriaza, *supra* note 24, p 487, argue that the 'derivative' obligation to punish those responsible for the violation of non-derogable rights (such as the right to life) is itself non-derogable on the basis that punishment is the only effective means to ensure such rights. This assertion is not settled law and is not supported by fact. In certain cases, prosecution may lead to war or conflict, which in turn will lead to further violations of the rights Roht-Arriaza claims punishment will protect. In other cases, in which it is simply impossible to prosecute for practical reasons, the reform of the criminal justice system may do more to protect non-derogable rights than punishment.

43 Orentlicher, *supra* note 1, p 2596, asserts that 'a prerequisite of any law requiring prosecution of particular offences is that the national judiciary must be capable of handling the burden imposed by that law'.

44 Orentlicher, *supra* note 1, p 2600, asserts that, 'treaties should be interpreted in a manner that avoids imposing impossible obligations or duties, whose discharge would prove harmful'.

45 This includes domestic judges reviewing an amnesty in their own country, as well as foreign judges and judges of international bodies reviewing amnesties of other states.

46 Such as those outlined in 'Legitimate grounds for failing to prosecute' above.

47 See 'State obligations under international law'.

48 For example, the Rwandan government may be able to justify a failure to punish on the basis that it is objectively impossible to fairly investigate, prosecute and convict more than a very small percentage of the hundreds of thousands of perpetrators, both in custody and at-large.

49 Some authors support this test. See Douglas Cassel, 'Lessons from the Americas: Guidelines for International Response to Amnesties for Atrocities', *Law and Contemporary Problems*, 59(4) p 219. However, Orentlicher, *supra* note 1 at note 260, rejects popular ratification of amnesties, arguing that constitutions are inherently anti-majoritarian and are designed to protect vulnerable minorities (such as victims) against expedient or unjust decisions taken by the majority. This argument is unconvincing, because Orentlicher herself concedes (p 2610) that a majority of legislators (and by extension, a majority of the population) may be entitled to adopt a treaty that permits derogation from constitutionally protected rights under certain narrowly defined circumstances. Popular ratification of a decision to grant amnesty under circumstances of grave threat or impossibility of performance is, therefore, analogous to a democratic legislature ratifying a treaty that permits derogation from international obligations. Furthermore, while constitutions with a bill of rights tend to protect the rights of minorities, they do not always defer to them. Courts regularly uphold laws that adversely affect one section of the population, providing the government is able to articulate just and rational reasons for its policies.

50 A similar approach is articulated by Robert Weiner, 'Trying To Make Ends Meet: Reconciling the Law and Practice of Human Rights Amnesties', *St Mary's L.J.* 26, p 857.

51 See Cassel, *supra* note 49.

52 On this basis the Spanish government would not be required to uphold the legality of the Chilean amnesty in so far that it grants amnesty to persons criminally responsible for the deaths of Spanish citizens, even if it were to meet the requirements set forth here. It should be noted that the Chilean amnesty does not satisfy several of the requirements set forth in this paper.

53 Such as those claims pursued in terms of the Alien Tort Claims Act, 28 U.S.C. 1350.

54 See 'Legitimate grounds for failing to prosecute'.

55 An additional implication of this approach is that domestic courts should refuse extradition requests made by international or foreign courts, provided all requirements listed above are satisfied.

56 Such as providing full disclosure about the

crimes for which amnesty is sought or agreeing to assist in providing reparation to victims.

57 One danger of this approach may be that militaries will attempt to create disruption in circumstances in which a member is facing prosecution abroad so as to attempt to demonstrate they do pose a substantial threat to the nation. A court should carefully consider the objective threat posed, not the impression of a threat created by a military for tactical purposes.

58 Cassel, *supra* note 49 at 205, argues that it is unacceptable for international mediators not to be guided by the requirements of international law in the brokering of settlements.

SECTION 2
The philosophical framework of the Commission
Chapter 5

1 Stuart Hampshire, *Innocence and Experience* (Cambridge: Cambridge University Press, 1989, pp 72-8).

2 The idea of 'political death' is similar to the notion of 'social death' deployed by Orlando Patterson in *Slavery and Social Death* (Cambridge: Cambridge University Press, 1982).

3 I here react to the discussion of Kanan Makiya, Charles Maier and Yael Tamir at the International meeting on truth commissions organised by the World Peace Foundation. See Henry J Steiner (ed), *Truth Commissions, A Comparative Assessment: World Peace Foundation Reports* (Cambridge: Cambridge University Press, 1997, p 31).

4 I concur with Larry May's view that most of our responsibilities are shared ones, rather than unique to an individual. See Larry May, *Sharing Responsibility* (Chicago and London, 1992, p 19). My own views on the irreducibly social nature of human action is found in Rajeev Bhargava, *Individualism in Social Science* (Oxford: Oxford University Press, 1992).

5 Of course, this is entirely consistent with the view that members of such a collectivity are responsible in varying degrees, depending largely on the amount of power exercised by them.

6 Jeffrie Murphy and Jean Hampton, *Forgiveness and Mercy* (Cambridge: Cambridge University Press, 1988, p 15).

Chapter 6

1 Jose Zalaquett is a Chilean human rights lawyer who served on the Chilean National Commission for Truth and Reconciliation. He has been a leading voice in the debate on truth commissions as a means of promoting accountability for state crimes.

2 Aryeh Neier, *War Crimes: Brutality, Genocide, Terror and the Struggle for Justice* (New York: Times Books, Random House, 1998, p 107).

3 Martha Minnow, *Between Vengeance and Forgiveness* (Boston: Beacon Press, 1998, p 12). Minow contends that vengeance needs to be 'tamed', 'balanced' and 'recast' into a form of judicial retribution. Forgiveness, in turn, is an ideal that few achieve, making coexistence and reconciliation more adequate goals. See my essay, 'Getting on with life' in this volume.

4 Quoted in an extended essay on restorative justice: Jennifer J Llewellyn and Robert Howse, 'Restorative Justice: A Conceptual Framework'. Unpublished manuscript. Llewellyn and Howse criticise Marshall's definition as being too open-ended. It, nevertheless, provides a useful basis for discussion.

5 *Ibid*. Llewellyn and Howse argue that notions of retributive and restorative justice share a common conceptual ground in their commitment to establishing or re-establishing social equality between perpetrator and victim. For them, 'retributive justice is, at its root, concerned with a restoration of equality in relationships'. When this is extended to the 'restoration of social equality', they argue that one is able to 'grasp the way in which restorative justice theory and retributive theory diverge from their common conceptual ground'. The question is to what extent the ethical worth of individuals is undermined by imprisonment and punishment associated with retribution. It is perhaps this that distinguishes it most clearly from restorative justice.

6 HLA Hart, 'Positivism and the Separation of Law and Morals'; Lon Fuller, 'Positivism and the Fidelity to Law – A Reply to Professor Hart', *Harvard Law Review*, 71 (1957) p 58.

7 Fuller, p. 642-3. Pertinent to Fuller's point on 'continuity' was the insistence of the National Party at the time of the Constitutional Assembly in 1993 that the interim constitution be adopted by the tricameral parliament. While seeking to make a political point in this

regard, their concern was also to insist on the legitimacy of the white regime as a result of the Statute of Westminster in 1910. In brief, they insisted that there was continuity between the old and the new – discontinuity was not happening. The ANC conceded the point and the interim constitution was effectively 'rubber stamped' in a final session of the apartheid parliament.

8   Ronald Dworkin, *Law's Empire* (Cambridge, Mass: The Belknap Press of Harvard University Press, 1986, p 413). In his celebrated debate with HLA Hart, Lon Fuller had similarly focused on the concept of 'purpose' in law, suggesting the need to show judicial flexibility in moving beyond a positivistic application of law. 'Positivism and Fidelity to Law – A Reply to Professor Hart,' *Harvard Law Review*, 71 (1957), p 58.

9   *TRC Report*, Vol 1, Ch 5, para 80f.

10   *Carcer enim ad continendos homines non ad puniendos haberi debet*. Dirk van Zyl Smit, *South African Prison Law and Practice* (Durban: Butterworth, 1992).

11   A Sanders (ed), *Southern Africa in Need of Law Reform* (Durban: Butterworth, 1981).

12   J Consedine, *Restorative Justice: Healing the Effects of Crime* (Lyttleton: Ploughshares Publications, 1994); LM Muntingh, 'Community Service Orders: an Evaluation of Cases Supervised in Cape Town Between 1983 and 1994' (Pretoria: HSRC, 1996); Portfolio Committee on Correctional Services, Budget Report, South African National Assembly, 1996/7.

13   Lon Fuller, *The Morality of Law* (New Haven: Yale University Press, 1969, pp 209-10).

14   Karl Jaspers, *The Question of German Guilt* (New York: The Dial Press, 1947). First published as *Die Schuldfrage: Zur Politischen Haftung Deutschland* (Heidelberg: Verlagen Lambert Schneider, 1946).

15   Luc Huyse, *Young Democracies and the Choice Between Amnesty, Truth Commissions and Prosecutions*. A Policy Study on Development and Cooperation (Law and Society Institute, University of Leuven, 1998, p 7).

16   Antjie Krog, *Country of my skull* (Cape Town: Random House, 1998, p 16).

17   Minow, 1998, p 15.

18   Judgement, AZAPO and Others v The President of the RSA and Others, 1996 (8) BCLR 1015 (CC), para 18.

19   This follows a proposal by Joy Liddicott, a legal adviser with the Department of Justice in the United Kingdom, as a basis for a theory of restorative justice. See *Criminal Justice Quarterly*, 5 (1993).

20   John Braithwaite, *Restorative Justice: Assessing an Immodest Theory and a Pessimistic Theory* (Australian Institute of Criminology, Australian National University, 1998). Llewellyn and Howse, in turn, identify the difficulties involved in the incorporation of restorative dimensions of justice into established criminal justice systems.

21   Neier, 1998, pp 42-3.

22   Richard Goldstone, 'Foreword' in Minow, p xiii.

23   *TRC Report*, Vol 1, Ch 4, para 64f.

24   Nicholas Tavuchis, *Mea Culpa: A Sociology of Apology and Reconciliation* (Stanford: Stanford University Press, 1991, p 17).

25   Tina Rosenberg, *The Haunted Land* (London: Vintage, 1995, p 351).

26   Minnow, 1998, p 88.

27   Howard Zehr, 'Restorative Justice: When Justice and Healing Go Together', *Track Two*, 6(3 & 4) (December 1997), p 20.

28   In a Cambridge University address, *Saturday Argus*, 13/14 February 1999.

29   *Sunday Independent*, 21 February 1999.

Chapter 7

1   See Appendix to this volume, p 304.

2   See Ch 6, note 14 supra.

3   *TRC Report*, Vol 1, Ch 4.

4   *TRC Report*, Vol 1, pp 79-82.

5   *TRC Report*, Vol 1, p 67.

6   *TRC Report*, Vol 1, pp 73-7.

7   *TRC Report*, Vol 1, p 77.

Chapter 8

1   Kader Asmal, Louise Asmal and Ronald Suresh Roberts, *Reconciliation Through Truth: A Reckoning of Apartheid's Criminal Governance* (Cape Town: David Philip, 2nd edn, 1997, p 214).

2   The restrictive terms of reference of the Harms Commission that unsatisfactorily investigated hit-squad activities during the 1990-1994 political transition, influenced the drafters of the 1995 Act in the decision to avoid tying the moral and political hands of the Commissioners. See Asmal, Asmal and

Roberts, *Reconciliation Through Truth* (2nd edn, 1997, p 25) quoting the Act (the Commission is mandated to investigate 'gross violations of human rights, including violations that were part of a systematic pattern of abuse').

3   The Act, Section 4.

4   Commentators of assorted political persuasions concede the need for updating the laws of war. See, e.g., George H Aldrich, 'The Laws of War', *Netherlands International Law Review*, 23, (1996), pp 221-6. Aldrich cautiously advocates a 'third Hague Peace Conference' to update the work of the previous two, albeit he does so from the rather partial perspective of a former 'lawyer for the United States government'.

5   General Constand Viljoen, leader of the parliamentary right wing and formerly a general in the apartheid military, told the Commission that 'neither side will really pass the full test of a just war, at least in the classical sense of the theory', while also asserting, oddly, that if the apartheid/anti-apartheid struggle was a war, it was so unique a war 'that the traditional just war theory cannot easily be applied'. Testimony at a public discussion on the just war debate and reconciliation held on Tuesday 6 May in the Old Town House, Frans Hals Room, Green Market Square, 6 May 1997. (Transcript available from the Commission's web site: www.truth.org.za) Conspicuously absent from these contradictory utterances is any attempt to evaluate the applicability of just war theory as it has evolved since its 'classical' positivist period.

6   Alan Sigg, a witness at the just war hearings, who was seconded to the Commission by the Swiss Ministry of Foreign Affairs, committed this solecism, holding just war doctrine inapplicable since apartheid had 'nothing to do with war. It [was] an internal conflict.' In fact, since the 1977 Geneva Protocols, the laws of war extend into internal conflicts. Testimony at a public discussion on the just war debate and reconciliation held on Tuesday 6 May in the Old Town House, Frans Hals Room, Green Market Square, 6 May 1997. (Transcript available from the Commission's web site.) In fact, since the 1977 Geneva Protocols, the laws of war extend into internal conflicts.

7   See, e.g., WV O'Brien, *The Conduct of Just and Limited War* (New York: Praeger Publishers, 1981). O'Brien laments (calling it an 'aberration') that Article 1(4) 'qualifies national liberation movements as per se belligerents under the protocol designed for international conflicts'. But he can hardly deny the reality of this development.

8   Dinstein, p 69.

9   GAID Draper, 'Wars of National Liberation and War Criminality', in Michael Howard (ed), *Restraints on War* (Oxford: Oxford University Press, 1970, p 135).

10 We make this argument in greater detail in Asmal, Asmal and Roberts, *Reconciliation Through Truth: A Reckoning of Apartheid's Criminal Governance* (Cape Town: David Philip, 2nd edn, 1997).

11 Draper, in 'Wars of National Liberation and War Criminality', objects to this development, but does nor deny it. The inclusion of liberation movements in the protective ambit of Protocol I, he says, 'has obtruded discrimination into Protocol I. It may be seen as a vestigial and modified remnant of the old 'just war' theory. The nature of the 'cause' for which an entity resorted to armed force, may, by selective criteria, eg, race, convert that entity to a lawful participant in international armed conflicts.' *Ibid.* p 150.

12 George I Mavrodes, 'Conventions and the Morality of War,' *Philosophy and Public Affairs*, 4(2) (Winter 1975), pp 117, 128.

13 See Elizabeth Anscombe, 'War and Murder' in *War and Morality* Richard A Wasserstrom (ed) (Belmont, California, 1970, p 52); John C Ford, 'The Morality of Obliteration Bombing', *Ibid.* p 19-23; Paul Ramsey, *The Just War* (New York, 1968, pp157-8).

14 See generally, Richard Falk, Gabriel Kolko and Robert Jay Lifton (eds), *Crimes of War: A Legal, Political-documentary and Psychological Inquiry into the Responsibility of Leaders, Citizens, and Soldiers for Criminal Acts in War* (New York: Vintage Books, 1971).

15 Constand Viljoen, testimony at a public discussion on the just war debate and reconciliation held on Tuesday 6 May in the Old Town House, Frans Hals Room, Green Market Square, 6 May 1997. (Transcript available from the Commission's web site).

16 Draper, 1970, p 156.

17 Rodney G Allen, Martin Cherniak and George Andreopoulous, 'Refining War: Civil Wars and Humanitarian Controls', *Human Rights Quarterly*, 18 (1996), pp 747, 751.

18 In his just war testimony to the Commission, Professor Andre du Toit recognises this ('even if both sides participate in the same war, even if both sides commit similar acts of shooting, bombing and killing, morally speaking they cannot be equated'), but then erroneously confines this insight to the just cause analysis (*jus ad bellum*), segregating it from the just conduct of war (*jus in bello*). Testimony at a public discussion on the just war debate and reconciliation held on Tuesday 6 May in the Old Town House, Frans Hals Room, Green Market Square, 6 May 1997. (Transcript available from the Commission's web site.) We acknowledge that the *jus in bello* analysis is conceptually separate from that of *jus ad bellum*, but we deny that the justice of the cause is hermetically irrelevant to this second stage of analysis. The justice of the cause does not forgive all and every evil in the conduct of the war, but it does influence that analysis, especially given the convention-dependent nature of the laws of war and apartheid's grave violations of those conventions.

19 *International Military Tribunal,* 9, p 323. Proceedings, 8-23 March 1946.

20 *Trials of Criminals Before the Nuremberg Military Tribunals,* 11, p 852.

21 United States of America v Otto Ohlendorf *et al, Trials of Criminals Before the Nuremberg Tribunals,* Vol 4, p 411.

22 *Ibid.*

23 Michael Walzer, *Just and Unjust Wars: A Moral Argument with Historical Illustrations* (New York: Basic Books, 1977). Walzer's text is unambiguously the most influential postwar work on just war theory.

24 See Gordon Graham, 'Terrorists and Freedom Fighters', *Philosophy and Social Action,* 11 (1985), pp 43-54. Without necessarily endorsing Graham's conclusions, we would note that he engages in the sort of just war debate that would have been edifying for the Commission, investigating for instance whether there can be a bias-free basis for distinguishing terrorists from freedom fighters and exploring the sorts of conventions and

types of moral reasoning that might assist in answering such questions.

Chapter 9

1 Typified by the National Party Government publication *South Africa and the Rule of Law* (Pretoria, 1968).

2 Besides those such as Beinart and Cowen in the 1950s, the leading exponents of this view are AS Mathews *Law, Order and Liberty* (1971) and *Freedom, State Security and the Rule of Law* (Cape Town: Juta and Co., 1986) and John Dugard *Human Rights and the SA Legal Order* (Princeton: Princeton University Press, 1978).

3 See, for example, Raymond Suttner 'Law, Justice and the Nature of Man: Some Unwarranted Assumptions', *Acta Juridica* 173 (1973).

4 See particularly *SALB*, 7(1, 2 & 3) (1981).

5 For a very good overview, see Clive Thompson 'Trade Unions using the Law' in Hugh Corder (ed) *Essays on Law and Social Practice* (1988) Chap 13.

6 For a review in the late 1980s, see Hugh Corder and Dennis Davis 'Law and Social Practice: an introduction' in Corder (ed) *Op cit* note 5, Chap 1

7 For a descriptive analysis of these events, see, for example, Hugh Corder and Dennis Davis 'The Constitutional Guidelines of the ANC: A Preliminary Assessment', *SA Law Journal,* 106 (1989), pp 633-48.

8 Act 34 of 1995.

9 *TRC Report*, Vol 1, Ch 7, pp 174-200.

10 AZAPO v TRC 1996 (4) SA 562 (C).

11 See AZAPO v President of the RSA 1996 (8) *BCLR* 1015 (CC).

12 These legal disputes were all played out in the Magistrates Court in George, and so have not been officially reported, except in the *TRC Report*, Vol 1, p 197.

13 *TRC Report*, Vol 1, p 180.

14 See, for example, Niewoudt v TRC 1997 (2) SA 70 (SEC) and TRC v Du Preez 1996 (8) *BCLR* 1123 (C).

15 Reported as Du Preez v TRC 1997 (4) *BCLR* 531 (A).

16 Further details of the impact of the Du Preez decision can be found in the *TRC Report*, Vol 1, pp 185-6.

17 Those involved were Capt Dirk Coetzee and Joseph Mamasela.

18 Such as the non-certification of the initial draft of the final Constitution and the order to him to appear in the court in the case involved the setting-up of a commission of inquiry into the SA Rugby Football Union.

Chapter 10

1 Bonnie Gangelhoff, 'Re-opening an Old Mystery', *Newsweek,* 1 March 1999.

2 'Interest in Hit-squad Amnesty Hearing Grows as Revelations Are Made', South African Press Association, 21 April 1998.

3 *TRC Report,* Vol 1, Ch 8.

4 AZAPO v TRC 1996 (4) SA 562 (C). See also AZAPO v President of the RSA 1996 (8) *BCLR* 1015 (CC). See also, Hugh Corder, 'The Law and Struggle: The Same but Different', Ch 9 in this volume.

5 'Mandela Acknowledges Apartheid Criminals May Go Unpunished', 17 June 1998, South African Press Association and Associated Press.

6 *TRC Report,* Vol 4, Ch 4.

7 'Judiciary's Application of Security Legislation Slated', South African Press Association, 26 October 1997.

8 Jose Zalaquett, Conference statement in the course of 'Justice in Transition: Dealing With the Past' (Cape Town: IDASA, 1994). Quoted by Antjie Krog in 'The South African Road' in *The Healing of a Nation* (Cape Town: Justice in Transition, 1995).

9 'ANC Seeks to Interdict Truth Report', *Mail & Guardian,* 29 October 1998.

10 Wally Mbhele, 'ANC, TRC Clash Over Final Report', South African Press Association, 9 October 1998.

11 'ANC Accuses TRC of Criminalising Apartheid Struggle', South African Press Association, 27 October 1998.

12 Lynne Duke, 'ANC Seeks to Enjoin Abuse Data', *The Washington Post,* 29 October 1998.

13 'Mandela Backs Finding of TRC on Human Rights Abuses', South African Press Association, 21 October 1998.

14 Suzanne Daley, 'South Africa Gambles on Truth, Not Justice', *International Herald Tribune,* 28 October 1996.

Chapter 11

1 John D Caputo, *Against Ethics* (Bloomington & Indianapolis: Indiana University Press, 1993, p 12).

2 Caputo, *1993,* p 12.

3 John D Caputo, *Deconstruction in a Nutshell: A Conversation with Jacques Derrida* (New York: Fordham University Press, 1997, pp 16-17).

Chapter 12

1 Piet Meiring, *Chronicle of the Truth Commission,* (Vanderbylpark: Carpe Diem, p 29).

2 *The Star,* 29 February 1996.

3 H Russel Botman, Robin M Peterson, *To Remember and to Heal,* (Cape Town: Human and Rousseau, 1996, p 8).

4 Quoted from a R&R Committee discussion paper, January 1998.

5 Botman, Peterson, 1998, p 22f.

6 Quoted from an R&R Committee discussion paper, January 1998.

7 Quoted by Charles Villa-Vicencio in an article in *The Sunday Independent,* 7 June 1998.

8 Meiring, 1999, p 357.

9 Meiring, 1999, p 371.

10 Meiring, 1999, p 376.

11 *TRC Report,* Vol 5, pp 316f, 439f.

12 *The Sunday Independent,* 2 August 1998.

SECTION 3
What the commission sought to achieve

Chapter 13

1 TRC Act, Section 3.

2 *TRC Report,* Vol 3, p 203.

3 *TRC Report,* Vol 2, p 336.

4 *TRC Report,* Vol 2, pp 171 and 335-6; Vol 3, p 231. See also the ANC submissions to the TRC in August 1996 and May 1997.

5 PEBCO Three: Sipho Hashe, Qaqawuli Godolozi and Champion Galela.

6 Motherwell Four: Amos Themba Faku, Mbambala Glen Mgoduka, Desmond Mapipa and Charles Jack.

7 *TRC Report,* Vol 2, pp 224-5; Vol 3, 117.

8 *TRC Report,* Vol 3, p 118; Vol 2, p 272.

9 Timothy Garton Ash, *The File: A Personal History* (London: Flamingo, 1998, p 12).

10 Svetlana Aleksiyevich, 'Russia: The Play of War' in *Index on Censorship,* 5 (1996), p 154.

11 Michael Ignatieff, 'Articles of Faith', *Index on Censorship,* 5 (1996).

12 *Ibid.* pp 113.

13 *Ibid.*

Chapter 14

1   *TRC Report*, Vol 1, p 114.

2   *TRC Report*, Vol 1, p 131.

3   *TRC Report*, Vol 5, p 435. See also Vol 5, Ch 8.

4   See Antjie Krog, *Country of my skull* (Johannesburg: Random House, 1998); *TRC Report*, Vol 5, Ch 4.

5   *TRC Report*, Vol 1, p 60. See also Vol 1, pp 60-5, 69-70, 94-102; Vol 5, pp 196-8, 212, 274-6.

6   *TRC Report*, Vol 1, p 34.

7   *TRC Report*, Vol 1, p 62. See also Vol 4.

8   *TRC Report*, Vol 1, p 131; Vol 4, Vol 5, pp 359-62, 384-6.

9   *TRC Report*, Vol 4.

10 Anthony Kenny, 'Ludwig Wittgenstein: Why Do we Philosophise if it is only Useful Against Philosophers?' *Times Higher Educational Supplement*, 19 May 1987.

11 P Bate, *Strategies for Cultural Change* (London: Butterworth/Heinemann, 1980).

12 L Martel, *Mastering Change: The Key to Business Success* (London: Grafton Books, 1986, p 16).

13 Bate, 1980, p 16.

14 Thomas Kuhn, *The Structure of Scientific Revolutions* (Chicago: Chicago University Press, 1962, p 7).

15 J Huey, 'Nothing is Impossible', *Fortune Magazine*, 23 September 1991, p 91.

16 Bate, 1980, p 35.

17 There were, of course, also many people, especially from the Afrikaans-speaking communities, who reacted with criticism and denial to these painful truths. On resistance to the TRC among Afrikaners, see Willie Esterhuyse, 'TRC cartoons and the Afrikaner community' in WJ Verwoerd and M Mabizela (eds), *The TRC Through Cartoons* (Cape Town: David Philip, 1999).

18 JA Conger, 'Inspiring Others: The Language of Leadership', *Academy of Management Executive*, 5(1) (1991), p 31.

Chapter 15

1   Mahmood Mamdani, 'A Diminished Truth', *Siyaya*, 3 (Spring 1998), pp 38-40.

2   Martha Minnow, *Between Vengeance and Forgiveness: Facing History after Genocide and Mass Violence* (Boston: Beacon Press, 1998, p 4).

3   Desmond Tutu, 'The Truth and Reconciliation Commission', in CW Du Toit (ed) *Confession and Reconciliation* (Pretoria: Research Institute for Theology and Religion, 1998, p 3).

4   *TRC Report*, Vol 1, Ch 4.

5   *TRC Report*. Vol 1, Ch 5; Vol 5, Ch 9.

6   Judith Shklar, *The Faces of Injustice* (New Haven: Yale University Press, 1992, pp 46-7).

7   See *A Crime of Silence: The Armenian Genocide. Report of the Permanent People's Tribunal*, 13-16 April 1984, (London: Zed Books, 1985); Daine Kupelian *et al.*, 'The Turkish Genocide of the Armenians: Continuing Effects on Survivors and their Families Eight Decades After Massive Trauma', in Yael Danieli (ed) *International Handbook of Multigenerational Legacies of Trauma* (New York: Plenum Press, 1998).

8   See Iris Chang, *The Rape of Nanking: the forgotten holocaust of World War II* (New York: Basic Books, 1997).

9   See Barbara Heimannsberg and Christoph Schmidt (eds), *The Collective Silence: German identity and the legacy of shame* (San Francisco: Jossey-Bass Publishers, 1993).

10 A key difference is, of course, that the soldiers are often not only bystanders but the main perpetrators themselves, as the TRC has shown in the South African context. Here I am using Giotto's image of injustice in the first place as a striking picture of (official) responses to past injustices, not to describe the various actors involved in the injustices themselves.

11 See Michael Simpson, 'The Second Bullet: Transgenerational Impact of the Trauma of Conflict Within a South African and World Context' in *Danieli*, (1998, pp 487-511); M Symonds, 'The "Second Injury" to Victims', *Evaluation and Change* (1980), pp 36-8.

12 Thabo Mbeki, 'Culture: The Barrier Which Blocks Regress to Beastly Ways' in *Africa: The Time Has Come, Selected Speeches* (Cape Town: Tafelberg, Mafube, 1998, p 259).

13 Mbeki, 1998, p 259.

14 WB Yeats, *Selected Poetry* (London: Pan Books, 1974, p 104).

15 Donald Shriver reminds us of the wisdom and respect of the three men who came to Job's blistered side: 'They raised their voices and wept aloud ... They sat with him on the ground seven days and seven nights, and no

one spoke a word to him, for they saw that his suffering was great.' *Job* 2:12-13, quoted in Shriver, 'Long Road to Reconciliation: Some Moral Stepping Stones', published paper, p 1.

16   Speech in National Assembly, 15 April 1997, quoted in *TRC Report*, Vol 1, p 134.

17   Paul Ricoeur, 'The Memory of Suffering', *Figuring the Sacred* (Minneapolis: Fortress Press, 1995, p 290).

18   Elie Wiesel, 'For the dead and the Living' in *New Leader* (17-31 May 1993), pp 13-14.

19   *TRC Report*, Vol 1, Ch 4.

20   Yael Danieli (ed), *International Handbook of Multigenerational Legacies of Trauma* (New York: Plenum Press, 1998, pp 4-6, 71, 145, 150, 179, 194, 205).

21   See AZAPO v President of the RSA 1996 (8) *BCLR* 1015 (CC).

22   *Insig*, November 1998, p 6.

23   Johan Snyman, 'Interpretation and the Politics of Memory', *Acta Jurudica* (1998).

24   Snyman, 1998, pp 327-8.

25   Emily Hobhouse, *Boer War Letters*, 1984, pp 406-7, quoted in Snyman, p 329.

26   Hobhouse, pp 406-7, quoted in Snyman, p 329.

27   Hobhouse, 1902, pp 350-5; SB Spies, *Methods of Barbarism? Roberts and Kitchener and Civilians in the Boer Republics, January 1900-May 1902* (Cape Town: Human & Rousseau, 1977).

28   Ricoeur, 1995, p 290.

29   Antjie Krog, *Country of my skull* (Johannesburg: Random House, 1998, p 237).

30   Henry Shue, *Basic Rights* (Princeton: Princeton University Press, 1980, pp 18-19).

31   See Rajeev Bhargava's contribution in this book. Also Ashvai Margalit, *The Decent Society* (Cambridge. Mass.: Harvard University Press, 1996).

32   See Susan Mendus, 'Human Rights in Political Theory' in David Beetham (ed), *Politics and Human Rights* (Oxford: Blackwell, 1995, pp 10-24). I concur with her interpretation of human rights as primarily 'bulwarks against evil' and not 'harbingers of goods', and agree that 'the political impetus for human rights comes from the recognition of evil as a permanent threat in the world', pp 23-4.

33   Jonathan Allen, 'Balancing Justice and Social Unity: Political Theory and the Idea of a Truth and Reconciliation Commission', University of Toronto Law Journal, vol 49 (1999), pp 315-353. In this paper Allen confirms the significance of the TRC's focus on past injustices by referring to Wolgast's important point that 'the sense of injustice is prior to any particular conception of justice that we may articulate; a conception of justice is a response to and more or less successful articulation of our sense of injustice'. See Elizabeth Wolgast, *The Grammar of Justice* (Ithaca: Cornell University Press, 1987).

34   *Sunday Independent*, 15 November 1998.

35   6-12 November 1998.

Chapter 17

1   Decision of Gcinikhayae Makoma (0164/96) *et al.* (11 June 1998) ('St James Massacre').

2   Decision of David Petrus Botha (0057/96) (5 September 1997).

3   Decision of Vusumzi Samuel Ntamo (4734/97) *et al.* (28 July 1998) ('Amy Biehl').

4   Decision of Jean Prieur du Plessis (0151/96) (6 December 1996).

5   Decision of Brian Victor Mitchell (2589/96) (9 December 1996) ('Trust Feeds Massacre').

6   Decision of LH Froneman (0395/96) *et al.* (30 July 1997).

7   No state court has ruled its own government's amnesty illegal, although some courts have held that its country's amnesty does not apply to certain types of violations. In the most confrontational ruling by a domestic court against its own country's amnesty, a lower court in Chile ruled in 1995 that amnesty could not be granted for acts that constitute war crimes under the Geneva Conventions. This ruling was short-lived, however, as the Chilean Supreme Court quickly overturned it a few months later. See Derechos Chile, 'High Court Amnesties Human Rights Case: Overturning Lower Court Ruling on Geneva Conventions.' (http://derechoschile.com/english/news/19960131.htm) (31 January 1996).

8   The Spanish courts investigating human rights abuses in Argentina and Chile have proceeded despite the amnesties passed in both of those countries. For a brief discussion of these prosecutions, see Richard J Wilson, 'Spanish Criminal Prosecutions Use International Human Rights Law to Battle Impunity in Chile and Argentina,' KO'AGA

RONE'ETA ser. iii (1996) (http://www.-derechos.org/koaga/iii/5/wilson.html).

9   Aryeh Neier, *War Crimes: Brutality, Genocide, Terror and the Struggle for Justice* (New York: Times Books, 1998, pp 103-7).

10   In fact the Constitutional Court in its decision upholding the amnesty provisions conceded the strength of the third criticism, noting that the amnesty violated some of the rights of victims recognised in the South African Constitution. See AZAPO vs President of South Africa, CCT 17/96, 1996 (4) SALR 671 (CC) paras 9-10.

11   After it was promulgated, the Uruguayan amnesty was the subject of a countrywide referendum. A majority of those who participated in the referendum voted for the amnesty.

12   Of course, the decision to grant amnesty in South Africa was not the result of a democratic process, but came out of the multi-party negotiations that formed the basis for the transition to democracy. The South African public was thus never given an opportunity to decide whether an amnesty should be granted, as the Uruguayan public eventually was in the form of a post-amnesty referendum.

13   Of course how much this legislative process really does reflect the will of South Africans is an important question. Even if we accept that it does, it does not address the claim that the amnesty is illegitimate because it substantially infringes the individual rights of victims.

14   The argument that increased truth is a form of justice is reflected in international tribunal decisions that obligate a state to at least investigate certain violations. See Velasquez Rodriguez Case, Inter-Am. Ct. HR (ser. C) No 4 (1988) (judgement). On truth telling as a form of justice, see Ruti Teitel, 'From Dictatorship to Democracy: The Role of Transitional Justice,' in Harold Hongju Koh and Ronald C Slye (eds), *Deliberative Democracy and Human Rights* (Yale University Press, 1999).

15   See, e.g., Neil J Kritz (ed), *Transitional Justice*, Vol II, pp 391-2 (noting that Uruguayan amnesty law provides for investigations, but in practice few were conducted).

16   I have elsewhere discussed the quality of the truth produced by the amnesty hearings See Slye, 'Amnesty, Truth, and Reconciliation: Reflections on the South African Amnesty Process,' in Rotberg & Thompson (eds), *Truth Versus Justice: The Moral Efficacy of Truth Commissions in South Africa and Beyond* (forthcoming, 1999).

17   These are not the only requirements that an applicant must meet in order to be granted amnesty. For a list of other requirements, see Promotion of National Unity and Reconciliation Act, Section 20.

18   For an example of denial of amnesty based on a failure to fully disclose, see Cases of Mpayipheli William Faltein (0120/06) (amnesty denied on 23 January 1997); and Gerhardus Johannes Nieuwodt (3920/96) (amnesty denied on 20 November 1997).

19   The immediate source for this requirement in the South African amnesty is the Norgaard Principles. The Norgaard Principles were drafted by the former President of the European Commission of Human Rights, CA Norgaard, in the context of the political transition in Namibia. The principles are based on a comprehensive survey of state practice in defining and applying the political offence exception to extradition law.

20   See Article 20(3), which directs the committee to 'refer' to a number of criteria in determining whether an act is associated with a political objective, including the motive of the person committing the act, the context in which the act took place, whether the act was committed in the execution of an order or with the approval of a political organization, and the relationship between the proportionality of the act to the objective pursued.

21   There are some exceptions to this general assertion. There are a few cases in which following orders has been accepted as a defence, most notably in the Argentinean legislation that halted the post-transition trials in the 1980s. In 1987, the Argentinean government passed what is colloquially known as the 'Due Obedience' law, which provides an absolute defence of following orders to subordinate military officers accused of war crimes or crimes against humanity. See Neil J Kritz, *Transitional Justice*. Vol III, pp 507-8.

22   Decision of Johan van Eyk (0070/96) *et al.* (22 August 1996) ('Fidelity Guards').

23   See Decision of Jeffrey Theodore Benzien (5314/96) (17 February 1999) (police officer

granted amnesty for torturing and killing political opponents).

24 See generally Eugene de Kock, *A Long Night's Damage: Working for the Apartheid State* (Saxonwold: Kontra Press, 1998).

25 See Case of BH Jwambi (0126/96) (amnesty denied on 21 August 1997), in which members of the ANC were involved in acts of violence that the amnesty committee concluded were not political; and case of Derrick Tshidiso Kobue (0142/96) (amnesty denied on 13 March 1997), in which a political activist killed a policemen who had intervened in an argument between the applicant and the applicant's girlfriend.

26 See, e.g., Donald G McNeil Jr, 'Four Slain in South Africa, Raising Fear of More Violence,' *New York Times*, 10 March 1999, A5 (reporting on the murder of four politicians in the Western Cape).

27 For a general discussion about the danger of amnesties on political legitimacy and the rule of law, see Graeme Simpson, 'A Culture of Impunity,' *The Johannesburg Star*, 24 January 1997 (arguing that 'successive amnesties may send out wrong signals: encouraging rather than alarming criminals').

28 The words in quotations are based on my recollection of the conversation, and is not meant to be a direct quotation.

Chapter 18

1 *TRC Report*, Vol 1, p 5.

2 *TRC Report*, Vol 1, p 7.

3 See the Postamble of the Interim Constitution (Act 200 of 1993).

4 See AZAPO v President of the RSA 1996 (8) BCLR 1015 (CC).

5 See Jorge Correa, 'Dealing with Past Human Rights Violations: the Chilean Case after Dictatorship', in Neil J Kritz (ed) *Transitional Justice*, Vol II, pp 478-94.

6 See Priscilla Hayner, 'Reconciling Truth with Justice: Forecasting the Factors that Effect a Stable Peace'. Research paper presented at Woodrow Wilson International Center, March 1997.

7 See also *TRC Report*, Vol 1, Ch 5-7; Charles Villa-Vicencio, 'A Different Kind of Justice: The South African Truth and Reconciliation Commission', *Contemporary Justice Review*, 1, pp 407-28.

8 See Promotion of National Unity and Reconciliation Act (No 34 of 1995) (the Act), sections 18(1) – 22(2).

9 See WJ Verwoerd, 'Justice After Apartheid? 'Reflections on the South African TRC', paper delivered at the Fifth International Conference on Ethics and Development, Madras, India, 1997, p 5.

10 Verwoerd, 1997, pp 6-7.

11 In MR Rwelamira and G Werle (eds), *Confronting Past Injustices* (Durban: Butterworths, 1996, p xii).

12 See section 20(3) of the Act.

13 See Convention Against Torture and Other Cruel, Inhuman or Degrading Treatment or Punishment, 1987; Vienna Declaration of Torture, 1993 – both have been signed by South Africa.

14 *TRC Report*, Vol 5, Ch 5.

15 *Sunday Independent*, 17 May 1998.

16 The *Sowetan*.

Chapter 19

1 The requirements for amnesty are discussed more fully in an earlier essay included in this volume by Ron Slye.

2 See also George Bizos, *No One to Blame? In Pursuit of Justice in South Africa* (Cape Town: David Philip & Mayibuye Books, 1998, pp 39-100).

Chapter 20

1 Richard Wilson, 'The Sizwe Will Not Go Away: The Truth and Reconciliation Commission, Human Rights and Nation-Building in South Africa', *African Studies*, 55(2) (1996), pp 14-18.

2 Jonathan Allen, 'Balancing Justice and Social Unity: Political Theory and the Idea of a Truth and Reconciliation Commission.' University of Toronto Law Journal, vol 49 (1999), pp 315-353.

3 *TRC Report*, Vol 5, p 366.

4 Alex Boraine *et al, Dealing with the Past* (Cape Town: IDASA, 1994, p 15).

5 Donald Shriver, 'Long Road to Reconciliation: Some Moral Stepping Stones'. A paper delivered at Oxford University, 14-16 September 1998 on 'Burying the Past: Justice, Forgiveness and Reconciliation in the Politics of South Africa, Guatemala, East Germany and Northern Ireland'.

6   GH Mead quoted in Shriver, 1998.

7   Rajeev Bhargava, 'Is the Idea of a Truth Commission Justified?' A paper delivered at an international seminar on Justice, Truth and Reconciliation in Transitional Societies, Geneva, 9-12 December, 1998.

8   *Cape Times,* 16 February 1999.

9   Dan Stein, 'Psychiatric Aspects of the Truth and Reconciliation Commission in South Africa,' *British Journal of Psychiatry,* 173 (1988) p 456.

10 In *Africa News,* January 1998.

11 *TRC Report,* Vol 5, p 350.

12 Stein, 1988, p 455.

13 Martha Minow, *Between Vengeance and Forgiveness* (Boston: Beacon Books, 1998, pp 12, 120).

14 George Bizos, *No One to Blame? In Pursuit of Justice in South Africa* (Cape Town: David Philip & Mayibuye Books, 1998, p 238).

15 In Gilles Deleuze and Felix Guattari, *Anti-Oedipus: Capitalism and Schizophrenia* (London: Athlone Press, 1984, p iii).

16 Leon Jaworski, *After Fifteen Years* (Houston: Gulf Publishing Company, 1961).

17 Jacques Pauw, *Into the Heart of Darkness* (Johannesburg: Jonathan Ball, 1997, p 190).

18 Pauw, 1997.

19 Bizos, 1998, p 182.

20 In his 'Andries Van Riet Address', to the 30th Annual Convention of the South African Property Owners' Association, June 1997.

21 Part of the *Molo Songololo* submission to the TRC Athlone Youth Hearings, 22 May 1997.

22 *TRC Report,* Vol 1, Ch 5, para 80.

23 Albie Sachs, 'Reparation: Political and Psychological Considerations', *Psycho-Analytical Psychotherapy in South Africa,* 2, (Summer 1993), p 23.

24 Jeffrie G Murphy and Jean Hampton, *Forgiveness and Mercy* (Cambridge: Cambridge University Press, 1988, pp 30-1).

25 In *Journal of Democracy,* 4(1) (January 1993).

Chapter 21

1   *TRC Report,* Vol 1, p 1.

2   *TRC Report,* Vol 1, p 5.

3   *TRC Report,* Vol 5, p 125.

4   *TRC Report,* Vol 5, pp 238-49.

5   *TRC Report,* Vol 5, p 308.

6   *TRC Report,* Vol 5, p 252.

7   *Cape Times,* 20 October 1998.

8   *Cape Times,* 20 October 1998.

9   *Cape Times,* 24 April 1998.

Chapter 22

1   DJ Goldhagen, *Hitler's Willing Executioners* (New York: Vintage, 1995). In addition, GS Paulsson, 'Hiding in Warsaw'. Unpublished D.Phil thesis, University of Oxford, 1998.

2   *TRC Report,* Vol 5, p 260.

3   *TRC Report,* Vol 5, p 276.

4   *TRC Report,* Vol 5, p 276.

5   *TRC Report,* Vol 5, p 274.

6   *TRC Report,* Vol 5, p 275.

7   R Baumeister, *Evil: Inside Human Violence and Cruelty* (New York: WH Freeman, 1997).

8   J Duckitt, *The Social Psychology of Prejudice* (New York: Praeger, 1992).

9   *TRC Report,* Vol 5, p 294.

10 D Foster, 'Perpetrators of gross violations of human rights', *Journal of Community and Health Sciences,* 4(2) (1997), pp 1-34.

11 D Foster and D Skinner, 'Detention and Violence: Beyond Victimology', NC Manganyi & A du Toit (eds) *Political Violence and the Struggle in South Africa* (London: Macmillan, 1990, pp 205-33).

12 P du Preez, *Genocide* (London: Bayers/Bowerdean, 1994).

13 *Ibid.,* p 108.

14 J Gordin, 'Beyond mere Blames: Commissions' Report Forges a Moral Framework for the Future', *The Sunday Independent,* 4 April 1998, p 11.

15 E de Kock, *A Long Night's Damage* (Saxonwold: Contra Press, 1998).

16 P Gobodo-Maikizela, 'Eugene de Kock: Understanding Apartheid's Crusader Using Psychoanalytic Group Relations Theory'. Paper presented at the International Psychoanalytic Conference, Cape Town, 4 April 1998.

17 *TRC Report,* Vol 4.

18 S Lamb, *The Trouble With Blame* (Cambridge, Mass: Harvard University Press, 1996).

19 Baumeister, 1997.

20 T Scheff, *Bloody Revenge* (Boulder: Westview Press, 1994).

21 DJ Stein, 'The Neuro-biology of Evil: Psychiatric Perspectives on Perpetrators'. Paper presented at the Conference on Mental Health beyond the TRC, Medical Research Council, Bellville, 7-8 October 1998.

22 L Nicolas, 'Perpetrators and PTSD'. Paper presented at 4th PsySSA Annual Congress, University of Cape Town, 9-11 September 1998.
23 Baumeister, 1997.

Chapter 23

1   J Ellul, *Violence: Reflections From a Christian Perspective* (New York: Seabury Press, 1969, p 97).
2   L Gilbert, 'Urban Violence and Health – South Africa 1995' in *Social Science & Medicine*, 43(5) (1996), pp 873-86.
3   D Lisak, J Hopper & P Song, 'Factors in the Cycle of Violence: Gender Rigidity and Emotional Constriction', *Journal of Traumatic Stress*, 9(4) (1996), pp 721-43.
4   T De Ridder, personal communication in Cape Town, South Africa, 30 July 1998.
5   D Bar-On *et al*, 'Four Encounters Between Descendants of Survivors and Descendants of Perpetrators of the Holocaust: Building Social Bonds Out of Silence', *Psychiatry*, 58 (1995), pp 225-45.
6   F Kaslow, 'A Dialogue Between Descendants of Perpetrators and Victims – Session Two' *Israel Journal of Psychiatry and Related Sciences*, 34(1) (1997), pp 44-5.
7   J Collet, 1990. *A Time to Plant: Biography of James Lydford Collet, Settler* (Cape Town: Creda Press, 1990, p 44).

Chapter 24

1   The Act S3(1) (c).
2   The Act S1(1) (xiv).
3   The Act S4(f).

Chapter25

1   Gobodo-Madikizela, *Cape Times*, 3 December 1996.
2   Minutes of From Truth to Transformation Conference, April 1998.
3   J. Herman, *Trauma and Recovery* (New York: Harper Collins Publishers, 1992).
4   See parliamentary debate, 25 February 1999.
5   Proposal prepared by Andrew Shackleton and Michelle Fief, 22 February 1999.
6   Alex Boraine. See minutes of From Truth to Transformation Conference, April 1998.

SECTION 4
After the Commission
Chapter 26

1   Francis Wilson, 'The Current Relations of Poverty', keynote address at the National Povery Summit, June 1998.
2   *TRC Report*, Vol 5, p 318.
3   Gustavo Gutierrez, *We Drink From our Own Wells* (Maryknoll: Oribis Books, 1985).

Chapter 27

1   *TRC Report*, Vol 4, p 58.
2   *TRC Report*, Vol 4, p 58.
3   *TRC Report*, Vol 4, p 58.
4   While the wages of whites in the gold mines in 1911 were 11,7 times higher than those of Africans, white wages were 20,9 times higher in 1971. M. Lipton, *Capitalism and Apartheid (Cape Town:* David Philip, 1985, p 410).
5   *TRC Report*, Vol 4, Ch 2.
6   *TRC Report*, Vol 4, Ch 2.
7   *TRC Report*, Vol 4, Ch 2.
8   *TRC Report*, Vol 5, p 318.
9   *TRC Report*, Vol 5, p 318.
10 This first view was supported and articulated in the submissions of the ANC, SACP, COSATU, the Black Management Forum and myself.
11 The second view was supported in the submissions of the different business organisations, big corporations and by Mike Rosholt of Barlow Rand and Anton Rupert of Rupert International.
12 *TRC Report*, Vol 4, p 54.
13 M Mamdani, 'Reconciliation Without Justice', *Southern African Review of Books*, Nov/Dec 1996.
14 *TRC Report*, Vol 4, p 43.
15 K. Galbraith, *The Age of Uncertainty*, 1977, p 257.
16 *TRC Report*, Vol 4, p33.
17 *TRC Report*, Vol 4, p 34.
18 *TRC Report*, Vol 1, Ch 2.
19 *TRC Report*, Vol 1, pp 148-149.
20 *TRC Report*, Vol 1, Appendix to Ch 4, p94.

Chapter 28

1   See, for example, Thomas Karis and Gwendolyn Carter (eds), *From Protest to*

Challenge: A Documentary history of African Politics in South Africa, Vols 1-5 (Stanford: Hoover Institution Press, 1972); Tom Lodge, *Black Politics in South Africa Since 1945* (Johannesburg: Ravan Press, 1983); Julie Frederickse, *The Unbreakable Thread: Non-racialism in South Africa* (London: Zed Books, 1990).

2   Jacques Derrida, 'The Laws of Reflection: Nelson Mandela, In Admiration', in Jacques Derrida and Mustapha Tlili (eds), *For Nelson Mandela* (New York: Seaver Books, 1987).

3   See Chapter 9 in this volume by Hugh Corder.

4   See, for example, Jacques Derrida, *The Other Heading: Reflections on Today's Europe* (Bloomington: Indiana Press, 1982); Iris Marion Young, *Justice and the Politics of Difference* (Princeton: Princeton University Press, 1990).

Appendix
Key sections from Chapter 4
The Mandate, *TRC Report*,
Volume I

These sections from the Mandate chapter are included to facilitate readers who may wish to consider the key principles underlying the findings of the TRC regarding apartheid, its *inclusive* definition of victims of gross human rights violations and its *restrictive* definition of combatants as informed by International Humanitarian Law. In each case the numbers below correspond to the paragraphs in Volume 1, Chapter 4 of the *TRC Report*.

56 The mandate of the Commission was to focus on what might be termed 'bodily integrity rights', rights that are enshrined in the new South African Constitution and under international law. These include the right to life[2], the right to be free from torture[3], the right to be free from cruel, inhuman, or degrading treatment or punishment[4] and the right to freedom and security of the person, including freedom from abduction and arbitrary and prolonged detention[5].

57 But bodily integrity rights are not the only fundamental rights. When a person has no food to eat, or when someone is dying because of an illness which access to basic health care could have prevented – that is, when subsistence rights are violated – rights to political participation and freedom of speech become meaningless.

58 Thus, a strong argument can be made that the violations of human rights caused by 'separate development' – for example, by migrant labour, forced removals, Bantustans, Bantu education and so on – had, and continue to have, the most negative possible impact on the lives of the majority of South Africans. The consequences of these violations cannot be measured only in human lives lost through deaths, detentions, dirty tricks and disappearances, but in human lives withered away through enforced poverty and other kinds of deprivation.

59   Hence the Commission fully recognised that large-scale human rights violations were committed through legislation designed to enforce apartheid, through security legislation designed to criminalise resistance to the state, and through similar legislation passed by governments in the homelands. Its task, however, was limited to examining those 'gross violations of human rights' as defined in the Act. This should not be taken to mean, however, that those 'gross violations of human rights' (killing, torture, abduction and severe ill treatment) were the only very serious human rights violations that occurred.

State and non-state actors

77   Thus, the Commission adopted the view that human rights violations could be committed by any group or person inside or outside the state: by persons within the Pan Africanist Congress (PAC), the IFP, the South African Police (SAP), the South African Defence Force (SADF), the ANC or any other organisation.

78   It is important to note, however, that this wider application of human rights principles to non-state entities is a relatively recent international development. Traditionally, human rights focused on relations between state and citizens and on protecting the individual from the power of the state. Private non-state entities were not subject to the same restrictions and scrutiny. The traditional exceptions to this have been found in the area of war crimes and crimes against humanity which, even under the traditional definition of human rights, can be committed by any individual or entity.

79   The Act establishing the Commission adopted this more modern position. In other words, it did not make a finding of a gross violation of human rights conditional on a finding of state action. This extended view of human rights prohibitions reflects modern developments in international human rights law. It also contributes to national unity and reconciliation by treating individual victims with equal respect, regardless of whether the harm was caused by an official of the state or of the liberation movements.

80   At the same time, it must be said that those with the most power to abuse must carry the heaviest responsibility. It is a matter of the gravest concern when the state, which holds the monopoly of public force and is charged with protecting the rights of citizens, uses that force to violate

those rights. The state has a whole range of powerful institutions at its disposal – the police, the judicial system, the mass media, Parliament – with which it may denounce, investigate and punish human rights violations by private citizens or non-governmental groups. When this power is used to violate the rights of its citizens, as described in the report of the Chilean commission, their normal vulnerability is transformed into utter defencelessness.

81 This sensitivity to the unequal power relationships between state and non-state agents should be seen as an attempt to help lay the foundation for the rehabilitation of state institutions in order to hold present and future governments accountable for their use and abuse of power. It is thus central to the effort to prevent future violations of human rights.

Defining gross violations of human rights

82 The Act did not provide clear guidelines for the interpretation of the definition of 'gross violations of human rights'. In order to determine which acts constituted gross violations of human rights, it was important to interpret the definition and to consider whether there were any limitations excluding particular acts from this definition. The Act used neutral concepts or terms to describe the various acts that constituted a gross violation of human rights. For example, 'killing' and 'abduction' were used rather than murder or kidnapping. Clearly, the intention was to try to avoid introducing concepts with a particular content in terms of the applicable domestic criminal law. This was to avoid equating what was essentially a commission of enquiry with a court of law. If the full array of legal technicalities and nuances had been introduced into the work and decision-making functions of the Commission, its task would have been rendered immensely complex and time-consuming. It would also have contradicted the clear intention that the Commission should fulfil its mandate as expeditiously as possible. It could also have opened the way for a repetition of past injustices, with victims of the political conflict being excluded by legal technicalities from claiming compensation for their losses. Thus, it was clear that the underlying objective of the legislators was to make it possible for the Commission to recognise and acknowledge as many people as possible as victims of the past political conflict. This objective, in its turn, was central to the Commission's overall task to promote national unity and reconciliation.

83 Two distinct enquiries were envisaged by the Act insofar as it concerns the question of gross violations of human rights:

a) Was a gross violation of human rights committed and what is the identity of the victim? (Section 4(b))

b) What was the identity of those involved in such violations and what was their accountability for such violations? (Section 4(a)(iii), (v))

84   The first is a factual question about the conduct involved: in other words, does the violation suffered by the victim amount to one of the acts enumerated in the definition? This enquiry does not involve the issue of accountability. The question of whether or not the conduct of the perpetrator is justified is irrelevant. This is in accordance with the intention to allow as many potential victims as possible to benefit from the Commission's process.

85   The second enquiry is stricter and more circumscribed, involving technical questions like accountability. Findings emerging at this level of enquiry may have grave implications and impinge upon the fundamental rights of alleged perpetrators. This enquiry involves, therefore, both factual and legal questions.

86   Hence, the Commission could find that a gross human rights violation had been committed because there was a victim of that violation. It had, however, to apply a more stringent test in order to hold a perpetrator accountable for that violation.

88   As a consequence, the position adopted by the Commission was that any killing, abduction, torture or severe ill-treatment which met the other requirements of the definition amounted to a gross violation of human rights, regardless of whether or not the perpetrator could be held accountable for the conduct.

Armed conflict between combatants

91   The political conflicts of the past were not only of a 'civilian' nature. Several of the political groupings had an armed wing. The state used its armed forces to put down resistance and to engage in military actions in the southern African region. The Commission had particular difficulty in attempting to define and reach consensus on its mandate. Some argued that all killed and injured combatants should be included as victims of gross human rights violations. Others wanted to maintain a distinction between those defending the apartheid state and those seeking to bring it down. It was noted that members of the armed forces involved in these combat situations did not expect to be treated as victims of gross violations of human rights. This was illus-

trated in the submissions of political parties such as the NP and the ANC, which did not identify their members killed in combat as victims. In the end, the Commission decided to follow the guidelines provided by the body of norms and rules contained in international humanitarian law.

92 Armed conflicts between clearly identified combatants thus provided the only exception to the Commission's position that victims of gross violations of human rights should include all who were killed, tortured (and so on) through politically motivated actions within the mandated period.

94 International humanitarian law attempts to provide as much protection as possible to those faced with the harsh realities of armed conflicts, irrespective of what caused them. It therefore places limits on the means and methods used in warfare, declaring certain acts impermissible, while other acts, even some of those involving killing, are not regarded as violations. To understand this distinction, the two key concepts of 'combatant' and 'protected person' need to be clarified.

98 However, when a combatant uses force in an armed conflict against a protected person – that is someone who does not or who can no longer use force (and thus cannot defend himself or herself) – such acts break international humanitarian law, and those responsible must be held accountable. The laws of war provide minimum protections that apply in all armed conflicts. These protections are found in Common Article 3 of the four 1949 Geneva Conventions ...

99 Historically, when such violations have occurred in an international, as opposed to internal, armed conflict they constitute 'grave breaches'[6] which may be prosecuted by any state. This distinction between international and internal armed conflicts is less relevant today, as the laws of war have evolved to regulate more closely the use of force in all situations of armed conflict.

100 It is, furthermore, very important to note that the Geneva Conventions, both in their terms and as they have been interpreted, are inclusive in the protections they offer. In other words, if there is doubt about whether a particular person is entitled to certain protections provided by the Conventions, then it is presumed that such individual should be protected. (See Protocol I, Article 45.1, 50.1).

101 It must also be emphasised that the concepts of combatant and protected person are not necessarily opposites. When a combatant is wounded or surrenders, he or she becomes a protected person without losing combatant status. In other words, in order to decide whether someone was killed or injured as a combatant, two questions must be asked: first, was the person a member of an organised or regular armed force, and second, was the person in or out of combat?

102 The practice followed by the Commission was in accordance with these two considerations. The Commission also adopted the principle of giving the benefit of the doubt to those whose status as combatants or protected persons was unclear...

Victims of the armed conflict

103 Soldiers on either side of the political divide, whether they were permanent force soldiers, conscripts or volunteers, as well as their families and loved ones, were of course victims in a more general sense. They were victims of the armed political conflict of the past and their deaths, injuries and losses should be remembered and mourned.

104 In a number of cases that came before the Commission, however, the decision was more complex.

105 In respect of the first consideration – namely, whether the person was a member of an 'organised force ... under a command responsible to [a] Party to the conflict'[7] – the Commission was faced with the problem of how to categorise members of a variety of more or less organised armed groupings. These ranged from relatively well to poorly organised self-defence units (SDUs), self-protection units (SPUs) and vigilante groupings, under varying degrees of control by the ANC, the IFP, the state or other political formations. Some units were well trained and ostensibly under military control, although at times they operated on their own initiative. Others were little more than bands of politically motivated youth, acting on example and exhortation. Many SDUs, for example, were 'acknowledged' by MK, and even given some weapons and training, but were far from its chain of command.

106 The Commission had great difficulty in dealing with these cases. In the end, given the lack of information on the degree of control and the nature of the combat situation, it decided to employ the narrow definition of combatants. This meant that, in general, cases involving

members of the above organisations were treated in the same way as non-combatants (as described above). However, where clear evidence emerged, on a case-by-case basis, of direct military engagement by members of these groupings, they were regarded as combatants.

108 Thus the Commission made a conscious decision to err on the side of inclusivity – finding that most killings and serious injuries were gross violations of human rights rather than the result of the legitimate use of force. Where the evidence of a combat situation was clear, however, the traditional laws of war were applied.

1 See *TRC Report*, Vol 1, pp 64-5; 69-78.
2 *SA Constitution*, Section 11; *International Covenant on Civil and Political Rights (ICCPR)*, Article 6.
3 *SA Constitution*, Section 12(1)(d); ICCPR, Article 7.
4 *SA Constitution*, Section 12(1)(e); ICCPR, Article 7.
5 *SA Constitution*, Sections 12(1)(a),(b) and 35(1)(d); ICCPR, Article 9.
6 *Geneva Convention* I, Article 50; Protocol I, Article 85. 'Grave breaches' include the following acts against persons or property protected by the Convention: wilful killing, torture or inhuman treatment, wilfully causing great suffering or serious injury to body or health.
7 *Additional Protocol* 1, Article 43, para 1.

Index

Rebeiro, Dr and Mrs 193, 195
recidivism 70
recognition: of (past) injustice
155-65
insufficiency of 156
by perpetrators 24-5, 52, 63, 66,
67
of victims 24, 25, 27, 53, 135,
156, 158
reconciliation 39-41, 76, 121,
210-18, 264, 268, 277-86
achievement/non-achievement of
9, 40, 214
acknowledgement and 196, 228
aesthetics of 116
amnesty linked to 79
beyond the TRC event 114, 122,
214, 228
committee needed for 156
constitutional commitment to
17-18
cost of 154
criticism of 212-13, 216-18
definition 129-30
emotional levels 279
ethics of 115, 116
and Eucharistic redemption 113,
117, 118
individual/interpersonal 39, 40,
157, 216-19, 228, 279
and justice 23-4, 76, 130
limitations 280-81
mediation process needed 156,
251
national 39, 277-86
as objective 23, 36, 39-41, 113
performance of 117 *bis*
pluralistic 283
political 280-81, 283
preceding transition 281
process of 30-31, 114
punishment and 186
and religious component of TRC
129-30, 131
restorative justice and 23
rite of 117
sacrifice of victims and 119
spiritualisation of 280
statist view 279-80
success (or lack of) 9, 40, 214
symbolism of 114, 116, 117
TRC as model for 122
and transformation 144, 145,
153-4
and truth 39-41, 65-7, 79, 105
understanding and 85, 228-9
yardstick 157
reconciliation model 15
Reconstruction and Development
Programme 157, 191, 198
reconstruction of society 21, 191,
264
record of truth 144, 145
recurrence, prevention of x, xii, 20,

68, 70, 144, 228
international law 49
state obligation 49, 50, 53
redemption and TRC 113, 117,
118, 119
redistributive measures 268
redress 48
rehabilitation 27, 84, 239-40
international law 49
rehabilitative justice 73
religion
anti-apartheid role 115
role in apartheid 126
role in TRC process 123-31
religious component of TRC 130-31
remembrance 18, 29, 41, 53, 127-8,
159
forgetting and denial versus
158-60
religion of 127
selective 157, 161-3
of victims 163-5
see also memory
remorse 66, 77, 171
reparation(s) xiii, 21, 27, 172,
189-91, 239-49, 253-5
amnesty and 189-90
amount of 190
assessment of need 246
community involvement 255
at community level 188, 190-91,
254
eligibility for 79
expectations 156, 168, 197, 242
framework for 27
and healing 239-41, 249
individual financial 190, 254
international law 49, 51, 53
magnitude gap 221-2, 229, 241
monetary 241, 242, 244-4
pension option 53, 247, 248
by perpetrator/apartheid benefi-
ciary 40, 215
proportionality 188, 245
recommendations 75, 156
responsibility of state 73, 102
responsibility of whites 191
restorative justice and 23, 68, 69,
70, 73
service option 244
and suffering 197-8
symbolic 188, 191, 241, 254
symbolic value of concrete 172
urgent interim 172
Reparation and Rehabilitation
Committee 6, 82, 103, 125, 190,
239-40
'closed list' approach 243
Reparation and Rehabilitation
policy 243, 247
repentance 131, 268
reprisal against civilians 97
reprisals, legitimate: doctrine of 96-7
residential segregation 80

Resistance Movement *see* liberation
movement(s)
resistance theory 285
resistance to change 17
resources
(non-)equitable access to 150,
215
stewardship over 261
responsibility x, xiii, 33, 36, 53,
66-7, 93, 178
acceptance by ANC 20, 79
acknowledgement 67
collective/shared 20, 65-7, 71, 79
ethics of 121
gradations of 71
individual x, xiii, 33, 36, 53,
87-93, 95, 178
of leaders for actions of followers
78, 83
moral 20, 79, 112
shared 74, 136
of state and non-state agents
305-6
of supporters and beneficiaries of
apartheid 171
restitution proposals 267-8
restoration of society 72
restorative justice xx, 13, 23-6,
68-76, 110
restorative and retributive justice
component 28-30
restorative truth 144
retaliation, doctrine of 96
retributive emotions 63
retributive justice 15, 23, 25, 28, 65,
73, 110, 186, 213, 215, 272
see also revenge
revenge/vengeance x, 73, 116, 186,
227
revenge killings 224, 226
revisionism x; *see also* denials
revolution, legal path to 281
rich and poor *see* poor and rich
right of access to court 71, 102, 110,
194
right to conduct struggle 90
right to a fair trial 177
right to judicial protection 177
right to justice 177
right to organise 76
right to rebel against tyranny 98
right to a remedy 177
right wing, political 22, 227, 283
rights
TRC mandate definitions 304-5
victims' against accuseds' 78
see also human rights and under
perpetrators; victims
Ribeiro family 101
Rodriguez, Velasquez 48
rogue elements, responsibility for 83
Rome Statute 4
Roodeplaat Research Laboratory
226

CARVING A NICHE

MCGILL-QUEEN'S/ASSOCIATED MEDICAL SERVICES STUDIES
IN THE HISTORY OF MEDICINE, HEALTH, AND SOCIETY

SERIES EDITORS: J.T.H. CONNOR AND ERIKA DYCK

Volumes in this series have received financial support from Associated
Medical Services, Inc. Associated Medical Services (AMS) is a Canadian
charitable organization with an impressive history as a catalyst for change
in Canadian healthcare. For eighty years, AMS has had a profound impact
through its support of the history of medicine, the education of healthcare
professionals, and by making strategic investments to address critical
issues in our healthcare system. AMS has funded eight chairs in the history
of medicine across Canada, is a primary sponsor of many of the country's
history of medicine and nursing organizations, and offers fellowships and
grants through the AMS History of Medicine and Healthcare Program
(www.amshealthcare.ca).

Carving a Niche

The Medical Profession in Mexico,
1800–1870

LUZ MARÍA HERNÁNDEZ SÁENZ

McGill-Queen's University Press
Montreal & Kingston • London • Chicago

© McGill-Queen's University Press 2018

ISBN 978-0-7735-5297-5 (cloth)
ISBN 978-0-7735-5302-6 (paper)
ISBN 978-0-7735-5298-2 (ePDF)
ISBN 978-0-7735-5299-9 (ePUB)

Legal deposit first quarter 2018
Bibliothèque nationale du Québec

Printed in Canada on acid-free paper that is 100% ancient forest free
(100% post-consumer recycled), processed chlorine free

This book has been published with the help of a grant from the Canadian
Federation for the Humanities and Social Sciences, through the Awards to
Scholarly Publications Program, using funds provided by the Social Sciences
and Humanities Research Council of Canada. Funding has also been received
from the J.B. Smallman Publication Fund, Faculty of Social Science, University
of Western Ontario.

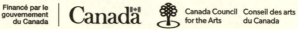

We acknowledge the support of the Canada Council for the Arts, which
last year invested $153 million to bring the arts to Canadians throughout
the country.

Nous remercions le Conseil des arts du Canada de son soutien. L'an dernier,
le Conseil a investi 153 millions de dollars pour mettre de l'art dans la vie
des Canadiennes et des Canadiens de tout le pays.

Library and Archives Canada Cataloguing in Publication

Hernández Sáenz, Luz María, 1952–, author
Carving a niche: the medical profession in Mexico, 1800–1870/
Luz María Hernández Sáenz.

(McGill-Queen's/Associated Medical Services studies in the history
of medicine, health, and society; 47)
Includes bibliographical references and index.
Issued in print and electronic formats.
ISBN 978-0-7735-5297-5 (cloth). – ISBN 978-0-7735-5302-6 (paper). –
ISBN 978-0-7735-5298-2 (ePDF). – ISBN 978-0-7735-5299-9 (ePUB)

1. Medicine – Mexico – History – 19th century. 2. Medicine – Practice –
Mexico – History – 19th century. 3. Medical education – Mexico –
History – 19th century. I. Title. II. Series: McGill-Queen's/Associated
Medical Services studies in the history of medicine, health, and society; 47

R465.H47 2018   610.97209'034   C2017-906244-1
                                               C2017-906245-X

This book was typeset by Marquis Interscript in 10.5/13 Sabon.

To my husband Andrew

To my parents

Contents

Tables and Figures

TABLES

FIGURES

Acknowledgments

The many years of research behind this work would not have been possible without financial assistance, the input of other researchers and colleagues, and the support of friends and family to whom I am profoundly grateful. I want to first thank the Associated Medical Services Ltd for the Hannah Grant-in-Aid that allowed me to initiate my research and fund my first research trips. The University of Western Ontario's internal grants also contributed to the initial stages of research and allowed me to clearly define the direction this project would take. The bulk of this work was financed by the Social Science and Humanities Research Council of Canada, to which I am most indebted. In addition, the University of Western Ontario Faculty of Social Sciences has generously funded my attendance at numerous conferences, which has given me the opportunity to disseminate my findings and exchange ideas with colleagues of other universities. Finally, I want to acknowledge the assistance of the J.B. Smallman Publication Fund and the Faculty of Social Science, the University of Western Ontario.

My research took me to numerous archives in Mexico, France, and England, where I found archivists willing to help me navigate each institution's collections and protocols and made my visits as productive as possible. I owe special thanks to archivists and staff at Archivo Histórico de la Facultad de Medicina, Archivo Histórico de la Secretaría de Salud, Archivo Histórico de la Ciudad de México, Archivo Histórico de la Academia de Medicina, and Archivo General de la Nación in Mexico City. Their professionalism and kindness not only aided my research and expedited my work but made it most pleasant. Outside the capital, archives in Yucatán, Querétaro, San

Luis Potosí, Zacatecas, Mérida, and Tlaxcala were equally supportive. The personnel of the Archivo General Municipal de Puebla and
the state archives of Jalisco, Guanajuato, and Veracruz went beyond
the call of duty to facilitate and promptly photocopy or digitalize the
material I requested. Foreign archives and libraries were just as efficient and solicitous. I fondly remember the Archives du Service de
Santé and Bibliothèque de l'Académie de Médicine in Paris, and the
Museum of the Foreign Legion in Aubagne, with their fabulous collections and patient personnel who made me feel welcome, and the
Bibliothèque Nationale, Archives Nationales, and Wellcome Institute
with their knowledgeable and polite staff.

During these years, I met colleagues and specialists in various
fields who contributed to shaping my historical approach and have
become good friends. Sandra Torres Ayala is one of them. I want to
thank her for her help with my research, valuable ideas, company
during our research trips, and friendship. Another good friend is
Jorge Zacarías Prieto, whose encyclopedic knowledge of the Faculty
of Medicine archive (UNAM) and his assistance when I needed specific information or photocopies were invaluable. Other friends and
colleagues have contributed in different ways. In Mexico, the inde-
fatigable Linda Arnold generously shared her files, clarified some
obscure legislation, and helped me fill important gaps in my work.
Thanks to Susan Deeds, whose friendship, advice, and social gatherings remind me that a visiting historian is not isolated in Mexico
City. I greatly appreciated the support from and interesting conversation with Rolando Neri, former director of the Archivo Histórico de
la Facultat de Medicina, UNAM. In Canada, eight colleagues and
friends deserve special mention. Shauna Devine gave me the strength
to persevere and continue with this work. She was kind enough to
read my manuscript, gave me invaluable feedback, and most important, offered me her friendship. The input of Kim Clark and Tracey
Adams from their respective anthropological and sociological disciplines aided the organization and development of this project.
Thanks for the enjoyable lunches we shared while we discussed our
research. I am also grateful to my friend Eli Nathans, who generously read and commented on an early draft of the manuscript, and
has always given me valuable feedback. Special thanks to Sam Clark
for his advice, support, and pleasand conversation. And I am indebted
to my friend Stephanie Gunter, who corrected grammar mistakes
and made valuable suggestions, to my ex-student and friend Riley

Nowokoski, who helped me with the tedious work of formatting tables and footnotes and often answered software queries, and to Austen Smith, for her assistance in the elaboration of the index.

Finally, I want to thank my family and friends who, in one way or another, and sometimes unknowingly, have participated in this long journey. My parents, who have always supported my endeavours and offered me a home in Mexico City; my sisters, Magui and Cati, who often provide transportation, run errands, and support me in any way they can; and my brother Federico and cousins Sergio and Roberto, who always show interest in my work. A special thanks to my cousin Elena and her husband, Chavo, for their hospitality and for making my frequent trips to Puebla most enjoyable. I am forever grateful to my dear husband, Andrew, for his proof reading and valuable suggestions as I struggled with the final stages of this project, for having endured throughout these years my long research trips during the short Canadian summers and my seemingly unending effort to bring this project to completion; and to my miniature schnauzer Kahlua, who sat patiently during my long hours at the computer and is the only one not afraid to let me know when it is time to stop. Thank you all for your constant support and contribution to this book.

Luz María Hernández Sáenz
London, Ontario

List of Terms

acequia principal	main canal
actos	university debates
acuerdo	agreement
agua de sosa	soda water
alcalde mayor	mayor
alcalde primero	mayor
anatomía	dissection
atribución	duty
Audiencia	highest tribunal in New Spain
avisos al público	public notices
ayuntamiento	municipality
bando	official proclamation
beneficencia	public welfare
cabildo	municipal government
Casa de Contratación	Board of Trade
casa de enseñanza	educational institution
cátedra	course
catedrático	professor
cirujano dentista	dental surgeon
comisionado	appointed delegate
consejo de beneficencia	welfare board
consejo de Salubridad	health board
Consejo Superior de Salubridad	main health board
conservador	keeper
consulado	trade board or guild
consultor	director (army)

contrata	tender
converso	converted Jew
corregidor	magistrate representing the crown
cortes	parliament
criollo	Mexican child born of Spanish parents
cuartel	city section
cuerpo de sanidad militar	military sanitary corps
curandero	healer
delegado de sanidad	health delegate
diputación provincial	provincial representation
escribano	secretary
específico	prepared medicament
espurio	son of a priest
establecimiento	establishment
fiscal	officer
fuero	privilege
Instrucción	directions
jefe superior politico	superior political chief
junta de caridad	charity committee
junta de censura	censorship board or committee
junta departamental	departmental board
junta consultiva de sanidad militar	military health board
junta de sanidad	health board
junta subalterna de sanidad	subordinate health board
junta superior de socorros	central aid committee
junta superior gubernativa de cirugía	superior surgical governing board
lazarettos	quarantine stations
limpieza de sangre	purity of blood
matrona	midwife
obrajes	small textile factories
obras pías	charitable endowments
officiat	French four-year medical program
paila	soap manufacturer
pardo	an individual of African descent
partera	midwife
peninsular	individual born in Spain

poblano	resident or originary of Puebla
Poder Conservador	central conservative power
policía	public health in the widest sense
policía de salubridad pública	public health and welfare
policía de salubridad y comodidad	general welfare of the population
practicante	intern
Protomedicato	colonial medical and public health board
protomedicato supremo de salud pública	supreme protomedicato of public health
protomédico	physician member of the Protomedicato
provincial	head of religious order or province
regidor	municipal official
romancistas	romance surgeons
sangrador	bleeder
sumidero	site where human waste was deposited
tarifa	list of licensed practitioners
tienda	surgery
título	section (of a document)
vecino	resident
visitador de aduana	customs inspector
visita de sanidad	sanitary inspection of arriving vessels
vocal	council or board member

CARVING A NICHE

Introduction

1813 was an ominous year for licensed physicians and surgeons in Mexico. The country was fighting for its independence from Spain and refugees fleeing the combat areas crowded the capital, contributing to water pollution and the spread of disease. In May a "fevers epidemic" descended on Mexico City claiming thousands of lives and forcing medical practitioners to work long hours risking and, in some cases, losing their lives. The same year, in an effort to erase medieval institutions, Spain ended the medical practitioners' monopoly and long held professional rights by abolishing their ancient guild, the Protomedicato, and substituting it with health boards under direct government supervision.

The deadly epidemic of 1813 brought the clash between old values and new ideologies to a head. On one hand was the Protomedicato, the colonial past, and the traditional privileges and social status enjoyed by its members. On the other hand was the vision of a more democratic society based on personal merit, and a government that oversaw public health. Although the 1813 legislation proved to be temporary, it became clear to medical practitioners that, to defend their interests and maintain their elite position, adaptation and reform of the Protomedicato would be imperative. They faced significant obstacles. First, they were handicapped by their small numbers (only seventy-three appear in the 1822 Mexico City official list), a result of the elitist view of university education and the high costs of obtaining a licence. Second, demand for their services was limited as few could afford the fees of a licensed practitioner. Third, the state of medical knowledge at the time made their treatment of limited effectiveness. Finally, in Mexico's multicultural society, most preferred home remedies and the services of traditional healers that better addressed their medical and religious beliefs. Change and reorganization would have to wait until the end of the war.

Following independence (1821), the top practitioners began to debate medical reform. Professional survival, modernization, and control over other medical fields were their goals. The first formal step came in 1831 with the union of the fields of medicine and surgery and the creation of a public health board that filled the role of the colonial Protomedicato. Two years later a modern medical curriculum became part of the legislation and reformers established an autonomous medical school. The crowning achievement, the establishment of the academy of medicine in the 1860s brought the national and international acknowledgement so much sought by local practitioners. The foundations were then set to embrace the age of bacteriology. This fascinating, critical and convoluted period, 1800 to 1870s, is at the heart of the current study.[1]

This work follows the trajectory of medical practitioners in their efforts to earn professional and scientific recognition, monopolize medical knowledge, and establish the basis of a modern profession. Placing this process in a national and international context, it explores the changes that health-care occupations underwent as the country transitioned from a colonial, corporative society to a liberal, independent republic. Their efforts, tightly interwoven with the political and economic context of these eventful years, mirror the growing pains of the young republic.

By placing the development of Mexico's medical practitioners in the fluid political context of the time, I delve into the effects that liberalism had on health care practitioners, public health, medical education and society. I argue that the liberal changes that ultimately resulted in Mexico's independence from Spain brought elite physicians and surgeons to collaborate in order to find a place in the new republic. The subsequent political reorganization of the country allowed, and forced, reformers to reorganize the medical profession and introduce educational reforms. Shaped by the evolving politics of the time, reform was a slow, difficult, and unique process that fused France's medical model and Spain's legacy.

The period under study, 1800 to the 1870s, is crucial for the understanding of the professionalization of medicine and the transformation of medicine into a science. During the eighteenth and nineteenth centuries, medicine evolved from an "art" often linked to superstition, religion, and even magic, to a "science" based on scientific principles, careful observation, and experimentation that produced visible results. The last stage of medical professionalization would come with the triumph of bacteriology and is, therefore, beyond the scope of this study. Most authors agree that a modern profession requires possession of a skill based on theoretical knowledge; control over the transmission of this knowledge; ability to offer a skilled, specialized service; monopoly over practice; and professional associations to promote research and solidarity and defend common interests. The nineteenth-century Mexican "medical profession" did not yet fulfill these premises, but some of them, such as control over medical education and the establishment of a professional association, were in gestation, and others, such as the agreement on licensing requirements and the view of all licensed healers as part of a whole, were already in place. As the renowned medical historian Henry E. Sigerist stated, medical history must include the context in which it was practised.[2] Professions in general are part of the world that surrounds them, and do not necessarily have to fit into present-day definitions. Andrew Abbott describes nineteenth-century professions as "peculiar social creatures" that "stood outside the new commercial and industrial heart of society. They were organized in a collegial manner that was distinctly anachronistic." In Europe – he specifically refers to France – professions were more hierarchical, but he sees such hierarchy not as the result of capitalist forms of organization, but as a holdover "from the Old Regime," their "civil servant quality" making them an oddity in the modern world.[3] The early nineteenth-century Mexican medical profession may be placed in this category. Thus, I use the term *medical profession* throughout this work to refer to this "peculiar social creature" formed by the various health-related branches that claimed to have some specialized knowledge or skills and, despite their occupational, social, economic, and even racial differences, were joined under similar rules and legislation.

As Toby Gelfand has pointed out, the evolution of the medical profession runs parallel to the history of medicine, but it is shaped by complex and local cultural factors.[4] In Mexico, the first stage of this process – approximately the first two-thirds of the century – presents unique characteristics that derived from the country's colonial past and its tumultuous history. The analysis of this stage is vital to the understanding of the future medicalization of mainstream society and the hierarchy of health-care providers. The status of the practitioner, based as much on social and economic factors as on specialized knowledge during colonial times, gradually came to rest exclusively on individual knowledge and skill in the late nineteenth century. Access to such knowledge and the ability to acquire expertise became indispensable to the survival of the various branches that formed the medical profession, and control over access to and recognition of such knowledge was necessary to ensure the privileged status of the physicians within the profession. Just as important to this process was the merging of the traditional spheres of medicine and surgery that ended the traditional antagonism between physicians and surgeons and made their areas of expertise complementary.

Various factors make the Mexican case unique. Since the 1520s, New Spain had been a Spanish colony influenced by Hispanic culture and institutions.[5] Among the latter was the Royal Tribunal of the Protomedicato, an umbrella organization that oversaw health-care practitioners of the various "branches" of medicine – physicians, surgeons, pharmacists, phlebotomists, bonesetters, and, later, midwives – and advised on health-related matters. The capitals of the two main Spanish viceroyalties, Mexico City and Lima, each saw the appointment of a *protomédico*, or first physician, in the sixteenth century. The first in a long line of protomédicos, Pedro López in Mexico and Hernando de Sepúlveda in Lima, received their appointments in 1527 and 1537, respectively. By the following century, the Protomedicato had consolidated its position as the first authority in the area of health care. As a royal tribunal, it had the right to decide medical cases and punish and fine infringements. It was also empowered to authorize medical textbooks, examine and license all practitioners, and enforce health-related measures.[6] The Protomedicato was closely tied to the Faculty of Medicine in both New Spain and Peru. In the former, the most senior members served as first and second protomédicos, while the third protomédico was selected by the viceroy from the same faculty. In Peru, the professor of Prima de medicina was also the Protomedicato's president.[7] However, the Protomedicato was far from being the centralized body representing, let alone controlling, all medical practitioners in the viceroyalty. It lacked enforcement powers, and it was handicapped by the confusing legislation that left its territorial jurisdiction open to debate and by the intervention of high government officials in the fulfillment of its duties. Nonetheless, the unification of all health-care occupations under the Protomedicato, the government recognition of all "medical branches" as part of a whole, and the Protomedicato's character of royal tribunal distinguished the "medical system" of the Spanish Empire from those of, say, England, France, or the Netherlands, and set the basis for professional unification and monopoly.

Closely related to the Protomedicato was the Royal and Pontifical University of Mexico. As its name indicates, in colonial times the university was a Crown institution, unable to modify its regulations, and therefore its curriculum, without the king's permission. Also, as a colonial institution, it was a secondary centre of learning and not a priority in Madrid. The university had been established in the sixteenth century and its regulations received royal approval in 1646. These included instructions for internal governance and the official curriculum that, in the case of medicine, was based on Hippocratic and Galenic medicine. A century later, these regulations and curricula remained in place, and faculty and administrators waited in vain for reform. Unable to effect any formal changes, in the latter part of the eighteenth century some faculty members began informally to introduce more current authors, and students gradually started to debate and be examined on the works of Herman Boerhaave, Gerhard Freyherr Van-Swieten, Lorenz Heister, and Xavier Bichat, among others.[8] During the years following independence, the university's regulations remained in force, the Faculty of Medicine maintained its monopoly over formal medical training, and the completion of the university's medical program continued to be a requirement for obtaining a physician's licence. Therefore, it is not surprising that, after independence, faculty, younger practitioners, and political reformers demanded modernization of the curriculum, updating of the medical program, and an overhaul of university education.[9]

Along with its legal and administrative framework, Spain exported its religious and racial prejudices to the colonies, crystallized in the *limpieza de sangre*, or purity of blood, regulations. The origins of the limpieza de sangre requirement for appointment to official posts and acceptance into universities, religious orders, and guilds date back to the fifteenth century. In 1449, the municipal government of Toledo issued the first piece of legislation, the Sentencia Estatuto, to prevent *conversos* (recently converted Jews) from holding office or benefices in the city. Its goal was to keep key government and

religious posts in the hands of "old Christians," as many of these
were occupied by conversos. As the century progressed and religious and social tensions increased, purity of blood requirements
were adopted in other areas and expanded to exclude Muslims and,
later, Protestants, Catholic heretics, and non-conformists and to
include first- and second-generation ancestry.[10]

Like all Spanish institutions exported to the Americas, the concept
of purity of blood was adapted to the realities of a conquered and
multicultural society and to include (or exclude) Indigenous peoples,
free and enslaved Africans, and their offspring. In the Iberian peninsula limpieza de sangre marginalized religious and racial minorities;
in the Americas, it buttressed the pre-eminence of a Spanish minority
over an Indigenous and mixed-blood majority. As in Spain, purity of
blood was required to obtain a higher civil and military post, enter
religious orders and most guilds, and attend university, although this
was not always the case. As Adam Warren and José R. Jouvé Martin
find, in Peru, men of African descent practised surgery and, later,
medicine legally. One of these "black doctors," José Manuel Valdés,
became first protomédico in post-independence Peru.[11] Similarly, in
New Granada (Colombia), medical practitioners were, according
to José Celestino Mutis, "pardos and 'lower class people,'" and the
Protomedicato of Havana recognized practitioners of African
descent.[12] Further research is needed on the racial background of
health-care practitioners in other areas of the Spanish Empire. As
opposed to Peru, New Spain seems to have adhered closely to the
regulations, at least in the case of physicians. The Protomedicato
files indicate that limpieza de sangre was a requirement for medical
licences, but that the requirements were more lenient for surgeons.
Nonetheless, I have not encountered the mention of African descent
in any medical or surgical licences issued in the late eighteenth century. When José Mariano Martínez Peredo, after finishing his medical studies, applied for a licence, the Protomedicato launched an
investigation that revealed him to be the son of a mulatta slave. To
make matters worse, the applicant was an *espurio* (son of a priest).
He was denied the licence.[13] Another case involved a Cuban surgeon, recognized by the Havana Protomedicato, but refused a licence
by the Mexico City protomédicos for his *pardo* (African descent)
background.[14] Consequently, in New Spain, the reputation of a
licensed physician rested not only on his "special" medical knowledge and privileged socio-economic position (as it did in other

countries), but also on his "racial superiority" as attested by his medical degree and licence. The importance of race in determining social status and hierarchy in New Spain and post-independence Mexico is the key to understanding the tensions between physicians and surgeons in the late colonial period and the racial and social prejudices that shaped the organization and hierarchization of healing practitioners after independence.

Another factor relevant to the relations between physicians and surgeons in the Spanish Empire was the educational and social distinctions between surgeons who had attended university (so-called latin surgeons) and those who had apprenticed in their trade (*romancistas*, or romance surgeons). The former had access to more prestigious posts, served as consultants to the protomédicos, and were closer to physicians in education and status than was the case in other countries, resulting in less bitterness and antagonism between them. The latin surgeons' education, purity of blood, and social status also separated them from the *romancistas*, who were closer to the humbler phlebotomists, creating two tiers of surgical practice. Regarding New Spain, surviving documents do not reflect much tension between physicians and surgeons until the latter part of the eighteenth century, when competition for patients, the arrival of European military surgeons, and the incipient nationalism of *criollo* (American-born Spanish) practitioners intertwined.

The arrival of European military surgeons was a result of Spain's efforts to defend its empire. The reorganization of the Spanish army and navy began in the early eighteenth century, and by mid-century military reform had reached the colonies with the creation of local militias organized around a core army. An offshoot of this innovation was the establishment of the Real Escuela de Cirugía (Royal Surgical School) in New Spain, whose objective was to train local personnel to serve under *peninsular* (Spanish) military surgeons. The peninsular surgeons had been trained at Spanish and other European surgical colleges, and some of them were licensed to practise both medicine and surgery and to treat civilians when no other practitioner was available. As Europeans, they considered themselves (and were perceived as) racially, socially, and professionally superior to colonial practitioners. Adding insult to injury, military medical personnel were beyond the jurisdiction of New Spain's Protomedicato. The new arrivals were deeply resented by the local practitioners, who disliked their superior airs and, understandably, considered them unfair competition. In the words of the last protomédico, "Those [practitioners] who were shielded by military privileges ... and protected by their co-nationals pretended to be great physicians, made a great deal of money, and returned to their land to enjoy it."[15] The animosity between the peninsular military surgeon Antonio Serrano, director of the Royal Surgical School, and the protomédicos went beyond professional differences and a clash of personalities; it reflected the resentment that had been brewing for years among the criollos. In New Spain, tensions between physicians and surgeons previously had been curbed by the similarities between physicians and latin surgeons, and by the considerable occupational, racial, and status gaps between physicians and romancistas. Professional differences came to the fore with the arrival of the peninsulares; after independence, the better trained and more racially "pure" local latin surgeons would claim their place at the side of the physicians.

The Napoleonic invasion of Spain in 1808 precipitated a chain of events that heralded the end of the Spanish Empire. In 1810, rebellions against Madrid broke out in the American colonies, and in 1812 the liberal parliament issued the first Spanish constitution. Although enforced only briefly (1813 to 1814, and reinstated in 1820), the constitution had long-reaching consequences in the colonies, and in Mexico promoted the union of medicine and surgery. The collaboration of physicians and surgeons was triggered by the threat of the *juntas de sanidad* (health boards) established by the 1812 Constitution that gradually encroached on the practitioners' privileges and practice. Only after independence would elite practitioners be able to participate in the reform of their profession.

The long struggle for independence accentuated criollo resentment and resulted in the masses' growing hostility toward peninsulares. The possibility of a friendly parting of the ways between Spain and its colony had ended with the high-handed responses of royalists to local elites' aspirations of participatory government at the onset of the war. Fear of the mixed-blood masses had kept New Spain's elites loyal until political events in the two countries united local and peninsular loyalists and rebels under the banner of the royalist commander, Agustín de Iturbide. Mexico became an independent country in 1821, after an eleven-year war of independence that accentuated regional political divisions, devastated its economy, and affected its overall administration. Years of political turmoil, economic distress, and social change followed, influencing both the pace of reform and the development of the medical profession. Of significant importance for the time under study was the federalist-centralist struggle that determined the power and jurisdiction of the national government, impeded the standardization of public health policy and educational requirements, and prevented a national professional monopoly. Officially, the political system determined the territorial reach of legislation; practically, the realities of a weak central state, a constant state of turmoil, and the centrifugal forces of provincial regionalism prevented union and collaboration.

Another important factor affecting the medical profession was the rivalry between a politically, economically, and socially powerful church that monopolized higher education, and a weak state of dubious legitimacy and usually on the verge of bankruptcy. The contest was not resolved until the 1867 triumph of the liberal republic and a secular society. The struggle between church and state slowed change, especially in medicine. Professionalization included control over education (higher education was monopolized by the church until 1830s) and practical training at hospitals, most of which were under the control of the church, to validate licensed practitioners and a hierarchical professional organization. These conflicts of interest, all intricately connected, had to be resolved before reformers agreed on an overarching reform. It is in this context that medical practitioners worked to raise their public image, reorganize themselves as a cohesive group, and enforce a monopoly over medical practice. Their efforts mirrored those of political reformers trying to impose a secular society and capitalist values on a reluctant majority, and ran parallel to those of politicians seeking to draw up legislation and set the basis for the country's administration while simultaneously trying to promote a moribund economy. The dire political and economic context weighed heavily on professional and educational reforms, and hindered practitioners' efforts to unify their profession and create a national health board.

The first formal step towards forming a modern profession came with the union of physicians and surgeons in 1831. Two years later, legislators ordered the closure of the National University (previously Royal and Pontifical University) and the Surgical School, and enshrined into law a modern medical curriculum shaped after France's model. A new paradigm was now officially in place. A few years later, the Surgical School was absorbed by the newly founded

Colegio de Medicina, which then came to control medical education. Its monopoly over medical education and the physicians' tight
control of licensing distinguished Mexico from the decentralized
educational and licensing systems of other countries. Despite legislation, the medical profession did not rest on a solid basis. The efforts
of medical reformers and educators to create an overarching system
encompassing medical schools, hospitals, and public health, and to
claim scientific national and international recognition would have to
wait thirty years more.

The reforms undertaken during the period under study followed
the example of France. Spain's refusal to accept independence as a
fait accompli and the Crown's attempts to recover its former colony
in 1829 fuelled political differences and further alienated the local
population, which demanded the expulsion of all Spanish residents.
Intellectuals and politicians rejected colonial institutions as retrograde, and considered the Spanish past the cause of the country's
misfortunes.[16] Thus, they looked towards "the civilized (European)
countries" for inspiration to organize the new nation. Contemporary
writings indicate that, among these countries, France was the most
favoured, especially in the field of medicine.[17] This is hardly surprising, as Paris was then at the forefront of medical research and boasted
the best training in the field. As a result, whenever possible, Mexican
and other Spanish-American practitioners furthered their studies in
France and returned eager to follow the teachings of the Paris clinical school. In Colombia, for example, returning physicians brought
French anatomo-clinical practices that they implemented in classrooms and hospital wards.[18] Other factors also attracted Mexican
reformers: France had undergone political turmoil and revolution
before the reorganization of its medical education and licensing system, and French academies and scientific organizations were open to
relations with their Mexican counterparts. Consequently, in Mexico
and Spanish America the reorganization of health-care practitioners
and medical training followed the French model.

The present work analyzes the development of the medical profession and the different factors that shaped it. It challenges such traditional interpretations of Mexico's medical history as the dichotomy
of colonial obscurantism versus post-independence enlightened liberalism, which is usually equated with modernity; the praised contributions of "liberal" reformers as opposed to those little publicized of
their "conservative" counterparts; and the political stance of some

practitioners. It also stresses the valuable contributions made by foreign practitioners that are often ignored in traditional Mexican historiography. Some issues discussed may sound familiar to the reader, such as the difficult advance of medical knowledge, the medical profession's insistence on monopoly over practice, and government efforts to balance health and environmental issues with immediate economic and political events. The intersection of war, political fragmentation, and epidemics, a topic as important in 1813 Mexico City as it is now, underscores the efforts and successes of contemporary physicians and authorities and may mirror those of modern healthcare practitioners presently dealing with similar circumstances. This study explores the relationships between professional monopoly, marginalization of medical sub-fields, and race and gender that continue to be relevant in our multicultural societies. It also seeks to answer questions that have received little attention. Why was political and health-care centralization crucial to achieving the professionalization of medicine? If all Latin America was influenced by French medicine, why is Mexico's case unique? Such topics are indispensable to understanding the history of medical professionalization in Mexico. They are also linked to overarching and current themes of control, power, monopoly over practice, medical knowledge, and public trust in the medical profession.

These themes will interest not only Mexican and Latin American specialists but also social scientists who have an interest in the development of the medical profession and its sub-fields. The broad field of public health, its administration, and policies regarding water and air pollution will appeal to those interested in environmental history. Similarly, the efforts to prevent and contain disease and the vaccination campaigns will interest anthropologists, sociologists, and historians with a focus on epidemics and their consequences on society. Those concerned with race, class, and gender will find the professional hierarchy and the challenges that women and minorities faced within the medical profession most telling. French influence on Mexican medicine and the active role of French military personnel will be surprising to many readers and will raise questions about nationalism and the legacy of France's cultural expansionism. Chapters 4 and 5 will appeal to specialists in the history of education and academic organizations. In a larger context, this work will be useful to scholars interested in nineteenth-century liberalism and its effects on government, education and society, state-building, cultural imperialism, the many facets of nationalism. Finally, the present analysis of the Mexican medical profession's difficult path to professionalization will prove valuable to scholars, regardless of their discipline, for comparative purposes.

The almost insurmountable obstacles medical professionals faced may be recognizable to medical historians: the struggle to elevate medicine to the status of science, to differentiate themselves from healers without formal training, and to provide the best possible education to future generations, among others. These obstacles were aptly described on 8 September 1839, when faculty and students of the recently established Colegio de Medicina in Mexico City met at the main hall of the National University for the first student award ceremony. Professor Manuel Carpio addressed the audience to describe the challenges as well as the rewards of professional life. He explained his hopes that the prizes about to be handed out would inspire students to work tirelessly and would encourage them to embrace the path of the physician that he described as "a sad path in society, a path filled with thorns and covered by sand where only a few flowers grew; his [the physician's] real reward for his exertions being the intimate satisfaction of trying to work for the welfare of humanity ... [satisfaction] that will increase when he realizes that there were many grateful and just men in Mexico who by their esteem and appreciation encourage us [practitioners] in our tediousness and disappointments."[19]

After encouraging those present to continue their studies, he warned them that "a physician has sacred and tremendous obligations that he cannot expect to fulfill without untiring study of books." He also warned his audience against adhering to "exclusive [medical] systems" because "one system follows another," as had been the case with John Brown's theories "that had reigned tyrannically" for a short time before being substituted by "others." He concluded his remarks by expressing his hopes for the future of medicine in Mexico.[20]

Carpio's words reflect both the limited professional expectations of a nineteenth-century physician and the shaky theoretical ground that supported contemporary medicine. As a founder and promoter of the medical school, he was aware of the difficult years that lay ahead for medical educators, practitioners, and students. At the time, the school could not expect much from a weak and nearly bankrupt government whose priority was political survival. For students, a medical degree implied considerable financial sacrifices, time-consuming work, moderate financial rewards, and very limited possibilities for further study. Aside from hospital positions, demand for costly medical services was limited to those fortunate enough to afford them. Intellectual stimulation was also limited, as there were no funded research institutions or laboratories. The obstacles in the path of graduating physicians were not so different from those their forefathers faced in colonial times.

The challenge for those who spearheaded reform was to enact the changes that would allow them to find a place in the new legislative, administrative, and political space, while also maintaining the professional hierarchy of colonial times and ensuring their own place at the apex of that hierarchy. Accordingly, the main focus of the analysis is the role played by a small, select, and influential group of physicians and surgeons that I term the "medical elite" or "medical leadership." Members of this group shaped and enforced, within their power, the reforms necessary for the survival of health-care occupations in the liberal environment of independent Mexico. Neither all health-care occupations nor all medical and surgical practitioners were active participants in the reorganization or contributed to the transition from colony to nation, and not all of them benefited from such changes. It was the top physicians and surgeons, the medical leadership, who set the pace of this transition and led the efforts to modernize the main medical "branches" of medicine and surgery. They collaborated with the state authorities to ensure legal recognition of their professional rights and position, tried to ensure their privileged places by establishing a medical school to monopolize and control specialized medical knowledge, and sought to gain recognition as the guardians of such knowledge by forming an academy. Their efforts were not completely successful, but they did prepare the terrain for those who came after them.

The process of medical professionalization in Mexico shares some similarities with the experiences of other nations. One was the prevalence of illegal healers and the medical practitioners' efforts to prove their professional superiority. As Mathew Ramsey has shown, in France the number of illegal healers outstripped those of formally trained practitioners up to the twentieth century.[21] In the United States, the decentralization of education and licensing also made it almost impossible to curb illegal practice. Regardless of training and licensing, the main reason for the profession's inability to enforce its monopoly over practice derived from its inability to translate medical knowledge into superior therapies, or to provide and control the medicaments necessary to address patients' complaints. In this sense, nineteenth-century practitioners were still helpless, their success dependent not only on medical discoveries, but also on the development of allied sciences. Furthermore, physicians' fees were usually high and beyond the reach of most of the population. In Mexico, as in other Spanish-American countries, the situation was aggravated by poverty, the extreme scarcity of formally trained practitioners, especially in the countryside, and by the country's multicultural roots. In colonial times, Indian towns abided by a different set of rules and were not subject to the Protomedicato.[22] Local healers flourished, and traditional multicultural practices persisted. As a result, monopoly rested merely on legislation and its enforcement, rather than on the public's preferences. The physician had a long way to go to prove his professional superiority to the public.

Of special interest is the case of France, the country that served as a model for Mexico's medical reforms. The French reorganization of medical education and practice was precipitated by the ideology of the French Revolution and the Napoleonic regime. The changes were not only radical, but also took place within a short period, and may be compared to the reforms resulting from Mexico's wars of independence and the 1833 legislation on education. Therefore, of great relevance for the present analysis are the works of French medical historians Toby Gelfand, David Vess, George Weisz, and John Harley Warner, among others.

Gelfand contrasts the deplorable state of eighteenth-century medicine with the pragmatic and innovative approach of surgery that ultimately served as the model for its reform, an argument that, although recently challenged, may be applied to the Mexican case.[23] David Vess takes the same contrasting approach but focuses on the crucial role played by military medicine in the reorganization of medicine and medical education. His *Medical Revolution in France, 1789–1796* offers some parallels with the innovations brought by military medical personnel to New Spain, the establishment of formal surgical teaching, and the army's semi-official training of surgical personnel.

The importance and implications of the Paris clinical school have attracted the attention of Russell C. Maulitz and John Harley Warner. The former focuses on Xavier Bichat to explore the development of

pathological anatomy and its implications for the notions of diagnosis and disease. Pathological anatomy provided a guide to deci-
pher the body and the basis for the future union of medicine and
surgery.[24] Unlike Gelfand and Vess, Maulitz traces its roots back
to the *ancien régime* and sees continuity, rather than change. The
development of pathological anatomy is of utmost importance
in understanding the centrality of the Paris clinical school in the
Western world and is of special relevance to Mexico, since the country embraced French medical practice so ardently. Furthermore,
Maulitz's emphasis on continuity, as opposed to Gelfand's and Vess's
stress on change, resonates in the Mexican context.

Warner concentrates on the transfer of French ideology and techniques, the so-called Paris clinical school or Paris school, to the
United States. His work centres on the experiences of the American
students who attended the famous school and their influence on
American medicine. He examines the appeal of Paris and its clinical
instruction for foreigners and the challenges that American and
British students faced. His study of the life and experiences of foreign students proved to be of great value to the present study, because
Mexican students in France left no comparable records with which
to evaluate their experience. Warner concludes that, although the
initial enthusiasm of returning physicians gradually vanished, the
Paris clinical school had an important influence on antebellum medicine and left a long-lasting legacy on American medicine.[25] The differences between the two countries are striking: although a much
smaller number of Mexican physicians travelled to Paris to "perfect
their studies," their crucial contributions to local medicine and education are undeniable, as shown by the medical education curriculum and by public health administration and legislation.

The topic of legal and illegal medical practitioners, covering
roughly the same time as the above works, has been approached by
Mathew Ramsey. Despite the prestige of Paris as the centre of clinical
teaching, Ramsey shows that, throughout this period, illegal practice
predominated, especially in rural areas, as the result of traditional
beliefs, scarcity of practitioners, popular resistance to accepting scientific medicine, and inability to pay costly fees. These factors worked
against physicians' effort to monopolize practice.[26] Ramsey's conclusions may be extended to Mexico, where a multicultural society,
poverty, and scarcity of licensed medical personnel made the problem more intractable. At the other end of the spectrum, George Weisz

analyzes the role played by the French Academy of Medicine in the development of France's national medical elite.[27] Unlike the present study, Weisz's work extends to the twentieth century, a period in which medicine became recognized as a scientific and modern profession. Despite important differences in their origins and political and cultural contexts, the French and the Mexican academies shared basic similarities, such as their unifying role at the national level and their contribution to raising professional prestige. Furthermore, the Mexican academy, founded in 1866 as a medical society, was an offshoot of the French Scientific Expedition to Mexico; it not only conformed to the French model, but half of its founding members were also French.

In Britain and the United States, medical professionalization followed a very different path, which, although less relevant to the present study, is nonetheless useful for comparative purposes. In Britain, where the medical profession was closely wedded to liberal principles, Gelfand describes "a much more gradual evolutionary process."[28] There was no unification in training or licensing, and the borders of medicine, surgery, and pharmacy were often bridged, as the excellent study of the Royal Infirmary of Edinburgh by Guenter B. Risse illustrates.[29] The first attempt to regulate professional education was the Apothecaries' Act of 1815, which recognized the role of scientific courses and clinical training. This was followed by the 1858 Medical Act, which introduced a single register for practitioners whose training had been legally recognized, while continuing the division between medicine and surgery. Loose enforcement allowed the inclusion of illegal practitioners, however, making the Act highly ineffectual. Professional unification had to wait until the 1880s, when examinations and certifications of the various training institutions were regularized.[30] An important, although dated source on this topic is M. Jeanne Peterson's *The Medical Profession in Mid-Victorian London*, a study on the changes taking place in hospitals and medical education, the efforts of the elite practitioners to regularize and control their less powerful brethren, and the beginnings of general practice and hospital specialization.

The United States followed a similar but more extreme pattern. During the mid-nineteenth century, the country lacked a uniform system of training and licensing, partly a result of the weak control of the federal government over the states. Thus, medical schools and private training proliferated with most uneven results, producing many practitioners who lacked proper training. The emergence of numerous medical theories and therapeutic systems such as homeopathy and Thomsonianism added to the confusion.[31] This situation continued until the 1880s, when the Supreme Court granted the states the right to license their own practitioners. It may be said that medical professionalization in the United States developed following the law of supply and demand, bearing few similarities to Mexico's "top-down" organization. Furthermore, in the United States, the licensing and organization of medical education and hospital teaching took place after the triumph of bacteriology and, therefore, was more influenced by German medicine than was the Mexican case. It is not surprising, therefore, to find more affinities between Mexican and French medicine and practitioners than between Mexico and the Anglo-Saxon countries.[32] Contemporary practitioners were aware of such affinities, as are present-day historians interested in the topic.

In Mexico, the area of the history of medicine is as broad as it is varied, encompassing more than 500 years, a variety of belief systems, and a multicultural society. Thus, although research has increased rapidly, the field remains wide open. Among the works directly relevant to medical professionalization during the nineteenth century is the grandiose *Historia de la Medicina en México* by Francisco de Asís Flores y Troncoso (1886), a comprehensive and informative work that covers pre-Hispanic, colonial, and nineteenth-century medicine and includes first-hand accounts of the author's contemporaries, personal experiences, and information on the medical school that, at the time, was common knowledge. Its main weakness is a lack of citations, a conscious (and unfortunate) decision by Flores y Troncoso, who did not want his work to appear "presumptuous." A second but not less important criticism is its outdated approach, a result of the author's education (he was a student of the well-known positivist educator Porfirio Parra). The work follows the "theological," "metaphysical," and "positivist" stages that reflected the linear development of medicine from obscurantism to scientific reality. Despite these considerable problems, *Historia de la Medicina en México* remains an important source that continues to shape the perceptions of the nineteenth-century history of medicine in Mexico.

Flores y Troncoso's contemporary, Nicolás León (1859–1929), native of the state of Michoacán, physician, linguist, anthropologist, writer, and internal pathology professor at the Morelia University, was also an important contributor to the topic under study. In addition to works on local and pre-Hispanic history, botany, and languages, León is the author of two brief historical descriptions of his state's medical world, *Apuntes para la historia de la medicina en Michoacán* (1886) and *La Escuela de Medicina de Michoacán* (1910), probably the first provincial medical description in Mexico. He also contributed a history of obstetrics in Mexico that gives interesting details on obstetrical education and practice in the capital during the last decades of the nineteenth century.[33] More recent authors have analyzed the same topic in a more critical fashion. Among them is Ana María Carrillo, who has recently written about the marginalization of midwives and the medicalization of obstetrics.[34]

Among the next generation of historians writing about nineteenth-century medicine is José Joaquín Izquierdo Raudon (1893–1974), a Puebla physician specialist in physiology and author of approximately three hundred medical and historical articles and eight books. Among the latter is *Raudon, cirujano poblano de 1810*, a biography of his great-grand-uncle. It portrays the surgical world of the late colonial period and, according to the author, the struggle of a provincial surgeon against the powerful, elitist, and retrograde Protomedicato. His work on the physician Luis Montaña (1755–1820), which includes a preface by Henry E. Sigerist, with whom the author corresponded for twenty years, follows the same line of thought: the enlightened practitioner, promoter of science against a traditionalist medical faculty. Izquierdo was, like Flores y Troncoso, a positivist; his linear view of history reflects his unquestionable faith in science and his desire to find a place for local medicine in European and world science. His works, nonetheless, represent a great contribution to the field of nineteenth-century medicine and place him among the main provincial historians of the time.[35]

Another great contributor to the history of nineteenth-century medicine is the physician Francisco Fernández del Castillo (1899–1983), whose short and descriptive work on the history of the Mexican Academy of Medicine and his volume containing the 1836–1956 indexes of the academy's journal (now outdated, as both were written in the 1950s) are of great value for those interested in the origins and life of the academy. His two-volume anthology, a posthumous collection of writings on the most diverse medical topics, includes some articles on the nineteenth century. Unfortunately, as with Flores y Troncoso, the latter lacks citations. Despite such problems, Fernández del Castillo's writings have been of great value to this study as sources of reference.

The above three authors share similar characteristics: they were practising physicians, believed in the advance of science, and tried to raise Mexican medicine to what they considered undeniably superior foreign standards; to them, the history of medicine proved the unstoppable advance of science. Recently, other scholars have approached the nineteenth century from different points of view. Among them is Fernando Martínez Cortés, who has concentrated on the history of the public health board. His first volume briefly discusses the Facultad Médica, the Protomedicato's successor, centring on the first fifty years of the Consejo Superior de Salubridad or public health council.[36] Based on the historical archives of this council, this study is especially relevant because it was through the Consejo Superior, or public health board, formed by physicians and pharmacists, that the medical elite reaffirmed their authority over public health and controlled professional licensing. In a second volume, co-written with his daughter Xóchitl Martínez Barbosa, the author provides the chronological follow-up covering the health board's reorganization during the Porfirio Díaz regime (1884–1910).[37]

Two analyses of related topics are the recently published study of Porfirian Yucatán by David Sowell's *Medicine on the Periphery: Public Health in the Yucatán, Mexico, 1870–1960*, and Claudia Agostoni's *Monuments of Progress: Modernization and Public Health in Mexico City, 1876–1910*. In the former, the author traces the unique evolution of Yucatán's public health system, from its establishment as an independent organization to its nationalization when the 1917 Constitution enshrined health as a national right. *Monuments for Progress*, also a valuable contribution to the history of public health, analyzes efforts by the Díaz regime to modernize the capital in accordance with contemporary positivist beliefs. Modernization, therefore, meant turning it into a hygienic city and changing the disorderly and unclean practices of its inhabitants. In agreement to my findings on the earlier part of the century, Agostoni sees modernization coming from above, an imposition on the popular classes. This work links Porfirian public health policies with the late colonial ones, prompted by the Enlightenment, but fails to discuss the crucial developments of the post-independence time, reaffirming the need for further study of this important period.

Another important contribution is the series Archivalía Médica, published by the Universidad Nacional Autónoma de México's Department of History and Philosophy of Medicine. The series includes short biographies on such key medical figures as Manuel Carpio, credited with the introduction of the stethoscope in Mexico, and the well-known ophthalmologist Rafael Lucio, as well as other medical practitioners who participated in politics: the substitute president and physician Valentín Gómez Farías; the surgeon and congressman Miguel Muñoz; and the politician, physician, and director of the medical school Casimiro Liceaga.[38] Each of these titles provides a brief biographical introduction followed by facsimile and typed versions of select primary documents of great value to researchers. Other more recent publications have greatly contributed to our understanding of nineteenth-century medicine: Martha Eugenia Rodríguez and Jorge Zacarías Prieto have increased our knowledge about the medical school and the maternity hospital;[39] Ana María Carrillo has summarized nineteenth-century relations between the medical profession and the state in her excellent article, "Profesiones sanitarias y lucha de poderes en el México del siglo XIX"; Rolando Neri Vela has researched the development of ophthalmology;[40] and various authors have written important medical history studies on the states of Puebla,[41] Guadalajara,[42] Guanajuato,[43] and Michoacán.[44] Worthy of mention is also the original analysis of Nora E. Jaffary, *Reproduction and Its Discontents in Mexico: Childbirth and Contraception from 1750 to 1905*, which traces how the views of childbirth and reproduction and the legislation and ethical perceptions surrounding them evolved from colonial times to the Porfiriato. Despite these valuable contributions, numerous topics have not been properly researched, and many questions remain unanswered.

The literature on Latin American countries is in a similar situation. Probably the closest publications to the topic at hand are Adam Warren's *Medicine and Politics in Colonial Peru* and José R. Jouve Martín's *The Black Doctors of Colonial Lima*. Warren focuses on the opportunities that the Bourbon reforms opened to local physicians who wished to secularize medical care, claim their expertise on medicine, and impose their own medical culture over that of the church. Their achievements were undermined in post-independence Peru, when they became dependent on shifting politics and politicians.[45] The last period discussed draws interesting parallels to the unstable political situation of post-independence Mexico and its consequences for the medical profession.

The most recent publication on Peruvian physicians is José R. Jouve Martín's work on the "black doctors" of Peru, an original monograph that examines the characteristics that allowed the licensing of Afro-Peruvian physicians during the first years of the nineteenth century, the important role they played during those years, and their legacy to the profession.[46] Unlike New Spain's medical elite, the Peruvian Protomedicato did not maintain strict racial controls over the profession. Like Warren, Jouve Martín covers the transition between colony and independent country that the present study analyzes and, although the topic is unique to Peru, it offers some contextual parallels to, as well as striking differences from, the case of Mexico.

Also of great importance is the excellent study by Steven Palmer, *From Popular Medicine to Medical Populism*, which stresses the commonalities and collaboration between formal and popular medicine and the relations between medical professionalization and nation building in Costa Rica. Palmer considers healers as intermediaries between formal and popular medicine and contributors to the formation of a local medical profession. The work brings to the fore differences from the Mexican case. For example, the colonial medical backgrounds of the countries differ. In the early nineteenth century, Costa Rica lacked licensed practitioners and, therefore, a Protomedicato to defend professional interests and monopoly. Furthermore, as the only health-care practitioners, healers were indispensable, resulting in a more lenient attitude among authorities. This situation is comparable to that encountered in the peripheral areas of Mexico, but not to that in the capital. Costa Rica also differs in the political and social context that shaped the development of the profession.

As to Mexico, to my knowledge there is no comprehensive analysis of the early nineteenth-century medical profession, as most authors concentrate either on colonial times or on the Porfiriato. It is this gap in the literature that motivated me to write this work. The present study adds to the historiography by examining the development of the medical profession in Mexico City and its surrounding area from the last years of the colonial period (approximately 1800) to the fall of the Second Empire.[47] I have chosen to conclude in the 1870s for several reasons. In that decade, most Mexican health

*

practitioners could look back on their achievements with satisfaction. With the only exception of phlebotomists and, to a lesser degree, midwives, they had established themselves as experts in their field by accumulating enough knowledge to differentiate them from the non-medically trained. Physician-surgeons had control over their training (despite requiring final government approval) and had formed professional organizations that confirmed them as a distinct group with unique and specialized scientific knowledge. The following decades would witness rapid scientific, political, and socio-economic changes. Bacteriology began to revolutionize medical therapies, opening a new chapter in medical history. From a political point of view, Mexico was about to begin a thirty-year dictatorship that would bring relative stability, the first stage of industrialization, and economic growth. The resulting socio-economic changes would transform education, professional practice, and the government's health-care priorities. Formal training expanded to include nurses, and medical specialties flourished. The crucial importance of this stage requires and deserves a separate analysis.

Four main themes intertwine throughout this volume. The first is continuity: I argue that educational programs and legislation developed gradually and were the result of collaboration between individuals and institutions, a view contrary to that of the traditional literature, which portrays sudden change, individual action, and clashes between factions and institutions as the triggers of change.[48] The second theme is the importance of the Paris school and French public health organizations, as well as the key and often-ignored role of foreign (mainly French) practitioners and their contributions to the modernization of the Mexican medical profession. The third persistent theme is competition. In colonial times, locals competed with Europeans and physicians with surgeons; the various "branches" of medicine competed among themselves for status, patients, and recognition; after independence, the top layers resolved their differences by merging and then availing themselves of their privileged position to prevent competition with the rest of the practitioners; licensed practitioners competed against illegal healers; teaching institutions competed against one another; and, in a more general way, the state and the church competed against each other. The fourth and final overarching theme refers to the ambiguous role of government in the modernization and reorganization of the profession, in ensuring the physician-surgeon's place at the apex of the

professional hierarchy, in legitimizing reforms by means of legislation, and often in hindering reforms.

In summary, this work concentrates on licensed medical practitioners: their efforts to form a modern profession, to be recognized
as such, and to carve their place in post-independence Mexico in
the period from 1800 to the 1870s. The monograph is not a medical history per se, nor does it delve into an in-depth analysis of
illegal practice, a fair study of which requires a separate work.
Thus, I approach *curanderos*, or folk healers, and quacks (who, I
recognize, were in the majority) through the lens of the medical
establishment, as competitors and as an obstacle to their monopoly
over medical practice.

This project is based on sources gathered at archives in Mexico
(mainly Mexico City), France, and England. The main but not the
only archives consulted in Mexico City were the Archivo Histórico
de la Facultad de Historia y Filosofia de la Medicina, which contains
the Protomedicato and medical school records, as well as other valuable documents on medical practice and education; the Archivo
Histórico de la Secretaría de Salud, where I consulted the records of
the Facultad Médica and Consejo Superior de Salubridad, as well as
information on hospitals and the practice of medicine; the Archivo
Histórico de la Ciudad de México, which contains municipal government records since colonial times, as well as information on epidemics, hospitals, and *policía*. These archives are well organized and
indexed, and their helpful and knowledgeable staff facilitate the
work of the researcher. The same can be said of the Archivo General
de la Nación, where information on the Protomedicato, medical
school and curricula, provincial medical education, and the Spanish
Empire, among other topics, may be found. The main challenge for
the researcher is the extremely large body of documentation and the
confusing organization caused by the constant administrative
changes of the time (education, for example, depended on different
ministries) during the years under study.

Municipal and state records in the states of Puebla, Jalisco,
Veracruz, Guanajuato, and Morelia were also mined for information
that was complemented by short trips to archives in Tlaxcala, Toluca,
Mérida, Aguascalientes, and Zacatecas. In my experience, the earlier
part of the nineteenth century continues to be the most challenging
for the researcher. In some archives, information on the matter at
hand is easily accessible; in others, documentation remains to be

catalogued and research tools compiled. In some cases, one must sort through boxes of loose pages that may or may not include information on the topic of interest. The result is a very interesting but slow process that demands time and funding, and partly explains the relatively small number of publications on the period.

In addition to Mexican archives, I consulted the Archives Nationales, Archives du Service de santé (Hôpital militaire du Val de Grâce), Archives de la Académie de Médecine, and the Bibliothèque Nationale in Paris, and the Service historique de la Défense in Vincennes. The sources found were of great value in understanding the collaborative efforts of medical and foreign practitioners during the French occupation of Mexico. In London, the Wellcome Institute holds limited but rare early nineteenth-century documents unavailable in Mexico that were of great value to my research.

This work is divided into five thematic chapters. The first chapter, "The Juntas de Sanidad and the Protomedicato," deals with the juntas de sanidad from their creation in 1812 to their abolition in 1836. The chapter focuses on the juntas' rivalry with the Protomedicato and its consequences for the profession and its representative body. The creation of the juntas de sanidad was a result of the political events taking place in Spain: the Napoleonic invasion and subsequent formation of liberal *cortes* (parliaments) that proceeded to enshrine a series of liberal reforms into a constitution, the first of its kind in the country. The juntas de sanidad were a result of tradition, a continuation of the temporary colonial boards established to deal with epidemics that required the presence of the clergy and were founded on the principle of Christian charity. They were also innovative. The juntas reflected the increasing concern of European countries for public health as a matter of political and economic concern. Furthermore, they were the result of a more democratic system that empowered municipalities to oversee disease prevention and public welfare and promoted human intervention to combat disease. The juntas de sanidad reflect the clash between new egalitarian values and a traditional and elitist colonial system, and the competition for control over professional and public health matters. During the following two decades, the juntas competed with the Protomedicato for control over public health and medical practice, encroaching on its jurisdiction, challenging its authority over professional issues and public health, and contributing to the erosion of its prestige in the capital and the provinces. Such a challenge, I argue,

placed the Protomedicato on the defensive and promoted the formation of a common front of physicians and surgeons and the reorganization of the main branches of medicine. This chapter examines
their struggle for control and emphasizes the social and political
context: criollo nationalism, the erosion of Mexico's City authority
over the provinces, and the growing regionalism of the post-independence years that foreshadowed the federalist-centralist tensions
to follow. In summary, the juntas de sanidad played a crucial role by
triggering the collaboration between physicians and elite surgeons
and the reorganization of the medical profession.

The second chapter, "Union and Control: Professional Reorganization and the New Nation," focuses on the realignment of the different medical fields, a result of the political reorganization in the
post-independence years. I argue that the professional alliance of
physicians and surgeons was prompted by their desire to defend
their interests from the juntas de sanidad. By spearheading reform
and ensuring their control over education and licensing, physicians
and elite surgeons sought to confirm and continue their privileged
place in the medical pyramid. The hierarchization of the health-care
occupations was shaped by colonial traditions, class, race and gender prejudices, and access to education. The chapter is divided into
seven sections. The first examines three reform proposals, while the
second focuses on the physician-surgeon alliance. The following
three sections analyze the impact of reform on the phlebotomists,
dentists, and midwives, respectively. The next section refers to foreign practitioners, and the final one looks at the challenge that charlatans and curanderos posed for licensed medical practitioners. The
realignment of the top professional echelons and their control over
other practitioners were of crucial importance for the development
of educational reforms, medical practice, future specializations, and
for the profession in general.

The third chapter, "The Medical Profession and Public Health,"
examines the role played by the Protomedicato's successors, the
Facultad Médica, the Consejo Superior de Salubridad, and the
Consejo Central, as professional bodies and public health boards. In
this chapter, I argue that the latter role gradually increased in importance, resulting in the ultimate separation of professional issues from
the public health field. During the time under study, physician-surgeons controlled these organizations and staked their place as
experts on all health-related issues and as medical professionals. The

first section of the chapter examines the Facultad Médica as the national reincarnation of the colonial Protomedicato in the post-independence period. The Facultad Médica inherited its public health responsibilities from the juntas de sanidad, not the Protomedicato, but remained primarily a professional organization. The second and third sections examine the establishment of the French-inspired Consejo Superior the Salubridad, its financial difficulties, and its uneasy alliance with government authorities. The fourth and fifth sections explore the wide range of the Consejo's mandate and the overlapping areas of professional monopoly and public health. The final section examines the short life and legacy of the Consejo Central, the first organization to approach public health from a national point of view. Intrinsic to this chapter are the political background (the federalist-centralist struggle and the inability of the central government to impose its public health initiatives), the influence of France, the adaptation of French models to local reality, and changes in the approach to public health.

The fourth chapter, "Training Future Generations: Medical Education," focuses on the struggle of the medical elite to reform and control medical education. It traces the proposals for reform and the development of the medical curriculum as inspired by the French *officiat*, the establishment of the medical school and its struggle to survive and fulfill its mandate, and the school's central role in the development of the medical profession. I argue that the growing importance of owning and transmitting the knowledge that separated medicine from other health-care-related occupations prompted the medical elite to work, against all odds, for educational reform and the establishment and consolidation of a medical school. Such reform was the result of negotiation and compromise and not, as many authors imply, the sudden, enlightened reform imposed by a small group of liberal politicians This chapter is divided into nine sections that form part of three main topics. The first topic gives a short political context and then follows the reforms that took place after independence and culminated in the foundation of the Establecimiento de Ciencias Médicas in 1833. The second topic examines the medical school per se, its curriculum, struggle for survival, rivalry with other teaching institutions, and the problems of teaching medicine without sufficient funding and infrastructure. The final part offers a brief comparison with the obstacles faced by provincial medical schools (in Morelia, Puebla, and Guadalajara) and the role of the capital's medical school in the formation of the profession's identity and professional network. This chapter underlines the continuity of medical education reform, the adaptation of foreign models, institutional competition, and the faculty's perseverance and commitment to achieve its goal.

The fifth and final chapter, "In Search of Recognition: The Establishment of the Academy of Medicine," concentrates on the top medical practitioners' efforts to form an academy, a learned organization that would allow them to discuss professional interests, debate ideas and experiences, and disseminate medical knowledge. It traces their pursuit from the first years after independence until the 1870s, and describes the various academic organizations, their achievements, and their contributions to the development of the medical profession. The chapter is divided into six parts. The first two focus on the short-lived academies formed between 1822 and 1860 and their publications as part of a continuum that, I argue, illustrates the profession's gradual maturing. The following two sections concentrate on the political and international circumstances that resulted in the foundation of the organization that would become the Academia de Medicina de México. The final two sections deal with the academy's immediate predecessors, the Sección de Medicina and the Sociedad Médica de México, their organization, and the extraordinary collaboration between French military practitioners and their Mexican colleagues. This chapter emphasizes the influence of France on Mexican medicine, the crucial role played by the French military medical corps in the foundation of a long-lasting academy, and its consequences for the Mexican medical profession. I question the traditional idea of nationalism as defined by the dichotomy characteristic of political and military history by arguing that support for the French initiative was considered by some as proof of national loyalty and pride. Similarly, I differ from authors such as Paul N. Edison and Lewis Pyenson who consider the French Commission Scientifique a failed attempt of France's policy of cultural expansion.[49] Instead, I approach the topic from the Mexican point of view and argue that Mexican practitioners welcomed French medical personnel and worked with them collegially as researchers and scientists. Furthermore, the endorsement of France gave the new academy credibility, fostered collaboration, facilitated connections with the European scientific world, and increased local practitioners' self-confidence. The establishment of the academy on firm ground was the crowning achievement of a medical leadership that had struggled for fifty years to reorganize the medical hierarchy, to provide modern scientific education for new generations, and to create a scientific organization that gave credibility to their efforts.

This work explores the changes that the medical profession underwent from the beginning of the nineteenth century until the Porfiriato (the Porfirio Díaz regime, 1876 to 1910). It places the development of Mexico's medical practitioners in the fluid political context of the time and delves into the effects that liberalism had on health-care practitioners, public health, medical education, and society. This analysis challenges traditional interpretations of nationalism and the application of liberalism, the view of a linear advance to modernity, and the role of liberal politicians. In offering this alternative view, I hope to contribute to the understanding of nineteenth-century medical and Mexican history and to promote further debate not only on the professionalization of medicine in Mexico and other Latin American countries and the role the state played in it, but also on the effects of liberal ideology on nineteenth-century society, science, and culture.

I

The Juntas de Sanidad
and the Protomedicato, 1800–1836

By the end of the colonial period the health boards not only over-saw public health but had also taken over most of the Protomedicato's responsibilities. The physicians' views on the marginalization of the Protomedicato were summarized by its president, Manuel de Jesús Febles, in an emotional speech to a gathering of almost two hundred practitioners and pharmacists: "The health boards that were formed as ordered by provincial regulations and should have been dissolved … became more influential than the Protomedicato and appropriated responsibility for all areas concerning public health and hygiene, leaving this body [the Protomedicato] without its main tasks."[1]

Although Febles's claims were well founded and the health boards brought change to a head, the Protomedicato's decay may be traced back to colonial times, the result of evolving ideologies, a changing society, and political reforms. This chapter analyzes the decline of the Protomedicato, the establishment of the juntas de sanidad in the different political contexts of Mexico City, Puebla, and Veracruz, and the clash between traditional values and liberal ideology in the organization of medical practice and public health. The chapter is divided into five sections, which explore the historical context of the Protomedicato; the establishment and beginnings of the capital's junta de sanidad and its political context; the different development of the Puebla and Veracruz juntas; and the struggle between the Mexico City junta de sanidad and the Protomedicato for control over all health-related matters, a struggle that the Protomedicato could not win.

BRIEF HISTORICAL CONTEXT

The effort to oppose the Napoleonic invasion of Spain in 1808 resulted in the formation of liberal cortes that gradually came to be consolidated in the Cortes of Cádiz. Their aim was to rule in the monarch's absence, but their liberal members availed themselves of the situation to enact a series of reforms that were formalized in the 1812 Cádiz Constitution. This constitution, the first of its kind in Spain, envisioned a more democratic society, elected representatives at the local level, and a less centralized power. Municipal governments were empowered and charged with more responsibilities, among which was public health. To oversee the public's welfare, the constitution ordered the creation of juntas de sanidad formed by medical practitioners, church representatives, and local residents. The juntas were not completely innovative: temporary juntas de sanidad had been organized to coordinate charitable and medical efforts in times of epidemics. However, the 1812 Constitution made them permanent and dependent on a democratic *cabildo* (municipal government), reflecting not only new egalitarian values, but also the growing concern for public health in European countries. In New Spain, the Cádiz Constitution was enacted in 1813, but was in place for only fourteen months; it was reinstated in 1820, shortly before independence. The juntas de sanidad remained for fifteen years until a centralist regime, seeking to redefine jurisdictional bounds and centralize authority, issued new legislation, and the juntas de sanidad became *juntas de caridad* (charity boards). Despite their short life, the juntas de sanidad had long-lasting consequences, not only in public health, but also for the medical profession in general. Without a clear-cut mandate, the new organizations challenged the traditional jurisdiction of the Protomedicato and interfered with medical practice, with different results according to region.

In New Spain, as in other Spanish American colonies, the Royal Tribunal of the Protomedicato had been responsible for licensing all health-care practitioners, enforcing professional monopoly, preventing illegal practice, and maintaining medical and professional standards.[2] It had also served as an advisory body on health-related issues since the sixteenth century. As did other colonial institutions, however, the Protomedicato lacked both a clear geographical jurisdiction and the means to enforce its regulations.[3] By the late eighteenth century, the increasing power of the state, the questioning of authority that characterized Enlightenment ideology, the new emphasis on practical as opposed to theoretical knowledge, and a more critical view of traditional medicine loosened the Protomedicato's control over medical practice, undermining the foundations of its authority and bringing its traditional privileges under attack. In 1805, the Protomedicato lost its independence when new legislation required the presence of an *oidor* (judge) or civil authority to proceed against any individual, reform that sought to organize the judicial system and curtail the privileges of traditional corporations. Seven years later, the Cádiz Constitution stripped the Protomedicato of its status as a tribunal and deprived it of its contentious privileges, leaving all cases of illegal medical practice and malpractice in the hands of a judge.[4] These provisions (and the Cádiz Constitution) were revoked fifteen months later, but the Protomedicato's prestige never recovered.

In Spain, the Enlightenment had resulted in the revision and modernization of university curricula and the creation of the more "practical" military surgical colleges of Cádiz, Madrid, and Barcelona. In New Spain, a petition to offer anatomical courses at the Royal Indian Hospital resulted in the establishment of a royal surgical school, the Real Escuela de Cirugía (1767), staffed by peninsular military surgeons. Although not a military school, the Escuela de Cirugía's main aim was to train local surgeons to serve under Spanish medical military personnel.[5] Formal education raised the status of colonial surgeons and diminished the distance that separated them from physicians, at the considerable price of subservience to their peninsular colleagues and loss of control over surgical education that was placed in the hands of Spanish military practitioners. The gap between physicians and surgeons was also reduced by the arrival of Spanish and foreign military surgeons who accompanied the armies and held degrees from the prestigious Spanish colleges and other European institutions. In most cases, they were authorized to practise both medicine and surgery and take civilians as their private patients. Their privileged position, the favour they enjoyed from the royal authorities, their popularity with the public, and their often patronizing and arrogant attitude caused resentment among local practitioners who, not unreasonably, saw them as unfair competition. Furthermore, as military officials, they were beyond the Protomedicato's jurisdiction. The rivalry was most pronounced between European practitioners and local physicians, as both belonged to the same social and racial strata and competed for the same patients. Such rivalry is reflected in the antagonistic relations between the peninsulares appointed by the Crown on the one hand, and the Protomedicato and the criollo faculty of the Real y Pontificia Universidad on the other. Their differences went beyond professional boundaries and personal animosities, and clearly reflected a strong nationalist component.

In 1790 the proposal of the Irish military practitioner Daniel O'Sullivan to teach a course of "medicine and other sciences" was flatly refused by the Protomedicato, and when he applied for the post of mathematics professor (mathematics was a requirement for medical studies) he was rejected because regulations forbade foreigners from occupying public posts.[6] The same year, the Faculty of Medicine cancelled the *acto* (debate) in which O'Sullivan was to participate, arguing that he was not part of the university body. The Protomedicato's decision was unreasonable, born of its desire to protect the criollo professional monopoly. O'Sullivan held a doctorate from the University of Toulouse, belonged to prestigious scientific academies in Edinburgh and Cadiz, and had worked in Edinburgh, London, and Paris. In New Spain, he had served in the hospitals of Jesús Nazareno, San Juan de Dios, and the military hospital of San Andrés, where he substituted mercury treatments for innovative and more benign methods to treat venereal disease. O'Sullivan appealed to the king who, not surprisingly, sided with him.[7] O'Sullivan was not alone.

The director of the newly established Botanical Gardens, Martín Sessé, and its botany professor, Vicente Cervantes (both peninsulares) had experienced similar problems. The medical faculty had refused to incorporate their courses into the university and accept them within the university fold, arguing that, on granting them the privileges reserved for the university faculty, the Crown had violated the institution's regulations. In August 1788, under government pressure, both were reluctantly sworn in as *catedráticos* (professors or faculty members) but continued to be excluded from faculty meetings and activities.[8] The Protomedicato used a similar approach and resisted the royal order to admit Cervantes and Sessé as part of the examining board of Pharmacy, because such an appointment "opposed the laws … [and was] incompatible with the national custom ruling this Tribunal." Instead, the protomédicos accepted them only as *alcaldes interinos* (internal officials) without power to participate in the examinations. In 1789, Viceroy Revillagigedo ordered the tribunal to comply and appointed Sessé third protomédico.[9] Not surprisingly the appointee refused the honour, explaining his local colleagues had received him with "repugnance" in response to his peninsular origins.[10] The recalcitrant position of the criollo faculty must be understood not only as a defence of professional privileges, but also as a conscious effort to keep control of the university and their profession strictly in criollo hands in a time when locals were purposely being displaced by peninsulares in government and church positions.

Mexico's wars of independence (1810–21) changed the medical profession. The capital's control over the provinces loosened and its legitimacy as representative of a higher authority disappeared. The war overstretched military resources and increased the need for military surgeons, opening professional opportunities and establishing the bases for long-term changes in the profession. The government's financial straits adversely affected university medical education: in 1810, the building of the Real y Pontifícia Universidad de México was turned into a military barracks and faculty ceased to be paid. Some professors continued to lecture in their private residences and offer lessons at local hospitals, but registrations plummeted; it was the beginning of the end of the Faculty of Medicine.

After independence, the short-lived empire of Agustín de Iturbide (1822–23) was followed by a few years in which the liberal ideals of democracy and legal equality seemed within reach. The withdrawal of royal officials had opened political and military posts that the criollos had coveted for years, and social mobility became feasible for mixed bloods, as the importance of race slowly began to recede. In 1823, a constitutional congress began the task of drawing up legislation for the new country. To that end, congressmen formed committees to deal with the main issues that preoccupied the legislators, while the disposition of less pressing concerns, such as public health, education, and medical reform, were left for later. The result was the liberal Constitution of 1824, which set the guidelines for a federalist democratic republic and maintained the public health provisions set by the Cádiz Constitution in 1812.

POLITICS, PUBLIC HEALTH, AND THE JUNTAS DE SANIDAD

The liberal reforms enacted in Spain in 1812 were an indirect result of the political and legislative changes triggered by the Napoleonic invasion of the country: the king's forced abdication, the imposition of Joseph Bonaparte, and the formation of cortes or parliaments to rule in the absence of the king.[11]

In New Spain, the events taking place in the mother country caused consternation and uncertainty. The news of the abdication of Charles IV in favour of Napoleon's brother arrived in July 1808. In response, two groups began to emerge. The first, following the Spanish example, favoured autonomy or the creation of a provisional government that would rule temporarily in the name of the king; the second, formed mainly by the peninsular elite, preferred to continue with the status quo, to wait and see.[12] Unsure of how to act, New Spain's viceroy, José de Iturrigaray, called a meeting of Mexico City's notables, raising concerns among the most conservative elements, who suspected his close ties to the francophile ministry of Manuel de Godoy in Spain and therefore a liberal, pro-French stance. The situation facing rulers and ruled brought to the surface political, social, and racial divisions among colonial elites and forced them to engage in a discussion of the origins of political power and the colonies' rights to representation. The discussion first centred on a legal point, whether the king's abdication of the Spanish throne included his abdication as king of New Spain. The priorities then shifted to a political point, the locus of authority in the absence of the monarch. Both issues would divide liberals and conservatives, criollos and peninsulares, during the coming years and prepare the path to independence.[13]

In August 1808, the arrival of two representatives of the junta of Seville seeking recognition (as well as the amortization monies awaiting shipment in Veracruz) prompted a second meeting of Mexico's elites, with the majority of attendants, but not the viceroy, leaning toward the requested recognition.[14] The confusion reigning in the peninsula became clear when a representative of another junta (Oviedo) arrived shortly after with the same request. Recognition was denied to both parties, and the viceroy, still unsure how to proceed, expressed his wish to call a meeting of the cities. Although such an initiative conformed to Spanish tradition, the conservative Audiencia (the highest tribunal in New Spain) read it as a move toward independence and a result of Iturrigaray's personal ambition. A conspiracy took shape, and on 16 September it removed Viceroy Iturrigaray and placed the government in the hands of the ultra-conservative merchant Gabriel del Yermo. The conservatives were now in control, but their actions had undermined the legitimacy of royal authority and increased criollo discontent. Thus, the struggle for the political control of the viceroyalty had begun. For the next two years, the reins of government would be in the hands first of Yermo, then of Archbishop Francisco Javier Lizana y Beaumont, and finally of the Audiencia. Ineffectual government and the illegal and highhanded actions of the conservative elite alienated liberals and nationalist criollos alike and eroded the government's credibility and legitimacy.

In the meantime, Spain wrestled with its own demons. The rivalry of the juntas gradually ceded to cooperation that resulted in the establishment of a central organization based in Cádiz, the Junta Central de España e Indias that, in 1808, came to be recognized as the regency.[15] Influenced by the latest democratic ideas, the Junta Central called on Spanish towns, provincial juntas, and the general population to send their representatives to Spain's parliament, the Cortes, an invitation that was extended to the colonies in February 1810. Once in session, the Cortes, now in charge, appropriated legislative rights and drew up a liberal constitution to curb the powers of the Crown. The Cádiz Constitution, promulgated in March 1812, would remain in place for two years; the Constitution arrived in New Spain at the beginning of September 1812 and was promulgated three weeks later. The Cortes continued its regular sessions until May 1814, when, with the return of the ultraconservative Ferdinand VII to the throne, it was dissolved and the Constitution abolished.[16]

Although not thoroughly enforced and lasting just over a year, the Cádiz Constitution triggered long-lasting political, administrative, and social changes throughout New Spain. Traditionally, Mexico City had been the centre of political power and the administrative seat of the viceroyalty. Officially, power was centred in the viceroy, the king's representative, who was responsible for all New Spain. The Cádiz Constitution ended this arrangement by abolishing the office of viceroy, which now became a *jefe político supremo* (supreme political chief), and giving more independence to the provinces, which now were granted their own *diputaciones provinciales* (provincial representation) and placed under a *jefe superior político* (superior political chief). Also, in the name of democracy, the Constitution empowered the *ayuntamientos* (municipalities) and their cabildos as the people's representatives. Cities and towns of more than a thousand inhabitants were authorized to establish their own elected cabildos. Despite its lax enforcement, the new

legislation multiplied the number of municipal governments and
granted more independence to provinces and towns at the cost of
traditional powers, diminished the authority of the viceregal officials, diluted royal power in the colony, and prepared the terrain for
the centralist federalist struggles of post-independence Mexico.[17]

To clarify the role of the new administrative bodies, the Cortes
issued the *Instrucción para el gobierno económico político de las
provincias* outlining the new regulations (proclaimed in New Spain
on 23 June 1813).[18] Its first chapter, "On the Ayuntamientos' Responsibilities," entrusted the *policía de salubridad y comodidad* (general
welfare of the population) to the municipal and provincial governments. At the time, the term *policía* had an extremely broad and
unrealistic meaning encompassing anything that affected human
health and welfare in the widest sense. As a result, the ayuntamientos became responsible not only for the good condition and cleanliness of streets, hospitals, jails, markets, and other public places, but
also for the removal of anything that might "alter" the public's
health. They were also to ensure that sufficient good-quality food
and water were available, that the streets were lighted and safe, and
that public places were "beautiful." If these provisions failed to ward
off disease, the ayuntamiento concerned had to report it immediately to the jefe político so that adequate measures could be taken.
The decree also entrusted statistical records to the ayuntamientos,
which became responsible for records of births, marriages, deaths,
and epidemics.[19] This new focus on statistics, characteristic of the
late eighteenth and early nineteenth centuries, was partly the result
of the new emphasis on observation and efforts to discover the natural laws that controlled disease and epidemics.

The same regulations ordered the yearly appointment of a junta
de sanidad in each municipality comprising the *alcalde primero*
(mayor), who would be its president, the eldest parish priest, one
or more medical practitioners, one or more *regidores* (aldermen),
and one or more *vecinos* (residents), depending on the town's size.
Appointments were left to the municipal governments, which could
increase the number of members and reappoint them as they saw fit.
Provincial juntas de sanidad, placed under the responsibility of the
jefe político of the area, would mirror the organization of the municipal health boards. Their job was to coordinate the tasks of the local
juntas de sanidad under their jurisdiction, decide how to prevent and
combat epidemics at the provincial level, and serve as collecting centres for data gathered by subordinate juntas.

Although far from innovative, the new juntas de sanidad differed from their predecessors in some important ways. Colonial juntas de sanidad had been temporary organizations formed by order of the viceroy or royal representative in times of epidemics and dissolved shortly after. Now, juntas de sanidad would be permanent bodies whose members would be renewed annually and depend on the democratically elected ayuntamientos (or on the political chief at the provincial level), and their objectives were expanded to include measures to prevent disease. In accordance with the miasmatic theories of the time that identified environmental factors as the causes of disease, they were endowed with broader and permanent responsibilities. However, these as well as the juntas' prerogatives were not clearly delineated in the *Instrucción*, which simply subjected them to "existing regulations," with any major decision having to be reached in agreement with the local authorities.[20] Thus, the mandate and exact jurisdiction of the juntas remained undefined, leaving the door open for both the expansion of their aims and prerogatives, and potential conflict with existing organizations and authorities. The juntas had a second, political objective: to counteract the traditional privileges of the Protomedicato.

As the juntas de sanidad were closely linked to the ayuntamientos, their survival and efforts to assert themselves as public health organizations became intricately linked to the power struggle between traditional and democratic authorities and between the centre and the periphery. The juntas' obligations often replicated those of the Protomedicato, clergy, and royal officials, so that their success depended not only on local political forces but also on their ability to find a niche for themselves in an already crowded space. The historical context and the local politics of each city would shape the role and evolution of each junta de sanidad and the cabildo on which it depended. In Mexico City, both faced the combined challenges of political uncertainty, epidemic disease, and financial crisis.

THE CABILDO, THE VICEROY, AND MEXICO CITY'S JUNTA DE SANIDAD

The liberal creation of permanent public health boards with duties that overlapped those of the Protomedicato effectively ended the latter's monopoly over health-related matters. Gradually, the juntas widened their prerogatives and jurisdiction at the expense of an increasingly vulnerable Protomedicato. The contest between both bodies was most evident in Mexico City, the viceroyalty's main city and centre of power.

The overthrow of Viceroy Iturrigaray had been planned and executed by the city's merchant and peninsular elite, who continued to control the government until 14 September 1810, when Francisco Xavier de Venegas, the new viceroy appointed by Spain's Junta Central, arrived to fulfill his mandate. The conservative Venegas, an enemy of the reforms being enacted in Spain, refused to implement the freedom of the press decree issued by the Cortes in November 1810 and delayed the enactment of the Cádiz Constitution until public pressure forced his hand.[21] Although the public and the authorities greeted the constitution's arrival in the capital with public celebrations and rejoicing, both Venegas and his successor hindered the constitution's enforcement. Reluctantly, however, Venegas ordered preparations for the election of the Mexico City cabildo, which took place in November of the same year and resulted, as the viceroy and the conservatives had feared, in a clear liberal criollo majority. Refusing to share power, in late December, before the cabildo members could take possession of their posts, the viceroy, alleging voting irregularities, annulled the election and ordered the traditional hereditary cabildo to remain in power.[22]

In March 1813, Venegas was recalled to Spain and replaced by Félix María Calleja del Rey. As conservative as his predecessor, Calleja gave only lip service to the constitution. Nonetheless, in accordance with the legislation, municipal elections took place, which confirmed the outcome of the previous elections. Calleja was forced to accept the results, but kept the cabildo under a tight rein, unlawfully forcing it to accept the conservative intendant Ramón Gutiérrez del Mazo as its head. Soon thereafter, the viceroy confronted the municipal body, accusing some of its members of lending their support to the rebels and demanding a list of "principal individuals" sympathetic to the rebel cause. The cabildo refused, but the battle lines between the conservative royalists (mostly peninsulares) and the reformist criollos were now clearly drawn.

During the next year and a half, the Mexico City cabildo sought to establish its legitimacy in an uphill battle against Calleja, the Audiencia, and the merchant elite. As all well knew, the cabildo's existence undermined the authority of the viceroy.[23] Thus, the former fought for its survival and the latter to safeguard his power. Mexico City, the seat of viceregal authority, became the centre of opposition to criollo autonomy and the rebel cause as well as the source of the autonomist movement unofficially represented by its elected cabildo.

In addition to having to face Calleja's opposition, the unenviable task of the municipal authorities was further complicated by the conditions resulting from war, limited funds, and, in 1813, a devastating epidemic. The concentration of military forces and the arrival of numerous families fleeing the fighting in the provinces exerted great pressure on the capital's infrastructure and resources, resulting in food scarcity, overcrowding, and increasingly unsanitary conditions, all of which facilitated the arrival of "fevers" that soon reached epidemic proportions. The symptoms – high fever, strong headaches, sharp pain in the shoulders and legs, and occasional vomiting – puzzled medical professionals.[24] Some believed it was the dreaded *matlazáhuatl* (typhus), but most experts disagreed, and not finding a better diagnosis, declared it an epidemic of "mysterious fevers."[25] On 18 May 1813, to deal with the dangerous situation, the viceroy ordered the establishment of a provisional junta superior de sanidad for the Province of Mexico and appointed Intendant and Jefe político Gutierréz del Mazo as its president and viceregal representative.[26] He was to serve with Dr José Miguel Guridi y Alcócer, the archbishop's representative; Juan Ignacio Vertis, the regidor and representative of the provincial *diputación*; the Count of la Cortina; the *maestre escuela*[27] of the metropolitan church; Dr Juan José Gamboa, a vecino; and the practitioners Antonio Serrano, honorary physician of His Majesty's Chamber and director of the School of Surgery, and Rafael Sagaz, ex-*catedrático* (professor) of the same school, both of whom were peninsular military surgeons as well as loyalists. Neither local practitioners nor a representative of the Protomedicato was included.[28] The capital, on the other hand, would have to wait another year for a municipal junta de sanidad.

In its meeting of 13 April 1813, two months before the arrival of the detailed *Instrucción* issued by the Spanish Cortes, Mexico City's first elected cabildo set the guidelines for the management of public health. It interpreted the new legislation as a mandate to establish a commission responsible for *sanidad y comodidad* (health and welfare), which included general public health (in streets, theatres, markets, and so on) as well as personal and property safety. However, the same minutes clarified that *sanidad* remained under the direct care of the municipal government itself, which, in the event of an epidemic or the fear of it, would take the necessary measures to deal with the problem.[29] As a result, the cabildo was responsible for efforts to combat the 1813 epidemic.[30] These were entrusted to the well-known criollo physician Luis Montaña and coordinated by the Protomedicato, the recognized health-care authority, which in the absence of a junta de sanidad organized aid and medical care throughout the city.[31] Their efforts would run parallel and sometimes in opposition to the measures dictated by the viceroy and enforced by the provincial officials and their junta de sanidad.

The task facing the authorities was immense. The city was on the verge of bankruptcy and its democratically elected cabildo lacked both power and authority. By mid-April, with the fevers now reaching the suburbs, the impecunious cabildo was forced to canvass for donations, and the underfunded and crowded hospitals refused to receive epidemic victims. Two months later, the cabildo had exhausted all its resources and had to depend on private charity. Nonetheless, the viceroy refused its requests to free the monies of the abolished Inquisition to cover the needs of the population. Instead, to marginalize the cabildo's efforts, Calleja established a junta de caridad directly under his control to distribute food, clothing, and medicines obtained on credit. Desperate, the cabildo contacted potential donors such as the Real y Pontificia Universidad and the wealthy widow of the Marquis of Vivanco, but their donations proved insufficient. Food scarcity, inflation, and poor sanitation added to the city's woes. Military actions resulted in the paralysis of trade, which tripled food prices and increased the cost of aid to the poor; the problem of sanitation became more acute as many workers died, others fled, and the municipality was unable to purchase the necessary number of carts for waste collection. The municipal government's penury also affected the maintenance of the canals, with the result that, by the end of the year only the main ones continued to be drained with borrowed monies. Mercifully, the epidemic lasted only a few months, ending in August of the same year. Although of short duration, it left an astounding death toll of 20,385 (out of a population of approximately 124,000).[32] The city's resources were completely exhausted but, as Timothy Anna states, "proud and self-assured, desperately trying to prove the validity of its constitutional mandate, the cabildo ... decided that all income from municipal properties outside the city limits would be diverted directly to this task [paying the loans contracted due to the epidemic]."[33]

The city was just recovering from the epidemic when, in early 1814, news of an outbreak of smallpox reached the authorities. This time the cabildo adhered to the *Instrucción* and on 20 April appointed a municipal junta de sanidad that included two criollo physicians, the conservative but nationalist José Ignacio García Jove, first protomédico, and the aforementioned Luis Montaña.[34] The junta wasted no time, and at the end of April Montaña presented a report (*Informe a la Junta de Sanidad*) on how to distribute the smallpox vaccine more effectively. Inoculation had been introduced in New Spain since the eighteenth century and practised in times of epidemic since at least 1779.[35] In 1797 the city published "instructions" or guidelines to prevent smallpox from spreading that included enforcing quarantine when inoculation, that had been introduced "voluntarily and happily," was not enough to contain the epidemic.[36] However, it was not until 1804 that the vaccine was officially introduced in Mexico by the Spanish Royal Philanthropical Vaccine Expedition led by the physician Francisco Xavier Balmis. The expedition, the first global immunization campaign left La Coruña in November 1803 with twenty-two non-immune orphans aged three to nine who were gradually vaccinated during the voyage, transferring the vaccine by arm-to-arm inoculation. The expedition reached Mexico in June 1804, remaining until February of the following year, immunizing the population and setting up the necessary infrastructure to continue doing so in the future.[37] The municipal governments were made responsible for vaccination and a *conservador* (keeper) of the vaccine appointed in each town. The Mexico City conservador in 1814 was the military surgeon and future politician Miguel Muñoz, who received the vaccine fluid from Balmis. At the time the vaccine had to be imported from Europe and was transmitted "brazo a brazo" (arm-to-arm) as the other two contemporary methods – drying the fluid in threads or keeping it between two crystals – were unreliable.[38] Muñoz was responsible for ensuring the vaccine fluid was available.

Montaña's report to the junta de sanidad and cabildo proposed an offensive approach, suggesting that the authorities not wait for the public to demand the vaccine but instead reach the vulnerable young by contacting *casas de enseñanza* (educational institutions), *obrajes* (small textile factories), and shops. Interested individuals, regardless of gender, should learn how to vaccinate and to recognize the "good" vaccine.[39] The report also proposed taking vaccinated children (to be used as a source of the vaccine) to all city areas and avoid waiting for the "common people" to request the vaccine ("*conducir niños vacunados a las casas de vecindad y a todos los barrios para no atenernos a la decision del pueblo*").[40] In another meeting, Montaña suggested ascertaining the degree of opposition to the vaccine among the people and the names of the opponents, gathering exact statistics and addresses of those vaccinated and following each case for ten days to determine the effectiveness of vaccination; he also urged use of the pulpit and confessional to persuade the public.[41] The following day, the junta de sanidad discussed the important issue of *lazarettos* (quarantine stations) and praised Pedro Romero de Terreros, count of Regla, for his offer to cover the necessary expenses for their establishment.[42] Another item on the agenda was Montaña's recommendation, as a preventive measure, to fumigate the city with nitro and sulphur, substances that were inexpensive and could be easily obtained from the powder factory.[43]

In May 1814, Marshal of Castille Francisco de Paul Gorraez y Medina, writing on behalf of the provincial junta de sanidad, requested funds from the authorities to prevent further spreading of the epidemic.[44] He also praised the efforts of the junta municipal de sanidad, which had given "proof of its zeal, good judgement [*tino*] and efficiency."[45] On 7 May six children, who had already been vaccinated, were inoculated with natural smallpox in the presence of three practitioners and the main city functionaries to produce "pus" for the initial vaccinations. The children remained at the facility during "the natural time of the (skin) eruption" and were visited regularly by the junta de sanidad.[46] The same month, two *Avisos al Público* (public notices) were published to promote vaccination and dispel fears about it, and the viceroy ordered the publication of directions on how to vaccinate or, if vaccine fluid was not available, to inoculate.[47] These directions, published in consultation with the provincial junta de sanidad and paid for with public funds, were to be distributed "in all the districts of the viceroyalty."[48] Statistics were not neglected, and the junta stressed the need to report the type of illness as well as the number of casualties, recoveries, and deaths to hospitals and other authorities. To this end, a form with the heading *Parte de Sanidad Pública* (public health report) was printed for distribution to all relevant authorities. It was divided into three sections – smallpox, *dolor de costado* (usually pneumonia), and "fevers" – each with four separate columns to indicate the number of existing patients, patients admitted during the week, patients released, and deaths.[49] Throughout the crisis, the Protomedicato played a secondary role as a consultant to the junta de sanidad. It provided the names of licensed medical practitioners, and two protomédicos served in the junta as members, but the campaign's coordination and final decisions remained in the hands of the junta de sanidad.

In May when the hard work of the junta de sanidad was beginning to pay off, royal orders arrived from Madrid – the constitutional experiment was over. Ferdinand VII, who preferred an absolutist form of government, had abrogated the Cádiz Constitution as well as the constitutional ayuntamientos. In Mexico, Viceroy Calleja promptly complied but allowed the members of the cabildo to remain at their posts for five more months to organize the celebrations of the king's restoration. After their term ended, the more pliable members of the pre-constitutional hereditary cabildo returned to government.[50] Probably in response to the threat posed by the smallpox epidemic, the Mexico City junta de sanidad continued to function, and a strong vaccination campaign under the supervision of the regidor, or alderman, of each district got under way. The junta de sanidad intensified the propaganda campaign, publishing a thousand copies of a booklet paid for by its own members. To ensure that the vaccine reached everybody, two runners were hired to carry the live fluid throughout the city. By August the efforts of the authorities had paid off – the disease was under control and the junta de sanidad had met its objectives.[51] At that point, the municipal junta de sanidad apparently ceased to function, as it disappears from the cabildo records. Mexico City would not have another junta de sanidad until 1820, after the rebellion of Rafael del Riego in favour of a liberal government forced the hand of Ferdinand VII.

The Mexico City cabildo had avoided conflict with the Protomedicato by appointing García Jove and Montaña to the junta de sanidad, but the signs of future tensions were already visible. In May 1813, when the capital suffered from the "mysterious fevers" epidemic, Rafael Marquez, a cabildo member, lodged a formal complaint against Montaña for his refusal to allow surgeons to treat epidemic victims, since it would amount to allowing them to practise internal medicine. Montaña's attitude was described as "capricious" (*puro capricho*) and against "the welfare of humanity," considering, Marquez argued, that there were not enough physicians to meet the emergency. Furthermore, Montaña's reasoning made no sense to

Marquez, as in his view there were physicians "infinitely more ignorant" than the "knowledgeable surgeons." Such a position, shared by
others, threatened the privileges of the local physicians and the Protomedicato's monopoly. Montaña offered to renounce his appointment, which the cabildo seriously considered; it also debated giving
itself the right to appoint any practitioner, physician, and surgeon to
oversee medical care in a given district. It was finally decided to try
to reason with Montaña on this urgent matter. As Montaña continued in his post, we may assume that, at least in the short term, the
differences were resolved.[52] But the issue remained and resurfaced in
1814 when the first protomédico, García Jove, launched a similar
complaint against the surgeons' role during the smallpox epidemic.
This time the unfavourable balance of power between the protomédicos and the civil authorities became patent when Gutiérrez del
Mazo, as president of the junta superior de sanidad, ordered all
practitioners, "regardless of degrees and licences," to render their
reports using the forms previously distributed.[53] Although the abolition of the Cádiz Constitution restored the Protomedicato's authority over all medical-related issues, the damage to its prestige was
apparent. A few years later, when the Constitution was reinstated, a
weaker Protomedicato would face a more liberal and independent
cabildo that would be less accommodating.

REGIONALISM AND PUBLIC HEALTH:
JUNTAS DE SANIDAD IN PUEBLA AND VERACRUZ

While the Mexico City junta de sanidad was established in the midst
of the capital's political, nationalistic, and professional tensions, juntas in other cities were born and developed in different circumstances.
A case in point is Puebla, where the local junta de sanidad enjoyed a
safe distance from viceregal intrigues and professional associations.
The tenuous control of the Protomedicato over the province's junta
and practitioners, and the Puebla authorities' support for the local
junta allowed this to successfully challenge the protomédicos.

At the beginning of the nineteenth century, Puebla had great economic importance as the result of its agriculture, industry, and trade.
Located in a central area between Veracruz and Mexico City, Puebla
was the obligatory stop for immigrants and merchants and a key
point for trade between the Pacific and south, and between the central and northern areas. Nonetheless, Puebla was not a political or

military base for the royalists, and the viceroy resided at a safe distance that prevented him from interfering directly with local matters.

For the medical profession, the relations between the city's practitioners and the Protomedicato had not always been friendly. The protomédicos had opposed establishment of a surgical school in Puebla's Hospital of San Pedro and had a long history of conflict with local pharmacists. In 1782, the inspection carried out by the future protomédico José Ignacio García Jove had caused such indignation that the pharmacists launched a formal complaint accusing him of extortion.[54] The same problem came up in 1805 when the pharmacists initiated a process against the Protomedicato's inspector Bartolomé Moreno, asking for his removal and for indemnification for the "scandalous" sums he had extracted from them.[55] Therefore, for *poblanos* (residents of Puebla), the local junta de sanidad not only empowered the municipal government but also gave more independence to local practitioners. It is not surprising, therefore, that the junta de sanidad continued to function in Puebla even after the viceroy abrogated both the Constitution and the *Instrucción*.

In his biography of surgeon Juan Nepomuceno Raudón, José Joaquín Izquierdo states that, in view of an imminent epidemic, the ayuntamiento established a junta de sanidad on 16 January 1813.[56] The initiative did not originate in the cabildo, however, but with a petition presented on 12 January by practitioners Mariano Anzures y Ceballos, Mariano Revilla (or Rivilla), José Maria Horta, and Juan del Castillo, and pharmacist Antonio Cal, who were concerned about the danger posed by the "mysterious fevers" epidemic. Their petition pointed out the importance of public health and the many "abuses" in medical practice (a reference to illegal medical practice) that, in their view, justified the establishment of a junta de sanidad as it was done in the (European) "civilized countries," to serve "God and humanity."[57] The junta was established before the *Instrucción* reached Mexico, and therefore did not adhere to the new regulations, but it set the basis for its successor, which would be installed a year later.

Like Mexico City, Puebla was facing a serious epidemic (possibly typhus), probably as a result of the battles taking place in the Cuautla area at the time.[58] The Puebla junta de sanidad proceeded to divide the city into sixteen nine-block sections or *cuarteles*, with each block under a *junta subalterna* (subordinate junta) and a *comisionado*, or delegate. It also requested that the authorities assign prisoners to clean the streets "that for their great filth are sustaining the epidemic."[59] Medical practitioners Revilla and del Castillo drew up a set of instructions on the appropriate nourishment to be administered to the sick, the best treatment of those convalescing, and the proper sanitation for dwellings. These were published and distributed to all comisionados. The junta de sanidad also selected pharmacies to dispense medicaments to the poor (paid for by the municipality), oversaw the establishment of the provisional hospital of San Xavier, and ordered the opening of four cemeteries with "ditches four *varas* deep"[60] to dispose of corpses. As in Mexico City, the mysterious fevers were under control by August. San Xavier closed its doors and its patients were transferred to a local hospital. The Puebla junta de sanidad rendered a report of its activities in October, praising its members, the juntas subalternas, local practitioners, and charitable individuals who had contributed generously to defeat the epidemic that had seized the city. Almost 49,000 people had contracted the disease and more than 7,000 had died, among them the junta de sanidad secretary, Lieutenant-Colonel José María Lafragua.[61] The cost to the government was calculated at 44,227 pesos, 6 reales, and 6 granos, and the junta emphasized that the pharmacies filling the prescriptions for those in need had kept the most "scrupulous" accounting of income and expenses.[62] On 8 November 1813, once the epidemic was over and the junta had fulfilled its duty, its members asked the municipal government for further instructions. Although dependent on the cabildo, the junta wondered if it should continue with its functions or be dissolved.[63] The response of the cabildo is unclear but presumably the junta ceased to function before the end of December.

On 26 January 1814, in accordance with the *Instrucción*, a new junta de sanidad was installed that included practitioners Mariano Anzures and Mariano Revilla and pharmacist Antonio de la Cal among its members.[64] The main task ahead was to deal with a potential smallpox epidemic. The dreaded disease had already been reported in nearby Córdoba, Jalapa, and Veracruz, so the new junta wasted no time in initiating a vaccination campaign. Not taking any chances, the junta requested that Governor Intendant Ramón Días Ortega instruct police and military officials "to collect" the children who should be vaccinated and order military commanders and civilian administrators to aid "the propagation of the vaccine." The junta also proposed training sufficient personnel to ensure the vaccination of the population and ordering nearby towns and villages to send two or three children to be vaccinated and "transport" the vaccine fluid back to their towns.[65]

The results, however, do not seem to have been completely satisfactory, as the following month the junta pressed to prevent those who were sick with smallpox from leaving their villages and children who had not been vaccinated from travelling to infected villages. On 24 February, the junta proposed the publication of a *bando*, or official proclamation, reminding the population of their obligation to report smallpox cases and warning parents that if they neglected to take their sick children to the lazarettos, the authorities would do so by force.[66] Probably as a result of these measures, from January to 3 March, 824 children were vaccinated in the city, 325 in Amozoc, and 907 in "different departments." Still dissatisfied with the results, the junta asked, and apparently obtained, thirty soldiers to gather children who had not yet been vaccinated.[67] Another 1,400 children were vaccinated the following week, and by the end of the month the junta reported a total of 8,825 vaccinations. In August, with the emergency over, vaccinations were scheduled every ten days "to maintain the seed."[68] Thanks to the combined efforts of the junta de sanidad, local health-care providers, and the civilian and military authorities, the forced vaccination campaign had prevented a serious smallpox epidemic.

The cabildo records indicate that, despite royal orders to the contrary, the junta de sanidad, backed by the local authorities and practitioners, continued to function without interruption. During this period the junta served as a coordinating and information centre for the province until it was officially re-established 1820.[69] On 15 September 1814, the junta received reports of "a true nervous typhus" from the town of San Pablo and "a devouring plague of putrid fevers" in Santa María Quecholán.[70] Two months later, on 24 November, its members learned of yellow fever cases in the town of Acacingo, and shortly after, a local physician reported the dreaded disease had reached Puebla in "cotton bundles" transported from the port of Veracruz.[71] In June 1815, the junta received acknowledgment for the vaccine fluid it had sent to Mexico City and "its happy effects," and two years later, upon the request of the bishop, it sent a local physician to the town of Yanquimecam in the jurisdiction of Tlaxcala to treat the victims of "putrid and malignant fevers."[72]

In addition to combating the ever-present illnesses, Puebla's junta de sanidad was rapidly becoming the municipal and provincial medical authority. When the hospital of San Pedro established an obstetrics course, its instructor, Mariano Anzures, notified the junta members, and when in 1814 Mexico City requested more "fresh pus" (for vaccination), the municipal government forwarded the petition to the junta as the recognized authority on the matter.[73]

After the 1820 restoration of the Cádiz Constitution, the Puebla junta de sanidad proceeded to draw up its own regulations on health and sanitation in the widest sense and to appropriate the right to police medical practitioners. The junta took on responsibility of enforcing professional monopoly, avoiding encroachment of medical branches on each other's field of practice, ensuring that no "abortive, narcotic, corrosive or similar substances be prescribed," and that all practitioners signed their prescriptions. In a clear contravention of the Protomedicato's traditional jurisdiction, the junta also empowered itself to review the qualifications of "military medical personnel with degrees from Spanish colleges" who wished to practise in Puebla. The junta also became responsible for inspection of hospitals and public and charitable institutions, overseeing the quality of food and drink, preserving "the most interesting branch of the vaccine," and compiling of birth, death, and marriage statistics. To fulfill its many responsibilities, the junta met twice a month unless an epidemic or some other emergency required more frequent meetings.[74] After independence the Puebla junta de sanidad continued to be backed by the state authorities who, in 1827, appointed it "protector and keeper" of the state's vaccine and assigned 450 pesos to the task. The junta then appointed a practitioner and an assistant at the cost of 250 and 150 pesos respectively, and covered the cost of the necessary needles, paper, and books with the remaining 50 pesos. The junta de sanidad was to meet each three months to discuss the reports gathered by the municipal juntas and as often as needed in the case of an epidemic.[75] As it had with vaccination, by the end of the decade, the Puebla junta de sanidad had effectively displaced the Protomedicato as an advisory body and a licensing and public health authority in the state.

In gradually appropriating the rights and responsibilities that had belonged to the Protomedicato, Puebla's junta de sanidad had the support of the municipal and provincial governments, which saw the new legislation as a way to loosen their dependence on the capital and reaffirm local interests, its attitude a reflection of the incipient provincial federalism that would characterize independent Mexico. For the poblanos, the municipal junta de sanidad symbolized independence from Mexico City and its institutions (among them the Protomedicato), a symbol they chose to preserve, even when legislation no longer required it. Such an attitude hindered the national implementation of national health-related regulations and standards during the rest of the century.

Like Puebla, Veracruz also adopted the *Instrucción*, but the challenges the city faced were different. Veracruz was the main port of the viceroyalty and the connecting point to Spain. As such, the city was key to transatlantic trade and therefore of immense economic, political, and military importance for the empire. Veracruz was also famous (or infamous) for its unhealthy environment, its well-deserved reputation derived mainly from its frequent yellow fever epidemics and its endemic malaria, and for being the port of entry of other diseases such as smallpox and measles. Therefore, the port was much feared not only by Europeans but also by visitors from the highlands, who saw in its dunes, oppressive heat, humidity, and stagnant waters the images of disease and death. Such fears became real more than once, when arriving Spanish troops were decimated by disease.[76] Indeed, by the turn of the nineteenth century, Veracruz's devastating yellow fever epidemics and unhealthy reputation were such that the authorities considered relocating the population and destroying the city.[77]

Nonetheless, Veracruz's municipal government undertook preventive policies and public health measures that were of prime importance not only for the health of the local population but also for the welfare of the whole viceroyalty. Outbreaks of smallpox in Cuba in 1790, 1793, and 1796 had prompted the viceregal authorities to order the establishment of temporary juntas de sanidad to prevent the landing of infected ships in their effort to ward off disease. When a yellow fever epidemic appeared in Spain in 1801, the viceroy adhered to the traditional quarantine and isolation measures and ordered the establishment of permanent juntas de sanidad in all ports.[78]

Veracruz's unique circumstances shaped the composition and objectives of these early juntas. Since the arrival of the Spanish armies in the mid-eighteenth century, military medical personnel had served in local hospitals that catered to the needs of the army and navy and had also been entrusted with the required sanitary inspections. The public health issue loomed large in the minds of the local business community, as the attendance of local merchants, representatives of the Mexico City trading houses, and the local *consulado* (trade board) at regular junta de sanidad meetings attests.[79] The various and often conflicting interests of the mercantile community, medical practitioners, and local and viceregal authorities frequently resulted, however, in disagreements and lack of action. Often, the Veracruz juntas found themselves in the middle of the debate between "contagionists" and "hygienists." While the former, following common sense, located the sources of infection in incoming vessels, the merchant community opposed any measures to quarantine vessels and merchandise. Instead, leaning on hygienists' views, merchants pressed for environmental improvements such as draining stagnant ponds, widening streets, and relocating corpses buried in the churches.[80] The constitutional junta would inherit similar debates and challenges from its predecessors.

The first constitutional junta de sanidad in Veracruz was installed in March 1814 "in fulfilment of the *Political Regulations of the Provinces.*" Among its members were the military practitioners José de Ynoyos and Florencio Perez Camoto, both peninsulares.[81] According to its regulations, the junta's purpose was to prevent contagious ailments and epidemics by carrying out "operations" (inspections) in vessels, lazarettos, and neighbourhoods, and to "'propagate' and conserve alive the precious gift of the vaccine."[82] Of all its responsibilities, the most onerous and controversial was the *visita de sanidad*, or sanitary inspection of arriving vessels.[83] These visitas were not new. In 1764, after two small vessels had arrived from Caracas carrying smallpox victims, Viceroy Marquis of Cruillas had ordered that such an inspection be carried out on all incoming vessels.[84] The visita was a time-consuming and unpleasant affair that practitioners not only dreaded but tried to avoid at all costs. It implied boarding the incoming ship, questioning the captain and the crew, and, in suspicious cases, making a thorough inspection. If an ill crew member or passenger was found on board, the inspector had to decide whether to quarantine the ship or isolate the sick individual. It was a laborious task that cut into the assigned practitioner's time for his other obligations and private practice. The visita was the duty of the naval practitioners stationed in the port and was often a cause of arguments and disagreements among them. These reached such a point that, in 1808, the viceroy was informed that, in view of the reluctance of one practitioner, Francisco Hernández, to fulfill his duty, all practitioners had refused to carry out inspections.[85] In 1814, the sanitary inspections became the responsibility of practitioners associated with the constitutional junta de sanidad.

Shortly after its appointment and aware of the numerous responsibilities and difficulties it faced, the constitutional junta requested the appointment of a physician and an *escribano* (secretary) at government expense. The junta pointed out that the port was "the main and almost only point of entry" to the mainland and emphasized the utmost importance of its welfare. It also reminded the authorities of "the innumerable operations (inspections) carried out in ships, lazarettos and residential areas" entrusted to its medical practitioners and the impossibility of their carrying out such duties while fulfilling their jobs and other responsibilities as members of the junta. The junta also requested that, for sanitary inspections, practitioners be paid a salary higher than the monthly seventy-five pesos they normally received.[86]

In addition to the heavy responsibility of sanitary inspections, the junta de sanidad was in charge, as its predecessors had been since 1804, of "the most important task of distributing and keeping alive the precious gift of the vaccine."[87] Indeed, the two obligations were closely related, as smallpox frequently entered New Spain through its Caribbean ports. The "maintenance of the vaccine" was also of crucial importance to the rest of the viceroyalty, as the vaccine was not produced locally but had to be imported from Europe.

Veracruz's constitutional junta de sanidad continued working until the end of 1814, when it was dissolved in conformity with Madrid's orders. On its dissolution, the junta surrendered its archives to the local cabildo, which presumably then became directly responsible for public health.[88] Veracruz would have to wait six years to appoint its next constitutional junta de sanidad. As did its predecessor, the new junta would include a peninsular military practitioner, Miguel Sauch, among its members.[89]

After independence, in its session of March 1826, the junta de sanidad complained to the government that its work was hindered by the lack of clarity in defining its obligations and mandate. It therefore asked the municipal authorities to provide it with "all precedents on the matter" to draw up its regulations. It is unclear when they were drawn up, but the junta continued to serve as a health-related advisory body, counselling the government on public health measures necessary to improve the health of the population.[90] A month later the junta was authorized to add four individuals to its membership and, at least during the following few years, the Veracruz junta seems to have played an important role in the authorities' efforts to combat disease.[91]

Clearly, the responsibilities, power, and development of juntas de sanidad varied, depending on local circumstances. In Mexico City, the first constitutional junta became a pawn in the autonomist royalist struggle. It was not until 1820, with a self-assured cabildo standing on firmer ground, that the junta showed its independence and began to claim its place in the public health area. In Puebla, the junta de sanidad flourished with the blessing and support of the local authorities, who wished to emphasize their independence from the overbearing centre. In Veracruz, the importance of the city as the main entry port to New Spain attracted the attention of the viceregal authorities and led to the establishment of a permanent junta de sanidad before 1813. Its role as a naval base resulted in the appointment of peninsular military practitioners to carry out duties that should have fallen to the municipal government, and the first constitutional junta continued to include, out of choice or necessity, military personnel to carry out part of its duties. Although the 1814 constitutional juntas de sanidad were short-lived, they temporarily altered the institutional, political, and professional balance in the field of public health and set a precedent for their 1820 successors. Regardless of their duration and specific obligations, the juntas de sanidad weakened the Protomedicato's professional monopoly, challenged its role as the primary public health authority, and contributed to its demise.

THE PROTOMEDICATO VERSUS THE MEXICO CITY JUNTA DE SANIDAD

The lessons learned from the establishment of the permanent juntas de sanidad were not lost on the Protomedicato and the physicians it represented. It was well aware of the new challenges it faced. Throughout the Western world, the status of surgery was rising at the expense of that of medicine, and the dividing lines between the two branches of medicine were becoming increasingly blurred. In Mexico, the monopoly enjoyed by physicians and the Protomedicato's credibility had been increasingly undermined by the conflicting legislation issued since the turn of the century.[92] The wars of independence had overstretched government resources to the detriment of medical education and had forced physicians to fall back on a hospital apprenticeship system. It had been a hard blow for the proud physicians, who had always based their claims of professional superiority on a university education.[93] Nonetheless, the protomédicos struggled to maintain their traditional position. They continued to meet regularly, serve as experts in all health-related matters, offer their knowledgeable advice to other cities and, as already mentioned, they collaborated closely with the municipal and viceregal authorities to contain the deadly 1813 and 1814 epidemics that affected Mexico City.

The existence of the Protomedicato depended on the preservation of the status quo, but, ironically, the Protomedicato was undergoing profound changes. Little is known about its internal functioning and even less about the ideology and politics of its members.[94] Most authors portray the Protomedicato as a conservative, monolithic institution that stubbornly opposed innovation, but they fail to place it in its historical context or to consider the composition of its membership. During the last years of the colonial period, the Protomedicato began to undergo important changes triggered by the arrival of new members who belonged to a younger generation. In 1812, the second protomédico, Juan Vicuña, died and was succeeded by his younger colleague, José María Gracida y Bernal, who occupied the post for only three years before dying suddenly in 1815. He in turn was followed by the conservative Luis Montaña, who died in 1820 at the age of sixty-five. In 1823, the septuagenarian first protomédico, José Ignacio García Jove, who was well known for his defence of criollo interests and had been accused by his critics of "denouncing all Spaniards as if he were Moctezuma's heir and had his crown stolen from his temples," died.[95] It was the changing of the guard, as the last colonial protomédicos were succeeded by younger individuals with different training and a liberal ideology, individuals who did not identify with the struggles and objectives of their predecessors.[96]

García Jove's replacement, Manuel de Jesús Febles, was an 1812 graduate of the Escuela de Cirugía who also held a doctorate in medicine;[97] Casimiro Liceaga, an independence sympathizer who completed the surgical program at the Escuela de Cirugía in 1815 and received a doctorate in medicine in 1819, replaced Montaña as second protomédico;[98] and Joaquín Guerra, who gained his doctorate in 1820, became the third protomédico. Febles and Liceaga participated in politics, served as congressmen, and were key participants in the reform of the medical curriculum. Thus, the importance of these changes cannot be overstated. The Protomedicato may have been rooted in Hispanic tradition and conservatism, but by 1820 the protomédicos were ideologically and professionally different from their colonial predecessors and, contrary to traditional belief, showed themselves, as well as many of the physicians they represented, to be not only open to change but eager for reform.

The situation of the surgeons had also changed, but in a different and more advantageous way. Surgical education was in only slightly better condition than medical education, as the quality of training at the Escuela de Cirugía had deteriorated for lack of funding. The Hospital Real de Naturales (Royal Indian Hospital), where the Escuela de Cirugía was located, had also declined as the number of its patients dwindled and its resources dried up. At the same time, the professional opportunities for surgeons had improved. The war had increased the need for surgeons, and although local surgeons were usually employed to fill the gap left by the insufficient number of European practitioners, the army offered recent graduates employment as well as the chance for professional and financial improvement. It was an attractive proposition, and some surgical students requested permission to shorten their internship or simply abandoned their studies to join the army. As military practitioners, local surgeons had the opportunity to observe and learn from their usually well-trained European superiors. Surgeons sent to practise in isolated posts had to treat medical and surgical cases and military and civilian patients alike, thus gaining valuable experience, often at the expense of their patients. Military practitioners enjoyed another advantage: their common experiences developed camaraderie among those who served, and military medical personnel developed friendships as well as valuable political and military networks that would serve them well after independence.[99] Civilian surgeons also benefited from the reduction in their number and the increased demand for their services as so many of their colleagues followed the armies.

Despite these achievements, surgeons continued to face serious handicaps. For example, even latin surgeons had not completely escaped identification with untrained bleeders. As well, many practising surgeons had attended the Escuela de Cirugía but had failed either to graduate or to complete their studies and, similarly to most phlebotomists, lacked the necessary official credentials. They might have enjoyed more demand for their services, but academically, socially, and professionally they remained in a position inferior to that of the university-trained physicians.

As well, new threats loomed on the horizon, of which protomédicos and physicians were well aware. Egalitarian ideals allowed ambitious people of mixed blood to join the criollo ranks, undermining the racial hierarchy that buttressed the physicians' dominant position. At the same time, the demand for more democratic institutions endangered their traditional rights and privileges. In addition, the growing political power of the army challenged the established order and enhanced the division between military and civilian practitioners. But the most immediate danger came from the reinstated juntas de sanidad that, from 1820 on, threatened the independence of the medical and surgical elite by increasing the chance of direct intervention by local governments.

At the end of May 1820, the news of the Constitution's reinstatement was enthusiastically received in Mexico. Once more, cities elected municipal officials, and the constitutional cabildos proceeded to appoint juntas de sanidad. The newly formed Mexico City junta de sanidad met for the first time on 11 July 1820.[100] It scheduled its meeting for Tuesday afternoons to prevent conflict with the attendants' morning occupations and set as its first priority the appointment of a commission to draw up its regulations.[101] Among the commission's members were the university professor Manuel de Jesús Febles, soon to become a protomédico, and the young military surgeon Francisco Montes de Oca, later professor of surgery. The commission's proposal, presented on 22 August, identified the junta de sanidad's two main objectives as the prevention of disease and the provision of aid to the citizenry in times of illness. As the first aim, the prevention of disease, was closely related to the precepts of public hygiene, the commission proposed to leave this area in the hands of the appointed medical practitioners. Aiding the population in case of disease, however, fell under the principles of "humanity and Christian charity," and the commission recommended leaving this task in the charge of those individuals the junta considered best suited for it.[102] It is impossible to know the degree of influence Febles and Montes de Oca exerted on the writing of this proposal, but clearly its intention was to guarantee medical and surgical practitioners control over medical matters. In the end, however, the junta does not seem to have endorsed the proposal.

It did not take long for Mexico City's junta de sanidad to begin its tasks. In July 1820, the town of San Juan Acatlán was the first to

report "an epidemic of fevers," which soon reached the capital,
peaking in October and November and lasting until March of the
following year. The junta de sanidad addressed the problem by printing and distributing a thousand copies of a treatise on preventive
measures and treatment.[103] By conforming to legislation and taking
charge of disease prevention, the junta for all practical purposes
assumed responsibility for the extremely broad area of public health,
which included "the atmosphere, streets and plazas, buildings, fountains, food and even the practice of all the branches of medicine,
surgery and pharmacy."[104] The population soon recognized the
junta as the organization in charge of public health and began to
bring their complaints on policía matters. The Canoa Street residents brought to its attention the garbage accumulated in the street,
and the neighbours of San Hipólito hospital complained about the
sewage that leaked from its building and made the street impassa-
ble.[105] Gradually, the juntas increased their jurisdiction, a trend that
may be compared to the expansion of the French health boards'
duties. It was not by coincidence that contemporary French hygienists served as a model and were cited by the junta members during
their discussions; the influence of the French hygienist movement on
Hispanic juntas was patent.

Conflict between the junta de sanidad and the now-empowered
cabildo on the one hand, and the physicians represented by the
Protomedicato on the other, rapidly surfaced. In October 1820, José
Bernardo Baz, a member of the junta de sanidad, proposed the establishment of a *junta de censura* (censorship committee) that would be
responsible for judging and prosecuting medical malpractice and
illegal practice and for rewarding professional excellence. This
would be formed by nine practitioners divided into three groups
(medicine, surgery, and pharmacy) and its decisions would be final,
except in criminal cases when the accused had the right to appeal
after being sent to criminal court. There would be one such committee in each political department. Baz was an admirer of François-
Emmanuel Fodéré's *Medicina legal e higiene pública* and supported
his argument with a long quote from this work, an indication of the
increasing influence of French authors in Mexico.[106] Fodéré considered public health a responsibility of the government that should act
through its health boards; physicians should serve only as the latter's
advisers.[107] Baz's proposal received support from a cabildo member
who pointed out that the Protomedicato had been abolished by the

Spanish Cortes. Not surprisingly, the junta's three practitioners backed the Protomedicato and strongly opposed the initiative, claiming it was "contrary to justice" and pointing out "the notorious offence to the Protomedicato by depriving it of the authority granted by the law to correct or punish the members of its corporation."[108] In response to the difference of opinion, and wishing to prevent a heated and acrimonious argument, the junta agreed to inform the protomédicos of the proposal. The latter's response came as no surprise: the junta de sanidad, the protomédicos argued, lacked the expertise necessary to police the profession and rule over health matters, and the busy schedules of its members prevented them from acquiring it. The result was that the medical professionals appointed to serve in the junta de sanidad were forced to "carry out all its responsibilities." Furthermore, the protomédicos believed the junta's work would be fruitless, because the measures agreed upon and its proposals were usually unenforceable for lack of municipal funds.[109] Although Baz's proposal was not accepted, it was a clear reminder of the new political vision, the diverse goals and mentalities of the two bodies, the tensions between them, and the declining authority and credibility of the Protomedicato.

Indeed, the junta de sanidad continued to encroach on the traditional rights and obligations of the Protomedicato, which was now on the defensive. On 17 July 1821 (just two months before Mexico proclaimed its independence), the Mexico City ayuntamiento, on the basis of decisions of the junta de sanidad and in conformity to the Cádiz Constitution, ordered practitioners to clearly stipulate the number, weight, and measurement of required medications in Spanish instead of Latin and to sign their prescriptions.[110] Availing itself of the tensions between the Mexico City cabildo and the royal authorities, the Protomedicato complained to the viceroy, Francisco Novella, who was also head of the provincial junta superior de sanidad in charge of the Province of Mexico. Novella backed the Protomedicato, but his response indicates that his main concern was the independence shown by the municipal cabildo and its junta de sanidad, not the encroachment on the protomédicos' jurisdiction. Not intimidated, however, the Mexico City cabildo challenged Viceroy Novella by reminding him of the legislation recently issued by Madrid.[111] Much had changed in only seven years.

The situation of the Protomedicato did not improve after independence. Another clash between Mexico City's ayuntamiento and the Protomedicato took place in 1822, when the latter forbade the foreign physician John Woodbury to sell *agua de sosa* (soda water). The *alcalde mayor* (mayor), Francisco Fagoaga, refused to allow the Protomedicato to intervene in the matter, stating in no uncertain terms that the municipal authorities had the duty to watch over public health, which included food and beverages. The protomédicos, he added, should limit themselves to overseeing medical and pharmaceutical professional practice. As Fagoaga explained, his decision was based on a report by the commissioned pharmacists Vicente Cervantes, Manuel Cootero, and Andrés del Río, who, after careful analysis, had concluded that agua de sosa was neither harmful nor deadly. Furthermore, their conclusion was supported by "the civilized countries," where agua de sosa was not considered a medicinal substance, despite its benefits. Fagoaga thus declared the Protomedicato's claims unfounded and stated that consenting to them would result in requiring the protomédicos to inspect all food and beverages. Therefore, using his authority and fulfilling his duty to protect the "personal liberty and safety" of the municipality's residents, Fagoaga authorized Dr Woodbury "to use his machines" and sell his agua de sosa as long as he conformed to municipal health regulations. He also warned Woodbury "not to obey other orders but those communicated by me or my superiors" in the future.[112]

Despite Fagoaga's insistence that the Protomedicato limit itself to "the duties under its jurisdiction" and to oversee medical professional practice, the new regulations of the junta de sanidad (1820) empowered it to police the practice of medicine, surgery, and pharmacy and to act against abuses committed in *beneficencia* (welfare houses or establishments).[113] Thus, in 1824, the junta began to debate the illegal practice of medicine, ways to prevent patients from requesting the services of unlicensed practitioners, and the establishment of an obstetrics school and a maternity hospital, all areas that supposedly fell under the Protomedicato's jurisdiction.[114] Under regulations introduced in 1826, the junta broadened its responsibilities to include not only the prevention of illness and the organization of aid during epidemics, but also the inspection of buildings, fountains, plazas, foodstuffs, beverages, and "even the practice of medicine, surgery and pharmacy and all their branches." The new regulations divided the junta into two sections, one composed mainly of medical practitioners responsible for "public hygiene," and the other in charge of welfare and matters related to Christian charity and "humanity." The division forecasted the parting of the ways between medicine and religion, science and charity that would soon take place.

The structure and procedures of the junta reflected the democratic ideals of the time. Henceforth, the junta's members were to be selected annually by freely elected municipal governments. With the sole exception of the president, the regulations did away with the hierarchical division of its members, "who would take their seats indistinctly and without formalities." Even the time and day of the sessions would now be decided by a majority of votes, and all members would be free to participate in the discussion on equal terms.[115] The many physicians and surgeons who served at the junta de sanidad and their yearly rotation reflect its inclusiveness as well as the professional opportunities that such an onerous service entailed (see table 1.1). For some young practitioners, whose names would later be included among the main medical educators and reformers such as Manuel Andrade, Ignacio Torres and Leopoldo Río de la Loza, a post as the junta's adviser implied a further step in their professional careers. For others, such as the foreigner John Woodbury, it was an attempt to secure professional recognition from the authorities and find acceptance amongst his new colleagues.[116]

The role and importance of the juntas de sanidad increased during the 1820s and early 1830s. During the 1833 cholera epidemic in Mexico City, the municipal junta de sanidad organized aid and medical services, kept the public informed, and oversaw the transportation and burial of victims of the epidemic.[117] It also coordinated the repeated fumigations with vinegar, sulphuric acid, ordinary and sublimated camphor, soda muriate, chlorinated water, lemons, and "aromatic herbs purchased from the Indians" ordered by the physician Cornelio Gracida. The 550 pesos cost for the substances, the required carbon, transportation of the necessary materials and labour were subsidized by the municipal government, which also paid for a third fumigation of the Santiago cemetery.[118] Despite the important public health role of the juntas de sanidad, they, like the Protomedicato, eventually fell victim to innovative legislation. The laws issued in 1836 affected public health and the licensing of medical practitioners. Public health became the responsibility of a new body, the Facultad Médica del Distrito Federal y Territorios, and the juntas de sanidad became juntas de caridad (charity boards), caring for the welfare of the poor and occasionally inspecting hospitals and charitable institutions.

The constitutional juntas de sanidad shattered once and for all the Protomedicato's monopoly on health-related issues. They had been a

Table 1.1 Practitioners and pharmacists appointed to the Mexico City Junta de Sanidad

1820	Manuel de Jesús Febles, José María Vara, Francisco Montes de Oca
1821	(Joaquín) Guerra, Manuel de Flores y Heras, Joaquín Piña, José María Amable
1822	Cornelio Gracida, Sebastián Morón (pharmacist)
1823	José María Ballesteros
1824	Juan Balenchana, Francisco Montes de Oca, Joaquín Piña
1825	José María Vara (renounces), replaced by Francisco Montes de Oca
1826	José María Vara (refuses), John Woodbury, Joaquín Piña, José María Varela
1827	José María Benitez, Manuel Meneses, Félix Velasco, Miguel Nájera (pharmacist), José Crespo (pharmacist)
1828	Casimiro Liceaga, Manuel Basconcelos, José Ruiz, Francisco Rodríguez Puebla, José María Osorio, Joaquin Altamirano, Miguel Salvatierra, José María Torices, Félix Velasco, Francisco Montes de Oca
1829	Isidoro Olvera, Manuel Carvallido, Miguel Salvatierra, Leopoldo Río de la Loza, José Aramburo, Cervantes (Vicente Cervantes' son, also a pharmacist)
1843	Manuel Andrade, Ignacio Torres

product of the liberal ideals of the Cádiz Constitution and, as such, depended on democratically elected municipal governments. Unlike the Protomedicato, the juntas were not elitist bodies representing the interests of a select group, and medical practitioners served in them in a merely advisory capacity. The same liberal ideology and political priorities that inspired their establishment eroded the prestige and power of the Protomedicato. It was clear that the prevailing balance between the various colonial institutions was coming to an end, opening new spaces in the political, social, and professional spheres. The liberal reforms imposed by the new constitution, with its emphasis on a democratic system, triggered the realignment of forces; democracy would come at the expense of traditional privileges, monopolies, and corporations like the Protomedicato. The reforms came as a wake-up call for physicians, weakened by declining numbers and the growing number of licensed and unlicensed surgeons. A new realignment was imperative to strengthen their position. It would require concessions, negotiation, and the reordering of the professional hierarchy. The surgeons were open to suggestions.

Union and Control:
Professional Reorganization
and the New Nation, 1800–1860

When the physician John Woodsbury was appointed to the Mexico City junta de sanidad, the local physicians serving in the same board launched a formal complaint. Woodbury had to reply to the charges against him: lacking the necessary credentials and being a foreigner (and thus disqualified to serve in an official capacity). He presented proof of his studies in the "medical and surgical college of the state of New York's West District," an official letter of naturalization issued by the Mexican government, and letters attesting to his professional services.[1] His reply reflects the difficulties that an outsider faced when trying to join the medical practitioners' brethren. Woodbury was not alone, and as more foreigners entered Mexico and provincial practitioners applied for licences, the capital's medical elite had to redefine the terms in which the newcomers, provincial colleagues, and the future generations would be accepted into the profession.

This chapter focuses on the reorganization of the medical profession. The alliance of physicians and surgeons secured their position at the apex of the new hierarchy and their control over the "lesser" branches of medicine. By mid-century physician-surgeons had gained recognition as health-care specialists, but their efforts to enforce a monopoly over medical practice were not successful, as numerous non-licensed practitioners continued to offer their services to the population. The first part of this chapter examines and compares four proposals for change submitted by the Protomedicato; the civilian surgeon and critic Miguel Muñoz; the director of the surgical school, Antonio Serrano; and the military surgeon, Pedro del Villar; and illustrates the authors' different points of view and objectives.

The next two sections focus on the formal merging of medicine and surgery based on the 1831 legislation and the implications of that merger. Those sections are followed by an analysis of the effects of the 1831 legislation on the "minor" branches of medicine: phlebotomy, dentistry, and midwifery. The final part of the chapter concentrates on the efforts of the physician-surgeons to rein in competition from foreign and illegal healers or charlatans. Throughout the chapter, the main topics of continuity, competition, and control intertwine with the factors of race, gender, and nationality.

The long years of war changed Mexico as much as they changed the medical profession. The capital's control over the provinces loosened and its legitimacy as representative of a higher authority disappeared. The withdrawal of royal officials opened political and military posts to the criollos and, as the official racial distinctions were eliminated, the chances of socio-economic mobility increased and became a reality for many. The turmoil of Iturbide's empire (1822–23) was followed by a few years in which the liberal ideals of democracy and legal equality seemed within reach. In 1823 an elected congress began the task of drafting the country's constitution. To this end, various committees were formed to deal with the main issues that preoccupied the legislators, and those interested were consulted and given the opportunity to participate. The result was the liberal constitution of 1824, which established the guidelines for a federalist democratic republic and influenced the reorganization of the medical profession. The less pressing issues of public health, education, and medical reform continued to be discussed, but remained undecided for almost a decade.

Throughout the colonial period, the Protomedicato had ensured the racial purity and social standing of the medical elite. Unlike in Peru, no individuals of African background had been allowed to practise medicine or surgery legally, but the wars brought numerous changes that contributed to break down racial and social barriers. The physicians' wishes to strengthen their position, the students' need to attend classes at different institutions, the erasing of racial hierarchies after independence, and the medical services rendered during the wars of independence allowed the entrance of a limited number of practitioners of lower socio-economic standing into the medical elite. Nonetheless, economic and social factors continued to work against this limited democratization and, during the first part of the century, the profession remained firmly in criollo hands.

FOUR PROPOSALS FOR CHANGE

Independence offered the chance to reorganize the nation and achieve the secular society and prosperous country envisioned by contemporary liberals. However, numerous obstacles, ranging from the devastated economy to the lack of political experience and the difficulty of fulfilling the expectations of a multiracial and multicultural society, hindered achievement of these goals. Liberal principles demanded the replacement of the colonial privileges, hierarchies, and monopolies, now relics of the past, by more egalitarian views and democratic ways. The physicians recognized the imminent danger and, in an effort to maintain their privileged position at the apex of the medical hierarchy, accepted the urgency of reform. Unfortunately, the post- independence consultation and collaboration that resulted from the enthusiasm and idealism of legislators and reformers would soon give way to political priorities and more inflexible positions.

Under the leadership of the protomédicos, the main physicians met on various occasions to discuss their future within the medical hierarchy and their role in the new nation. Their meetings resulted in a proposal entitled (in its short form) *Memoria Sobre la Necesidad y Utilidad de reunir el estudio de medicina de la Universidad, el de Cirujía del Hospital de Naturales, y el de Botánica del Jardín de palacio en un Colegio de Medicina y Ciencias Naturales* (Treatise on the need and utility of uniting the university medical studies, the surgical studies taught at the Indian Hospital, and those of botany taught at the Botanical Gardens in a College of Medicine and Natural Sciences) presented by the Protomedicato to the "Sovereign Congress of the Heroic Mexican Nation" in June 1823.[2] The proposal consisted of a series of reforms to the system rather than revolutionary changes. It began by portraying the dismal conditions of medical and surgical education in Mexico. The university was in decline, lacking funding and a proper space in which to teach the courses indispensable to a good practitioner. The surgical school, it continued, was in an even worse condition, with just one professor, aided by an assistant or dissector, teaching all the courses and taking care of administration. Its base of support, the Hospital de Naturales had lost part of its income in 1814 when the half-real contribution paid by the natives was abolished. Soon after, the legal distinction of "Indian" ceased to exist and the hospital lost its raison d'être. Its closure in February 1822 placed the future of the surgical school in jeopardy.[3]

In addition to an inadequate education, the proposal explained, local practitioners enjoyed almost no financial rewards for their labours and were viewed with disdain by the public. To make matters worse, the *vulgo acomodado* (literally "ordinary people of means") preferred foreign practitioners, regardless of their qualifications. Despite this "deplorable" situation, the protomédicos argued somehow contradictorily, local students continued to be trained and examined, and local physicians such as Dr Luis Montaña, "whose name will always be the glory and honour of Americans," excelled at their profession.[4] Thus, the protomédicos proposed to create a new body, a *tribunal general de salud pública* (public health tribunal), which would be endowed with wider jurisdiction and greater powers than the Protomedicato. The new tribunal would be "a permanent centre of physicians" and, following liberal ideals, would be based on the equality and union of all practitioners for their own benefit and that of the public. Although physicians and surgeons had been trained differently, the forced attendance of both groups at an *escuela médico-quirúrgica* (medical surgical school) would gradually "equalize" their knowledge, leaving only a division between physicians and pharmacists. Part of the required funds would come from the usual sources – examinations, licensing, and pharmacy inspections – and the rest would be subsidized by government monies earmarked for the botanical gardens and the salaries of the university and surgical school medical faculties, complemented by the income derived from the properties belonging to the Hospital de Naturales.[5]

The idea of uniting both branches of medicine under one organization was not without precedent. In Spain, clinical training for physicians became mandatory for university graduates in 1795, and two years later a decree ordered medical students to study two years of "practical medicine" before applying for licensing. The reforms started by Charles IV's minister Manuel de Godoy were taken further by the liberal and francophile Mariano Luis de Urquijo. During his brief ministry (1799–1801), Urquijo suppressed the Protomedicato, substituting it with the Junta General de Gobierno de la Facultad Reunida, or "General Committee of United Faculties," formed of senior physicians and surgeons, and granted graduates of the medical surgical colleges permission to practise medicine and surgery.

Urquijo, however, was followed by a conservative minister who immediately undid the reforms, restoring the Protomedicato and the division between the two branches of medicine.[6] From then on, medicine and surgery would be united and separated, depending on the politics of those in power. Conservatives opted for tradition, division, and the ancestral Protomedicato; liberals, instead, adhered to the French model, which preferred the union of both branches. Some critics condemned the conservatives for their support of medieval *fueros* (privileges), while others identified liberals with revolutionary and Napoleonic France to the detriment of any efforts to bring about innovation. Napoleon's troops entered the Iberian peninsula in 1807, and in 1811 Spain's new ruler, Joseph Bonaparte, established a Supreme Council of Health that, following the French example, reunited medicine, surgery, and pharmacy, a move that was welcomed by Spanish reformers. Simultaneously, and ironically, in the areas beyond French control, the progressive Cortes also united the various branches of medicine but re-established the Protomedicato.[7]

The defeat of Napoleon and the return of the Spanish king Ferdinand VII ended reform. Medicine and surgery were separated once more, and the medical university faculties were ordered to function under the legislation in place in 1804. Emphasis was placed on political stances, and the progressive education plans presented by some universities were rejected. There matters rested until the rebellion of Rafael del Riego in 1820 returned the liberals to power. The new regime centralized education once more, established a special school of health sciences, and erased the distinction between physicians and surgeons for the next two years. The return of Ferdinand VII in 1823 marked the end of reform, as well as the separation of medicine and surgery in Spain for years to come.[8]

In Mexico, the dizzying and often contradictory political and legislative changes in the mother country prevented any long-lasting reforms from taking place. Of more consequence were the various changes to military medical regulations affecting the armies, which contributed to confusion and promoted animosity between physicians and surgeons, a situation further complicated by the military civilian dichotomy, racial prejudice, and nationalistic feelings. Under the Reales Ordenanzas of 1795, graduates of the Spanish royal surgical colleges licensed to practise medicine could treat military patients afflicted with "internal" or medical diseases. Two years later, a royal decree authorized them to treat civilian as well as military patients and to practise freely among the civilian population "because they were the only ones in attendance."[9] In any case, the protomédicos' 1823 proposal to join medicine and surgery implied continuity rather than a radical break with the past, echoing the reforms previously imposed in Spain but adhering to the innovative French model so much mentioned in contemporary proposals. It also recognized that in practice, both branches of medicine were already merging.

In fact, the Protomedicato proposed to discard its old name and adopt a more democratic attitude to ensure its survival, a privileged place for the physicians in the professional hierarchy, and an adequate source of funding, but it was the surgeons, rather than the better organized physicians, who had the most to gain from the proposal. Surgeons lacked an organization that would prioritize their interests over those of the other medical fields; furthermore, surgery was a more heterogeneous branch, with a wide range of practitioners divided between civilians and military officers and different educational and socio-economic levels. This lack of uniformity weakened their cause.

With the submission of his *Memoria Histórica*[10] to the Mexican Congress in 1823, surgeon and congressman Miguel Muñoz may be considered the (unofficial) speaker for the civilian surgeons. Most of the *Memoria Histórica* is a defence of surgery and an attack on "physiological empirical medicine" that betrays the frustration felt by some contemporary surgeons at being relegated to a secondary place. Starting with classical Greece, Muñoz follows the main medical and surgical developments, with comments on the contributions of prominent authors up to contemporary times. He does not hide his contempt for medicine "that had little to offer" and for local physicians, accusing them of never producing anything worth reading. Even the eminent Luis Montaña, "who achieved perfection in other branches of medicine," comes under attack for his neglect of anatomy, the fundamental basis of medicine, and for his incomplete study of "the science of man."[11] With such terminology, the long list of French works he includes, and his praise for a country that "will swell with pride for having produced Bichat, Chausier and Brousais [*sic*], founders of the new and exact medicine," the influence of French thinking on Muñoz becomes obvious.[12] The surgeon's admiration for French medicine is not surprising, as the anatomo-clinical approach of French practitioners had raised the status of surgery and ultimately contributed to the merging of both branches. The French model, therefore, was of special interest to educated Mexican surgeons such as Muñoz, who felt they deserved the same recognition as their medical colleagues. Other commonalities between Mexico and France, such as the army's urgent need for trained personnel as a result of war, the egalitarian ideals of the reformers, and the central role of the state, made the French model especially appealing to local practitioners.

In France, reform had been intimately linked to the ideals and events of the Revolution and to the needs of the Napoleonic wars. Almost all universities had been abolished as part of the effort to erase privilege and social differences. Equality and liberty demanded the same opportunities and the freedom to practise any trade, so in 1790 all requirements and training were thrown out the window – medicine became just another trade, to be performed by anybody who paid for a licence. The price of this reform was rapid lowering of standards of medical education and practice. But revolutionary ideals had to bow to military pragmatism when the French armies began their conquest of Europe. War required able surgeons for the care of the volunteer soldiers, so medicine and surgery were united and medical training was reinstated around state-run teaching hospitals. The result was hands-on training and the flowering of the anatomo-clinical medicine (known as the Paris clinical school) that placed early nineteenth-century France at the forefront of the medical world.[13]

Knowing that anatomy and surgery were indispensable for the advance of medicine, Muñoz proposed the establishment of a government-controlled junta de salud pública and, as in France, a "surgical-medical school" in Mexico City and every provincial capital. Unfortunately, Muñoz stopped short of giving any details as to their organization or funding. He warned, however, that if the separation of medicine and surgery continued, American (that is, Mexican) physicians would continue to "practise empiricism" and to be "mere echoes" of foreigners, to the nation's dishonour.[14] Muñoz's proposal may have echoed the union of surgery and medicine as practised in the French écoles but it was also heir to Spain's attempts to unite both branches of medicine.

The proposals of Muñoz and the protomédicos have more commonalities than differences. Both asked for the union of medicine

and surgery, and envisioned one profession and one educational curriculum. Reform, for Mexico, would mean a break with the colonial
past and the traditional hierarchical divisions based on race and
privilege that were intricately linked to the professional pyramid.
Practitioners wished to follow the example of *la culta Europa*, a
term that referred mainly although not exclusively to France, the
inspiration and model of contemporary Mexican medical reformers.[15] At the same time, physicians and surgeons struggled for control over the rest of the profession.

Not all surgeons agreed with Muñoz's unified vision, preferring
instead the traditional separation of the two medical branches. One
of those who opposed the merging of medicine and surgery was
Antonio Serrano, director of the Real Escuela de Cirugía. Serrano
was a peninsular military surgeon, a graduate of the Colegio de Cádiz
who had been sent to Mexico in 1795 to fill the post of "anatomical
dissector and second professor" of the surgical school.[16] His appointment was controversial, as the committee and royal authorities
shunned local applicants in favour of a peninsular military surgeon.
Protests followed and in the end, the Crown sent Serrano as its own
appointee.[17] According to his own account, Serrano had accepted the
post reluctantly, as an act of duty to his king. Once in Mexico,
Serrano's doubts were neither dispelled nor alleviated, as he encountered hostility from the local practitioners, who resented both him
and his appointment, as contrary to the surgical school's own regulations.[18] It was not long before Serrano found himself involved in a
bitter struggle with the Protomedicato over the control of surgical
licences and fees. His numerous petitions to Madrid fell on deaf ears
and his efforts on behalf of the school received little recognition.
Nonetheless, Serrano served Spain and later Mexico loyally and
fought continuously for "his" school's welfare and independence.

In 1822, Serrano presented a proposal to Congress, hoping to
obtain from the Mexican government what he had not obtained
from Spain – namely, an independent, well-funded surgical institution with the ability to license its own graduates. His project, therefore, was a new version of those submitted to the Spanish Crown in
previous years.[19] Unlike Muñoz and the protomédicos, Serrano
envisioned a *junta superior gubernativa de cirugía* (superior surgical
governing body) or *protomedicato supremo de salud pública*
(supreme protomedicato of public health), a body that would oversee a medical-surgical college attached to a hospital and be inspired
by the Spanish surgical colleges. This body would be composed of

the college's director, three of its professors, and the main army surgeon, though it is not clear if he intended an exclusively military organization or one for both military and civilian practitioners.[20] Serrano's proposal was more conservative than those of Muñoz and the protomédicos, as it adhered to the traditional division between medicine and surgery. He also intended that surgery take precedence over medicine. In this respect, Serrano's plan reflected his age, traditional views, and past struggles on behalf of the surgical school.

The sad condition of surgical education and the unfortunate looting of the Escuela de Cirugía during the Parián riots[21] were probably behind the 1829 proposal submitted by military surgeon Pedro del Villar.[22] Like Serrano, del Villar bemoaned the "lack of protection [of] medical sciences" and made clear that his proposal referred only to surgery, his "first profession."[23] After condemning the Protomedicato for its negligence and the excessive costs of licensing, del Villar proposed its substitution by a *junta consultiva de sanidad militar* (military health board) formed by all medical branches, the establishment of a national surgical school under its control, and the introduction of training in the promising field of obstetrics. By entrusting examinations and licenses to the junta consultiva de sanidad militar, del Villar hoped to ensure that military practitioners had control over both surgery and obstetrics. Although his proposal focused only on surgical education, del Villar's mention of a single body representing the various medical branches hinted at the possibility of union. Del Villar based his argument on the high costs of licensing, the greed of the Protomedicato, and the inability of the protomédicos to carry out examinations in a field they did not know.[24] Such charges were, however, false or at least inaccurate – the protomédicos Manuel de Jesús Febles and Casimiro Liceaga had degrees in both medicine and surgery, and the Protomedicato could do little about the costs of licensing, since all reforms had to come from the government. Mistaken though del Villar's complaints may have been, they nevertheless reflected the growing animosity between local physicians and surgeons, as well as the Protomedicato's poor public image in post-independence Mexico.

A MARRIAGE OF CONVENIENCE

While congressmen, physicians, and surgeons debated the options of professional and educational reorganization, the union of medicine and surgery was becoming a reality. Military practitioners posted in

isolated areas became physicians and surgeons more out of necessity
than as a result of legislation to this effect. Similarly, the lack of physicians in provincial cities and towns allowed surgeons (or even barbers) to fill the gap. The wars of independence increased the need for
medical personnel and contributed to blur divisions still further. In
the capital, the closure of the university hindered the teaching of
theoretical courses, causing some students to drift to the Royal
Surgical School and others to avail themselves of the hospital apprenticeship open to them.[25] For all practical purposes, in the 1820s
medicine and surgery were becoming one. Since the beginning of the
century, numerous students had entered medicine after completing
their surgical degrees. Ignacio Durán, Casimiro Liceaga, Ignacio
Erazo, Manuel Robredo, and José Ferrer, all future professors of the
medical school, were only a few of those who chose to pursue both
medical areas.[26] Others attended university to obtain the degree of
latin surgeon. In 1831, the capital had fourteen physician-surgeons,
thirty physicians, thirty-two latin surgeons, and eighty-three surgeons or a total of 159 licensed practitioners.[27] Almost a third of
them were either physician-surgeons or surgeons who, having
attended university, were familiar with theoretical medicine. It is
impossible to know how knowledgeable of medical theories the
remaining eighty-four surgeons were, but as the proposals submitted
by surgeons Miguel Muñoz and Pedro del Villar indicate, at least
some of them were well versed in theoretical medicine.

The first official step toward the formal union of medicine and
surgery was the 30 December 1830 law on the new requirements for
the practice of medicine in the Federal District and Territories. It
required medical students to take a minimum of three courses at the
Escuela de Cirugía (renamed National Surgical School after independence) to apply for final examinations, while surgical students
had to take a minimum of three medical courses at the National
University.[28] Furthermore, from then on, all surgical students would
have to hold an arts degree.[29] Current students were not included,
and the law did not specify when the new regulations would be
enforced. This piece of legislation was followed by the Law of
21 November 1831, which decreed examinations in medicine and
surgery for all students. Interns were allowed extra time to take their
examinations in both areas, and licensed individuals in either branch
with at least four years of practice were given the chance to take an
exam at no cost in the other required area without further studies.

Thus, in Mexico City, the division of medicine and surgery officially ended.[30] Other cities and states soon followed.

In 1833, for example, the government of Michoacán asked the state Congress to pass a law ending the "damaging distinction" between medicine and surgery. It blamed "the ignorance of the Spanish government for dividing the two inseparable branches of this science," and cited the example of the capital. The proposal asked for the union of medicine and surgery and for the creation, as in Mexico City, of a *facultad médica* or regulating body as required by "the honour and the enlightenment of the state."[31] Such a union had been theoretically achieved in the curriculum planned for the first medical course to be offered in the city of Morelia in 1830. However, as the course offered was a *cátedra de medicina*, or medical course taught by a trained physician, the official union of both branches had to wait until 1847, when the Facultad Médica was transformed into the Establecimiento Médico Quirurgico (Surgical Medical Establishment).[32]

In Puebla, the state Congress received a similar petition on 11 March 1834. The signatories were eight practitioners of "medical surgery" – the physicians José Mariano Gallegos, Antonio Almorín, and Nicolas Seoane (who had been in practice for fifteen years), the physician-surgeon Pedro Calderón (examined in accordance with the 1831 law), and three interns, Manuel Seoane, Mariano Escalante, and Luis Guerrero, who were still to be examined.[33] The petitioners asked for the end of the division between physicians and surgeons, which was "as ridiculous as it was hateful and unfounded." They based their argument on the fact that surgeons had "as their main objective to cure the most grave ailments of viscera and entrails, of the external organs and finally of all the animal economy ... leaving to physicians the most simple cases."[34]

In the state of Jalisco, surgeons also asked for recognition. In 1824, Ignacio Moreno, main surgeon of San Miguel hospital in the state capital, Guadalajara, compared the duties of the surgeons to those of the hospital's physician to argue against the supposed inferiority of surgery. A surgeon, he claimed, invested more time, dedication, and effort than did the physician and was at greater risk of infection. If the surgeon himself "reunited surgery and medicine," he had to dedicate more time to his studies because his field of practice became wider. Moreno also noted that he had "incomparably" more responsibilities than the physicians due to the number of patients under his care, the number of personnel in his charge, and the numerous certificates he had to issue for judicial purposes.[35] Despite Moreno's views, the union of medicine and surgery was not decreed in Jalisco until 13 March 1837, and it did not become a reality until 1839, when the required clinical courses began to be taught at the Hospital de San Miguel.[36]

As compromise was reached, surgeons became physicians and physicians began to practise surgery officially and legally, the old colonial medical hierarchy was erased, and a new one created. Union worked to the advantage of well-educated and licensed surgeons, who raised their academic and professional credentials, distancing themselves from their less educated colleagues and the bleeders and improving their public image and professional status. Physicians gained by merging with the increasingly important area of surgery and expanding their field of work. They also increased their numbers, political strength, and ties with the army. Such advantages came at the expense of sharing the exclusive control they had enjoyed over the profession by accepting into their midst well-educated surgeons. The pact, sealed in 1831, placed the physician-surgeons in charge of the profession.

In theory, the medical profession had been transformed. Physicians and surgeons had united as *médicos cirujanos* to lead the other practitioners, with pharmacists and chemists tagging along. Although it is not easy to evaluate the impact of these changes on most practitioners, the official government lists of licensed practitioners in Mexico City for the years 1822, 1831, and 1835 indicate some general trends.[37] From 1822 to 1831, before union took place, the number of physicians and surgeons increased from 73 (27 physicians and 46 surgeons) to 160 (45 physicians, 32 latin surgeons, and 83 surgeons), or an increase of more than 100 per cent.[38]

The reasons for such an increase are complex, but they seem to be related to opportunities for socio-economic mobility the new nation offered in its initial years and the increasing importance in education. As Michael P. Costeloe explains, while racial prejudices had not disappeared, these were of less importance for mestizos and "did not prevent someone of mixed or non-European blood from entering the ranks of the *hombres de bien*."[39] Jaime E. Rodríguez O. goes further, stating, "Economic, rather than racial, factors constituted the main determinants of social status. While colonial Mexicans regarded being white as a positive characteristic, the records of New Spain provide

Table 2.1 Number of registered practitioners
in Mexico City

	1822	1831	1852	1866
Physician	27*	31	7	–
Physician-surgeon		14	96	135
Latin surgeon	9**	32	–	–
Surgeon	37	83	18	–
Phlebotomist	25	5	6	–
Pharmacist	NA	31	33	33
Midwife	NA	NA	7	24

*Seven physicians listed as having a doctorate

**One surgeon listed as "doctor"

Sources: Lista de facultativos, 1822. AHCM,
Ayuntamiento, Policia, Salubridad, vol. 3668, exp. 14;
Febles, Esposicion, 8–10; Almonte, Guía de forasteros;
AGN, Segundo Imperio, vol. 59, exp. 17; Maillefert,
Directorio del comercio del Imperio Mexicano.

numerous examples of upwardly mobile people of color who attained elite status by making money and then claiming to be white."[40] The new opportunities were also the result of the changing values of the time. Gradually, tradition, privilege, and ancestry were giving way to personal merit and skills. Education and training were gaining importance by the turn of the nineteenth century, as is obvious in the writings of reformers such as José Luis Mora and Lucas Alamán. The liberal emphasis on education and the widening opportunities may have encouraged youngsters to continue their education.

The difficult economic situation of post-independence Mexico surely made the possibility of work in a medical area (or any other field) attractive. Life was not easy, and among the "middle sectors" of society, poverty was widespread; many retained their middling social position more as the result of their race and status than of their financial situation.[41] Wasserman calculates that in Mexico City, professionals, preceded by high government and church officials and wealthy merchants and miners, comprised the elite and upper middle class (about 20 per cent of the population). They were followed by a lower middle class of artisans, small shopkeepers, and skilled workers with very limited resources.[42] Medicine and surgery offered individuals of the middle socio-economic level the chance to improve or at least maintain their privileged position.

Knowledge of medicine or surgery guaranteed a place in the military or state militias. As the army was more forgiving when it came to degrees and professional licences, it offered a chance for professional and economic improvement. At the outbreak of the Mexican American War, there were almost twenty thousand permanent troops and more than ten thousand active militia reserves in the country.[43] The number of troops increased during the War of Reform and the French Intervention, augmenting the demand for medical personnel. Backed by the military, some individuals claimed a place within the profession, and a few of them continued practising surgery in agreement to military appointments obtained in colonial times. For example, in 1841, the Toluca municipal authorities accepted as valid Antonio Cano's 1819 appointment of *practicante* (intern) ratified by the director of military surgery, Juan Nieto Samaniego, in 1822, entitling him to practise surgery among military and civilian patients.[44] In an uncertain economy like that of post-independence Mexico, work and the opportunities for advancement as a military practitioner, especially during the early years, must have been appealing to many.

Interestingly enough, after 1831, the number of practitioners listed with the municipal authorities remained largely unchanged. The 1835 list includes 22 physicians, 33 physician-surgeons, and 65 surgeons, and the 1852 list registers 7 physicians, 96 physician-surgeons, and 18 surgeons. The total number of practitioners in 1835 was 120, and 121 in 1852.[45] Fourteen years later, there were 135 physician-surgeons registered in Mexico City.[46] Although these numbers include only those practitioners who resided in the city, registered with the municipal authorities, and presumably not in the military, the demand for medical services seems to have remained static.

The same can be said for the pharmacists, with thirty-one registered in 1831 and thirty-three in both 1852 and 1866. The midwives, on the other hand, increased from seven in 1852 to twenty-four in 1866.[47] It must be emphasized that these figures indicate the lowest number of practitioners, as others may not have registered, and military practitioners are not included. Therefore, these figures are far from conclusive and deserve further research (see table 2.1).

Other trends are also obvious from the official lists of practitioners. The first is the classification of the medical fields, which confirms the narrowing gap between the younger physicians and the best-educated surgeons. The 1822 list divides physicians according to their degrees of bachelor or doctor, and the surgeons' names are

Table 2.2 Physicians and surgeons
registered in Mexico City

Year	Total
1822	73
1831	160
1835	120
1852	121
1866	135

Sources: Lista De Facultativos, 1822;
Febles, Esposicion, 8–10; Lista de los
profesores, 1835, 15; Almonte, Guía
de forasteros, 1852; AGN, Segundo
Imperio, vol. 59, exp. 17; Maillefert,
Directorio del comercio del Imperio
Mexicano

preceded by the abbreviations "Sr" (Señor) or "Br" (Bachiller), the latter indicating they were latin surgeons. Thus, seven out of twenty-seven physicians held a doctorate, while the rest had a bachelor's degree, and nine of the forty-six surgeons are listed as latin surgeons (table 2.2). In the colonial context, university education indicated not only knowledge of medical theories but also "pure" Spanish ancestry and the ability to cover (or know somebody who would pay) the costs of their university studies, examination, and graduation ceremonies. The local medical and racial hierarchy forced the Royal Surgical School to be more lenient in this respect: limpieza de sangre requirements were only loosely enforced, costs were much lower, and there were no costly graduation ceremonies.[48] Nonetheless, its students claimed criollo status. In this regard, Mexico's situation was very different from that in contemporary Peru where, as described by José R. Jouve Martín, Afro-Peruvian surgeons were officially accepted and reached the highest echelon of the profession.[49]

The 1831 listings reflected Mexico's efforts to distance itself from the colonial past and its adoption of liberal ideology. The divisions were now based on professional education, with less attention to socio-economic (and racial) considerations. However, it is worth noticing that the new emphasis on education continued to favour the urban, mostly criollo socio-economic minority. Access to education (and therefore to social mobility) was intrinsically linked to personal finances, race, place of residence, and, of course, gender.

The list divides physicians into thirty-one "professors licensed in Medicine" (two of them foreigners) and fourteen "professors examined in Medicine and Surgery." Of 115 surgical practitioners, 32 were "latin surgeons and surgeons with a bachelor's degree in Philosophy" and the remaining 83 were "surgeons."[50] Thus, in the short term, "union" did not mean consolidation but further divisions. In addition to the obvious increase in the number of practitioners, other preliminary conclusions may be drawn from these lists. First, by the time legislation merging both branches of medicine was issued, almost a third of physicians (fourteen out of forty-four) already held surgical degrees. Second, in less than ten years, the percentage of surgeons who had attended university had risen from 20 to 27 per cent. Clearly, the professional and social gap between the surgical elite and the physicians was rapidly closing.[51] Third, as was the case with other professions, medicine and surgery continued to be dominated by the better-off criollo minority.

The 1831 legislation ordered practitioners to register the licence issued by the Protomedicato, or its successor the Facultad Médica, with the municipal authorities of the town where they wished to practise. It appears that this provision was not immediately enforced, as it was reissued in 1835.[52] The list published that year following these requirements is telling. First, it includes a total of eighteen physicians described as *"profesores de medicina,"* twenty-seven physician-surgeons, and sixty-five surgeons, and it does not distinguish between latin surgeons and the rest.[53] Second, it shows that after four years, only ten individuals (four latin surgeons and six surgeons) had taken advantage of the legislation to become physician-surgeons, of whom four were probably fulfilling official requirements: José Becerril and José Piña became members of the Facultad Médica in 1831, while Agustín Arellano and Manuel Carpio had been appointed to teach at the recently founded medical school. It is also telling that none of the physicians, not even the president of the Facultad Médica, Joaquín Villa, was listed as a médico cirujano. As previously stated, the 1835 list includes only those practitioners who conformed to the law and registered with the municipal authorities, and it is surely incomplete. Nonetheless, it is clear that at least forty-four surgeons had ignored the legislation and declined the opportunity to become physician-surgeons. Five of them – José María Gutiérrez Guzmán, José María Hidalgo, José María Lizaula, Joaquín Salas, and, ironically, even Miguel Muñoz, who had worked for the union of medicine and surgery – remained listed as surgeons as late as 1852.[54] Thus, although the difference between physicians and surgeons had been erased at the stroke of a pen, a separation between the two branches of medicine continued.

Indeed, in 1852, the merger was not yet complete as, in addition to ninety-six physician-surgeons, that year's *Guía de Forasteros* listed eighteen surgeons and seven physicians. Five of the latter also appear in the 1831 official list of practitioners, indicating that they had graduated before the merger took place.[55] The sixth, Luis Antonio Garrone, had studied in Sardinia at the Royal Academy of Turin and had obtained a licence to practise in Mexico in 1842.[56] It is unclear where or when the seventh physician, Manuel María Castro, graduated. As well, five of the eighteen surgeons listed in 1852 had been practising since 1835. Of the other thirteen, at least one, Ignacio Cañamares, was a military surgeon and anatomy professor in the *cuerpo de sanidad militar* (military sanitary corps) in 1832.[57] The records do not specify if the remaining twelve were also army surgeons.

Although in the long run, the merging of surgeons and physicians benefited both professions, other practitioners did not fare as well. Control of all the medical branches was now in the hands of the physician-surgeons, their power buttressed by a superior education and social status. The gap between them and the lower ranks widened as the marginalized phlebotomists, dentists, and midwives, unable to exert control over their education and licensing, lost ground.

THE PHYSICIAN-SURGEONS AND "THE OTHERS": PHLEBOTOMISTS AND BARBERS

As the nineteenth century advanced, the number and professional status of the phlebotomists or bleeders rapidly decreased. Traditionally, phlebotomists, like most surgeons, had learned their trade by apprenticeship and did not require any formal training. Phlebotomy, like other health-care occupations, had its own hierarchy, with licensed and professionally successful individuals at one end of the spectrum and surreptitious bleeders who offered their services in markets and streets at the other. Well-established phlebotomists had their own *tiendas* or surgeries. A 1790 survey indicates there were at least eighty-six of these surgeries in Mexico City, fifty-seven of them owned by licensed individuals. The largest belonged to José Albino

Figure 2.1 "Extraction of a stone from the head." Tile decoration on a wall of the Hospital of San Pablo in Mexico City.

Carbajal, José Grajales, and Andrés Isaguirre. Carbajal employed one official and four apprentices in his shop located on Joya Street, Grajales owned a shop on Tacuba Street and employed two officials and two apprentices, and Isaguirre's Palma Street shop had one official and three apprentices.[58] The number of bleeders practising in Mexico City at the end of the colonial period is unknown. The (incomplete) 1811 *Padrón*, or survey, of Mexico City residents refers to 218 "barbers" and twenty-seven apprentices but does not differentiate between bleeders and barbers (although many may have been both).[59] Other bleeders worked in hospitals, jails, and convents or joined the army, and at least some of them made house calls to accommodate their patients' preferences.[60]

During the colonial period, phlebotomy was recognized as an integral part of therapy and phlebotomists as its specialized "technicians." Bleeders also pulled teeth and carried out minor operations that sometimes encroached on the surgeons' work field. The examinations of José Morales Montoro and Julián Acosta indicate the knowledge and skills a phlebotomist was expected to have at the time. A phlebotomist examination consisted of two parts, theory and practice. Montoro's theoretical exam took place in 1692 at the residence of the first protomédico. The applicant was asked the location of various veins, how to bleed them, and the type of lancet required, as well as the reasons to refuse treatment, despite a physician's orders. The latter question illustrates the trust placed in a phlebotomist's abilities and his professional independence. The practical exam took place the following day at the Hospital del Amor de Dios, but neither the examination itself nor its result was entered in the record.[61] The examination of Julián Acosta, which took place sixty-six years later, in 1758, included forty-five "and other various" questions on veins, arteries, bleeding methods, and bleeding and tooth-extracting instruments. One of the examiners was a licensed phlebotomist considered an expert on the field who acted as the protomédicos' consultant.[62] As these rare documents indicate, although occupying one of the lower echelons of the healing profession, phlebotomists were considered expert "technicians," and their licensing examinations required the presence of one of their own, a specialist in the field. Furthermore, phlebotomists not only enjoyed the right to voice their professional opinion but also had an obligation to do so if they felt bleeding was not in the patient's best interest.

References to barbers, surgeons, barber surgeons, or the more technical term *phlebotomist*, used interchangeably in contemporary documents, reflect the ill-defined occupational specialties characteristic of the time, as well as the wide range of services these individuals offered. To differentiate between bleeders and barbers, Viceroy Miguel Joseph Azanza ordered bleeders to place a "blind" and a plaque outside their surgeries, and barbers to have a curtain and a vessel outside their shops. According to the same order, no barbers were allowed to meddle in bleeding, and no bleeders could practise without a licence.[63] Despite viceregal dispositions, bleeders continued to occupy a grey area between barbers, bleeders, and surgeons that allowed them to move within these three occupations. Adding to the confusion, in 1804 the *Ordenanzas para Colegios de Cirugía* divided latin, or university-trained, surgeons from their "romance" counterparts, who were described as *sangradores* (bleeders) and now required a minimum three-year apprenticeship before examination.[64] Legislation, therefore, offered ambitious phlebotomists such as Miguel Muñoz the opportunity to reach the surgeons' level.

As formal education and scientific medical knowledge gained in importance in Mexico, phlebotomists began to slip from the ambiguous place they had occupied in colonial times. The union of physicians and surgeons in 1831 aimed to raise the status of surgeons, further distancing them from phlebotomists. No longer did the licensing regulations require an examination of the phlebotomist, only a written application, a baptismal certificate, and a certificate of apprenticeship.[65] As the gap widened, the chances to move from phlebotomy to surgery diminished. At the hospitals, the phlebotomist's work was now assigned to hospital staff or to eager medical students fulfilling their internship, whose duties included applying caustics, leeches, and bleeding.[66] Phlebotomists, excluded from the alliance between physicians and surgeons, lost their traditional independence as well as their voice in the qualifying process of their own profession. The surviving documents do not indicate any reaction on their part, perhaps as the result of their lack of a representative body, the dwindling number of licensed individuals, and the fact that the new legislation had no immediate consequences. In addition, the phlebotomists' social position and educational background placed them at a disadvantage in challenging the leadership of the medical profession.

In 1835 the Facultad Médica had to decide on the phlebotomists' licensing requirements, which had gone unmentioned in the 1831 regulations. After a thorough discussion and despite their belief that no individual should be examined in phlebotomy alone, its members agreed to follow tradition and continue examining candidates. The decision was enshrined in regulations drawn up in 1841 that limited examinations of phlebotomists to basic anatomical knowledge of their area and the "theory of minor operations" they were allowed to perform.[67] To dispel any doubts about the phlebotomists' field of work, the 1841 Regulations stated that they were allowed to pull teeth and apply simple cuppings; only under a physician's orders were they to bleed and apply leeches, wet cuppings, and strong caustics.[68] The recognition of a phlebotomist's expertise in his area and his right to oppose the orders of a physician were a thing of the past. Instead, the nineteenth-century phlebotomist was henceforth completely subject to the physician-surgeon, becoming a low-level technician in charge of minor and less financially rewarding tasks.

An 1854 *Dictámen* (resolution) confirmed previous regulations and tightened control by adding that "only" under a physician's orders could phlebotomists bleed or apply leeches, wet cuppings, or caustics, or "cure teeth," and "under no circumstances were they allowed to apply chloroform."[69] At the time, the use of chloroform was still a novelty that involved considerable risk to the patient but showed great potential. The 1854 regulations ensured that only physician-surgeons had access to such an innovation. As a result of these changes, the decrease in the number of licensed phlebotomists, although not necessarily of unlicensed bleeders, comes as no surprise. The 1852 *Guía de Forasteros* lists only six bleeders, as opposed to the twenty-five licensed phlebotomists included by the Protomedicato in 1822, and the eighty-six surgeries that existed in the late eighteenth century; by 1866, the phlebotomist had disappeared from the list of official medical practitioners.[70] Bleeders continued to ply their trade, but only as marginal practitioners increasingly alienated from mainstream medicine.

THE RISING FIELD OF DENTISTRY

The weakening of phlebotomy as an independent occupation allowed the fragmentation of its services and opened a space for the new and upcoming area of dentistry that, in the early nineteenth century, was almost unknown in Mexico. Dentistry, however, followed a different path, as its first practitioners were foreigners trained abroad who kept in touch with the scientific and technological advances on their field and targeted the better off classes.

The first mention I have found of a dentist dates back to 1786, when the French dentist Claudio Marion was called as a witness in an Inquisition case. Unfortunately, the document does not provide any details of his trade. Eight years later, the dentist Juan de Gaeta, a native of Salerno (Italy), applied to the Protomedicato for a licence.[71] During the next two decades, dentists and dentistry disappear from the medical records and the only documented cases related to tooth extractions refer to barbers or phlebotomists. No dentists are included in the official lists of practitioners, nor were there any regulations for training or licensing in this area. However, occasional advertisements in newspapers and references in surviving documents show that a few dentists, all of them foreigners, continued to offer their services.[72]

It was not until the 1842 Regulations required all foreign practitioners to register with the local authorities that six dentists, all of them foreigners, applied for a licence to practise their trade. Applicants had to present proof, first, of being Roman Catholic, second, of having obtained naturalization, and third, of training in their craft. In addition, they had to include three testimonies of good conduct. The documentation accepted by the Consejo Superior de Salubridad (health board) in charge of licensing reflects the low regard in which this new area of medicine was held. Of the six applicants, only two included proof of their training. One, a Frenchman named Francisco Lacoste, who had "professed the art" for six years, included a letter signed by the renowned physician-surgeon (M.) Goupilleau;[73] the other, Antonio Labully, also a Frenchman, included testimony of his two-year training under Gabriel Villette, a French surgeon residing in Mexico.[74] The remaining applications mention the applicants' training only in passing. Ironically, to obtain his licence the candidate had to prove his knowledge and skill in an area that was foreign to his examiners. That the latter might not be qualified to judge did not seem to have been a matter of concern for the health board. Their examinations, as those of the phlebotomists, were limited to the "anatomical area each must know" and to the theory of the minor operations they were allowed to practise.[75] Unfortunately, no examples of such examinations are included in the files.

Two other Frenchmen were successfully examined on 24 August 1841. Eugenio Crombé (or del Cambre), who had practised "for more than six years" and planned to remain in the country with his Mexican wife and two children, and José Magnin.[76] The Consejo Superior de Salubridad also received an application from an American, Jorge A. Gardiner. As in the case of the two French applicants, Gardiner's dossier includes only the testimonies of three witnesses and no mention of his training. Nonetheless, all three applicants received licences. Within two years, two more Frenchmen, Pierre Boisson and Beloni René Vadie, and the Englishman Guillermo Seager obtained licences to practise dentistry without any proof of training.[77]

The contrast between the documentation required of applicants for a medical or pharmaceutical licence and that accepted from the dentists is most telling. The Consejo Superior de Salubridad followed strict guidelines in the case of the former, but when it came to the dentists it seems to have been more interested in their religion and "civic and moral conduct" than in their qualifications or skills.[78] To the medical elite, a dentist was not much different from a phlebotomist specialized in teeth extraction. In fact, the licensing records of both were entered in the same registry.[79] In 1842, the Consejo admonished Jorge Gardiner for claiming to cure scurvy and other mouth inflammations and for advertising himself as a *cirujano dentista* (dental surgeon). Gardiner's detailed response offers a fascinating glimpse of the challenges a dentist faced as well as the dismal condition of his patients. Gardiner first described the nature of the problem: the so-called scurvy was inflammation of the gum to the point that there was constant bleeding and suppuration caused by the accumulation of tartar or pieces of broken teeth that remained inside the gum. Such a problem arose mainly from lack of hygiene and could be easily addressed. He then explained that he treated this condition by ridding the teeth of the accumulated tartar, extracting the teeth roots when necessary, and prescribing the necessary mouth rinse.[80] Unmoved, the Consejo insisted that Gardiner keep "within the limits" of his field.[81] The Consejo's patronizing attitude probably stemmed from the view that caring for teeth was below a physiciansurgeon's station and from the fact that medical practitioners failed to recognize the health implications of good dental hygiene as well as the field's lucrative potential. Besides, the limited number of practitioners and their status as foreigners ensured their subordination to the medical elite.

The surviving records indicate that, in 1841, five dentists received permission to work in Mexico City and three more were licensed during the following two years.[82] The *Guía de Forasteros* for 1852 lists only five dentists in the capital, all of them foreigners.[83] Two years later, the Consejo Superior de Salubridad issued licences to the Cuban Juan Havá, the Frenchman Juan Trancoz, and the first two Mexican dentists, Mariano Chacón and Benito Acuña, both of whom had been trained by the Englishman Guillermo Saeger.[84]

In 1854, the municipal authorities asked the Consejo to clarify the rules on the practice of dentistry, midwifery, and phlebotomy. As the 1841 Regulations had not included dentists or "the operations they were allowed to perform," an appointed commission studied the matter and drafted the necessary guidelines. These were sent to the governor of the Federal District on 20 December 1854 for approval, before being published in the newspapers. According to the new rules, dentists were authorized to "clean, file, cauterize, fill (with lead), straighten, move, extract and replace a healthy tooth in the same alveolus from which it had been mistakenly extracted," the latter referring to cases in which the wrong (healthy) tooth had been extracted instead of the damaged one.[85] Such guidelines conformed to what some authors describe as "systematic conservation of teeth": the removal of tartar, filing of sharp edges, and filling of cavities by various methods.[86] According to the same rules, dentists could also treat the "posture of isolated teeth" and provide "complete artificial dentures." They were prevented from the "mechanical destruction of the dental pulp," because such an operation was "extremely painful and ineffective,"[87] and were absolutely forbidden to employ chloroform, which the commission believed was a dangerous substance not suitable for all patients. If a patient wanted to be treated "in the state of unconsciousness produced by the inhalation of this substance," it would have to be administered by a physician who had "a deeper knowledge of this substance and its effects"[88] – an ironic statement, considering the use of chloroform was still in its infancy and physicians were just as prone as dentists to unfortunate accidents.[89] The exclusion of dentists (and phlebotomists) ensured the physician-surgeons' monopoly over an innovative substance with great therapeutic and lucrative potential.

Despite the limitations imposed upon them, dentists gradually carved a niche for themselves by adopting new technologies, offering a wide range of new services, and targeting the higher-income strata. In 1831, Ricardo Skinner advertised his services in the *Diario del Gobierno de la República de México*. These included supplying false teeth at ten, eight, or five pesos, depending on their quality, placing gold fillings or gold coverings at a cost of three pesos, and offering the free extraction of molars to patients who came to his surgery at 5 Segunda Calle de Plateros. He also sold powders to clean teeth and a substance to cure and restore the gums.[90] His fees indicate that the advertisement was directed at "the better classes," those whom Michael Costeloe describes as "*hombres (y mujeres) de bien*" who read the newspaper, cared for their appearance, and could afford his services.[91]

Although the medical elite treated dentists and phlebotomists with a similar patronizing attitude, there were glaring differences between the two. An important difference between dentistry and phlebotomy was the national and racial background of their practitioners. During the first part of the nineteenth century, all licensed dentists were foreigners of European background – Frenchmen, Englishmen, or Americans, racially superior individuals in the eyes of Mexican society. Phlebotomists were different: for them, as colonial documents indicate, purity of blood requirements were lax, allowing *castas*, or mixed-bloods, to enter the trade. Indeed, most licensed phlebotomists were of mixed blood, and the proportion was surely higher still among illegal bleeders. There is no indication that the situation changed after independence; on the contrary, the end of legal racial distinctions facilitated the entrance of mixed bloods, while the diminishing status of phlebotomy must have dissuaded criollos from entering this minor branch of medicine. Such a situation worked to the advantage of dentists and contributed to marginalizing phlebotomists, who continued to be identified with the mixed-blood illegal bleeders and barbers who served the lower social strata.

Generally, dentists claimed an education based on contemporary scientific medicine and a better training than the phlebotomists, as was the case with Francisco Lacoste, who had learned his trade from a respected surgeon. Their mother tongues (English or French) allowed them to keep up with the latest works on their field, which were usually published in (or translated to) these languages, as the services they advertised showed. In addition, the hands-on nature of their practice required the use of specialized instruments and chemical substances (used for enamel fillings, dentures, etc.) and evolving modern technology that would identify them with the modern professions and ultimately allow them to create their own separate medical field. As opposed to phlebotomy, dentistry was an innovative, forward-looking area.

Finally, dentists rode the hygienist wave of the time, their services reflecting the growing concern for cleanliness and personal appearance. As Michael Hau indicates, in the nineteenth century "society grew increasingly body-conscious," and men and women became more concerned with their physical appearance and health. This awakening of body consciousness was partly the result of the increasing availability and diffusion of drawings, anatomical models, and textual descriptions, as well as the birth of photography, which allowed the visualization of disease, degeneration, and health.[92] The public became more aware of physical shortcomings and the opportunities to address them. Instead of simply extracting teeth when pain was unbearable, as any barber or phlebotomist would do, the dentist tried to prevent the problem, to heal the tooth, or in a worst case scenario replace it, increasing his clientele and the length and value of his services. Aesthetics and hygiene distinguished dentistry from phlebotomy. In Mexico, the expanding middle class and the moneyed elite, more in contact with foreign trends, were willing and able to pay to improve their appearance and look after their health. Thus, the increasing number of newspaper ads recommending the virtues of health and beauty products such as *l'Eau dentifrice* and the *Poudre dentifrice* manufactured by Maison Botot, the *Ferro Quevenne*, an iron supplement, and *Vinaigre de Toilette de Jean Vincent Bully* recommended for "hygienic purposes" and tired muscles.[93] By offering new types of services and catering to male and female vanity, dentistry would prove a most lucrative field indeed, and the demand for dentists ultimately would result in the establishment of a specialized school, Escuela de Odontología, in 1904 and an independent area of health care.[94]

MIDWIVES: EDUCATION, GENDER, AND MARGINALIZATION

The third minor branch of medicine, the "art" of midwifery, was the only medical field that had traditionally been in the hands of women. As such, it has attracted the attention of historians since the early twentieth century. The first work on colonial and nineteenth-century midwifery, the descriptive work *La obstetricia en México,* written by Nicolás León, was published in 1910. Its main value resides, as with Flores y Troncoso's work, in the author's first-hand knowledge of the persons and events he describes.[95] More recently, historians have sought to analyze the development of obstetrics and its practitioners in a more critical manner, using two main approaches. The first argues that regulation of midwifery paved the way for women's entrance to the medical profession. According to Lee M. Penyak, "Midwives slowly gained respect, assumed key positions in hospitals, and were perceived as professionals by government officials and tax assessors."[96] The recent study of reproduction and childbirth by Nora E. Jaffary considers midwives as dominant in their field, with physicians making few inroads before the turn of the twentieth century.[97] Other scholars, such as Ana María Carrillo and Mercedes Alanís-Rufino, see instead the professionalization of the midwife as her subordination to male medical practitioners and the medicalization of childbirth.[98] Carrillo goes further, stating that after exerting control over the training and licensing of midwives, the medical elite marginalized and gradually excluded them from the field of obstetrics. On the basis of my research of the first seventy years of the nineteenth century, I concur with Carrillo. By controlling midwifery's training and licensing requirements, the medical elite ensured their subordination and guaranteed the physician-surgeons' monopoly on this increasingly profitable field. Although midwifery may have gained some social and professional recognition and opened a path to medical careers to a select few, as Penyak states, the goal of the medical elite was to eliminate direct competition. The medical establishment's control over the midwives' education and licensing resulted in the formalization of a two-tiered system: a lower, less prestigious, and profitable level for midwives, and a higher, better paid, specialized tier for male practitioners to serve the moneyed patients and attend more difficult and costly cases.

The Protomedicato showed no interest in midwifery before the eighteenth century. The field remained unregulated in Spain until 1750, when it began to attract the attention of surgeons. At the time, new regulations issued by the Spanish Crown required midwives to have a minimum of four years of training under a licensed surgeon, proof of purity of blood, and a certificate of good conduct issued by a priest or government official. If the applicant was married, she also required her husband's permission.[99] In Mexico, the laws were ignored for the remainder of the century, as the first midwife, Angela María Leite, was not licensed until 1816.[100] Two years later, Francisca Ignacia Sánchez became the only other midwife to be licensed in colonial times.[101]

It is no coincidence that the first efforts to regulate midwifery occurred as surgeons became interested in obstetrics, a potentially broad and profitable field of practice. In 1787 obstetrics became part of the curriculum at the Royal College of San Carlos in Cadiz, where the military surgeons sent to Mexico were trained.[102] Their interest in the area is illustrated by the ten works on the matter included in the personal library of Florencio Pérez Camoto, a surgeon serving in the port of Veracruz.[103] By the late eighteenth century, the criollo elites had begun to solicit the services of physicians and surgeons during childbirth. Demand was met by surgeons such as the Frenchman Carlos Lloret, one of the first to introduce this trend in New Spain, Agustín Francisco Guerrero y Tagle, and Miguel Muñoz, who were considered specialists in this field.[104] The opening of obstetrics to male practitioners brought midwives (called *matronas* or *parteras*) under the scrutiny of the medical hierarchy, which became increasingly critical of the "ignorant *matronas*" whose "inexperienced hands ... in many cases murder the most precious part of society."[105] The opinionated charges of physicians and surgeons are not only suspect for the vested interest they had in the matter, but their views and impartiality are also challenged by the attitude of contemporary government officials. During late colonial times, midwives were often called as expert witnesses at trials, and their opinions weighed heavily in the judges' decisions and sentencing.[106] The practice continued after independence, and in 1841 Leopoldo Río de la Loza lamented how "shameful it is that in cases of pregnancy [and] rape the highest tribunals, the criminal judges, and the military authorities pass sentences based on the report of an ignorant midwife."[107] Thus, at least up to the middle of the century, the criticism from medical practitioners seems to be more the result of conflicting professional interest than of dismal standards among the midwives.

The first institution to offer formal training to midwives was the Hospital de San Pedro in Puebla, which established a midwifery course in 1814.[108] Mexico City lagged behind. The need to establish such a course was discussed by medical practitioners and municipal authorities on various occasions, but local politics and professional bickering got in the way. In 1824 the junta de sanidad debated establishing an obstetrics course for women as well as a small maternity hospital, and estimated the total cost would be 1,525 pesos, the bulk of it a one-time expense. Although some money was earmarked for this purpose, the project never materialized.[109] A second proposal to offer an obstetrics course was put forward by the above-mentioned military surgeon Pedro del Villar, as part of his 1829 plan to establish a military surgical school. Although del Villar insisted on the need to provide such a course for midwives, his main goal was to offer it to surgeons as part of their curriculum. Like others before it, however, del Villar's proposal never came to fruition.

Nineteenth-century writers condemned midwives for their ignorance and recklessness, but they were given few chances to improve.

In Mexico City, an operations and obstetrics course was not offered until December 1833. According to Nicolás León, in 1833 or 1834 midwives could take an obstetrics course at the Convent of Betlemitas, but as the government requested the classroom for other purposes, the women's classes had to continue at the professor's residence.[110] The licensing dossier of Juana García Cabezón includes a certificate signed by Pedro del Villar indicating she had attended his course during 1834, "all the time it was opened to the persons of her gender."[111] It is unclear if the course for midwives was interrupted after 1834. According to Nicolás León, the first student who attended courses at the Escuela de Medicina and obtained a licence was Carlota Romero, examined in 1842,[112] and the records of Atanasia Recuero and Teresa Zamora (licensed in 1829 and 1837 respectively) do not specify where courses were taught.[113] We do know, however, that when classes at the medical school resumed in 1838, Pablo Martínez del Río was appointed principal obstetrics instructor, José Ferrer Espejo adjunct, and Ignacio Torres substitute.[114] We may assume, therefore, that from then on, courses were taught at the medical school, although as late as 1846 midwives were examined at the residence of the medical school's president.[115]

The 1842 regulations ensured the subordination of midwifery to the main medical fields. The obstetrics course was divided in two separate sections, one for medical students and another for midwives; entrance requirements and course content reinforced the academic gap between male and female students. Males who attended the obstetrics course had completed high school, were familiar with subjects such as botany, chemistry, and anatomy, had completed four years of the medical program, read French, and had some knowledge of English. Obstetrics, moreover, was considered a "specialty" within the male students' field, a complement to their broader medical knowledge. Student midwives, on the other hand, were asked only for proof of literacy and knowledge of the four basic rules of arithmetic.[116] The literacy requirement may have slightly raised the midwives' standards, but the medical elite made sure the wide gap between midwives and physician-surgeons was clear. The choice of textbooks reflected the same policy: medical students were assigned J. Jacquemier's two-volume *Manuel des accouchements et des maladies des femmes grasses or accouches*, Jules Hatin's 700-page *Cours complet d'accouchements et de maladies des femmes et des enfants*, or P. Cazeaux's 1,000-page *Traite théorique et pratique de l'art des*

accouchements. Midwives used Pedro del Villar's translation of a
French basic work or *cartilla* that in 1858 was substituted with
Ignacio Torres's *Manual de Partos dedicado a las Parteras*, a basic
work expressly written for her female students. The latter was later
changed to the Spanish translation of Prosper Garnot's *Leçons élé-
mentaires sur l'art des accouchements: à l'usage des élèves sages-
femmes*.[117] Originally, each course was taught in a different semester
but, when necessary, the duration of the obstetrics course for males
was extended "for obvious reasons" at the expense of that taught
to women.[118] The 1842 regulations expanded the duration of the
course for medical students to an academic year (January to October)
but did not modify the women's course. Fifteen years later, the newly
appointed obstetrics professor Ignacio Torres requested a clarification of his obligations, stating that he considered one semester sufficient for male students, as obstetrics "was merely a specialization."
The school's director disagreed, stating that, given the text used,
fifth-year medical students required at least a full year of instruction,
and women half that time, as theirs was "only an elementary
course."[119] By controlling knowledge, the medical elite widened the
gap between aspiring physician-surgeons and midwives and reinforced their overall control over obstetrics.

Although, in theory, obstetrics courses raised the professional
standards of midwives, in practice the scope of midwives' work
became narrower as the century progressed. Traditionally, midwives
had offered prenatal care and advice, presided over childbirth, were
in charge of postnatal care of mother and child, and served as expert
advisers in court cases. In 1854, the Consejo Superior de Salubridad
agreed to allow matronas to perform the "perforation of the tumour
formed by the water at the time of parturition," to extract the afterbirth, and "to compress the 'aorta' in case of bleeding after the expulsion of the afterbirth" only if the circumstances required it. Specifically,
the midwife might intervene only if the birth was delayed because the
woman's water did not break or there was a risk of a fatal hemor-
rhage and the physician could not arrive promptly. Otherwise, these
operations should be performed by physicians who, having a deeper
medical knowledge, were better able to undertake them.[120] By the
1880s women taking courses to become midwives were warned by
the obstetrics instructor, Professor Rodríguez, that "they were not
more than specialized nurses and that it was illicit for them to pre-
scribe any remedies or even worse operate on a woman either in

labour or after birth."[121] Thus, midwives were gradually pushed into the most time-consuming and least profitable tasks.

The difference in earnings is illustrated by the *Tarifas de Facultativos* issued in Mexico City in 1840. A physician charged 50 pesos for a simple childbirth and visits during the first nine days, 100 pesos for the manual extraction of the infant, 150 pesos for the turning of the child, and 200 pesos if the birth required forceps. The *Tarifas* clarified that the figures were based on "ordinary services" for an individual with capital of 20,000 pesos or an annual income of 1,000 pesos, a far cry from the earnings of poor and rural families.[122] The physicians' high income is confirmed by an 1838 tax assessment by which each "profession and lucrative occupation" was assigned a minimum and maximum amount of tax, based on average professional income. The scale assigned to physician-surgeons, between 5 and 100 pesos, was second only to that assigned to lawyers, 10 to 800 pesos.[123] The document does not include midwives, but more than fifty years later, in 1898, seventy-six midwives paid a total of 121.50 pesos in taxes or an average of 1 peso and 59 cents.[124] As a matter of comparison, in 1838 escribanos were assessed between 5 and 100 pesos, male school teachers 1 to 25 pesos, and, as a reflection of the prevalent gender inequality, female teachers between 4 reales and 6 pesos.[125]

The monthly salaries paid in 1866 to the maternity hospital's medical personnel confirm the income difference between physicians and midwives. The partera Adelaida Zuleta earned 40 pesos and the subdirector, José Espejo, 60 pesos. As the post of subdirector was occupied by the obstetrics professor who received a salary of 125 pesos from the medical school, the 60 pesos may be considered as a complement for his extra duties. The difference becomes more pronounced when one reads the hospital's regulations. Espejo was in charge of the obstetrics clinic (part of his obligations as professor) and afternoon rounds, and he and the director were on call if needed in difficult cases. In addition, Espejo, like all his colleagues, had a private practice. Zuleta's obligations included full-time work at the hospital, availability for twenty-four hours a day, and residence at the hospital. In addition, she could not leave the hospital without the subdirector's express consent.[126]

Gender set midwives apart from other practitioners and continued to reinforce their inferior position to the better-trained physician-surgeons. In a time when the intellectual capacity of women was questioned, parteras had to prove themselves in a male medical world that prevented them from obtaining the academic and scientific credentials required to rise in the medical hierarchy. For example, female applicants to the obstetrics course, and consequently those applying for a licence, had to be between eighteen and thirty years of age (no age limits were set for male students). The reasons for this requirement were simple (in view of the Escuela de Medicina's faculty): a woman younger than eighteen "should not be given this type of knowledge" because morality might be offended, and at such a tender age she did not have enough maturity for "the arid nature of the material." On the other hand, women older than thirty without previous education were too old to acquire the necessary knowledge; only women who had a "more polished education," a rare occurrence among midwives, could overcome such a problem.[127]

There are numerous examples of the patronizing attitude of instructors, practitioners, and government officials towards midwives and their patients. María Loreta de Jáuregui's 1836 student record indicates that she acquired "the necessary knowledge in obstetrics that, according to her gender, may be expected."[128] The director of the medical school, Ignacio Durán, was no exception, as his correspondence with various Puebla officials illustrates. In 1866, the prefect of Puebla asked the director of the School of Medicine to support his project of bringing women from the villages to the capitals of the departments (as the states were then called) to be trained as midwives. Director Durán thanked the prefect for his interest but refused to back his plan. In his view, it would be difficult to find the necessary instructors in all departments and too expensive to bring the women to the capital, and the costs of examination and licensing in Mexico City would be beyond their reach. Furthermore, he could not make any exceptions and allow them to be examined in Puebla, as it would be unfair to physicians and pharmacists (he did not mention phlebotomists or dentists), who lacked similar opportunities. In addition to the above arguments, Durán believed that midwives "do not have the influence it is assumed on the life of mothers and children," because their functions were limited to the most basic care, which was all that women of the "last social class" required. These women were always attended by mothers or other women with experience and, in any case, out of economic need could not remain at rest for the required nine days. If they had a difficult labour, he reasoned, they should go to a physician. On the other hand, women of a higher class (presumably the only ones who really mattered) were always in a physician's care, and the midwife limited herself to waiting, in case "the necessary manoeuvres to extract the infant mortified the mother if done by a male" and later helped with the child during its first days of life.[129] The director's telling response indicates not only the low regard in which physicians held midwives at the time but also a complete disregard for the welfare of poor and rural women unable to pay for their services.

Gender influenced the quality of education and training that aspiring midwives received while, at the same time, making their services indispensable, as many women preferred to be examined and assisted by a female. Thus, the medical establishment accepted midwives as minor practitioners in a field that was gradually becoming more medicalized. As assistants, they were responsible for the longer and more tedious stages of childbirth, leaving to the physician-surgeon the most complicated and profitable tasks of obstetrics.

In addition to their supposed gender inferiority, Mexican midwives faced racial and social prejudices. In her study of Mexico City women, Silvia Marina Arrom concludes that during the nineteenth century women did not work out of choice but out of need. As a result, most working women were Indigenous or mixed-bloods belonging to the lower socio-economic strata, while the better off "Spanish" (white) women were in the minority.[130] We may assume, therefore, that most legal and illegal midwives were either Indigenous or mixed-blood and that the public's racial perception of the partera was correct. Liberalism in post-independence Mexico did not erase racial discrimination, so the colonial "racial stigma" of the midwife continued to work against her image and status as a medical practitioner.

An 1865 report of the Department of Guanajuato stated that, in an effort to "save the art of obstetrics from society's scum," the physician Rafael Domínguez offered a free course and paid from his own purse for the examinations of six *señoras* (a term applied to women of a "better" class) from the city of León. The departmental *consejo de beneficencia* (welfare board) commended the practitioner's actions, while Domínguez praised the señoras who had laid aside the prejudices that prevented "distinguished persons" from practising "such an important profession." The local authorities welcomed the training of the six señoras, whom they contrasted to the "despicable women called parteras." The enthusiasm of the authorities surely derived from the social and racial background of the students, not their economic status, as Domínguez had to offer some of the women financial help to conclude their training and subsidize their stay in the capital while they took their exams.[131] It is impossible to determine the racial background of the señoras, but the racial prejudices implied in the document are clear.

As Arrom explains, contrary to present-day beliefs, during the time under study Mexican women were not empowered by work, as society considered it a man's role to support his wife and dependents. Instead, working women considered employment a "misfortune" and were aware their contemporaries saw them with a mixture of pity and distrust. It comes, therefore, as no surprise that most contemporary working women were either single or widows.[132] The poverty of the above six señoras and their need to work is made clear in the document. Unfortunately, with only a few exceptions, little is known of the midwifery students' economic situation. We do know that Teresa Zamora, applied for a licence in 1837 for financial reasons (two years before, she had applied for a phlebotomy licence but was rejected because the regulations did not include women) and that Carlota Romero began to study obstetrics only after she became a widow.[133] In 1864 Julia Caro requested financial aid to take her final exam, but her request was denied "to prevent similar requests in the future."[134] As Ignacio Durán recognized the same year, midwifery students were poor.[135] Nonetheless, these women had some basic education and were able to attend courses and pay for their training and licensing. According to the 1842 regulations, the medical school charged three pesos per course, four for the annual examinations of phlebotomists, dentists, and midwives, and four pesos for their final examination, but the record of Juana García Cabezón indicates a charge of twenty pesos for her final exam.[136] In addition, licensing cost sixteen pesos. Therefore, the regulation of midwifery contributed to the hierarchization of its female practitioners, as parteras unable to afford licensing were marginalized from their licensed colleagues; the difference was accentuated by racial and class prejudices.

In addition to financial circumstances, contemporary social prejudices about women and work contributed to limit the number of licences issued during the first thirty years. The increase in the number of licensed midwives after the 1860s reflects the opening of opportunities in the field, the increasing need of credentials (at least in urban settings), and a gradually changing mentality towards women and work. During the first part of the century and despite the efforts of the medical authorities to regulate midwifery, few parteras applied to obtain a licence. Only five women were licensed in the 1840s, among them Agatha Carolina Letellier, the first foreign midwife licensed in Mexico. Born in Berne, Switzerland, she obtained her degree as *sage-femme* in Paris in 1838. When she applied to be examined in Mexico, she was thirty-two and a resident of Veracruz. With her credentials, she was not required to attend the obstetrics course.[137] Twelve licences were issued in the 1850s and twenty-nine in the 1860s. Although chronological gaps in the records seem to indicate these are incomplete (only one midwife was licensed in each of the years 1845, 1858, and 1859, and no licences were issued in 1847, 1848, 1850, 1851, 1852, and 1856), other documents confirm the data entered in the records.[138] The 1852 *Guía de Forasteros* lists only seven parteras (two of them foreigners), while the 1866 official list of medical practitioners includes twenty-four midwives, including the foreigner Maria Pene Abadie.[139] The limited number of midwifery licences issued may have forced the authorities to relax the enforcement of regulations. An exception was made in the case of Luz Gutiérrez, seemingly the only woman to be examined in both obstetrics and phlebotomy. After attending the required obstetric courses at the medical school, Gutiérrez took her obstetrics examination on 1 February 1858, and her phlebotomy exam three days later. Her file includes a special permission from the Ministry of Justice, Ecclesiastical Affairs and Public Instruction to enable her to practise phlebotomy as well as documentation of "her literary career" (obstetrics courses attended and approved), but it lacks any documentation on her phlebotomy training.[140] In 1860 thirty-four-year-old Antonia Barrientos was granted an exception from the age requirement to take her examination; no explanation is included in her file.[141] Four years later, thirty-four-year-old Andrea G. Caballero requested to be exempted from the same regulation, and the Escuela de Medicina concluded that the applicant was "an individual of clear intelligence and her culture would allow her to learn" and to fulfill her duties as a midwife, and she should be accepted. The Ministry of Justice and Public Instruction concurred and gave its approval.[142] There was a noticeable increase in the number of applicants in the 1860s, when twenty-nine licences were issued (three of them to foreign women). The number of licensed midwives continued to increase during the last three decades of the century, averaging 6 a year or a total of 168 from 1870 to 1898.[143]

Unfortunately, with few exceptions, we know little about the women who obtained their midwifery licences, as their records include very limited information. One of these exceptions is Teresa Zamora, who first applied for a licence as a phlebotomist in 1832. At the time, she had been employed at the Hospital de San Andrés for at least three years, carrying out "operations of the commonly called minor surgery." Unable to achieve her wishes, she applied again, this time backed by letters from the hospital's administrator, Antonio Gutiérrez, and her tutor, the obstetrics professor Ignacio Torres, who was in charge of the surgical ward. Gutiérrez's letter stated that she had learned to apply leeches, wet cuppings, and blisters "at the side of his main interns and under the direction of the physicians Francisco Rodríguez Puebla and his successor Luis Poza." She also worked in the women's surgery and syphilitic wards, where she learned to apply external medicaments and to treat ulcers, "to which she has been dedicated with the singular application of her gender." Gutiérrez ended by commenting on Zamora's "impeccable" conduct. In her original application, Zamora also included the motive for her request – that she needed a phlebotomy licence to support her parents and herself. Unprepared for such an application, the Facultad Médica, after debating the issue, decided to examine her as a midwife and to request permission from the authorities for her phlebotomy exam.[144] Zamora then applied herself to learning obstetrics and, after attending the required courses, obtained her licence in 1837. A remarkable woman ahead of her times, Zamora was commended by *El Mosquito Mexicano* as "useful and intelligent [knowledgeable] in her field" and an example of a professional midwife. Following the regulations, Zamora displayed the corresponding placard outside her residence, located in the Callejón del Espíritu Santo.[145]

A short biographical sketch of Carlota Román, an Indigenous midwife from Puebla, was included in Nicolás León's work. After becoming a widow, Román attended the obstetrics course in 1853 and received her licence in 1855. León enthusiastically describes her as a "distinguished matrona," an extraordinary woman who never forgot her mother tongue Nahuatl and was also able to "perfectly" translate French. Her abilities and discretion, León adds, "endeared her to all social classes," an interesting comment that refers to her racial and social background. Román was appointed midwife of the

Maternity Hospital in 1861 and presumably served in this capacity (León is not sure whether the hospital opened or for how long it functioned). The same author also claims that she "gave lessons of obstetrics to women and medical students," but he does not give further details, and the medical school archives do not have any record of these activities.[146]

In summary, up to 1870, a woman who wished to be a licensed midwife had not only to attend and pay for the same required courses, examination, and licensing expenses as male practitioners, but she had to overcome deeply rooted social prejudices and accept the limitations of her degree and the impossibility of furthering her education. If the applicant did not reside in Mexico City, she (like male health-care applicants) would have to arrange, at extra cost, to be examined locally or to travel to the capital for the examination, an option that was beyond the financial reach of most midwives. There was, moreover, little sympathy from the medical elite for those unable to afford such expenses. The attitude of the medical authorities was, therefore, contradictory: they lamented the high number of unlicensed parteras but refused to facilitate their licensing. Once licensed, a midwife had to challenge conventions and attend patients day and night.[147] It is therefore not surprising that more women registered for obstetrics courses later on in the century as work opportunities opened in hospitals. For the midwives, the results of professionalization were, at best, mixed. While in theory professionalization raised standards and defined women as professionals, in practice it restricted their field of work, subjected them to the control of the better-trained practitioners, pushed them into the most tedious and less profitable aspects of childbirth, and further marginalized those unable to fulfill license requirements. Thus, the large majority of midwives continued to practise illegally, and many women had to depend on "the nosy, ignorant and fearless midwife ... with her semicircular chair" that Guillermo Prieto remembers in his *Memorias*.[148] The most affected were the poor. Well-off families could always call on a better-qualified male practitioner in difficult cases. The medical leadership ensured that midwives remained as inferior manual labourers, allowing physicians to keep tight control over this lucrative area of medicine. The few midwives who furthered their careers did so only after 1870 by giving up midwifery and joining the ranks of the physician-surgeons.

FOREIGN PRACTITIONERS
AND UNFAIR COMPETITION

When it came to illegal practice, the physician-surgeons were especially concerned with foreigner practitioners. Since colonial times, foreigners had been a constant irritant for local practitioners. In the eighteenth century criollo physicians and surgeons had resented the military medical personnel arriving with the royal armies who, taking advantage of confusing legislation, soon began to offer their services to civilians.[149] Military personnel were, despite the Protomedicato's objections, beyond its jurisdiction. When in 1809 surgeons Florencio Pérez Camoto and his colleague Joaquín Ablanedo were accused of practising medicine despite holding only a surgical degree, the Crown responded ambiguously that they had "freedom to practise medical surgery." Legislation further confused the issue. The Reales Ordenanzas of 1795 allowed graduates from the Spanish surgical colleges to treat military patients who suffered from "internal diseases" – permission that in 1799 was extended to the civilian population "in the absence of other practitioners."[150] As already mentioned, in Spain, medicine and surgery were united in 1799 and separated in 1801. A few years later both areas were merged again briefly before being separated in 1814. As a consequence, European military practitioners could easily justify their right to practise medicine and surgery and treat military as well as civilians, and do so with the blessing of the army. Not surprisingly, the protomédicos decried the situation, complaining that European practitioners "of intolerable arrogance ... scoffed and insulted" their local colleagues.[151]

Equally disturbing were the practitioners who accompanied the entourages of viceroys and royal officials and enjoyed their patronage. It was unfair competition, claimed the locals, as the European background and training of the newcomers placed them in a more advantageous social and professional position. Two of the many available examples show their concerns were well founded. In 1794 the Protomedicato received complaints against the Swiss physician Pedro Puglia. The controversial Puglia was not only practising medicine illegally, but he was charging patients exorbitant fees. He had arrived under the mantle of Viceroy Revillagigedo and established himself in northern New Spain (where there were few, if any physicians) with the support of the governor of Nuevo León, the intendant of San Luis Potosí, and the regidor of Ayacapixtla, who were also his patients.[152] The Piedmontese Domingo Melica, who also practised without a licence, was the physician of the exclusive convent of Capuchinas in Querétaro, and had the support of the city's *corregidor* (royal magistrate).[153] The root of the problem lay in the shortage of medical personnel, but, as the local practitioners argued, racial and national prejudices facilitated the success of foreign practitioners.

The enthusiasm of the better-off classes for foreign physicians continued after independence, as did the demand for medical practitioners. The constant need for military surgeons, the limited number of graduates in medicine and surgery due to the difficulties and costs of completing the program, and the growing number of foreigners arriving in Mexico (who were also potential patients) offered foreign practitioners ample opportunities to practise, to the chagrin of their Mexican colleagues. Such opportunities were enhanced by the Protomedicato's decline after independence and its inability to enforce regulations, by the relative independence of the provinces that, in need of practitioners, shunned regulations, and by the absence of uniform legislation across Mexico. To address the situation, colonial laws were adapted to the new circumstances, but change was slow to come.

When in 1827 the French pharmacist Próspero Fayet enquired about a licence to practise pharmacy, he was told that, "for the time being," foreigners should abide by the (colonial) laws still in force.[154] Before independence, non-Spaniards who wished to live and work in New Spain had to obtain naturalization documents or a special permit known as *gracias al sacar,* and an immigration permit from the Casa de Contratación (Board of Trade) in Spain. It was prohibited for foreigners to engage in commerce, especially if it involved precious metals or cochineal, and, except for army personnel, to reside in seaports. Once in New Spain, foreigners wishing to practise any branch of medicine had to obtain a licence from the Mexico City Protomedicato.[155] Fayet's inquiry prompted the Protomedicato to request from the national government an updating of the law. The first official regulations were issued in August of the same year: foreigners already practising legally could continue to do so, and those who wished to practise were now required to present their degrees or any relevant documentation, take an examination, and hold or obtain naturalization papers. All applicants should be Roman

Catholic, and only those "known and credited for their fame" would be exempt from examination by the Protomedicato.[156]

More detailed requirements were spelled out in the 21 November 1831 law: foreigners who wished to practise in the Federal District and Territories had to undergo an examination in the Spanish language and to register their licence with the municipal government.[157] Another law issued five days later imposed a fine of 500 pesos or one year's imprisonment to foreign practitioners practising illegally.[158] A decade later, the 1842 Reglamento added that foreign applicants had now to provide personal identification, an authenticated diploma, and a baptismal or birth certificate, speak "intelligible Spanish," and present proof of a two-year residence in Mexico before taking their examination.[159] Only if the Consejo Superior de Salubridad[160] found the applicant's qualifications sufficient could it wave an examination and register the original diploma.[161] But the lack of a national regulatory system and the continuous changes in legislation, the numerous jurisdictional rivalries, and the centralist federalist seesaw hindered enforcement and often placed the medical elite and its representative body at odds with various authorities.

While the physician-surgeons recognized the danger foreign practitioners represented, they also understood the advantages to be derived from collaborating with them and benefited from their knowledge, expertise, and links to the international medical community. A considerable number of foreign practitioners who abided by the regulations found a good reception, enjoyed a comfortable standard of living, and worked side-by-side with their Mexican colleagues. Worthy of mention are Severino Galenzowski and Pedro Vander Linden (Van der Linden or Vanderlinden), who joined the medical leadership and became important contributors to the development of medicine and medical education in Mexico.[162] Galenzowski was born in "a province of Poland called Ukrania" in 1801. He attended the University of Wilna (Lithuania), graduating in 1824. After teaching for four years he undertook a study trip to Germany, France, England, and Italy "to increase his knowledge." On his return to his native city, the war between Poland and Russia forced him to flee to Warsaw, where he first worked in a hospital and then joined the Polish army. Fearing reprisals by the victorious Russians, Galenzowski left his country once again, this time for Berlin. After a short stay he continued to Guttenberg, Hanover, and finally Hamburg, where he was hired by the German American

Mining Company. He arrived in Mexico in 1834 and established himself in the Mineral de Angangueo, a mining town in Michoacán. As did many other foreigners, he later moved to Mexico City, where he was a founder of the first academy of medicine, collaborated with its journal, and in 1837 became its president. Galenzowski remained in Mexico the rest of his life.[163]

The Belgian Pedro Vander Linden graduated from the University of Bologna in 1827 and practised his profession in Paris for a short time. After returning to Brussels he formed part of the local health board, worked in a military hospital, and was appointed director of the cholera hospital. He then joined the army, was present during the 1830 July Revolution in Paris, and participated in the "campaign against Holland."[164] Vander Linden arrived in Mexico in the early 1830s. He practised medicine in Guadalajara and in 1837 was appointed professor of the new course of surgery and obstetrics at the Hospital de Belén. The same year he joined the Mexican army and in 1840 became director of the local military hospital. He obtained the rank of colonel, and in 1845 was appointed general inspector of the sanitary corps. Vander Linden was responsible for drawing up the first modern medical military regulations in Mexico, the 1846 *Reglamento del Cuerpo Médico Militar,*[165] which outlined the duties of the medical personnel in detail and laid out precise rules for the functioning of military hospitals.[166] The *Reglamento* was approved by President Antonio López de Santa Anna and later served as a prototype for future regulations. During the Mexican American war, Vander Linden took part in the bloody battles of Angostura and Cerro Gordo, during which he personally tended to the wounded. In Cerro Gordo he was taken prisoner and served as intermediary between the Mexican army and General Zachariah Taylor. Vander Linden continued serving in the medical military corps for ten years and retired in 1858, remaining in Mexico until his death.[167]

While numerous practitioners like Galenzowski and Vander Linden obeyed the letter of the law, others did not. Diverse political and professional jurisdictions and the lack of a centralized regulatory system make it difficult, however, to assess the Consejo Superior's success (and that of its predecessors) in bringing foreigners under its jurisdiction. The problem is compounded by the continuous and often contradictory legislation issued at all levels of government and the often-incomplete archives. Although any figures are at best a guess, some trends are noticeable. We know that, in 1831, when the first medical licensing regulations of an independent Mexico were issued, the Facultad Médica received at least eight applications from non-Hispanic practitioners (including pharmacists) and that no fewer than twenty-two more applications had been received by 1843. In summary, from 1831 to 1843, a minimum of thirty foreign practitioners regularized their credentials in Mexico City.[168] It is impossible to determine the number of foreigners practising medicine in the provinces.

The records indicate that Mexico attracted practitioners from diverse European countries and the United States, but most non-Hispanic applicants seem to have been French nationals, whose predominance may be explained by several factors. First, during the last decades of the eighteenth century, the Family Pact between Spain and France and the close relations of the two countries allowed Frenchmen to join the Spanish armies, facilitated the arrival of French practitioners at the service of viceroys and higher officials sent to New Spain, and contributed to the immigration of refugees fleeing the French Revolution.[169] Second, in the post-independence years Mexico received a growing number of French immigrants, among whom were the Arnaud brothers – the first of the well-known *Barcelonettes* – who arrived in 1821.[170] They were followed by other enterprising merchants from the same region who became well established and attracted and aided many of their co-nationals. In 1838 there were approximately four thousand French citizens residing in Mexico who controlled twenty-one wholesale and more than four hundred retail businesses.[171] Undoubtedly, these immigrants offered an attractive market for the services of French practitioners in search of professional improvement. Third, at the time, France was experiencing what George D. Sussman has described as a perceived "glut of medical practitioners," a result of the reorganization of medical education in France and the presence of many officiers de santé, trained during the Napoleonic wars. Believing rightly or wrongly that there was no market for their services, many such practitioners looked for greener pastures.[172] Fourth, cultural affinities between France and Mexico, such as the same religion and closely related languages, made it easier for applicants to conform to the requirements set by Mexican law. Finally, after independence Mexico, like the rest of Latin America, became openly francophile. The elite's admiration for France, especially for French medicine, eased the integration of the newcomers into the better-off classes and practically ensured them a clientele.

It did not take long for newly arrived practitioners with French credentials to become acquainted with the local elite, who soon contracted for their services.[173] Among them were Pablo Alejandro Lefevre (or Lefebre), who held doctorates from the University of France in both medicine (1821) and surgery (1824). He had attended courses and worked with such luminaries as François Chaussier, François Victor Joseph Broussais, Jean Louis Marc Alibert, François Magendie, and Alexis Boyer, who praised him for his dedication and skills and considered him to be among "the most distinguished physicians of Paris." Lefevre had practised surgery at the Hôpital de Charité, and his dossier included a letter of recommendation signed by the king's first physician, Baron Portal. He was a member of numerous academies and scientific societies, such as the Royal Academy of Medicine in Paris, Society of Medicine, Surgery, and Pharmacy of the Department of Eure and the Medical Circle of the Wassy District in Haut Marne, the Linnean Society of Paris, and the Arts Athneaum. His dossier reflects an organized and meticulous man who carefully abided by the rules. His detailed documentation was translated into Spanish by Mariano Cal (a well-known pharmacist of Puebla), and the translations were verified by two French-speaking individuals. It is therefore possible to retrace his steps from France to Mexico; his journey illustrates the experiences of a practitioner immigrating to Mexico. On 10 March 1827, Lefevre obtained his French passport that describes him as being 1.69 metres in height and having brown hair, blue eyes, a high forehead, long nose, brown beard, and a reddish complexion. Two days later he presented himself to the Havre General Trade Agency of the United States of Mexico, property of the merchant Tomás Murphy, where he purchased his ticket and had his documentation checked. He sailed on the *Amable Victoria* on 16 March and registered with the Veracruz authorities on 25 May. Lefevre immediately presented his documentation to the local authorities and was given permission to carry weapons for personal use. His passport was stamped in Córdoba (Veracruz) five days later, before he continued to Orizaba (Veracruz), where he practised his profession until 20 November. His next stop was Puebla, where he obtained permission to practise both medicine and surgery in May 1828. In 1831 the Protomedicato granted

Lefevre a licence to practise his profession, one of the last licences issued by this body.[174] Lefevre married and remained in Mexico for some time before moving to Tenancingo, Puebla, where he continued to practise and began to research the "botanical geography" of the different climatic zones.[175]

Although other applicants such as Louis Estevan Blaquiere, a graduate of the "University of France," José María Sentis, who held a degree from Montpellier, and Eustaquio Dujat, who had studied at the Faculté de Paris, had less impressive credentials than Lefevre, they obtained permission to practise their profession and contributed to the promotion of French medicine in Mexico.[176] Even some individuals with dubious degrees, such as the *officier de santé* (sanitary officer) Juan Roumingas, could hope for professional improvement. Availing himself of the merging of medicine and surgery and the confusing French and Mexican regulations, Roumingas requested to be examined in medicine. He admitted he had not studied chemistry, natural history, or physics, but argued that, as an officier de santé, he had been examined and licensed in both medicine and surgery. In this case, the Facultad Médica agreed and granted him a medical examination.[177] Pedro Gouze attempted a similar ruse, and the Facultad Médica originally denied his application, but he persisted and was finally examined and licensed in 1841.[178] On the other hand, José Furey Saurinet, who presented a diploma of doctor in medicine from the University of France, failed to persuade a single examiner of his competence.[179]

In time, complaints about foreign practitioners became fewer and farther apart, an indication that the problem of unlicensed foreigners had been brought (or was perceived to have been brought) under control. With tighter regulations in place, foreign practitioners must have realized that it was to their advantage to work within the system rather than against it, and opted to acquire the necessary licence to practise their profession in peace; the same regulations probably gave local physicians a feeling of control. Furthermore, as Mexican practitioners stood on a firmer ground, their professional self-confidence increased, as the following chapters will show. By mid-century, a new generation of more self-confident practitioners unconnected with the national and professional tensions of the late colonial period were working side-by-side with their foreign counterparts. After collaborating for at least three decades, Mexican and foreign practitioners had learned to accept each other as colleagues rather than rivals.

THE ENFORCEMENT OF MONOPOLY:
CHARLATANES AND *CURANDEROS*

As a result of their non-Mexican status, foreign practitioners could be co-opted into joining the fray, but healers who continued to challenge professional monopoly posed a more serious problem for the licensed practitioners. This heterogeneous group known as *charlatanes* (quacks) or *curanderos* (healers) included unlicensed practitioners of any kind; practitioners of syncretic medicine (a combination of Indigenous, African, and Hippocratic beliefs) inherited from colonial times that is presently identified as "popular" medicine; and Indigenous healers. In other countries licensed practitioners faced the same problem. Mathew Ramsey's examination of popular medicine in France indicates that throughout the nineteenth century charlatans were in the majority among rural practitioners.[180] In nineteenth-century Colombia the situation was similar. As David Sowell explains, popular healing practices and beliefs, common in colonial times, were marginalized by science and the professionalization of medicine: "The state-assisted process pushed earlier practices into the layers of popular, folk and traditional medicine now referred to as *medicina tradicional.*" This type of medicine and its practitioners prevailed in rural and urban areas.[181] In Peru, the popular support for the curanderos became clear in the case of Dorotea Salguero. Her imprisonment in 1828 brought to the fore the clash between scientific and popular healing practices. The discussion was aired in the newspapers and gave critics the opportunity to attack and ultimately demand the closing of the Protomedicato.[182] Clearly, the competition between licensed practitioners and curanderos was not unique to Mexico.

"Every day the Department gets worse because far from decreasing, the number of charlatanes increases" bemoaned Leopoldo Río de la Loza in his 1843 report to the Consejo Superior de Salubridad.[183] The "ignorant curanderos, who apply ridiculous remedies, carefully keeping them a mystery," irritated licensed professionals, who saw them not only as a danger to society but also as competition.[184] Licensed practitioners were also suspect of unorthodox treatments and those who practised them. If such treatments had any value, they believed, they should be applied only by licensed physicians. Phrenology was one such suspect innovation. In 1835 Licenciado Ramón Pacheco published *Experiencia sumaria del sistema del Dr Gall* (Summary of Dr Gall's system) that he dedicated to the director and professors of the medical school.[185] The latter's response is unclear, and phrenology seems to have been accepted only gradually. In 1846 Roberto Whoit applied to open a phrenology school in Mexico City, but the Consejo Superior, under the control of physician-surgeons, rejected his petition, arguing that "the teaching of phrenology to the public was dangerous as it went against dogma and might alter social order." As a dangerous field, phrenology should be kept in the hands of professionals.[186] Not surprisingly an article in the 1847 issue of the *Phrenology Journal and Magazine of Moral Science* stated that there were "few cultivators of phrenology" in Mexico, but local practitioners who had studied in France and some English physicians who resided in the country were disseminating its principles. The same article bemoaned the existence of so many charlatans who claimed to practise the field.[187] Phrenology was not the only new field with dubious practitioners. Another one was homeopathy, which will be treated in the following chapter.

Eliminating illegal medical practice was not an easy task. Licensed practitioners were a small minority, and contemporary medicine was still trying to claim a place among the sciences and prove its therapeutic superiority over the healers it decried. In addition to the shortcomings of contemporary medicine, other important factors hindered monopoly, such as an insufficient number of qualified practitioners, the high costs of medical treatment, and the inability to restrict access to medicinal substances. In its difficult task of safeguarding the interests of its licensed brethren, the medical elite had no other choice but rely on legislation. It was the continuation of a struggle that dated back to colonial times, and still remains unresolved.

Numerous colonial laws and decrees had forbidden the practice of medicine by unlicensed individuals. After independence, various pieces of legislation, such as the already mentioned 1831 law establishing the Facultad Médica, supported the exclusive right of licensed medical personnel to practise medicine or any of its branches.[188] In 1842, the Ministry of Justice issued a law sentencing vagrants and unlicensed medical practitioners to military service.[189] This piece of legislation seems to have had multiple objectives: to rid the streets of unwanted individuals, to increase the number of recruits, to incorporate individuals with medical skills into the army, and probably the least important in the government's eyes, to protect licensed practitioners. It is doubtful that any of its goals were achieved.

There was no easy answer to the imbalance between demand for practitioners and their supply, as both were closely connected to the cost of medical services and the preferences of the population. In Cuauhtitlán, for example, there were no physicians, surgeons, or pharmacists, only "amateur women who practise the art of childbirth and are necessary in the town."[190] Cosamaloapan (Veracruz) had a similar problem in 1854. When the local health board ordered José María Castelán to stop practising medicine, the Veracruz government contacted the minister of public instruction in Mexico City. Castelán did not have a medical licence, but the town lacked "curanderos or amateurs" to serve the population. The minister's pragmatic response, that in view of the circumstances Castelán should be allowed to practise, indicates that, unlike the Consejo Superior de Salubridad, he placed the population's needs over the physicians' interests.[191] In summary, there was an undeniable scarcity of qualified physicians and other medical personnel, but at the same time few could afford a physician. Furthermore, few were convinced Western medicine was the best approach, as Indigenous medical beliefs persisted unabated for various reasons. In colonial times, natives continued to prefer their own traditional therapies; there was no manpower to control illegal practice; and more important, only Spanish officials, who had no jurisdiction over Indian towns, had authority to sanction illegal medical practice.[192] As a result, the problem of illegal practice was especially acute in smaller towns and rural areas, where fewer patients were able to cover a doctor's fees, and more patients, attached to their native roots, consulted traditional healers. The medical elite, therefore, faced the same challenge as liberal reformers, to incorporate rural areas into the process of modernization they so strongly advocated.

To address this problem and exclude illegal practitioners, the Consejo Superior, as representative of the medical profession and citing the cantonal physicians in the "civilized nations," asked the governor of the Department of Mexico to set aside funds for the establishment of "district physicians." The proposal, undoubtedly inspired by the French cantonal physician project in the Bas-Rhin

(Lower Alsace), described the urgent need for practitioners in the rural areas, the inadequacy of hospitals, and the dubious medical opinions of unqualified personnel in criminal cases.[193] It asked for twenty district physicians to be posted in as many towns that lacked a practitioner. Each appointee would receive a small subsidy of between twenty-five and forty pesos and, "trusting in his philanthropy," would fulfil his other duties without pay. The latter included attending the needs of the poor, "propagating" the vaccine, looking after the wounded, carrying out autopsies, and any other responsibility entrusted to him by the Consejo Superior. To complement their inadequate salary, the appointees would be allowed to freelance among propertied patients. The proposal was published in the *Periódico de la Academia de Medicina de Mégico* with a footnote explaining, however, that it could not be carried out at that time.[194] There is one glaring difference between the French experiment and the Mexican proposal. While the former included the training of local healers to serve the needs of the population, the Mexican proposal adhered strictly to professional monopoly and insisted on the appointment of licensed physicians exclusively. Once more, professional interests overrode the needs of smaller towns and rural areas.

The physicians' unbending attitude towards healers was not only unrealistic but sometimes strained relations with local authorities. When a Taxco judge enquired about the legal status of unlicensed practitioners in an area that lacked licensed medical personnel, Manuel Robredo, the Consejo Superior's secretary, was uncompromising: the laws should be upheld, and the "knowledgeable healer" in question should obtain a licence. Otherwise, it was up to the town to contract for the services of a duly recognized physician.[195]

The medical elite's protective attitude to their monopoly and their position on unlicensed practitioners is illustrated by the case of Doña Antonia Hernández from Río Frío, who in 1864 requested permission to treat venereal disease. At the time, Mexico was occupied by thousands of foreign troops, and venereal disease had reached epidemic proportions. Doña Antonia's petition was reviewed by the Consejo Superior de Salubridad, which represented the medical profession and its interests. José María Reyes, the Consejo's secretary, dismissed the application. Doña Antonia lacked not only the "long and profound knowledge in the diverse medical branches" but also the proper licence to practise medicine, and given that "even the very subaltern practitioners of dentistry, midwifery, and phlebotomy were required a licence," it was impossible to accede to her petition. Furthermore, her sudorific treatment was not adequate for all kinds of venereal ailments as the common people believed, and such an approach could be dangerous when not applied by a qualified physician.[196] Doña Antonia insisted, and two years later the municipal government endorsed her petition but requested further information before deciding. To gather it, the authorities proposed to allow Doña Antonia to try her treatment on a group of syphilitic patients in the local hospital. The physicians assigned refused, arguing that in good conscience they could not "compromise their conscience and their profession's dignity" by participating in secret treatments at the hands of "an incompetent individual."[197]

Closely related to the supply and demand of practitioners was the cost of medical services, which in 1840 varied from 1 peso for a "basic" visit to 32 pesos for spending the night at a patient's side. These rates were based on a patient with yearly revenue of 1,000 pesos or capital of 20,000 pesos – wealth that only a minority enjoyed.[198] As the costs in this case had been calculated for a tax assessment, one may assume that the amounts indicated are on the lower rather than the higher end of the spectrum. In his study of contemporary life in Mexico, Mark Wasserman estimates the average daily salary of a skilled worker to have been between fifty cents and 1 peso, with unskilled labourers earning half that amount. Wasserman calculates that only a third of the capital's population had full-time employment.[199] One may then conclude that the physicians recognized that only a minority of the population could enlist their services, and that for most of the population, barely able to cover the most basic expenses, medical treatment was an unaffordable luxury. It is true that, on licensing, medical practitioners took an oath to serve the poor at no cost, but it is most doubtful that most of their work was pro bono. The result was a limited market, especially for the more costly services of licensed physicians, and a large demand for those of illegal healers, dealers in herbal medicines, and lower-ranking practitioners who presumably charged less.

The intrusion of the juntas de sanidad into the traditional jurisdiction of medical practitioners helped to unite the elite practitioners in defence of their interests. The union was facilitated by the surgeons' rising status and the opportunities for social mobility that resulted from the same liberal ideas that inspired the juntas, and by the upheaval of the independence wars. Tradition could not be erased at the stroke of a pen, and the fusion of both branches took years to become a reality. After all, not all surgeons were eager to become physicians, and physicians do not seem to have been interested in a surgical degree. Union enabled physicians and well-educated surgeons to strengthen their position at the apex of the medical hierarchy and guaranteed them control over the minor branches of the profession. The new agreement was reached with the support of the government, which believed in a liberal and more democratic society. Democracy, however, did not include everybody, and the minor branches did not necessarily benefit from the arrangement. More strict educational requirements hardened the divisions between medical branches, hindered the possibility of upward professional mobility, and either limited or denied formal education to minor medical fields, marginalizing them and bringing them under the tight control of the medical elite. In the case of the phlebotomy, requirements were lowered to distance its practitioners from the licensed surgeons. The result was the demise of the professional phlebotomist before bleeding became anachronistic and the merging, once more, of the bleeder and the barber. Midwives were also negatively affected. They received a most basic training, faced strict professional limitations, were limited by gender prejudices, and were reduced to assisting the physician-surgeons as childbirth became medicalized. On the other hand, those with a more solid medical background benefited. Dentists joined the ranks of the lesser practitioners, but their foreign and more scientific training, their national origins, as well as their ability to take advantage of new technology, and the emphasis on physical appearance gradually set them apart and allowed them to gain their independence. Many foreigners opted to join the ranks of legal practitioners and profited from their decision. An unknown number remained at the margins of the profession, practising as charlatans beyond the law. Illegal practitioners continued to flourish, favoured by popular beliefs and medical traditions among the population and by the more accessible cost of their services. The realignment of health-care practitioners that resulted from the physician-surgeon alliance required a different representative organization and regulations. A decade after independence, the Protomèdicato had become obsolete, so its abolition by the law of 21 November 1831 came as no surprise.[200] It was mostly a symbolic act, as the Protomedicato, with some changes, was reborn as the more democratic Facultad Médica del Distrito Federal y Territorios.

The Medical Profession and Public Health, 1831–1872

In 1845, after receiving complaints regarding the washing of animal skins in the main irrigation ditch, the local authorities sought the Consejo Superior de Salubridad's advice. After an inspection of the site and a thorough debate, the members of the Consejo, all medical practitioners, found no reason "to forbid the washing of skins because, although this activity is supposedly harmful to public health ... the simple washing of skins does not impair the residents' health. The situation in which the tanners find themselves forces them to use the main ditch and, as there are no health-related consequences, the committee agrees [with the tanners]."[1]

As this case illustrates, the physician-surgeons, represented by the health board, had regained their position as arbiters of public health.

This chapter discusses the successful efforts of the physician-surgeons, through their representative organizations, to reclaim both the place usurped by the juntas de sanidad and their authority over all health-related matters. During the time under study, medical practitioners had control over professional practice and education. They also confirmed themselves as experts on health-related issues, raising the prestige of medicine and their own claims as a profession. However, the distance between professional concerns and public health widened, and the two were finally divided at the end of the century.

The chapter is divided into six sections. The first three deal with the organization and contributions of the Facultad Médica and the Consejo Superior de Salubridad, and their uneasy collaboration with government authorities. The following two sections describe the challenges these organizations faced in public health and control of medicinal substances. The final section analyzes the first effort to create a national public health organization and its legacy.

In 1828 the presidential term of Guadalupe Victoria drew to a close, and Manuel Gómez Pedraza, representing the centralist faction, was elected as his successor. Unhappy with the results, the federalist faction rose in rebellion. In October the disturbances reached Mexico City, where the Motín de la Acordada (28 October 1828) decided the fate of the republic. The defeated candidate, hispanophobe Vicente Guerrero, became president, confirming the failure of democracy in post-independence Mexico.[2] The anti-Hispanic feelings and resentment of the population, fanned by the populist speeches of the radical politician and future president Valentín Gómez Farías, erupted into mob violence, or what Timothy Anna describes as "the closest thing to anarchy" the capital had experienced in 150 years.[3] The mobs sacked and burnt the Parián, the main market dominated by Spanish merchants, and adjacent buildings. The authorities were unable to impose order for four days. The riots shook the elite and middle levels of society, and contributed to the voluntary exile of numerous Spaniards.[4] Spain's misguided and ineffectual effort to reconquer Mexico the following year confirmed local fears, increased resentment against the mother country, ended all possibility of diplomatic reconciliation, and justified the radicals' decision to expel all Spaniards from Mexico.

In this context of increasing radicalism and anti-Hispanism, the medical elite proceeded to reorganize its representative organization. The Protomedicato, the main defender of the physicians' privileges, had become an anachronistic symbol of the Spanish past, an institution based on old hierarchies, racial prejudices, and privilege that offended liberal egalitarian and democratic principles. At the same time, the juntas de sanidad had gained power at the Protomedicato's expense and were now threatening the practitioners' professional independence. Aware of their predicament, the medical elite, formed now by physicians and surgeons, responded by adapting to the political context of independent Mexico and forming a new representative organization that better reflected the republican system of government. Other countries reacted differently. Peru opted for a change of name, relabelling the Royal Protomedicato as the Protomedicato General del Estado without changing its structure or the profession's organization.[5] In Colombia, the 1826 Plan of Studies established the Universidad Central de Bogotá, and its Faculty of

Medicine took over the responsibilities of the Protomedicato.[6] The end of the Protomedicato (or its change of name) symbolized the medical profession's break with the colonial past, but, at least in Mexico, it did not mean physicians had renounced a deeply rooted organization and hierarchy or their claim as the ultimate authority on public health issues.

THE PROTOMEDICATO'S SUCCESSOR: THE FACULTAD MÉDICA, 1831–1841

The Protomedicato was replaced with the Facultad Médica, which, according to the law of 21 November 1831, "will substitute for the Protomedicato in 'all its attributes' not contrary to the present system of government and legislation" and, until the sanitary code is finished, "will exercise the same functions that correspond to the Protomedicato" in the Federal District and Territories. The change, therefore, was more of form than of substance – the transformation of the Protomedicato into an association more attuned to liberal ideology.[7]

The choice of name is unclear. We know that, in February 1826, Congress was discussing the creation of a "Facultad de medicina de la federación." Although this referred to a teaching institution, the ninth article of the proposal being discussed stated that it was "with the understanding that the new establishment must replace the Protomedicato in all its obligations ... if compatible with the law."[8] As the Facultad Médica was not a teaching institution, the choice may have been influenced by the French *facultés*, described by Mathew Ramsey as *aggrégations* or organizations whose main function was the control of professional privileges.[9] Although more democratic than its predecessor, the Facultad Médica was far from being an independent and representative organization, as it was ultimately dependent on government legislation and geographically restricted to the capital.

Immediately after the dissolution of the Protomedicato, Mexico City practitioners in each of the main medical fields met separately at the government's request to select four representatives. It was a watershed for the profession, and Manuel de Jesús Febles underlined its importance in his final speech as a protomédico, reminding his colleagues that their votes were crucial, "as the fate of the profession, or more specifically of humanity, depended on the election that

will take place," and urging his colleagues to act with "union, cir-
cumspection, and prudence ... [to achieve] the betterment of the
heroic Mexican Nation to which we all have the honour to belong."[10]
Twelve names were selected and sent to the Supreme Government
(the president or his representative) for the appointment of a president, secretary, *fiscal* (officer), and treasurer. The three main branches
of medicine had been consulted and given the chance to participate
in the process as prescribed by the law, but by allowing physicians
and surgeons to elect members in two different categories and then
uniting both as one (physician-surgeons), the same law ensured their
majority and primacy. It also consolidated their union by ordering
that in future, only physician-surgeons (and pharmacists) would
be appointed.[11]

Thus, the Facultad Médica had a larger numerical representation
than did the Protomedicato and opened its doors to elite surgeons
who, with the physicians, were now at the helm; at the same time,
it excluded the "lesser" practitioners, formalizing their marginalization and subservience. The physician-surgeons' position was
buttressed by reserving to them the posts of president, secretary,
and fiscal and leaving that of treasurer to the pharmacists. In this
way, the physician-surgeons maintained not only a majority but
also the main posts. Those not elected as officials (five physician-
surgeons and three pharmacists) served either as *vocales* (members)
or as substitutes.[12]

The Facultad Médica also enjoyed the privilege of selecting its
own president. His duties included representing the organization
and presiding over meetings, examinations, and pharmacy inspections. If he became unable to discharge any of his duties, he could
appoint a representative to take his place. He was followed in order
of importance by the secretary, who was in charge of administration,
organized the agenda for the meetings, kept the minutes, reported on
decisions and communications received, followed up the correspondence received, and updated five registries – "Minutes," "Resolutions," "Examinations," "Licences," and "Pharmacy Inspections."
The secretary was also responsible for taking the oath of elected
vocales, licensed practitioners, and graduating students. The third
post was that of fiscal, who ensured the fulfillment of professional
requirements and government laws and regulations by all practitioners, reviewed and approved applications, enforced internal discipline, and looked into complaints. The treasurer was in charge of the

Facultad Médica finances, keeping a record of income and expenses, and rendering an annual report in the first yearly meeting. Most telling is the post of *portero flebotomista*,[13] described in the last article of the regulations, whose duties included cleaning the meeting room, handing out correspondence, remaining at the door during meetings and pharmacy inspections to carry out any tasks requested by the vocales, and "obeying the president's orders."[14] Thus, the only phlebotomist included was to serve as a cleaner and errand boy at the orders of his superiors, a clear step down from the consultative place at examinations and professional recognition phlebotomists had enjoyed under the Protomedicato.

In addition to professional restrictions and the informal requirement to reside in the capital (members had the obligation to attend meetings regularly), financial considerations contributed to limit participation in the Facultad Médica. Many practitioners were either unwilling or unable to serve when the only remuneration offered was, as in colonial times, minimal. A member received 6 pesos for taking part in an examination in medicine or surgery, 3 pesos for one in midwifery, and 2.5 pesos for each pharmacy inspection, but he was not remunerated for his attendance at weekly meetings and extraordinary sessions, for research, or for consultation on specific matters, all of which were compulsory.[15] The result was that, after the initial enthusiasm for the new organization, posts were rotated among a few ambitious individuals, dedicated practitioners, and those unable to refuse their appointment.

The first officials of the new organization were the physicians Joaquín Villa, José Gracida, and Mariano Sierra, latin surgeon Manuel Carpio, surgeons Francisco Montes de Oca and Joaquín Piña, and pharmacists José Maria Vargas and José Crespo.[16] All appointees had received their licences before 1822, reflecting a clear preference for well-established individuals with at least ten years' experience.[17] This would change over the next few years. In 1835, the Facultad Médica consisted of fourteen members: four physicians, five physician-surgeons, four pharmacists, and a phlebotomist. Joaquín Villa, Mariano Sierra, and José Lemus occupied the posts of president, secretary, and treasurer, respectively, while physicians Cornelio Gracida (José Gracida's son), José María Ballesteros, and José Barela, physician-surgeons Joaquín Piña, José Becerril, Ignacio Durán, and José María Martínez del Campo, and pharmacists José Crespo, José Bustillos, Ignacio Baz, and Marcos Arellano were vocales.[18] Four years after its establishment, the Facultad Médica's key posts remained in the hands of established practitioners trained in colonial times, but six of their younger colleagues (Ballesteros, Barela, Durán, Bustillos, Baz, and Arellano) had joined as members. The younger practitioners were not wedded to the colonial past and therefore more open to reform. Durán, for example, would later become the director of the Escuela de Medicina. This new generation would leave its mark on the profession.

The Facultad Médica functioned first and foremost as a professional organization. Fifty-two of the ninety-one articles of its regulations dealt with its internal organization, duties, responsibilities, and privileges, the frequency and length of meetings, the specific duties assigned to each official, and the right to select its own president. Of the remaining thirty-nine articles, thirty-seven dealt with professional examinations, the licensing of physician-surgeons and pharmacists, and the enforcement of the professional monopoly. Two final articles, almost an afterthought, were dedicated to phlebotomists and midwives, who did not require any formal training to obtain a licence.[19] Thus, as discussed in the previous chapter, the regulations, written by the physician-surgeons, ensured their place at the top of the medical hierarchy and their distinction from the "inferior" medical branches.

Although the 1831 legislation stated that the Facultad Médica "would substitute for the Protomedicato in all its attributes," its territorial and jurisdictional mandate was narrower. Under Mexico's federal system of government, the Facultad Médica remained a departmental institution with its mandate and membership limited to the capital and Territories; the proclamation of a centralist republic in 1836 brought no changes in this regard. Its official mandate was more geographically limited than that of its predecessor, and neither the law that created it nor its regulations assigned it an advisory or public health role.[20] In 1834, when the national government was trying to decide on the fate of the newly established medical school, the Facultad Médica was not consulted. Instead, the national government appointed its own experts.[21] The regulations also remained silent on the important area of public health, probably because this fell under the jurisdiction of the juntas de sanidad.[22] The lack of records makes it unclear what, if any, role the Facultad Médica played in these matters. When the cholera pandemic reached Mexico in 1833, acting president Valentín Gómez Farías resorted to military surgeon Pedro del Villar, and the physician-chemist Leopoldo Río de la Loza, who were not members of the Facultad Médica. Del Villar was asked to draw up "clear and easy-to-follow" national preventive and therapeutic guidelines, and Leopoldo Río de la Loza was commissioned to analyze the "atmospheric air" to determine the origins of the epidemic.[23] In Mexico City, the surgeon Francisco Montes de Oca and the physician Joaquín Piña, both members of the municipal junta de sanidad, wrote a brochure on the matter, which the junta published. The junta then took charge of the situation, coordinating medical services and aid for the needy, a clear indication that public health remained under its mandate.[24]

The Facultad Médica does not seem to have played a role in public health until 1836, after the bases for a centralist system of government had been established and the juntas de sanidad eliminated. Under its auspices, twenty-four prominent medical men met on 18 November 1836 in the conference room of the Mexico City ayuntamiento to discuss and prepare a report on fevers, preventive methods, and general rules for their treatment. Among those who attended were the well-known physicians Ignacio Erazo and José María Vértiz, both professors of the medical college; Agustin Arellano, a professor at both the university and the medical college; the well-known practitioner Louis Jecker;[25] and the renowned military surgeon Pedro Escobedo, consultor (adviser) to the medical military corps.[26] Unfortunately, the records of the meeting have been lost.

Most of the Facultad Médica's time was dedicated to enforcement of the new regulations on medical education, licensing, and professional monopoly. Its responsibilities included professional examinations and licensing of students, recent graduates, and established practitioners who had not fulfilled the requirements set out by the 1831 legislation. As the accreditation process became more thorough, the number of local, provincial, and foreign applicants grew, and the workload of the Facultad Médica members increased. They had to review each application, organize and carry out the necessary examinations, and issue the corresponding licence.[27] Especially time-consuming were the applications of foreign practitioners, "special cases" not foreseen by the regulations, and requests for exceptions from legislation. All supporting documentation had to be carefully reviewed and thoroughly discussed before a decision could be made, as in the case, discussed below, of Rafael de la Garza, a Mexican practitioner who had studied medicine in France.[28]

Despite the considerable work involved, neither the 21 November 1831 legislation nor the regulations mention a source of funding for the Facultad Médica or a salary for its members, who apparently were supposed to serve pro bono. Like the Protomedicato before it, the new organization had no fixed location and no government allowance. It was supposed to meet at its president's residence and finance itself from examination fees, pharmacy inspections, and fines. It was up to its members to cover any shortfall.

The work of the Facultad Médica was interrupted shortly after it began by the controversial 1833 educational reforms spearheaded by acting president Valentín Gómez Farías (see chapter 4). These abolished the Facultad Médica and reassigned its duties to the professors of the recently formed Establecimiento de Ciencias Médicas (Medical Sciences Establishment). The decree to this effect, signed by the governor of the Federal District, José María Tornel, was issued on 21 December 1833 and published "in all accustomed places."[29] Gómez Farías's experiment ended a few months later when President Antonio López de Santa Anna returned to his post. In August 1834, another decree cancelled the 1833 reforms and the posts they created, re-established the abolished institutions, and reinstated their suspended faculty and employees. Although the latter bando did not mention the Facultad Médica, it stated that, for the time being and pending an inspection, the Establecimiento de Ciencias Médicas would limit itself to instruction (*por ahora se mantendrá en la parte instructiva*).[30] Consequently, during the following years, the Facultad Médica continued to perform its duties as the medical profession overseer and representative by default.

Meanwhile, the country's political and administrative context was changing, and these changes affected medical practice regulations. The 1836 Constitution issued under provisional president José Justo Corro proclaimed a centralist republic and reorganized the political make-up of the country. Known as the Siete Leyes, the new legislation established a centralist republic with a Poder Conservador, or central body, to oversee the executive, legislative, and judicial branches. The states became "departments" headed by governors, and the Federal District was incorporated into the Department of Mexico. Each department was divided into districts under the authority of prefects and subdivided into *partidos*, or sub-districts, under sub-prefects.[31] Shortly after, the *Reglamento provisional para el gobierno interior de los Departamentos*, reminiscent of the 1813

Instrucción of colonial times, ordered the establishment of *juntas departamentales* (departmental boards) formed of six elected members and seven substitutes serving a four-year term. These boards were responsible for initiating legislation on taxes, public education, industry, commerce, and municipal administration. Their duties included establishing primary schools, ensuring the improvement of public education and welfare institutes, gathering statistics, and, in collaboration with the governor, drawing up departmental public health regulations.[32] Enforcement of the new legislation was not immediate. The Constitution gave Congress three months in the second year of its sessions (1838) to decide on the departmental divisions, while the juntas departamentales had the rest of the year to subdivide their departments into districts and partidos.[33] Implementation was further slowed by public resistance to the new constitution, the dismal state of the treasury, and mounting foreign debt that culminated in the 1838 invasion of Veracruz by the French navy.

The Facultad Médica del Distrito Federal y Territorios was not affected by the Siete Leyes administrative changes until August 1840, when, to conform to recent legislation, it changed its name to the Facultad Médica del Departamento de México. In its new version, the Facultad Médica was no more than a provisional body with two main objectives: to produce a sanitary code and to draw up medical education regulations to be integrated into the unfinished general education curriculum. In the meantime, the Facultad Médica was to continue the role of its predecessor until a professional body with national jurisdiction could be organized. The choice of Casimiro Liceaga, the Escuela de Medicina's director and former protomédico; Manuel de Jesús Febles, the senior member of the university medical faculty, who had also served as the last president of the Protomedicato; and Joaquín Villa, the experienced member and last president of the Facultad Médica del Distrito y Territorios to lead the new provisional organization indicates the government's objectives and priorities at the time.[34] It was imperative to incorporate medical education and the medical profession in general into the centralist political framework.

The Facultad Médica continued working to fulfill its goals, but despite daily meetings, the medical education curriculum could not be completed on time. At the beginning of October 1840, Liceaga contacted the authorities, requesting an extension as well as permission to initiate medical courses in accordance with the existing guidelines;[35] both requests were granted. By 25 November, however, the departmental authorities were losing patience and ordered the Facultad Médica to render its report before 23 December, otherwise government officials would draw up the regulations themselves.[36] The sanitary code was sent to the departmental government at the beginning of December, and the proposed medical curriculum and licensing requirements were handed in before the deadline.[37] The latter were discussed by the departmental junta headed by Governor Luis Gonzaga Vieyra and approved on 23 December as *Orde-namiento de arreglo de los estudios médicos, y exámenes de pro-fesores y policia en ejercicio de las facultades de medicina en el Departamento de México* (Regulations for the organization of medical studies and professional examinations, and public health under the Department of Mexico health boards; henceforth *Orde-namiento*).[38] Despite the theoretical power of the central govern-ment over the departments as defined by the Siete Leyes, the regulations (and presumably the sanitary code) remained a depart-mental effort sanctioned by the local governor. The Facultad Médica (as the central government) fancied itself the ultimate authority on health-related issues empowered to dictate national professional standards, but its ability to impose its mandate remained wishful thinking. Having fulfilled its task, the short-lived Facultad Médica del Departamento de México was dissolved to give way to the Consejo Superior de Salubridad del Departamento de México.

ADOPTING AND ADAPTING FROM THE FRENCH: THE CONSEJO SUPERIOR DE SALUBRIDAD, 1842–1865

During the following months, the *Ordenamiento* drawn up by the Facultad Médica was revised by the medical school faculty and the newly formed Consejo Superior de Salubridad and reissued with some changes on 12 January 1842 as *Reglamento de Enseñanza y policía médicas* (henceforth *1842 Reglamento*).[39] It must be empha-sized that, although the departmental authorities sanctioned and formalized both the *Ordenamiento* and the *1842 Reglamento*, the two sets of regulations were drawn up by the physician-surgeons themselves. It is unclear how many individuals collaborated, but the final drafts of the *1841 Ordenamiento* were discussed by fifteen members of the medical school faculty, who met in December 1840

Table 3.1 Professional and public health boards, 1600s to 1880

Protomedicato (1600s–1831)

Juntas de sanidad (1813–14, 1820–38)

↓

Facultad Médica del Distrito y Territorios (1831–42)

↓

Consejo Superior de Salubridad (1842–65)

↓

Consejo Central de Salubridad (1866–67)

↓

Consejo Superior de Salubridad (1867–1917)

---

at the request of Liceaga.[40] Their collaboration indicates that by 1840 the Facultad Médica was not the only organization uniting the medical profession and that its position was now being challenged by the medical school. It also shows that only a select minority played a role in formulating the regulations that would control all medical fields.

As was the *Ordenamiento*, the *1842 Reglamento* was divided into three sections, or "chapters." The first two focused on medical education and examinations and will be discussed in the next chapter. The third dealt with the newly formed Consejo Superior de Salubridad del Departamento de México.[41] The *1842 Reglamento* made clear distinctions between medical education, professional issues, and public health, and reflected the growing gap separating them. The physician-surgeons tried to ensure their control over the profession and to enforce their monopoly by including admission to professional examinations and licensing as public health responsibilities of the Consejo Superior, but the departmental government disagreed. Instead, it ordered that the required documentation be received and judged by a government official appointed by the department's governor, not by the Consejo Superior itself. In this way, the communication explained, "vices" or abuses by the Consejo Superior would be prevented.[42]

The Consejo Superior was established as the main public health authority in the department and as head of the subordinate consejos in smaller towns. Like the Protomedicato and the Facultad Médica before it, however, its mandate and geographic reach were not always clear. As the main board of health in the capital of a centralist republic, the Consejo Superior should have enjoyed national, overarching jurisdiction. The reality, however, was different, and the central government knew it could hardly claim control over the whole national territory. The Consejo Superior remained, as did the central government, a departmental body that, while claiming superiority over other similar organizations, did not enjoy power over them – a situation that did not prevent it from patronizing provincial organizations and practitioners. The Consejo's attitude is patent in its 1842 letter to the Dirección de Sanidad de Puebla expressing its surprise at the latter's decision to examine José Guadalupe Figueroa, who lacked the botany course required by the 11 January 1842 legislation. Indignantly, the Dirección replied that Figueroa had been licensed much before the "supreme decree" was issued and had been, therefore, considered exempt from it. Otherwise, he had fulfilled all requirements specified by law. The communication closed by stating it was a reply to the Consejo's letter of reproach.[43]

The organization of the Consejo Superior was similar to that of the Conseil de Salubrité de Paris (Paris health council), after which it seems to have been modelled, but their historical, national, and municipal context and objectives were different. In France, the Napoleonic regime revived the centralized authority of the pre-revolutionary monarchy and awoke a fervent nationalism among its citizens, who were willing to work with and for the government to promote the welfare of the citizenry and the greatness of the motherland. As opposed to the Consejo Superior, the Paris health council enjoyed strong political and financial backing of both the municipal and the national government. After all, French national leaders believed in the close connection between a healthy population and a powerful state. Established as an advisory municipal body, the health council's objective was to advise the Paris municipal government on "police" matters such as air and water pollution, the sanitary condition of markets and slaughterhouses, and epidemic diseases. Its responsibilities rapidly grew to include inspection and recommendations to improve sanitary conditions in public places, revision of applications for industrial buildings, gathering of statistics, and research. As its duties expanded, its membership grew to encompass physicians, chemists, scientists, and individuals with technical and administrative skills such as engineers, architects, and public servants. Its interdisciplinary character resulted in innovative research and the publication of a mounting number of reports that made it the national and international leader in public health. These reports began to be published in the *Annales d'hygiene publique et de médecine légale*, which came to be recognized as the most prestigious publication of its kind.[44] Soon the Paris Conseil's name came to be linked to those of the most prominent scientists, physicians, urban planners, administrators, and engineers of the time, men who belonged to the most renowned scientific institutions of France (the Institute of France, the Royal Academy of Medicine, etc.) and willingly lent academic support and contributed to its prestige.[45] In summary, the success of the Paris council was mainly due to the conditions prevalent in the country at the time, a strong centralized government, the wish to improve public health to strengthen the state, and the position of Paris as a centre of medical innovations – conditions that Mexico lacked.

Like the Paris health council, the Consejo Superior's members were divided into three categories: titular, adjunct, and honorary. Titular and adjunct members were appointed by the government and departmental junta from a list of candidates drawn up by the Consejo itself, served for a term of five years, and could be reappointed. The Consejo was presided over by the governor of the department, but was free to elect its own officials, thus enjoying limited independence.[46] The Consejo differed, however, in two important and interrelated points from its French counterpart – its objectives and the composition of its membership. As already mentioned, the Paris health board was an advisory body on public health matters formed by an interdisciplinary membership. Instead, in Mexico the Consejo Superior was established as a professional board first, and a public health organization second. Thus, it remained firmly under the control of the medical profession, with three physicians, a pharmacist, and a chemist as titular members. To become a titular or an adjunct member, the candidate had to have a medical or medical-surgical degree and be a graduate of the Establecimiento de Medicina. If he had not been trained in the capital, he had to hold a bachelor's degree in philosophy. The same regulations stipulated that pharmacists be at least thirty-five years of age and have a minimum of ten years of professional experience in the Department of Mexico to become members. The same age requirement and six years of professional experience applied to chemists.[47]

Titular members were assigned a yearly salary of 500 pesos (which they did not always receive), and adjunct members were paid only when carrying out pharmacy inspections (from the fees collected).[48] Regulations were more lax for honorary members, who served pro bono. The latter included the medical school director and the professors of hygiene and legal medicine, "ex-titular" members, and any deserving individual appointed by the titular members such as the pharmacists José María Vargas and Domingo Lazo de la Vega.[49] Individuals representing other disciplines could only be appointed honorary members. Among those chosen were José Manuel Herrera, chemistry professor at the Colegio de Minería; Joaquín Velásquez de León, professor of zoology and geology at the same institution; the writer José María Lacunza; and the lawyer Bernardo Couto.[50] These regulations guaranteed the medical elite's control over all health care areas, narrowed the Consejo's approach to public health, and hindered its diversification.

The incentives to serve in the Consejo Superior were limited. Salaries were not always forthcoming, and members could only expect limited recognition. Unlike the prestigious *Annales d'hygiene publique et de médecine légale*, published by the Paris board, the Consejo Superior had no journal in which to publish its members' work, nor was it recognized for its research internationally or even nationally. All in all, such conditions limited the pool of practitioners willing to serve on it. Those who did formed a select group that exerted control over the various medical branches, set professional guidelines, licensed and represented all practitioners, and served as their intermediaries with the authorities.

AN UNEASY ALLIANCE: FUNDING, CONTROL, AND INTERFERENCE

The collaboration between the medical elite and the government was a result of necessity that often produced benefits to both. To claim its place in the new country, the former needed the government's legislative support. For the latter, the collaboration of the medical profession was indispensable in matters related to public health and medical emergencies such as epidemics and war. Thus, both parties collaborated continuously and closely, but tensions between them were unavoidable. The root of the problem was the different interpretation that each party gave to the role and purpose of the Consejo Superior and the Facultad Médica before it. The government saw them as providing valuable, sometimes indispensable services, but nonetheless as dependencies subject to its authority. As such, they occupied a place in the bureaucratic hierarchy and were subject to the orders and whims of their superiors. The practitioners saw things differently. They considered both the Facultad Médica and the Consejo Superior as professional associations that, having been entrusted with overseeing the welfare of society, deserved leeway to carry out their tasks. Their decisions, after all, were based on the officially recognized medical knowledge and expertise of their members. Three main factors influenced the Consejo Superior's relations with the government: funding, government indifference, and the authorities' interference in their decisions, especially on the touchy issues of licensing and professional monopoly.

Funding was a key factor in relations between the Consejo Superior and the government, as the continuous scarcity of funds hindered the Consejo's work, limited the number of potential practitioners willing to serve, and frustrated its members. While its predecessor, the Facultad Médica, was forced to rely on the same sources of income as the Protomedicato – professional licensing and examination and pharmacy inspection fees, and the monies from fines charged for illegal practice, pharmacy violations, and similar transgressions – the Consejo Superior, at least in theory, received a government subsidy. Nonetheless, in contrast to the Conseil de salubrité de Paris, which enjoyed the generous financial support of national and municipal authorities, the Consejo Superior was underfunded, a fact that limited its activities and membership. The 1841 provisional legislation that established the Consejo Superior assigned it "direct" and "indirect" sources of funding, the former referring to the same funding that the Facultad Médica and the Protomedicato before it had enjoyed (licensing fees, pharmacy inspections, and fines). To these were added "indirect" sources that were as varied as they were confusing: an (indeterminate) amount to be set by the governor of the department, a meat tax that previously had been assigned to the Junta Superior de Sanidad, a tax levied on cows milked in the city (previously assigned to an obstetrics course that had not yet materialized), a tax on cemeteries (2 pesos per body buried in a private tomb or sepulchre), and one-third of the medical school professors' salaries when their courses were taught by substitute instructors, who received a lesser pay.[51] As a result of such a patchwork, the

Consejo Superior did not enjoy a fixed subsidy; the amount it received (or was supposed to receive) varied yearly, and the various sources of funding made collection difficult and unreliable. The meat tax, for example, imposed on all cattle and pigs slaughtered in the capital and its surrounding jurisdiction was to be shared with the Huehuetoca sewage works and the chamber of deputies, but the law did not specify the percentage to be allocated to each party. To complicate matters, in 1839 a new law had allocated the proceeds of the same tax to the Banco Nacional, while its collection remained in the hands of the city customs. In January 1844 the Consejo Superior wrote to the departmental authorities in charge of collecting the tax reminding them to remit their share, but to no avail as, according to its 1849 report, the Consejo had not yet received the meat tax allowance assigned by law.[52] The tax on the milking of cows posed a similar problem. In 1822, when it was originally established, opposition from cattle owners forced the municipal government to desist temporarily from attempting to collect it. Persistence seems to have paid off, as in 1842 and 1843 the Consejo Superior received 600 and 200 pesos, respectively. The latter was only a partial payment, and by the end of the year the Consejo tactfully reminded the municipal government to send the rest – clearly, public health was not the municipal government's priority.[53]

The Consejo Superior did not depend solely on municipal officials for funding. It collected cemetery fees directly, but the results were similar. The convents of Balvanera, la Encarnación, la Enseñanza, San Lorenzo, Santa Clara, Santa Inés, San Bernardo, and Corpus Christi, as well as the colleges of San Ignacio and Belén refused to pay cemetery fees unless so ordered by the archbishop, and the Santa Paula cemetery managed to obtain a tax exemption.[54] The Consejo Superior appealed to have the exemption rescinded, but the matter remained undecided eight years later.[55]

In short, confusing legislation, the attitude of government authorities, bureaucratic inefficiency, lack of an efficient collection system, and the dismal state of the treasury all meant that the Consejo Superior would suffer from chronic lack of funds that prevented it from fulfilling its obligations. In response, the Consejo was forced to limit its budget to the minimum; sometimes individual members contributed from their own pockets to cover the most basic expenses. During its first year, the treasurer counted only 103 pesos 2 reales, of which 42 pesos had already been disbursed and 55 were used to pay for the official seals, leaving only 6 pesos 2 reales, which were not enough to cover the expenses of the parchment for and printing of medical degrees, let alone other necessary expenses such as the most basic furniture, reactive substances, weights, measures, and other instruments indispensable for pharmacy inspections.[56] In 1842, the Consejo Superior enjoyed a total income of 1,679 pesos, derived from examination and licensing fees (772 pesos), pharmacy inspections (147 pesos), the cow milking tax (600 pesos), and burial tax (160 pesos), plus a modest amount (6 pesos) left by the Facultad Médica. Although considerably increased during the second year, such funds were still not enough to cover the Consejo Superior's many obligations, including its members' wages.[57] It was, therefore, not unusual for members to fulfill their obligations without receiving remuneration, and by September 1852, the government owed fourteen present and past members of the Consejo Superior a total of 8,891 pesos. These included the considerable sums of 1,909, 1,887, and 1,088 pesos belonging to Ignacio Baz, Leopoldo Rio de la Loza, and the estate of Joaquín Villa, who had died in 1845 while fulfilling his duties as vice president.[58] Such a situation reduced potential membership, as only a limited number of practitioners could, or would, work without pay. On the verge of bankruptcy, governments had to make hard choices, but contemporary budgets indicate that public health and the welfare of most of the population were not priorities.

It was not only insufficient funding that strained relations between the Consejo Superior and government officials, it was also the latter's indifference to the Consejo's objectives and needs.

To carry out the annual inspection of the pharmacies that were part of its obligations, the Consejo Superior required a local pharmacopeia or official guide of medicinal substances. Such a pharmacopeia was of special interest to both the Consejo and the pharmacists, who also needed a manual of local medications to fulfill requirements. At the request of the government, a Mexican Academy of Pharmacy was formed with the express purpose of writing the *Farmacopea Mexicana* to serve both purposes, but a lack of funds prevented its publication. In 1841, wishing to see their work published, the academy members donated the 500 pesos needed, but the money, in copper coins, was requisitioned by the government, leaving the *Farmacopea* unpublished.[59] Although the Treasury ministry had agreed to pay back the 500 pesos collected, new legislation stopped the payments. An article in the *Periódico de la Sociedad Filoiatrica* lamented that "the only corporation of this type that concluded its tasks in only three years faces challenges that cannot be solved without the aid of the government."[60] The *Farmacopea Mexicana* remained unpublished for five more years, making pharmacy inspections more challenging and forcing the Consejo Superior de Salubridad to rely on the "*Código de Paris*, Sougbeiran [*sic*], or la *Razonada.*"[61] The *Farmacopea Mexicana* was finally published in 1846.[62]

Another cause of tension was the decision of the governor of the Department of Mexico to tax the activities of illegal practitioners in 1844. In response to this measure, the Consejo argued in a strong letter that such a measure would amount to an official authorization by the cash-strapped government to practise medicine without a licence.[63] It was a serious matter for the Consejo Superior and the practitioners it represented, as such tax not only contravened the law but in fact prevented their enforcement of professional monopoly, one of their main objectives.

The Consejo's disenchantment with the authorities' indifference and the difficult financial position becomes obvious in the first two reports rendered by its secretary, Leopoldo Río de la Loza. The first report, dated 31 March 1841, was an enthusiastic account of the first three months' activities. After being installed on 21 January of that year, all members had taken the oath, selected the vice president, secretary, and adjuncts, and appointed a commission to draw up its internal regulations. Other commissions were struck to draw up a sanitary code and the *tarifa*, or list of licensed practitioners. The regulations' first draft was discussed shortly after, and delivered to the governor and departmental junta on 22 February. The customs inspectors (*visitadores de aduana*) had also taken the oath and were ready to start work. In addition, the Consejo Superior had written eight *acuerdos* (reports), answered two consultations, given nineteen expert opinions, and examined three aspiring practitioners. The report's enthusiasm was tempered only by the admission that the new organization could not cover its most basic expenses.[64]

Nine months later, Rio de la Loza rendered his second report. Gone is the secretary's initial enthusiasm and optimism. The Consejo Superior had inspected seven pharmacies, but the resistance of the owners and the lack of government support had forced them to suspend inspections. Having no guidelines yet, its members had not yet carried out the inspection of workshops, temples, and theatres. As to the vaccine and the sanitary code, nothing concrete had been done. Proposals to better preserve the vaccine and carry it to a wider number of children had been presented to the authorities, who had not yet replied. In view of such indifference, the Consejo Superior's reluctance to begin the onerous work of compiling a sanitary code is understandable. The report referred to the "general disenchantment" of the members and reminded the audience of the difficulties of discharging their duties in view of the government's lack of funding.[65] Not surprisingly, in June 1842 Río de la Loza handed in his resignation. The authorities, however, did not accept it, and he reluctantly remained as titular member until 1844, when he was finally allowed to resign.[66] His successors seem to have grappled with similar problems.

The authorities' indifference did not necessarily mean that either the Consejo Superior or the Facultad Médica before it enjoyed the freedom to act, as their decisions were sometimes overridden by government officials. Such an attitude of those in authority reflected the larger political context in which rules and laws were easily broken to buy political support and satisfy personal whims. Patronage was not new in Mexico – examples of it abound in the colonial period – but government favouritism diminished the credibility of public health authorities and sometimes put the public at risk. Such interference resulted in tensions and controversy, and hindered the work of the Consejo. Clearly, the Consejo Superior never exerted complete control over its own decisions. Unable to counter superior orders, it had to bend to government decisions, even when these went against its best judgment. The public was aware of the situation, and applicants often sought to speed up or override the decisions of the Consejo by seeking government intervention. Such was the case of José Pascual Querejazu, who was appointed honorary surgeon of the Army Ambulance in 1847 in view of "the interesting services" he had rendered in the army and his internship at the military Hospital de San Andrés. At the same time, the executive ordered the Consejo Superior to license him as a physician-surgeon able to practise throughout the country. It is unclear if the presidential order was obeyed, as in 1855 the magistrate of the Supreme Tribunal of Justice ordered the Consejo Superior to include Querejazu (who was his brother-in-law) in the list of official physicians.[67] The treatment of Susana Villaret provides another instance of intervention by superior officials: in June 1854 the Ministry of justice told the Consejo

Superior of "His Most Serene Highness, President Santa Anna's" decision to exempt Villaret from the obstetrics course required by law and to give his approval for her examination. To add insult to injury, Villaret was to be examined and licensed for free.[68]

Like the Consejo Superior, the Facultad Médica had been similarly treated by the authorities. In 1833 Rafael de la Garza, a Mexican citizen and holder of a French medical degree, applied for a licence (without examination) to practise in Mexico. He had served as a member of Mexico's legation in Rome and had important connections in the government, as the dedication of his thesis to Vicente Rocafuerte, Mexico's chargé d'affaires in London and Miguel Ramos Arizpe, minister of justice and ecclesiastical affairs, indicates.[69] At the time, many Mexican physicians travelled to France after completing their studies in Mexico, but few boasted a French degree. His dissertation, "Quelques considérations générales sur l'empoissonnement" (Some general considerations on poisoning), indicates de la Garza trained with some of the luminaries of contemporary French medicine – Mathieu Joseph Bonaventure Orfila, Jean Cruvelhier, François Joseph Victor Broussais, and Anthelme Richerand, among others.[70] Thus, de la Garza's case was exceptional and, most important, he was aware of his privileged and unique position. Without precedents or specific regulations on the matter, the Facultad Médica treated de la Garza as a foreigner and required him to be examined. Offended, de la Garza appealed to the ministers of state and foreign relations, who ordered the Facultad Médica to issue him a licence without further delay. The latter refused, the conflict escalated, and the resulting stalemate lasted until acting president Valentín Gómez Farías suspended the Facultad Médica members dealing with the case and called for the substitutes. Knowing that its credibility was at stake, the Facultad Médica refused to comply, arguing that no substitutes had been appointed. After seven months of wrangling, six members agreed to abide by the authorities' orders, and the remaining two resigned. The government had triumphed at the expense of the Facultad Médica's prestige and credibility.[71]

In this regard, there was no difference between federalist or centralist, liberal or conservative officials and, despite changes of government, the abuse of authority continued. In October 1856, provisional president Ignacio Comonfort authorized Augusto Teodoro Staum to practise medicine and surgery in all of Mexico for a term of two years.[72] Two years later, the Ministry of Justice informed the

Consejo Superior that President Benito Juárez had granted Tomás Federico Fuller permission to practise as a physician-surgeon in Pachuca and its surrounding area. According to this communication, Fuller had been examined in Veracruz and his certificate had been lost by the ministry in charge under Comonfort's presidency.[73]

Sometimes government intervention opened the door to experimental and dangerous therapies. In 1858, after a thorough discussion, the Consejo Superior denied Rafael Castrejón's application to apply electricity to "nervous illnesses," a decision that was soon overridden by government officials. Without further consultation, and to the chagrin of the Consejo Superior, the Ministry of Development authorized Castrejón, who did not hold a medical degree, to apply his electricity treatment under the supervision of a licensed physician.[74]

However, government authorities did not always choose to override the Consejo Superior's decisions, and by going to the political authorities, applicants risked antagonizing it. In 1841, the Puebla physician Rafael Gutiérrez Martínez contacted the Supreme Executive Power, complaining that his Puebla licence had not been accepted by the Consejo Superior and asking to be included in the official list of practitioners. He had a medical and a surgical degree from Havana and Louisiana, respectively, and, as his documentation showed, had been licensed as a physician-surgeon by the Puebla Dirección de sanidad. Unfortunately for the petitioner, this time the Supreme Executive Power does not seem to have interfered on his behalf. Annoyed, the Consejo Superior responded that it had "seen with displeasure Gutiérrez's petition because it was offensive to those who regulated medical practice in the department." The letter added that the applicant would be registered when he fulfilled all requirements; in the meantime, he was prohibited from practising in the Department of Mexico. The secretary copied the Supreme Government in his response.[75]

One of the most consequential cases of government patronage was that of the Catalonian José Carbó. In 1854, Carbó requested a licence and permission to open a homeopathy school. Realizing the potential for competition that a different healing approach entailed, the Consejo Superior members turned him down, patronizingly stating that "homeopathy was not medicine"[76] – not for the first time, as it had previously prohibited the Spaniard Narciso Sanchís "to heal with homeopathic methods."[77] In Mexico, as in other countries, physicians opposed homeopathy because its principles differed from and often contradicted those of scientific medicine. It is not clear when homeopathy first reached Mexico. As in other Latin American countries, it arrived by way of Spain, and in 1839 it was already a topic of interest among Mexican practitioners.[78] One of the first homeopaths in Mexico was Ramón Comellas, an ex-faculty member of the University of Valencia and founder of the Instituto Médico Valenciano, who arrived in 1851. His *Reseña sobre la Homeopatía dedicada a los Mexicanos* was the first publication in Mexico explaining the main homeopathic principles that challenged contemporary medical principles. This was a time when different healing approaches such as phrenology and electrical and water therapies were being explored, competing with traditional medicine.[79] The popularity of homeopathy rested on its more gentle approach (as opposed to the more radical and painful procedures of allopathic medicine) and its lower cost to the patient. According to David Sowell, the belief that disturbances of the "vital force" caused illness appealed to those who were not attracted by the purely scientific and secular approach of medicine.[80] Not surprisingly, the Consejo Superior tried to use its authority to marginalize unorthodox methods and their practitioners, such as Narciso Sanchís and José María Carbó. The Consejo, however, was unaware of Carbo's connections. During the 1854 yellow fever epidemic, he had worked tirelessly among the troops housed in San Juan de Ulúa, thus winning the president's gratitude. Availing himself of the circumstances, Carbó took his appeal to President Santa Anna, who ordered the Consejo Superior in no uncertain terms to issue the licence. Carbó received his permission, but it is unclear if he ever opened his school.[81] Regardless, we do know that homeopathy flourished in Mexico with the blessing of the authorities. In 1858 the Spanish physician Pascual Bielsa began to publish articles on homeopathy in the local newspapers and, despite many challenges, three years later he and Pablo Fuentes established the short-lived Mexican Homeopathic Association, the first of its kind in the country. Nine years later, the first homeopathic pharmacy, located at 13 San Francisco Street, opened its doors.[82] Nonetheless, as in the rest of the countries, the medical elite consistently opposed homeopathy and its practitioners. In 1871 the Consejo Superior opposed the application of Julián González to open a homeopathic dispensary.[83] Twenty years later, the homeopaths resorted again to the central government officials who favoured their cause and, with the support of the minister of state, Manuel Romero Rubio, the National Homeopathic Hospital was officially inaugurated in 1894 with the attendance of President Porfirio Díaz, Minister Romero Rubio, and the governor of the Federal District, José Ives Limantour. The following year a presidential decree authorized the foundation of the Escuela Nacional de Medicina Homeopática (the first of its kind in the world) and its granting of the degree of surgeon-homeopath.[84] Later, homeopaths would be similarly favoured by successive governments, forcing the formal recognition of homeopathy, despite opposition of the medical profession.[85] While the popularity of homeopaths was partly due to their low cost and gentle treatments, the consolidation of homeopathy as a medical option was the result of the national authorities' support. In the case of homeopathy, government decisions trumped the cherished monopoly of medical practitioners.

The combination of government meddling, neglect, and lack of funding translated into lax enforcement of legislation, which was detrimental to public health and a waste of precious time and valuable resources, which neither the Consejo nor the government had. It also diminished the stature of the Consejo Superior and its members and eroded their credibility in the public eye. The frustrations resulting from dealing with a bankrupt government and inept bureaucrats, as well as the immense workload as official advisers to the departmental and national governments, coordinators of health-related measures in emergencies, and members of a professional board, meant that few individuals were interested in joining the Consejo Superior. Those practitioners who served in it or in its predecessor may have enjoyed leadership roles and exerted control over the profession, but they did so at a very considerable financial and personal cost.

Despite many frustrations and limited funding, the Consejo Superior continued to function regularly until 1864, when it was replaced by the imperial Consejo Central de Salubridad. Unfortunately, the minutes of its meetings disappear from the records in 1858. Clearly, its work was not interrupted, as professional licences and other isolated documents prove.[86] The lack of records may be explained by the political turmoil of the times. In 1859 Mexico was in the midst of the bloody War of Reform between liberals or federalists and conservatives or centralists; the conservative defeat was followed by a five-year French Intervention. During these chaotic years, the

Consejo Superior sessions may have become less frequent, or records may have been relocated for safeguarding and later lost. Nonetheless, the Consejo Superior must be credited for its perseverance and hard work in such difficult circumstances.

THE VAST FIELD OF PUBLIC HEATH

The Facultad Médica and the Consejo Superior were responsible for policía or public health, a still poorly defined area of immense reach. Its vastness and the lack of infrastructure to deal with issues that would presently fall under diverse government agencies hindered the Consejo's work and often prevented it from fulfilling its mandate. Since 1820, policía had been entrusted to the juntas de sanidad, which continued to function until the creation of the centralist republic in 1836. Therefore, the role of the Facultad Médica in public health was negligible during the first years. It was not until 1836 that the Facultad, as representative of the medical profession, was asked by the Mexico City authorities to appoint a commission to study the causes and treatment of the serious fevers that affected the population. The Facultad rapidly complied, appointing well-known physicians Manuel Carpio and José María Vertiz, the surgeons Ignacio Erazo and Tomás Guapillo, and the British physician Guillermo Schiede.[87] The Consejo Superior, on the other hand, had been conceived as a public health board that would inherit the mandate of the juntas de sanidad, abolished by the Reglamento para el Gobierno Interior de los Departamentos, or 20 March 1837 law. As already mentioned, this law confirmed the municipal government's public health obligations but placed medical aspects, preventive measures, and general public health directly in the hands of municipal and local governments. It also abolished the juntas de sanidad (the Mexico City junta de sanidad records end, without further explanation, in 1839). Thus, the Consejo Superior responsibilities consisted of the broad categories of government consultant, inspector, coordinator of vaccination efforts, and all other health-related measures.[88] Later, the Consejo Central would enjoy an even broader mandate, becoming the head of a centralized public health network at the national level. In some cases, such as the sale of medications and pharmacy inspections, public health issues overlapped with professional concerns; in others, the gap between both areas was patent. Nevertheless, the Consejo Superior's role as expert authority and government adviser enhanced its position and the credibility of the practitioners it represented and legitimized the position of medical practitioners as experts in their field. Such benefits came at the price of time-consuming work and considerable effort on the part of Consejo Superior members. A few examples illustrate the wide range of cases that came to the Consejo's attention.

Two years after its establishment, the Consejo Superior was consulted on the best way to dispose of organic and inorganic waste, manage the disposal sites, and avoid contamination. After a commission studied the matter, following contemporary miasmatic beliefs, it recommended combustion as the best method to destroy noxious substances. This method had the advantage that the high temperature would purify the atmosphere, ridding it of "swamp emanations." The *sumideros* (sites where human waste was deposited) should be deep and located at the city's southeast and southwest to prevent them from contaminating the dominant south and northern winds that carried "healthy fluids" from the vegetable gardens. The side facing the city should be fenced, and a line of trees should be placed on the north side to oxygenate the atmosphere and prevent the gases from reaching the capital.[89]

A few years later, when the governor of the Federal District ordered the construction of privies, sewers, and drains, the Consejo Superior objected, arguing that in the crowded multi-residential buildings, the sewers would emit putrid miasmas and mephitic gases into the rooms each time their covers were opened to either clean them or empty bedpans and other waste. Carbonic and "sulphidric" acid, nitrogen, and putrid emanations would then escape and contaminate the atmosphere. To support their argument, the Consejo members referred to two examples cited by the famous Paris hygienist Alexandre-Jean-Baptiste Parent-Duchâtelet: a ship carrying human waste going from La Rochelle to Nantes and another one with the same cargo from the Island of Guadeloupe. In both cases the crews had fallen seriously ill of an "adynamic" fever, leading to the conclusion that its cause was the putrid ferments of the cargo.[90]

The Consejo Superior was not the only official body grappling with these problems. In Guanajuato, the municipal authorities were discussing Doña Ana Soto's petition to keep open the pig slaughterhouse she had in her residence. To make her case, the petitioner argued that the "civilized European nations allowed slaughterhouses within the cities" and referred to the conclusions of the Paris health board. Irritated, the authorities responded they were well aware of "the principles adopted by Paris and the fact the Parisians were not affected by the slaughterhouses' putrid exhalations." However, as Doña Juana wanted to slaughter pigs in Guanajuato and not in Paris, she should abide by local laws. Her petition was denied and she was given five days to move the slaughterhouse outside the city.[91] As these cases indicate, the Consejo as well as the public adhered to the hygienist beliefs of the time and kept abreast of public health developments in France.

In 1855 the Mexico City municipal government consulted the Consejo Superior on a more complex case regarding the *acequia principal* (main canal), used simultaneously for transportation and sewage. Canoe owners who used the canal to transport merchandise complained about debris in the main canal and the loss of water space to tanneries and woodworking shops, which encroached on the canal and threw their refuse – fecal matter, wood, skins, and blood residue – into the water, often blocking the canal and causing it to overflow onto streets and into lower apartments. The city authorities wished to assess the health risks and the feasibility of prohibiting the washing of skins in the main canal. After careful study, the Consejo advised against prohibition because, in its opinion, such activities did not impair the neighbours' health (!), although "they might imply other unhealthy activities."[92] A few years later its successor, the Consejo Central, adopted a different attitude when it studied a similar problem in the canal of Santo Tomás. The process involved in skinning and cleaning the leather was unpleasant and odorous and the tanning shops were unhealthy. The worst part was the "fermentation" of the skin followed by its tanning (interleaving the skins with bark and tannin). The disposal of water and solids "corrupted" the waters of the canal, "kept a pestilent atmosphere, and turned it into a permanent focus of infection." The imminent danger of the situation compelled the Consejo Central to appoint a commission in charge of drawing up the necessary regulations. Furthermore, it strongly recommended not discharging the water used in the process into the canal; instead, liquids should be placed in barrels and used as fertilizer on agricultural land, and solid refuse should be burnt.[93] Whether, despite its concern and good intentions, the Consejo Central accomplished its goal is most doubtful.

When conflict arose, the Consejo Superior seems to have placed the interests of its own members ahead of the public welfare. For example, the residents of the towns of Tlascuac, Callejón de las Cabezas, and Necatitlán filed a complaint against a factory of "chemical products" located in the area, noting that in the previous two years the building had caught fire twice, resulting in victims of smoke inhalation and the death of an employee, and expressing the fear that a larger fire could reach the powder deposit located "not far" from the laboratory. In addition to the potential danger, the strong and unpleasant smells caused by the gases inconvenienced the residents, "harmed their stomachs," and endangered their health. The complainants requested that the laboratory be relocated to an unpopulated area. The factory was owned by the renowned physician and chemist Leopoldo Río de la Loza, a prominent citizen, professor of the medical school, and an active member of the Consejo Superior, having served as secretary and treasurer.[94] The complaint seems to have been ignored, however, as there is no record of any subsequent action taken in this regard. However, another case on a similar matter had different results. In 1852 the municipal authorities requested the Consejo Superior's opinion on whether the metallurgic work at the Casa del Apartado produced noxious gases harmful to the surrounding area. After an inspection, the Consejo recommended employing a qualified chemist and redesigning both the chimneys (to allow the remaining gases to escape) and the pipes (to improve the extraction of vapours from the sulphuric acid chamber). Following these recommendations, the municipal authorities issued the relevant orders.[95] It is clear that the Consejo was selective in its responses and that at least in the above-mentioned case, it chose to ignore a valid complaint rather than affect the personal interests of one of its own.

Workplace accidents were considered a public health matter, so in 1844 the frequent accidents taking place in the *tocinerías* (establishments where *tocino* or fried pork fatback was prepared and sold) were brought to the attention of the Consejo Superior, which appointed a commission to look into the matter. The commission recommended adopting a preparation method that did not require steam or, if this was impracticable, compelling employers to build rails around the boilers to prevent workers from falling into them. To ensure enforcement, the Consejo Superior volunteered to carry out the necessary inspections.[96] Also work related were the inspections of cigarette factories and the recommendation that the paper used to roll the cigarettes be changed, as it had harmful effects on the workers. The Consejo was also asked to inspect the metal-working shops of the women's Arts and Trades School to determine if the work involved was "appropriate to their gender."[97]

Closer to the Consejo's area of expertise was the report by the prison physician José Mária Barceló de Villagrán on "the various occasions" when he had been called to examine the bodies of individuals who had perished inside a *temazcal* (Indigenous steam bath), a matter, he felt, that the Consejo should explore. [98] Apparently the latter did not consider the issue worth its attention, and only on 18 December 1855, more than a year later, did the Consejo finally decide, upon learning about the "arsenic baths" that the *temazcal* in question was offering, to carry out an inspection as soon as possible.[99]

The coordination of emergency responses also fell under the Consejo Superior's mandate. When a cholera epidemic threatened the city in 1850, the Consejo Superior appointed committees to enforce sanitary measures, organized a *junta superior de socorros* (central charity committee), and worked closely with the governor and the municipal government to put in place the necessary sanitary measures. In addition to ordinary weekly meetings, Consejo Superior members held fifteen extraordinary sessions to prepare for the dreaded epidemic.[100] After the arrival of the first cholera victim at the Hospital de San Andrés on 1 May, the Consejo called an emergency meeting, in which it decided to continue with the preventive measures already in place, such as cleaning drains, removing refuse daily, readying lazarettos, and overseeing the remuneration of the practitioners assigned to care for epidemic victims. Within two days, members had compiled a list of items that should be prohibited, and on 11 May they discussed the advisability of declaring a "choleric state" in the capital, deciding to wait a few more days.[101] In July they agreed on fumigating cemeteries with a mixture of lime or "soda chloride" and coffee grains diluted in water.[102] Related themes, such as cholera regulations, cemetery and hospital inspections, and the merits of the remedy known as *raíz del indio* (root from the *Aristolochiaceae* family), were discussed in successive meetings.[103]

Collaboration among states in matters of public health was not unusual, and in times of crisis the Consejo Superior was contacted by other cities. In 1850 the prefect of Morelia inquired about the medicinal value of ether, alkali, and camphorated *aguardiente* (an alcoholic drink derived from sugar cane)[104] in cases of cholera. The pragmatic response was that the tea in question should be used only if there were no physicians available as, "generally, such a method could not be recommended."[105] As to the enquiry of the Puebla health board on the best treatment for cholera, the Consejo recommended a concoction of opium, ether, alcohol, and other antispasmodics, as well as astringent substances, as the remedy that produced "the best results."[106] By the end of August 1850, the state of alert was lifted and the Consejo began to gather the casualty reports of hospitals, cemeteries, and municipal governments to prepare a statistical summary. It also prepared annotated meteorological observations carried out during the epidemic, which were sent to the Sociedad de Geografía y Estadística (Geography and Statistics Society) for publication.[107]

Epidemics were not the only emergencies that preoccupied the Consejo Superior. In 1844, when a rebellion broke out in the city, the Consejo received 1,000 pesos to organize three emergency hospitals for the victims. Volunteers included its vice-president, Joaquín Villa, medical school professors Leopoldo Río de la Loza, Miguel Francisco Jiménez, Agustín Arellano, Pablo Martínez del Río, Ladislao de la Pascua, and Francisco Vertiz. They were assisted by nine Sisters of Charity, hospital staff, and female volunteers who contributed by sewing linens, pillows, and blankets.[108] The Consejo Superior's role earned it the praise of the authorities, who the following year entrusted it with safekeeping the surgical instruments used in military hospitals during the war and their return to the Ministry of War and Navy.[109]

In 1854 the Consejo Superior called an extraordinary session to prepare for an imminent civil war.[110] Its members approved the maintenance of a medicine chest for each four city blocks with "all the necessary items" for first aid; this would be entrusted to an "inspector," who would also be charged with calling the closest physician in case of casualties. If wounded in the proximity of the Hospital de San Pablo, the only establishment that accepted this kind of cases, the victim should be taken there immediately. It was also agreed that physicians who took care of casualties would be paid for their services from the fines collected for "police" or sanitary infractions.[111]

Finally, it is worth mentioning the role played by the Consejo Superior and its successor, the Consejo Central, as forensic medicine experts. Since colonial times, practitioners had been asked for their professional opinion in cases of battery, rape, and murder, and hospitals had carried out autopsies to determine the cause of death for legal purposes. Some cases also entailed medical malpractice: for example, in 1856 the midwife Manuela Guardiola was accused of causing Dolores Abascal and her child serious harm due to her ignorance; after confirming that Guardiola lacked the required credentials, the Consejo Superior reported her to the government, which ordered her apprehension and began proceedings against her.[112] Others, more complex, required careful research. In 1852 the judicial authorities of the District of Morelos requested the Consejo's expert advice on the nature of certain powdered herbs. The case involved a woman by the name of Ana María who, tired of being mistreated by her husband, decided to poison him. She mixed the powders acquired from a Juan Miguel (probably a healer) in her husband's food, but unfortunately he and his father switched plates. The latter became ill after the meal and died three days later. Having been questioned, Juan Miguel admitted his guilt in providing the powdered bark of two local trees. The task of determining if the powders in question were indeed poisonous was entrusted to the physician Luis Hidalgo y Carpio, considered a specialist in forensic medicine (among other areas). Hidalgo y Carpio acquired two medium-size chickens to test the powder. He administered two *drachmas* (one-eighth of an ounce) of powder in four dosages to the first one with no consequences. The second chicken was given the same amount in a single dosage, with similar results. Hidalgo y Carpio concluded the powders were harmless but cautioned that in some cases substances affected animals and humans differently.[113] In the nineteenth century, legal medicine was still in its infancy and lacked sophistication, so, although licensed practitioners complained that legal decisions were often based on the opinion of bleeders, midwives, or curanderos, it is not clear that their own opinions were more informed. Nonetheless, between 1842 and 1846 the Consejo Superior worked on at least forty-three legal cases encompassing injuries, poisonings, and murders.[114] Its successor, the Consejo Central, would go further when, at the request of the judicial authorities, it exhumed cadavers on three occasions, examined them "following all the rules of the art," and helped "to rectify certain decisions."[115]

PROFESSIONAL MONOPOLY, HERBS, AND MEDICINAL SUBSTANCES

The Consejo Superior, like the Facultad Médica before it, considered professional monopoly a priority. Both knew that monopoly over practice depended largely on their ability to control the sale of medicinal substances, a responsibility that conformed also to their role as public health authorities. The issue was complex because it implied control over the sale of herbs, medicaments, and the establishments that sold them. Medicinal herbs were available in markets, stores, and pharmacies, and the control of their sale required constant inspections, which neither the Facultad Médica nor the Consejo Superior was able to carry out. In 1843, the Consejo Superior appointed a commission to advise on the best way to prevent the damage caused to the public by the sellers of plants and other substances. The commission reported that, since "time immemorial," small shops known as *herbolarias* had sold *pepita de San Ignacio* (*Hura polyandra* seeds), *piñoncillo* (fruit from a *Euphorviaceae* family bush), hemlock, substances with "energetic actions," and other curative plants to people who "lacked any scientific knowledge."[116] A law of 24 January 1842 banned such stores but, the report admitted, they had the advantage of providing, at minimum prices, fresh products that otherwise would lose all or part of their curative virtues.

After some debate, the Consejo Superior came up with four recommendations: first, to make the sale of medicinal plants conditional on the Consejo's authorization; second, to draw up a list of the plants that could be legally sold and make it available "to all those interested"; third, to have an appointed commission inspect the stalls of licensed sellers; and, fourth, to issue legislation to forbid the unlicensed sale of medicinal plants and substances. Such recommendations, however, were wishful thinking, impossible to enforce when supply could not be controlled, and there was no clear definition of what qualified as a medicinal substance – as illustrated by the already discussed attempt on part of the Protomedicato to stop the sale of agua de sosa in 1818 (see chapter 1). As the same report pointed out, herbs represented an inexpensive alternative to practitioners' fees, they could be gathered easily, and their sale could not be controlled. As to the constant inspections of the numerous legal and illegal shops and stalls that would be required, the municipal authorities lacked not only the resources but also the will to carry them out.[117] Thus, the status quo persisted. Herbs and their derivatives continued to be readily available, peddled in markets and stores.

Yet another problem was the sale of medicinal preparations, many of them imported, that could be acquired in the most surprising places, such as the store of a Luis Benign, the *Carnicería Francesa* (a

butcher shop), which sold "illicit pills and powders," and the home
of an enterprising individual who sold Morrison pills to the public.[118] The sale of medicaments at pharmacies without medical prescription was an equally important issue, especially in the case of
dangerous or poisonous preparations. The problem was not new,
but the growing use of mineral and chemical substances in medicinal
preparations made it all the more pressing. In 1832 two Facultad
Médica members, physician Cornelio Gracida and pharmacist José
(María) Vargas, concerned with the indiscriminate sale of drugs in
numerous stores and the availability to the general public of dangerous substances that could cause "the most grave results," had proposed to address this problem with several suggestions that were
fully endorsed by those attending the meeting. First, a list of licensed
practitioners residing in the capital should be drawn up and circulated among the city's pharmacists, pursuant to a regulation supposedly in effect since colonial times. Second, pharmacies should fill
only dated prescriptions signed by a licensed practitioner, another
requirement that dated back to pre-independence years. Third, pharmacists should retain the medical prescriptions of dangerous drugs
and stamp other prescriptions before returning them to the buyer.
Fourth, only pharmacies should be allowed to sell medicines. Fifth,
all local and imported medicinal substances, including *específicos*
(prepared medicaments), should first be approved by a pharmacist
appointed by the Facultad Médica, and only pharmacies should be
allowed to sell such medicines to the public. Finally, individuals who
broke the law should be punished "accordingly."[119] These measures
aimed not only to increase the public's safety but also to ensure the
licensed practitioners' monopoly over medical practice.

In 17 July 1835 the Mexico City ayuntamiento acted upon these
recommendations by ordering practitioners, including phlebotomists, to present their licences, which, after being sanctioned by the
Facultad Médica, would be registered with the local municipal government. A list of licensed practitioners and their addresses, updated
every January, would then be posted in all pharmacies, which would
despatch only dated prescriptions signed by listed practitioners.[120]
The results of this legislation seem to have been unsatisfactory, as
eight years later the Consejo Superior had to remind pharmacists,
once more, not to fill the prescriptions issued by unlicensed individuals.[121] The 1835 law may not have achieved its objective, but it set

the basis for a formal registry of licensed practitioners and a tighter control over medical practice.

Nonetheless, the illegal sale of medicinal substances and dangerous chemicals continued. In 1842 the Consejo Superior received a letter from a Dr Trivece regarding a woman treated with morphine acetate by another practitioner – a treatment that almost killed the unfortunate patient. Trivece expressed his surprise at the use of such a poisonous substance that, according to him, was never used in European hospitals, and he suggested an inquiry be launched into the pharmacy that had sold it.[122] Another disquieting incident was reported three years later. A student of the National College of San Gregorio purchased a liquid that burned through his clothes and caused him a large blister. Alarmed, the director of the college sent a servant to the store to buy more of the liquid, to prove that such a dangerous substance could be easily acquired. He then contacted the Consejo Superior, which conducted an investigation into the matter before "raising its weak voice" to the governor, and requesting that the retail sale of sulphuric, nitric, and muriatic acid, iodine chlorate, mercury oxide, lead and copper acetate, silver nitrate, and arsenic and its compounds be limited to pharmacies.[123] The assumption was, of course, that such substances should be prescribed only by licensed practitioners.

The problem did not go away, however, and further legislation was required to recognize illegal practice as a serious public health issue. To prevent quacks from compromising the "health, life, and sometimes the honour" of families, the 1865 imperial regulations made the Consejo Central responsible for providing pharmacies, judges, and tribunals with a current list of licensed practitioners while the latter were to punish any infringement. The illegal sale of medicines had become a crime.[124] The inability to control medicinal preparations (be they herbs or chemical substances) was not only a serious public health matter; it was also linked to professional monopoly, an issue of great concern to all licensed practitioners. It was in their own interest that pharmacies be managed by licensed pharmacists who filled prescriptions only from licensed and supposedly competent practitioners. Nonetheless, some establishments continued to operate without a properly trained pharmacist, and many continued to sell medications regardless of who prescribed them. Little could be done without an effective system to control and track wholesale acquisitions and retail sales, and the personnel to enforce regulations.

Sometimes the Consejo Superior had to deal with an exceptional case, such as the Hospital de San Pablo's pharmacy. As the hospital, the pharmacy was under the administration of the Sisters of Charity, who lacked both formal training and a licence to practise pharmacy. After an inspection, the Consejo Superior reported that labels were misplaced on some flasks, the pharmacy lacked an aerometer (indispensable for the preparation of medications),[125] and the sisters lacked the pharmaceutical knowledge required by law. The inspectors had witnessed the preparation of a poisonous and strong mixture of *nuez vómica* (*Strychnos nux vomica*) and seeds by one of the sisters, and "such considerations" prompted the Consejo "to reflect on the laws that have always prohibited women from preparing and selling medicaments." As most women did not know Latin, they were unable to fill prescriptions and lacked "the scientific knowledge that only those who have studied the profession have," an interesting observation since, for almost twenty five years, it had been illegal to write prescriptions in this language. Practice was not enough, the Consejo Superior believed, as "many medicines were very different but had similar names." It failed, however, to mention that women had no such knowledge because they were prevented from studying pharmacy, even though, as the sisters had showed, they were perfectly capable of learning the trade. The report ended with the suggestion that the sisters limit themselves to hospital administration, stop working at the pharmacy, and employ a licensed pharmacist.[126] Despite the Consejo Superior's grumbling, the sisters continued to run their pharmacy in contravention of gender prejudices and training requirements.[127]

It was a losing battle – the control of medications continued to elude the Consejo Superior. As time passed, more mineral medications such as mercury, silver nitrate, and liquid ammoniac acetate became common, and imported pharmaceutical substances began to flood the market and be openly advertised.[128] The journal published by the French army in Mexico, *L'Estaffette*, for example, carried numerous advertisements of the most varied remedies: Bristol pills for dyspepsia, liver ailments, and migraines, Agua de Orezza for stomach ailments and weakness, and Mr Dublanc's Preparations for chronic lung affections and skin and urinary tract diseases, which were sold at the establishment of E. Maillefert.[129] Only the arrival of the modern pharmaceutical companies closely linked to the medical establishment and a stricter control over the establishments that sold medicaments would allow tighter control of the sale of medications. Indeed, the issue has not yet been completely resolved, as stalls and stores in Mexico continue to sell medicinal plants and preparations, and restricted drugs are still available in some pharmacies.

THE FIRST NATIONAL APPROACH
TO PUBLIC HEALTH, 1865–1867

In May 1863 the republican government of Benito Juárez fled the capital, which was then occupied by the victorious conservatives backed by the French expeditionary forces. An elected group of notables temporarily took charge of the government until an empire could be formally established. With the establishment of the Regency, the political context changed once again. In theory, Mexico was now an empire with a central government, its territory divided into twenty-two departments, six territories, and one District of Mexico.[130] In reality, it was a fragmented country, its borders defined not by administrative divisions but by the latest military actions, the capital's hold on the rest of the country decreasing with distance. Nonetheless, the imperial authorities undertook a redrawing of the country's political, administrative, economic, and social landscape. On 1 December 1865 the Law of General Police of the Empire replaced the Consejo Superior with a Consejo Central de Salubridad en la Capital del Imperio or Imperial Capital Central Public Health Council (henceforth Consejo Central), responsible to the Ministry of Government.[131]

The Consejo Central, officially inaugurated on 3 January 1866, was composed of five titular and eight adjunct members; there is no mention of honorary members. Appointed as titular members were the physician-surgeons José María Reyes, Manuel Berganzo, and Manuel María Carmona, and the pharmacists Francisco González and Rafael Martínez, while the practitioners Aniceto Ortega, Domingo Aramburu, Lauro María Jiménez, Francisco Armijo, Angel Iglesias, and Agustín Andrade, and the pharmacists Maximino Río de la Loza and Evaristo Bustillos served as adjunct members.[132] The Consejo Central was part of a general administrative and legislative reorganization undertaken by the empire during 1865 and the beginning of 1866 to create "an organic imperial law" to coordinate the tasks and jurisdictions of the different ministries.[133]

The Law of General Police of the Empire involved important changes. First, it interpreted the term *policía* according to its traditional meaning; public health referred to "general police," which included police forces, the environment – that is, the urban landscape in the form of buildings, streets, parks, and so on – and public health in its present-day meaning. Thus, the law was divided into three different *títulos* or sections: the first and second sections dealt with policing in the modern sense, and with the order and maintenance of cities and towns, including regulations on weapons, public entertainment, gambling, urban lightening, business establishments (public baths, bakeries, and factories), and carriages, while the last section referred to the *policía de salubridad pública* (literally, public health police). According to the last, the newly established Consejo Central was to coordinate public health across the empire, have a direct mandate over the capital and its department (now called Departamento del Valle), and be responsible only provisionally for the professional aspects – medical practice, pharmacy inspections, licensing, and so on – while a separate sanitary code was issued.[134] The law also established a *junta subalterna de sanidad* (subordinate health board) in the capital of each department, a *delegado de sanidad* (health delegate) in each town, and *juntas de sanidad* (health boards) in the ports. Both the juntas subalternas and the juntas de sanidad were conceived as fairly independent bodies that would report regularly to their superior, the Consejo Central. This network was to coordinate all public health matters, gather data, and provisionally oversee professional licensing. The Consejo was also to draw up the regulations of its dependencies and a sanitary code, create statistical tables from the data gathered from the departments, and advise the juntas subalternas. Its ultimate goal was the centralization and uniformity of all health-care-related areas in the empire.[135] Although this was never achieved, it was the first time that public health was envisioned as a national issue and its authorities given a clear, official mandate over the whole country.

The third and last section of the 1865 law was divided into four chapters. All chapters described in detail the many obligations of the Consejo Central and its subordinate juntas and delegates. When listing the *atribuciones*, or duties, of the Consejo Central, the first chapter dedicated two out of twenty-one subsections to licensing, reviewing, and approving candidates' requirements and taking the necessary oath. The remaining atribuciones refer exclusively to public health. The second chapter, *Ejercicio de la Medicina* (medical practice), was a single article divided into twelve parts dealing with medical practice, which was now placed beyond the exclusive control of the medical elite. Pharmacy licences now required the signature of both the Consejo Central representative and the political prefect, and violations were punishable by the judicial authorities. Thus, the Consejo Central was viewed as an expert body, as an adviser of the political authorities, and illegal practice was no longer simply a matter of professional monopoly but a serious issue affecting public health.[136] The third chapter, "Medidas de Salubridad" (health measures), included separate sections on issues as diverse as vaccination, cemeteries, garbage and its collection, markets, baths, drinkable water, slaughterhouses, hospitals, prisons, factories of chemical products, and *pailas* (soap manufacturers). The final chapter, "Disposiciones Generales de Salubridad" (general provisions for public health), included guidelines on match, steel, and powder factories, beer making, preparation of dangerous chemical substances, and the sale of white phosphorus, as well as recommendations in case of emergency. Attached was a detailed alphabetical list of dangerous, unhealthy, or "uncomfortable" establishments that were covered by article 159 of the same law. Each establishment was classified according to these three categories, and qualified as first or second class according to its potential for harm. Establishments that purified oils by means of sulphuric acid were qualified as "dangerous" and "uncomfortable," of the second class, as a result of their foul smell. Manure deposits were "unhealthy and uncomfortable," of the first class. Ceramic manufacturers were "uncomfortable," of the second class, for their smoke, while the cooking of animal heads in cauldrons belonged to the same category for the resulting smoke and bad smell.[137] Clearly, these regulations placed much greater emphasis on public health than did previous ones.

In addition to the priority placed on public health, the new regulations changed the composition of the Consejo Central's membership to reflect medical developments and increasing professional specialization. Chemists acquired a larger presence that reflected the growing importance of chemistry in medical science and the development of drugs and industry in general, and a new specialty, veterinary medicine, was included for the first time. All in all, the medical profession maintained its control over the new organization, but its power was diluted by a higher proportional presence of pharmacists, chemists, and veterinarians. Titular positions would now be filled by three physicians and two pharmacists, while two pharmacists, two chemists, two veterinarians, and six physicians would serve as adjunct members. In the departments, the juntas subalternas were to be formed by three titular members (one of them a pharmacist) and four adjunct members that included a pharmacist and a veterinarian. These modifications reflected the acceptance of medicine as a science and its dependence on chemistry, whose practitioners now required representation. At the same time, specialties were beginning to be recognized, as rapid medical developments forced practitioners to concentrate on specific fields.[138] One was veterinary medicine. At the time, Mexico had at least one veterinary school. The Escuela Nacional de Agricultura established by President Santa Anna in 1853 seems to have included veterinary medicine among its subjects, although it is unclear if it continued to be offered, but the Escuela Especial de Agricultura advertised its theoretical and practical courses in veterinary medicine in 1866.[139] Nonetheless, this area was not recognized in local medical discourse until the arrival of the French military veterinarians. Two of them, Eugenio Beygeyre and M. Leguistin, were among the founders of the future academy of medicine and published their works in the *Gaceta Médica*.[140] This fragmentation of medicine into different specialties made the traditional division between physicians and surgeons totally obsolete. It also demanded a new terminology that reflected the increasing complexity of contemporary scientific medicine.

The Consejo Central presented its impressive report in January 1867, less than five months before the fall of the empire. According to this report, the Consejo had drawn up its internal regulations using those of its predecessor as a model. These had been revised and modified by the imperial authorities and were now in effect. Twenty departments now had functioning juntas subalternas.[141] The report indicates that the Consejo Central saw disease prevention as its main objective. To this purpose, it had drawn up regulations on the wholesale and retail sale of medicinal substances, but it had not neglected the inspection of tanneries, starch factories, markets, and chocolate manufacturers.[142] It had also drawn up or reviewed regulations for starch factories, leech nurseries, and slaughterhouses, as well as for burials and the cleaning of sewers and privies.

The Consejo Central had also gathered careful statistics on the causes of death in Mexico City and requested, with little success, all

juntas subalternas to do the same. The results, it hoped, would help
to address public health problems and prevent unnecessary deaths.
In the capital, the mayor aided the task by passing a bylaw requiring
practitioners to issue death certificates specifying cause of death. The
surrounding areas were a different matter. The Consejo Central was
aware of the challenges that the gathering of such data presented,
especially in small towns and haciendas where there were no qualified practitioners. Thus, in the interest of statistical accuracy, those
whose cause of death was not clear (either because they had died
without a physician or they had been under the care of a curandero)
were recorded as "unclassified." The data gathered in 1866 indicate
that almost half the casualties (3,457 out of 7,866 deaths) were children younger than ten, and mortality was higher during the summer
(June to August). The report classified illnesses into two main categories, general and infectious ailments. The first was subdivided into
ten groups: diseases of the head, chest, digestive system, and genital-
urinary system, "elephantiasis of the Greeks" (lymphatic filariasis),
chlorosis (anemia also known as "green sickness"), "alcholosis,"
scurvy, scrofula (tuberculosis), and syphilis. Infectious diseases were
divided into typhoid, smallpox, intermittent fevers (malaria), and
yellow fever. Chest and digestive tract ailments were the most lethal
general diseases, and typhoid and smallpox the most deadly infectious ailments. Along with the statistical information, the report
made some recommendations to reduce mortality, such as building
more orphanages and hospitals, enforcing public health regulations,
cleaning the city carefully, drying swamps and marshes, and vacci-
nating the population.[143] The Consejo Central's ambitious attempt
to gather similar statistics and reports for the whole country was,
however, frustrated by lack of funds, inexperience, war, and the
rapid disintegration of the empire. Only Puebla seems to have complied, sending a report on the medical organization of the department and the condition of its streets, public buildings, charitable
institutions, and hospitals.[144] The document ended by stating that
the Consejo Central members had adhered to the law, acting diligently and in good faith for the welfare of the population, a clear
effort to disassociate the organization and its members from political events and the rapidly disintegrating empire.[145]

The Consejo Central's secretary rendered his report five months
before the collapse of the empire. As the French troops began to
withdraw, the territory under imperial control shrank and economic

resources evaporated. On 23 February, *El Diario del Imperio* announced the arrival of Maximilian in Querétaro in a last-ditch attempt to stem the tide that threatened to engulf him.[146] It was to no avail, and in July the capital was once more under the control of Juárez and his republicans. In an effort to erase the memory of the empire, changes were undone, records were destroyed, and Mexico returned to pre-imperial practices. The Consejo Central ceased to exist, and new appointees rushed to occupy their posts at a Consejo Provisional (provisional board). A "definite" Consejo Superior de Salubridad del Departamento de México was appointed in May 1868 under the previous *1842 Reglamento*. In addition, the republican government disavowed the licences issued by the empire, and practitioners had to apply (and pay) again to practise their profession legally.[147] It was a step back in the public health area, as outdated regulations were put in place, the Consejo became once again a professional and public health board, and its mandate was restricted to the capital and surrounding area.

In 1872, a new *Reglamento del Consejo Superior de Salubridad* was issued by the governor of the Federal District. This time, the Consejo Superior would be formed of "proprietary" and adjunct members, with three physicians, one pharmacist, and one veterinarian in the former category, and four physicians, two pharmacists, and one veterinarian in the latter. At least for the time being, physicians continued to form a majority, but the objectives of the organization had changed. The new Consejo Superior was stripped of its role as a licensing authority and overseer of professional monopoly, becoming exclusively a public health board. Finally, professional matters were separated from public health issues. Five years later, the Consejo was placed under the jurisdiction of the Junta Directiva de Beneficencia Pública, but the arrangement lasted only two years.[148] The Consejo Superior continued its activities until 1891, when new medical developments, political changes, and the exigencies of international trade prompted the government of Porfirio Díaz to draw up a national sanitary code and reorganize the Consejo as a national public health board.[149]

The merging of medicine and surgery and the political transformation of Mexico made the reorganization of the medical profession and its leadership imperative. The Protomédicato, a symbol of professional elitism and "colonial obscurantism," gave way to the

Facultad Médica, a supposedly more democratic body better attuned to the times. The Facultad led the efforts to modernize the profession, allowing the medical elite to maintain control over all licensed health-care providers and all branches of medicine to identify as part of a whole. Thus, through the Facultad Médica the medical elite drew up professional regulations, designed a medical curriculum that would ensure the profession's survival and guaranteed it a place among the sciences. The Facultad also influenced legislation and government decisions in the public health area.

After ten years, the Facultad Médica, having fulfilled its role, was replaced with the Consejo Superior de Salubridad del Departamento de México. The new body was inspired by the Paris health board but lacked the financial and political backing that the French enjoyed. Unlike the Paris health board, the Consejo Superior's regulations, drawn up by medical practitioners, prioritized its character as a professional body over its role as a public health organization. Nonetheless, the two roles reinforced each other and contributed to raise the professional status of medicine and its practitioners. Gradually, urban sanitation and industrial concerns came to claim most of the attention of the Consejo Superior members, and at the same time the medical school began to claim its place as a centre of medical discourse and debate. The trend became obvious in the regulations of its successor, the short-lived imperial Consejo Central, whose main responsibility was public health.

Both the Facultad Médica and the Consejo Superior required government support to achieve their objectives, and the authorities needed a public health board and expert advisers. But their relationship was far from smooth. Financial dependence on a penniless government and frequent political changes hindered the work of both organizations, which found government intervention a constant irritant. Practitioners did not object to the government's "right" to head the Consejo Superior or to sanction the appointment of its officials – such was the price of official recognition and legal authority. They expected, however, that the agreement spelled out in the regulations would be respected by the same officials who sanctioned it. These differing visions were incompatible and often resulted in tensions and even open clashes that hindered the public health organizations' work and undermined their standing and authority. Nonetheless, despite disagreements and numerous obstacles, both the Facultad

Médica and the Consejo Superior enhanced the prestige of the medical profession, aided its continuation and development, and helped to carve its niche in independent Mexico.

Their successor, the Consejo Central, was born out of a somewhat anachronistic legislation based on the traditional concept of policía and was to function, temporarily, as a professional organization. Nonetheless, the new law fleshed out public health concerns, updated regulations to include Mexico's budding industries, and described in more detail the Consejo Central's obligations. The new Consejo was designed mainly as a central public health organization, the centre of a network that reached the whole country and was part of government administration. For the first time, public health was envisioned as a concern of the national government, placed beyond the control of a medical elite and ultimately separate from professional matters. Although the Consejo Central's short life and the lack of archival materials prevent a fair evaluation, it clearly set precedents for the 1872 public health regulations, the Porfirian Consejo Superior de Salubridad, and the first Sanitary Code (1891).

4

Training Future Generations:
Medical Education, 1800–1870

Concerned about the "atmospheric emanations" of San Andrés hospital's amphitheatre and their effect on patients and staff, the medical school director, José Ignacio Durán, decided to suspend the *anatomías* (dissections) temporarily. However, in 1853, after the medical school was relocated to a less-than-suitable building, Durán was forced to reconsider and ask the hospital to allow, once more, the "cadaveric operations" necessary to fulfill the curriculum. At the same time, he requested the hospital's statistics and "necrological records" to determine the autopsies' effects on its patients. The hospital administrator opposed the request and referred it to the archbishop in charge. The director then contacted the local authorities. Thus started a copious correspondence between the school, the hospital administrator, the archbishop, and the local government to reach an agreement.[1] The resulting documentation reflects the medical school's difficulties in attempting to offer a full curriculum, the need for a centralized infrastructure, the important role played by government officials and clergy in the development of medical education, and the perseverance of the medical faculty.

This chapter deals with the medical elite's struggle, first, to design and teach a modern curriculum, and second, to control medical education. The modernization of education had two main objectives: to place the physician-surgeons on firmer professional ground and to maintain their place at the top of the medical hierarchy. The chapter covers the fifty-year period that followed independence. It argues that, far from being a sudden innovation, the reforms of medical education were part of a gradual process that can be traced back to the eighteenth century and that continued throughout the nineteenth century. The establishment of the medical school and its survival against almost insurmountable odds was a collective effort, a task the physician-surgeons had to undertake to ensure their professional survival. The reforms were the result of debate and negotiation. The interested parties, united in their rejection of the colonial past and with bitter memories of the independence wars, searched for more modern models to shape education and build the new nation. Medical practitioners found their ideal in France, a country that in their eyes shared similarities with Mexico and was at that time the main European centre of medical research. Despite their best efforts, Mexican reformers were not able to duplicate the French system. Medical education in nineteenth-century Mexico might have been inspired by the Paris school of medicine but continued to be rooted in its Hispanic past.

In nineteenth-century Mexico, the ongoing struggle for political power, the efforts to create a secular society, and the state's attempts to assert its power shaped medical education. Traditionally, historians identify the most conservative elements with those who believed in a strong central government (centralists), had the support of the elite, the church, and the military, and resided in the capital. Their rivals, labelled liberals or federalists, believed in a weaker national government and stronger state powers, and identified with the provinces (or states) and the emergent middle class. This dichotomous image is far from accurate, as personal beliefs and interests sometimes defined political stance, and differences were not always stark. Chronologically, the centralists enjoyed the upper hand, with some exceptions, until 1855. Thereafter, the pace of reform quickened, and the insoluble differences resulted in a bloody civil war, followed by French intervention in support of an imperial government. Traditional historiography considers the fall of the empire (1867), the indisputable victory of republicanism, and a loose federal system the beginning of modern Mexico. However, political differences were not always as clear-cut as this brief description suggests, nor was the chronology as precise.

Five pieces of legislation are of utmost importance in understanding the links between political events and the development of medical education. The first is the 1833 Plan for Education Reform, issued under the acting presidency of Valentín Gómez Farías, a radical liberal credited with the creation of the medical school. The reforms were short-lived, but left an important precedent for future medical programs. The second piece of legislation is the 1843 General Studies Plan (or Baranda Plan). Drawn up by a centralist government and enforced at the local level by departmental committees, it aimed to raise standards and achieve national uniformity.[2] Despite its laudable purposes, the plan found few supporters outside the capital, as the departments resented the central government's intrusion into their affairs. The third legislative act was a follow-up law (1846) that sought to placate provincial critics by granting provincial governments "the necessary freedom to organize public education in their respective territories," and allocated funds for this purpose.[3] The fourth law, issued in 1854 by the Santa Anna dictatorship, was a new educational plan for the country, the *Reglamento General de Estudios* – better known as the Lares Plan. Although the regime fell a few months afterward, the Lares Plan influenced provincial medical education. The fifth set of education reform laws was drawn up by the liberal government that followed the Santa Anna regime and included important changes such as the closing of the National University of Mexico (1857) and a short-lived Law of Public Instruction. The next set of legislation followed in December 1865, when the imperial government of Maximilian of Habsburg issued its own educational regulations, limiting professional education to the main cities. The detailed Law of Public Instruction did not affect medical education in the capital, nor did it survive the empire. On the return of the republicans in 1867, legislation was changed once more, as the Barreda Law (1868) modified the general curriculum to reflect positivist beliefs.[4] The new law affected preparatory studies but did not change the medical curriculum per se. Thus, although national legislation provided the general context, local politics, legislation, practitioners, and specific circumstances defined the path of medical education and the local development of the medical profession.

   This chapter is divided into ten sections. The first two set the political and historical context of educational reform. The third section follows the proposals and debates that resulted in the 1833 educational reform to illustrate the gradual pace of reform. The fourth and fifth sections are analytical and comparative, and show reformers' inability to erase the colonial past and their adaptation of French models to local realities. The following three sections – on institutional rivalry, the medical school's funding and relocations, and the lack of infrastructure to teach the school's curriculum – focus on the obstacles the medical school and its faculty faced and their responses. A short overview of provincial medical education is included to offer some perspective on the challenges that other cities faced. The final section provides a more human side and examines the Escuela de medicina's contribution to the formation of a group that shared the same specialized knowledge, objectives, duties, and risks.

COLONIAL PRECEDENTS

In the eighteenth century, the functioning of the human body was not completely understood and a direct relation between theoretical medicine and medical treatment had yet to be established. Consequently, the assumed superiority of the colonial physician lay not only in his academic knowledge and his ability to translate it into effective therapies, but also in his social status as a university graduate. A university degree meant more than a command of abstract knowledge handed down since classical times; it acknowledged the holder as a member of an exclusive academic corporation with access to privileges that set him apart from the rest of society. In Mexico, a university degree also implied that the holder was part of a privileged, "racially pure" group with sufficient wealth (or connections) to afford the expenses of a higher education. The required *actos* or university debates were as ceremonial as they were academic, and the expensive and very public graduation ceremonies acknowledged the graduate's admission into a select social and intellectual brotherhood. Thus, the professional credibility of a colonial physician rested not only on his knowledge of theoretical medicine and his professional skill but also on his social status.

During the late eighteenth century, the traditional values that had supported social and professional hierarchies began to be questioned, and corporative privilege started to give way to individual merit. In the realm of science, observation and experimentation undermined classical medical knowledge and raised the importance of practical skills over abstract theories. The transformation was most evident in France, where the anatomo-clinical school shook the foundations of traditional medicine and set it on a new course. This emphasis on practical skills worked against the physicians, who had to shift their attention to hands-on training. The same trend helped to raise the status of surgeons, who now became aware of the importance of a solid academic base that would legitimize them professionally and isolate them from untrained practitioners. The Real Escuela de Cirugía partially filled the latter's needs, but further reform would have to wait until Mexico achieved its independence.

The wars of independence accelerated the disintegration of the social and intellectual foundations that had supported the medical hierarchy and brought drastic changes to medical and surgical education. To combat the rebels, the government was forced to overstretch its financial resources and re-evaluate its priorities. The Real y Pontificia Universidad, a symbol of the past, was among the institutions most affected by these events. In 1810, a viceregal order turned its building into a military barracks, a reflection of the increasing opposition to corporations and elitism bred by liberal ideas. Classes suffered and registrations at the medical faculty plummeted, with only six physicians graduating during these turbulent years.[5] Some professors continued to lecture in their private residences, and students were allowed to complete their studies under the guidance of a physician.[6] Keen students had no choice but to complement their hospital education with private lessons and classes at the Real Escuela de Cirugía. In the words of a contemporary, "the study of Medicine decayed much and physicians almost had to be educated in private Academies."[7]

Forced to channel financial resources into the war effort, the government ceased to pay the university's traditional subsidy and pressured faculty members to contribute 10,000 pesos to the royal cause. Moreover, the university had to "loan" 9,000 pesos to the government, which never paid the agreed interest, let alone the principal.[8] The university recovered its building only in 1816, after paying 500 pesos for the relocation of the barracks, but the harm was done and the Faculty of Medicine never recovered from this blow.[9] For the next fifteen years, medical students continued to avail themselves of the limited number of courses offered by the university and surgical school, hospital practical training, and, depending on individual resources, private instruction. Although hardly conducive to professional improvement, such an educational patchwork allowed students to familiarize themselves with both medicine and surgery and facilitated the merging of both medical branches.

While the university was struggling to survive, the Escuela de Cirugía had its own problems. The university's woes and the great demand for military surgeons pushed the number of registrations up from 70 in 1806 to 86 in 1813, and to 112 in both 1816 and

1817.[10] Clearly, not all students completed the program: in 1816, eighty-one students took examinations at different levels, but only ten completed their studies. Nevertheless, between 1810 and 1819, the Escuela de Cirugía produced eighty graduates and partially trained a much larger number of surgeons.[11] Although the number of students certainly increased, the school's resources did not.

Until 1818, students had received free education, partly subsidized by the Hospital Real de Naturales (and therefore by Indian tribute),[12] but as the hospital's income declined until it practically disappeared, the Escuela de Cirugía had to find other sources of income. Madrid paid the salaries of its director (who was also the main professor) and dissector, but the school needed to cover the preparation and cleaning costs involved in dissections and the salaries of at least an intern and a servant. The situation became so dire that, in 1818, after various requests, Director Antonio Serrano obtained royal permission to charge students a small fee to cover the most basic expenses.[13] Such financial constraints were behind Serrano's continuous requests that the Escuela be granted the right to license its own graduates. The first of such petitions, written in 1804, fuelled animosity between the nationalist first protomédico, José Ignacio García Jove, and the peninsular Serrano. Their exchanges are worth mentioning, as they have often been accepted at face value and cited as proof of the decadence of medical education in Mexico. Most critics have ignored the other factors that were at stake, such as the struggle for control over medical and surgical education and the nationalistic and political context of their disputes.[14] The ultra-nationalistic García Jove was not about to yield to a "foreigner," nor was he willing to accept the Protomedicato's loss of control over licensing and renounce one of the few sources of income the proto-médicos enjoyed.[15] The overarching conflict between medicine and surgery and between theoretical versus practical medical education thus was complicated by nationalistic feelings and the desperate financial situation of both teaching institutions.

THE SLOW AND GRADUAL PATH TO REFORM, 1822–1833

The end of colonial rule offered the opportunity to destroy the old structures and set the basis for a modern and progressive state. Physicians and surgeons seized this chance to push for medical education reform. The government did likewise. Legislators and politicians attending the first Congress assembled in independent Mexico (1822) made education a main item on the agenda, but their vision was different: for them, the education of the masses was an indispensable requirement for the imposition of a democratic system of government. Higher education had a different purpose, to raise Mexico to the level of the "civilized countries" they so much admired.[16] Legislators thus sought to design a comprehensive program that incorporated basic and higher education and fulfilled political and nationalistic goals. Such an approach failed, however, to recognize the unique needs of medical education and its place in the area of health care. It also ignored the importance of medical training for the welfare of the population and the connection between a healthy population and the creation of a strong state. Thus, for some politicians, the reform of medical education was only a small part of a general overhaul of the educational program designed to impose liberal ideologies, erase the colonial past, and promote progress as understood at the time. For more conservative reformers, it was a way to recognize and improve traditional institutions and to assert their preference for gradual change. However, medical education reform was not a priority, so it was usually underfunded, and the authorities were either reluctant or unable to cover the costs of proper installations and equipment. The ultimate result was less than satisfactory training for local practitioners and the hindering of medical development. Not surprisingly, those physicians who were able to afford it travelled abroad to "perfect" their studies.

Practitioners approached the issue from a different point of view. They realized that, in Mexico, war and political change had created a vacuum that allowed the enforcement of radical changes in medical education. Here was their opportunity to update the medical curriculum and raise professional standards. Physicians and surgeons were also aware that the monopoly over this knowledge and its transmission ensured their privileged position in the medical hierarchy. Thus, each branch of medicine considered educational reform an opportunity either to retain or to seize control of the profession; the ensuing struggle would not be resolved until 1831 with the physician-surgeon alliance. During the first decade after independence, the reorganization of education was shaped by the different and often conflicting approaches of politicians and practitioners and by the tensions within the latter group. Furthermore, it was not long before politicians used medical education, a pawn in the struggle for political control, for their own objectives.

In the 1820s, medical reformers faced two options: revamp the university curriculum or establish a separate medical school. All proposals submitted opted for the latter but disagreed on its organization and on the role the university should play. For physicians, direct control over all branches of medical education was crucial, if they were to maintain their position of leadership within the profession. Their own academic and professional superiority rested on the premise of their superior knowledge and the assumption that other health-care practitioners received only the instruction necessary to practise within the boundaries of their field. Surgeons disagreed and sought a system that would provide them with theoretical knowledge and raise their professional status. The reformers' different goals and the government's limited resources hindered advances and increased tensions among all participants.

In Mexico, reform of medical education and practice was part of the general reorganization of the country as an independent nation with a republican system of government. It was in this fluid political context that Mexican reformers tried to incorporate the new emphasis on observation and experimentation, and the anatomo-clinical approach that was transforming medicine into a modern science. The process, therefore, was slow and tortuous, the result of a continuous clash of interests and beliefs. Mexican practitioners followed medical developments taking place in France with great interest, as they appreciated the similarities between the two countries. In France, as in Mexico, war and political turmoil had caused a vacuum that permitted the state-led modernization of medical education and practice. Moreover, the central role played by the state in France, not unlike the traditional system in place in Mexico, did not escape the attention of reformers, who looked toward the French model and wanted to emulate it. They were well aware that the support of the state was indispensable and collaboration imperative, not only to achieve change but also to shape it.

In January 1822 the constitutional Congress struck a committee to prepare an educational plan.[17] At first, the efforts were characterized by democratic enthusiasm as both committee and Congress welcomed suggestions and invited interested parties to participate in the debate. They requested information from the rectors of the University of Mexico, the University of Guadalajara, the colleges of San Ildefonso, San Juan de Letrán, and San Gregorio, the Protomedicato, the director of the Botanical Garden, the president of the Academy of Jurisprudence, and the *provinciales* (heads) of religious orders. Soon after, the commission contacted the directors of the Colegio de Minería (mining college) and the surgical school, and a month later sent a reminder to all those previously contacted.[18] Unfortunately, the legislators' enthusiasm for democracy and educational improvement soon ran its course as political interests began to dominate; as Anne Staples accurately notes, "Education became a political weapon of groups that struggled for power."[19]

Those willing to participate responded to the committee's call (see table 4.1). The author of the first proposal presented to the committee was Antonio Serrano, director of the Escuela de Cirugía. Serrano, a Spanish military surgeon and advocate of the primacy of surgery over medicine, was probably reacting to the ongoing congressional debates on the abolition of the half-real tax that supported the Hospital de Naturales, seat of the surgical school.[20] He proposed the establishment of a college of "medical surgery" under the jurisdiction of either a "superior surgical governing board or supreme protomedicato of public health" formed by a president (the college director) and four directors (three college professors and the first military surgeon). He believed the size and "other advantages" (installations and probably patients) of the Hospital de Naturales made it the best location for the new military medical college. The army would be responsible for the salary of the first surgeon and his assistant (as in colonial times); the subsidies assigned to the hospital, the fees charged for the examinations of surgeons, phlebotomists, and dentists, as well as "any other fund that is not incompatible" would cover the remaining expenses. This, of course, was not Serrano's first petition to the authorities, nor did it differ from previous ones. For almost twenty years he had been trying to free the school from the Protomedicato's jurisdiction, efforts that had caused him numerous confrontations with the protomédicos. The proposal seems to have fallen on deaf ears, as the Congress closed down the Hospital de Naturales shortly thereafter and transferred its few patients to other hospitals to save itself the salaries of the few hospital employees.[21] The minimal savings achieved by this measure had drastic consequences for the surgical school, which was now deprived of a teaching hospital and cadavers for study. The decision also made the reform of surgical education more urgent.

Table 4.1 Medical education reform: Proposals and legislation, 1820–1870

1822	*Proyecto para establecer un colegio de cirugía médica* (Proposal to establish a medical surgical college), presented by Antonio Serrano *Memoria* (Treatise), presented by the Protomedicato
1823	*Memoria histórica* (Historical treatise), presented by Miguel Muñoz *Proyecto de Reglamento General de Instrucción Pública* (Public instruction regulations proposal)
1826	*Plan General de Instrucción Pública* (General plan for public instruction proposal)
1829	*Proyecto de reforma del Establecimiento Nacional de Cirujia* (Proposal to reform the National Surgical School), presented by Pedro del Villar
1833	General education reform legislation creates the Establecimiento de Ciencias Médicas –enforced
1834	*Plan Provisional de arreglo de estudios* (Provisional education plan) – enforced
1835	Official reinstatement of the National University The Establecimiento de Medicina becomes Colegio de Medicina
1838	*Proyecto Orgánico de la enseñanza médica* (Medical education organic project), presented by Casimiro Liceaga on behalf of the Medical College faculty
1840	*Sistema de educación médica* (Medical education system), presented by Manuel de Jesús Febles to the Mexico City municipal government
1842	*Reglamento de Enseñanza y policía médicas* (Medical education and public health regulations), issued by the Mexico City municipal government – enforced
1843	*Plan General de Estudios de la República Mexicana or Baranda Plan* (General studies plan) – enforced.
1846	23 October law grants more freedom to provincial governments on education – enforced
1854	*Reglamento General de Estudios or Lares Plan* (General education program) – enforced
1855	Colegio de Medicina becomes Escuela de Medicina
1857	*Ley de Instrucción Pública* (Public instruction law) National University closure – enforced
1865	*Ley de Instrucción Pública del Imperio* (Imperial public instruction law) – enforced
1867	*1857* legislation reinstated.
1868	*Ley Barreda* (Barreda law) Republican government reorganizes education according to positivist principles

Sources: AGN, Justicia e Instrucción, vol. 13, exp. 1, ff. 1–12; *Memoria*; Muñoz, *Memoria Histórica*; Proyecto de Reglamento General de Instrucción Pública, 1823; Proyecto sobre el Plan general de instrucción pública, 1826; AGN, Justicia e Instrucción, vol. 13, exp. 12, ff. 142–4; Bando of 21 October 1833; Bando of 26 October 1833; Plan Provisional para el arreglo de estudios, 1834; *Suplemento*; AGN, Justicia e Instrucción, vol. 14, exp. 20, ff. 152–67; AGN, Justicia e Instrucción, vol. 15, exp. 2, ff. 6–36v; AGN, Justicia e Instrucción, vol. 14, exp. 45, f. 334; vol. 15, exp. 27, ff. 222v–3; *Reglamento de Enseñanza y policia médicas*, 44; Plan general de estudios, 1843, Decree of 18 August 1843; Mendoza Cornejo, *Ciento setenta años* 135, 157–63; Plan general de estudios, decree of 19 December 1854; Ley de Instrucción Pública del Imperio, 27 December 1865; Meneses Morales, *Tendencias educativas*, 188, 244–5.

The same year, the Protomedicato sent its own proposal, the already mentioned *Memoria* (see chapter 2).[22] Following the French example, the *Memoria* proposed a medical and natural sciences college under the aegis of a general public health tribunal, thus effectively uniting medical and surgical studies. To be admitted into the program, a candidate would require a bachelor's degree in philosophy and a certificate of good conduct. The proposed curriculum included courses on chemistry, botany, pharmacy, anatomy, physiology, general pathology, hygiene and "legal" (forensic) medicine, surgical operations, and practical or clinical medicine, which would be credited toward a university medical degree (table 4.1). After completing the program, the aspiring practitioner would be examined on his knowledge of medical theory. The exam would follow university tradition: the applicant would open the work of "a select author" at random and give a thirty-minute presentation covering the relevant medical and surgical theories and answer all questions asked. The next day, the candidate would prove his practical skills by undergoing a hands-on examination on "the most difficult surgical operation available" and responding to examiners' questions.

On financing the new college, the *Memoria* showed more initiative than other proposals. In addition to the traditional examination and pharmacy inspection fees, it proposed to apply *contratas* (tenders) on medicinal substances for pharmacies and municipal hospitals managed by the proposed general public health tribunal for the maintenance of the medical college. If necessary, these funds could be complemented with the profits of a printing press and any other sources "compatible with [the college's] objectives."[23]

By placing medical education under the jurisdiction of a proposed public health tribunal the protomédicos sought to strengthen their own and the physicians' positions. The proposal would increase the jurisdiction of the Protomedicato to include the medical program offered by the University of Guadalajara as well as the one proposed by Puebla, thus reaffirming its position as the national health authority. It was an attempt to reinvent and revamp the Protomedicato by reclaiming the legal status as a tribunal it had lost in 1812, giving it financial independence, and officially sanctioning it as the country's highest authority in the health care area. Although undoubtedly self-serving, the *Memoria* indicates the protomédicos' desire to reform medical education and their willingness to dissociate themselves from the university and its uncertain future. One of the proposal's signatories was the first protomédico and retired professor, José Ignacio García Jove. A representative of the Protomedicato's "old guard," García Jove was then in his seventies and in poor health (he died shortly after), so the degree of his input is questionable. Nonetheless, his signature indicates he supported the document.[24] The *Memoria* was also signed by the much younger protomédico Manuel de Jesús Febles, later a member of the Facultad Médica, who would contribute enormously to educational reform and collaborate with the government in the organization of the Consejo Superior de Salubridad.

Congressman and surgeon Miguel Muñoz firmly refuted the *Memoria* and presented to Congress his own *Memoria historica*.[25] Muñoz illustrated the possibilities that were opening to hardworking individuals at the time. Born into a poor family, Muñoz had worked since an early age to help his widowed mother. He obtained his phlebotomist's licence in 1798, continued his education at the Escuela de Cirugía, and obtained his surgeon's degree in 1807.[26] He also designed various ophthalmological instruments and an orthopaedic prosthesis that contributed to improving his professional and socio-economic status.[27] Given his background, neither his distaste for elitist, university-trained physicians nor his belief in the superiority of surgery, is surprising; both are reflected in the *Memoria histórica*, which may be described more as an attack on traditional medicine than a plan for reform.

Muñoz favoured a college under the supervision of a junta or committee to ensure an "intelligent" (knowledgeable) staff and the best textbooks. He did not provide specific details on the college's organization or its internal administration; neither did he describe its curriculum, except that it should have a strong clinical component. Muñoz agreed with Serrano on the priority of surgical over medical instruction, but, unlike Serrano, he envisioned an independent civilian institution that would produce practitioners with a well-rounded knowledge, or what he described as "the science of man."[28] The *Memoria historica* illustrates Muñoz's familiarity with Western authors and his admiration for French medicine, which he repeatedly praised. It also illustrates the rapidly closing gap between medical and surgical knowledge and their practitioners.

While individual practitioners presented their visions of medical education, legislators worked on broader educational reform. In 1823, ministers Lucas Alamán and Pablo de la Llave appointed a commission headed by Jacobo Villaurrutia to draw up a public education plan. The result, the *Proyecto de Reglamento General de Instrucción Pública* (Proposal for the general regulation of public Instruction; henceforth *1823 Proyecto*), was presented to Congress in December 1823. It divided education into three levels – primary, secondary, and superior – and centralized its administration. The section titled "Pharmacy, Surgery, and Medicine" included 47 articles (out of a total of 207) and, following the French example, proposed establishing "special schools" in the capital and provinces to teach the three branches of medicine and issue the corresponding degrees. The program consisted of twelve courses; eleven would be taught at the schools and the remaining one, forensic medicine, at the university, the only institution that could issue doctoral degrees. Interested students would require the degree of *bachiller* from the National University as well as knowledge of French, Greek, Latin grammar, logics, experimental physics, and chemistry "of the animal, vegetable and mineral kingdoms." The *1823 Proyecto* also provided for the establishment of a midwifery school, clarifying that, until this was established, women would be taught at the medical school. Two old Protomedicato rivals, Antonio Serrano and the director of the botanical garden Vicente Cervantes, collaborated with the authorities on the *1823 Proyecto*. Although the final draft did not conform to Serrano's earlier proposal, his endorsement indicates his flexibility and willingness to cooperate in drawing up a workable plan. The above proposals to modernize medical education and the *1823 Proyecto* illustrate the different views and objectives of medical and surgical reformers and their willingness to expose and debate their ideas. They also reflect the democratic ideals of those in power and their hopes for the new nation during the first post-independence years.

Regardless of its merits, the timing of the *1823 Proyecto* doomed any possibility of its success. In early 1824, Mexico was declared a federalist republic, so the power of the central government over the provinces (now states) was severely limited, making the *Proyecto*'s national scope obsolete.[29] Medical reformers and legislators would have to go back to the drawing board. On 14 February 1826, a commission charged with drawing up a proposal for the reform of medical education in the context of a federalist and more radical system of government presented its work to Congress. Its eleven-course curriculum was almost identical to the program of the *1823 Proyecto*, modified only to fit the new circumstances.[30] To reduce expenses, the new proposal stated that the eleven instructors teaching at the school would form a "Facultad Médica de la Federación" in charge of health-related issues in the capital and its territories. An important innovation was that instructors would no longer be required to hold a doctorate (and therefore to have attended university); furthermore, although the document continued to refer to the courses as *cátedras*, it uses the term *professor* as opposed to the more traditional *catedrático*, a word linked to university education and the colonial past.[31] The intentions of the new proposal, a reflection of government priorities, are clear: to erase the memory of colonial times and disassociate itself from surviving colonial institutions, the university and the surgical school (which the document does not even mention), to modernize the medical program, and to achieve reforms in a time of budgetary constraints. The change in tone foreshadows future and more radical changes and illustrates the evolving ideology of the reformers. The 1826 proposal was another step towards reform and, although it remained only a proposal, it influenced future reforms and legislation.

The 1826 medical education proposal was inserted with some modifications into a general education plan presented in October of the same year under the title *Proyecto sobre el plan general de instrucción pública* (henceforth *1826 Plan general*). This new and more detailed plan also divided education into three levels, making each a requirement of admission to the next; the highest educational tier would be formed by medicine (which included surgery and pharmacy), theology, civil and ecclesiastical jurisprudence, and military science.[32] Reflecting a concern for higher education, the *1826 Plan general* also included the establishment of a "general academy" to improve the secondary and higher levels of education, and an Academy of Sciences to both evaluate textbooks and produce a national scientific publication. The eleven-course medical curriculum presented seven months earlier was trimmed to eight courses and as many instructors. The *1826 Plan general* neither specified the roles reserved for the surgical school and the university Faculty of Medicine nor proposed to abolish them, mentioning only their funds.[33] Although, like its predecessor, the *1826 Plan general* never materialized, it illustrates the slow pace of reform, the collaborative effort of physicians, surgeons, and legislators, and the continuity between early proposals and the 1833 educational reform.

Two years later, with the reform of medical education looming, Escuela de Cirugía graduate and military surgeon Pedro del Villar presented a detailed proposal to improve the surgical school. Following in the footsteps of Serrano, del Villar proposed an *establecimiento nacional de cirujía* (national surgical establishment) under the academic and administrative direction of the military sanitary corps director (*consultor*) – who at the time was del Villar himself. The aim of this independent military institution and replacement of the decadent Escuela de Cirugía would be to place military surgery on firmer ground by adding chemistry, botany, physiology, *materia médica* (pharmacology), and obstetrics to the anatomy and operations courses already offered. Under the general category of "surgery," students would learn anatomy and physiology in the first two years. The former would be taught in the morning and the latter in the afternoon to make the most of the limited space available, each class to last two hours. The third year included *materia médica*, surgical therapeutics, and presumably midwifery, which would be taught in a separate area.[34] From April to the end of September (the period between courses) second- and third-level students would attend chemistry and botany lessons. To restrict the number of students, registrations would take place every three years, because "it is better to have ten well-trained students than thirty ignorant ones."[35] After completing all courses, the aspiring surgeon would begin a two-year internship, the last requirement to complete the program. The *establecimiento nacional de cirujía* would have the right to examine and license its graduates and to collect the pertinent fees.[36] Both del Villar and Serrano aimed to create an independent military surgical school and a surgical program backed by theoretical courses, prioritized surgery over medicine, and kept both branches separate. The two proposals were ignored, and the army continued to offer its own medical training, a parallel system that would challenge all efforts to streamline medical education and practice for years to come.[37]

The proposals illustrate the views of the various interested parties and the tensions among them. First, there is a noticeable difference between the proposals put forward by medical or surgical practitioners on the one hand, and those drawn up on behalf of the government on the other. The former approached medical education reform as an intrinsic part of professional modernization, underlining the importance of clinical medicine and the proposed institution's need of an attached teaching hospital. Their focus was on theoretical and practical instruction to be provided at independent teaching institutions directed by specialized professionals, without great concern for the larger context of general education. Rooted in the practitioners' world, the teaching institutions proposed would be funded by resources already earmarked for health-related matters, licensing and pharmacy inspections fees, hospitals' properties and other resources, and even a monopoly over medical supplies.

The reforms proposed by the Protomedicato, Serrano, Muñoz, and del Villar betray the physician-surgeon rivalry, now entangled in a military-civilian dichotomy. As military surgeons, Serrano and del Villar concentrated on raising the status of surgery and adhered to its traditional separation from medicine. Both sought to establish independent military surgical schools beyond the reach of civilian institutions and authorities. Although Miguel Muñoz's *Memoria histórica* is far from being a surgical education proposal, it agreed with the vision of the well-rounded surgeon knowledgeable in medicine and, following French terminology, in the "science of man."[38] The protomédicos, on the other hand, envisioned a medical school that included surgical training under the direction of a physician-controlled body – the continuation of the colonial Protomedicato. Their intentions were clear: to improve education and to continue in control of the medical hierarchy. Ironically, by calling for the union of the three main medical branches, theirs was the most forward-looking proposal.

For the legislators, the reform of medical education was a part of an overall education project that classed medical, legal, and theological studies together as "higher education," and separated medical studies from the world of science to which it belonged. Thus, medical education became one of many areas to be financed from a general education fund that was usually insufficient to cover necessary expenses. The educational reforms of the 1830s followed this approach and resulted in a medical school with insufficient funding, unpaid faculty, and inadequate hospital infrastructure. The tensions between both approaches would continue to hinder the medical elite's efforts to improve education and to raise Mexican medicine to the level of a "civilized nation."

THE 1833 EDUCATIONAL REFORMS:
CHANGE OR CONTINUITY

Most authors consider the 1833 education reform as the watershed that separates colonial obscurantism from modernity in Mexico.

Flores y Troncoso describes 1833 as a "memorable year" for Mexican science, a year that "must be written in golden letters in the annals of Mexican medicine." He adds, it was "the immortal" [Valentín] Gómez Farías, the "most courageous champion of the Reform," who single-handedly brought down "the ancient and legendary edifice of old and routine metaphysical knowledge."[39] The same theme has been repeated numerous times. Elí de Gortari, for example, credits Gómez Farías with "instilling in the youth the spirit of research and of doubt ... instead of dogmatism and debate."[40] Ignacio Chávez states, "The government of Valentín Gómez Farías created the Establecimiento de Ciencias Médicas where he reunited the careers of physician and surgeon and formed an advanced program of eleven courses."[41] More recent authors follow the same approach. Ann Staples refers to "the renovation of the medical studies, that gave the most spectacular leap from 1833 on, occupies a distinguished place in the history of Mexican education ... from being the least prestigious [medicine] became the first in innovation and creative spirit. It opened the door to scientific modernity, the experimental method and to a better communication with the European medical community."[42] Martha Eugenia Rodríguez concurs: "Academic medical education in México, that goes back to the sixteenth century, begins its modernization in the first third of the nineteenth century ... with the educational reform undertaken by Vice-president Valentín Gómez Farías, physician and liberal who put an end to institutions established in colonial times."[43] Even Ernesto Meneses Morales, who points out "the continuity of ideas and participating individuals," states that Gómez Farías reorganized education within a general plan and created a general directorate of public education.[44]

The simplicity and dichotomy of this approach is troublesome for many reasons. First, it reflects the traditional simplistic, black-and-white view of contemporary politics.[45] Second, it assumes the reforms represented a sudden break with the past, a view that is contradicted by the numerous proposals submitted and the consultative nature of the process. Third, it implies the legislators' imposition of a curriculum on a field beyond their area of expertise and ignores the important role played by practitioners, reformers, and university representatives in the process of reform.

The first point calls for a closer, politically unprejudiced analysis of the 1833 and 1834 reforms and their consequences. The traditional interpretation of the 1833 medical education reforms reflects the dualistic approach cultivated by nineteenth-century political historians. Conservative ideology and colonial institutions are equated to obscurantism, or what the positivist Flores y Troncoso describes as "metaphysic." "Liberals," on the other hand, represent the modernity and progress of the positive era. Twentieth-century authors followed the same general dichotomy, concentrating on the achievements of liberal historical figures. Thus, Gómez Farías has been praised as the "patriarch of the reform,"[46] or the enlightened politician who brought about the reform of medical education, while Santa Anna has been vilified for his decision to cancel such reforms. But the historical context indicates that much more was at play.

The political events of 1833 do not need to be recounted in detail. In 1832, Antonio López de Santa Anna became president of Mexico, but, claiming ill health, returned to his Veracruz hacienda in April of the following year, leaving the government in the hands of his vice president, Valentín Gómez Farías.[47] The radical Gómez Farías, surrounded by a like-minded Congress, proceeded to reorganize the country. The brunt of the reforms was felt by the military and the church, powerful corporations that opposed the reformers and offended liberal principles. Congress tried to bring the military under control by eliminating its *fueros* (privileges) and creating local militias to counterbalance its power. The church required a different approach. Reformers focused on its wealth, with two aims in mind: to undercut its authority and to bring much-needed funds into the government's coffers. Corporations closely connected with the church, such as the National University, were seriously affected by these reforms. The reform of education was as much about weakening the church by seizing its educational institutions as it was about modernizing the curriculum. The problem of financing was solved by forcing the university and its colleges to underwrite the costs of educational reform. The innovative nature of the medical education reforms so praised by de Gortari, Chávez, Staples, Rodríguez, and Meneses Morales, among others, is contradicted by the many congressional debates and proposals of the previous years. So is the praise given the legislators for approving reforms that had been in the works for almost a decade. To appreciate the nature and evolution of these reforms, one must scrutinize the 1833 changes and compare them to previous proposals.

The decree of 19 October 1833 centralized education by establishing the Dirección de Instrucción Pública del Distrito Federal y

Territorios, a directorate of public education presided over by the vice president. It also abolished the National University and placed its building and properties under the control of the new director- ate.[48] Another decree (26 October 1833), reminiscent of the 1826 general education plan, divided education into three levels: primary, preparatory, and higher studies. From an organizational point of view, the latest program was the logical continuation of previous proposals. It added "preparatory studies" and "ideological studies and humanities" to the higher education subdivisions proposed in 1826, and kept the remaining four with slight modifications. Theol- ogy became "ecclesiastical studies," military science changed its name to "physics and mathematics," civil and ecclesiastical juris- prudence adopted the simpler label of "jurisprudence," and medi- cine became "medical science." The university and its colleges were replaced by six new teaching institutions now called *establecimien- tos* (establishments) to erase any links with the former institution. The Establecimiento de Ciencias Médicas was assigned the old con- vent of Belén, the last location of the surgical school that the same reforms abolished, leaving it as the only institution teaching a medi- cal program in the capital.[49]

Academically, the 1833 medical program had great similarities to the proposal presented in 1826. Only the natural history course was moved "down," becoming a requisite for acceptance. Other courses required to enter the program were "elements of arithmetic," alge- bra, geometry and logic, physics, botany, and chemistry, as well as two courses of Latin and one of French.[50] A brief comparison with previous proposals illustrates the evolution, rather than revolution, in medical education.

In its 1823 *Memoria*, the Protomedicato had proposed a six-year program with successive courses of (presumably basic) chemistry and botany during the first year, pharmacy and chemistry applied to medicine in the second, and anatomy and physiology in the third. Medical students would spend their fourth year studying two courses, hygiene and forensic medicine, and general pathology. The final two years would be dedicated to "external clinic" (surgical clin- ical studies) and "internal clinic" (medical clinical studies), respec- tively.[51] It is worth noting that this proposal focused exclusively on medical education, as the protomédicos had no power or jurisdic- tion over other areas or levels of education (table 4.2).

Table 4.2 Medical education programs, 1823–1833

1823 Memoria	1826 Plan General	1833 Program	1834 Plan Provisional
Anatomy	General and descriptive anatomy	General and descriptive anatomy	General and descriptive anatomy
Botany			
Medical and surgical clinic	Surgical clinic	Surgical clinic	Surgical clinic
	Medical clinic	Medical clinic	Medical clinic
Pharmacy	Theoretical and practical pharmacy	Theoretical and practical pharmacy	Theoretical and practical pharmacy
Physiology	Physiology and hygiene	Physiology and hygiene	Physiology and hygiene
Hygiene and forensic medicine	Forensic medicine	Forensic medicine	Forensic medicine*
	Natural history		
Surgical operations	Surgical operations and obstetrics	Surgical operations and obstetrics	Obstetrics
General pathology	Surgical pathology	Surgical pathology	Surgical pathology
	Medical pathology	Medical pathology	Medical pathology
Chemistry			
			Hippocratic medicine*

*Courses taught at the National University

Sources: *Memoria*, 1823; Proyecto sobre el plan general de instrucción pública, 1826; Bando of 26 October 1833; Plan provisional para el arreglo de estudios, 1834.

The main difference between the Protomedicato's *Memoria* and the *1826 Plan General* presented by the appointed congressional commission was to move chemistry and botany to the secondary level of education, making them, along with physics (not mentioned by the protomédicos), requisites for admission. Other changes included adding natural history, relabelling the pharmacy course as "theoretical and practical pharmacy," and reshuffling other courses; legal medicine became a subject on its own, and hygiene was added to physiology. Finally, obstetrics was incorporated into the surgical operations course. Unfortunately, the *1826 Plan General* did not specify the order in which the courses would be taught, but we may assume it was similar to the previous one[52] (table 4.2).

The 1833 medical curriculum had few academic innovations, deviating only on two points from the previous proposal: *materia médica* was added to the program and natural history was "demoted" to *estudios preparatorios,* the second educational level.[53] Thus, the 1833 program was very much like the *1826 Plan General* proposed to Congress, which itself was based on the program suggested by the Protomédicos in their 1823 *Memoria.* The 1833 medical program was the result of a gradual evolution and the collaborative efforts of practitioners, reformers, and the university Faculty of Medicine represented by Manuel de Jesús Febles, rather than of a confrontation between a retrograde university and some enlightened reformers, as portrayed by traditional historiography[54] (table 4.2). From the beginning, physicians and surgeons were asked to present their views and have input into the process; some practitioners, such as Miguel Muñoz and Manuel Carpio, were members of Congress and participated in the debates.[55] The supposed sudden break with the past is a myth, further challenged by the appointment of Casimiro Liceaga as director of the new Establecimiento de Ciencias Médicas. As a university graduate, holder of a doctorate in medicine, catedrático of Hippocratic medicine, and one of the last protomédicos, Liceaga was indeed an odd choice for an institution seeking to make a clean break with the past.

President Santa Anna's return to the capital in May 1834 marked the end of the educational (and other) reforms. They were officially abolished in July, the educational institutions that had been shut down in 1833 were reinstated, and the new "establishments" were abolished. On 13 November 1834 the government announced a *Plan Provisional de Educación,* explaining that, as the previous reforms were impracticable, "His Excellency the President" had requested a group of "notoriously learned persons" to present a new education proposal agreeable with the allocated funding and the teaching of modern science (table 4.2).

Only the Establecimiento de Ciencias Médicas survived this round of legislation. After an inspection by an appointed committee, the new institution reopened with the name of Colegio de Medicina, to indicate its attachment and subjection to the reinstated university.[56] The medical curriculum was reworked to allow the incorporation of forensic medicine, Hippocratic medicine, and natural science as university courses, and, once again, entry to the program required a baccalaureate in philosophy. The five-year program was divided into three years of theoretical studies that earned the student the degree of bachelor in medicine, and two years of higher university courses and clinical practice (table 4.2). The Colegio de Medicina would grant the bachelor of medicine degree and the university the degrees of *licenciado* (master's degree) and *doctor*, a compromise that did not satisfy either institution but that both were forced to accept. After fulfilling these requirements, the applicant could apply to the re-established Facultad Médica for his licensing examination.[57]

The changes were more of form than of substance; the guidelines of the medical curriculum already had been set, as the 1838, 1843, and 1854 programs indicate. There would be some fine-tuning, courses would be updated, and textbooks would be changed, but, broadly speaking, the same program would remain in place until the late nineteenth century, when the new principles resulting from the acceptance of the new science of bacteriology demanded a thorough reform.

ADAPTING THE PARIS SCHOOL

The curriculum offered at the Establecimiento de Ciencias Médicas and its successors was clearly shaped after the French *officiat*, a four-year medical program[58] that enabled its graduates to practise medicine under certain restrictions. Originally designed to provide basic medical and surgical knowledge to army practitioners, it was later adapted to serve the needs of low-income and provincial students who could not afford expensive city life and more costly universities in Paris, Montpellier, or Strasbourg. It allowed interested individuals to attend instead any of twenty-two less costly *écoles preparatoires* located throughout France.[59] In Mexico, animosity toward the National University and its sad condition made the officiat most attractive to reformers.

Important differences between the programs offered in France and in Mexico were their length and intensity. The officiat consisted of twenty-three courses on eleven different topics, as well as two semesters of dissections (which the Mexican curriculum excluded).[60] These translated into a minimum of three and a maximum of five daily sixty- or ninety-minute classes, six days a week – three and a half to six and a half hours of instruction a day, depending on the semester and year.[61] In contrast, in Mexico, the 1838 provisional curriculum of the Colegio de Medicina consisted of three annual courses (and a clinical course) during the second, third, and fourth years and only two during the first and fifth years. Each course amounted to three hours of instruction a week (classes were one hour in length) except for the daily clinical courses. Thus, Mexican students received only between twelve and fifteen hours of classes a week. Although Febles had proposed daily courses, the Colegio de Medicina firmly resisted, arguing it was impossible to prepare daily lectures, especially for the anatomy course. The difference may well have depended on the number of faculty available to teach in the respective countries' institutions: since 1823, the Paris École de Santé had had fifteen academic posts, while in 1838 the Colegio de Medicina counted only nine instructors. Although instructors at the French school had to supplement their insufficient income with private practice, in Mexico during the initial period the catedráticos received only irregular compensation, if any, for their classes, and were understandably reluctant to commit more time to instruction at the expense of their private practices (table 4.3).[62]

Despite these adjustments, reformers tried to adhere to the teachings of the Paris school, as the textbooks required by the 1833 program show. These included *Nuevo manual de anatomía* (Madrid, 1820), a Spanish translation of Jacques Pierre Maygrier's *Manuel de l'anatomiste,* for the anatomy course; Francois Magendie's *Précis élémentaire de physiologie* and Etienne Tourtelle's *Histoire philosophique de la médecine* for the physiology and hygiene course; the *Nouveaux éléments de pathologie médicochirurgicale* by Louis Charles Roche for both internal and external pathology; the Spanish translation of Jacques Coster's text *Manual de operaciones quirúrgicas* (Madrid, 1830) and *Manuel d'obstétrique ou traité de la science et de l'art des accouchements* by Antoine Louis Dugés for surgery and obstetrics; *Manuel complet de médicine légale* by Joseph Briand was the textbook of forensic medicine; and for the internal and external clinic, Alphonse M. Tabernier's *Manuel de clinique chirurgicale* and the Spanish translation of Louis Martinet's work (*Compendio de clínica médica*, Gerona, 1827). The texts for theoretical and practical pharmacy and for *materia médica* were the *Journal de chimie médicale de pharmacie et toxicologie*[63] and Jean Baptiste Grégoire Barbier's *Traité élémentaire de matière médicale.*[64] Later, textbooks changed to reflect the curriculum's modifications and updating. In 1845 we find, among other changes, the 1840 Spanish translation of Joseph François Malgaigne's work, *Manual de medicina operatoria* as the required textbook for the surgery course taught by José María Vértiz; Eugène Soubeiran's *Nouveau traité de pharmacie: théorique et pratique* as the choice for the

Table 4.3 The *Officiat* and the 1834 curriculum

	Officiat (semester courses)	1842 Regulations issued by the Mexico City Municipal Government (year courses)*
FIRST YEAR	Anatomy and dissections Physiology Medical chemistry** Medical natural history** Pharmacy	Anatomy Physiology and hygiene
SECOND YEAR	Anatomy and dissections Pathology Internal pathology External clinic Physiology	Anatomy Pathology 1 Pharmacy Clinic 1
THIRD YEAR	Internal pathology External pathology Internal and external clinic Operatory medicine (Surgery) Obstetrics	Pathology 1 Pathology 2 Clinic 2 Operatory medicine (Surgery)
FOURTH YEAR	Pathology Medical clinic Operatory medicine (Surgery) Obstetrics *Materia medica*	Pathology 2 Clinic 1 Operatory medicine (Surgery) Therapeutics and *Materia medica*
FIFTH YEAR		Obstetrics and child illnesses Forensic medicine Clinic 2

*These are the first regulations that specify the courses taught at each level.

**Courses taught in Mexico at the secondary or preparatory level

Sources: Palluault, "Medical Students in England and France 1815–1858: A Comparative Study," 34–6; *Reglamento de estudios médicos*.

combined course of natural history and pharmacy; and J.L. Lassaigne's *Dictionnaire des réactifs chimiques employés dans toutes les expériences* for Leopoldo Río de la Loza's chemistry course. The internal clinic was now based on M.A. Raciborski's *Précis pratique et raisonné du diagnostic* (probably one of its Spanish translations, *Resumen práctico y razonado del diagnóstico*), which continued to be used in 1855.[65] This year more changes had taken place: students were reading, among others, the works of Jamain, Bérard, Richard, and Bouchardat;[66] and Ladislao de la Pascua and Leopoldo Río de la Loza were using their own textbooks, *Introducción al estudio de la física* (1853) and *Introducción al estudio de la química* (1850) in addition to the French texts (Nicolas Deguin's *Cours élémentaire de physique* and Jules Theóphile Pelouze and Edmond Frémy's *Abrège de chimie: Chimie organique*).[67] In summary, twenty years after the Escuela de Medicina's founding, the large majority of the courses were based on French authors, the exception being the Polish Raciborski, the Spanish Pedro Mata,[68] and the two Mexican authors. As late as 1874, the Escuela de Medicina's students continued to learn medicine from French authors, with the exception of Wagner and Uhle's *Handbook of General Pathology*[69] and the two textbooks that Leopoldo Río de la Loza and Luis Hidalgo y Carpio wrote to complement the French works they used.[70]

The choice of the officiat as a model, the textbooks selected, and the emphasis on the Paris school are not surprising. The latter's influence started early in the century. Among its first promoters was Manuel Carpio, a great admirer of Laennec and Bichat and a founder of the Establecimiento de Ciencias Médicas. In 1823, after spending time in Paris "perfecting his studies," he published a Spanish translation of an article on the *pectoriloquo* (stethoscope).[71] It is difficult to assess the impact of his translation, but his later publication "Heart Sounds" in the first volume of the *Periódico de la Academia de Medicina de Mégico* (1836) indicates that his interest in the topic continued.[72] Thus, we may infer he communicated his enthusiasm for Laennec's teachings to colleagues as well as students. Carpio was one of the first promoters of the Paris school but he was not the only one. As the writings and medical education proposals presented by his contemporaries illustrate, practitioners were well versed in French medicine. In the already mentioned 1823 *Memoria Histórica*, surgeon Miguel Muñoz praised Bichat and the "Paris pathological and physiological innovations" when he proposed to study "the science of man."[73] Only three years later, various practitioners established an academy of practical medicine "to promote the advances of all medical branches, especially pathology."[74] The presence of French physicians and surgeons like Louis Estevan Blaquiere, Pablo Lefevre, Gabriel Villette de Terze, and Juan Louis Chavert reinforced this trend. Blaquiere held the degree of doctor in medicine from the Paris Academy[75] and had decided to move to Mexico to carry out research; Lefevre's impressive credentials included doctorates in medicine and surgery from the University of Paris issued in 1821 and 1825 respectively, and membership in arts, agricultural, and industrial academic societies, and various official commendations (see chapter 2);[76] and Villette had attended the University of Paris and obtained his doctorate in medicine in 1825.[77] He and his colleague Theodore Leger, also a Paris graduate, published the first public health journal in Mexico in the 1830s.[78] Chavert held degrees from Paris and Louisiana and, as an expert on yellow fever, in 1822 he had been commissioned by the Mexican government to research a cure for this dreaded disease. The results of his work, translated into Spanish by Casimiro Liceaga, were published in Mexico under the title *Reflexiones medicas y observaciones sobre la fiebre amarilla en Veracruz*.[79] French practitioners directly influenced the medical school. When it opened its doors in 1833, two of the ten faculty members had first-hand experience with the Paris school, and the Swiss Louis Jecker held a French medical degree.[80] Two years later, Villette de Terze took over from Ignacio Erazo as obstetrics professor and Jecker continued teaching surgery.[81] In 1846, seven out of eleven instructors had attended the Paris school (two of them, Agustín Andrade and Pablo Martínez del Río, held Paris doctorates), and in 1855 half of the faculty had travelled to Paris.[82] Among the latter was Gabino Barreda, who would later reorganize higher education according to positivist ideology. As late as 1874, instructors educated in the Paris school continued to teach at the Escuela de Medicina.[83]

In Mexico, the impact of the Paris school was profound and long lasting. Not only did the Paris school define the medical curriculum, but the textbooks used forced students to immerse themselves in its teachings. John Harley Warner's analysis of the Paris school legacy in American medicine gives us a point of comparison. Warner found that approximately a thousand American practitioners had travelled to Paris between 1815 and 1850s. Although important conduits of French medicine to their country, the Paris school students were selective in the practices and experiences they sought to spread. Their enthusiasm for research often dampened in a sometimes hostile environment; and their Paris school teachings were gradually absorbed into the large body of general medicine. Nonetheless, they created an interest in French texts, which began to be translated into

English, and in European instruments, which were first imported and then locally manufactured. The main obstacle the returnees encountered, it seems, was cultural, as American society shared few commonalities with French culture. The large role of the French state, the centralization of teaching and hospitals, the monopoly of practice, and the emphasis on morbid anatomy ran counter to the most cherished values of their fellow Americans.[84] In summary, although their contribution laid the basis of postwar medicine, its effects were gradual and low key. In contrast, the Mexican case shows that, although relatively few Mexican practitioners travelled to Paris, the impact of French medicine was immediate and dramatic. The Paris school reached Mexico in the early 1820s and its influence increased in the following decades, when the medical education curriculum was in its formative years and continued until at least the last quarter of the nineteenth century. The medical program was fashioned after the officiat, articles on France's medical and public health innovations, statistics, and hospitals appeared regularly in local medical journals (see chapter 5), and French texts continued to be used throughout the nineteenth century. Unlike the American case, cultural prejudices were never an issue, and Paris school students proudly flaunted their knowledge and experiences. By 1886, as attested by the work of Flores y Troncoso, physicians continued to view *la culta Francia* as a main centre of medical education and research.

STRUGGLE FOR SURVIVAL: THE MEDICAL COLLEGE, THE SURGICAL SCHOOL, AND THE NATIONAL UNIVERSITY, 1833–1857

By turning the clock back and abolishing the reforms of the previous year, the 1834 legislation gave a last breath to the dying Escuela de Cirugía and brought to the fore the rivalry between military and civilian medical education. Since independence, the school's directors had fought for the Escuela's survival. Serrano had tried everything within his power to convince the authorities of the urgent need for and benefits of a surgical school but had failed. The surgical school's precarious situation was aggravated during the Parián riots of December 1828, when the mob sacked and destroyed its already sparse equipment; only the instruments and records that Serrano had taken home for cataloguing survived the disturbance. In July

1830, Serrano's successor, Juan Santibáñez, requested 400 pesos to replace the lost equipment as well as the 500 pesos "mentioned in the chambers by the minister of relations" to cover the school's expenses and his own salary.[85] The dismal condition of the Escuela de Cirugía described by Santibáñez is confirmed by the short inventory Serrano took soon after the riots. The ten-page list referred mainly to school records and legislation, with only three pages dedicated to furniture and instruments, some of them replacements for those lost, donated by Serrano himself.[86]

The abrogation of the 1833 educational legislation resurrected the defunct school, once again frustrating the physicians' quest for unification and monopoly. Tensions increased when Santibáñez's successor, the latin surgeon Miguel García, reignited physician-surgeon antagonism by asking the Facultad Médica to exempt his students temporarily from the required medical examination. García argued, not unreasonably, that the suspension of medical courses at both the Colegio de Medicina and the university prevented students from fulfilling such a requirement. Therefore, he requested they be examined as surgeons (and presumably be allowed to practise as such) and be given an extension to comply with regulations. Tactlessly, García pointed out that, as the courses offered by the Colegio de Medicina in 1836 had not been officially sanctioned, they "lacked legality."[87] It was not the first time García had gone head-to-head with the Colegio de Medicina. Two years before, he had written to the authorities claiming his post of "national professor of surgery" entitled him to the appointment of anatomy professor at the Colegio de Medicina. He resented the appointment of the foreigner Guillermo Cheyne when he had served as a substitute professor for years, without any payment. To add insult to injury, when Cheyne refused the post, it had been offered to the Swiss Louis Jecker. García's claims and resentment must be placed in perspective: in colonial times the Escuela de Cirugía's preference for peninsulares had been notorious, a situation that continued after independence; it took more than fifty years before the Escuela de Cirugía had its first local professor, the criollo Juan Santibáñez.[88]

Stung by the claims that "its" Colegio de Medicina stood on shaky legal ground, the Facultad Médica reacted aggressively. First, it refused García's request on the grounds that the intimate connection of all medical branches made it impossible to isolate surgery and allow students to take an examination only in the surgical field (as

had been done only four years before). As to García's claims regarding the medical program, the Facultad Médica counterattacked by
accusing him of not holding a proper appointment and by stating
that "his" Escuela de Cirugía had ceased to exist by virtue of the
1833 educational reforms.[89] As the 1834 legislation had excluded
all medical institutions, the 1833 reforms had remained in place and,
consequently, the surgical school did not legally exist.[90] But the
government disagreed with such an interpretation and, opposing
objections raised by the physicians, declared both institutions "not
incompatible" and ordered the Colegio de Medicina to return the
equipment received from the Escuela de Cirugía as a result of the
1833 reforms.[91] The Escuela de Cirugía was proving to be a thorn in
the side of the medical leadership and an impediment to the completion of their plans.

The death of Miguel García in late 1837 changed the prevailing
situation. The directorship of the Escuela de Cirugía now went to
Manuel Andrade, a younger French-educated physician-surgeon
more attuned to the times.[92] Andrade faced problems similar to
those of his predecessors. In 1838 he requested the reimbursement of
143 pesos of his own money spent to cover the Escuela de Cirugía's
expenses; a few months later, he was still waiting to be paid.[93] The
national government eventually authorized the payment, but it is
unclear if Andrade ever received it.[94] Later in the year, the Escuela de
Cirugía was closed definitively and Andrade was appointed substitute professor of anatomy[95] at the reopened Colegio de Medicina.[96]
He was soon given a permanent position in the new institution, and
continued teaching for at least seven years.[97] In theory, the closure of
the Escuela de Cirugía was the final chapter in the merging of both
branches of medicine and a victory for the medical leadership. In
practice, surgical instruction continued in the Hospital de Instrucción
(Teaching hospital) of San Hipólito and other military hospitals,
ensuring the separation of physicians and surgeons for years to
come. The battle for control over medical education and the physician-surgeon rivalry was not over yet.

The other institution that prevented the medical elite from having
a monopoly over medical education was the National University.
The decision to reopen the medical school after the university was
reinstated triggered a struggle for control between the institutions.
The Faculty of Medicine was going through trying times. Accused
of obscurantism and inertia, it saw its prestige and reputation fall

Table 4.4 Medical and surgical teaching institutions, 1580–1910

UNIVERSITY

Facultad de Medicina de la Real y Pontificia Universidad de México, 1580–1821
(Faculty of Medicine, Royal and Pontifical University of Mexico)

↓

Facultad de Medicina de la Universidad Nacional de México, 1821–57
(Faculty of Medicine, National and Pontifical University of Mexico)

SURGICAL SCHOOL

Real Escuela de Cirugía (Royal Surgical School), 1767–1821

↓

Escuela Nacional de Cirugía (National Surgical School), 1821–38

MEDICAL SCHOOL

Establecimiento de Ciencias Médicas (Medical Science Establishment), 1833–34

↓

Colegio de Medicina (Medical College), 1834–55

↓

Escuela de Medicina (Medical School), 1855–1910

↓

Escuela de Medicina is incorporated into the university, 1910

---

to new lows during the 1820s, as it remained powerless to effect any changes. Its negative image, as well as that of the university that housed it, deserves scrutiny. Surviving records indicate that, although unable to make formal changes to its curriculum, the Faculty of Medicine included modern authors in debates and examinations. In 1813, Dr Zurita y Miranda debated the physiology principles of Carlos Dumas; six years later, Agustín Arellano (later professor of the Establecimiento de Medicina) was the first to defend Xavier Bichat's *Physiology* and the last to debate the Hippocrates *Aphorisms*. By 1822, the works of Anthelme Richerand, Bichat, and John Brown, as well as the subjects of chemistry and physics, had found their way into final examinations.[98] The traditional names of the cátedras had not changed but their content certainly had, and by 1830 the four-year program included physiology, hygiene, external and internal pathology, therapeutics, *materia médica*, anatomy and operations, dissections, and botany. Attendance at the courses of legal medicine and Hippocratic medicine and two years of clinical training at a hospital or under a licensed physician completed university medical training.[99]

Despite its best intentions, the Faculty of Medicine had trouble offering a full program. When the substitute professor of anatomy and surgery died in April 1826, his position remained vacant for three years. The situation was not unique, as the Faculty of Arts had the same problem with the vacant chair of philosophy. The problem stemmed from the government's indecision on who should replace the colonial officials on the appointments committee and most importantly, its reluctance to make any changes until the education reform was in place.[100] A few years later, a similar problem arose when the government procrastinated in deciding among the three candidates for the post of anatomical dissector. Unable to act, and unsettled because "the students are lacking in this branch of instruction," the university continued, unsuccessfully, to press the minister in charge for a decision.[101] As these examples illustrate, the maligned Faculty of Medicine was not always to blame for the shortcomings of the education it offered.

For years, medical faculty and practitioners had petitioned the authorities for a medical school, and the 1833 legislation had given them just that. As the only survivor of the 1834 educational reforms, the Colegio de Medicina found itself in a unique position, and its first years were plagued by bureaucratic impediments resulting from both government inefficiency and lack of funding. These problems were intertwined with the larger issue of dividing a medical program between two institutions that were competing for supremacy. Thus, the Colegio de Medicina's privileges and responsibilities had to be curtailed to accommodate those of the Faculty of Medicine, and vice versa. The struggle between both institutions is illustrated by the three designations given to the medical school. In 1835 the Establecimiento de Medicina became a college, Colegio de Medicina, to indicate its ties to the National University. However, the regulations issued by the municipal government of Mexico City in 1842 (drawn up by the physician-surgeons themselves) refer to it as "school" or Escuela de Medicina because its faculty considered it an independent institution and not a university college. From then on, the school used this name (Escuela de Medicina) in its official documentation and letterhead. Nonetheless, during the following years the terms *establecimiento*, *escuela*, and *colegio* continued to be used interchangeably in official documents and legislation, a reflection of the lack of clarity in the medical school's situation. For example, the Baranda Plan (1843) refers to the Establecimiento de Medicina and mentions a colegio not yet built, while the Lares Plan (1854) refers to the institution both as school and college.[102] In summary, medical practitioners who had petitioned repeatedly for a medical teaching institution suddenly found themselves with a medical school, a university medical faculty, and a surgical school, none of which had enough resources and infrastructure to offer a proper program.

The struggle between the Colegio de Medicina and the university took place at a time when liberal ideology was considered the only path to progress and when the presumed need to erase the erroneous ways of the past prevented flexibility and compromise. As José Luis Mora, the chief architect of educational reform, later wrote, "The university was declared useless, non-reformable and harmful ... [It] was concluded that it was necessary to abolish it."[103] The fate of the university had been decided by the 1830s, but most conservative politicians preferred that it die a natural death, a death by attrition that would exculpate them from purposely causing it. Their more radical colleagues, however, had no qualms about closing it twice in 1833 and 1857.[104]

In 1834, the problem at hand was to harmonize the needs and responsibilities of the new Colegio de Medicina and the long-established Faculty of Medicine, now forced to collaborate on the same medical program. France offered a precedent. An option open to French medical students was a four-year program offered at the university Faculté de Médecine with higher entrance qualifications (a baccalaureate), a more in-depth and prestigious program, more thorough examinations, and a written essay or thesis. This stream required a much higher monetary investment and a longer time commitment. The medical degree granted by the Faculté de Médecine, the *Doctorat*, entitled its holder to obtain a government post or professorial position, and opened the door to membership in academic societies.[105]

In Mexico, this option was attractive to those who believed there was a place for university education. It would raise standards by requiring a bachelor's degree, offer the opportunity to include university studies in the medical curriculum, and provide a tangible difference between graduate and postgraduate university degrees. Nonetheless, prevalent ideologies, the institutional and historical context of each institution, and different goals hindered collaboration. The Colegio de Medicina offered the medical elite (now formed by physician-surgeons) the opportunity to control the knowledge that defined medicine as a profession and was its basis. This monopoly ensured the continuation not only of the profession as such but also of the hierarchy among the different medical branches. The Faculty of Medicine and the university approached the same issue from a different angle. With an aging faculty, a declining number of students, and a hostile political environment, the National University had to prove its relevance and its value to society. Thus, the Faculty of Medicine focused on admission requirements, the teaching of some (but not necessarily all) medical courses, and the ability to grant degrees. The requirement of a bachelor's degree to enter the medical program was important because it raised university attendance and reinforced the value of higher education, something the university and its colleges badly needed. The Faculty of Medicine did not oppose a medical school per se. After all, its representative, Manuel de Jesús Febles, had been part of the 1834 committee that advised the government against the new school's closure. The surviving records register only its insistence on being an active participant and on teaching part of the curriculum, preferably on the university's premises. Such insistence is understandable: as the highest teaching institution, the university maintained its right to conduct the highest-level courses. Finally, the granting of degrees and their recognition (as a requirement for teaching posts or government jobs) was crucial, as without it the university lost its *raison d'être*. But radical reformers had no room for university studies and had already discarded this option, and with it any possibility of postgraduate studies. To them, politics had priority over the pursuit of science and knowledge.

The 1833 educational reform was a wake-up call for the university, whose faculty showed great willingness to collaborate with the government after its reinstatement.[106] To accommodate the new legislation, the university and its colleges revamped their programs and regulations and published them in January 1835 under the title *Suplemento a las Constituciones de la Nacional y Pontificia Universidad de Mégico*. Concerning medical studies, the *Suplemento* specified that university studies aimed to "complete and perfect" the teachings of its colleges, adding that only the university could grant degrees.[107] Once again the issue of medical education was on the table and new projects came to the legislators' attention.

In October 1835 a proposal to establish a *colegio de medicina* in the convent of Belén was presented to Congress on behalf of the acting president, Miguel Barragán.[108] The authorship of the document is not indicated, but its tone and detailed explanations suggest it was drawn up by Colegio de Medicina faculty. It proposed a four-and-a-half-year program, to be taught at the new colegio, which would now come with an adjoining hospital. The proposal was fleshed out to include a detailed curriculum, the faculty's ranks and salaries, and sources of funding. Registration requirements would be modified to ensure independence from the university; as a conciliatory gesture, during the first four years, applicants would be required to hold a bachelor's degree in philosophy but thereafter, certificates of the required courses issued by any institution would suffice. In addition, the college would be empowered to grant its own degrees. The proposal also called for a national and centralized medical degree system, presumably through the Colegio de Medicina, and for the establishment of a *sociedad de medicina* with national and foreign members "for the advances of this science." To fund the proposed college and society, the project earmarked the properties of the Hospital de Belén, the Hospital de San Juan de Dios, and the Espíritu Santo convent and temple. If such revenue proved insufficient, it would be supplemented with as many properties of the ex–Royal Indian Hospital as necessary. The cost of such a grandiose project must have made Congress balk, as the proposal was still being debated in March 1837.[109]

The following year, Casimiro Liceaga, who remained as director of the still-closed Colegio de Medicina, presented a *Proyecto Orgánico*, or comprehensive plan, drawn up by the college's faculty as a requirement for its legal standing and opening. Not surprisingly, the Proyecto Orgánico tried to ensure the Colegio de Medicina's independence. It objected to the teaching of forensic medicine at the university by arguing it lacked the facilities for the necessary demonstrations on cadavers (though it failed to clarify that the proposed site for the medical school did not have them either). It also opposed the provision that only holders of a doctorate be appointed as instructors at the Colegio de Medicina, a requirement that was of vital importance to the university. Such opposition underlined the difficulties of reconciling the objectives of both institutions and the impossibility of collaboration. The Proyecto Orgánico included the medical school provisional regulations (a total of twenty-five articles), which were accepted as temporary by the Ministry of the Interior.[110] Faculty appointments were then regularized, and the Colegio de Medicina, which had been closed since 1836, finally reopened in 1838. Two years later, a comprehensive educational plan was still in the works. Simultaneously, the Facultad Médica, as representative of the medical profession, was working on the regulations for the medical school, the medical profession, and the public health council (see chapter 3).[111] Jurisdictional confusion and competition, characteristic of contemporary legislation, contributed to confound all parties involved and resulted in bickering and tension.

In a last-ditch attempt to link the Colegio de Medicina's studies with those of the university, Manuel de Jesús Febles, university catedrático and Facultad Médica member, presented a proposal for "an organic system of medical education." Febles proposed to re-examine the courses to be taught by the Faculty of Medicine to correct any problems and to improve the program. If the medical college availed itself of the Hospital de San Andrés to teach some of its courses, the university could do the same. He pointed out that the Colegio de Medicina's limited resources would benefit from those available at the university, adding that the latter had recently spent 800 pesos to acquire up-to-date medical texts and "more than a hundred" pesos to purchase a private library; it had also ordered from France "an anatomical body" and the necessary instruments for its courses. Both institutions, Febles suggested, could pool their resources to offer a better program to their students. Collaboration would bring other benefits, such as the prestige the college would derive from the National University, a nationally and internationally recognized institution. Febles also reminded the authorities that only by allowing traditional graduation ceremonies and the pursuit of the higher degrees of licenciado and doctor would physicians be encouraged to achieve excellence.[112] These degrees would enhance the status of the Colegio de Medicina's faculty, who were being criticized for "not being catedráticos." To this end, the university had recently modified its regulations and lowered the costs of its degrees. The proposal was dated 18 November 1840 and sent to the Junta Departamental de Mexico.[113]

Two more reforms confirmed the legislators' position on education and foreshadowed the end of the university. The first, a comprehensive education program, was issued on 18 August 1843 by the minister of justice and public instruction, Manuel Baranda. The Baranda Plan gave the upper hand to the medical school by granting it the right to teach all medical courses and to conduct all examinations. It kept the traditional degree system in place, but limited the National University's role to the ceremonial granting of degrees previously authorized by the Colegio de Medicina and the Consejo Superior de Salubridad. Another innovation was the creation of a Junta Directiva General de Estudios composed of the rectors of the university and its two colleges, the directors of the Colegio de Medicina and Colegio de Minería, the president of the Lancasterian Schools Company,[114] and three individuals appointed by the government. The choice of terms is interesting. The traditional university colleges (San Juan de Letrán and San Ildefonso) were headed by "rectors," while the more scientifically oriented medical and mining colleges had "directors," widening the gap between the latter two and the university. The Junta Directiva acted as a combination of financial administrator, academic coordinator, curriculum and textbook inspector, and liaison with "scientific establishments and societies in Europe and the United States." In the last role, the junta could "decree scientific expeditions to broaden natural science and archaeological knowledge." To supplement the funding already in place, a 6 per cent tax of all Mexico City inheritances was allocated to the colleges (with the only exception of the Colegio de Minería).[115] In summary, the Baranda Plan placed the medical program under the control of the Colegio de Medicina and assigned the university a merely symbolic and administrative role. It maintained the latter's ceremonial degree-granting right, but made the licenciado and doctor degrees irrelevant, as they ceased to be requirements for a government or professorial post. As a small concession, the university was given the opportunity to participate in scientific and archaeological research, which apparently never materialized. The Baranda Plan remained in place for the next eleven years.

In 1854, the minister of justice, ecclesiastical affairs, and public instruction, Teodosio Lares, announced another, more detailed and inclusive *Plan General de Estudios*, the last educational plan under a centralist government and therefore with a national reach. The Lares Plan divided education into different stages: primary, secondary, or preparatory, and a third level of higher studies that was further sub-divided in two.[116] One stream provided the indispensable knowl-edge for "certain careers" that were subject to academic degrees, such as philosophy, medicine, jurisprudence, and theology, and the other, "special studies," was designed for those who wished to pur-sue the more technical areas of mining, commerce, or agriculture. The medical program now lasted eight years and was divided into three years of preparatory studies and five of medical studies per se. After concluding the fourth year of the program (or first year of medical studies), students obtained a bachelor's degree in philoso-phy, and after completing the sixth, a bachelor's degree in medicine. The latter degree was indispensable to continue to the seventh year, after which the applicant could apply for his professional examina-tion at the Colegio de Medicina and obtain a "professor's degree" (and automatically receive a licenciado degree from the university). Those who wished to obtain a doctorate would have a further year to take the required courses on *moral médica* (medical ethics), his-tory of medical sciences, public hygiene, and pathological anatomy (which had not yet been established). By reinstating postgraduate degrees, the Lares Plan opened once more the possibility of special-ized studies and research.

The Lares Plan, more conservative than its predecessor, returned the exclusive control over examinations, accreditation of require-ments, and granting of degrees to the National University and rein-stated the university's role in the medical program at the Colegio de Medicina's expense. It also dedicated a section to the latter's academic ceremonies and "exercises," the election of its faculty, and its inter-nal administration. Lares gave priority to the National University, declaring it "central" and placing provincial universities under its jurisdiction, a reflection of the centralist system of government in place.[117] The Lares Plan was issued on 19 December 1854. A few months later, the fall of the Santa Anna regime and the installation of Ignacio Comonfort's federalist system of government made it obsolete. Nonetheless, its organization of educational levels made it a precursor of future reforms.

After the return of the liberals and the adoption of a more liberal and anticlerical approach, the National University was closed in September 1857, leaving the medical school, now officially renamed Escuela de Medicina, in control of medical education. The Escuela de Medicina faculty had won out over the university, but the latter's elimination came at the high cost of sacrificing the chance of further studies and research. The mandate of the medical school was limited to the transmission of the necessary knowledge to practise medicine, and made no provisions for specializations or research. Practitioners wishing to pursue further studies would have to do so abroad; research was not promoted but left to the individual, who could expect neither government support nor encouragement. Later government legislation made half-hearted efforts to address this problem without any satisfactory results. Mexico would be a consumer rather than a producer of medical knowledge for years to come.

THE MEDICAL SCHOOL GROWING PAINS: FINANCIAL DIFFICULTIES AND RELOCATION

The copious legislation issued from 1833 to 1860 did not ensure the future or the quality of medical education, and the medical school continued to face numerous challenges. The main obstacles hindering a good medical education during these years were financial and a lack of adequate and permanent facilities. All educational reform proposals shared a common weakness, their proposed source of funding. The *1823 Proyecto* included a rosy report of the income and properties of the capital's "scientific institutes." The final balance sheet listed the university as having a yearly income of 14,130 pesos (6,517 pesos from its properties and 7,613.3 from a government subsidy), even though the government had ceased to pay the subsidy after 1810. The amount owed was included in a separate column and added to the calculations, distorting the result. In an even worse situation was the Academia de San Carlos, which had loaned 119,883 pesos to the national government and 22,500 pesos to the municipal government (out of a total sum of 233,734 pesos it was owed). As in the case of the university, amounts to be collected were included in the final calculations, resulting in a total of 675,105 pesos under the column "capital that must exist" (the sum of amounts derived from properties, yearly subsidies, and debts owed), an amount that was, to say the least, wishful thinking.[118]

The *1826 Plan General* faced similar challenges. It referred vaguely to funds that "up to the present have been destined to education" (schools, colleges, and the National University), adding that the remaining costs would be covered by the government with the chambers' approval, but there is no mention of either costs or available amounts.[119] Not surprisingly, as time went on and the country's financial situation deteriorated, educational reform became more elusive.

The liberal politicians' commitment to education seems to have been skin deep when one considers the financial resources dedicated to education. In January 1828, when Congress approved the budget for the period of 1 July 1827 to 30 June 1828,[120] the national government was divided into five ministries: Internal and External Relations, Justice and Ecclesiastical Affairs, War, Navy, and Treasury. Education depended on the Ministry of Internal and External Relations, which had a total budget of 476,566 pesos. From this amount, the university, San Ildefonso College, and San Juan de Letrán College were assigned 17,051 pesos. The botanical gardens received 2,849 pesos, and the Escuela de Cirugía 1,500 pesos, making a total of 21,400 pesos, or 4.5 per cent of the ministry's budget. At the same time, the Conservatorio de Antigüedades Mexicanas received 7,282 pesos, the Instituto de Ciencias y Literatura 6,000, and the Academy of San Carlos took the lion's share with 24,000 pesos (probably justifiable in view of the amount owed by the government), making a total of 7.8 per cent of the budget. For all the talk about the urgent need to educate the populace, the budget earmarked only 3,000 pesos for the Lancasterian schools, the only providers of basic education to be included. In summary, the ministry dedicated 0.6 per cent of its resources to primary education and 12.3 per cent to higher education. Contrast these amounts with the salary of 12,000 pesos for the extraordinary plenipotentiary minister, the 20,000 pesos for "extraordinary expenses," and the whopping 100,000 pesos for "external relations secret expenses."[121] Even this is not the whole story. The entire Ministry of Internal and External Relations received only 3 per cent of the national budget. The most expensive ministry was War, with 64.5 per cent of the budget (10,039,953 pesos), followed by Treasury with 22.2 per cent (3,457,893 pesos).[122] Such amounts, of course, were only on paper – more a wish list than reality – and clearly, at least in the case of the university and the colleges, the assigned subsidies were not being paid. Nonetheless, the approval of the 1828 budget reflected the priorities of legislators and politicians and the obstacles educators had to face.

In 1833, the Dirección de Instrucción Pública and its dependencies were assigned sources of funding that included certain church properties (the convent and temple of San Camilo and its properties, the Hospital de Belén, and the Hospicio de Santo Tomás and its orchard)

– from which the amounts of 8,000, 6,000, and 3,000 pesos were earmarked for the establishment of schools, the Instituto de Ciencias, Literatura y Artes, and the Federal District Lancasterian schools, respectively – as well as the earnings from the Hospicio de Pobres (poorhouse), the Hospital de Jesús with its temple and urban properties (already assigned to primary education by the law of 22 May 1833), and the funds of the National University and its dependencies. The decree, however, did not specify the exact amounts involved or how funds would be distributed among the different educational institutions, a troublesome point that did not bode well.[123] Furthermore, closer scrutiny of the sources assigned indicates that they were insufficient to undertake the ambitious plans the legislators had for public education.

As far back as 1823, reformer and politician José María Luis Mora, then director of the Colegio de San Ildefonso, had stated that its "deplorable financial situation" prevented him from including in his proposal a very necessary course of Spanish grammar. According to the same report, the college, which was owed nearly 55,000 pesos by different sources, could not cover its own expenses.[124] Another college dependent on the university was San Juan de Letrán, which seems to have been in an even worse situation. The writer and politician Guillermo Prieto, referring to the 1830s, describes San Juan de Letrán's two courtyards as "sombre and in ruins." One had "filthy horse sties and a black, smelly dark room [*antro*]" or kitchen, where one could barely make out in the dark "a hunchback and ragged witch who was the cook." The condition of the library was not much better, "buried in dust, with broken shelves and cobweb curtains over the dirty window panes."[125] Although Prieto's opinionated descriptions may be taken with a grain of salt, the San Juan de Letrán College was a most doubtful asset.

The university's economic situation was also grim. In 1825, the rector unsuccessfully requested from the central government the payment of "the exorbitant amount of 66,058 pesos, 5 reales, 2 granos" owed by the national Treasury.[126] The debt continued to mount and was never paid by the government. If the university and its colleges are indicative of the various sources of funding dedicated to public education, it is hard to believe they could have covered the costs of the six new educational establishments, their equipment, and staff.

As to the Establecimiento de Ciencias Médicas, it is most doubtful that it would have received the necessary funding to fulfill its mandate. The costs of medical education were rapidly increasing; no longer could medical students content themselves with a few medical volumes and a small number of instruments. Teaching modern medicine implied the considerable initial costs of creating the necessary facilities, amphitheatres, laboratories, anatomical collections, and other equipment. The amphitheatre was set up "at great expense" shortly after the medical school's establishment, but the laboratories, library, and pathological collections had to wait. Other expenses included the instructors' salaries (at least 14,500 pesos a month), the upkeep of buildings and equipment, and, ideally, the maintenance of a student residence.[127] According to the Colegio de Medicina's director, Casimiro Liceaga, when the Establecimiento de Ciencias Médicas first opened, instructors faced "an extreme scarcity" of the necessary teaching material and had to contribute their own instruments and books, and purchase "some items" necessary for their courses.[128] In April 1834, while the reforms were still in force, salaries ceased to be paid, foreshadowing the obstacles the new institution would soon face.[129] From a financial point of view, the 1833 reforms thus suffered from the same shortcomings as previous and succeeding ones.

The 1834 legislation cancelling the educational reforms had serious implications for the Establecimiento de Ciencias Médicas. As the 1833 reforms became a thing of the past and all institutions reverted to their previous sources of funding, the medical school was left out in the cold. The government decided it should continue to operate but assigned it no funding. Fearing its eventual closure, the professorial staff volunteered to teach without pay while the situation was sorted out. Thus the Colegio de Medicina reinitiated its activities without official sources of funding, recognition, or faculty posts. Not surprisingly, critics questioned its legality and the irregular position of its staff.[130] It would not be long before these irregularities came back to haunt it.

In 1836 Liceaga was still requesting payment of salaries owed to his staff since 1834. Adding insult to injury, in the same year the surgical school reopened and the Colegio de Medicina had to return its equipment, losing the instruments necessary to teach the anatomy course.[131] Tired of governmental indifference and arbitrary policies and deeply resenting the government's decision to reopen the surgical school, the whole faculty resigned in 1836, forcing the institution's indefinite closure.[132] Aware of the need to provide medical education, the medical leadership pursued the case and, two years

later, with the support of the minister of the interior, José Joaquín
Pesado, the college was able to initiate classes under provisional
regulations.[133] At the time, new legislation was in the works to
accommodate the new centralist political system, so reforms and a
permanent curriculum had to wait. The 1841 *Ordenamiento de
Estudios Médicos*, issued by the president of the Junta Departamental
of Mexico City and later sanctioned by the national government,
regularized (at least in theory) the medical school's situation. It recognized the Colegio de Medicina as a dependency of the Department
of Mexico and assigned a salary of 1,200 pesos to each of its professors and 2,000 pesos to its director.[134]

Despite the new legislation, the legality of the Colegio de Medicina
and its employees' salary claims continued to be questioned. In
1841, Director Liceaga was still requesting the amounts owed to
his staff from the Ministry of Treasury. The response of Joaquín
Obregón, a ministerial employee, illustrates the bizarre situation the
Colegio faced. Obregón first claimed he had no information on the
1834 legislation that had cancelled the 1833 educational reforms.
To enlighten him, Liceaga sent a newspaper containing the legislation in question. Obregón responded that such legislation did not
mention anything about funding and, most important, a law issued
in 9 August 1836 had prohibited "all innovations" until the Colegio
de Medicina was reorganized; the 1838 faculty appointments were,
therefore, illegal. As the medical school was a new establishment, he
added patronizingly, it lacked properties and capital, but no law
ordered the Treasury to cover its expenses.[135] The minister of the
interior intervened in favour of the college, but Obregón stood
his ground, also dismissing the 1841 *Ordenamiento*, which, as the
product of a departmental government, did not concern him or his
office.[136] Obregón's long and arrogant response ended by stating
that, if the professors were so concerned about "the harm caused to
the students, the detriment to the sciences, and the ignominy caused
to the nation" derived from the closure of the medical school, they
should continue to work without pay "for the short time" it would
take to reorganize education. In this way, they would also avoid
increasing the heavy burden of the already overtaxed national
Treasury.[137] Obregón did have a point, and his argument reflected
the lack of jurisdictional clarity and bureaucratic chaos characteristic of the time. To address the problem a law was issued on
8 November 1843 declaring higher education institutions "national"

and directly dependent on the Supreme (national) government.[138] It is not clear when or how the tug-of-war between the ministry and the Colegio de Medicina ended and the college's faculty members began to be paid. Nor do we know how regularly salaries were paid, but in 1851, faculty were still owed at least 50,000 pesos.[139]

The central government assumed responsibility for faculty salaries but did not solve the financial problems of the Colegio de Medicina. Eight years after its establishment the school had not yet received the 600 pesos the government had allocated for its library, which remained closed. The Consejo Superior de Salubridad was informed, and promised to "take the necessary steps."[140] In 1842, the pharmacy course still lacked a proper place to teach the practicum component so classes continued to be merely theoretical.[141] Professor Leopoldo Río de la Loza tried to alleviate the problem by arranging for students to fulfill the practicum at various pharmacies and in his own laboratory when he took over the medical chemistry course. Gradually, at his own expense, he began to acquire the instruments, equipment, and material necessary for the classes.[142] Three years later, the minister of justice and public instruction announced the arrival of "ninety-one boxes with machines and instruments and all the necessary items for a physics cabinet and a medical chemistry laboratory" at great cost, and added that installation costs still had to be covered (the minister did not clarify where these would be installed, as by that time the Colegio de Medicina had been asked to vacate its premises in the Espíritu Santo building).[143] Most instruments, laboratory equipment, and other materials had to be imported from Europe or the United States and transported first by sea and then by land to Mexico City. This was a slow and costly process for the medical school. Customs requirements, paperwork for tax exemptions at the port of entry, and the dismal state of the roads made transportation slow and difficult, and the purchased items often arrived broken or damaged beyond repair.[144]

As noted, the Baranda Plan, issued in 1843, assigned higher education institutions the income from the properties, capital, *obras pías* (charitable endowments), and rents they held and the revenue collected from a tax of 6 per cent on all inheritances and legacies that went to a common fund. In addition, each institution would receive the registration, course, examination, and degree-granting fees (now regulated by the same legislation) of its students. While these dispositions benefited the university and its colleges, which enjoyed property and capital endowments, the Colegio de Medicina would have to content itself with its share of the common fund (which would be increased gradually to address the differences) and the fees charged to its students.[145] These provisions were confirmed by the 1854 Lares Plan, which continued to allow educational institutions to keep properties and legacies they held "and might acquire," as well as "those funds that may be assigned by the public instruction inspector," but placed responsibility for the collection and administration of funds on each institution.[146]

Despite the efforts of the government, the school, and individual instructors, institutional facilities were far from ideal. In 1855, faculty members concluded that "the decadence of pharmacy was so notorious that it demanded a rapid remedy." The situation could be alleviated only by teaching the practical component as ordered by law, something that represented "considerable expenses and presented difficulties."[147] However, the situation did not improve, and soon a more radical regime nationalized institutional properties. It was an uphill battle, but the Escuela de Medicina and its faculty were determined to win. It would take perseverance and patience by the faculty, as well as financial support from the government, help from benefactors, and the personal contributions of local physicians to acquire the necessary equipment and books, set up the laboratories, and build up the school's anatomical collections.[148]

In addition to insufficient resources, continuous relocations plagued the Colegio de Medicina during its first twenty years. This situation stemmed from the government's perpetual penury, which resulted in a hand-to-mouth existence, its instability, which forced it to adopt short-term solutions for political expedience, and its ability to commandeer properties at will. In 1833 the Establecimiento de Medicina was assigned the convent of Belén, a building that had belonged to the Bethlehemites, a religious order specializing in hospital care. The order had been dissolved in 1820 and Belén occupied, first by the nuns of Nuestra Señora de Guadalupe and their students and then by the Lancasterian school.[149] In 1829 the building was turned into a military school, and in 1833 it was assigned to the Establecimiento de Ciencias Médicas, which started courses in May 1834.[150] Soon after, the irregular situation of the medical school jeopardized its rights over Belén and its professors' generous offer to work pro bono worked against a speedy resolution of its status and funding. In 1836, with classes at the medical school suspended indefinitely, the government ceded the convent building to the nuns of Nuestra Señora de Guadalupe; the Colegio de Medicina was asked to vacate its premises in mid-July.

The closure of the Colegio de Medicina from 1836 to 1838 did not help its cause. It is not clear when the medical college relocated or for how long. Before its move, the faculty had contemplated moving to the San Juan de Letrán College, but the school was finally relocated to the ruined Espíritu Santo convent.[151] In December 1843, following the publication of the Baranda Plan and to the dismay of faculty and students, the federal government issued a decree placing the Colegio de Medicina under the jurisdiction of San Ildefonso College and ordering its relocation once more.[152] Contemporary documents fail to clarify the reasons for the faculty's great reluctance to accept such change, but their main objection seems to have been the loss of their independence. Medical students complained bitterly about the strict discipline of San Ildefonso and its "lack of hospitality" toward them.[153] San Ildefonso was the law and ecclesiastical studies college, so one may assume that its regulations were indeed stricter than those of the medical school. After all, medical students have never distinguished themselves for their discipline, and the dissection and hospital work required of them lowered their status and made them "suspicious" in the eyes of society.[154] Resentment by the San Ildefonso's faculty and student body is understandable, as they were forced to share their premises and gained nothing in return. Politics may have also played a role, as San Ildefonso's rector, Sebastián Lerdo de Tejada, a fervent federalist, may have resented the imposition of a centralist administration. It was not an ideal situation, and Congress was forced to rectify it in July 1845 by annulling the merger of the two institutions.[155]

The Colegio de Medicina was then moved to the San Juan de Letrán College. Once more, the arrangement was less than satisfactory, as residential and classroom space was limited, but it continued until 1851, when the Colegio de Medicina decided to purchase its own building. Informal discussions with the minister of justice and public instruction about the purchase of the ex-convent of San Hipólito had taken place since 1845 but had come to nothing. In 1848 during the United States invasion of the capital, San Hipólito had been turned into a military hospital, and in 1851 the federal government decided to turn part of the building into a military barracks. Finally, the Colegio de Medicina faculty members agreed to apply their unpaid (and seemingly uncollectible) salaries toward the acquisition of the building.[156] Their generosity is beyond question, but clearly, given the existing conditions, it was the only way they could receive some remuneration from the bankrupt government. The location was not ideal, as the building was in bad condition and required repairs before classes could start. Nonetheless, options were limited, so papers were signed, the transaction finalized, and the Colegio de Medicina relocated for what it seemed would be the last time. Professors and students settled down and classes continued until August 1853, when they were forced once again to move. Availing himself of a law that empowered the government to requisition buildings that had served for military purposes, President Santa Anna ordered the building turned into a military barracks to house the rapidly increasing number of recruits.[157] It was the first stage of the dictatorship that characterized Santa Anna's last years in power.

The refusal of the medical school to be relocated to San Ildefonso forced it to share space with San Gregorio College and hold some of its classes on the university premises until 1854, when the school was able to acquire the old Inquisition building on the Plaza de Santo Domingo in exchange for the amount paid for San Hipólito. The Colegio de Medicina moved once more, for what would be the last time. The following year the medical school opened a student residence that functioned in that capacity for more than twenty years, a small victory in a very long war. More than twenty years after its founding, the Colegio de Medicina finally had a permanent location, a testimony to the perseverance and single-mindedness of its director and faculty.

The description of the medical school published by the physician Mariano Brito, attaché to the Mexican legation in France in 1862, illustrates the hard-won improvements in medical education. The Escuela the Medicina was by then permanently located in the three-storey ex–Inquisition building. According to Brito, the first level was occupied by the administrative offices and "a luxuriously decorated" room for public exams. The second floor housed the amphitheatres, the pharmacology, chemistry, and pharmacy laboratories, a library, and a physics and still-incomplete natural history showcase. The legal medicine laboratory, the dissections room with various tables, the great amphitheatre for the anatomy and physiology courses, and the anatomy museum, with a rich collection of surgical, anatomy, and obstetrical instruments manufactured by Charière, occupied the third floor.[158] Such a glowing description must be taken with a grain of salt, as only two years later Director Durán obtained from the Regency funds for some "most urgent" repairs. These included placing an "economical stove" in the kitchen to prevent smoke from filling the dining room, enlarging the bull's-eye (rounded window) to allow more light into the room, and fitting a stove into the chemistry laboratory to evaporate the gases emitted during class. Durán also requested funds for painting the building and for curtains and the fixtures necessary to decorate and illuminate the balconies.[159] The Escuela de Medicina still had a way to go, but it now had a permanent domicile and the necessary facilities, and, most important, it had survived its most challenging financial period.

THE MEDICAL SCHOOL TEACHING CHALLENGES: CLINICAL TEACHING AND MORBID ANATOMY

The lack of a permanent location seriously impaired the ability of the Escuela de Medicina faculty to offer a good medical program during the first twenty years. The damage was compounded by lack of a centralized hospital infrastructure to support the program's clinical and anatomical components, which were essential to a program modelled after the Paris school. In France, secularization of hospitals and reorganization of medical studies had taken place within a short time. The demands of war had forced the state to adopt radical measures that would ensure the training of competent medical personnel for hundreds of casualties. The abolition of medical faculties and other "privileged" associations, the focus on surgery, and the emphasis on clinical training shifted the locus of education to the hospital and the amphitheatre. The creation of a central health school formalized the close relation between theoretical and practical teaching and the interdependence of school and hospital.[160] The hospital, therefore, became "the core of medicine not only for treatment of the sick and disabled but also of medical instruction and research."[161]

In Mexico, the secularization of hospitals was gradual and piecemeal, slowly depriving them of their sources of funding and leaving them at the mercy of bankrupt municipal, state, and national governments. Hospitals and their properties became pawns in the governments' struggle to dominate the church and build a secular society, a struggle in which the losers were those who could not afford medical care. Furthermore, there was no central body to over-see the institutions' administration, ensure their welfare, and coordi-nate their tasks. The efforts to secularize hospitals had begun at the turn of the nineteenth century, when the Spanish Crown ordered the closure of the Hospital de Montesclaros in Veracruz and replaced it with the military, and completely secular, Hospital de San Carlos.[162] In 1804 Madrid ordered the nationalization of real estate and capi-tal of charitable endowments and legacies (*obras pías*) that, although not completely obeyed, seriously affected hospitals. Another royal decree, issued in 1820, ordered the suppression of hospitaller orders (Bethlehemites, Saint Hypolite Order of Charity, and the Order Hospitaller of San Juan de Dios)[163] and the secularization of their hospitals. Hospitals dependent on bishoprics, secular associations, or private endowments were not affected. Aware of the unstable political environment (a few months later Mexico declared its inde-pendence), Viceroy Juan Ruiz de Apodaca enforced the orders only in Mexico City, where hospitals and their properties came to depend on the municipal government.[164]

During the next twenty years, congressional debates and reforms concentrated on political issues and administration, paying only marginal attention to health-care institutions. According to an 1843 report, an 1831 law earmarked 80,000 pesos from the annual 100,000 peso sales tax assigned to the Mexico City municipal gov-ernment for hospitals and prisons. However, in the last fifteen-year period, the municipal government had received only 100,000 from the sales tax.[165] A later decree, "that was like a flame that consumed the properties," appropriated the properties that had belonged to hospitaller orders and ordered the Treasury to pay interest on them (presumably to support the hospitals).[166] A year later, the centralist legislation known as *Bases Orgánicas* acknowledged the state's obli-gation to "create funds for educational and public health and chari-table institutions [*beneficencia pública*]" and to "establish and regulate welfare and correctional institutions."[167] This was followed by another law (5 May 1845) that returned unsold properties and ordered reimbursement, plus interest, to the hospitals for those properties already sold; a year later neither provision had been enforced.[168] Not surprisingly, the municipal government requested, unsuccessfully, to be relieved from its obligations to the hospitals.

The next crucial piece of legislation affecting hospitals was the *desamortización* law proclaimed in June 1856 by the liberal government of Ignacio Comonfort.[169] It prohibited religious and civil institutions or corporations from owning or administering real estate not directly related to their daily operations, and therefore included hospital properties administered by municipal governments. Issued under the pretext of breaking up large, supposedly idle properties and promoting private landholdings and a free market economy, its main objective was to weaken the church. Although two years later, the conservative government of Félix Zuloaga returned the properties not yet sold, the damage was irreparable. The political see-saw continued, and in 1859 the more radical government of Benito Juárez ordered the nationalization of all properties administered by the clergy, including hospitals and their adjacent buildings.[170] This measure was followed by the creation of a central administrative body, the Dirección General de Fondos de Beneficencia Pública or Directorate of Public Welfare Funds, responsible for the secularized institutions. The experiment was short-lived, as a year later Juárez abolished the underfunded directorate and returned the hospitals to the care of the municipal governments.[171] None of the above legislation mentioned an obligation of the state to provide for the health care of the population. Instead, contemporary documents continued to allude to the traditional Christian concepts of charity and appeal to moral obligations. Their references to patients as "miserable," "*desgraciados*" (wretched), and "*humanidad doliente*" (suffering humankind) confirm the continuation of traditional beliefs about the sick and the poor.

The effects of the desamortización laws on the hospitals were disastrous. The national government had neither the means to subsidize nor the infrastructure to administer the confiscated funds and properties, so the hospitals were left without resources. The Jesús, San Andrés, and San Pablo hospitals illustrate the effects of the piecemeal and often misinformed legislation of the time. The Hospital de Jesús, the first to be established in Mexico, was founded by Hernán Cortés in 1522 with the name of Nuestra Señora de la Concepción de Jesús. In his will, the conqueror left sufficient properties and funds to provide for its indefinite support. Despite being privately endowed, the hospital and its properties attracted the attention of reformers.[172] In 1833, Valentín Gómez Farías decreed the nationalization of its properties to help subsidize his education reforms, but the law was declared null after the return of President Santa Anna, and the properties returned to their owner in 1835.[173]

As an 1843 inspection report indicates, the hospital was able to keep high standards as a result of its economic independence. The inspection committee declared the Hospital de Jesús "the best." It housed a maximum of forty patients of both genders, was clean, and offered "exact" (good) service; it had its own pharmacy and boasted two large water tanks on the roof that provided hot water for baths and a deposit of cold water that was pumped to the kitchen, wards, and employee residences. Its wards had iron beds, wool-filled mattresses, and linen bedding, and patients received a hospital garment on their arrival. The hospital staff consisted of a physician and his assistant or *practicante mayor* (who was also a licensed physician), a main nurse "who is usually a medical student," and four interns or medical students who resided in the hospital until they completed their studies. The last were in charge of applying caustics and leeches, bleeding the patients, and administering the medicaments. The medical staff was assisted by *mozos afanadores* (a combination of nurse and servant) charged with cleaning, preparing baths, and other minor tasks. There was also a doorman to ensure visitors adhered to the visiting schedule and did not introduce alcoholic drinks, fruits, or other "harmful matters" to the building. The hospital had also a private section that charged patients four reales a day, and another one of private rooms at the cost of 45 pesos a month.[174]

The glowing report on the Hospital de Jesús contrasts with the dismal impression that the Hospital de San Andrés left on the visiting committee. The latter is described "as a turbulent prison to afflict the suffering mankind [*humanidad doliente*]" with dirty wards, filthy boards serving as beds, lumpy mattresses and pillows, and small pieces of cloth as sheets. The wards were overcrowded and lacked any privacy. The committee added that the hospital's diminished properties, small pension and revenue it received from the Santa Paula cemetery were insufficient to cover its needs.[175] San Andrés first opened its door in 1788 and a few years later had expanded to accommodate 1,000 beds. Its financial woes had started a few years after the death of Archbishop Alonso Núñez de Haro y Peralta, its founder and financial supporter. In 1806–07 the hospital was forced to make a "loan" to the Spanish Crown that unbalanced its budget. The wars of independence and the dismal economy of the post-independence years affected its properties' revenues at a time when the expulsion of the hospitaller orders increased the number of patients. In addition, the hospital was forced to subsidize the care of most of its patients – soldiers and prisoners – as the military and the government rarely covered the fees. The hospital continued to be administered by the archbishopric until its secularization in 1861.[176]

San Andrés was not the only hospital affected by the government's financial and political decisions, and by the mid-nineteenth century the Hospital de San Pablo was undergoing serious financial difficulties. San Pablo had been established in 1847 to receive the capital's military casualties during the United States invasion of Mexico. Since its founding, the hospital had been entrusted to the Sisters of Charity, who served in it until their expulsion in 1874. Despite its limited budget, San Pablo made ends meet, thanks to the sisters' careful administration but, after being placed under federal administration in the 1850s, its financial situation deteriorated. A letter, written in May 1861 by Sor Micaela Ayans, San Pablo's administrator, illustrates the effects of the government's short-sighted policies:

> This hospital opened its doors on 23 August 1847 and received all those in need ... but since approximately six years ago [1856] it began to experience scarcity, its staff has not been paid, food and medicine are [obtained] on credit, it is impossible to provide clothing for the patients or to repair the buildings. On 15 April, fifteen interns left because they had not been paid. Physicians and staff are now owed eighteen months' salary. Since April, the hospital owes Leopoldo Río de la Loza for all its pharmacy supplies, and it owes Antonio Escandón 4,100 pesos for meat and 3,200 for bread, and 79 pesos for medicines to Cervantes. Last month's expenses amounted (excluding salaries) to 1,381 pesos, but I received only 450 pesos ... Antonio Escandón refused to give me more credit, but after begging him I convinced him to wait a few more days. Each time is "more impossible" to satisfy such debts. When the federal army entered the capital, the hospital filled with soldiers suffering from typhus that only in the month of January cost the hospital 710 pesos and 75 cents. I delivered the bill to the president of the Republic, who gave it to the treasury minister, but I have not been reimbursed yet. The battle of Tacubaya left so many wounded that we had to place mats between the beds and in the middle of the wards. They have not paid me anything for this either ... [W]hen the municipal government was in charge, it provided me with everything, but since the hospital was placed under the Dirección de Beneficencia, it is the

opposite; nobody trusts me and I experience more hardship and worries and I have to beg for charity with supplications and promises to pay that I believe impossible to fulfill.[177]

Sor Micaela also complained about the Dirección de Beneficencia's lack of funds and indifference, and asked the authorities to place the hospital under the charge of the municipal government once again. The letter was sent to the municipal authorities, but her request was denied in May 1862.[178]

The root problem of the dismal conditions that prevailed at San Pablo and San Andrés was the same: lack of funding. The secularization of hospitals and appropriation of their properties may have brought needed funds to government coffers, but it also saddled the state with a heavy financial burden. It was short-term gain for long-term pain – pain felt by all those who required medical services. The government of Maximilian of Habsburg (1864–67) tried to improve the situation by centralizing public health-care institutions under a Consejo General de Beneficencia (Welfare General Board) presided over by Empress Carlota. Public health and welfare were of special interest to the imperial government, and centralization was a step in the right direction, but the regime's short life and its deteriorating financial situation prevented any worthwhile results.[179]

The gradual secularization of Mexican hospitals and their properties followed political motivations and paid little attention to educational needs. The governments of the time, fighting for survival, had neither interest nor means to improve hospital services, so hospitals languished, doing the best they could with whatever funds they could obtain. In view of the circumstances, their reluctance to serve the needs of the Escuela de Medicina comes as no surprise. To the latter, hospital access was imperative, as clinical medicine allowed students the opportunity to observe different illnesses and, at least in theory, acquaint themselves with ordinary and extraordinary cases. Faculty and students were well aware of the problem, as indicated by an anonymous article in an 1838 issue of the *Periódico de la Academia de Medicina de México* requesting the establishment of "a certain number of beds" to allow students "to see and touch the symptoms and signs of disease." The same article reminded its readers that, in the "Mexican Republic, there was not one complete college destined to the teaching of medicine."[180] The lack of a proper

Figure 4.1 Hospital of San Pablo's central patio. Mexico City.

hospital infrastructure represented a serious obstacle for the teaching of a program based on the Paris school.

Mexican hospitals were not only inadequate for meeting educational objectives, they were often less than enthusiastic about on-site teaching. In 1835, Ignacio Torres complained that his students had been barred from entering the Hospital de San Andrés when they tried to attend his surgery course.[181] In 1851 the clinical medicine course was jeopardized when the Hospital de Jesús and the Hospital de San Andrés refused to allow any type of instruction, alleging "it was not convenient that the patients be disturbed with the explorations that were required," as they caused them "extreme harm."[182] It took negotiations and pressure from officials to change their policy. The only hospital willing to cooperate, the municipal Hospital de San Pablo, was considered unsuitable because its patients were "surgical cases."[183] The obstetrics course faced a greater challenge, as the lack of a maternity hospital prevented students from acquiring practical experience.[184] Instead, obstetrics instructors had to limit

Figure 4.2 Corridor and wards of the Hospital of San Pablo, Mexico City.

themselves to theoretical classes and classroom demonstrations on dummies, forcing faculty to recognize in 1855 that the education imparted by the Escuela de Medicina had not reached "the degree of perfection that could be wished," and "one of the most imperfect" courses was obstetrics, which limited itself to theory.[185]

The hospitals were not at fault. In addition to being overcrowded, suffering from insufficient resources, and lacking the necessary installations, they had been established as charitable institutions, not as teaching hospitals, and as such their main obligation lay with their patients. Furthermore, there was no coordinating central body and each institution depended on different authorities: Hospital de Jesús on a private foundation, San Andrés on the archbishopric, and San Pablo on the federal or municipal government. Such a decentralized system hindered cooperation in the best of the cases. Some hospitals reluctantly cooperated, but those students who misbehaved and antagonized hospital staff did not help the situation. In 1850 the Hospital de San Pablo administrator made a formal complaint about the interns, who, after "enjoying themselves in their room," had threatened a member of the staff with knives.[186] Poorly paid and overworked personnel understandably had no time for such antics.

Despite the numerous obstacles, Miguel Francisco Jiménez, professor of clinical medicine and director of the Hospital de San Andrés medical ward, offered a course like those he had attended at the Paris school.[187] Among others, students had the opportunity to observe the case of Manuel Esteva, a fifty-year-old man described as a street seller of "roasted heads" who had a "large thorax, thin members and a very reduced intelligence." The patient originally complained of fever, headaches, and a sore body. Later, he felt an acute pain on the left of his back that made him cough and prevented him from breathing properly. Jiménez's examination revealed "yellow and glutinous sputum," shortness of breath, and pain that increased when the patient coughed. Auscultation gave Jiménez more clues: a dull sound from the scapula's angle to its base, "complete lack of breathing" in the lower part of a lung, and a crackling sound that helped the practitioner determine the extent of the damage. He completed the examination by taking the patient's pulse and (skin) temperature and then diagnosed him with "left pleuro-pneumonia." The next day, following Gabriel Andral's teachings, he examined the patient's sputum under a microscope to confirm his suspicions.[188] His diagnosis was now more specific: a partly "hepatized" inferior lobe (hardened pulmonary tissue similar to the liver's surface) and false membranes in the pleura, and an infarct in the remaining part of the lobe. After Manuel Esteva, died his autopsy confirmed a "hepatized" and a partly useless lobe.[189]

Another subject of Jiménez's clinical lessons was Antonio Campos, a thirty-one-year-old baker of "lymphatic constitution" and "without personal or family pathological history worth mentioning." Campos suffered from a strong pain in the right part of his back that hindered his breathing, a continuous cough and fever, and bloody sputum. Bleeding, purging, dieting, and ointments had brought him some relief, but after three weeks the symptoms returned to the point that he could not work. He had lost his appetite and his feet began to swell. Jiménez and his students examined him, measuring the thorax and feeling the intercostal spaces, and carefully comparing the right and the left hemithorax. Percussion and auscultation followed, comparing the sounds of the lower and higher parts of the thorax. The "solid" sound, the absence of breathing noises, and voice resonance indicated that "the lung did not exist" and had been substituted "by another body that fills the cavity and is impermeable to air." The "convexity" observed when the patient was measured indicated the presence of pleural discharge of undetermined nature. Jiménez diagnosed "hydro-thorax in the right side" and, on the basis of persistent fever and weakened condition of the patient, he concluded the discharge was purulent (empyema). To ensure students learned to distinguish empyema cases from "simple hydro-thorax" he made them examine thirteen patients with similar symptoms and follow their cases.[190] As Martínez Cortés indicates, the classes taught by Jiménez centred on "pure" clinical medicine: the patient was first questioned, then examined, his body was explored by the practitioners, and, in case of death, the clinical diagnosis was confirmed by anatomo-pathological findings.[191] Against formidable odds, professors disseminated their medical knowledge among their students. The conditions were far from perfect, but the teachings of the Paris school were passed on to future generations.

If clinical medicine was central to contemporary medical education, so was practical anatomy the basis of nineteenth-century medicine. As Florent Palluault accurately states, it "united the exploratory skill of the surgeon to the pathological expertise of the physician" and opened the door to other medical areas.[192] Dissections were indispensable to any nineteenth-century medical program, because they allowed students to familiarize themselves with organs and tissues, observe the ravages of disease, and learn surgical skills. In France, the officiat program offered anatomy and dissections courses in its first and second years. The Mexican curriculum included "descriptive anatomy" in its first year and "anatomy" in the second, but it did not specifically mention dissections, the cornerstone of French medical training.[193] As the above cases indicate, this does not necessarily mean that dissections were absent from the program, simply that they were not its foundation. The reasons were surely pragmatic. An intensive dissections course required close cooperation between hospitals and the medical school. The Escuela de Medicina did not have the necessary infrastructure in place, and classes had to be taught when and where possible. Mexican hospitals lacked adequate amphitheatres, as did the medical school during the first decades. On the opening of the Establecimiento de Ciencias Médicas, the convent of Belén had been equipped with an amphitheatre, but this was not rebuilt in Espíritu Santo: "The furniture and equipment that had formed part of the amphitheatre [in Belén], built at so much expense, lay on a pile, as did the furniture that had belonged to other classrooms."[194] The amphitheatre's "atmospheric emanations" were also a cause of concern, and in 1853 the Escuela de Medicina's director requested San Andrés hospital's mortality statistics to study the matter.[195] The situation seems to have gradually improved, as illustrated by the autopsies conducted in the 1850s at the same hospital.[196] However, the school did not have a proper amphitheatre until its final establishment at the ex-Inquisition building.

It was not only the lack of a dissecting room that hampered the medical school's ability to offer this important component of the program regularly; the Escuela de Medicina was also seldom able to secure the necessary cadavers for anatomical demonstrations. The problem lay in the limited number of available bodies, the fact they had to be shared with private courses taught at the hospitals, and the difficulties of preservation and transportation within a limited time;[197] the bodies were stored in the hospitals' usually unsuitable facilities for days, and there was no coordinating system to speed paperwork, to inform those interested, and to facilitate transportation.[198] Professors had to improvise. When in 1840 the anatomy professor Manuel Andrade had to suspend his lessons at the Hospital de San Andrés for lack of cadavers, he proposed to add extra classes whenever possible to fulfill the course requirements.[199] Eleven years later, the medical school's director, Ignacio Durán, wrote to the executive requesting his intervention to procure the necessary cadavers for dissection. The request was sent on to the minister of relations, who forwarded it to the "Commission of Hospitals," which then consulted with the municipal government and the archbishop in charge of the Hospital de San Pablo. After this long bureaucratic process, the medical school was given access to the cadavers of the prisoners who died in the hospital. They would be transported to the medical school amphitheatre after the autopsy (if this was required) at the expense of the school, which would be responsible for taking the remains to the cemetery.[200] A few years later, the governor of the Federal District, Juan J. Baz, directed a similar order to all hospitals and prisons.[201] It is clear that the prevailing conditions hindered the medical school faculty from providing a hospital-based program centred on clinical practice and practical anatomy. Frequently, faculty were forced to emphasize theoretical instruction over practical skills and classroom over hospital teaching, deviating from the practical instruction model that inspired their curriculum. Provincial education faced larger challenges.

MEDICAL EDUCATION IN THE PROVINCES:
A COMPARISON

Mexico City practitioners were not the only ones interested in establishing a medical school. Their efforts were being duplicated, with different degrees of success, by colleagues in provincial capitals. Provinces (or states) were influenced by the same ideologies and national policies, but the development of medical education in each of them was shaped by local circumstances. A detailed description of the development of medical education in provincial capitals is beyond the scope of this work, but a general description of its evolution in three main cities – Morelia, Guadalajara, and Puebla – provides some context for the topic and illustrates the difficulties of enforcing a national standard for medical education and consequently for the profession.

In Morelia (present-day capital of the state of Michoacán), the establishment of medical courses was first proposed to congress in 1824 but the idea was rejected for lack of resources. Five years later, at the initiative of the state's provisional governor and physician Juan Manuel González Urueña, congress approved the creation of a "school of medicine" in Morelia. Classes began in 1830 with two courses offered at the Hospital of San Juan de Dios: descriptive anatomy, taught by Mariano Ramírez, and medical and surgical pathology, taught by González Urueña himself. After four years, classes were moved to the Coliseum (now Ocampo Theatre) to accommodate demand and, echoing the changes taking place in Mexico City, the "school" changed its name to Facultad Médica de Michoacán. Unfortunately, during the first years, dissections were not carried out and instructors had to complement their lectures with an anatomical atlas.[202]

In 1847, after the central government issued the 1846 law to placate provincial opposition to the controversial Baranda Plan of 1843 and provinces were granted more freedom to reorganize education, Governor Melchor Ocampo ordered the incorporation of the Facultad Médica into the Colegio de San Nicolás and changed its name to Escuela de Medicina.[203] His motives were undoubtedly financial, as the subsidy for medical studies came from the educational funds targeted for primary education. To comply with the Baranda Plan, the Morelia school offered, physiology, botany, pathology, anatomy, *materia médica*, and pharmacology, among other courses. Instructors' reports reflect the difficulties of teaching such courses with the limited resources at hand, as well as the obstacles faced by students and faculty. Exceptions had to be made for students who did not fulfill the requirements, higher courses had to be adapted, and textbooks were sometimes scarce or unavailable.[204] Three years after its founding, in 1850, the state congress appointed a commission to evaluate the school. Its report was far from positive, describing a lack of resources and proper infrastructure, and led to the government's decision to close the institution after registered students completed their studies.[205] When the medical school reopened in 1858 the political context had changed. The liberal triumph had resulted in the nationalization of church property and the secularization of the Hospital de San Juan de Dios. The school, renamed Establecimiento de Instrucción, was relocated to the secularized hospital now renamed Hospital Civil. Change came once again in 1861 but the hospital and its school were reopened in 1867, after the fall of the Second Empire.[206] As it was the case in other cities, in Morelia the establishment of medical education was spearheaded by local physicians and politicians, and shaped by political events and local circumstances.

Guadalajara (capital of the state of Jalisco) was unique among provincial capitals for its university. The University of Guadalajara had been officially established in 1792, but its regulations, and therefore its curriculum, were not sanctioned until 1817, only four years before Mexico's independence. Therefore its medical program, unlike the one offered in Mexico City, included modern authors such as Herman Boerhaave, Gerhard Freyherr Van-Swieten, and Lorenz Heister.[207] After independence, Guadalajara distinguished itself for its liberal ideology and preference for federalism, a result of the distance that separated it from Mexico City and the rivalry between both cities. Immediately after Mexico was proclaimed a federal republic in 1824, local legislators proceeded to draw up the legislation for the "Free and Independent State of Jalisco." This included a radical educational reform that the state congress approved in 1826. The university, described as "a gothic building that served as leverage to tyranny," was abolished and replaced with an Instituto del Estado, or state institute, divided into eleven "sections."[208] Its ninth (surgical) section included descriptive and practical anatomy, theory and practice of pathological anatomy and surgery, and the tenth (medical) section offered clinical and legal medicine courses.[209]

Following the 1833 and 1834 educational reforms in the national capital, the government of Jalisco issued its own educational reform (September 1835) that aimed to raise literacy and improve higher education. The reform did not alter medical education radically but provided for the creation of an academy to promote science and the publication of a scientific journal.[210] The program was never put in place, as shortly after its approval the government was replaced by a more conservative regime. In 1837, under the new government, a surgical course promoted by the conservative physician Pablo Gutiérrez and the Belgian surgeon Pedro Vander Linden (a Santa Anna supporter) was inaugurated at the Hospital de Belén, and the university was reopened. The new course, based on the Paris school, was divided into theory and practice that included "bandages," surgical clinic, and obstetrics. Its findings and statistics were published in the first volume of the *Anales de la Sociedad Médica de Emulación de Guadalajara* (1839).[211] In 1839, a recently created Faculty of Medicine, Surgery, and Pharmacy began courses at both the university premises and the local hospital, and six years later it offered a five-year program that included seventeen courses.[212]

In 1846, as United States troops marched into Mexico and the central government weakened, Jalisco rebelled against the regime and appointed the federalist Juan Nepomuceno Cumplido as provincial governor. One of Cumplido's first acts was the closing of the university and the reinstatement of the State Institute (renamed Instituto de Ciencias de Jalisco), which now became responsible for medical education. The first measure caused such a negative reaction among the population that the government was forced to reinstate the university the following year.[213] During the next twenty years medical education bounced between the Instituto de Ciencias and the university, as they were closed and opened according to the regime in power. After two more closures in 1853 and 1857, and the triumph of Benito Juárez and his liberal, federalist followers, the University of Guadalajara was finally abolished in December 1860. An advertisement of its courses on clinic and surgery at the Hospital de Belén shows the program was still being taught during its last year.[214] Following the lead of the Juárez government in Mexico City, Jalisco issued its own educational reform (Plan General de Educación) in 1861, which created schools of higher education, among them a school of medicine. Its six-year medical program included medical physics, mineral and organic chemistry, botany and zoology, general and descriptive anatomy, physiology and hygiene, elements of general pathology, external and internal pathology, surgery, *materia médica* or pharmacology, and therapeutics, obstetrics, and forensic medicine. As in Mexico, students were required to have a working knowledge of French. The school also offered training for midwives and phlebotomists but left course content and length to the instructor's discretion.[215] To facilitate hospital courses, the Hospital de Belén received new regulations, and its building was gradually renovated. Although the regulations clearly outlined the obligations of students and professors on the one hand and hospital staff on the other, tensions over jurisdiction and patient availability continued, to the program's detriment. It is worth noticing that despite the advances of the medical-surgical program, Guadalajara did not have a maternity ward until 1874.[216]

Like Guadalajara, Puebla, the capital of the state of Puebla, had offered surgical and obstetrical instruction since the beginning of the nineteenth century. In 1822, during the short-lived empire of Agustín de Iturbide (1822–23), Puebla's municipal government submitted a proposal to establish a medical school, but the Protomedicato, whose authority was being challenged by the Puebla junta de sanidad, opposed it. The Puebla medical school would have to wait twelve years more. In 1834, after the capital's educational reform was in place, the Puebla medical school opened its doors with a five-year program drawn up by local practitioners but fashioned after the French-inspired 1833 Mexico City curriculum. Courses included descriptive and general anatomy during the first year, physiology and hygiene during the second, and "operations" and obstetrics, *materia médica* and forensic medicine during the third. The last two years were dedicated to clinical medicine and surgery, medical and surgical pathology, and botany. The textbooks employed indicated the influence of the Paris school: Antoine Laurent Jessie Bayle's *Traité élémentaire d'anatomie* and A. Richerand's *Phisiology*, as well as the works of Johann Friedrich Meckel Jr, Xavier Bichat, François Magendie, François Chaussier, and François Victor Joseph Broussais.[217] In 1838, the school began to offer courses in phlebotomy and four years later opened its pharmacy program, which resulted in the graduation of twenty-seven phlebotomists and ten pharmacists during the following twelve years.[218]

In June 1842 the government of the Department of Puebla issued new regulations for the study and practice of medicine, *Reglamento para el estudio y ejercicio de las ciencias médicas,* to conform to the Baranda Plan. The *Reglamento* added new courses to the program, eliminated the bachelor of arts requirement, and changed their nomenclature (*materia médica* became pharmacology, "childbirth" obstetrics and internal and external clinics became medical and surgical clinics).

After the announcement of the Lares Plan (1854), the Mexico City Escuela de Medicina was asked to report on the Puebla institution. To this purpose, director Casimiro Liceaga and vice-director Ladislao de la Pascua travelled to Puebla. Their unfavourable report cited a limited number of students and inadequate facilities. Costs seemed unjustifiable and the central government ordered its closure, which was prevented only by the latter's fall and its replacement by a federalist regime. Enjoying more independence, the state of Puebla now embarked on reforms. The local Dirección de Sanidad (medical and public health board) became the Academia de Ciencias Médicas, and the medical program increased from five to seven years and required eleven courses. In 1864 the Puebla medical school came to the attention of the central authorities (now the imperial government of Maximilian of Habsburg) that had undertaken, once again, the task of reorganizing education. After an evaluation of conditions, costs, and outcomes, the school was closed in 1864.[219]

As the cases of Morelia, Guadalajara, and Puebla illustrate, provincial medical education followed chronological patterns, teaching trends, and financial difficulties similar to those experienced by the capital's Escuela de Medicina but were dependent on both provincial (or state) and national governments, authorities, and legislation. They had fewer resources and students and functioned in more traditional societies. In 1850 the Morelia chemistry and external pathology courses had only two students each. When their duties at the lazaretto prevented the students from attending the latter course regularly, the professor cancelled the course entirely, to assist the numerous cholera patients.[220] Furthermore, Mexico City authorities and medical and public health officials were often unsympathetic to provincial initiatives that they considered a challenge to their authority. The schools' apologists cited the urgent need for practitioners, but the expenses incurred were hard to justify when so few students completed their studies. Up to the 1860s most provincial medical schools were not cost effective. Their establishment and resilience can be explained only by regional pride and the centrifugal forces that characterized Mexican politics at the time.

THE INNER CIRCLE AND THE FORMATION
OF A PROFESSION

The establishment and maturing of the medical school were due to the work, determination, and perseverance of a select group of practitioners. As one reads the surviving documentation, the same names come up again and again. Unfortunately, the archives concentrate on the formal work, meetings, and regulations of the time and disclose little, if anything, about the private lives and personalities of those who donated their time, and often their money, to achieve the ends they pursued. The individuals who worked for the transformation of medical education and health-care reform in general formed a cohesive group, despite their generational, professional, and political differences. Such cohesiveness may be explained by the limited number of practitioners, their common professional interests, and their similar socio-economic and educational backgrounds.

According to the *Manual de geografía y estadística de la República Mexicana*, published in 1857, Mexico City then had approximately 185,000 inhabitants.[221] Anne Staples estimates that, at the primary level, there were 123 schools and 11,549 students.[222] On the basis of these estimates, it can be calculated that not more than 10 per cent of the total population attended (but did not necessarily complete) primary education, and even fewer continued to the secondary level. On the other hand, in 1840, the medical school had 98 students, 50 of whom were registered in their first year of studies and 5 in their fifth year;[223] the following year, the student population had increased to 134, with 48 in first year and 5 in the fifth and last year (table 4.5).[224] Sixteen years later, in 1857, the medical school had a total enrolment of 229 students, of whom 12 graduated that year.[225] An 1866 report rendered to the Public Education Ministry indicates that, from 1857 to 1866, the school issued a yearly average of nineteen medical and two or three pharmaceutical degrees (table 4.6).[226] Other documents confirm such exclusivity. According to the municipal records, in 1822, Mexico City counted 27 physicians and 46 surgeons; by 1831, the numbers had increased to 44 physicians and physician-surgeons and 115 surgeons.[227] Licensed medical practitioners, therefore, formed a very small and select group of the population.

These small numbers resulted in a close community of colleagues in which students and faculty knew each other well and formed close ties. Some of them were related, like Casimiro Liceaga, his nephew Francisco, and his grand-nephew Eduardo; Manuel Andrade

Table 4.5 Escuela de Medicina: Registrations and examinations, 1840 and 1841

Academic year	Students registered in 1840	Students examined in 1840	Students registered in 1841	Students examined in 1841
1st year	50	29	48	30
2nd year	16	16	28	16
3rd year	23	20	14	12
4th year	4	2	20	16
5th year	5	4	5	3
Total	98	71	134	77

Source: Periódico de la Academia de Medicina de Mégico 5 (1840): 112 and 359.

Table 4.6 Escuela de Medicina: Number of graduates, 1857–1866

Year	Physicians	Pharmacists	Total
1857	12	3	15
1858	10	4	14
1859	25	1	26
1860	27	2	29
1861	23	2	25
1862	18	–	18
1863	10	3	13
1864	20	3	23
1865	23	2	25
1866	19	3	22
Total	187	23	210

Source: AHFM, EM-FMYA, leg. 133, exp. 57.

and his son Agustín; and the brothers José María and Francisco Vértiz. Others were or became close friends, such as Luis Muñoz and José María Vértiz, who travelled together to Europe to pursue their medical studies.[228] Five years of medical training developed strong ties between faculty and students. Ignacio Durán had been a student of Casimiro Liceaga and Manuel de Jesús Febles at the university, graduating in 1824 and shortly thereafter becoming Febles's substitute in the *prima de medicina* course. In 1838, when the medical school reopened under the directorship of Liceaga, Durán was appointed adjunct professor, and seven years later he became its vice-director. His career reflects the transition between post-independence university training and "modern" nineteenth-century education. Durán was a participant in the struggle to provide the medical education that would ensure the continuation of his profession. In 1846 he became the director of the medical school he had helped to establish, and a mentor to the following generations. Eduardo Liceaga was one of his protégés. Durán allowed the young man, who had just lost his father, to live in a spare room at the school's premises and tried to help him obtain funding to complete his studies. He also introduced his student, new to the capital, to his extended family and circle of friends, making sure he was included in family gatherings and weekend meals. This helped Liceaga to develop a network of friends and acquaintances that would prove invaluable in his personal and professional future.[229]

During the first two decades after independence, physicians and surgeons served in public posts that allowed them to contribute to the legislation of the new country and further their professional interests. In 1825 Casimiro Liceaga occupied the post of senator and was twice a congressman for his native state of Guanajuato. He also served as a member of the Facultad Médica and was instrumental in drawing up the medical curriculum in 1833. Ignacio Erazo, Miguel Muñoz, Manuel de Jesús Febles, Pedro Escobedo, and Manuel Carpio were also congressmen and senators and took part in the reorganization of education. Manuel Andrade was part of the departmental congress in 1846, and Durán was one of Mexico's representatives in Italy and France.[230] Later on, Miguel Francisco Jiménez formed part of the interim government before the arrival of Maximilian of Habsburg.

Military service was another tie that united physicians, promoted cohesion, and furthered the interests of the profession. Casimiro Liceaga, Ignacio Durán, Pedro Escobedo, Pedro del Villar, José Ferrer Espejo, and Luis Hidalgo y Carpio served as military practitioners. Liceaga had joined the insurgent forces during the independence wars and entered Mexico City with the victorious army of Iturbide, and his connection with the army continued after independence as he worked to improve its medical system.[231] Ignacio Durán had served in the military too, having been part of a volunteer royalist infantry regiment during the wars for independence and in 1833 secretary of the medical corps.[232] Pedro Escobedo occupied the important post of *consultor de sanidad militar* (literally director of military health) in 1832 and in 1836, surgeon Pedro del Villar became the first consultor of the military sanitary corps.[233] A few years later, their younger colleagues Luis Hidalgo y Carpio and José María Barceló y Villagrán joined the sanitary corps and participated in the 1846 war against the invading armies of the United States, in which Barceló y Villagrán was taken prisoner.[234] Military as well as government posts developed closer ties among medical practitioners, put them in close contact with powerful figures, and facilitated their participation in the reform of medical education and public health.[235]

Other practitioners served temporarily in cases of emergency such as the 1847 defence of Mexico City, a cause that rallied students and faculty. In 1847, as the American troops marched towards the capital, students and staff collected among themselves a total of 238 pesos and 2 reales towards the war effort, and the professors of clinical medicine and chemistry, Miguel Francisco Jiménez and Leopoldo Río de la Loza, donated four quintals of refined saltpeter. More important, seventy-three students and eighteen faculty members volunteered to fight, and four students and two of their professors offered their services as medical personnel. With the enemy approaching, the first priority was to arm the twenty-seven volunteers who had no weapons, so, with the government's permission, the money collected was applied to this purpose. On 3 May classes were suspended to be continued "as soon as the circumstances allowed it," and five days later, volunteers led by faculty began military training in the university's patio. The unit was led by "Captain" Miguel Francisco Jiménez, "Lieutenant" Leopoldo Río de la Loza, "Sublieutenants" Francisco Vertiz and Francisco Ortega, and "Sergeants" Felipe Castillo and Rafael Lucio.[236] Among its ranks was Francisco Mellet, who years later would become director-in-chief of the medical military corps. The unit joined the Hidalgo battalion, formed by civil servants and employees, and its volunteers saw action in the bloody battle of Churubusco in August of the same year.[237] Such an experience undoubtedly solidified friendships among medical students and strengthened their relations with faculty.

Other experiences also brought physicians and medical students closer together, professionally and personally. In the nineteenth century, the practice of medicine entailed serious risks, which faculty and students shared equally. In 1847, while colleagues and students participated in the military defence of the capital, anatomy professor Manuel Andrade took charge of the Hospital de San Pablo, which was established to care for the war's casualties. With the Sisters of

Charity as its nurses, the hospital opened its doors just in time to receive the wounded from the battles of Churubusco and nearby San Angel.[238] Andrade's contribution proved to be the most costly: the following year he died as a consequence of typhus contracted in the hospital while he attended sick soldiers.[239] A more tragic example is the Battle of Tacubaya. In April 1859, after a bloody battle between liberals and conservatives, four medical students volunteered to assist medical personnel caring for the casualties. When the victorious soldiers arrived with orders to eliminate all enemies, two of the students managed to flee by jumping over a fence, but the other two, Juan Díaz Covarrubias and Ildefonso Portugal, and the surgeons Gabriel Rivero, director of the medical corps, Manuel Sánchez, Alberto Abad, and Juan Duval were executed.[240] But practitioners were at risk not only in times of war; Eduardo Liceaga recalled in his memoirs that his best friend and closest companion, Juan Jaime, contracted typhus when attending the clinical medicine courses at the Hospital de San Andrés. Away from his family, Juan Jaime became the Escuela de Medicina's responsibility. Director Durán isolated him and considered hiring a nurse but, despite the enormous risk, Liceaga and his fellow-student José Amézquita volunteered to look after their friend. Liceaga confesses that, in addition to his worry about the health of his friend, he lived in fear of contracting the terrible disease. Juan Jaime died a few weeks later.[241] The continuous danger of contagion and the risks of tending to the wounded were factors that differentiated medicine from other professions. The experiences in the classroom and the amphitheatre, the close collaboration between students and faculty in times of crisis, and their common duties, dangers, and responsibilities developed close friendships and tightened the links that joined present and future practitioners. The Escuela de Medicina united the capital's physician-surgeons, and its pivotal role in developing an inner circle cannot be underestimated. The crucial role of the school as the centre of this circle is illustrated by its tradition of taking charge of the funeral arrangements and costs of its deceased faculty members and by the attendance at such funerals of the student body.[242]

In addition to professional interests and shared hazards, some practitioners were united by common personal interests, such as music, literature, or the arts, which cemented friendships and enabled them to develop ties with important political figures who later served their interests or those of the profession. Ignacio Durán was a passionate musician and composer who, with his colleague Aniceto Ortega, also a composer, was one of the founders of the Sociedad Filarmónica Mexicana. Such an endeavour attracted important figures such as Manuel Ortiz de Montellano, subsecretary of public instruction; Manuel Siliceo, well-known politician and minister of development in the 1850s; and the millionaire Ramón Romero de Terreros.[243] Some years before, Manuel Carpio, Juan N. Navarro, and the aspiring physician Joaquín Navarro, who shared a love for literature, had joined the Academia de Letrán. Other attendants at its meetings were José Joaquín Pesado, a close friend of Carpio's who was instrumental in the 1838 reopening of the medical school, the powerful politician José María Tornel, and José María Lacunza, who later occupied influential government posts.[244]

Despite disagreements and different views on how to achieve their goals, the leadership of the profession worked together during these years. The medical school faculty contributed the salaries owed toward the purchase of a building for the school. Clearly, it would not have been easy to collect such amounts from a bankrupt government, but the gesture indicates solidarity and belief in their mission. On numerous occasions, faculty members contributed materials and instruments to teach classes and cover basic expenses. Practitioners occupied posts knowing the chances of payment were slim or served on committees voluntarily. Notwithstanding personal animosities, such an attitude reflects cooperation and a sense of purpose and contradicts the traditional perception of a clash between the university's obscurantism and the medical school's modernity. This image, repeated by numerous scholars, is not just inaccurate; it is simply false. Casimiro Liceaga and Manuel de Jesús Febles may have represented two rival institutions competing for resources and a place in the new educational system, but both had formed part of the Protomedicato during its last years, they were colleagues at the university, and they collaborated throughout their lives. Liceaga continued to be an active member of the university community until his death, and both served and collaborated as members of the Facultad Médica. They represented the interests of different institutions and had different views, but in the end both pursued the same objective – the improvement of medical education. Only the latter can explain Febles's decision to donate the 1,000 pesos he was owed for serving as member of the Consejo Superior to the medical school, then under the directorship of Liceaga.[245]

In summary, their limited number, similar socioeconomic backgrounds, professional education, common interests, and privileged economic position distinguished physicians as an exclusive group that provided services indispensable to government and society. Within the larger group, a determined minority seized the leadership and struggled for years to achieve its vision. In the end, their hard work, personal sacrifices, and perseverance allowed them to shape medical education and the future of the profession. To the medical leadership, the reform and control of medical education was vital for professional survival and the continuation of the existing hierarchy – thus, their persistence in establishing a medical school and their decision to support it, despite sudden political changes, government inefficiency, and the authorities' arbitrary decisions. For politicians, medical reform was part of a larger educational project with political and economic objectives, an "organic plan" that had to meet these objectives and reconcile various interests. Despite their different goals, government and physicians knew collaboration was imperative to achieve their goals. Government officials consulted with medical practitioners, who responded willingly, serving in committees, presenting proposals, and helping to draft legislation. The numerous education projects and the resulting legislation reflect such collaboration, indicate the gradual evolution of medical education reform, and disprove the traditional image of sudden innovation. In 1833 the medical elite achieved its immediate goal, the establishment of a medical school with an updated curriculum based on the Paris school.

The medical school's program and the proposals for medical reform illustrate the great influence France had on medical education in Mexico. They also indicate the selective choices reformers made. As they did not (or could not) imitate French medical education blindly, they adapted it to suit Mexican realities and their own interests. They adopted the French officiat but rejected higher university degrees, so as not to hinder their own monopoly over education, and they incorporated most of the courses offered by the écoles preparatoires, but omitted the dissections course for pragmatic reasons.

The medical leadership's need for control and independence ensured the survival of the medical school against immense odds. To achieve their objectives, the leaders first concentrated on the issue of monopoly. Thus, we see their opposition to the Escuela de Cirugía and its insistence on the separation of medicine and surgery, which would have hindered their exclusive control. The antagonism between the medical college and the surgical school went beyond institutional jealousy: it was a competition for scarce funds, limited space, students, and even dissection material. It was ultimately a battle for survival. The struggle ended in 1838 with the closure of the surgical school, but the physicians' victory was incomplete, as the army continued training its own practitioners.

The conflict with the university Faculty of Medicine stemmed from the same issues of control and independence, buttressed by the contemporary disdain for traditional corporations. Collaboration was impossible, because it curtailed the independence of the medical school and its control over education. Thus, the latter rejected accommodation and did everything within its power to exclude its rival. By the late 1850s, the medical leadership had achieved a monopoly over (civilian) medical education, but at a hefty price. By eliminating the Faculty of Medicine, they had forfeited the possibility of higher studies and of research, which were left to individual initiative – to practitioners with enough time and resources to undertake them. Nonetheless, by the end of the period under study, the medical school founders had achieved their goal: providing the best formal medical education available in the country, an education based on the Paris school.

In Search of Recognition:
The Establishment of the Academy
of Medicine, 1820–1827

In 1827, the French physician resident in Mexico Juan Luis Chavert published his work on yellow fever. The result of more than five years of research, the work was translated into Spanish by Casimiro Liceaga and was dedicated to President Guadalupe Victoria. Chavert, a graduate of Montpellier who arrived in Veracruz in 1817, was one of the first French practitioners, but certainly not the only one, to choose Mexico as his residence.[1] The collaboration between Mexican and French practitioners can be traced back to the late colonial period. French physicians were among the founders of the first medical associations and the present-day Academia de Medicina that are the focus of this chapter. The views of contemporary Mexican practitioners regarding their role were accurately summarized by Manuel Carpio in an article published by one of the first short-lived medical academies: "Our scientific relations with France are much more intimate because they are easier than [those] with the rest of Europe, therefore we will preferably speak of French and Mexican medicine, mentioning briefly ... [the medical beliefs] in other countries."[2]

This chapter analyzes the long and winding path that resulted in the establishment of the first permanent medical academy in Mexico. The first section examines the short-lived academies or societies founded between 1820 and 1860 and their legacy. The second section analyzes the academies' publications as a mirror of the development of medicine in Mexico and the growing self-assurance of its practitioners. The final section concentrates on the unusual circumstances that resulted in the establishment of the Sección de Medicina and its successor, the Sociedad de Medicina (1866), which became the Academia Nacional de Medicina de México (1887), and the role played by the French army in its initial years.

Since colonial times, the medical elite had exchanged ideas and participated in university debates, or *actos*. In 1774 the university held a public debate on Albrecht von Haller's *De Sensibilité*, and Friedrich Hoffman's *Pathology* was debated in 1785.[3] Although far from a free exchange of ideas, such debates allowed physicians to present and explore contemporary theories and ideas with their colleagues. The demise of the university, precipitated by the wars of independence and the post-independence period, deprived practitioners of both the venue and the infrastructure for such exchanges. · Rapid nineteenth-century medical developments increased the urgent need for a scientific academy, recognized nationally and internationally, to communicate and discuss the new ideas. The importance of such an organization, when the only way to make contact was either by letter or publication, cannot be understated. Regular meetings served not only to communicate innovations, but also to discuss personal experiences, weave a professional network, and develop professional self-assurance. Academies also allowed participants to claim their place among those who had specialized knowledge and separated them from laymen. In Mexico, efforts to establish a permanent academy of medicine ran parallel with the struggle of the medical elite to provide and control medical education and be recognized as specialists in health-related matters. Mexico was not unique among Latin American countries. The nineteenth century saw the establishment of medical academies in, for example, Argentina (the Academia Nacional de Buenos Aires, 1822), Brazil (the Royal Medical and Surgical Society, 1829), Cuba (the Academia de Ciencias Médicas, Físicas y Naturales, 1861), and Colombia (the Sociedad de Medicina y Ciencias Médicas de Bogotá, 1873, which became the Academia Nacional de Medicina de Colombia in 1887).[4] Peru founded a short-lived Sociedad Médica de Lima in 1854 and the Academia Libre de Medicina de Lima in 1884, which became a national academy in 1888.[5] Each of these organizations was the result of local circumstances, but the objectives and political and military context of the Mexican case make it unique.

THE FIRST ACADEMIES, 1820–1860

Medical academies (study groups under a professor equivalent to modern-day seminars) had existed in Mexico since colonial times. In the middle of the eighteenth century, Nicolás Torres, professor of *method medendi* (therapeutics) at the Real y Pontifícia Universidad de México, established one in his residence, with "enormous benefits" to the attending students; half a century later, in 1808, attendance at the academy that met at the home of the president of the Protomedicato, José Ignacio García Jove, became obligatory for medical students.[6] Similarly, an academy of surgery was formed after independence. It included theoretical lessons taught at the university that were complemented by practical instruction at the Hospital de San Andrés under the guidance of surgeon Pedro Escobar. Surgical instruments and other course expenses were paid by army surgeon José Ruiz, who wished to promote the surgical techniques of Dominique Jean Larrey and Guillaume Dupuytren.[7] The medical education programs drafted in the 1830s continued to refer to such academies, which were described as "establishments of instruction for those who want to pursue a profession."[8]

The changes brought by independence were conducive to the establishment of another type of academy, defined as either "a scientific, literary, or artistic society" or "a junta or meeting of academics."[9] Such societies aimed to improve knowledge and to act as guardians of the profession's exclusive knowledge, and they were indispensable for the profession's credibility and legitimacy. From a more pragmatic point of view, academies offered practitioners a forum and facilitated professional ties among colleagues. The earliest attempt at such an association was the Academia de Medicina Práctica de México, formed in Mexico City in 1825 "to promote the progress of all branches of medicine, especially Pathology." Its regulations stipulated that membership consisted of core (*socios de número*), honorary, and correspondent members. The first group consisted of physicians, surgeons, and pharmacists who resided in the capital and were appointed by the academy. Their obligations included fulfilling "the assigned tasks and commissions" and attending all monthly meetings and extraordinary sessions.[10] Honorary members were expected to be present at biannual meetings and had the right, but not the obligation, to attend the regular first-Monday-of-the-month sessions. The last category, correspondent members, was reserved for provincial practitioners, who reported on local "medical topography," epidemic ailments, and other relevant information. When joining the academy, all members had to either present a *Memoria,* a report or an ailment's "curious history," or to donate instruments, books, or other items worthy of the institution.

Members paid a one peso fee per trimester, and when the institution could not cover its expenses they were to make a voluntary contribution.[11] Unfortunately, little evidence remains of the activities and legacy of the Academia de Medicina Práctica, which is mentioned only in passing by some authors, including Francisco de Asís Flores y Troncoso and José Alvarez Amézquita et al. (table 5.1).[12] We know, however, that the academy was hard at work in the year of its establishment: in the midst of an ongoing measles epidemic and upon the request of the federal government, it published a *Memoria Instructiva sobre la enfermedad epidémica del sarampion* (Instructive treatise on the smallpox epidemic).[13] Written by surgeon Pedro Escobedo and physicians Francisco Rodríguez (Puebla) and Francisco Alvarado, the work included information about the course of the illness, preventive measures, and home treatment for those who lacked either a physician or the means to pay for medical treatment. The *Memoria Instructiva* seems to be the only surviving work of the academy, which disappears from the records soon after its publication.[14]

It was ten years before another similar organization, the Academia de Medicina de Mégico, was established in the capital. Citing an unpublished manuscript of Dr Nicolás León, Alvarez Amézquita et al. state that the academy was formed in 1836 after the failure to re-establish the medical school. In a 1839 speech Manuel Carpio, professor of philosophy and hygiene at the university, stated that the Academia "had more than three and a half years of existence," which would place its opening in 1835.[15] To add to the confusion, the minutes of the academy's 20 January 1840 session clearly stated that article 25 of the (1838) medical school provisional regulations ordered the faculty to form "a society of medicine with its own regulations."[16] Article 25 reads: "The professors will form a Society of Medicine with its own regulations for the improvement of this science. Such society will admit national and foreign members that for their reputation or services deserve such distinction."[17]

By 1838, after the Academia Medicina de Mégico had been functioning for at least three years, legislation sought to either tie it to the Colegio de Medicina and thus bring it under government control, or replace it with a new organization. The following year, the authorities were pressuring the academy to add its members to the medical school faculty, "as prescribed in the regulations."[18] Although the official minutes indicate the academy's membership was formed in large part by the medical school faculty, its members preferred to be

Table 5.1 Academies of medicine in Mexico, 1800–1887

Academia de Medicina Práctica de México (1825–?)
Academia de Medicina de Mégico (1835?–43)
Academia de Medicina de México (1851–?)
Unión Médica de México (1856–58?)
Sección de Medicina de la Comisión Científica y Literaria de México (1864–66)
Sociedad Médica de México (1866–73)
Academia de Medicina de México (1873–87)
Academia Nacional de Medicina de México (1887–present)

independent of the school.[19] After careful deliberation, the commission in charge concluded that the regulations did not specify that members of the academy had also to belong to the medical school and that few, if any advantages of mutual membership would derive to both organizations. The commission argued that the two were of "a different nature due to their origin and existence, obligations and rewards." Most important, the school would take precedence, which would result in its overriding the academy's regulations and purpose, and members would lose their freedom to exert control over their academy's regulations and fate.[20] There were also pragmatic concerns, such as the role to be played by non-faculty academy members added to the professorial staff, the uncertainty of attracting professors willing to serve in both organizations, and the extra duties their fusion would involve. It is worth noting, however, that the academy's independence was feasible only because it received no financial assistance from government – there was, after all, a silver lining to the authorities' financial neglect of such organizations.

At a time when practitioners lacked governmental support to carry on research and develop professionally, the Academia de Medicina de Mégico, described as "a literary corporation whose only goal was to promote scientific advance," played a crucial role.[21] It had an organization similar to that of the Academia de Medicina Práctica, with core, honorary, and correspondent members. Ordinary sessions took place regularly at its permanent location at the convent of Belén (also location of the medical school) and, when necessary, members were called to extraordinary sessions. The meetings served as a forum to discuss national and international medical developments, current epidemics, and diseases, as well as the cases of individual patients and their best course of treatment. For example, at the 18 November 1839 session, those in attendance discussed their observations of hemorrhages, tumours in the knees, and the use of mercury to treat erysipelas (a skin infection).[22] On 16 March 1840 the discussion centred on a smallpox epidemic then under way, its prevention, and most promising treatments, as well as the practitioners' personal experience in cases of complication. Pedro Escobedo reminded his listeners of surgeon Miguel Muñoz's recommendation of cold baths to fight smallpox. His colleague Manuel Carpio disagreed, arguing that the lack of a proper scientific testing method precluded any conclusions on the matter. Escobedo insisted, however, that during the first stage of the illness, warm baths and good ventilation were always "useful." As a consensus was not reached, the president called on all members to gather data so the issue could be further discussed at the following meeting.[23]

Outstanding practitioners were invited to join as correspondent members. Thus, in the 18 November 1839 session, the names of Guillermo Cheyne and his brother Jorge, both residents of Guanajuato, were put forward by Severino Galenzowski, Manuel Carpio, and Pablo Martínez del Río.[24] The Londoner Guillermo Cheyne arrived in Guanajauto in 1827 as the physician of a mining company. He had trained at the Royal College of Surgery and attended the University of Hesse, where he obtained the degree of "doctor in medicine, surgery, and the art of midwifery." Soon after, his brother joined him in Guanajuato. Both physicians were highly regarded by the local political authorities and had offered their services pro bono in times of crises.[25]

By 1840, the academy had established a web of correspondent members throughout Mexico, allowing Leopoldo Río de la Loza to gather information from Puebla, Veracruz, Guanajuato, and Morelia on the smallpox epidemic.[26] In addition to individual correspondents, the academy had cordial relations with the Sociedad de Emulación de Guadalajara, a similar organization presided over by the physician, politician, and University of Mexico graduate Pedro Tames. In 1839, the academy sent its Guadalajara counterpart copies of its journals and diplomas for its members and, when it required data on the smallpox epidemic, its members contacted their Guadalajara colleagues.[27] Medical academies and societies were important centres for the communication and exchange of ideas and experiences, not only among practitioners residing in the same city, but between colleagues who lived in different geographic areas. Furthermore, academies, as centres of specialized knowledge, lent professional legitimacy to their members.

In this recently formed academy, links with internationally renowned practitioners and associations were vital for national and international recognition. Thus, the Academia de Medicina de Mégico reached out to famous foreign practitioners who were at the forefront of medical developments. In 1839 Ignacio Durán, Manuel Robledo, and José Terán proposed inviting the renowned physiologist François Magendie, the genito-urinary surgeon Philippe Ricord, and a Dr Ponzi from Rome to become correspondent members. For their part, Carpio, Martínez del Río, and Galenzowski put forward the names of the plastic surgeons Friedrich Johann Dieffenbach from Hamburg and a Herr Fricke from Berlin. All such proposals were unanimously endorsed.[28]

In addition to the invitations extended to well-known individuals, the academy reached out to similar organizations in other countries. Of utmost importance were ties with medical organizations of the "civilized countries," which would amount to an international seal of approval and legitimacy. In this, the academy availed itself of its foreign members to approach organizations overseas. When the already mentioned Luis Estevan Blaquiere, a French physician and member of the academy resident in Mexico, travelled to Europe, he carried introductory letters and copies of the academy's journal. Blaquiere's first stop was the United States, where he presented a letter with a copy of the publications to both the New York Medical Surgical Society and the Philadelphia Medical Society. On his arrival in France, he contacted the Académie Royale de Médecine, the Societé d'Emulation, and the Societé de Médecine de Paris, as well as "a society in Strasbourg." He also sent letters of introduction to medical societies in London, Berlin, Turin, Vienna, and Pavia, among others, taking the precaution of delivering them personally to their countries' respective ambassadors in Paris. Also, as soon as diplomatic relations between Mexico and Spain were established in December 1836, Blaquiere approached the Madrid academy.[29]

On his return to Mexico, Blaquiere reported that the French organizations had responded immediately, "praising our articles and encouraging our efforts." The Académie Royal de Médecine had assured corresponding membership reciprocity, and Strasbourg had gone further by sending membership diplomas to five members of the Mexican academy. Madrid had also responded enthusiastically, and the academy at Pavia, which was then part of the Austrian Empire, had stated its desire to initiate relations as soon as it obtained permission from Austrian authorities.[30] On the other hand, Blaquiere complained, England, Prussia, Austria, and the United States "did not dignify us with a response." He concluded his report by stating that there were more *elementos de simpatía* between Mexico and France than between Mexico and any other nation. Blaquiere's experience undoubtedly brought the Mexican organization closer to its French counterparts and increased its members' admiration and esteem for France. Not surprisingly, in presenting his *Extrait de Mes Tablettes d'outre-mer* to the Medical Society of Toulouse in March 1851, Dr Dencausse noted that all scientific books in Mexico were French, and that Mexican medicine reflected the French school.[31]

Despite the government's lack of support, the Academia de Medicina de Megico published its journal for seven years. Exactly when and why the academy ceased its activities is unclear, but the 1842 legislation organizing medical education and practice may have been a factor. The academy's efforts were continued by another organization originally established in 1840, called the Sociedad Filoiátrica de México. Again, there is confusion about dates of formation. Alvarez Amézquita et al., quoting Nicolás León as their source, say this organization was formed in 1844 by some members of the extinct Academia de Medicina. The Sociedad Filoiátrica, Amézquita continues, lasted only two years, leaving the second volume of its journal unpublished.[32] Yet a bound manuscript in the Nicolás León library indicates the organization was established in 1840 or 1841 at the latest.[33] The manuscript's introduction, written by Juan N. Navarro on 2 November 1840, states the founders' objective was "to illustrate themselves in this society, that one day will be part of Mexico's history of medicine." The Sociedad Filoiátrica was formed by younger members, a coming and more critical generation that sought a better future for its profession.[34] According to *Revista Médica,* the Sociedad Filoiátrica published its journal through 1844 and at least part of 1845, so one may assume that it lasted for at least five years.[35]

In 1851, another attempt was made to organize an academy, the first meeting taking place at the residence of Leopoldo Río de la Loza on the evening of 30 November (table 5.1). He reminded the twenty-seven practitioners present that "medical corporations have

followed each other ... each serving as the basis for the next one."
The new Academia de Medicina de México elected Río de la Loza as
its president and Gabino Barreda as its secretary, both professors
of the medical school.[36] Unfortunately, this organization was more
ephemeral than its predecessors, publishing its *Periódico de la
Academia de Medicina de México* for only one year. Mexico's practitioners refused to accept defeat, however, and yet another academy
was established in 1856 under the name of La Unión Médica de
México, this time under the leadership of Gabino Barreda. Once
again, it is unclear why or when it ceased to function – its journal,
La Unión Médica de México: Organo de la Academia de Medicina,
was published from 1856 to 1858 – but its fate was undoubtedly
affected by the political turmoil of the time. Its successor, the
Sociedad de Medicina, Mexico's first permanent medical professional organization, would be founded seven years later under
exceptional circumstances.

The above organizations were short-lived but not irrelevant. They
functioned as the only venues where medical practitioners could
meet to discuss medical issues and their professional experiences. By
opening membership to their provincial colleagues, the Mexico City
membership sought to create a national professional network at a
time when political and economic conditions prevented enforcement
of national policies and professional uniformity. The academies'
publications are of great historical importance, because they trace
the development of Mexican medicine and its practitioners from
imitation and mere importation of European medical writings to
research-oriented articles of local interest written by more self-
confident authors proud of their achievements.

DISSEMINATING INFORMATION:
MEDICAL JOURNALS, 1820–1860

All the above early academies shared the common goal of promoting
and diffusing medical knowledge and research for the improvement
of the profession by means of their publications. The first and lon-
ger-lasting of these publications was the *Periódico de la Academia de
Medicina de Mégico* published by the Academia de Medicina de
Mégico from 1836 to 1840, and again, under the directorship of
Manuel Carpio, in 1843. Later attempts, such as the *Periódico de la
Academia de Medicina de México* (1852), under the leadership of

Leopoldo Río de la Loza, or *La Unión Médica de México: Organo de la Academia de Medicina*, issued when the academy reorganized itself as the Unión Médica de México (1856–58) under Gabino Barreda, were shorter-lived.

The objectives, content, and authorship of these publications reflected both the continuity and the evolution of the medical profession in Mexico. They were written and read by mainstream practitioners and represented the views of the medical establishment. They focused on medical topics, dedicating a smaller section to contemporary issues of interest to their medical readership that was merely informative, the editors prudently refraining from criticizing government health-care initiatives or policies. In some exceptional cases, the local interests of the capital's medical elite were defended, as in two articles published in 1843 attacking the Dirección de Sanidad de Puebla for its decision to license two practitioners not approved by the capital's medical authorities.[37] This was clearly a matter of competing jurisdictions, and the local medical establishment did not shy away from defending its interests in writing.

The journals' objectives and content must be analyzed on the basis of the generational differences of the authors. The physicians who collaborated on articles published in these journals may be divided roughly into three generational groups that sometimes overlapped. The first was formed of physicians and surgeons who had been educated during the wars of independence or shortly afterwards – men born at the turn of the nineteenth century, such as Casimiro Liceaga, Manuel Carpio, Tomás Guapillo, José María Espejo, José Manuel González Urueña, and José Manuel Romero. They knew first-hand the difficulties a medical student faced when the university was occupied by the army, epidemics descended on the city, and the economic situation deteriorated day by day. They had lived through trade embargos, interruptions of transatlantic crossings due to war, and political censorship – factors that had restricted their ability to follow the developments of European medicine as closely as they would have liked. Thus, the main objective of these early journals was not to publish local research but to disseminate foreign medical literature.

The second group of authors, born between 1805 and 1820, faced a different scenario. Post-independence Mexico offered hope but only a limited improvement in conditions to those who wanted to pursue a medical career. Lack of funding, government indifference and inefficiency, and the retirement and deaths of university medical faculty had left noticeable gaps in their education. Deprived of its hospital and in serious financial trouble, the Escuela de Cirugía had little else to offer, and the slow start of the Establecimiento de Ciencias Médicas was as frustrating as it was discouraging. Many physicians of this generation were trained mainly by apprenticeship, learning from physicians and surgeons who had access to a hospital and were willing to tutor them. Some were apprenticed in army hospitals. Ramón Alfaro, for example, was forced to interrupt his studies in 1831 and was unable to continue them when the Establecimiento de Medicina opened its doors. He had to finish his training as a surgeon at a Toluca military hospital, and was later licensed as a physician in accordance with the 23 November 1831 law.[38] A few in this generation were fortunate enough to travel to France and learn from the great Parisian practitioners. Manuel Andrade, José María Vertiz, Ignacio Erazo, Leopoldo Río de la Loza, Manuel Robredo, and Gabino Barreda, all professors at the medical school, belonged to this group.

The last group was composed of practitioners born after 1820. Their struggle was different, as they had access to formal medical training. Nonetheless, their education left much to be desired as a result of the medical school's frequent closings and relocations and unsatisfactory installations and equipment. This was a more self-assured and critical generation, frustrated by limited opportunities to keep up with the latest medical developments and profoundly influenced by French medicine – the future ophthalmologists Agustín Andrade and Rafael Lavista; Eduardo Liceaga, who distinguished himself in the public health field; and the military practitioner Francisco Montes de Oca are amongst them. They were later followed by practitioners with a sounder education and better professional organization, heirs to the struggle of previous generations.

The first journal, the *Periódico de la Academia de Medicina de Mégico* published from 1836 to 1843, provided the pattern for those that followed. Its first volume consists of two sections, "Academic Works" and "Diverse Notes," to which a third section, "Documents Related to the Life of the Academy," was added the following year. "Academic Works" occupies most of the space and consists of articles written by local physicians or translations from other publications, some of which do not indicate the author's name or do not specify if the name given belongs to the author or the translator. All articles submitted were reviewed by an editorial committee that on occasion requested corrections, and had to be officially accepted by a majority.[39]

The first volume of the *Periódico de la Academia de Medicina de Mégico* contains sixty-nine articles under "Academic Works" and only three in the second section, "Diverse Notes."[40] During the following years, the journal published between fifty and sixty-five articles a year, except for 1840, when only forty-two were published. Themes vary immensely, and often the same author writes about completely different topics. In 1836, Luis Estevan Blaquiere collaborated on four pieces on the bilateral method to operate for kidney stones, painful menstruation, a lead and opium treatment for pneumonia, and ovarian dropsy; González Urueña wrote on the treatment of burns; Andrés del Río contributed a piece on Mr Mattensi's experiments with a "torpedo";[41] and Manuel Andrade described Parisian hospitals in two different articles.[42] Subsequent volumes of the *Periódico* were equally eclectic, reflecting the authors' many interests and their practice of general, as opposed to specialized, medicine.

The second section, "Diverse Notes," also underwent changes as more articles were gradually inserted. This included news about the medical school, a circular of the Consejo Superior de Salubridad, the obituaries of colleagues, and the above-mentioned articles on the decision of the Dirección de Sanidad de Puebla. However, the section's objective, to include information on non-medical issues of interest to the medical profession, was sometimes obscured by the inclusion of purely medical themes, such as an article on "cold tumours" and another on tracheotomy, that seem to belong to the "Academic Works" section. The last section of the journal was reserved for the minutes of the Academia de Medicina's meetings.

The contribution of foreign practitioners residing in Mexico cannot be overstated. Louis Estevan Blaquiere, Louis Jecker, Cristiano Julio Guillermo Schiede, Gabriel Villete, German Federico von Uslar, and Severino Galenzowski were enthusiastic members of the Academia de Medicina de Mégico and important contributors to the first medical journals. Of the sixty-nine articles published in 1836 under "Academic Works," thirty-four were written by foreigners (some of them translations from articles published abroad); another thirty-one were composed by Mexicans, and four were anonymous (table 5.2). Seven of the foreign collaborators resided in Mexico City, and at least four of them – Schiede, Blaquiere, Jecker, and Galenzowski – were actively engaged in the academy's regular sessions. Juan McCartney was also an active member but did not contribute to the publication. Schiede contributed five articles on diverse topics: a treatise on diabetes, observations on epidemic, and *materia médica* or pharmacology. Blaquiere wrote four pieces on lithotomy, dysmenorrhea, a lead and opium treatment for pneumonia, and hydropsia in the ovary. Jecker contributed with three articles on lithotomy, malformation of female genitourinary organs, and children's pneumonia. Galenzowski's article deals with ablation of the inferior left half jaw. Among the non-resident foreign authors included were P.A. Piorri, a contributor to the *Dictionnaire des Sciences Médicales* published in Paris; François Lallemand, a Montpellier physician; and a Dr Weber (probably Hermann Weber). Piorri's articles explore "acute spontaneous arthritis," Lallemand's seems to be a summary of his *Des pertes séminales involontaires* about to be published in Paris (1838),[43] and Weber's dealt with calomel as a treatment for typhoid infections. Among the main Mexican contributors were Manuel Carpio with fourteen articles, Manuel Andrade with four, and Ignacio Erazo and Pablo Martìnez del Río, who wrote two each. Their topics included childbirth, use of ammoniac in apoplexy, use of purgatives in typhoid fevers, diabetes, *coqueluche* (whooping cough), effects of typhoid infections on the stomach, Bright's disease, and cleft lip operation. In total, the 1836 volume included the work of nine Mexican practitioners and twenty-one foreigners, as well as four unsigned works that include articles published in foreign journals (table 5.2). The volume includes also the obituary of one of the contributors, Guillermo Schiede.[44]

The following year, the number of Mexican contributors decreased to eight, but the trend was similar: of sixty-three articles in the "Academic Works" section, forty were by eighteen foreign practitioners, twenty-one by eight Mexicans, and two anonymous (table 5.2). Manuel Carpio continued to be the most prolific of all, writing nine articles; Jecker contributed eight, Galenzowski seven, and Manuel Andrade five. Adolfo Hegewich and Gabriel Villette wrote four each, and Uslar and Pablo Martínez del Río three. Clearly, foreign practitioners living in Mexico played a key role in the launching of the country's first medical journal.[45] In 1839, eighteen foreigners and fourteen Mexicans contributed to the journal with twenty and seventeen articles respectively; nineteen more were anonymous, mostly translations from foreign works, with the authors of three identified only by their initials. In 1840, the journal contained forty-two articles in its "Academic Works" section by thirteen Mexicans (twenty-two articles) and only five foreigners (five articles); fifteen articles were anonymous (two signed with initials). Among the foreign authors, only Luis Blaquiere resided in Mexico. The number of articles written by each author had diminished considerably, the maximum being three pieces by both Ramón Alfaro and Manuel Robredo (table 5.2).[46]

The journal was then discontinued for two years, but a final volume appeared in 1843, with contributions by sixteen foreign and thirteen Mexican authors (fifteen and thirty-one articles respectively), and seven anonymous articles, apparently reprints from other publications (tables 5.2 and 5.3). The only foreign author residing in Mexico was again Blaquiere, who contributed one article. Among the Mexicans, Luis Hidalgo y Carpio and Leopoldo Río de la Loza wrote six articles each, Agustín Andrade and Manuel Robredo three each, and Miguel Francisco Jiménez and José María Terán two each. Surprisingly, the formerly prolific Manuel Carpio, now the publication's director, contributed no articles to this final volume of the *Periódico de la Academia de Medicina de Mégico*.[47]

The reasons for the decreasing collaboration of foreigners in the last two volumes or the interruption in the journal's publication are not clear. A factor to be considered is the expulsion of French citizens following France's invasion of Veracruz in 1838. With the scarcity of practitioners and the high regard in which French physicians were held, it is unclear how many were affected. We do know that Blaquiere, Hegewisch, MacCartney, Villette, and Galenzowski continued to attend meetings regularly and be active participants. Neither the academy's regulations nor the minutes of its sessions make any reference to the authors' nationality, but it may have been decided to give preference to local contributors, or perhaps a younger generation was beginning to take charge. What is clear is that, by 1839, there was tension among the members. A disagreement between Manuel Andrade and Rafael Martínez caused the latter to suddenly renounce his post as secretary.[48] The position was then occupied by Julián Sobrino, who published an angry refutation of Andrade's claim that Sobrino was to blame for some mistakes in the publication.[49] A year later, in the 7 December 1840 session, the academy was informed in writing that Villette was renouncing his membership as the result of his numerous occupations, so his name

Table 5.2 *Periodico de la Academia de Medicina de Mégico*: Articles published under "Academic Works" section, 1836–1843

Year of publication*	Foreign authors	Mexican authors	Anonymous articles	Total
1836	34	31	4	69
1837	40	21	2	63
1838	26	20	14	60
1839	20	17	19	56
1840	5	22	15	42
1843	15	31	7	53

*Some articles were written by more than one author.
Source: Fernández del Castillo, *Bibliografía*.

was immediately erased from the list.[50] Thus internal fighting among the membership may have contributed to the two-year gap in the journal's publication and the academy's demise.

Notwithstanding such disagreements and the motives behind the changes in authorship, physicians were gradually asserting control over their academy and its journal. Although in 1840 many of the articles published continued to be translations of European publications, a larger number of local practitioners contributed with articles about their own work. Thus, the Academia de Medicina de Mégico and its journal helped to build the profession's self-confidence and the image of the practitioners themselves.

The successor of the *Periódico de la Academia de Medicina de Mégico* was the short-lived and more critical *Periódico de la Sociedad Filoiátrica*. The first attempt to publish the journal goes back to November 1840, as indicated by a manuscript (probably a draft) under the same title. Its introduction states a physician should not be content with possessing knowledge, because "his noble position forces him to publish his writings" and demands from him the "difficult and precarious art of writing." The journal presumably intended to give physicians the opportunity to "dedicate themselves to writing." Thus the editors invite their colleagues to contribute to the publication, begging at the same time for the reader's forgiveness for the lack of variety in the first issue and its "many defects." The rest of the manuscript includes the translated biographies of famous European physicians and the signatures of Juan N. Navarro, Rafael Lucio, G.J. Bustamante, Francisco Ortega, Aniceto Ortega,

and Patricio Balbuena as translator.[51] All the signatories had been
born between 1819 and 1825 and were still students, a younger generation eager to promote the last European innovations and improve
the Mexican medical establishment.

It was not until 1844, however, that the *Periódico de la Sociedad
Filoiátrica* appeared in print. Very different from the 1840 manuscript, the printed version sought to reach fellow practitioners (the
organizers were now licensed physicians) and raise awareness of
medical-related issues and the role practitioners played in society.
The editors mention "the unfortunate ending" of the journal of the
Academia de Medicina de Mégico, "the only one of its kind." To fill
the void, the editors promise to include unedited *memorias* (observations) on local medical cases, articles on forensic medicine and public health, and the most outstanding pieces published in French and
English journals. Among the articles in the now-bound volume are
local news and (mostly critical) commentaries on contemporary
issues, such as the obstacles pharmacists faced in publishing their
Farmacopea Mexicana due to governmental policies.[52] In a bitter
article on "clinical teaching," the young professor José María Reyes
vents his frustration at the "obstacles that hindered clinical learning."[53] He points a finger at professors who failed to fulfill their
duties, the hospital system, and the students' conduct, as well as at
inefficient administration and government stinginess. Reyes followed
up with another piece in which he proposes solutions to correct such
problems.[54] The Escuela de Medicina was not the only body criticized; the Consejo Superior de Salubridad was also reproached for
its "useless efforts" to improve hospitals and prisons, and the government for ignoring the "enlightened writings" it had received.[55]

Most of the articles in the *Periódico de la Sociedad Filoiátrica*
are authored works, and pieces that were extracts of a foreign work
are so identified in their title – for example, "Bibliographic Extract
on the Work of Mr Abercrombie on Stomach Illnesses," "Extract
on Surgical Operations: Results of Statistical Studies in the Paris
Hospitals," or "Examination of Phrenology in Gall, Spurzheim, and
Broussais Doctrines." Among the contributors are well-established
practitioners such as Manuel Carpio, and younger colleagues such
as Miguel Francisco Jiménez, and the future professors Ladislao de
la Pascua and José María Barceló de Villagrán, who would soon
make a name for themselves. The *Periódico de la Sociedad Filoiátrica*,
however, was unable to survive for more than a few months.[56]

In 1851, a reorganized Academia de Medicina de México made another attempt to publish a medical journal, the *Periódico de la Academia de Medicina de México*.[57] Leopoldo Río de la Loza and Gabino Barreda, the academy's president and vice president, respectively, became its editors. In its only volume, it follows the same organization as the *Periódico de la Academia de Medicina de México*. Under "Academic Works" are fourteen articles, five of which are anonymous, eight written by six Mexican physicians, and one a reprint of a foreign author (tables 5.3 and 5.4). The section concentrates exclusively on medical articles, such as "Heart Hypertrophy," by Juan N. Navarro; "Arterial Diameter," by Martín Alfaro and Marcelino Palacios; "About Chloroform," by Ramón Alfaro; and "Extraction of Strange Bodies," by Gabino Barreda; there is also an article on the curative method for myopia by a Dr Turnbull. Six Mexican practitioners collaborated on the publication.[58] The second section, "Diverse Notes," consists of eleven anonymous articles on miscellaneous medical-related topics, such as the birth of live quintuplets, a new anti-syphilitic, the uses of cod liver oil, and the speech given at the medical physics ceremony. The volume also contains the minutes of the academy's sessions held between November 1851 and September 1852, and an anonymous text, with its own pagination, entitled "Elements of Internal Pathology," divided into three chapters about the "first, second, and third class of illnesses" and presumably written as a text for medical students.[59]

Five years later, a new Academia de Medicina launched yet another journal, *La Unión Médica de México: Organo de la Academia de Medicina*, under the directorship of Gabino Barreda. The journal, which was published only in 1856–58, contains twenty-nine biweekly issues in two volumes. The first volume has forty-nine articles under "Academic Works" and thirty under "Diverse Notes." A third section, "Documents Related to the Life of the Academy," is reserved for the minutes of the academy's meetings. Although the *Unión Médica* is similar in organization to previous journals, its content in each section is different. "Academic Works" is dedicated in its entirety to the research and discussions carried out by the academy's members, and all articles are now signed (tables 5.3 and 5.4). The topics continue to be as varied as the writers. Miguel Francisco Jiménez contributes an article on liver abscess, Manuel M. Carmona writes on blood transfusion studies, Gabino Barreda on observations on amputations in cases of dry gangrene, and Hidalgo y Carpio

Table 5.3 Nationality of collaborating authors in academic publications, 1836–1866

	1836	1837	1838	1839	1840	1843	1851	1856–58, vol. 1	1856–58, vol. 2	1864–65	1866
Foreign	21	18	15	18	5	16	1	–	1	15	6
Mexican	9	8	12	14	13	13	6	20	17	18	24

Source: Fernández del Castillo, *Bibliografía*.

on meningitis and forensic medical classification of wounds. Manuel Carpio and Ramón Alfaro, veterans of the first publication, collaborate with their disciples Rafael Lucio and Manuel Carmona on an article on chloroform. The second section, "Diverse Notes," is dedicated to foreign works, translations, extracts, and commentaries, and to local news of interest to the profession. Some of the articles in the first group indicate the author and the translator's name; among the local news stories are an article on the awards ceremony for the best students at the Escuela de Medicina and another on the use of chloroform in the Mexican army. The second volume includes twenty-five articles by seventeen local practitioners and one foreign author (another four were anonymous) and follows a rationale similar similar to that of the previous volume (tables 5.3 and 5.4). Thus, in the medical journals of the 1850s, there was a reversal of priorities. The publications became a forum for the research and professional experiences of local practitioners, and the dissemination of foreign medical developments took a second place, the result of a more self-assured generation of practitioners.

The publications of the three early academies may be the best known, but they were not the only ones. Two other medical journals that contributed to the transmission of medical knowledge and the development of professional ties among practitioners are worth mentioning: *Higea Periódico de la Salud* and *Revista Médica*. The former was the result of the efforts of two French physicians resident in Mexico, Theodoro Leger and Gabriel Villette, who either wrote or edited all its contents.[60] This biweekly publication, which first appeared on 15 April 1833, may be described as a public health journal focusing on general "hygiene," in which objective it differs from the other medical-related publications discussed above.[61] Its first number concentrates on scarlet fever, but the rest focuses on a then-raging epidemic of *cholera morbus*. In June and July of the same year the authors dedicate three issues to "private hygiene" for the benefit

Table 5.4 Academic medical journals, 1855–1866: Articles in "Academic Works" sections

Year of publication	By foreign authors	By Mexican authors	Anonymous	Total
1851[a]	1	8	5	14
1856–58[b] (vol. 1)	–	48	1	49
1856–58[b] (vol. 2)	1	25	4	30
1864[c]	19*	52	5	81
1866[c]	8	53	1	62

[a]*Periódico de la Academia de Medicina de México*

[b]*La Unión Medica de Mexico: Organo de la Academia de Medicina*

[c]*Gaceta Médica de México.*

*In addition, five articles were co-authored by French and local physicians.

Source: Fernández del Castillo, *Bibliografía*

of citizens, "young wives," and authorities. The 1 July issue includes a description of a necropsy, and the following two numbers, 15 July and 1 August, concentrate on cholera and its treatment. Both authors were firm believers in the miasmatic theory and conclude that prevailing atmospheric conditions in Mexico prevented population growth. Subscriptions to *Higea Periódico de la Salud* were available in Mexico City and state capitals, and the journal could also be purchased at Villette's residence, at 23 Donceles Street. It is unclear how many issues were published, but the cost of a subscription, a steep sixteen pesos a year, surely contributed to its demise.[62]

Revista Médica began to be published on 1 February 1851. Its aim, as the introduction indicated, was to present "material that has seen the light in Europe," so that colleagues unable to acquire foreign medical journals could obtain information at low cost. To provide a sense of mission and collegiality, the introduction ends with the hope that the need to promote "the most useful science" will be recognized by medical practitioners, who deserve to be awarded "the title of friends of humanity." The contents confirm the editors' intentions to disseminate international medical research and relevant news by including how to prepare the pills of Mr D'Avoine, statistics of the French medical profession, prizes awarded in Paris to medical students, and whooping cough observations made in Glasgow. Despite the journal's emphasis on foreign content, its editors welcomed original material and observations from any Mexican practitioner "who wished to so honour" their journal. The prolific writer Miguel Francisco Jiménez was one who accepted the invitation, contributing an article on contemporary medical conditions; there are also articles on the interrupted renovations of Mexico City's mental hospital, the National University, the mining school, and the hospital de San Pablo[63] (table 5.4).

Revista Médica is unique in its editors' assurance that they will indicate (and therefore acknowledge) the sources of all foreign works published. The price of this monthly publication was two reales in Mexico City and twenty-two reales in other cities (due to postage), paid in advance.[64] In the capital, readers could subscribe at the Escuela de Medicina's bookstore, located on San Francisco Street, "next to number 12."[65] Once again, it is not clear how many issues of this publication saw the light, but, as its editors explain, its publication required a sacrifice that could be lessened only by a robust number of subscriptions. It is unknown how many subscriptions were sold, but the short life of the publication indicates they were insufficient.

During the first half of the nineteenth century, medical societies and their publications played a crucial role in the development of a modern medical profession in Mexico. Although sporadic and short-lived, these organizations and journals served as points of contact for practitioners of the main medical branches, the only avenue by which contributors could connect with their colleagues, and a place that united practitioners and readers as members of the same profession. The perseverance of contemporary practitioners indicates their awareness of the great importance of an academy in their professional development, their claim as owners of specialized knowledge, and their legitimacy as scientists. Thus, these academic organizations must be considered not as failed attempts but as steps on a long path toward domestic and international professional recognition, and the development of a modern medical profession in Mexico.

THE FRENCH COMMISSION SCIENTIFIQUE

The next and ultimately successful attempt to create an academy of medicine was the result of the unique political situation in Mexico in the 1860s and France's efforts to expand its influence and culture across the Atlantic. Ironically, the only government support to form a local association to promote medical knowledge came from the

French, not the Mexican authorities, and the groundwork was carried out by the French army of occupation. An in-depth analysis of the scientific "commissions" of France's Second Empire is beyond the scope of this work, but a short discussion of their origins and motives is necessary to understand their role in the establishment of a permanent academy of medicine in Mexico, and their impact on the medical profession. The best-known of the commissions is the Commission Scientifique du Méxique, formed in Paris in 1864 by order of Napoleon III, with the objective of replicating the achievements of Napoleon Bonaparte's Egyptian expedition of 1798–1801. The commission was placed under the auspices of the Ministry of Public Education, and, on 27 February 1864, Minister Victor Duruy underlined the benefits of the enterprise placed under his care: "By the time our soldiers leave this land [Mexico], they will have left glorious memories and our *savants* will have conquered it by science. There is no doubt that, thanks to their works, branches of our knowledge will be known and understood ... and that new facts will produce new and fertile ideas that will enhance our great studies."[66]

The official *Projet de Règlement* drawn up by Duruy further specified the goals of the Commission Scientifique as "*faire connaître à tous les points de vue le Méxique proprement dit et les contrées qui se rattachent à cet antique centre de civilisation indigene*" (to make known all aspects of Mexico itself and the lands around this ancient centre of civilization).[67] To achieve this aim, the commission was divided into four committees: Natural Sciences and Medicine; Physics and Chemistry; History, Linguistics, and Archaeology; and Political Economy, Statistics, Public Works, and Administration. The committees, responsible to Duruy, were formed of French scientific, artistic, and political luminaries and charged with setting goals and approving research proposals. The Natural Sciences and Medicine Committee consisted of the zoologist Henri Milne Edwards; the botanist Joseph Decaisne, founder of the Botanical Society of France; the well-known naturalist Jean Louis Armand de Quatrefages de Bréau; and the surgeon Baron Hippolyte Larrey, president of the Académie Impériale de Médecine,[68] who drew up the guidelines for the medical subsection.[69]

The central committees communicated through a delegate "of French or any other nationality" resident in Mexico who would be in charge of organization at a local level, public relations, and liaisons with France. The research and field work would be carried out by *voyageurs* (travellers) of either "French or any other nationality" and by appointed *correspondants*. Among the latter were Léon Alexandre Hyppolite Coindet and the military practitioner Carlos Alberto Ehrmann, physician-in-chief of the Expeditionary Army in Mexico, as well as the civilian Denis Dumont. Later, some Mexicans were added to the list, such as the physicians Miguel Francisco Jiménez and Gabino Barreda, and the mining engineer Joaquín Velázquez de León. All appointments were made in Paris by the minister of public instruction.[70]

Some authors consider the Commission Scientifique an example of the cultural imperialism that would characterize European policies of the late nineteenth century.[71] The objective of the commission was to expand French culture to the glory of the motherland, and cultural imperialism is thus the best term to describe France's objectives. However, this view is one-sided, as it approaches the issue only from France's perspective. Furthermore, the commission's wide scope and diverse results make blanket statements about it not only risky but also inaccurate. A proper evaluation demands careful analysis of each group involved: its objectives, failures, and achievements. The intentions of the archaeological section – exporting valuable pre-Hispanic pieces to France, now seen as looting national archaeological treasures – cannot be equated to those of the medical section, which were the study of local disease and morbid conditions. Furthermore, the commission's successes and failures varied, depending on section and national perspective. In the field of medicine, France's long-term intentions undoubtedly were self-serving: to aid military conquest and promote French immigration. Nonetheless, medical research proved beneficial not only to Mexico but also to medicine in general. Since the Mexican government had always attached little importance to medicine, let alone medical research, many Mexican practitioners and scientists welcomed the French enterprise. In the end, the archaeologists did not export Mexican national treasures, and the physicians did not aid immigration, so from France's point of view the Commission Scientifique was a failure, but not necessarily from Mexico's, as the results of the medical section indicate.

LA COMISIÓN CIENTÍFICA, LITERARIA Y ARTÍSTICA DE MÉXICO

As the Commission Scientifique was being officially sanctioned in France, the commander-in-chief of the Expeditionary Army in

Mexico, General François Achille Bazaine, contacted the Mexican General Juan Almonte.[72] In a letter dated 20 March 1864, Bazaine explained that he was organizing a "scientific commission" based in Mexico City and consisting of Mexican, French, and foreign residents, to correspond with "all important points of the [Mexican] Empire." Its objectives would be to develop in Mexico the love of science, letters, and the arts, to establish "scientific commerce" between Mexico and France, to reinforce intellectual links beneficial for the interests of both countries, to encourage by means of its publications the progress of agriculture and industry, and to make public the wealth of the country and, therefore, to propitiate immigration. The letter added that the enterprise had the full support of the empire's minister of development, José Salazar Ilárregui, who, in collaboration with Colonel Louis Doutrelaine of the French engineer corps, had worked diligently to draw up a preliminary program and suggest a list of potential members. In the final paragraph, Bazaine asked Almonte to ensure that government functionaries lent their complete support to the enterprise and facilitated the work of its researchers.[73]

The following day, Bazaine sent a circular to the chief commanders of the French army in Mexico, announcing the establishment of the Comisión científica, literaria y artística de México, which would be divided into ten different sections.[74] The Comisión's mandate was to collect and coordinate "interesting objects" of the sciences, letters, and the arts, to place them in "its rooms of permanent exhibition," or to send them to France. The circular ended by making all resources of the military convoys and French military postal service available to carry the correspondence and packages sent to the Comisión's headquarters.[75] Six days later, Bazaine instructed Mr Budin, Treasury delegate, to set aside 1,000 pesos for the Comisión's organization, transportation, and research costs, and make them available to a Colonel Doutrelaine on request.[76]

It is not clear what motivated Bazaine: professional ambition, a wish to promote the status of the military, or simply his belief that science and art should be promoted in Mexico. Notwithstanding his motives, the result was the involvement of the military in France's efforts to gather information and expand its cultural influence. Unlike the Egyptian expedition, in which scientists and army personnel remained separate and often at odds, in Mexico the army and navy not only participated in the venture but were a crucial part of its personnel and played the most active role.

Three days after sending the circular to his chief commanders, on 24 March Bazaine wrote to the French minister of war acknowledging the latter's 24 February letter, announcing the organization of a scientific commission in Mexico based in France. Bazaine also informed him that, on his own initiative, he had already formed a scientific and literary commission composed of French military personnel aided by the top Mexican scientists and specialists. He included a description of its organization and sections, a list of its members, and a request for funds to ensure the work could be carried out properly.[77] This letter differed from his communications to Almonte and the chief commanders in tone and emphasis. It gave the impression that the commission would be entirely in the hands of French military personnel, with Mexican specialists playing only a secondary role. Furthermore, it mentioned nothing about promoting science and culture in Mexico, and implied that its only objective was the cultural and scientific benefit of France. In addition to being a good military leader, Bazaine seems to have been a good diplomat.

While Bazaine was organizing his Comisión científica, in France the minister of war was assuring Minister Duruy that the army would provide any "things and men" the Commission Scientifique might require. To this end, he requested information on the instructions given to the *voyageurs*, so that Bazaine could then select the individuals best suited to support the enterprise.[78] In April the French minister of war wrote again to Duruy, informing him about Bazaine's Comisión científica and explaining that it did not conform exactly to the guidelines set in Paris, an indication that Bazaine had his own motives for establishing the commission and had acted on his own initiative.[79] Despite differences in motives and objectives, the work of the two organizations merged. Members of the Mexican Comisión were appointed *correspondants* of the Commission Scientifique on Bazaine's recommendation, and the medical research carried out by the Comisión científica was forwarded to the Commission Scientifique, which accepted it as its own.

The Commission Scientifique seems to have given only marginal attention to medicine, as the general *Projet de Règlement* fails to mention any of the medical fields, listing instead the areas of geography, orography, mineralogy, botany, zoology, atmospheric phenomena, anthropology (the study of races), and history. It was only later, probably influenced by Bazaine's program, that Baron Larrey, the only medical man on the Natural Sciences and Medicine Committee of the Commission Scientifique, sent a guideline for its correspondents.[80] The Comisión científica, however, dedicated one of its ten sections to the research and study of medicine, surgery, hygiene, veterinary medicine, medical statistics, medical matters, and anthropology, its interest in medicine and allied sciences perhaps explained by the military priorities of the French army in Mexico.[81] The section reported to Colonel Doutrelaine, who forwarded its findings to Baron Larrey, who in turn presented them to the central committee meetings in Paris.

THE SECCIÓN DE MEDICINA AND THE SOCIEDAD MÉDICA DE MÉXICO, 1864–1865

In Mexico, the Sección de Medicina (medical section), the sixth section of the Comisión científica, was officially established on 30 April 1864. Bazaine appointed the capable Carlos Alberto Ehrmann as its president but made sure Mexican practitioners were evenly represented in the other posts. The recognized Mexican physician Miguel Francisco Jiménez and the Frenchman Julio Clement, a long-time resident of Mexico, were appointed first and second vice-president respectively; Agustín Andrade, a professor of the medical school, became first secretary; Carlos A. Schulze second secretary; and the well-known physician Rafael Lucio, treasurer. Mexican physicians were not only able to participate in the enterprise but were assured an active role and accepted as equals to their French counterparts.

There were twenty-nine founding members of the Sección de Medicina,[82] and at least five of them (Ehrmann, Coindet, Bergeyre, Liguistin, and Jiménez) were also correspondents of the Commission Scientifique. The original members were invited to propose the names of other practitioners, whose admission would then be decided by secret vote. By the end of the year, the Sección de Medicina's membership had increased to forty-seven, which included, among others, H. Libermann, correspondent of the Commission Scientifique, and Maximino Río de la Loza, whose brother Leopoldo was a member of the Comisión científica's physics and chemistry section.[83] Fifteen more members were accepted in 1866 (all of them Mexican), among them the well-known practitioners and Escuela de Medicina professors Lauro M. Jiménez, Leopoldo Río de la Loza, and Gumersindo Mendoza.[84] By the end of the empire, the Sección de Medicina – by then called the Sociedad Médica de México

– counted forty-eight members, forty-three of them Mexican and the rest foreigners residing in Mexico.[85]

In its first meeting, the Sección de Medicina organized itself into five subsections or specialties: Pathology, Hygiene, Legal Medicine, and Medical Statistics; Veterinary Medicine; *Materia Médica* and Pharmacology; and Physiology and Anthropology. The decision was reached by common agreement, and each subsection was left at liberty to choose the topics it would study. Members were free to express their own opinions, which would then be openly discussed in the meetings.[86] The freedom to select a topic of research mainly benefited local members, who, not being correspondents, did not have to adhere to a pre-arranged program. On the other hand, French members were bound by their superiors' orders and by the objectives of the Commission Scientifique, as drawn up by Baron Larrey's *Instructions*. Topics of research were divided into two main areas: "medical geography," or the influence of altitude, weather, and environmental conditions on illness and health, and the study of "fevers." "Medical geography" included anthropology, defined as the study of races and their "pathological aptitudes."[87] These topics often intertwined, as in the research of the correspondent Léon Coindet, *médecin major* in Tacubaya, author of the widely read *Les altitudes de l'Amérique tropical compares au niveau des mers du point de vue de la constitution médicale* (1861).[88] Coindet was also interested on "fevers," the topic that he chose for his dissertation, "Considérations sur les fièvres de l'Algérie," published in Paris in 1851.[89] Impressed, the *Commission* appointed him as correspondent as the result of his interest in and knowledge of medical topography, hygiene, and the "comparative physiology of races."[90] After the fall of the empire, Coindet published his experiences in the two-volume *Le Mexique considéré au point de vue médico-chirurgical*.[91] The same topics interested his colleague, Denis Jourdanet, also a correspondent and founding member of the Sección de medicina. Jourdanet was a pioneer in the study of the harmful effects of high altitudes on the human body (hypoxia) and the author of three works on Mexico and the effects of its climates and altitudes on population.[92] Both Coindet and Jourdanet published their findings on these topics in the *Gaceta Médica de México*, and the latter collaborated in two articles on yellow fever with his Mexican colleagues.[93]

The study of tropical "fevers" was of great importance to France's military and government, as they continued to embark on the colonization of Africa and Asia, and of no less interest to Mexico, whose population was constantly and seriously affected by epidemics. Yellow fever, described by Larrey as "the question that completely dominated the pathology of Mexico,"[94] was of special interest; the nomination of Fuzier, *médecin major* in Veracruz, as correspondent was made on the basis on his expertise in the pathology of the tropics: "Among our military he is the one that best knows about the illnesses of the hot lands."[95] Fuzier carried out hundreds of autopsies on yellow fever victims and kept detailed notes on his findings until he, himself, fell victim to the disease.[96] His detailed reports and findings were published in the 1863 issues of the *Recueil de mémoires de medicine de chirurgie et the pharmacie militaires.*[97] The French military were not the only ones interested in the study of these illnesses; the impact of malaria and yellow fever on the key port of Veracruz and other Gulf and Pacific ports, and consequently on Mexico's economy and welfare, was well known. In addition to these tropical diseases, other fevers were of interest to both countries. Typhus had also claimed thousands of victims, as had other "fevers" such as typhoid and respiratory diseases. Thus the interests of the Sección de Medicina members went beyond national and political boundaries and often overlapped. Ehrmann, Libermann, Jourdanet, and Claudel researched typhus, but so did Hidalgo y Carpio, Jiménez, and Garrone.[98] Freedom of research may have been somewhat restricted by the Commission Scientifique's guidelines and military priorities, but it was broad enough to allow the Sección de Medicina members to pursue their own interests.

One may argue that the articles published in its journal, once the Sociedad de Medicina became an independent organization, show a nationalistic slant. These include eleven articles on local flora and insects and their therapeutic uses, as well as a report on endemic illness in Guanajuato, written by Gabino Barreda. Also included are articles on the history of the Hospital de San Hipólito and on colonial medical practice in Mexico.[99] But, ironically, such "nationalistic" topics are the same as those that interested the Commission Scientifique and are listed in its guidelines.

From its inception, the Sección de Medicina met monthly on Wednesdays at 8:00 p.m. at the Escuela de Medicina installations. To pool resources, each member handed in a list of the books in his personal library. In addition, volunteers gathered a list of the works available at the Escuela de Medicina library, which was open to

Sección de Medicina members every day at 5:00 p.m. Members also agreed to prepare a bibliography of "useful" works not yet published in Mexico, presumably to acquire them. Thus, from its inception, the Sección de Medicina adopted the role of an academic organization that sought to further professional interests. Such a role required leadership of its members, who were expected to be at the forefront of medical research. It also implied that membership was a privilege, as reflected by the decision to forbid members to advertise their services in the newspaper.[100]

Under Ehrmann's leadership, meetings took place punctually and adhered scrupulously to the agenda. The committees took turns presenting their research on pre-arranged topics and discussing them with those in attendance. In the 26 July 1864 session, for example, the discussion centred on "hydrophile cotton" and its medical uses. Hidalgo y Carpio and Barceló de Villagrán, who had volunteered to test it among their patients at the Hospital de San Pablo, reported their findings.[101] At the same meeting, it was agreed that the "medical constitution" (birth, death, and morbidity statistics) be presented by the Hygiene, Legal Medicine, and Medical Statistics subsections and thoroughly discussed during the first session of each month.[102]

Three months after its establishment, the Sección de Medicina agreed to publish its works, "including the scientific part of its acts (meetings)," in a journal entitled *Gaceta Médica de México*. Members who wished to contribute financially to the publication were asked for their signatures to ensure their commitment. The costs, it was agreed, would then be divided by the number of contributors, who would share them "in complete equality," and any profits obtained would be dedicated to the improvement of the publication. To such ends, those in attendance appointed a committee and a treasurer, who would report to the membership every six months. At the following meeting, Miguel Francisco Jiménez and Julio Clement read the publication proposal in Spanish and French, respectively, and invited, also in both languages, all medical and veterinary practitioners to publish their research in the journal. To cover the initial costs of publication, each member was asked to contribute four pesos within two weeks. It was also proposed to sell each issue of the journal for the modest price of two reales. All motions were approved, and the first ongoing medical publication of Mexico was born.[103]

The *Gaceta Médica de México* was geared exclusively to the research and organization of the Sección de Medicina. As its predecessors, it was divided in two sections, "Academic Works" for articles submitted by its members or any other practitioner, and "Documents Related to the Life of the Academy," with the minutes of the sessions held – an odd choice of title, as the Sección de Medicina was not yet an academy. Later, in 1869, a "Diverse Notes" section would be added. In the first volume (1864–65), "Academic Works" contains eighty-one articles, nineteen written by fifteen foreigners, fifty-two by eighteen Mexican nationals, five co-authored by French and Mexican practitioners, and five anonymous works (tables 5.3 and 5.4).[104] The second volume (1866) is more modest, with only sixty-two articles in the "Academic Works" section. Seven of these were written by French practitioners, one by the Sardinian Luis Garrone, a resident of Mexico, one was anonymous, and the rest (fifty-three) written or co-written by Mexican practitioners (table 5.4). Thirty authors, twenty-four of them Mexican, contributed to the volume (table 5.3).[105] Most important, these pieces consisted of original research and observations, a far cry from the reprints that filled the first medical publications.

During its first two years, the *Gaceta Médica de México* was the result of the close collaboration of all the members of the Sección de Medicina. In the first volume, the most prolific contributor was Luis Hidalgo y Carpio, with fourteen articles. He was followed by Miguel Francisco Jiménez, who wrote seven articles and collaborated with Ehrmann on another, and by José María Reyes, who contributed six pieces. Among the French members, Léon Coindet was the main contributor with three articles, followed by Jourdanet, who wrote two and co-authored another two. In 1866, the *Gaceta Médica de México* included the work of only four French practitioners – Ehrmann, Liguistin, Jourdanet, and Tourainne – who managed to publish despite the increasingly restive military situation. Four articles were the result of the collaborative efforts of Mexican researchers. Luis Hidalgo y Carpio and M. Poza collaborated on two studies on meningitis, and Alfonso Herrera and Gumersindo Mendoza co-authored two articles on the medicinal uses of cantharides and *yoloxóchitl*, respectively (table 5.4).[106]

The third volume, covering 1867–68, contains fifty articles in the "Academic Works" section, written by Mexican practitioners, the only exception being a piece by Julio Clement, a long-time resident in Mexico. Familiar names such as those of Aniceto Ortega, Rafael Lucio, and Luis Hidalgo y Carpio were now joined by younger contributors such as Lino Ramírez, Rafael Lavista, and Sebastián Labastida.[107] The *Gaceta Médica de México* would continue to be published regularly and become the main national forum for the diffusion of medical research in Mexico.

At the urging of Ehrmann, in October 1865 the members voted to dissolve the Sección de Medicina and form the Sociedad Médica de México, thus severing ties with the Comisión científica and consequently the Commission Scientifique.[108] Ehrmann stepped down and Miguel Francisco Jiménez was elected president. The director of the Escuela de Medicina, Ignacio Durán, became vice-president, and Angel Iglesias and Aniceto Ortega first and second secretaries, respectively.[109] The motives behind this change were not recorded, but in hindsight they are clear. In his first annual report, Miguel Francisco Jiménez underlined the importance of preventing the "ardour and decision" that had prompted the creation of the Sección de Medicina to become "sterile and even to die" as a result of the "languid existence without future to which it was united," a reference to the Mexican and French scientific commissions. The tree had borne fruit, but its survival required complete independence from the disintegrating parent organizations.[110] Furthermore, such a decision adhered to the mandate of both the Comisión científica and the Commission Scientifique. Since the founding of the former, Bazaine and Doutrelaine had sought to engage dynamic local specialists as active collaborators who could eventually take over. As to the Commission Scientifique, one of its goals was the establishment of long-lasting organizations in Mexico that would collaborate with their French counterparts and serve as tangible proof of France's legacy in the country. Both objectives had been met.

FRIENDS AND FOES

Over the next two years, the Sociedad Médica de México's original membership of twenty-nine rapidly expanded, as twenty-six more practitioners joined. As the French military forces withdrew, the Sociedad counted thirty-nine members.[111] Thus, the willingness of local physicians to join an enterprise spearheaded by France and to collaborate with its military practitioners is undeniable. In response to his appointment as correspondent of the Commission Scientifique, Miguel Francisco Jiménez thanked the commission for "the distinction that you have afforded me" and assured its members that, having dedicated his life to medicine, he would always be most willing to collaborate on the progress of this science. With his letter, dated February 1865, Jiménez included three works, hoping they would contribute in a small way "to the noble ends" of the Commission Scientifique.[112]

Jiménez was not the only willing collaborator; other scientists showed similar enthusiasm. Engineer and politician Joaquín Velásquez de León thanked the Commission Scientifique for his appointment as *correspondant* and offered his full cooperation with an enterprise that, "recognizing the progress of science as the basis, will give beneficial and honourable results for the two empires of France and Mexico, so united by friendship." The acting president of the Sociedad Mexicana de Geografía y Estadística, Urbano Fonseca, went further, praising the Commission Scientifique's "illustrious and disinterested efforts to propagate science" and assuring its committee that its *dignes missionaries* would receive the full support of his organization.[113]

Such collaboration with the French was not simply a matter of diplomacy or expediency. The minutes of the Sección de Medicina indicate that its members not only discussed the topics set by the agenda, but also shared specific medical experiences, consulted with each other in complicated cases, and often sought their colleagues' advice.[114] When Ehrmann designed an apparatus to treat fractures of the neck of the femur, Hidalgo y Carpio tested it at the Hospital de San Pablo and then presented his report to other members.[115] A new procedure to close wounds presented by Julio Clement at one meeting roused such great interest that a committee was appointed to evaluate it and present a report. When the same practitioner, seemingly in the vanguard of surgical procedures, experimented with an innovative technique to operate for bladder stones with scissors instead of a scalpel, members attended what proved to be a successful operation; the patient, a child, recovered in a short time.[116] Indeed, the first two volumes of the *Gaceta Médica de México* (1864–65 and 1866) illustrate collaborations between local practitioners and their French colleagues. The introductory article in the first volume, entitled "Prospecto," was written by Ehrmann and Miguel Francisco Jiménez; Denis Jourdanet, Luis Garrone, and José María Barceló de Villagrán researched and wrote "Fiebre amarilla" (Yellow fever), and Jourdanet collaborated with José María Reyes on a third piece entitled "Profilaxia de la fiebre amarilla" (Yellow fever prophylaxis).[117] Thus, as intended by its founders, the Sección de Medicina and its successor became the forum where specialists met, discussed their research, and exchanged their experiences – the professional and academic organization that local physicians had longed to have for years.

Why, one may ask, did local practitioners so eagerly collaborate with their French military colleagues, who formed part of the army of occupation? Their motives, it seems, were as varied as the individuals who joined the Sección de Medicina, but there are common factors behind their decision, which must be examined and placed in historical context. First, it is important to stress that the political and nationalistic views of present-day Mexicans did not necessarily prevail at the time. The black-and-white contrast portrayed by most political and military histories may not have been as stark to those who lived through these events as it is to later writers, whose values and judgments were shaped by events that were then still in the future. In her excellent work on the Second Empire, Erika Pani concludes that many collaborators were savvy politicians and public servants who lent their support to the venture in a sincere effort to improve Mexico. After years of political turmoil, some of them considered a European-backed regime as a viable option; others, despite doubts or even opposition, felt that the country's cause could be better served by their collaboration with and input into the empire.[118] Still others, witnesses or participants in the Mexican-American war, may have seen it as the only way to stop United States expansionism. At least a few Sección de Medicina members, such as Miguel Francisco Jiménez, Pablo Martínez del Río, and Agustín Andrade, were enthusiastic supporters of the empire, but colleagues such as Rafael Lucio and Gabino Barreda clearly were not. It may be argued that, despite their political beliefs, most were simply scientists, dedicated physicians who preferred not to involve themselves in politics. Their duty as physicians was to care for the sick and the wounded, and their goal as medical men was professional improvement for their own and their patients' benefit.

The founders of the Sección de Medicina and its heir, the Sociedad Médica de México, were among the most renowned physicians in the country, committed men of science who excelled at their profession and were keenly interested in research and innovative therapies. Minister José Salazar Ilarregui, who collaborated with Colonel Doutrelaine in the planning and organization of the Comisión científica y literaria de México, expressed his satisfaction in his inauguration speech on "seeing so many Mexicans of different political opinions, distinguished by their talent and the depth of their knowledge but always in agreement when working to raise the fatherland to the rank reserved by Providence."[119] His statement is corroborated by surviving letters of acceptance sent to the Commission Scientifique. Leaving aside formalities, the appointees' excitement on having been selected by some of the most renowned European scientists was genuine. After all, France was still at the vanguard of scientific development, especially in the medical field, and such a distinction was a sign of international recognition and professional achievement, and a reason for nationalistic pride. Equally important, the correspondence indicates a sincere desire of the authors to promote scientific development in Mexico. In this context, the willingness of local practitioners to join the Sección de Medicina is not surprising, nor should it be condemned as treachery, but simply as their preference for science over politics. In summary, political beliefs cannot be dismissed as a factor, but they neither explain the physicians' decision to collaborate nor account for the success of both the Sección Médica and its successor the Sociedad Médica de México. One must, therefore, explore other factors.

Ironically, nationalism was behind the decision of some practitioners to collaborate with the French initiative. Gumercindo Mendoza and Alfonso Herrera agreed to be part of the Sociedad Médica de México and collaborated on articles for the *Gaceta Médica* to disprove the belief of the Commission Scientifique that there were no competent botanists in Mexico.[120] Theirs was an act of nationalism that sought to improve the image of Mexican science. A similar nationalistic feeling was expressed by Manuel S. Soriano in his speech at the 3 June 1868 session of the Sociedad Médica on the death of one of its members, Lino Ramírez. With pride, and in the grandiloquent style of the time, Soriano reminded attendees that Ramírez had represented the Sociedad Médica at the 1867 International Medical Congress celebrated in Paris, despite the fact that, "for anomalous circumstances," Mexico had not taken part in the 1867 World Exhibition: "Lino Ramírez is invited to take a seat among those knowledgeable men; his voice resounds in that temple, the summit of medical civilization, and his speech about liver abscesses is received with a clear demonstration of appreciation: the name of Mexico is registered in the records due to Lino

Ramírez; his own name remained there, at the side of Mexico's."[121]
The tragic events of 1867 had not dampened the Sociedad Médica's
enthusiasm for France, and the nationalism of its members is undeniable, even when viewed through a different lens.

Another contributing factor was Mexicans' admiration for France
and its cultural achievements, reflected in the fact that in 1863
Mexico was the sixth-largest importer of French publications, surpassed only by five European nations.[122] Such admiration was especially patent in the field of medicine. After independence, medical
education was patterned after the curricula offered in France, the
textbooks used were French, and Mexican physicians able to do so
travelled to Paris to further their knowledge. As in other Latin
American countries, a study visit to Paris confirmed a practitioner's
professional credibility and improved his professional standing.[123]
The deeply rooted admiration for *la culta Francia* that Dencausse
observed in 1851 prevailed, despite the political events of the 1860s,
as the monumental *Historia de la medicina en México* by Francisco
de Asís Flores Troncoso attests. Such infatuation with French medicine and science that persisted throughout the nineteenth century
cannot be easily dismissed when analyzing the collaboration between
Mexican and French practitioners.

In hindsight, the input of French medical personnel was invaluable in the establishment and formative months of the Sección de
Medicina. French military practitioners were not asked to collaborate; they were ordered to do so. And so they did, even though only
a few seemed to be interested in the project. Nonetheless, their contributions facilitated the work of the Sección de Medicina and lent it
credibility. Among these practitioners, one deserves special mention
for his outstanding contribution, without which the success of the
Sección de Medicina would not have been possible. Carlos Alberto
Ehrmann's role as promoter and president was remarkable in the
difficult political circumstances he faced. As a military man, Ehrmann
had the discipline necessary to establish the basis of the Sección de
Medicina, and as the chief physician of the army he enjoyed the
necessary authority over his subordinates to ensure their collaboration. He also earned the respect of his Mexican colleagues by his
hard work, his commitment to the task at hand, and his disposition
toward them. Thus, he ensured cooperation and goodwill. Aware of
his role as facilitator, Ehrmann laid the foundations of the Sociedad
Médica de México, passed the baton to the Mexican members, and

continued to attend meetings and contribute until his duties forced him to leave Mexico City. Numerous references to his contributions and integrity may be found in contemporary sources, of which the best example is the "Necrology" published on his death by the *Gaceta Médica de México* that he had helped to establish. This appeared in 1871, four years after the French army had left Mexico and at a time when there were no diplomatic relations between the two countries. It refers to Ehrmann's "high abilities, his exquisite knowledge, his gentlemanly character, and his justice toward the men and things of our country," and ends by stating that "the pleasant memory that his beautiful heart left here [in Mexico] among his friends make his loss twice as tragic."[124] The key role played by Ehrmann was complemented by that of his subordinates, who diligently gathered data and formed a network that set the nascent project on firmer ground.

The wish to form a stable and long-lasting medical academy was nothing new. Since independence, physicians had sought, unsuccessfully, to establish a permanent professional organization that would legitimize them as possessors of specialized knowledge, but their efforts had been repeatedly frustrated by financial shortcomings, political turmoil, and government indifference. The authorities had limited themselves to issuing legislation and had attempted to bring the existing association under their control, but they had never provided funds, encouragement, or infrastructure for research. It was an uphill battle for the medical leadership, and for forty years they saw their efforts frustrated. Nonetheless, the various short-lived associations gave them an intermittent focus around which they could group, discuss professional issues, and pursue their research. These early attempts, therefore, were an important contributing factor in the development of the profession and stepping stones to a longer-lasting organization.

As the century progressed and medicine began to claim its place as a science, the need for a medical academy became more urgent. The Sección de Medicina came to fill this void. As a French army initiative, it was endorsed and promoted by the authorities, supported by military manpower and logistics, and linked to what was perceived as a grandiose Commission Scientifique spearheaded by the French imperial government. Local practitioners and other medical specialists were presented for the first time with the opportunity to form a professional organization that was promoted and backed by those in

power. The Sección de Medicina offered them the chance to collaborate personally with experienced and well-trained French practitioners of international recognition, to engage in fruitful research and
debates, to establish relations with specialists in France and other
European countries, and to publish their work. As a branch of the
Commission Scientifique, the Sección de Medicina could claim credibility and international recognition and establish relations with
similar European organizations. To the individual practitioner, the
new organization also offered the chance to disseminate his work
beyond national boundaries and to gain international recognition; it
was a golden opportunity that many individuals seized. Although
many of these hopes were not realized at the time, the Sección de
Medicina proved a firm base on which a lasting professional organization could be built. As the only medical academic organization of
its type in the country's capital, its successor, the Sociedad Médica de
México, claimed a monopoly over medical knowledge and its position as the arbiter of such knowledge, and gave the medical profession the recognition it sought. The new organization sanctioned
medical practitioners as a recognized group with specialized medical
knowledge and expertise over all health-related matters. Its establishment was the crowning achievement of a now cohesive group of
practitioners who could consider themselves members of a "modern" medical profession according to contemporary standards.

Conclusion

In May 1877, the physician and congressman Adrián Segura, acting as representative of the Academia de Medicina de Mexico, petitioned Congress for a subsidy. He cited the Academia's contributions to society, its work evaluating the ongoing drainage of the Valley of Mexico, and the international recognition it enjoyed. Segura reminded his fellow congressmen that European academies had the financial support of their governments and that the Sociedad de Geografía y Estadística already enjoyed an annuity from the Mexican government. After a debate on the merits of the petition, Congress approved a subsidy of 5,000 pesos. Two months later, the Academia became the official consulting agency for the federal government on medical matters. The inauguration of its academic year was presided over by President Porfirio Díaz and Minister of Justice and Public Education Protasio Tagle.[1]

It had been a long journey. For fifty years, a small number of practitioners had struggled to find a place for their profession in the new republic. Their endeavour was rooted in colonial times, prompted by the intellectual, economic, social, and military changes of the Bourbon era that sought to tighten control of the Spanish Crown over the colonies. From an intellectual point of view, a growing emphasis on observation and experimentation would transform medicine from an art into a science and undermine the traditional medical knowledge that distinguished physicians from other health-care practitioners. From a social point of view, the position that Habsburg legislation had guaranteed to the medical practitioners as part of the privileged Spanish minority was being challenged. Economic growth and the outstanding performance of the mining and export sectors attracted immigrants, promoted socio-economic mobility, and loosened the established social and racial colonial hierarchy of the colonies, threatening the status of the Spanish elite. Militarily, European conflicts spilled over into Spain's American colonial possessions, requiring the organization of American militias to serve around a core of well-trained peninsular armies.

The resulting military reorganization of the Spanish Empire had important consequences for colonial medical practitioners. The peninsular armies brought with them medical personnel who challenged the local practitioners' monopoly and triggered a bitter rivalry between local physicians and peninsular surgeons. The establishment of a surgical school in Mexico City to train individuals to serve under peninsular medical practitioners increased the number of surgeons with formal training, facilitated class mobility, and reduced the gap between physicians and surgeons. Nonetheless, a clear line between the local surgeons – many of whom did not or could not boast an untainted Spanish lineage – and their peninsular superiors remained. Furthermore, as the supply of medical services increased, competition for the limited number of patients able to afford such services caused animosity and professional rivalry between European and local practitioners who, with the support of the Protomedicato, were determined to protect their interests.

The 1812 Cádiz Constitution and the establishment of permanent juntas de sanidad dealt a heavy blow to the medical elite's traditional privileges. These juntas, a result of modern liberal ideology, were dependent on municipal governments and empowered to watch over public health and the welfare of the population, thus overlapping the traditional jurisdiction of the Protomedicato. Lack of clarity in the legislation and the fluid political situation allowed the juntas to expand their reach at the expense of the discredited protomédicos. The contest for control was most visible in Mexico City, the seat of the Protomedicato, while in other cities the development of the juntas and their jurisdictional expansion depended on the support of the local government and their specific circumstances. When the juntas began to encroach on professional rights and threaten to regulate medical practitioners, the medical elite became alarmed. The Protomedicato could not protect the interests of licensed practitioners, and a realignment of forces was imperative.

The wars of independence disrupted the economy, exhausted the government's coffers, and changed its priorities, with serious consequences for the university and the surgical school. They also accelerated the erosion of social and racial distinctions and the chances of socio-economic mobility for mixed bloods, decreasing the gap separating medicine from surgery and physicians from surgeons. The merging of both medical branches in post-independent Mexico was the next logical step. Physicians benefited from the numerical strength of the well-educated surgeons and from the rising status of surgery, while ensuring their participation in a field that showed great potential. Elite surgeons gained by anchoring their education in theoretical medicine, raising their professional status, and distancing themselves from their poorly trained colleagues and the mixed-blood bleeders and barber surgeons. Together, they presented a common front better able to defend their professional interests.

Once their alliance had been sealed by legislation, the merged branches ensured their place at the apex of the profession by widening the gap that separated them from the lower practitioners. Education was the key. Their prominence in the Facultad Médica gave them the power to draw up training and licensing regulations and solidify their position. Surgeons without formal education were excluded, while phlebotomists lost the limited independence they had enjoyed in colonial times and saw their status downgraded by their lack of access to formal education. Midwives were also affected, as their education and tasks were limited to the tedious and less profitable aspects of childbirth. Dentists proved more difficult to control. In other countries, dentistry was recognized as a separate branch of surgery and its practitioners were often trained by renowned surgeons. The first dentists in Mexico were foreigners, from either Europe or the United States. They had been formally trained and were well acquainted with the latest innovations and technology in their field. Socially, their foreign nationality and white race placed them above the mixed-blood local barbers, their direct competitors. Furthermore, they benefited from the individualism characteristic of the time, the hygienist theories and emphasis on cleanliness then in vogue, and the growing interest in the welfare and beauty of the body, which increased demand for dentistry and its related services among the well-off classes. In summary, their formal education, forward-looking approach, and use of modern technology guaranteed the dentists' inclusion in the medical hierarchy. In a few years, dentists would strike out on their own and assert their independence as a separate and lucrative profession.

As reorganization required severing ties with the colonial past, the Protomedicato was discarded and the Facultad Médica, a similar organization more agreeable to republican ideas, created. The change required collaboration with the government, which officially sanctioned the Facultad Médica and legitimized the transition and reforms that kept the profession and its hierarchy in place. Historians usually dismiss the Facultad Médica for its provisional nature and relatively short duration. Nonetheless, it proved essential for the continuation of the profession. In addition to drawing up professional and medical education regulations that, with some changes, would remain in place until Porfirian times, it served as a base for a profession undergoing a crucial formative stage. In time, this important role passed to the medical school, which later shared it with the academy of medicine. The Facultad Médica was followed by the Consejo Superior de Salubridad, a combination of public health board patterned after the Paris Conseil de salubrité and the Protomedicato. The Consejo Superior functioned first as the administrative headquarters in charge of processing examinations and licences and watching over the professional monopoly, and second as a public health board. Despite its modern outlook, the Consejo Superior could not shake the tradition of the Protomedicato. It continued to be controlled by the physician-surgeons and to function mainly as a professional organization, enforcing monopoly and zealously guarding the elite's privileges. Only gradually did its public health duties begin to attract more of its attention. Instead, its successor, the Consejo Central, was established as a public health board with different objectives and priorities, and beyond the medical practitioners' control. Despite its short life, the Consejo Central foreshadowed the division between professional issues and public health that became a reality with the 1879 regulations.

The history of the Escuela de Medicina is well documented in its surviving archives. During its first two decades, the new institution faced immense difficulties. Lack of funding, government indifference, and forced relocations are part of this history. The school's survival is testimony to the perseverance and determination of the medical leaders, who, aware of the importance of medical education, contributed their efforts, work, and earnings to the education of the following generations and to the continuity of their profession. Gradually, the medical school took root and the number of students increased. Indeed, the students themselves must be commended for their interest in medicine and their willingness to adapt to difficult circumstances. Some of them, such as José María Vertiz, Miguel Francisco Jiménez, Rafael Lucio, and Eduardo Liceaga, flourished despite the difficult circumstances and, mainly through their own efforts, became excellent physicians and specialists in their field.

However, the medical elite wanted more than a teaching institution that would transmit knowledge from one generation to the next. Since the 1820s, top physicians and surgeons had yearned for a professional organization that would allow them the interchange of ideas and experiences. The first academies were short-lived, the efforts of their founders frustrated by lack of funds and political turmoil. Nevertheless, the energy and resources invested in establishing the various academies and publishing their journals attest to practitioners' interest in professional improvement and the value they attached to it. The resulting publications are testimony to the profession's development and growing self-confidence. The journals published by the first academy and by the Sociedad Filoiátrica reflect the profession's shaky position at the time and the frustrations of a generation that considered its medical education and professional future to be in jeopardy. Initially, the aim was modest: to circulate medical information. At first, the articles were mostly from foreign sources, but as the century progressed, journals included more Mexican content and by the 1850s local writers predominated. More self-asserted practitioners were no longer satisfied with being informed about international medical developments; instead, they aimed to exchange their own experiences and research with colleagues.

The set of circumstances resulting in the establishment of the Sociedad de Medicina, which would evolve into the present-day Academia Nacional de Medicina, were unique to Mexico. The practitioners' willingness to participate in the French-influenced initiative to form such a society should not surprise us. For the first time, they were being supported by the authorities and legitimized by both the local and a foreign government. Medicine and science for once prevailed over politics. The inauguration of the Sociedad de Medicina as an independent Mexican organization was the crowning achievement of the medical elite in the mid-nineteenth century. It gave them legitimacy, international connections with European organizations, and a well-deserved self-confidence they had sought since the beginning of the century.

Traditional Mexican history is divided into stages that are often analyzed separately. Of these, the most problematic is the nineteenth century, which has been subdivided into segments based on political and military events usually examined as unconnected episodes with little bearing upon one another. In this study, I have taken a different view, stressing continuity over sudden change and emphasizing the gradual transition of the medical profession from a colonial to a national context. Continuity, therefore, characterizes the legislation, events, institutions, and organizations that contributed to such transition. The juntas de sanidad created in 1812 were the next logical step from their temporary colonial counterparts, established to fight epidemics and disbanded shortly after these were under control. The new juntas de sanidad had their roots in the past but were also innovative: their mandate was expanded to include not only fighting disease, but also prevention. They also had a political role: to limit the traditional privileges and jurisdiction of the Protomedicato. The juntas de sanidad were, therefore, the product of a liberal ideology that gave more importance to public health in its effort to modernize society.

The gradual metamorphosis of the Protomedicato as a professional and a public health board followed a similar path. The Protomedicato was abolished to formally sever the top practitioners' links with the colonial past, and to erase their ties to privilege in a racially divided society that was at odds with the ideology of the new nation. The Facultad Médica, a very similar but more democratic organization with a wider representation, was formed to occupy its place. But in contemporary Mexico, democracy was not meant to include all. The top echelons of the profession gained better representation in the Facultad Médica, while the weaker, lower levels were further marginalized. The unshakeable liberal faith in formal education contributed to the survival of the colonial medical hierarchy, now strengthened by the physician-surgeons' control of medical education. Colonial social differences and racial distinctions became more flexible, but were not erased; they informally continued under the republican government and contributed to shape the fate of the lower echelons of the medical profession. The Protomedicato's role as a public health board is also characterized by continuity. During its last years, the Protomedicato lost its place as an arbiter of public health, but its successor, the Facultad Médica, recovered it when the juntas de sanidad were abolished in yet another legislative change.

The next incarnation of the Protomedicato, the Consejo Superior de Salubridad, was founded, like its predecessors, as a professional

body first and a public health board second, but this latter role gradually became more prominent as medical practitioners claimed
expertise over it. Gradually, the Consejo Superior came to be an
administrative centre that oversaw educational regulations and
licensing and dealt with public health issues. The emphasis changed
in 1866, when the Consejo Central, established as a public health
board beyond the control of the medical profession, was given a
clear mandate over policia and only temporarily put in charge of
licensing and education. For the first time, the separation between
medical practice and education on the one hand, and public health
on the other, was made official. Although the 1867 republican triumph over the empire turned the clock back temporarily to 1842,
the trend was clear and the division inevitable. The detailed Porfirian
public health legislation was heir to the Consejo Central's regulations as well as the result of its natural progression.

Continuity is also clear in the development of medical education. The much-trumpeted 1833 medical education reform was not
drafted by one reformer, nor was it the result of the forward thinking
of a small group of liberal politicians. Rather, the new curriculum
was the outcome of careful planning, long discussions, and the
input of interested institutions, physicians, surgeons, and educators.
Discussions began after independence and continued for ten years,
centred more on control over education than over the curriculum
itself. The various proposals presented illustrate a common objective, the different interests at stake, and the difficulties of reconciling
the obsolete health-care infrastructure of colonial times with a modern medical program. The novelty of the 1833 educational reforms
lay in their funding source, rather than their substance. Congress
solved the main obstacle to educational reform by forcing the church
to underwrite it, and cleared the way by closing-down the university
and its colleges. When the controversial reforms were cancelled, the
medical curriculum itself was left almost intact, proving that the
core of the issue was the contextual struggle for power and resources,
not the curricular reform itself. The medical education program
issued in 1833, with only minor updates in content and textbooks,
remained in place until the Pasteurian revolution made it obsolete.

The foundation of the Academia Nacional de México followed a
similar line. The ephemeral organizations that preceded it were part
of the continuous efforts of medical practitioners eager for scientific
recognition, and the first academies' objectives as well as the content

of their publications illustrate the gradual development of the medical profession in Mexico. Originally created to diffuse European medical developments and make foreign works available to their readers, the publications' content gradually shifted in favour of local articles. By the second half of the century, more Mexican practitioners were willing to publish their own research and experiences, and more readers were willing to read about them. Despite its unique origins, the Sociedad de Medicina was the logical outcome of previous efforts and the Academia Nacional de Medicina the result of a long struggle to create a nationally and internationally recognized professional body.

As well as continuity, the period under study is defined by continuous struggle and competition. The wars of independence and the organization of the new nation opened spaces and opportunities for various actors that competed among themselves for control over services, ideas, and resources. Competition is a constant theme in this analysis and is found not only within the medical profession, but also between licensed and unlicensed healers, between individuals with different visions, between the Protomedicato and the juntas de sanidad, and among the three educational institutions. The constant competition among political actors, the ensuing political instability, and the constant changes of legislation on which the profession was anchored are of utmost importance to understanding the latter's development. The competition between the Protomedicato and its successors on the one hand, and the provincial health boards and authorities on the other, was defined to a large degree by the ability of the political centre to impose its will on the rest of the country. In summary, the extremely fluid context that frequently frustrated the efforts of the medical elite is as important to the historian as are the developments that took place within the profession itself. The same chaotic context impedes the imposition of most theoretical models of professionalization that refer to modern professions in industrialized and politically stable societies.

Nonetheless, the model of competing occupations with a claim to special skills and specialized knowledge contesting for markets for their services might be applied to the 1830s reorganization of the medical profession in Mexico. For years, colonial physicians and peninsular surgeons competed against each other, their professional differences buttressed by their national origins – competition that some local surgeons continued after independence. Other important factors, however, were also at play. The narrowing gap between medicine and surgery, the wars for independence, the creation of a new nation, and the threat to the professional independence of physicians and surgeons propitiated their alliance. Union was the logical outcome. It guaranteed them control over access to medical knowledge, fields of practice, and licensing requirements, and considerably strengthened their position. After their merging, the physician-surgeons could draft regulations on medical education and practice and determine the working parameters of health-care workers. The dentists, who had some formal training, survived and flourished, and later formed an independent profession. The midwives, with access to limited education and hindered by their sex and mixed race, were accepted as minor, subordinate, lower-paid practitioners. The phlebotomists, deprived of formal training, gradually disappeared from the official list of practitioners, their responsibilities entrusted to medical interns and hospital staff. The bleeders survived, but as illegal practitioners marginalized from mainstream health-care occupations.

The general idea of competition for jurisdiction, resources, and "clients" (patients or recipients of services) may be expanded to include contemporary institutions and organizations. The juntas de sanidad challenged the Protomedicato's jurisdiction by expanding their services to the public, undermining its prestige. Supported by the liberal ideology that was at the root of their origins and more in tune with the times, the juntas gradually pushed their anachronistic rival aside. They were not the only ones. Other institutions competed for scarce government funds, professional prestige, and limited markets for their services. Since the late colonial period, the surgical school and the Protomedicato competed for the revenues derived from licensing. Such competition became more urgent during the war, as government resources dried up. The struggle continued after independence and was inherited by the university medical faculty, ending with the surgical school's demise. Similarly, the struggle for control over medical (and surgical) education began soon after independence, as the previously discussed proposals illustrate. The 1831 union of both medical fields did not end the competition for students and resources, and the founding of the medical college two years later brought yet another player to the field. The 1838 final closure of the surgical school left the two remaining institutions to contest for students, resources, courses, and prestige, a contest that was resolved in 1857 when the government ordered the closure of the university.

Competition went beyond the medical profession and its educational institutions to include struggles between church and state, the capital and the provinces, and federalists and centralists. These contests for power greatly influenced the development of the medical profession, health-care institutions, and professional education. In Mexico City and the provincial capitals, schools, universities, and hospitals became pawns of forces beyond their control. An analysis of the medical profession and related topics thus requires careful attention to the political and ideological context as much as to changes within the profession itself.

Continuity and competition did not exclude innovation and collaboration. European, especially French, medical theories, practices, and technologies were enthusiastically embraced. The influence of French medicine can be traced back to colonial times, when military medical personnel familiar with French medicine reached New Spain. Local physicians, yearning for reform, were open to new ideas, although these were not always applicable to the situation at hand. After independence, various factors contributed to the growing admiration for French medicine. One such factor was Mexico's alienation from Spain, a result of the long wars of independence, the reluctance of Spain to recognize Mexico's independence as a *fait accompli*, and Spain's efforts to recover its colony. The new nation rejected its colonial past and strove to erase its legacy, looking instead at the example of a "civilized country." Mexico, like most of Latin America, became a follower and admirer of France, a country that better reflected their political objectives and cultural aspirations. French influence may be found in most areas of life, from architecture to fashion, but in the medical field various factors contributed to emphasize the trend.

The end of the colonial period coincided with the high point of the Paris school, whose advances in medicine and anatomy placed France at the forefront of medical science. The reorganization of France's health-care professionals and medical education system as a consequence of revolution touched a chord among Mexican practitioners who saw similarities with their own situation. The French model, therefore, seemed the most appropriate to local medical reformers, who did not hesitate to incorporate the teachings of the Paris school into their medical program. The influence of the Paris school curriculum was reinforced by the textbooks chosen and the enthusiasm of faculty who had attended classes in France or held a French degree. Despite the many obstacles that the imposition of such a program implied for a poorly funded school that lacked the infrastructure to support the practical component, the Mexican medical education program was shaped by and adapted from French models.

Although its undeniable Hispanic roots made it a representative professional organization first and an advisory board second, the Consejo Superior de Salubridad was also shaped by the influence of France. Following the Protomedicato's tradition, the Consejo served the interests of the medical elite by ensuring the physician-surgeons' privileged position and setting clear divisions between the different health-care practitioners. However, the Consejo Superior was also a public health board, and its organization mimicked that of the Paris Conseil. The Consejo, therefore, may be described as the result of Spanish tradition, French influence, and Mexican reality.

Important contributors to the francophile attitude of Mexican physicians were the French practitioners who resided in Mexico, key collaborators in the establishment of academies and the development of a professional network among their colleagues. Chavert, Jecker, and Villette collaborated in the reorganization of medical education, aided the dissemination of the Paris school's innovations, and promoted personal and institutional relations with Europe. They also helped launch the publication of the first medical academy journal and contributed articles to it. Collaboration and interchange increased in the 1860s as Mexican practitioners and French military medical personnel worked together, formed an organization to discuss their ideas and research, and strengthened the scientific relations between both countries.

Also of great importance were France's contemporary policies of cultural expansion, which translated into its positive response to the opening of the first Mexican medical academy in the 1830s. When the newly established academy required recognition and legitimization from more established organizations, two renowned French academies stepped in and offered Mexican practitioners the sanctioning they sought. Later, France's cultural imperialism and its interventionist role in the 1860s would result in the establishment of a permanent academy of medicine and, despite the unfavourable political situation and interruption of diplomatic relations, the

strengthening of relations between the practitioners of both countries. In spite of political and military events, Mexican practitioners'
infatuation with France did not diminish, as illustrated by the proud
description of Lino Ramírez's attendance at the international medical congress celebrated in Paris in 1867 – the same year that French
troops withdrew from Mexico. Similarly, the first academy founded
by military surgeons in Mexico in 1868 was named Academia
Médico-Quirúrgica Larrey in honour of Napoleon's surgeon.
Mexico's enthusiasm for French culture continued unabated for
years to come, and academic collaboration and exchanges continue
to this day.

The central role of the state and contemporary politics in the
development of the Mexican medical profession is another overarching theme in this study. That role can be traced back to the
Hispanic past, when the Crown determined and legislated professional status, rights, and privileges. The colonial Protomedicato was
established by royal order, and the Crown, by means of its viceroy,
intervened in its organization, sanctioning the choice of protomédicos and selecting one of them. Similarly, university faculty, regulations, and decisions had to be approved by the monarchy. State
intervention did not stop after independence, as the government
continued to have the last word on university, Protomedicato, and,
later, Facultad Médica and Consejo Superior appointments. However,
the difference between the colonial period and the independent state
is of utmost importance. The prestige and permanence of the Spanish
monarchy had given way to weak, short-lived governments with
little credibility. Unfortunately for the medical leaders, their only
option was to resort to the state. The limited number of practitioners
and the inability to provide superior therapies and outcomes that
would ensure them the health-care market forced them to seek government support and sanction. Thus, the profession's organizational
changes and development of medical education during the time
under study were not achieved by market forces, as in the cases of
Britain and the United States, nor were they the result of medical
advancement. They were achieved by legislation.

As in France, and in contrast to the Anglo-Saxon countries, in
Mexico the state played a central and most crucial role in the development of professional regulations, monopoly, and a medical curriculum. In exchange for government backing and legislation, the
medical leadership offered collaboration. Such a quid pro quo was

not always smooth, with relations between the two sides depending on the situation at hand and the balance of power between them. Laws, of course, did not mirror reality; the latter usually took some time to catch up to legislation, and in some cases it never did. The medical school curriculum legislated in 1834 was not offered in its totality until the 1860s; the Consejo Superior's mandate went unfulfilled for lack of funding, bureaucratic obstacles, and political turmoil; and complete professional monopoly was impossible to enforce. Nonetheless, through legislation, the government shaped reforms, the success of which ultimately depended on a vision and forward-looking attitude that few politicians and bureaucrats had. The result was that relations between government officials and practitioners were often tense and were sometimes stretched to the breaking point, as indicated by the medical faculty's refusal to continue teaching until the school and their salaries were regularized. Nonetheless, both parties were aware of their interdependence and the benefits of collaboration. Medical practitioners might have been too few and lacked the power to ensure their privileged position, but they knew the services they offered were indispensable to the community, the military, and consequently the state. The various levels of government were often unable to enforce their own laws, but they could officially endorse change and set important precedents. The choice of France as a model for reform is thus far from surprising. It was a country with an interventionist state that better fit Latin American tradition and reality.

In 1877 the medical elite could look back with satisfaction. Since 1822 a small but determined group of practitioners had led the way, seizing the opportunity to modernize the profession and ensure their monopoly. Fifty years later, the medical school was on firm ground and properly funded; it offered a curriculum based on the Paris school, and its student body had grown to 221.[2] The Consejo Superior had been reorganized as a public health board with direct funding from the National Treasury, and its director, Eduardo Liceaga, was making a name for himself as a public health authority.[3] Four years before, the Sociedad Médica de México had become the Academia de Medicina de México, the country's main medical professional organization. It enjoyed international recognition and had forged relations with important academic organizations in Europe, the United States, and elsewhere in Latin America. The Academia had been placed under the auspices of the Ministry of

Justice and Public Education and honoured with the attendance of President Porfiro Díaz at the ceremony opening its academic year. Indeed, it had been a long and sometimes tortuous journey, shaped by the fluid politics of the time and slowed by political turmoil and financial shortcomings, but the medical profession could now say it had carved its own niche within the Mexican nation.

Notes

INTRODUCTION

1 Although the 1813 closing of the Protomedicato and the establishment of government-controlled health boards may be considered as the trigger of change, the decreasing gap between medicine and surgery that would characterize later reforms was obvious by 1800. My study ends in the 1870s when the Sociedad de Medicina, established in 1865, received official status as the Academia de Medicina de México (1877). The official recognition of the academy coincides with the beginning of the Porfiriato (the Porfirio Díaz regime), which brought important political changes and initiated an era of relative peace and modernization (or Westernization) and is considered as the beginning of modern Mexico.

2 Cited in Leavitt, "Medicine in Context."

3 Abbott, *The System of Professions*, 3–4.

4 Gelfand, "The History of the Medical Profession," 1:1119.

5 In colonial times, the viceroyalty of New Spain encompassed roughly present-day Mexico, the southern United States, Central America, and the Philippines.

6 Martínez Barbosa, "Atención y regulación médica," 134–6; Zavala Battle, "El Protomedicato en el Perú," 151–7.

7 Lanning, *The Royal Protomedicato*.

8 Hernández Sáenz, *Learning to Heal*, 26–9.

9 The Royal and Pontifical University's monopoly over medical education was broken briefly by the medical program offered at the University of Guadalajara. The latter was established in 1792 and was closed down in 1825.

10 Rawlings, *The Spanish Inquisition*, 50–3.

11 Warren, *Medicine and Politics in Colonial Peru*, 50–1; Martín, *The Black Doctors of Colonial Lima*.

12 Gardeta Sabater, "El Real Tribunal del Protomedicato," 223; Velasco Ceballos, *La Cirugía Mexicana*, 453–5.

13 AGN, Universidad, Doctores y Licenciados en Medicina, vol. 286, ff. 585–98.

14 Velasco Ceballos, *La Cirugía Mexicana*, 453–5.

15 Febles, *Esposición*, 4.

16 See, for example, José María Luis Mora's works, in *José María Luis Mora, Ensayos, Ideas y Retratos*.

17 Contemporary medical articles as well as private and official documents praise France and often mention it as a model. See, for example, the publications of the various academies of medicine.

18 Sowell, "Contending Medical Ideologies," 912.

19 Carpio, "Discurso," 81–6. All translations from Spanish are mine.

20 Ibid.

21 Ramsey, *Professional and Popular Medicine in France*.

22 AGN, Protomedicato, 1799, vol. 3, exp. 8, f. 155v.

23 Gelfand, *Professionalizing Modern Medicine*.

24 Maulitz, *Morbid Appearances*.

25 See Warner, *Against the Spirit of the System*. His argument has been countered by those who consider the German teaching and hospital system more influential.

26 Ramsey, *Professional and Popular Medicine*.

27 Weisz, *The Medical Mandarins*.

28 Gelfand, "History of the Medical Profession," 1:1134.

29 Risse, *Hospital Life in Enlightenment Scotland*.

30 Gelfand, "History of the Medical Profession," 1:1134–5.

31 Thomsonianism rejected formal medicine and its practitioners and promoted the use of herbs and other traditional medicines; see Gelfand, "History of the Medical Profession," 1:1137–40.

32 The historiography of nineteenth-century medical practice is as varied as it is fragmented, for lack of uniformity in practice. Sources on the topic include Ludmerer, *Learning to Heal*; Rosenberg, *The Care of Strangers* and *The Cholera Years*; and Shryock, *Medicine and Society in America*.

33 León, *La obstetricia en México, Apuntes para la historia de la medicina en Michoacán* and *La Escuela de Medicina de Michoacán*. The latter two have been reprinted by the state government of Michoacán and published under the title *Historia de la Medicina en Michoacán*. This includes a bibliographic introduction by Vázquez Gallardo and a biographic sketch by Somolinos de Ardois. More information on Nicolas León may be found in Saldaña, "Los Historiadores de la Ciencia y Michoacán," 58–72.

34 Carrillo, "Profesiones sanitarias y lucha de poderes," 149–68.

35 Izquierdo was one of the founders of the Sociedad Mexicana de Historia y Filosofía de la Medicina, and instrumental in the creation of the Department of Physiology at the National University of Mexico. He is also the author of *Las Primeras Academias de México* and *La Escuela Médica Quirúrgica de Puebla*. Gamboa-Ojeda, "Raudon, cirujano poblano"; Castañeda Lopéz and Rodríguez, "Henry Sigerist y José Joaquín Izquierdo."

36 Martínez Cortés, *De los miasmas y efluvios*.

37 Martínez Cortés and Martínez Barbosa, *El Consejo Superior de Salubridad*.

38 Martínez Cortés, *Carpio, Laennec y la Invención del estetoscopio*; Martínez Barbosa and Zacarías Prieto, *Rafael Lucio*; Malvido and Flores, *Documentos de Valentín Gómez Farías*; Cordero Galindo, *Vida y obra del doctor Miguel Muñoz* and *Casimiro Liceaga*.

39 Rodríguez Pérez, *La Escuela Nacional*; Rodríguez Pérez and Zacarías, *El Hospital de Maternidad e Infancia*.

40 Neri Vela, "La evolución de la oftalmología mexicana."

41 Zedillo, ed., *Antiguo Hospital de San Pedro*; Huerta Jaramillo, *Los boticarios poblanos*; Cortés Riveroll and Palacios García, *Historia de la medicina en Puebla*.

42 Oliver Sánchez, *Salud*.

43 Tucker Thompson, *Las otras guerras de México*.

44 Figueroa Zamudio, *La Enseñanza de la Medicina*; Martínez Cortés and Guzmán Ávila, *Ensayos sobre la Historia de la Medicina*.

45 Warren, *Medicine and Politics in Colonial Peru*.

46 Jouve Martín, *Black Doctors of Colonial Lima*.

47 The Second Empire, supported by Napoleon III and presided over by Maximilian of Habsburg, ended in April 1867.

48 Flores y Troncoso is a good example of this approach, but the same views may be found in José Joaquín Izquierdo's works on Luis Montaña and Juan Nepomuceno Raudón, and in more recent studies such as Malvido and Flores's *Documentos de Valentín Gómez Farias*.

49 Edison, "Conquest Unrequited"; Pyenson, *Civilizing Mission*.

CHAPTER ONE

1 Febles, *Esposición*, 5.

2 The Protomedicato of Peru, as that of New Spain, dates back to 1570. In 1639 its presidency was linked to the newly established chair of Prima de medicina. The Protomedicatos of Cuba, Santa Fe in New Granada, and

Rio de la Plata were founded in 1711, 1758, and 1770 respectively. The last was a dependency of the Peruvian Protomedicato. Zavala Batle, "El Protomedicato en el Perú," 2; Martínez Larrarte and Reyes Pineda, "El Protomedicato"; Gardeta Sabater, "El Real Tribunal del Protomedicato en la Audiencia de Santa Fe."

3   Lanning, *El Real Protomedicato,* 141.

4   Febles, *Noticia de las Leyes y órdenes de policia,* 2.

5   Hernández Sáenz, *Learning to Heal,* 89, 118.

6   Faculty meeting of 30 July 1795, AGN, Universidad, Libro de claustros, vol. 27, ff. 209–14.

7   Ibid., ff. 198–9v; Archer, "Combatting the Invisible Enemy," 54–5.

8   Faculty meeting of 26 August 1788, AGN, 1788, Universidad, Libro de Claustros, vol. 26, ff. 306–7v.

9   Tanck de Estrada, "La Colonia," 48.

10 Solicitud de Martín Sessé, 1792, AGN, Historia, vol. 460, exp. 24, ff. 239–41.

11 Anna, *The Fall of the Royal Government,* 37.

12 Ibid., 37–8.

13 Anna, *Forging Mexico, 1821–1835,* 43–4.

14 Amortization moneys refers to the capital that resulted from the loans and mortgages the church was forced to recall and send to Spain by royal order.

15 Anna, *The Fall of the Royal Government,* 37.

16 Benson, *Mexico and the Spanish Cortes,* 3–9.

17 *Instrucción para el gobierno económico político de las provincias*; Dublán and Lozano, *Legislacion mexicana.*

18 Ibid.

19 Ibid., chap. I, arts I, II, III.

20 Ibid., chap. I, art. IV.

21 The decree was issued on 10 November 1810 and reached the Mexico City cabildo on 21 January 1811. Venegas refused to implement it. Anna, *The Fall of the Royal Government,* 103–4.

22 Ibid., 111–13.

23 Despite recent legislation, Calleja was appointed viceroy of New Spain.

24 Cooper, *Las epidemias en la Ciudad de México,* 208.

25 Most authors now believe it was typhus, but Miguel E. Bustamante thinks it was malaria exacerbated by typhus, typhoid, and dysentery resulting from the poor conditions prevalent in the city. Bustamante, "Cronología epidemiológica," 417.

26 Del Mazo had also been imposed as head of the cabildo by Calleja.

27 Cathedral official in charge of teaching ecclesiastical studies.

28 Hernández Torres, "El sitio de Cuautla," 562.

29 Acta de Cabildo del 13 de abril de 1813, AHCM, Ayuntamiento. Actas de Cabildo, 1813, vol. 132A, f. 72.

30 Up to September, the cabildo minutes of 1813 do not mention a junta de sanidad. As the epidemic was over in August, it is doubtful that a junta was appointed after September. AHCM, Ayuntamiento. Actas de Cabildo, April to September 1813, vol. 132A, ff. 72–260v.

31 Following tradition, each registered practitioner was assigned to a city section and made responsible for the medical care of its population.

32 Anna, *The Fall of the Royal Government*, 4.

33 Ibid., 170.

34 The other members were the regidores Tomas Salgado and Manuel Teran and the citizens (*vecinos*) Conde de Basoco, Ciro de Villaurrutia, Antonio Velasco de la Torre, and Joaquin de Aldana. AHCM, Ayuntamiento, Policia. Salubridad. Epidemias. Viruela, vol. 3679, exp. 27, f. 1.

35 Inoculation or variolization refers to the transferal of matter extracted from a smallpox vesicle to the recipient to induce a mild case of smallpox. It resulted in lifetime immunity but it was not without risks. Vaccination refers to the transferral of the cowpox vaccine. Mark and Rigau-Pérez, "The World's First Immunization Campaign," 66; Smith, The "Real Expedición Marítima de la Vacuna," 10–11.

36 AHCM, Ayuntamiento, Policia, Salubridad, Epidemias, Viruela, vol. 3678, exp. 8.

37 Mark and Rigau-Pérez, "The World's First Immunization Campaign," 69–81.

38 Cordero Galindo, *Vida y obra del doctor Miguel Muñoz*, 1–3.

39 AHCM, Ayuntamiento, Policia. Salubridad. Epidemias. Viruela, vol. 3679, exp. 29, ff. 12–13v.

40 Ibid., f. 4.

41 Ibid., f. 12.

42 The Count of Regla was the owner of various mines and haciendas and one of the wealthiest men in the colony. He contributed to numerous charitable causes. For more on his remarkable life, see Couturier, *The Silver King*.

43 Ibid., exp. 29, ff.15–15v. The Royal Powder Factory was a Crown monopoly established in the late eighteenth century. Powder was used for military purposes, mining, and fireworks. Quiroz Zamora, *Historia de México*.

44 The Mariscal de Castilla was serving as alcalde of the Mexico City cabildo at the time. Anna, *The Fall of the Royal Government*, 124.

45 AHCM, Ayuntamiento, Policia. Salubridad. Epidemias. Viruela, vol. 3679, exp. 27, ff. 8–11v.

46 They were Francisco Barrola, fourteen years of age; Sóstenes Sotomayor, ten; Anselmo Sánchez, twelve; Mariano García, nine; Pedro Arteaga, ten; and Ricardo Ocio, nine. Cordero Galindo, *Vida y obra del doctor Miguel Muñoz*, X, 4 n.

47 *Aviso al Público*, 30 April 1814, and *Aviso al Público*, 17 May 1814, AHCM, Ayuntamiento, Policia. Salubridad. Epidemias. Viruela, vol. 3679, exp. 29, ff. 26 and 29.

48 Ibid., exp. 27, f. 54.

49 Ibid., exp. 29, f. 42.

50 Anna, *The Fall of the Royal Government*, 129.

51 Ibid., 162–75.

52 AHCM, Ayuntamiento, Policia. Salubridad. Epidemias. Viruela, vol. 3679, exp. 27, ff. 123v–4.

53 Ibid., f. 91.

54 Carta al asesor, 1782, AGN, Protomedicato, vol. 2, exp. 1, ff. 58–62.

55 Hernández Sáenz, *Learning to Heal*, 157.

56 Izquierdo, *Raudón cirujano poblano*, 208.

57 Libro de actas de la Junta de sanidad, 1813–33, AGMP, Ayuntamiento, Actas de Cabildo, vol. 78, exp. 885, ff. 200–395, 213–13v.

58 At the time, Cuautla was under siege by royalist troops. Hernández Torres, "El sitio de Cuautla," 551–64.

59 Izquierdo, *Montaña*, 208–9.

60 A *vara* is approximately 2.8 feet deep so the ditches were 10 feet 8 inches or 3.25 metres deep.

61 The report states there were 7,125 casualties from a total of 48,726 victims.

62 "Informe Instructivo sobre la epidemia de la fiebre," 29 October 1813, Fuente, *Efemérides sanitarias*, 49–50.

63 Ibid., 51.

64 Libro de las Actas de la Junta de sanidad, 1813–33, AGMP, Serie Expedientes, vol. 78, leg. 885, f. 246.

65 Ibid., 239–41.

66 De la Fuente, *Efemérides*, 51–2.

67 Libro de las Actas de la Junta de sanidad, AGMP, Expedientes, vol. 78, leg. 885, ff. 240–1.

68 Ibid., f. 251.

69 Reglamento de la junta de sanidad. Ibid., vol. 79, leg. 888, ff. 39–50.

70 Libro de las Actas de la Junta de sanidad. Ibid., vol. 78, leg. 885, f. 253.

71 Ibid., f. 279v.

72　Ibid., ff. 267v–80.

73　De la Fuente, *Efemérides sanitarias*, 58–9.

74　Libro de actas de la Junta de sanidad, A G M P, Expedientes, vol. 79, leg. 888, f. 42.

75　A G M P, Leyes y Decretos, 1827, ff. 179–81v.

76　Archer, "Combatting the Invisible Enemy," 49–92.

77　Cruz Velázquez, *Los Hospitales del Puerto de Veracruz*, 44.

78　Knaut, "Yellow Fever."

79　Ibid., 641.

80　Ibid., 636–7.

81　Junta Municipal de Sanidad de Veracruz, 1814, A H M V, Actas de cabildo, caja 109, exp. 145, ff. 243–302, f. 284v.

82　Ibid., f. 283.

83　So. Establecimiento de la Junta Sanidad en cumplimiento del Reglamento politico de las Provincias, 1814, ibid., caja 110, vol. 147, ff. 282–5.

84　Cruz Velázquez, *Los Hospitales del Puerto de Veracruz*, 74.

85　Informe del diputado de Sanidad, 1808, A G N, Protomedicato, vol. 1, exp. 4, ff. 92–116.

86　So. Establecimiento de la Junta Sanidad en cumplimiento del Reglamento politico de las Provincias, 1814, ff. 253–91; A H M V caja 110, vol. 147, ff. 282–5.

87　Ibid., f. 282v.

88　Ibid., f. 250.

89　So. creacion de la Junta de Sanidad, 1820, ibid., caja 130, vol. 174, f. 244.

90　A H M V, Actas de cabildo, caja 140, vol. 185, ff. 159–60.

91　Ibid., ff. 140–40v.

92　See chapter 2.

93　*Memoria.*

94　The minutes of their meetings have been lost.

95　Tanck de Estrada, "La Colonia," 47.

96　Vicuña was born in 1735 and graduated in 1774; Gracida y Bernal graduated in 1784; Luis Montaña was born in 1755 and received his doctorate in 1793; and García Jove graduated in 1772, so his approximate age at death was seventy-five. Their age varied between sixty and seventy-five.

97　Fernández de Recas, *Grados de Licenciados, Maestros y Doctores*, 209; *Diccionario Porrúa*.

98　Cordero Galindo, *Casimiro Liceaga*, 1–7.

99　There are numerous examples, such as Casimiro Liceaga and Ignacio Durán, later appointed directors of the medical school, and Pedro Escobedo, who was well acquainted with Valentín Gómez Farías and

Antonio López de Santa Anna. Oscoy and Fernández del Castillo, *Efemérides de la Medicina Mexicana*, 5; AMM, *La Revolución francesa y su interpretación médica.*

100 The junta de sanidad was formed by the alcalde primero Ignacio de Aguirrevengoa, who acted as president; regidores Juan Ignacio González Vertiz, Jose Manuel Velazquez de la Cadena, Miguel Calderón, Manuel Carrasco; and síndico Agustin de la Peña y Santiago; the clergyman Dr Jose Miguel Guide; the vecinos José Bernardo Baz, Jose Antonio Martinez de los Rios, and Ignacio Suarez; the physicians Manuel de Jesús Febles and Jose María Vara; and the surgeon Francisco Montes de Oca. Flores y Troncoso, *Historia de la Medicina*, 2:437; Actas de la Junta de Sanidad, 1820, 11 July 1820, AHCM, Ayuntamiento, Policia. Salubridad, Juntas de Sanidad, vol. 3685, exp. 7, ff. 1–2.

101 Actas de la Junta de Sanidad, 1820, AHCM, Ayuntamiento. Policia. Salubridad. Juntas de Sanidad, vol. 3685, exp. 7, ff. 1–2.

102 Ibid., ff. 1–8.

103 Anna, *The Fall of the Royal Government*, 173.

104 Ibid.

105 Actas de la Junta de Sanidad, 1820, AHDF, Ayuntamiento. Policia. Salubridad. Juntas de Sanidad, vol. 3685, exp. 7, ff. 3–4v.

106 Baz was referring to Fodéré's *Traité de médecine légale et d'hygiène publique ou de police de santé, adapté aux codes de l'Empire français, et aux connaissances actuelles, à l'usage des gens de l'Art, de ceux du Barreau, des jurés et des administrateurs de la santé publique, civile, militaire et de marine*. The first three-volume edition was published in Paris in 1798. A second, six-volume edition was published in 1813. AHCM, Policia. Salubridad. Juntas de Sanidad, vol. 3685, exp. 12, ff. 2–3.

107 La Berge, *Mission and Method*, 33, 137.

108 AHCM, Ayuntamiento. Policia. Salubridad, Juntas de Sanidad, vol. 3685, exp. 12, ff. 5, 12–15.

109 Ibid.; *Memoria*, 17.

110 The issue was debated at length by the junta de sanidad members; the physician Joaquín Guerra, who opposed the new regulation, was outvoted by his colleagues José María Amable and Joaquín Piña. AHCM, Ayuntamiento. Policía. Salubridad. Juntas de Sanidad, vol. 3685, exp. 14, ff. 14, 17.

111 Ibid., ff. 19–24.

112 Ibid., vol. 3686, exp. 38, ff. 12–13.

113 Ibid., exp. 44, f. 9.

114 Ibid., exp. 32, ff. 1–2 and 17v.

115 Ibid., exp. 39.

116 Ibid., exp. 38, ff. 10–15.

117 AHCM, Ayuntamiento, Policía, Salubridad, vol. 3668, exp. 19.

118 Actas de la Junta de sanidad, AHCM, Ayuntamiento. Policía. Salubridad.
      Junta de sanidad, vol. 3686, exp. 33, 48.

CHAPTER TWO

1 AHCM, Ayuntamiento, Policia. Salubridad. Juntas de Sanidad, vol. 3686,
    exp. 38.

2 The full title is *Memoria sobre la Necesidad y Utilidad de reunir el estudio
    de medicina de la Universidad, el de Cirujía del Hospital de Naturales, y el
    de Botánica del Jardín de palacio en un Colegio de Medicina y Ciencias
    Naturales, en que los catedráticos por el mismo sueldo que hoy les tiene
    señalado la Nacion, desempeñen las funciones y atirbuicones [sic] que
    hasta aquí ha tenido el Proto-medicato. Memoria.* This document has
    no pagination.

3 Zedillo Castillo, *Historia de un hospital,* 117–18.

4 *Memoria.*

5 Ibid.

6 Burke, *The Royal College of San Carlos,* 146–50.

7 Ibid., 170–1.

8 Ibid., 173–9.

9 Hernández Sáenz, *Learning to Heal,* 110–11.

10 The full title is *Memoria Histórica en la que se refieren el origen, pro-
    gresos y estado de brillantez del hombre físico entre los estrangeros y el
    empirismo con que se ejerce entre nosotros por falta de colegios especiales
    donde se estudie teorica y prácticamente.*

11 Muñoz, *Memoria Histórica.*

12 Ibid., 23.

13 Gelfand, *Professionalizing Modern Medicine,* 164–71.

14 *Memoria Histórica,* 29.

15 Carpio, "Cuadro del Estado Actual de la Medicina."

16 AGN, Ramo Hospitales, vol. 24, exp. 11, ff. 310–15.

17 The documentation on the long and confusing process is published in
    Velasco Ceballos, *La Cirugía Mexicana,* 151–97 and 223–96.

18 Not only Mexican applicants had been rejected but the king had made
    the appointment in contravention to the school's regulations. Ibid., 296.

19 See, for example, the letters of Serrano to Iturrigaray (1804) AGN,
    Protomedicato, vol. 3, exp. 15 and 16.

20 El Dr Don Antonio Serrano solicitando el establecimiento de un colegio de cirujía médica, 1822, AGN, Justicia e Instrucción Pública, vol. 13, exp. 1.

21 In early December, popular unconformity with the election of President Manuel Gómez Pedraza resulted in a series of riots. The Parián, the main Mexico City market, along with other central buildings, was sacked and burnt by the mob. The rioters entered the Escuela de Cirugía, destroying and stealing its limited equipment and instruments; only the items that Serrano was cataloguing at home were spared. The losses were later estimated by Serrano's successor, Juan Santibáñez, in the amount of 400 pesos. El catedrático substituto de la Escuela nacional de Cirujia sobre haber denegado el Hospital de Sn Andres los cadaveres necesarios para las lecciones de aql. establecimiento, 1830, AGN, Justicia e Instrucción, vol. 13, exp. 14, ff. 175–83v, f. 176.

22 Villar, *Proyecto*.

23 Villar obtained his medical degree in 1832. Gutiérrez Sedano, *Historia del Servicio de Sanidad Militar*, 1:128–9.

24 Villar, *Proyecto*.

25 Carreño, *Efemérides de la Real y Pontificia Universidad*, 2:847; *Memoria*.

26 The five practitioners graduated first as surgeons and then as physicians. The years of their graduation were Liceaga 1815 and 1818; Durán 1820 and 1826; Erazo 1825 and 1827; Robredo 1826 and 1829; and Ferrer 1818 and 1822. According to Cordero Galindo, Liceaga did not have a surgical degree, but Gutiérrez Sedano states he obtained his degree from the Protomedicato in September 1815. Cordero Galindo, *Casimiro Liceaga*, 3; Gutiérrez Sedano, *Historia del Servicio de Sanidad Militar*, 126–7; *La Revolución francesa y su interpretación médica*, 20; Oscoy and Fernández del Castillo, *Efemérides de la medicina*, 37; *Diccionario Porrúa*.

27 Febles, *Esposición*, 8–10.

28 After independence, royal institutions such as the Surgical School became "national institutions."

29 Law of 23 December 1830, Dublán y Lozano, *Legislación Mexicana*.

30 Decreto. 21 November 1831, AGN, Justicia e Instrucción, vol. 13, exp. 20, ff. 263–63v.

31 Expediente sobre unidad de las ciencias medicas y quirurgicas, AHCEM, Legislatura V, 1833–4, Varios, caja 5, carpeta 5.

32 Sánchez Díaz, "Las contribuciones michoacanas," 128, and 135–7.

33 Representación al Honorable Congreso del Estado, AHCEM, Legislatura V, 1833–4, caja 9, carpeta 15.

34 Ibid.

35 Razones que expone el ciudadano Ignacio Moreno, Cirujano mayor del Hospital Nacional de San Miguel para que no se le rebaje el sueldo de 1000 pesos que disfruta, 1824, AHEJ, Beneficencia, Legislación, caja 824.

36 Mendoza Cornejo, *Ciento setenta años de legislación*, 121–2.

37 It is important to stress that these lists refer only to licensed practitioners. Many others continued to practise illegally, so it is impossible to provide an accurate figure.

38 Lista de facultativos, 1822, AHCM, Ayuntamiento, Policía. Salubridad, vol. 3668, exp. 14; Febles, *Esposición*, 8–10.

39 Costeloe, *The Central Republic in Mexico*, 19.

40 Rodríguez O., "Down from Colonialism."

41 A good example is Guillermo Prieto and the difficult economic situation he lived in during his formative years. Prieto, *Memorias de mis tiempos*, 130–3.

42 Wasserman, *Everyday Life*, 37.

43 Ibid., 82.

44 Noticia de los Profesores de Medicina, Cirujia, Farmacia, Flebotomia, Dentistas, y Parteras que presentan sus titulos con arreglo a la Ordn. Superior que con fha 7 de Marzo incerta la Prefectura, 1841, AHSS, Salubridad Pública, Sección Ejercicio de la Medicina, caja 1, exp. 41.

45 Lista de los profesores de Medicina, Cirujia, Farmacia y Flebotomia, 1835, in Martínez Cortés, *De los miasmas y efluvios*, 15; Almonte, *Guía de forasteros*, 346–53.

46 AGN, Segundo Imperio, vol. 59, exp. 17.

47 Almonte, *Guía de forasteros*, 346–53; AGN, Segundo Imperio, vol. 59, exp. 17.

48 Velasco Ceballos, *La Cirugía Mexicana*, 366.

49 Jouve Martín, *The Black Doctors of Colonial Lima*.

50 Febles, *Esposición*.

51 Ibid., 8–10; Lista de facultativos, 1822, AHCM, Ayuntamiento, Policía. Salubridad, vol. 3668, exp. 14.

52 Law of 21 November 1831, Dublán y Lozano, *Legislación Mexicana*.

53 Lista de los profesores 1835, Martínez Cortés, *De los miasmas y efluvios*, 15.

54 Almonte, *Guía de forasteros*, 346–53.

55 They were José María Benítez, José María Castro, Mariano Dávila, Victorio Gracida, and Casimiro Liceaga, Almonte, *Guía de forasteros*, 349–50.

56 Luis Garrone, 1842, AHFM, Protomedicato, leg. 23, exp. 16.

57 Certificado, 1838, AHFM, Protomedicato, leg. 17, exp. 4, f. 3.

58 Expediente formado de oficio del Real Tribunal del Protomedicato sobre que los Maestros Flebotomianos matriculen sus aprendices y oficiales, AHFM, Protomedicato, leg. 2, exp. 16.

59 Padrón de la Ciudad de México 1811–12, AGN, Padrones, vols. 53–8, 60–4, and 66–78.

60 Causa formada contra Manuel Espinosa, 1791, AHFM, Protomedicato, leg. 3, exp. 10, ff. 1–15; Averiguación sumaria contra el barbero José María Orihuela, 1818, AHFM, Protomedicato, leg. 12, exp. 9, ff. 1–5.

61 The document is published in Fernández del Castillo, "Cirujanos y Barberos," 277–9.

62 Título de flebotomiano concedido a Julián Antonio de Acosta, 1758, AHFM, Protomedicato, leg. 1, exp. 2.

63 El Intendente de la Provincia sobre el mejor arreglo del oficio de Barberos, y examen de los Flebotomianos, 1798, AGN, Protomedicato, vol. 3, exp. 8, ff. 136–207v, f. 145.

64 Burke, *The Royal College of San Carlos*, 158.

65 *Reglamento de la Facultad Médica del Distrito y Territorios de la Federación*, 1832, AGN, Justicia e Instrucción, vol. 14, exp. 1, ff. 4–13v.

66 AHCM, Ayuntamiento, Hospitales, Hospital de San Andrés, vol. 2297, exp. 15; Solicitud de Da. Teresa Zamora pidiendo examinarse en Flebotomía, 1835, AHFM, Protomedicato, leg. 20, exp. 20.

67 Reformas al Ordenamiento de 4 de enero de 1841, art. 60, 1841, AHSS, Fondo Salubridad Pública, Presidencia, Secretaría, caja 2, exp. 25; Solicitud de Teresa Zamora, 1835, AHFM, Protomedicato, leg. 20, exp. 20, f. 10.

68 Dictámentes sobre dentistas, parteras y flebotomianos, 1854, AHFM, Protomedicato, leg. 31, exp. 30, f. 6.

69 Ibid., f. 4.

70 AGN, Segundo Imperio, vol. 59, exp. 17; Maillefert, *Directorio del comercio del Imperio Mexicano*.

71 Hernández Sáenz, *Learning to Heal*, 179.

72 *Diario del Gobierno de la República Mexicana*, Tuesday, 26 November 1839, vol. 15, no. 1672.

73 Francisco Lacoste, dentista aprobado, 1841, AHFM, Protomedicato, leg. 22, exp. 39.

74 Antonio Labully, dentista aprobado, 1841, AHFM, Protomedicato, leg. 22, exp. 36.

75 Reformas al Ordenamiento de 4 de enero de 1841, art. 60, 1841, AHSS, Fondo Salubridad Pública, Presidencia, Secretaría, caja 2, exp. 25.

76 Expediente justificativo del examen de Eugenio del Cambre, 1841, AHFM, Protomedicato, leg. 23, exp. 6; Eugenio Crombé aprobado en el arte de

dentista, 1841, AHFM, Protomedicato, leg. 22, exp. 12; Fernández del Castillo, "Los primeros dentistas graduados en México el año de 1841," 410.

77 Fernández del Castillo, "Los primeros dentistas," 410–11.

78 Dictámenes sobre dentistas, parteras y flebotomianos, 1854, AHFM-FEMYA, leg. 31, exp. 30.

79 Registro, AHFM-FEMYA, Libro Número 7, Sección de libros, 1841.

80 At the time, a tooth extraction consisted in breaking the tooth and leaving the root in place. Hoffmann-Axthelm, *History of Dentistry*, 330.

81 Consejo de Salubridad a Jorge Gardiner, dentista, 1842, AHSS, Salubridad Pública, Ejercicio de la Medicina, caja 2, exp.10.

82 Fernández del Castillo, "Los primeros dentistas," 410.

83 Consejo pide que dentista americano Jorge Gardiner no se anuncie en la plancha que tiene en su casa en clase de doctor en cirugia ya que solo tiene titulo de dentista, 1845. AHSS, Sección Presidencia, Ejercicio de la Medicina, caja 2, exp. 73; Almonte, *Guía de Forasteros*, 352.

84 Expedientes de D. Juan Havá, D. Juan Trancoz, D. Mariano Chacón, and D. Benito Acuña, 1854, in AHFM, Protomedicato, leg. 31, exp. 19, 22, 23, and 24 respectively.

85 Dictámenes sobre dentistas, parteras y flebotomianos, 1854, AHFM-FEMYA, legajo 31, exp. 30.

86 Hoffman-Axthelm, *History of Dentistry*, 287.

87 This painful type of treatment had been used in Europe and the United States since the early ninetenth century. The pulp cavity was trephinated and cauterized with a burning iron, arsenious acid, or sulfuric and nitric acid. The first root canal or extirpation of the pulp seems to have been carried out by Edward Hudson in 1809. Ibid., 311–13.

88 Dictámenes sobre dentistas, parteras y flebotomianos, 1854, AHFM-FEMYA, legajo 31, exp. 30.

89 In England, the anesthetic effects of nitrous oxide (laughing gas) and ether were well known by the turn of the eighteenth century. The first tooth extraction under ether took place in Rochester, NY, in 1842. Experimentation using nitrous oxide and ether in surgical and dental procedures continued during the 1840s, but they were gradually replaced by chloroform, as this was faster, had less unpleasant side effects, and was easier to use. Hoffman-Axthelm, *History of Dentistry*, 330–5.

90 *Diario del Gobierno de la República Mexicana*, 26 November 1839, 15:1672.

91 Costeloe, *The Central Republic in Mexico*.

92 Hau, *The Cult of Health and Beauty in Germany*, 2–4; Aguilar Ochoa, *La fotografía durante el Imperio de Maximiliano*, 15–18.

93 These and similar advertisements appeared regularly in *L'Estaffette*, the journal published by the French army in Mexico from 1863 to 1866.

94 Moll, *Aesculapius in Latin America*, 308–9.

95 León, *La obstetricia en México*.

96 Penyak, "Obstetrics," 1.

97 Jaffary, *Reproduction and Its Discontents*.

98 Carrillo, "Profesiones sanitarias y lucha de poderes," 2; Alanís-Rufino, "Una cuestión de parteras y médicos," 63–8.

99 Hernández Sáenz, *Learning to Heal*, 206.

100 Angela María Leite, 1816, A H F M, Protomedicato, leg. 10, exp. 12.

101 Francisca Ignacia Sanchez, 1818, A H F M, Protomedicato, leg. 12, exp. 15.

102 Burke, *The Royal College of San Carlos*, 97–8.

103 Lista de los libros del uso del Doctor Don Florencio Pérez Camoto que se remiten con su equipage a México, 1810, Inquisición, vol. 1449, ff. 141–9; Nota de los libros que contienen 2 cajones del uso del Dr D. Florencio Pérez Camoto, 1811, A G N, Inquisición, vol. 1453, ff. 117–18.

104 Velasco Ceballos, *La Cirugía Mexicana*, 186; Causa contra Maturino Carlos Lloret, 1764, A G N, Inquisición, vol. 1082, exp. 2, ff. 29–206; Fernández del Castillo, "Lo que México debe al cirujano Miguel Muñoz II," 1:652.

105 Villar, *Proyecto*, 1.

106 Hernández Sáenz, *Learning to Heal*, 207–8.

107 Quoted in Martínez Cortés, *De los miasmas y efluvios*, 145.

108 Cruz, *Historia de la Educación Pública en Puebla*, 1:28.

109 Actas de la Junta de Sanidad, 19 January and 7 February 1824, A H C M, Policía. Salubridad. Junta de Sanidad, vol. 3686, exp. 12, ff. 2–3.

110 León, *La obstetricia*, 268.

111 Examen de obstetricia de Da. Juana Garcia Cabezón, A H F M, Protomedicato, leg. 26 exp. 2.

112 León, *La obstetricia*, 269.

113 Solicitud de exámenes de Atanasia Recuero, 1829, A H F M, Protomedicato, leg. 13, exp. 24; Solicitud de Da. Teresa Zamora pidiendo examinarse en Flebotomía, 1837, A H F M, Protomedicato, leg. 20, exp. 20.

114 Flores y Troncoso, *Historia de la Medicina*, 3:141; León, *La obstetricia*, 261.

115 There is no explanation for the choice of location. Maria Josefa Belasco (1846), A H F M, Protomedicato, Leg. 28, exp. 19.

116 Flores y Troncoso states that midwives were also required to have knowledge of French. However, I have not found any indication of this requirement, and the textbooks assigned were either translations from French

works or texts in Spanish. Flores y Troncoso, *Historia de la medicina*, 3:573; León, *La obstetricia*, 268.

117 León, *La obstetricia*, 268.

118 El catedrático Don Ignacio Torres responde a la prevención sobre el curso de obstetricia, 1857, AHFM-FEMYA, leg. 123, exp. 22, ff. 1–18, f. 3.

119 Ibid., ff. 5–10.

120 Dictámenes sobre dentistas, parteras y flebotomianos, 1854, AHFM, Protomedicato, Leg. 31, exp. 30, f. 6.

121 Flores y Troncoso, *Historia de la medicina*, 3:576.

122 Tarifas de facultativos, AHSS, Salubridad Pública, Ejercicio de la Medicina, caja 1, exp. 23, f. 8.

123 Decree of 23 August 1838, AGN, Universidad, vol. 198, ff. 525–25v.

124 Penyak, "Obstetrics," 73n45.

125 Decree of 23 August 1838, AGN, Universidad, vol. 198, ff. 525–25v.

126 Gastos hechos en la Casa de maternidad por cuenta y orden de Su Majestad, AHAMM, vol. 2308, leg. 1, exp. 3; Reglamento, ibid., exp. 52; Reformas al Ordenamiento de 4 de enero de 1841, Art. 60, 1841, AHSS, Fondo Salubridad Pública, Presidencia, Secretaría, caja 2, exp. 25.

127 Doña Andrea G. Caballero solicita inscribirse en esta Escuela, á pesar de tener mas edad que la designada en el reglamento, 1864. AHFM-FEMYA, leg. 130, exp. 50, ff. 2–2v.

128 Examen de María Loreta Jáuregui, AHFM-FEMYA, leg. 19, exp. 27, ff. 1–6.

129 Sobre el establecimiento de una cátedra de obstetricia en Puebla, 1866, AHFM-FEMYA, leg. 133, exp. 29.

130 Arrom, *The Women of Mexico City*, 154–205.

131 AGGEG, Fondo Gobernación, Sección Secretaría, caja 342, exp. 1.

132 Arrom, *The Women of Mexico City*, 154–205.

133 Teresa Zamora, 1837, AHFM, Protomedicato, leg. 20, exp. 20, ff. 1–11.

134 Petición de Julia Caro, 1864, AHFM-FEMYA, leg. 131, exp. 49.

135 Ibid.

136 The receipt issued specifies "depósito e información para examen de obstetricia." Juana García Cabezón, 1844, AHFM, Protomedicato, leg. 26, exp. 2, ff. 1–8.

137 Agatha Carolina Letellier, AHFM, Protomedicato, Leg. 27, exp. 16.

138 The gaps may be partly explained by the frequent cancellation of courses as the result of political turmoil and foreign invasion, and the dismal state of the economy.

139 Almonte, *Guía de Forasteros*, 352–3; Lista de los médicos-cirujanos, farmacéuticos, dentistas y parteras residentes en la capital, 1866, AGN, Segundo Imperio, vol. 59, exp. 17.

140 Doña Luz Gutiérrez examinada en flebotomía y obstetricia, 1858, AHFM, Protomedicato, leg. 33, exp. 22.

141 The file mentions that a Francisca Flores had requested a similar permission but does not include any further explanation. Doña Antonia Barrientos, 1860, AHFM-FEMYA, leg. 35, exp. 22.

142 Doña Andrea G. Caballero solicita inscribirse en esta Escuela, á pesar de tener mas edad que la designada en el reglamento, 1864, AHFM-FEMYA, leg. 130, exp. 50.

143 This information was collected from the AHFM Protomedicato and FEMYA (Fondo de la Escuela de Medicina y Alumnos) collections.

144 Solicitud de Da. Teresa Zamora pidiendo examinarse en Flebotomía, 1835, AHFM, Protomedicato, leg. 20, exp. 20.

145 *El Mosquito Mexicano*, Friday, 7 May 1841, 9:37.

146 León, *La obstetricia*, 270–1.

147 *El Mosquito Mexicano*, Friday, 7 May 1841, 9:37.

148 Prieto, *Memorias*, 193.

149 Legislation was unclear and often contradictory, but for all practical purposes, military surgeons served the civilian population. Hernández Sáenz, *Learning to Heal*, 109–16.

150 Velasco Ceballos, *La Cirugía Mexicana*, 379.

151 Informe de los ministros del Real Tribunal del Protomedicato, AHSS, Salubridad Pública, Presidencia, Secretaría, caja 1, exp. 9.

152 Pedro Puglia, carta a conde de Revillagigedo AGN, Protomedicato, vol. 5, exp. 1 and 3, ff. 161–77; AGN, Historia, vol. 460, exp. 9–11, ff. 74–85.

153 Información de Domingo Ventura Melica, AHFM, Protomedicato, leg. 4, exp. 3, ff. 13–15; AGN, Protomedicato, vol. 2, exp. 6, ff. 227–8 and exp. 8, ff. 264–79.

154 Sobre solicitud del farmacéutico francés Prospero Fayet, AHFM, Protomedicato, leg. 18, exp. 2, f. 8.

155 Carlos IV a Branciforte, 1796, AGN, Protomedicato, vol. 3, exp. 8, ff. 182–4.

156 Sobre solicitud del farmacéutico francés Prospero Fayet, AHFM, Protomedicato, leg. 18, exp. 2, f.8.

157 Consulta al Consejo Superior de Salubridad, 1841, AHSS, Ejercicio de la Medicina, caja 3, exp. 1.

158 Espediente de D. Santiago Peysant, AHFM, Protomedicato, leg. 31, exp. 27, f. 3v.

159 Reformas al Ordenamiento de 4 de enero de 1841, AHSS, Salubridad Pública, Presidencia, Secretaría, caja 2, exp. 25.

160 The Consejo Superior de Salubridad was established in 1842 and will be discussed in the following chapter.

161 Ibid.

162 Hernández Sáenz, "'Pues no haviendolo aquí,'" 45.

163 Ocurso hecho por Severino Galezowski, 1836, AHFM, Protomedicato, leg. 20, exp. 14; Hernández Sáenz, "'Pues no haviendolo aquí,'" 45–6.

164 Belgium separated from the Netherlands and became an independent country in 1830.

165 The name of Servicio de Sanidad Militar (sanitary corps) was changed to Cuerpo médico militar (medical military corps) in 1846. Gutiérrez Sedano, *Historia del Servicio de Sanidad*, 75.

166 Reglamento del Cuerpo Médico Militar expedido en virtud del decreto de 12 de febrero de 1846, AGN, Folletería, caja 8, no. 306.

167 Pedro Vander Linden, Hoja de Servicio, AHSD, Archivo de Cancelados, XI/111/2-905; Oliver Sánchez, *Salud*, 155–6; Gutiérrez Sedano, *Historia del Servicio de Sanidad*, 45–8.

168 It is impossible to know how many Spanish-speaking applicants were foreigners, as many applications do not include origin. Therefore, only foreigners from non-Spanish-speaking countries are included. Applications for licences may be found at AHFM.

169 Aiton, "Spanish Colonial Reorganization," 269–80; Herr, *The Eighteenth-Century Revolution in Spain*, 79, 300.

170 The Arnaud brothers were the first of a large group of immigrants that arrived from the Barcelonnette valley in southeastern France. By the end of the century their descendants controlled a commercial, industrial, and banking empire in Mexico. Proal and Charpenel, *Los Barcelonnettes en México*, 15–23.

171 Costeloe, *The Central Republic in Mexico*, 13.

172 Sussman, "The Glut of Doctors in Mid-Nineteenth-Century France," 287–304.

173 Pablo Alejandro Lefevre, AHFM, Protomedicato, leg. 15, exp. 19; Pedro Estevan Blaquiere, ibid., leg. 16, exp. 2; José María Sentis, ibid., leg. 16, exp. 14; Eustaquio Dujat, ibid., leg. 22, exp. 7.

174 Pablo Alejandro Lefevre, AHFM, Protomedicato, leg. 15, exp. 19.

175 AHSS, Salubridad Pública, Ejercicio de la Medicina, caja 2, exp. 77.

176 Pedro Estevan Blaquiere, AHFM, Protomedicato, leg. 16, exp. 2; José María Sentis, AHFM, Protomedicato, leg. 16, exp. 14; Eustaquio Dujat, AHFM, Protomedicato, leg. 22, exp. 7.

177 Exámenes de la Facultad de Medicina, AHFM, Protomedicato, leg. 21, exp. 4, f. 10.

178 Expediente de D. Pedro Gouze, 1840, AHFM, Protomedicato, leg. 21, exp. 47.

179 José Furey Saurinet, 1841, AHFM, Protomedicato, leg. 23, exp. 14.

180 Ramsey, *Professional and Popular Medicine in France*.

181 Sowell, "Contending Medical Ideologies," 4.

182 Jouve Martín, *The Black Doctors of Colonial Lima*, 101–26.

183 Memoria de la Secretaria del Consejo Superior de Salubridad, 1842, AHSS, Salubridad Pública, Presidencia, Secretaría, caja 2, exp. 60

184 Rio de la Loza, "Exposicion que hizo el consejo superior de salubridad de Méjico," 448.

185 Flores y Troncoso, *Historia de la Medicina*, 3:378.

186 Martínez Cortés, *De los miasmas y efluvios*, 50–1.

187 W.M.M., "Phrenology in Mexico," 459.

188 The laws of 21 November 1831 and 17 July 1835, and the *1842 Reglamento* are some examples of such legislation.

189 The same law ordered enlistment for vagrants that, without legal rights, were supported by *apoderados*, or well-off honest men. Alvarez Amezquita et al., *Historia de la Salubridad y Asistencia*, 1:252.

190 Informe del Prefecto de Cuautitlan, AHSS, Fondo de Salubridad Pública, Ejercicio de la Medicina, caja 1, exp. 39.

191 AGN, Justicia e Instrucción, vol. 87, ff. 86–92.

192 Indian towns were governed by Indigenous officials; Spanish officials had no jurisdiction over them.

193 This program was put into place by Baron Lezay-Marnésia, one of Napoleon's prefects, in Lower Alsace in 1810. It successfully provided medical care to the area for most of the century. Sussman, "Enlightened Health Reform," 565–84.

194 "Exposición que hizo el consejo superior de salubridad de Méjico al E. Sr. Gobernador del departamento," *Periódico de la Academia de Medicina de Méjico* 5 (1840): 443–51; AHSS, Salubridad Pública, Presidencia, Secretaría, caja 2, exp. 17.

195 Consulta del Juez de paz de la cabecera de Taxco, 1845, AHSS, Sección Presidencia, Ejercicio de la Medicina, caja 2, exp. 66.

196 Doña Antonia Hernández de Riofrío solicitando permiso para curar las enfermedades venéreas, 1865. AGN, Gobernación, leg. 1716, exp. 3.

197 Doña Antonia Hernandez de Riofrío y Doña Lugarda Riofrío solicitan permiso para curar por un método especial a los enfermos del mal venéreo, 1866. AHFM, FEMYA, leg. 39, exp. 6.

198 Arancel para los honorarios de los profesores de Medicina, 1840, AHSS, Salubridad Pública, Ejercicio de la Medicina, caja 1, exp. 23, ff. 5–9.

199 Wasserman, *Everyday Life and Politics*, 39–40.

200 Law of 21 November 1831, Dublán y Lozano, *Legislación Mexicana*.

CHAPTER THREE

1 Reporte, 1845, AHCM, Policia. Salubridad, leg. 3668, exp. 30, f. 1
2 Fowler, *Tornel and Santa Anna*, 91–7.
3 Anna's quote is found in ibid., 94.
4 Sims, *Expulsion of the Spaniards from Mexico.*
5 Warren, *Medicine and Politics in Colonial Peru.*
6 Sowell, "Contending Medical Ideologies."
7 Law of 21 November 1831, Dublán y Lozano, *Legislación Mexicana.*
8 Meeting of 14 February 1826, Mateos, *Historia parlamentaria.*
9 Ramsey, *Professional and Popular Medicine in France*, 39.
10 Febles, *Esposicion.*
11 Later, the Facultad Médica expanded its membership to twelve individuals (eight physician-surgeons and four pharmacists), from whom four officials were elected every three years. Law of 21 November 1831, Dublán y Lozano, *Legislación Mexicana.*
12 Despite these regulations, in 1835 the Facultad was still distinguishing between *vocales médicos*, or physicians, and *vocales médico-cirujanos*, or physician-surgeons. Lista de los profesores de Medicina, Cirujia, Farmacia, y Flebotomia que tienen registrados sus títulos por el Exmo. Ayuntamiento, 1835, published in Martínez Cortés, *De los miasmas y efluvios*, 15, hereafter *Lista de profesores, 1835.*
13 Literally "phlebotomist porter or doorman."
14 Reglamento de la Facultad medica del Distrito y Territorios de la Federacion, 1832, AGN, Justicia e Instrucción Pública, vol. 14, exp. 1, 4–13v.
15 Law of 21 November 1831, Dublán y Lozano, *Legislación Mexicana.*
16 These are the only names included in the various sources. Febles, *Esposición*, 7.
17 With the only exception of Villa, all appointees appear in the 1822 list of practitioners published by the Protomedicato. It is unclear why Villa was not included, as he graduated in 1818. Flores y Troncoso, *Historia de la Medicina*, 2:206, 3:536; Lista de facultativos, 1822, AHCM, Ayuntamiento. Policía Salubridad, vol. 3668, exp. 14.
18 *Lista de profesores, 1835.*
19 *Reglamento de la Facultad Médica del Distrito y Territorios de la Federación*, 1832, AGN, Justicia e Instrucción, vol. 14, exp. 1, ff. 4–13v.
20 Ibid.
21 The appointed committee was formed by Manuel de Jesús Febles, Louis Jecker, Juan Luis Chavert, Guillermo Cristino Schiede, Joaquín Villa, and Dávila Arrillaga. Flores y Troncoso, *Historia de la medicina* 3:81.

22 Ibid.; Reglamento formado por la junta superior de sanidad del Distrito para gobierno de la junta municipal de sanidad de Mexico, 1833, AHCM, Ayuntamiento. Policía. Salubridad. Junta de sanidad vol. 3686, exp. 49.

23 Flores y Troncoso, *Historia de la Medicina* 3:273, 295.

24 Actas de la Junta de sanidad, AHDF, Ayuntamiento. Policía. Salubridad. Junta de sanidad, vol. 3686, exp. 33 and 48.

25 Louis Jecker was brother of the infamous Juan B. Jecker, whose claim precipitated the French intervention in Mexico.

26 The only document in this respect is a Facultad Médica's circular to the practitioners, but it is unclear on whose initiative it was sent or if it was influenced by political changes. Circular de la Facultad Médica, 1836, AHSS, Salubridad Pública, Presidencia, Secretaría, caja 1, exp. 42.

27 Law of 21 November 1831, Dublán y Lozano, *Legislación Mexicana*.

28 Ocaranza, *Historia de la Medicina en México*, 153–6.

29 Bando of 21 December 1833, AGN, Universidad, vol. 198, 497.

30 Bando of 2 August 1834, Dublán y Lozano, *Legislación Mexicana*.

31 This Constitution was promulgated on 1 December 1836, Dublán y Lozano, *Legislación Mexicana*.

32 This *Reglamento* was issued on 20 March 1837, Dublán y Lozano, *Legislación Mexicana*.

33 Law of 29 December 1836, Dublán y Lozano, *Legislación Mexicana*.

34 Martínez Cortés, *De los miasmas y efluvios*, 16.

35 Se concede a la Facultad Médica prórroga, 1840, AHSS, Salubridad Pública, Presidencia, Secretaría, caja 1, exp. 51.

36 Comunicación sobre reglamento para la enseñanza médica, AHSS, Salubridad Pública, Presidencia, Secretaría, caja 1, exp. 54, 5–9.

37 I have been unable to locate the Código Sanitario. All secondary sources consulted state it was never completed. However, a short note from the Facultad Médica to the departmental committee indicates that "the project of medical police" was sent on 3 December 1840. It may have been incorporated in the *Ordenamiento*. AHSS, Salubridad Pública, Presidencia, Secretaría, caja 1, exp. 58.

38 *Ordenamiento*, 1840, AHCM, vol. 3890, exp. 1.

39 *Reglamento de Enseñanza y policia médicas*, ASSA Fondo Salubridad Pública, Presidencia, Secretaría, caja 2, exp. 44.

40 The invitation, dated 30 November 1840, was extended to professors José María Varela, Manuel Carpio, José Martínez del Campo, Pedro Escobedo, Agustín Arellano, Ignacio Erazo, Marchos Arellano, Ignacio Torres, Leopoldo Río de la Loza, Francisco Rodríguez Puebla, Manuel Robledo

(o Robredo), José María Vargas, José María Terán, José Espejo, and Ignacio Durán. Martínez Cortés, *De los miasmas y efluvios*, 16.

41 *Reglamento de Enseñanza y policia médicas*, AHSS Fondo Salubridad Pública, Presidencia, Secretaría, caja 2, exp. 44.

42 AHSS, Salubridad Pública, Ejercicio de la Medicina, caja 1, exp. 53.

43 AHSS, Salubridad Pública, Sección Presidencia, Secretaría, caja 2, exp. 56.

44 The *Annales d'hygiene publique et de médecine légale* was established in 1829 by the leaders of the hygienist movement to publish the data gathered by the Paris Health Board. Its national and international circulation and its standing as the best publication on the topic contributed to the Health Board's international reputation. La Berge, "The Paris Health Council," 349.

45 Ibid., 339–52; Weiner, "Public Health under Napoleon," 271–84.

46 Although the regulations refer to a vice-president and secretary, the minutes of the Consejo Superior meetings mention only a secretary and a treasurer.

47 *Reglamento de estudios médicos, de examenes y del Consejo de salubridad del Departamento de México*, AHCM, Consejo de Salubridad, vol. 3890, exp. 1.

48 The titular members of the Conseil de Salubrité de Paris enjoyed a salary of 1,200 francs, while its adjunct and honorary members received no remuneration except for the satisfaction of seeing their names linked to a world-recognized organization and having their work published. La Berge, "The Paris Health Council," 339–52.

49 Ibid.

50 Actas del Consejo Superior de Salubridad, 1850, AHSS, Salubridad Pública, Presidencia, Actas de Sesion, caja 1, exp. 1.

51 *Reglamento de estudios médicos, de examenes y del Consejo de salubridad del Departamento de México*, AHCM, Consejo de Salubridad, 1842, vol. 3890, exp. 1.

52 Informe del Consejo Superior de Salubridad, 1844, AHSS, Salubridad Pública, Presidencia, Secretaría, caja 3, exp. 1.

53 Ibid.; Memoria de la Secretaría del Consejo Superior de Salubridad, 1842, AHSS, Salubridad Pública, Presidencia, Secretaría, caja 2, exp. 60.

54 Martínez Cortés, *De las miasmas*, 23;

55 Memoria de la Secretaría del Consejo Superior de Salubridad, 1842, AHSS, Salubridad Pública, Presidencia, Secretaría, caja 2, exp. 60.

56 Informe del Secretario sobre los trabajos del Consejo, 1841, AHSS, Salubridad Pública, Presidencia, Secretaría, caja 2, exp. 1.

57 Ibid; Memoria de la Secretaría del Consejo Superior de Salubridad, 1842, AHSS, Salubridad Pública, Presidencia, Secretaría, caja 3, exp. 1.

58 Martínez Cortés, *De las miasmas y efluvios*, 24.

59 From 1833 to 1837 the government resorted to copper coinage to cover its expenses. It was not the first time. Previous governments had done the same to a lesser degree. The problems caused by the copper coinage were compounded by the counterfeit coins that circulated freely. To correct the situation, in 1841 Santa Anna prohibited their circulation and the government purchased them at 50 per cent of their value. Arrangoiz, *México desde 1808 hasta 1867*, 379.

60 "Farmacopea Mexicana," 79.

61 The works mentioned are Eugène Souberian, *Nouveau traité de pharmacie: théorique e practique*, and the Spanish translation of the *Traité de pharmacie: practique e théorique* by N.E. Henry and G. Guibourt, published in Madrid as *Farmacia Razonada o Tratado de Farmacia Práctico y Teórico*. AHSS, Salubridad Pública, Presidencia, Secretaría, caja 2, exp. 1.

62 *Farmacopea Mexicana*.

63 Minutas de comunicaciones, 1844, AHSS, Salubridad Pública, Presidencia, Secretaría, caja 3, exp. 4.

64 Informe del secretario sobre los Trabajos del Consejo, 1841, AHSS, Salubridad Pública, Presidencia, Secretaría, caja 2, exp. 1.

65 AHSS, Salubridad Pública, Presidencia, Secretaría, caja 2, exp. 60.

66 AHSS, Salubridad Pública, Presidencia, Secretaría, exp. 57, and caja 3, exp. 2.

67 Pascual Querejazu. Permiso para ejercer en toda la República, 1855, AHSS, Salubridad Pública, Ejercicio de la Medicina, caja 2, exp. 38, ff. 1–9.

68 Actas de sesiones del Consejo Superior de Salubridad, 1854, AHSS, Salubridad Pública, Presidencia, Actas de Sesión, caja 1, exp. 6.

69 Vicente Rocafuerte was Equatorian, but the Mexican government had appointed him secretary of the legation sent to London. In the absence of the minister, Rocafuerte became Mexico's chargé d'affaires from 1827 to 1829. *Diccionario Porrúa*, 2:2486.

70 Orden a la Facultad Médica para que informe porque ha prohibido a Rafael de la Garza ejercer su profesión, 1833, AGN, Instrucción pública, vol. 13, exp. 28, f. 295.

71 Ocaranza, *Historia de la Medicina*, 153–6.

72 Acta de sesión extraordinaria del Consejo Superior de Salubridad, 21 October 1856, AHSS, Salubridad Pública, Presidencia, Actas de Sesión, caja 1, exp. 8.

73 Acta de sesión del Consejo Superior de Salubridad, 13 April 1858, AHSS, Salubridad Pública, Presidencia, Actas de Sesión, exp. 10.

74 Acta de sesiones del Consejo Superior de Salubridad, 22 June and 3 August 1858, AHSS, Salubridad Pública, Presidencia, Actas de Sesión, exp. 10.

75 AHSS, Salubridad Pública, Sección Ejercicio de la medicina, caja 1, exp. 53.

76 Acta de sesión, 28 November 1854, AHSS, Salubridad Pública, Presidencia, Actas de Sesión, exp. 6.

77 Correspondencia entre el Gobierno del Distrito y el Consejo de Salubridad, 1855, AHSS, Salubridad Pública, Ejercicio de la Medicina, caja 3, exp. 21.

78 Sowell states that homeopathy was introduced in Colombia in the late 1840s. Sowell, "Contending Medical Ideologies," 915; Dr Boret, "Noticia sobre la medicina Homeopática," 23–34.

79 Flores, *Historia de la Homeopatía en México*, 23–4.

80 Sowell, "Contending Medical Ideologies," 915.

81 Acta de sesión, 28 November 1854, AHSS, Salubridad Pública, Presidencia, Actas de Sesión, caja 1, exp. 6.

82 Flores, *Historia de la Homeopatía en México*, 25.

83 AHSS, Salubridad Pública, Ejercicio de la Medicina, caja 3, f. 26.

84 Flores, *Historia de la Homeopatía*, 41–3.

85 Presently, the Escuela Nacional de Medicina y Homeopatía is part of the Instituto Politécnico Nacional granting the degree of Homeopathic Physician-Surgeon.

86 The licences issued by the Consejo during these years are located at the AHFM, FEMYA, leg. 34–7.

87 AHSS, Salubridad Pública, Presidencia, Secretaría, caja 1, exp. 42.

88 The same year a junta de caridad (charity board) was established, separating public health from welfare issues. However, for the next months the terms *junta de caridad* and *junta de sanidad* were used interchangeably. Law of 20 March 1837, Dublán y Lozano, *Legislación Mexicana*; AHCM, Ayuntamiento, Policía. Salubridad, Juntas de Sanidad, vol. 3686, exp. 1–53.

89 Martínez Cortés, *De los miasmas y efluvios*, 91–2.

90 Ibid., 93.

91 AHUG, Salubridad y Asistencia, (1849) tomo 9, exp. 73.

92 AHCM, Policia. Salubridad, 1845, Policia. Salubridad, vol. 3668, exp. 30, 1–24v.

93 Memoria leida por el Secretario del Consejo Central de Salubridad, 17 January 1867, AGN, Folletería, caja 22, f. 686, 23–4.

94 Martínez Cortés, *De los miasmas y efluvios*, 88–9.

95 Ibid., 89–90.

96 Minutas de comunicaciones dirigidas al Consejo Superior de Salubridad, 1844, AHSS, Salubridad Pública, Presidencia, Secretaría, caja 3, exp. 4.

97 Ibid., 90.

98 Acta de sesión del Consejo Superior de Salubridad, 14 August 1854, AHSS, Salubridad Pública, Presidencia, Actas de Sesion, caja 1, exp. 6.

99 Acta de sesión del Consejo Superior de Salubridad Sesión, 18 December 1854, AHSS, Salubridad Pública, Presidencia, Actas de Sesion, exp. 7.

100 Actas de Sesion del Consejo Superior de Salubridad, 1850, AHSS, Salubridad Pública, Presidencia, Actas de Sesion, caja.1, exp.1.

101 Actas de Sesión Sesiones del Consejo Superior de Salubridad, 1 May to 29 October 1850, AHSS, Salubridad Pública, Presidencia, Actas de Sesion.

102 AHSS, Salubridad Pública, Epidemias, caja 1, exp. 28.

103 Actas de Sesión del Consejo Superior de Salubridad, 1 May to 29 October 1850, AHSS, Salubridad Pública, Presidencia, Actas de Sesion, caja 1, exp. 1.

104 It may also refer to brandy drops mixed in chamomile or orange-leaf tea. Gregorio López recommended using red wine and boiling it thoroughly. López, *El tesoro de medicinas*, 159.

105 Acta de sesión extraordinaria del 17 de julio 1850, AHSS, Salubridad Pública, Presidencia, Actas de Sesión, caja 1, exp. 1.

106 Ibid.

107 Actas de Sesión del Consejo Superior de Salubridad, 1 May to 29 October AHSS, Salubridad Pública, Presidencia, Actas de Sesión, caja 1, exp. 1.

108 Martínez Cortés, *De los miasmas y efluvios*, 101–3.

109 AHSS, Salubridad Pública, Presidencia, Secretaría, caja 3, exp. 27.

110 The Plan de Ayutla was proclaimed on 1 March 1854 against Santa Anna's despotic regime. It signalled the beginning of a revolution that overthrew the regime in August 1855.

111 Acta de sesión extraordinaria del Consejo Superior de Salubridad, 1 April 1854, AHSS, Salubridad Pública, Presidencia, Actas de Sesión, caja 1, exp. 6.

112 Actas de sesiones del del Consejo Superior de Salubridad, 15 and 29 June 1856, AHSS, Salubridad Pública, Presidencia, Actas de Sesión, caja 1, exp. 8.

113 Martínez Cortés, *De los miasmas y efluvios*, 125–6.

114 These figures are based on the holdings of the Archivo Histórico de la Secretaría de Salubridad. Police records were not consulted. Ibid., Medicina legal, caja 1, exp. 1–49.

115 Memoria leida por el Srio. El Consejo Central de Salubridad, 17 January 1867, AGN, Folletería, caja 22, f. 686, 25.

116 AHSS, Salubridad Pública, Ejercicio de la medicina, caja 2, exp. 44.

117 Ibid.

118 Reporte de la venta ilícita de píldoras y polvos en la Carnicería Francesa, and Acuerdo del Consejo para dictaminar sobre la venta de Píldoras de Morrison, AHSS, Salubridad Pública, Sección Inspección de Farmacias, caja 1, exp. 44 and 55.

119 Proposiciones de Cornelio Gracida y de Jose de Vargas, 1832, AHSS, Salubridad Pública, Presidencia, Secretaría, caja 1, exp. 33.

120 In addition, *regidores* (aldermen) became responsible for preventing the sale of liquours "offensive to health and public morals." Bando emitido por el gobernador del Distrito, 1835, AHSS, Salubridad Pública, Presidencia, Secretaría, caja 1, exp. 38.

121 Circular dirigida a los profesores farmacéuticos para que no surtan las recetas de los curanderos, 1843, AHSS, Inspección de farmacias, caja 1, exp. 40.

122 Carta que envia el Dr Trivece, 1842, AHSS, Salubridad Pública, Presidencia, Secretaría, caja 2, exp. 42.

123 Comunicación del Director del Colegio Nacional de San Gregorio, 1845, AHSS, Salubridad Pública, Inspección de Farmacias, caja 1, exp. 50.

124 *Ley sobre la policia general del Imperio.*

125 Aerometer was an instrument that determined the weight and density of gases.

126 Visita al Hospital de San Pablo, 1852, AHSS, Salubridad Pública, Inspección de Farmacias, caja 1, exp. 68.

127 After thirty-one years of invaluable service, the Sisters of Charity were expelled from Mexico in 1874 by the government of Sebastián Lerdo de Tejada. Alvarez Amézquita et al., *Historia de la Salubridad* 3:407–8.

128 *Farmacopea Mexicana*, 164, 166, 177.

129 Advertisements for these products appeared repeatedly in *L'Estaffette* (1866).

130 Each department was under the jurisdiction of a prefect. Militarily, the empire comprised eight "divisions" or districts. Maillefert, *Directorio del comercio del Imperio Mexicano*, 23–5.

131 It is unclear how much input the medical profession had in drawing up this legislation as not all physicians supported the empire. *El Diario del Imperio*, 1 December 1865, 2:293.

132 Also appointed were Gumersindo Mendoza and Alfonso Herrera, who refused to serve because of their many occupations. *El Diario del Imperio*, 9 January 1866), 3:308.

133 *El Diario del Imperio*, 1 November 1865, 2:253, 433.

134 Ley sobre la policía general del Imperio, *El Diario del Imperio*, 1 December 1865, 2:279, 593.

135 Ibid.
136 Ibid.
137 Ibid.
138 The division of the Sección the medicina into five areas of research (Pathology; Hygiene, Legal Medicine, and Medical Statistics; Veterinary Medicine; Materia Médica and Pharmacology; and Physiology and Anthropology) is a clear indication of growing professional specialization. Fernández del Castillo, *Historia de la Academia*, 24.
139 *El Diario del Imperio*, 24 December 1866, 4:507.
140 *El Diario del Imperio*, 3 January 1866, 3:304; Fernández del Castillo, *Historia de la Academia*, 21.
141 The juntas subalternas were established in Veracruz, Puebla, Tula, Tulancingo, Querétaro, Guanajuato, San Luis, Matehuala, Tamaulipas, Monterrey, Durango, Zacatecas, Aguascalientes, Fresnillo, Jalisco, Morelia, Toluca, Isla del Carmen, Yucatán, and Oaxaca. *Memoria del Consejo Central de Salubridad*, 4.
142 Hot chocolate was a very common beverage in Mexico. It was believed that its adulteration could have serious consequences.
143 *Memoria leida por el secretario del Consejo Central de Salubridad*, AGN, Folletería, caja 22, f. 686, 7–18.
144 Ibid.
145 Memoria leida por el Srio. El Consejo Central de Salubridad.
146 *El Diario del Imperio*, 26 February 1867, 5:646.
147 Medical practitioners had to pay the considerable amount of 32 pesos for the revalidation of their professional licences. AHFM-FEMYA, leg. 41, exp. 15.
148 Martínez Cortés, *De los miasmas y efluvios*, 167–8.
149 Martínez Cortés and Martínez Barbosa, *El Consejo Superior de Salubridad*, 15–19.

CHAPTER FOUR

1 AGN, Justicia e Instrucción Pública, vol. 56, ff. 63–7.
2 The legislation known as Bases Orgánicas (1843) divided the country in departments (as opposed to provinces or states) directly responsible to the central government. In 1855, the federalist government changed them into states.
3 Salas hoped to attract provincial support in the midst of political instability and the imminent US invasion of Mexico. See Mendoza Cornejo, *Ciento setenta años de legislación*, 135.

4 Meneses Morales, *Tendencias educativas,* 188, 244–5.

5 According to the university records, the graduates were Manuel de Jesús
Febles (later professor and Protomédico), José María Contreras y Canseco,
José Casimiro Liceaga (later director of the Establecimiento de Medicina),
José María de la Vara y Ortiz, Jose Rafael Calvillo Martinez Herrera,
and José Joaquín Guerra de la Fuente, AGN, Ramo Universidad, vol. 302,
ff. 42–3v.

6 Faculty meeting of 13 November 1810, AGN, Universidad, *Libros de
Claustros de 1801 a 1816,* no. 28, ff. 196v–7v, Carreño, *Efemérides,*
2:847.

7 Faculty meeting of 18 April 1839, Comunicaciones oficiales del Supremo
Gobierno y otras autoridades. Bandos 1823–50, AGN, Universidad,
vol. 198, ff. 99–100.

8 Faculty meeting of 17 February 1810, Carreño, *Efemérides,* 847.

9 Faculty meeting of 8 July 1816, ibid., 872.

10 Data for 1806 and 1813 are given by Valle, *La Cirugía Mexicana,* xv.
The numbers for 1816 and 1817 may be found in *Diario de México,*
11 December 1816; and *Noticioso General,* 19 November 1817, both
in AGN, Archivo Histórico de Hacienda, vol. 569, exp. 7.

11 Autos fhos en razón de recepta al Real Tribunal del Proto-Medicato, 1766,
AGN, Archivo Histórico de Hacienda, vol. 569, exp. 14, ff. 1–6; Velasco
Ceballos, *La Cirugía Mexicana,* 342; *Diario de México,* 11 December
1816; *Noticioso General,* 19 November 1817.

12 The Hospital Real de Naturales, or Royal Indian Hospital, was sustained
by the half-real contribution extracted from Indigenous subjects. The contribution was abolished in 1814 and then reinstated for a few years. The
hospital's income was considerably reduced, affecting the Escuela de
Cirugía. Zedillo, *Historia de un Hospital,* 117–18.

13 El Dir. de la Rl. Escuela de Cirujia sobre arvitrio para el servicio de la Rl.
Escuela, 1818, AGN, Archivo Histórico de Hacienda, vol. 569, exp. 7.

14 Velaco Ceballos, *La Cirugía Mexicana,* 199–206, 217–22, and 297–345.

15 The Protomedicato's only income derived from examinations, licensing,
and pharmacy inspection fees and fines for illegal practice.

16 Staples, *Recuento,* 15–32.

17 Among its members was José María Luis Mora, who would be instrumental in future educational reforms. Mora, 1822, *Obras completas,* 235.

18 Mora, *Obras Completas,* 8:66–7.

19 Staples, *Recuento,* 32.

20 Sesión del 20 de febrero de 1822, Mateos, *Historia parlamentaria,* ser. I,
vol. 1, t. 1, 240.

21 El Dr Don Antonio Serrano solicitando el Establecimiento de un colegio de Cirujía médica, 1822, AGN, Justicia e Instrucción, vol. 13, exp. 1, ff. 1–12; El Director de la Rl. Escuela de Cirujia sobre arvitrio para que sin gravamen de la Rl. Hda. le puedan costear practicantes para el servicio de la Rl. Escuela, 1818, AGN, Archivo Histórico de Hacienda, vol. 569, exp. 7.

22 The full title of this document is *Memoria sobre la necesidad y utilidad de reunir el estudio de medicina de la universidad, el de cirujia del hospital de naturales, y el de botanica del jardin de palacio en un colegio de medicina y ciencias naturales* and has been discussed in chapter 2.

23 Ibid.

24 García Jove's death was announced at the 19 June 1822 university meeting. Carreño, *Efemérides,* 2:883.

25 Muñoz, *Memoria historica.* This document has been discussed in chapter 2.

26 José Miguel Muñoz, 1807, INAH, Fondo Colección Antigua, leg. 4, exp. 13.

27 Neri Vela, "La práctica de la oftalmología," 185; Fernández del Castillo, "Lo que México debe al cirujano Miguel Muñoz," 1:636–44.

28 *Memoria historica,* 27–8.

29 Proyecto de Reglamento General de Instrucción Pública, 1823, AGN, Gobernación Legajos, leg. 18, caja 35, exp. 9; Tanck de Estrada, *La educación ilustrada,* 31.

30 These were general and descriptive anatomy, physiology and hygiene, surgical (external) pathology, medical (internal) pathology, *materia médica* (pharmacology), surgical clinical studies, medical clinical studies, surgical operations and obstetrics, natural history, theory and practice of pharmacy, and forensic medicine.

31 Congressional meeting of 14 February 1823, Mateos, *Historia parlamentaria.*

32 The intermediate level of "preparatory instruction for more in-depth studies" included grammar of old and modern languages, literature, history, logic, political economy, geography, law, and what we may assume were basic mathematics, statistics, physics, chemistry, mineralogy, geology, botany, agriculture, and zoology.

33 Proyecto sobre el plan general de instrucción pública, 1826. Mateos, *Historia parlamentaria.*

34 The consultor had the obligation of teaching the courses of physiology and *materia médica.*

35 Proyecto de reforma del establecimiento Nacional de Cirujía presentado por Pedro del Villar, 1829, AGN, Justicia e Instrucción, vol. 13, exp. 12, ff. 142–4.

36 Ibid.

37 The Escuela Práctica Médico Militar was not established until 1880.

38 *Memoria historica.*

39 Flores y Troncoso, *Historia de la medicina,* 2:457.

40 Quoted in Malvido and Flores, *Documentos de Valentín Gómez Farias,* xx.

41 Chávez, *México en la cultura médica,* 81–2.

42 Staples, *Recuento,* 123.

43 Rodríguez, *La Escuela Nacional,* 13.

44 Meneses Morales, *Tendencias Educativas,* 1:120.

45 I recognize that not all areas of education were affected in the same way; my analysis deals exclusively with the medical education reforms.

46 Fernández Ruiz, *Un Reformador y su reforma,* 147.

47 Some authors such as Will Fowler see this as a political manoeuvre, but Santa Anna's claim deserves further research and may be legitimate, as the capital was suffering the first cholera epidemic. Fowler, *Tornel and Santa,* 129–32.

48 These included the convents and temples of San Camilo and Espíritu Santo and their urban properties, the Hospital de Jesús and its temple and the properties owned by their previous owner, the Duque de Monteleone, that would be applied to primary education; the Hospital de Belen, the Hospicio de Santo Tomás with its orchard, the Inquisition building assigned to the San Carlos Academy, and the printing press established at the Hospicio de Pobres, Bando of 21 October 1833, Mateos, *Legislación Mexicana.*

49 The National Surgical School had been recently founded as the continuation of the Real Escuela de Cirugía and a dependency of the military medicine corps. Gutiérrez Sedano, *Historia del Servicio de Sanidad Militar,* 2:12–13; Bando of 26 October 1833, Dublán y Lozano, *Legislación Mexicana.*

50 Ocaranza, *Historia de la Medicina,* 157–9.

51 *Memoria.*

52 "Proyecto sobre el plan general de instrucción pública," 1826.

53 Bando of 26 October 1833, Mateos, *Legislación.*

54 Among these authors are Flores y Troncoso, *Historia de la Medicina;* Cárdenas de la Peña, *Historia de la Medicina en la Ciudad de México;* Fernández del Castillo, *Antología;* and Malvido and Flores, *Documentos de Valentín Gómez-Farías.*

55 Sesión del 14 de febrero de 1826, Mateos, *Historia parlamentaria.*

56 After the end of the reforms, the government ordered an inspection of the Establecimiento de Ciencias Médicas to determine its fate. The inspecting

committee was formed by university professor Manuel de Jesús Febles; surgeon Louis Jecker; physicians Juan Luis Chavert, Guillermo Cristino Schiede, and Joaquín Villa; and Dávila Arrillaga. The law of 17 November 1834 confirmed it as a *colegio* dependent on the university. Febles a Director del Establecimiento de Medicina, 1839, A G N, Universidad, Comunicaciones oficiales del Supremo Gobierno y otras autoridades y Bandos, 1823–50, vol. 198, f. 99 v; Flores y Troncoso, *Historia de la medicina,* 3:81.

57 Circular, 12 November 1834, *Legislación Mexicana.*

58 One year of instruction as well as another of hospital work were later added.

59 Palluault, "Medical Students," 34–6.

60 Although originally a three-year program, in 1820 it was expanded to four years. One year of instruction as well as another of hospital work were later added. Heller, *"Officiers de Santé,"* 28–30; Amette, *Code Medical,* 84–6.

61 Palluault, "Medical Students," 78–9.

62 Liceaga, "Reseña histórica del Establecimiento de ciencias medicas," 432.

63 Although contemporary documents refer to M. Chevallier as its author, the journal was published by the Societé de chimie mèdicale. During the 1820s Chevallier's name (probably the editor-in-chief or the organization's chair) appeared first, but the journal was a collaborative effort by Dumas, Fee, Guibourt, Julia de Fontanelle, Lassaigne, Orfila, Payon, E. Peligot, G. Pelletan, Pelouze, A. Richard, and Robinet. A decade later, Berard had taken Chevallier's place. *Journal de chimie médicale* 4 (1828), and 2nd ser., 3 (1837).

64 Rodríguez, *La Escuela Nacional,* 73–5.

65 Ibid., 79–80; Flores y Troncoso, *Historia de la Medicina,* 3:146–7.

66 Alexander Jamain, *Nouveau traité élémentaire d'anatomie descriptive et de préparations anatomiques* (Paris, 1853); P. Bérard, *Cours de physiologie* (Paris, 1848); Achille Richard, *Elements d'histoire naturelle* (Paris, 1831); and Apollinaire Bouchardat, *Elements de matière médicale et de pharmacie* (Paris, 1839). Rodríguez, *La Escuela Nacional,* 82–4.

67 Ibid., 82–3; Flores y Troncoso, *Historia de la Medicina,* 3:146–7.

68 Pedro Mata, *Tratado de medicina y cirugía legal* (Madrid, 1846).

69 Rodríguez refers to the author as Hule Wagner and does not provide a title. The text chosen by Gabino Barreda for his general pathology course was Emst Leberecht Wagner and Johann Paul Uhle, *Handbuch der Allgemeinen Pathologie,* originally published in 1862. Mexican students probably used a translation. Rodríguez, *La Escuela Nacional,* 93.

70 Ibid., 92–4.

71 The article had been originally published in the *Dictionaire des Sciences Medicales* by a Dr Marat. Sanfilippo and Flores, *Manuel Carpio*, 24.

72 Ibid., 5, 89.

73 Muñoz, *Memoria histórica*, 15–17.

74 *Bases Reglamentarias de la Academia de Medicina Practica de Mexico*.

75 Ocurso hecho por el Dr Luis José Estevan Blaquiere, 1831, AHFM, Protomedicato, leg. 16, exp. 2.

76 Ocurso hecho por el Dr Alejandro Pablo Lefevre, 1831, AHFM, Protomedicato, leg. 15, exp. 19.

77 Ocurso hecho por el Dr. Gabriel Villette, 1831, AHFM, Protomedicato, leg. 16, exp. 4.

78 *Higea*, 1:1.

79 AHFM, Protomedicato, leg. 15, exp.15. An original copy of the *Reflexiones médicas* is located at the Biblioteca Municipal de Morelia's Fondo Reservado.

80 Manuel Carpio, Ignacio Erazo, and Louis Jecker.

81 Rodríguez, *La Escuela Nacional*, 76.

82 Ibid., 73–82.

83 Miguel Francisco Jiménez, Rafael Lucio, Gabino Barreda, and Luis Muñoz. Ibid., 92–5.

84 Warner, *Against the Spirit of the System*.

85 El caterático substituto de la Escuela nacional de Cirujía sobre haber denegado el Hospital de San Andrés los cadáveres necesarios, 1830, AGN, Justicia e Instrucción, vol. 13, exp. 14, ff. 175–83, f. 176.

86 Inventario, 1829, AGN, Justicia e Instrucción, vol. 13, exp. 13, ff. 69–173v.

87 As the general education program to integrate the colegio and the university programs was under study, the medical curriculum was considered "provisional." El Director de la Escuela Nacional de Cirugía sobre que los cursantes del establecimiento puedan presentar examen solo en esta facultad, 1837, AGN, Justicia e Instrucción, vol. 14, exp. 46, ff. 343–9v.

88 Miguel García, comunicación 1835, AGN, Justicia e Instrucción, vol. 14, exp. 17, ff. 126–37.

89 García had been Serrano's substitute and had fought to substitute Santibánez after the latter's death but had not undergone the traditional competition for the post. Staples, *Recuento*, 135.

90 Sobre que no se admita a examen a ningun individuo de cirujano o medico siendo precisamente en ambas facultades, 1837, AGN, Justicia e Instrucción, vol. 14, exp. 36, ff. 300–4v.

91 Director del Colegio de Medicina al Ministerio de Relaciones, 1836, AGN, Justicia e Instrucción, vol. 14, exp. 29, ff. 244–5v.

92 García had refused to become part of the military sanitary corps. Gutiérrez Sedano, *Historia del Servicio de Sanidad*, 25.

93 Escuela de cirugía, AGN, Justicia e Instrucción, vol. 14, exp. 34 bis, ff. 292–3.

94 Documentos varios, AGN, Justicia e Instrucción, vol.14, exp. 44, ff. 331–3.

95 Substitute professors lectured when the main professor was unable to attend, receiving half of his salary. There were also adjunct professors, the last rank of the hierarchy. They received no pay but were usually promoted to substitutes after some time.

96 Documentos varios, AGN, Justicia e Instrucción, vol. 14, exp. 45, f. 334.

97 Flores y Troncoso, *Historia de la Medicina*, 3:68; Rodríguez, *La Escuela Nacional*, 77–9.

98 Libro de Actos de esta Nacional y Pontificia Universidad, 1804–37, AGN, Universidad, vol. 135, ff. 262v–64.

99 Comunicaciones oficiales del Supremo Gobierno y otras autoridades y Bandos, 1823–1850, AGN, Universidad, vol. 198, ff. 99–100v.

100 Faculty meeting of 15 April 1826, AGN, Universidad, Claustros plenos 1824–39, vol. 31, f. 45.

101 Faculty meeting of 12 November 1830, ibid., ff. 143–6.

102 I will refer to the medical school as Colegio de Medicina from 1834 to 1855, and as Escuela de Medicina from this year on.

103 Mora, *Obras completas*, 2:459–60.

104 After being re-opened by the Regency, the university was definitively closed by Maximilian of Habsburg in 1866.

105 Ramsey, *Professional and Popular Medicine*, 80, 109.

106 The reinstatement of the National University was officially confirmed by the law of 29 April 1835. *Suplemento a las Constituciones de la Nacional y Pontificia Universidad de Mégico.*

107 Ibid.

108 Miguel Barragán was elected acting president in January 1835 while President Santa Anna was on leave. Di Tella, *National Popular Politics*, 251–2.

109 El Srio. de relaciones Inicia el establecimiento de un Colegio de Ciencias Medicas en el Convento que fue de Belen, AGN, Justicia e Instrucción, vol. 14, exp. 20, ff. 152–67.

110 El Director del Establecimiento de Ciencias medicas remitiendo el proyecto organico de la Enseñanza medica, 1838, ibid., vol. 15, exp. 2, ff. 6–36v.

111 The 1841 Reglamento has already been discussed in a previous chapter. However, it is worth noting that although it referred only to the capital and its territories, its medical program referred to the medical school, a national institution dependent on the federal government. The situation was confusing even for contemporaries who had to debate who would be responsible for covering the latter's expenses.

112 Manuel de Jesús Febles, Plan para formar un sistema orgánico de enseñanza médica, AGN, Justicia e Instrucción, vol. 15, exp. 27, ff. 222v–3.

113 The first version of such regulations, *Ordenamiento de arreglo de los estudios médicos,* issued in January 1841, referred only to the Department of Mexico and its territories; the revised version, *Reglamento de Enseñanza y policía médicas,* sanctioned by the national government, was published a year later. Both have been discussed in chapter 3, Manuel de Jesús Febles a Junta Departamental, 1840, ibid., ff. 213–47v.

114 Schools that followed the Lancasterian method of basic education.

115 Plan general de estudios de la República Mexicana, decree of 18 August 1843, Mateos, *Legislación Mexicana.*

116 The secondary or preparatory level, taught in six years, consisted of basic grammar, geography, history, logic, mathematics, physics, chemistry, languages, and metaphysics. Plan general de estudios, Decree of 19 December 1854, Dublán y Lozano, *Legislación Mexicana.*

117 Ibid.

118 Estado Gral. que demuestra los fondos conque cuentan los establecimientos científicos de esta capital, 1823, AGN, Gobernación, vol. 18, exp. 9, ff. 141–9.

119 Proyecto sobre el plan general de instrucción pública, 1826; Mateos, *Historia parlamentaria.*

120 This was the first budget approved by Congress. Parliamentary session of 28 January 1828, Mateos, *Historia parlamentaria.*

121 Ibid.

122 Ibid.

123 Bando of 26 October 1833, Dublán y Lozano, *Legislación Mexicana.*

124 Mora, *Obras Completas,* 1:53 and 63–5.

125 Prieto refers to the years 1820 to 1840, Prieto, *Memorias,* 101-02.

126 Rector a Presidente Guadalupe Victoria, 1825, AGN, Universidad, vol. 68, ff. 261–7.

127 Each *cátedra* had been assigned a minimum of 1200 and a maximum of 1500 pesos, and the salaries of the director and vice-director were set at 2000 and 1500 respectively. The director was not part of the teaching faculty. Bando of 26 October 1833, Dublán y Lozano, *Legislación Mexicana.*

128 Exposición de Agustín Arellano al Sr. Director y Junta de Catedráticos de la Escuela de Medicina, AHSS, Salubridad Pública, Presidencia, Secretaría, caja 2, exp. 48.

129 Payments stopped three months before the 1833 educational reforms were abolished (July 1834) and one month before Santa Anna returned to the capital. Liceaga, "Reseña Histórica," 432.

130 El Director de la Escuela Nacional de Cirugía sobre que los cursantes del establecimiento puedan presentar examen solo en esta facultad, 1837, AGN, Justicia e Instrucción, vol. 14, exp. 46, ff. 343–9v.

131 Liceaga, "Reseña histórica," 435.

132 Comunicación del director del Establecimiento de Ciencias médicas al Ministro de Relaciones, 1836, AGN, Justicia e Instrucción Pública, vol. 14, exp. 29, ff. 243–7v.

133 Pesado was a close friend of Manuel Carpio, professor of the medical school. Durán, "Discurso," 357.

134 *Ordenamiento*, 1840. This document was discussed in chapter 3.

135 Contestaciones entre el Tribunal de rebision de Cuentas y este Ministerio por el nombramiento de Catedraticos del Establecimiento de Ciencias medicas, 1838, AGN, Justicia e Instrucción, vol. 15, exp. 3, ff. 37-49.

136 Decree of 8 November 1843, Dublán y Lozano, *Legislación Mexicana*.

137 Contestaciones entre el Tribunal de rebision de Cuentas y este Ministerio por el nombramiento de Catedraticos del Establecimiento de Ciencias medicas, 1838, AGN, Justicia e Instrucción, vol. 15, exp. 3, f. 46v; Joaquín de Obregon a Ministro de Justicia e Instruccion publica, 1841, AGN, Justicia e Instrucción, vol. 15, exp. 20, ff. 177–83.

138 Law of 8 November 1843, Dublán y Lozano, *Legislación Mexicana*.

139 Zacarías Prieto, Martínez Barbosa, and Ángel Rodríguez, *Los Recintos*, 11.

140 Liceaga, "Reseña histórica," 435.

141 Exposición de Agustín Arellano al Sr. Director y Junta de Catedráticos de la Esc. Medicina, AHSS, Salubridad Pública, Presidencia, Secretaría, caja 2, exp. 48.

142 Rodríguez, *La Escuela Nacional*, 66.

143 *Memoria del Ministro de Justicia e Instrucción Pública*, 1845.

144 Rodríguez, *La Escuela Nacional*, 67.

145 Plan general de estudios de la República Mexicana, 18 de agosto de 1843, Dublán y Lozano, *Legislación Mexicana*.

146 Decree of 19 December 1854. Ibid.

147 Martínez Barbosa and Zacarías Prieto, *Libro de Juntas*, 90.

148 Brito, *Description de l'École de Médecine*, 13.

149 Muriel, *Hospitales de la Nueva España*, 2:100.

150 Zacarías Prieto, Martínez Barbosa, and Ángel Rodríguez, *Los Recintos,* 3.

151 Ibid., 432; Decree of 5 December 1843, Dublán y Lozano, *Legislación Mexicana.*

152 Zacarías Prieto, Martínez Barbosa, and Ángel Rodríguez, *Los Recintos,* 9.

153 Memoria del Ministerio de Justicia e Instrucción Pública, 1845; Flores y Troncoso, *Historia de la Medicina,* 3:101–2.

154 See, for example, Waddington, "Mayhem and Medical Students," 45–64; Palluault, "Medical Students," 178–86.

155 Comunicación del Ministerio de Justicia e Instrucción, 1845, AHFM-FEMYA, Apéndice, exp. 238.

156 Orden suprema de que no se distraiga de su objeto el hospital de San Hipólito, AHCM, Ayuntamiento, Hospital de San Hipólito, vol. 2301, exp. 50; Rodríguez, *La Escuela Nacional,* 23; Zacarías Prieto, Martínez Barbosa, and Ángel Rodríguez, *Los Recintos,* 1–15.

157 The Ministry of War planned to increase the army to an incredible 90,000 men. Fowler, *Tornel and Santa Anna,* 263, Zacarías Prieto, Martínez Barbosa, and Ángel Rodríguez, *Los Recintos,* 12–13 and 243.

158 Zacarías Prieto, Martínez Barbosa, and Ángel Rodríguez, *Los Recintos,* 12–13.

159 Consulta al Supremo Gobierno la aprobacion de los presupuestos, 1864, AHFM-FEMYA, leg. 130, exp. 45.

160 Vess, *Medical Revolution,* 138–44; Maulitz, Russell C., *Morbid Appearances,* 39–40.

161 Vess, *Medical Revolution,* 138.

162 Hernández Sáenz, "Seamen, Surgeons and Empire," 21–36.

163 Hospitaller orders dated back to the time of the Crusades and dedicated themselves to hospital service.

164 Muriel, *Los hospitales,* 2:321–2.

165 Sobre visita al hospital de San Pablo, AHCM, Ayuntamiento, Hospitales, Hospital de San Andrés, vol. 2297, exp. 19.

166 According to the source, the decree was issued on 21 September 1842. Ibid.

167 Quoted in Muriel, *Hospitales,* 2:327.

168 Sobre visita al hospital de San Pablo AHCM, Ayuntamiento, Hospitales, Hospital de San Andrés, vol. 2297, exp. 19.

169 *Desamortización* referred to the sale of "manos muertas" (dead hands) or inalienable properties left in wills and legacies to charitable causes. This law became part of the 1857 constitution.

170 The law excluded the Sisters of Charity in charge of the administration of the general hospital of San Andrés (the largest in the city), the municipal

hospital of San Pablo, San Juan de Dios, and Divino Salvador (mental hospital for women). Muriel, *Hospitales*, 2:326–7.

171 Ibid., 327; Petición de la directora para que el hospital vuelva al cargo de la municipalidad, AHCM, Ayuntamiento. Hospitales. Hospital de San Pablo, vol. 2310, exp. 69.

172 At the time the estate belonged to the Duke of Monteleone, a descendant of Cortés, and was administered by the historian and politician Lucas Alamán.

173 Fernández del Castillo, "El Hospital de Jesús."

174 Contrato, AHCM, Ayuntamiento, Hospitales, Hospital de San Andrés, vol. 2297, exp. 15.

175 Ibid.

176 Muriel, *Hospitales*, 2:215–33.

177 Petición de la directora para que el hospital vuelva al cargo de la municipalidad, AHCM, Ayuntamiento, Hospitales, Hospital de San Pablo, vol. 2310, exp. 69.

178 Ibid.

179 Muriel, *Hospitales*, 2:340–2.

180 Liceaga, "Reseña histórica," 438.

181 Ignacio Torres, Comunicación 1835, AHFM-FEMYA, Sección Apéndice, leg. 56, exp. 1.

182 Jose Ignacio Duran a Ministro de Relaciones, 1851, AGN, Justicia e Instrucción, vol. 55, exp. 32, ff. 242–4.

183 Presidente de la comisión de hospitales a Ministro de Relaciones, 1851. AGN, Justicia e Instrucción, vol. 55, exp. 32, ff. 64–5.

184 The first maternity hospital was inaugurated in 1863 by Empress Carlota. León, *La obstetricia*, 269.

185 Martínez Barbosa and Zacarías Prieto, *Libro de Juntas*, 77–81.

186 Providencias dictadas para remediar algunos abusos que se han cometido en el de S. Pablo y de presos en S. Hipolito, 1850, AHCM, Ayuntamiento, Hospitales en General, vol. 2299, exp. 39.

187 Jiménez, "Abscesos del hígado: Lecciones de Clínica médica del Dr Miguel F. Jiménez," 49, 137, 158, 163, 179, 307, and 328.

188 According to Andral, a small amount of blood in the sputum indicated pneumonia. Martínez Cortés, "La clínica en México," 210.

189 Ibid., 209–11.

190 Ibid., 206–9.

191 Ibid., 206.

192 Pallualt, "Medical Students," 106.

193 Bando, 26 October 1833, Dublán y Lozano, *Legislación Mexicana*.

194 Liceaga, "Reseña histórica," 432; Decree of 5 December 1843, Dublán y Lozano, *Legislación Mexicana.*

195 Director de la Escuela a Ministro de Justicia, AGN, Justicia e Instrucción Pública, vol. 56, ff. 66–77.

196 Martínez Cortés, "La clínica en México," 206–7.

197 The law required an autopsy on anybody who died from wounds or under suspicious circumstances. The Escuela de Medicina was limited to bodies that were not autopsied or claimed by relatives.

198 El caterático substituto de la Escuela nacional de Cirujía sobre haber denegado el Hospital de San Andrés los cadáveres necesarios, 1830, AGN, Justicia e Instrucción, vol. 13, exp. 14, ff. 175–83, 176v.

199 Oficio del Dr Manuel Andrade explicando el motivo por el cual ha suspendido clases de anatomia, 1840, AHFM, FEMYA, Apéndice 124.

200 El Sr. director de la Esc. De Medicina exponiendo los inconvenientes que se presentan para establecer la catedra de clinica interna, 1851, AGN, Justicia e Instrucción, vol. 52, exp. 32, ff. 242–4; Se concede permiso a la Escuela de Medicina para que dé catedra de clinica en el Hospital de S. Pablo, 1851, AHCM, Ayuntamiento, Hospitales en general, vol. 2310, exp.14.

201 Rodríguez, *La Escuela Nacional*, 65.

202 León, *Historia de la medicina*, 115–16.

203 Staples, *Recuento*, 148.

204 AHUM, Gobierno, Instrucción Publica, Colegio de San Nicolas, caja 2, Catedras, Memorias de Regentes, Año: 1850–84; caja 6, Correspondencia, Año 1847–74.

205 Figueroa Zamudio, *La enseñanza de la medicina*, 140–4.

206 Arreola Cortés, *Historia del Colegio de San Nicolás*, 258–70.

207 Castañeda, *La educación en Guadalajara*, 188–93, 386–7.

208 Quote from Governor Prisciliano Sánchez, in Mendoza Cornejo, *Ciento setenta años*, 92.

209 Ibid., 96.

210 Ibid., 109–13.

211 *Anales de la Sociedad Médica de Emulación de Guadalajara* I.

212 Mendoza Cornejo, *Ciento setenta años*, 132–4; and Oliver Sánchez, *Salud*, 152–60.

213 Mendoza Cornejo, *Ciento setenta años*, 179.

214 Oliver Sánchez, *Salud*, 169.

215 Mendoza Cornejo, *Ciento setenta años*, 179.

216 Oliver Sánchez, *Salud*, 170–2.

217 Cortés Riveroll and Palacios García, *Historia de la medicina en Puebla*, 156–62.

218 Ibid., 174.

219 Informe sobre la Escuela de medicina de Puebla, AHFM-FEMYA, Sección Apéndice, leg. 4, exp. 402.

220 Cátedras del Colegio de San Nicolás, AHUM, Gobierno, Instrucción Pública, Colegio de San Nicolás, caja 2, Cátedras y Memorias, 1848–54; caja 6, Correspondencia, 1847–74.

221 Hermoso, *Manual de geografía y estadística de la República Mexicana*, 194.

222 Staples, *Recuento*, 234.

223 *Peródico de la Academia de Medicina de México* 5 (1840): 111.

224 At the end of the year a total of seventy-seven students took the yearly examinations; among the forty-eight first-year students only twenty-one ended the year successfully. *Peródico de la Academia de Medicina de México* 5 (1840): 359.

225 *La Unión Médica de México* (1856–8), 89.

226 Noticia remitida al Ministerio de Instrucción pública de los individuos que han recibido en esta Escuela en el decenio de 1857 a 1866. AHFM-FEMYA, leg. 133, exp. 57.

227 Lista de facultativos, 1822, AHCM, vol. 3668, exp. 14; Febles, *Esposicion*, 8–10.

228 Flores y Troncoso, *Historia de la Medicina*, 3:548.

229 Liceaga, *Mis Recuerdos de otros tiempos*, 37–9.

230 Flores y Troncoso, *Historia de la Medicina*, 3:500–2, 578–82.

231 Ibid., 503–6; Cordero Galindo, *Casimiro Liceaga*, 4–17.

232 As a result of the unique circumstances of independence (the merging of royalist armies and rebels), in post-independent Mexico both factions were considered contributors to independence. Flores y Troncoso, *Historia de la Medicina*, 3:738–40.

233 Ibid., 3:500–2, 510–11; Gutiérrez Sedano, *Historia del Servicio de Sanidad*, 1:128–30.

234 Ibid., 508–9, 740–2.

235 Ibid., 465, 500–2, 738–40; Martínez Cortés, *Carpio*, 18–19; Cordero Galindo, *Casimiro Liceaga*, 7.

236 Organización e instrucción de la compañía formada con los alumnos e individuos de la Escuela, AHFM, FEMYA, Apéndice, leg. 2, exp. 247.

237 Churubusco is approximately fourteen kilometres from downtown Mexico City. It is now famous for the 1847 battle. Prieto, *Memorias*, 335; Flores y Troncoso, *Historia de la Medicina*, 3:432.

238 Both areas are about twelve and fifteen kilometres from the hospital and are now part of Mexico City. AHCM, Actas de Cabildo. Borradores, vol. 477A, 13 de agosto de 1847.

239 Various sources state the patients were American soldiers, but I have found no documents that either confirm or contradict the patients' nationality. Somolinos Palencia, *La Revolución francesa*, 21.

240 After this episode Gral. Leonardo Márquez became known as "The Tiger of Tacubaya" and the victims as Martyrs of Tacubaya. Micheli-Serra, "Médicos y cirujanos," 79–84.

241 Liceaga, *Mis recuerdos de otros tiempos*, 3.

242 Flores y Troncoso, *Historia de la Medicina*, 3:509.

243 Ibid., 31–7.

244 Prieto, *Memorias*, 101–17.

245 Donación de los honorarios del Sr. Febles a la Escuela de Medicina, 1843, AHSS, Salubridad Pública, Presidencia, Secretaría, caja 2, exp. 59.

CHAPTER FIVE

1 Chavert, *Reflecsiones Medicas y Observaciones sobre la fiebre amarilla*.

2 Carpio, "Cuadro del Estado Actual de la Medicina," 1.

3 Solicitud de Joaquín Pío Muro para que se le nombre protomédico de merced, 1795, AGN, Hospitales, vol. 62, exp. 15, ff. 361–70.

4 Academia Nacional de Medicina de Argentina, http://www.acamedbai.org.ar/anm.php; Academia Nacional de Medicina de Brasil, http://www.anm.org.br; Funes Monzote, *Despertar de asociacionismo científico en Cuba*, 30; and Sowell, "Contending Medical Ideologies."

5 Academia Nacional de Medicina: Lima – Peru. http://www.acadnacmedicina.org.pe/resena.html.

6 Fernández del Castillo, *La Facultad de Medicina*, 276.

7 Fernández del Castillo, *Historia de la Academia Nacional*, 12; and *Antología de Escritos Histórico Médicos*, 2:986–7.

8 El Director del Establecimiento de Ciencias medicas remitiendo el proyecto organico de la Enseñanza medica, 1838, AGN, Justicia e Instrucción, vol. 15, exp. 2, ff. 6–36v.

9 *Diccionario de la lengua española*.

10 *Bases Reglamentarias de la Academia de Medicina Práctica de México*.

11 Ibid.

12 Flores y Troncoso, *Historia de la Medicina*, 3:344–5; Alvarez Amézquita et al., *Historia de la Salubridad*, 1:213.

13 Escobedo, Rodríguez, and Alvarado, *Memoria Instructiva sobre la enfermedad epidémica del sarampion*.

14 Eduardo Liceaga states that the Academia "existed between 1825 and 29." Alvarez Amézquita et al., *Historia de la Salubridad*, 1:213.

15 Ibid., 1:228; Carpio, "Discurso," 83.

16 Meeting of 20 January 1840, *Periódico de la Academia de Medicina de Mégico* 5 (1839): 355.

17 Proyecto de educación médica, AGN, Justicia e Instrucción, vol. 15, exp. 2, ff. 6–21.

18 *Periódico de la Academia de Medicina de Mégico* 4 (1839): 354–8.

19 Among the regular attendants to the weekly sessions and therefore core members were Manuel Andrade, Agustín Arellano, Manuel Carpio, Ignacio Durán, Pedro Escobedo, Casimiro Liceaga, Ladislao de la Pascua, Rendón, Manuel Robredo, José Manuel Romero, Leopoldo Río de la Loza, Sobrino, José María Terán, Ignacio Torres, Pablo Martínez del Río, and the foreign physicians Louis Jecker, Luis Estevan Blaquiere, and Severino Galenzowski. The latter two were the only practitioners not linked to the medical school. Meeting of 20 January 1840, ibid.

20 Ibid.

21 Meeting of 16 March 1840, *Periódico de la Academia de Medicina de Mégico* 4 (1839): 435–40.

22 Meeting of 18 November 1839, *Periódico de la Academia de Medicina de Mégico* 4 (1839): 271–4; Rodríguez, "La Academia Nacional de Medicina de México," 569–75.

23 Meeting of 16 March 1840, *Periódico de la Academia de Medicina de Mégico* 4 (1839): 435–40.

24 Prospective members had to be endorsed by at least three core members. Meeting of 18 November 1839, *Periódico de la Academia de Medicina de Mégico* 4 (1839): 271–4.

25 Ocurso hecho por Don Guillermo Cheyne, AHFM, Protomedicato, leg. 15, exp. 13.

26 Meeting of 6 April 1840, *Periódico de la Academia de Medicina de Mégico* 4 (1839): 470–1.

27 Meeting of 4 November 1839, *Periódico de la Academia de Medicina de Mégico* 4 (1839): 270.

28 Meeting of 18 November 1839, *Periódico de la Academia de Medicina de Mégico* 4 (1839): 271–4.

29 Diplomatic relations between Mexico and Spain were established in December 1836, so Blaquiere must have contacted the Madrid Academy in 1837.

30 Pavia was under Austrian administration from 1815 to 1859.

31 Dencausse, *Extrait de Mes Tablettes d'outre-mer*, 27.

32 Alvarez Amézquita et al., *Historia de la Salubridad*, 1:253.

33 The Biblioteca Nicolás León is part of the Department of the History and Philosophy of Medicine of the Universidad Nacional Autónoma de

México's Faculty of Medicine and is located at the old Inquisition building in Plaza de Santo Domingo (Mexico City).

34 *Periódico de la Sociedad filoiátrica*, October 1840 to July 1841 (manuscript), located at the Biblioteca Nicolás León.

35 *Revista Médica* consists of two volumes published by the Sociedad Filoiátrica. *Revista Médica*, 1 February 1851, 1.

36 *Periódico de la Academia de Medicina de México* 1 (1851): 1; Fernández del Castillo, *Historia de la Academia Nacional*, 15–18.

37 "Escuela de Medicina de México," 88; "Contestación al artículo inserto," 124.

38 Solicitud de Ramón Alfaro, 1837, AHFM, Protomedicato, leg. 17, exp. 18, ff. 5–5v.

39 The editorial committee was composed of three individuals who performed this role for a month.

40 Each volume includes one year's publications.

41 The article refers to experiments with electrical charges on the skin and their effects on various organs. *Periódico de la Academia de Medicina de Mégico* 1 (1836): 370–1.

42 Andrade was so impressed with the labour of the Sisters of Charity in France that, with the financial backing of Countess María Ana Gómez de la Cortina he arranged to bring the order to Mexico. The sisters arrived on 14 November 1844, escorted by Andrade himself. Fernández del Castillo, *Bibliografía General*, 23–32; Somolinos Palencia, *La Revolución Francesa*, 21; Muriel, *Hospitales*, 2:326.

43 Lallemand, *Des pertes seminales involuntaires*.

44 Fernández del Castillo, *Bibliografía General*, 23–4.

45 Ibid., 25–6.

46 Ibid., 28–9.

47 Ibid., 30–2.

48 Sesión del 18 de marzo de 1839, *Periódico de la Academia de Medicina de Mégico* 4 (1839): 480–2.

49 Sobrino, "Contestación al Sr Andrade," 158–60.

50 Meeting of 7 December 1840, *Periódico de la Academia de Medicina de Mégico* 5 (1840): 315.

51 *Periódico de la Sociedad Filoiátrica*.

52 The funds destined for its publications, in copper coin, were seized by the government with the promise of repayment, but they were not refunded. *Periódico de la Sociedad Filoiátrica*, 79–80.

53 Reyes obtained his teaching post in 1838.

54 Reyes, "Enseñanza clínica," 97–100, 172–5.

55 Martínez Cortés, *De los miasmas y efluvios*, 63.

56 *Periódico de la Sociedad Filoiátrica*, 1844.

57 Although the *Periódico de la Academia de Medicina de México* was dated 1851, it was published in 1852 or later.

58 Fernández del Castillo, *Bibliografía*, 32–3.

59 Ibid.; *Periódico de la Academia de Medicina de México*, 1851.

60 Theodore Leger held a degree of the Faculté de Paris and was licensed to practise as a physician surgeon in Mexico in May 1833. Gabriel Villette de Terze, a graduate of the University of Paris, received his Mexican licence in 1827. Alvarez Amézquita et al., *Historia de la Salubridad*, 1:228; AHFM, Protomedicato, leg. 16, exp. 4.

61 Alvarez Amézquita et al. state that this journal began publication in 1834, but the issues housed at the Wellcome Library (London, England) were published in 1833. Alvarez Amezquita et al., *Historia de la Salubridad*, 1:228.

62 The only eight issues I located are housed at the Wellcome Library.

63 *Revista Médica* of 1 February, 1 March, and 1 June 1851, respectively. Various issues of this publication are located at the Biblioteca Nicolás León, bound together with the *Periódico de la Academia de Medicina*, 2nd ser., 1843.

64 A peso had eight reales.

65 *Periódico de la Academia de Medicina de México*, 1 February 1851.

66 Duruy, "Report to the Emperor," 7.

67 *Commission Scientific du Mexique: Projet de Règlement*, AN, Instruction Publique, F17 carton 2909, dossier 6, 1.

68 Henri Milne Edwards (1800–1885) occupied the chair of Zoology at the Muséum d'Histoire Natural; Joseph Decaisne (1807–1882), botanist and agronomist, was the chair of Culture of the same museum and a founder of the Botanical Society of France (1854); Jean Louis Armand de Quatrefages de Bréau (1810–1892) was a member of French Academy of Sciences (1852) as well as the chair of Anthropology and Ethnology at the museum. In charge of the medical area was Le Baron (Hyppolite) Larrey (1808–1895), son of the famous surgeon of Napoleon I, Dominique Jean Larrey, and personal surgeon of Napoleon III. Osborne, *Nature*, 1–33.

69 Larrey, *Programme d'instructions sommaires sur la médecine.*

70 *Archives de la Commission Scientifique*, 1:11, 13–14, and 17.

71 Edison, "Conquest Unrequited."

72 Almonte was one of the three members who formed the Regency, but his appointment was mainly nominal.

73 "Minuta de comunicación del Gral. Bazaine al Gral. Almonte," 20 March 1864, 1:333–4.

74 These were: (1) zoology and botany, (2) geology and mineralogy, (3) physics and chemistry, (4) mathematics and mechanics, (5) astronomy, "world physics," geography, hydrology, and meteorology, (6) medicine, surgery, hygiene, veterinary medicine, medical statistics, materia médica, and anthropology, (7) general statistics, agriculture, industry, and commerce, (8) history and literature, (9) ethnology, linguistics, and archaeology, and (10) fine arts, painting, sculpture, architecture, engraving, and music. "Minuta de circular del Gral. Bazaine a los Jefes militares," 21 March 1864, 1:339.

75 Ibid.

76 "Minuta de comunicación del Gral. Bazaine al comisario Extraordinario de Hacienda," 30 March 1864, 1:361.

77 Bazaine a Ministre de la Guerre, 24 March 1864, AN, Instruction Publique, F17, carton 2911.

78 Commission Scientifique à Ministre d'Instruction, AN, Instruction Publique, F17, carton 2909, dossier 6.

79 Pièces relatives à la Constitution de la Commission, AN, Instruction Publique, F 17, carton 2909, dossier 1.

80 *Commission Scientific du Mexique: Projet de Règlement*, AN, Instruction Publique, F17 carton 2909, dossier 6, 1.

81 Bazaine a Ministre de la Guerre, 24 March 1864, AN, Instruction Publique, F17, carton, carton 2911.

82 In his chapter on the Sección Médica, Fernández del Castillo states that there were twenty-two founding members, ten Mexicans, ten Frenchman, one German, and one Italian. However, in appendix 2 of the same work, titled "Lista de socios de la Academia Nacional de Medicina by chronological order since its establishment," he lists twenty-nine on the date of the Sección de Medicina's foundation (30 April 1864). The data included in this work are based on the appendix list. Fernández del Castillo, *Historia de la Academia Nacional*, 21, and 197–8.

83 The president of this section was Ladislao de la Pascua, professor of the medical school. Bazaine a Ministre de la Guerre, 24 March 1864, AN, Instruction Publique, F17, carton 2911.

84 Fernández del Castillo, *Historia de la Academia Nacional*, 197–8.

85 The five foreigners were Julio Clement and Luis Garrone, long-time residents of Mexico; Federico Semeleder, who had been Maximilian's personal physician; Carlos Schultz; and Juan Fénélon.

86 Fernández del Castillo, *Historia de la Academia Nacional*, 23–4.

87 Larrey, *Programme d'instructions sommaires sur la médecine*, MSSA, Bibliotheque, carton 54, dossier 4.

88 This work was discussed by Dr Hermann Weber on the *Dublin Quarterly of Medical Science*. Weber, "Notes on the Climate of the Swiss Alps."

89 During his stay in Mexico, Coindet published his findings on both topics in the *Gaceta Médica de México* and the French military journal *Recueil de Mémoires de medicine de chirurgie et de pharmacie militaries*. The latter also published his correspondence with Baron Larrey on Mexico's medical and public health issues during the French occupation of the country. Coindet, *Considérations sur les fièvres*; and "Correspondance du Mexique," 231–7.

90 Membres de la Commission, AN, Instruction Publique, F17, carton 2909, dossier 5; Correspondents, AN, Instruction Publique, F17, carton 2911.

91 Coindet, *Le Mexique*.

92 Jourdanet had arrived in Mexico in 1842, where he married and carried out research on the influence of climate and altitude on humans. Seventeen years later he went back to France, where he remained five years and published *Du Mexique au point de vue de son influence sur la vie de l'homme* (Paris, 1861). His return to Mexico in 1864 resulted in another work, *Le Mexique et l'Amerique tropicale: climats, hygiene et maladies* (Paris, 1864). After the fall of the empire, Jourdanet returned to France permanently, where he continued his studies in hypoxia and collaborated with the physiologist Paul Bert. His best-known work, *Influence de la pression de l'air sur la vie de l'homme : Climats d'altitude et climats de montagne*, was published in 1875. Auvinet and Brinlet, "El Dr Denis Jourdanet," 426–9.

93 Jourdanet, "Comunicado sobre la respiración en las alturas"; "Consideraciones sobre el tifo"; and "Profilaxia de la fiebre amarilla" (co-written with Angel Iglesias and José María Reyes).

94 Larrey, *Programme d'instructions sommaires de la Médecine*, 369–80.

95 Correspondents. Affaires générales, undated, AN, Instruction Publique, F17, carton 2911.

96 Fievre jaune. Observations et autopsies, MSSA, Bibliotheque, carton 54, dossier 3.

97 *Recuil de Mémoires*, 3rd ser., 9 (1863).

98 Fernández del Castillo, *Bibliografía*, 38–41.

99 Ibid., 38–41.

100 *Academia de Medicina de Mexico: Libro de Acuerdos*, 1864–92. The first page of this handwritten (and incomplete) volume reads "Acuerdos de la Academia de Medicina de México consignados en este libro, segun los datos existentes hoy en el Archivo de la Secretaria y recogidos por su Srio.

el Dr Manuel S. Soriano en diciembre de 1881." It includes the years from 1881 to 1892 and is located at the archives of the Academia Nacional de Medicina de México.

101 *Academia de Medicina de Mexico: Libro de Acuerdos.*

102 Jiménez, "Clausura del año," 387.

103 Icaza and Cordero, "Extracto del Acta de su Fundación," 1–4; Jiménez, "Resumen."

104 Included is the Sardinian resident of Mexico Luis Garrone, who wrote two articles and co-authored a third one.

105 *Gaceta Médica de México*, 1 and 2.

106 Fernández del Castillo, *Bibliografía.*

107 Ibid.

108 In 1873, the Sociedad Médica de México became the Academia de Medicina de México.

109 Icaza and Cordero, "Extracto del Acta de su Fundación," 1–4.

110 Jiménez, "Resumen."

111 This number does not include the sixteen French military practitioners recalled to France. The empire ended on 17 June 1867.

112 Interestingly, Miguel Francisco Jiménez signed his letter as professor of the medical school and "president of the Academy of Medicine," notwithstanding that the Sociedad de Medicina was not formed until October of that year and changed its name to Academia de Medicina de México in 1873. Miguel Jiménez à Mexico, febrero 6 de 1865, AN, Instruction Publique, F17, Carton 2911.

113 Fonseca à Ministre de l'Instruction Publique, AN, Instruction Publique, F17, carton 2909, dossier 6.

114 *Academia de Medicina de México: Secretaría: Libro segundo bis.* Minutes from 10 October 1866 to 27 February 1867.

115 Ibid.

116 Jiménez, "Sesión de clausura del Año," 390.

117 *Gaceta Médica de México* 1 (1864–5).

118 Pani, *Para mexicanizar el Segundo Imperio.*

119 "Viendo tanto mexicano de diferentes opiniones políticas, distinguidos por la variedad de su talento, como por la solidez de sus conocimientos, pero siempre de acuerdo cuando se trata de trabajar en levantar la Patria al rango que le reserva la Providencia." Fernández del Castillo, *Historia de la Academia Nacional*, 20.

120 Mendoza and Herrera, "El Yoloxóchitl"; and "Cantáridas, insectos vesicantes indígenas."

121 Soriano, "Discurso biográfico del señor Don Lino Ramírez," 87–96.

122 These were Belgium, England, Germany, Sardinian States, and Switzerland. *Boletín de la Sociedad de Geografía y Estadística de México* 10 (1863): 69–70.

123 A prime example is Colombia, where Antonio Vargas and a select group of physicians trained at the Paris Medical School, founded the first medical journals, set the basis for medical training, and established the first medical association in the country. García, "Typhoid Fever in Nineteenth-Century Colombia," 27–45.

124 "Necrología del Dr Carlos A. Ehrmann," 184.

CONCLUSION

1 Fernández del Castillo, *Historia de la Academia Nacional*, 53–4.

2 Rodríguez, *La Escuela Nacional*, 54–5.

3 Martínez Cortés, *De los miasmas y efluvios*, 188–9.

Bibliography

ARCHIVES

Mexico

AANM	Archivo de la Academia Nacional de Medicina de México
AGEY	Archivo General del Estado de Yucatán
AGGEG	Archivo General del Gobierno del Estado de Guanajuato
AGHPEM	Archivo General e Histórico del Poder Ejecutivo de Michoacán
AGMP	Archivo General Municipal de Puebla
AGN	Archivo General de la Nación
AHAMM	Archivo Histórico de la Academia de Medicina de México
AHCEM	Archivo del Honorable Congreso del Estado de Michoacán
AHDF	Archivo Histórico del Distrito Federal
AHEJ	Archivo Histórico del Estado de Jalisco
AHEM	Archivo Histórico del Estado de México
AHEQ	Archivo Histórico del Estado de Querétaro
AHESLP	Archivo Histórico del Estado de San Luis Potosí
AHET	Archivo Histórico del Estado de Taxcala
AHEZ	Archivo Histórico del Estado de Zacatecas
AHFM	Archivo Histórico de la Facultad de Medicina
AHMG	Archivo Histórico Municipal de Guadalajara
AHMG	Archivo Histórico Municipal de Guanajuato
AHMM	Archivo Histórico Municipal de Morelia
AHMT	Archivo Histórico Municipal de Toluca
AHMV	Archivo Histórico Municipal de Veracruz
AHSD	Archivo Histórico de la Secretaría de Defensa

AHSS   Archivo Histórico de la Secretaría de Salud
AHUG   Archivo Histórico de la Universidad de Guanajuato

France

AN   Archives Nationales (Paris)
ASS   Archives du Service de Santé, Val de Grâce (Paris)
SHAT   Service Historique de l'Armée de Terre (Vincennes)
SHD   Archives du Val de Grace, Hopital militaire du Val de Grace
          (Paris)

England

WL   Wellcome Library. Archives and Manuscripts

LIBRARIES

BAMM   Biblioteca de la Academia de Medicina de México (Mexico, DF)
BANM   Bibliothèque de l'Académie Nationale de Médicine (Paris,
          France)
BETV   Biblioteca Ernesto de la Torre del Villar (Mexico, DF)
BIC   Biblioteca Ignacio Garcia Cubas, AGN (Mexico, DF)
BJGI   Biblioteca Joaquín García Icazbalceta (Mexico, DF)
BMLT   Biblioteca Miguel Lerdo de Tejada (Mexico, DF)
BNF   Bibliothèque Nationale de France (Paris, France)
BNL   Biblioteca Nicolás León (Mexico, DF)
BPM   Biblioteca Pública de Morelia (Morelia, Michoacán)
GSIC   Gerstein Science Information Centre, UT (Toronto, Ontario,
          Canada)
RL   Robarts Library, UT (Toronto, Ontario, Canada)
TL   Taylor Library, UWO (London, Ontario, Canada)
WEL   Weldon Library, UWO (London, Ontario, Canada)
WL   Wellcome Library (London, England)

BOOKS AND ARTICLES

Abbott, Andrew. *The System of Professions: An Essay on the Division of Expert Labor.* Chicago: University of Chicago Press, 1988.
Academia Nacional de Medicina de Argentina. http://www.acamedbai.org.ar/anm.php.

Academia Nacional de Medicina de Brasil. http://www.anm.org.br.

Academia Nacional de Medicina de México. http://www.anmm.org.mx/.

Academia Nacional de Medicina Peruana. http://www.acadnacmedicina. org.pe/resena.html.

Agostoni, Claudia. *Monuments of Progress: Modernization and Public Health in Mexico City 1876–1910.* Calgary, AB, Boulder, CO, and Mexico City: University of Calgary Press, University Press of Colorado, and Universidad Nacional Autonoma de México, 2003.

Aguilar Ochoa, Arturo. *La fotografía durante el Imperio de Maximiliano.* Mexico DF: Universidad Nacional Autónoma de México, Instituto de Investigaciones Estéticas, 1996.

Aiton, A.S. "Spanish Colonial Reorganization under the Family Compact." *Hispanic American Review* 12, no. 3 (1932): 269–80.

Alanís-Rufino, Mercedes. "Una cuestión de parteras y médicos: Mujeres en el Hospital de Maternidad e Infancia en la Ciudad de México, 1861–1905." *Boletín Mexicano de Historia y Filosofía de la Medicina* 12, no. 2 (2009): 63–8.

Almonte, Juan Nepomuceno. *Guía de forasteros y repertorio de conocimientos útiles, 1852.* México: Instituto de Investigaciones Dr José María Luis Mora, 1997.

Alvarez Amézquita, José, Miguel E. Bustamante, Antonio López Picazos, and Francisco Fernández del Castillo. *Historia de la Salubridad y Asistencia.* 4 vols. Mexico: Secretaría de Salubridad y Asistencia, 1960.

Alvarez Carrasco, Ricardo Iván. "Francisco Rosas: Médico y político, un gran olvidado." *Acta Herediana* 56 (April–September 2015): 70–80.

Amette, Amédée. *Code Medical on Recuiel des Lois, Décrets et Réglements sur l'étude, l'enseignment et l'exercice de la médecine civile et militaire en France.* Paris, 1859.

Anales de la Sociedad Médica de Emulación de Guadalajara I. Guadalajara, Mexico, 1839.

Andrade, Manuel. "Nota al secretario del Establecimiento de Ciencias Médicas." *Periódico de la Academia de Medicina de Mégico* 4 (1839): 86–7.

Anna, Timothy. *The Fall of the Royal Government in Mexico City.* Lincoln: University of Nebraska Press, 1978.

– *Forging Mexico, 1821–1835.* Lincoln: University of Nebraska Press, 1998.

Arce Gurza, Francisco. *Historia de las profesiones en México.* Mexico: El Colegio de México, 1982.

Archer, Christon I. "Combatting the Invisible Enemy: Health and Hospital Care in the Army of New Spain 1760–1810." *New World: A Journal of Latin American Studies* 2 (1987): 49–92.

Archives de la Commission Scientifique du Mexique: Publiées sous les auspices du Ministére de l'Instruction Publique. Paris, 1865.

Arrangoiz, Francisco de Paula. *México desde 1808 hasta 1867.* Mexico: Editorial Porrúa, SA, 1985.

Arreola Cortés, Raúl. *Historia del Colegio de San Nicolás.* Morelia: Universidad Michoacana de San Nicolás de Hidalgo, 1982.

Arrom, Silvia Marina. *The Women of Mexico City, 1790–1857.* Stanford, CA: Stanford University Press, 1985.

Auvinet, Gabriel, and Monique Brinlet. "El Dr Denis Jourdanet; su vida y su obra." *Gaceta Médica de México* 140, no. 4 (July–August 2004): 426–9.

Aveling, J.H. *English Midwives: Their History and Prospects.* London: J.A. Churchill, 1872.

Avenel, Jean. *La campagne du Mexique (1862–1867): La fin de l'hégémonie européenne en Amérique du Nord.* Paris: Ed. Economica, 1996.

Bartolache, José Ignacio. *Mercurio Volante 1772–1773.* Mexico: Universidad Nacional Autónoma de México, 1979.

Bases Reglamentarias de la Academia de Medicina Práctica de México. Mexico, 1826.

Bazaine, François Achille, Marshal. Minuta de circular a los Jefes militares, 21 March 1864. In *La Intervención Francesa en México según el archivo del Gral. Bazaine,* compiled by Genaro García. 2nd ed. 1:339. Mexico: Editorial Porrúa, 1973.

– Minuta de comunicación al comisario Extraordinario de Hacienda, 30 March 1864. In *La Intervención Francesa en México según el archivo del Gral. Bazaine,* compiled by Genaro García. 2nd ed. 1:361. Mexico: Editorial Porrúa, 1973.

– Minuta de comunicación al Gral. Almonte, 20 March 1864. In *La Intervención Francesa en México según el archivo del Gral. Bazaine,* compiled by Genaro García. 2nd ed. 1:333–4. Mexico: Editorial Porrúa, 1973.

Ben-David, J. "The Growth of the Professions and the Class System: Chapter II of Professions in the Class System of Present Day Societies." *Current Sociology* 12, no. 3 (1964): 256–7.

Benson, Nettie Lee. "Introduction." In *Mexico and the Spanish Cortes 1810–1822,* ed. Nettie Lee Benson, 3–9. Austin: University of Texas, Institute of Latin American Studies, 1966.

Bérard, Pierre. *Cours de physiologie*. Paris: Libraire de la faculté de médecine, 1848.

Berlant, Jeffrey I. *Profession and Monopoly*. Berkeley: University of California Press, 1975.

Bledstein, B.J. *The Culture of Professionalism*. New York: Norton, 1976.

Boletín de la Sociedad de Geografía e Historia de México. Mexico: Sociedad de Geografía e Historia de México, 1863.

Booker, Jackie R. *Between the Summit and the Sea: Central Veracruz in the Nineteenth Century*. Vancouver: University of British Columbia Press, 1990.

Boret, Dr. "Noticia sobre la medicina Homeopática." *Periódico de la Academia de Medicina de Mégico* 4 (1839): 23–34.

Bouchardat, Apollinaire. *Elements de matière médicale et de pharmacie*. Paris, 1839.

Boudin, M.M., coord. *Recueil de Mémoires de Médecine de Chirurgie et de Pharmacie militaires rédigé sous la surveillance du Conseil de Santé*, vols. 8–11. Paris, 1862–5.

Brito, Mariano. *Description de l'École de Médecine de Mexico et de quelques opérations faites avec l'écraseur de M. Chassaignac*. Paris, 1862.

Burke, Michael E. *The Royal College of San Carlos: Surgery and Spanish Medical Reform in the Late Eighteenth Century*. Durham, NC: Duke University Press, 1977.

Burleigh, Nina. *Mirage: Napoleon's Scientists and the Unveiling of Egypt*. New York: Harper, 2007.

Bustamante, Miguel E. "Cronología epidemiológica mexicana en el siglo XIX." In *Ensayos sobre la historia de las epidemias en México*, ed. Enrique Florescano and Elsa Malvido. 2 vols. Colección Salud y Seguridad Social, Serie Historia, 2:417–25. Mexico: Instituto Mexicano del Seguro Social, 1992.

Cárdenas de la Peña, Enrique. *Historia de la Medicina en la Ciudad de México*. Mexico: Colección Metropolitana, 1976.

Castañeda, Carmen. *La educación en Guadalajara durante la colonia 1552–1821*. Mexico: El Colegio de México, El Colegio de Jalisco, 1984.

Carpio, Manuel. "Cuadro del Estado Actual de la Medicina." *Periódico de la Academia de Medicina* 5 (1840): 3–14.

– "Discurso que pronunció el catedrático de Filosofía e Higiene." *Periódico de la Academia de Medicina* 4, no. 3 (1839): 81–6.

Carreño, Alberto María. *Efemérides de la Real y Pontificia Universidad de México*. 2 vols. Mexico: Universidad Nacional Autónoma de México, 1963.

Carrillo, Ana María. "Nacimiento y muerte de una profesión. Las parteras tituladas en México." *Dynamis: Acta Hispanica ad Medicinae Scientiarumque. Historiam Illustrandam* 19 (1999): 167–90.

– "Profesiones sanitarias y lucha de poderes en el México del siglo XIX." *Aesclepio* 50, no. 2 (1998): 149–68.

Carroll, Patrick E. "Medical Police and the History of Public Health." *Medical History* 46 (2002): 461–94.

Castañeda Lopez, Gabriela, and Ana Cecilia Rodríguez. "Henry Sigerist y José Joaquin Izquierdo: dos actitudes frente a la historia médica en el siglo XX." *Historia Mexicana* 57, no. 1 (July–September 2007): 139–91.

Chavert, Juan Luis. *Reflecsiones Medicas y Observaciones sobre la fiebre amarilla, Hechas en Veracruz de orden del Supremo Gobierno de la Federacion mexicana, y redactadas en Frances, por Juan Luis Chabert, Dr. en Med. de la facultad de Montpelier; medico en gefe antiguo de varios hospitales &c. Protomedico antiguo y miembro de la junta de sanidad y consejo de salubridad publica del Estado de la Luisiana &c &c Socio de la academia de medicina practica de Mexico*. Mexico, 1827.

Chávez, Ignacio. *México en la cultura médica*. Mexico D.F.: Edición del Colegio Nacional, 1947.

Chevallier, A. et al. *Journal de chimie médicale de pharmacie et toxicologie*. Paris, 1828, 1837.

Coindet, Léon. *Considérations sur les fiebres de l'Algerie*. Paris, 1851.

– "Correspondance du Mexique." *Recuil de mémoires de médecine de chirurgie et de pharmacie militaires*, 3rd ser., 8 (1862): 231–7.

– *Le Mexique considére au point de vue médico-chirurgical*. Paris: V. Rozier, 1867–9.

"Contestación al Artículo inserto sobre la Dirección de Sanidad de Puebla." In *Periódico de la Academia de Medicina de Mégico*, 2nd. ser., 1 (1843): 124–5.

Cooper, Donald B. *Las epidemias en la Ciudad de México 1761–1813*. Translated by R. Gómez Ciriza. Mexico: Instituto Mexicano del Seguro Social, 1980.

Cordero Galindo, Ernesto. *Casimiro Liceaga Médico Patriota*. Archivalía Médica no. 7. Mexico: Universidad Nacional Autónoma de México, Facultad de Medicina, Departamento de Historia y Filosofía de la Medicina, 2006.

– *Vida y obra del doctor Miguel Muñoz*. Archivalía Medica no. 6. Mexico: Universidad Nacional Autónoma de México, Facultad de Medicina, Departamento de Historia y Filosofía de la Medicina, 2003.

"Correspondance du Mexique." *Recuil de mémoires de médecine de cirugie et de pharmacie militaires*, 3rd ser., 8 (1862): 231–7.

Costeloe, Michael P. *The Central Republic in Mexico 1835–1846: Hombres de bien in the Age of Santa Anna*. New York: Cambridge University Press, 1993.

Cortés Riveroll, José Gaspar Rodolfo, and Indira Dulce María Palacios García. *Historia de la medicina en Puebla durante la intervención francesa*. Puebla: Benemérita Universidad Autónoma de Puebla, 2012.

Couturier, Edith Boorstein. *The Silver King: The Remarkable Life of the Count of Regla in Colonial Mexico*. Albuquerque, NM: New Mexico University Press, 2003.

Covarrubias, José Enrique. *Visión extranjera de México 1840–1867: El estudio de las Costumbres y de la situación Social*. Mexico: Universidad Nacional Autónoma de México, Instituto de Investigación José María Luis Mora, 1998.

Crossland, Maurice. "The *Officiers de Santé* of the French Revolution: A Case Study in the Changing Language of Medicine." *Medical History* 48 (2004): 229–44.

Cruz, Salvador. *Historia de la Educación Pública en Puebla, 1790–1982*. 2 vols. Puebla: Benemérita Universidad Autónoma de Puebla, 1995.

Cruz Velázquez, Romeo. *Los Hospitales del Puerto de Veracruz, 1760–1800*. Veracruz: Instituto Veracruzano de Cultura, 1998.

Dencausse, Pierre. *Extrait de Mes Tablettes d'outre-mer, Memoire sur des materiaux pour servir a l'histoire, la statistique et la topographie medicales de la ville de San-Luis Potosi et ses environs, dans la Republique mexicaine, lu a la Societe de medecine de Tolouse, en seance extraordinaire, le 22 mars 1851*. Tolouse, 1851.

Devine, Shauna. *Learning from the Wounded: The Civil War and the Rise of American Medical Science*. Chapel Hill, NC: University of North Carolina Press, 2014.

Diccionario de la lengua Española. 19th ed. Madrid: Real Academia de la Lengua Española, 1970.

Diccionario Porrúa de Historia, Biografía y Geografía de México. 5th ed. Mexico: Editorial Porrúa SA, 1986.

Di Tella, Torcuato S. *National Popular Politics in Early Independent Mexico, 1820–1847*. Albuquerque, NM: University of New Mexico Press, 1996.

Dublán, Manuel, and José María Lozano, comps. *Legislacion mexicana: Coleccion completa de las disposiciones legislativas expedidas desde la independencia de la republica*. Mexico DF, 1876–1904.

Durán, José Ignacio. "Discurso." *Periódico de la Academia de Medicina* 5 (1840): 352–61.

Duruy, Victor. "Report to the Emperor," 27 February 1864. In *Archives de la Commission Scientifique du Mexique. Publiées sous les auspices du Ministére de l'Instruction Publique.* Paris, 1865.

Edison, Paul N. "Conquest Unrequited: French Expeditionary Science in Mexico, 1864–1867." *French Historical Studies* 26, no. 3 (2003): 459–95.

El Diario del Gobierno de la República Mexicana. 1839.

El Diario del Imperio. Mexico, January 1865–June 1867.

Ellis, Jack D. *The Physician-Legislators of France: Medicine and Politics in the Early Third Republic 1870–1914.* New York: Cambridge University Press, 1990.

El Mosquito Mexicano. 1834–9.

Escobedo, Pedro, Francisco Rodríguez, and Francisco Alvarado. *Memoria Instructiva sobre la enfermedad epidémica del sarampion: Su orígen, método curativo y medios de preservarse de ella.* Mexico, 1825.

"Escuela de Medicina de México: Dirección de Sanidad de Puebla." *Periódico de la Academia de Medicina de Mégico*, 2nd ser., 1 (1843): 88.

Esquirol, J. *Dictionnaire des sciences médicales.* 2nd ed. Paris, 1822.

Etemad, Bouda. *Possessing the World: Taking the Measurements of Colonisation from the Eighteenth to the Twentieth Century.* Translated by Andrene Everson. New York: Berghahn Books, 2007.

Fabre, Albert, ed. *Histoire de la Médecine aux Armées.* Vol. 2, *De la Revolution française au conflit mondial de 1914.* Paris-Limoges: Charles-Lavauzelle, 1984.

Farmacopea Mexicana formada y publicada por la Academia Farmacéutica de la Capital de la República, México, 1846. Mexico, 1846.

Febles, Manuel de Jesús. *Esposicion que el Doctor y Maestro Manuel de Jesús Febles dirijió a los profesores de Medicina, Cirujía, Farmacia y Flebotomía al extinguirse el Proto-Medicato.* Mexico, 1831.

– *Noticia de las Leyes y órdenes de policia que rigen a los profesores del arte de curar. Dispuesta por Manuel de Jesús Febles.* Mexico, 1830.

Fernández del Castillo, Francisco. *Antología de Escritos Histórico-Médicos.* 2 vols. Mexico: Universidad Nacional Autónoma de México, Facultad de Medicina, Departamento de Historia y Filosofía de la Medicina, 1982.

– *Bibliografía General de la Academia Nacional de Medicina, 1836–1956.* Mexico: Academia Nacional de Medicina, 1959.

– "Cirujanos y Barberos." In *Antología de Escritos Histórico-Médicos*, 1:277–9. Mexico: Departamento de Historia y Filosofía de la Medicina, Facultad de Medicina, Universidad Nacional Autónoma de México, 1982

– "El Hospital de Jesús y su sentido histórico." In *Antología de Escritos Histórico-Médicos*, 2:766–1.

– *Historia de la Academia Nacional de Medicina de México*. Mexico DF: Editorial Fournier, SA, 1956.

– *La Facultad de Medicina según el archivo de la Real y Pontificia Universidad*. Mexico: Consejo de Humanidades, Imprenta Universitaria, 1953.

– "Lo que México debe al cirujano Miguel Muñoz II." In *Antología de Escritos Histórico-Médicos*, 1:645–52.

– "Los primeros dentistas graduados en México el año de 1841." In *Antología de Escritos Histórico-Médicos*, 1:410–14.

Fernández del Castillo, Francisco, and Hermilo Castañeda. *Del Palacio de la Inquisición and Palacio de Medicina*. Mexico: Departamento de Historia y Filosofía de la Medicina, Facultad de Medicina, Universidad Nacional Autónoma de México, 1986.

Fernández de Recas, Guillermo. *Grados de Licenciados, Maestros y Doctores en Artes, Leyes, Teología y todas facultades de la Real y Pontificia Universidad de México*. Mexico: Universidad Nacional Autónoma de México, 1963.

Fernández Ruiz, Jorge. *Un Reformador y su reforma: Semblanza biográfica de don Valentí Gómez Farías*. Mexico DF: Sociedad Mexicana de Geografía y Estadística, 1981.

Figueroa Zamudio, Silvia. *La Enseñanza de la medicina en Michoacán en el Siglo XIX*. Morelia: Universidad Michoacana de San Nicolás de Hidalgo, 2002.

Flores, Fernando Darío Francois. *Historia de la Homeopatía en México*. Mexico DF: Biblioteca de Homeopatía de México AC, 2007.

Flores G., Sonia, and José Sanfilippo B. *Anastasio Bustamante y las Instituciones de Salubridad en el siglo XIX*. Archivalía Médica no. 2, Nueva época. Mexico: Universidad Nacional Autónoma de México, Facultad de Medicina, Departamento de Historia y Filosofía de la Medicina, 1990.

Florescano, Enrique, and Elsa Malvido, eds. *Ensayos sobre la historia de las epidemias en México*. 2 vols. Colección Salud y Seguridad Social, Serie Historia. Mexico: Instituto Mexicano del Seguro Social, 1992.

Flores y Troncoso, Francisco de Asís. *Historia de la Medicina en México desde la época de los indios hasta la presente*. 4 vols., facs. ed. Mexico: Instituto Mexicano del Seguro Social, 1992.

Foderé, Emmanuel. *Traité de médecine légale et d'hygiène publique ou de police de santé, adapté aux codes de l'Empire français, et aux connaissances actuelles, à l'usage des gens de l'Art, de ceux du Barreau, des jurés et des administrateurs de la santé publique, civile, militaire et de marine, 1798*. 3 vols. 2nd ed. Paris, 1813.

Fowler, Will. *Santa Anna*. Lincoln: University of Nebraska Press, 2007.

– *Tornel and Santa Anna: The Writer and the Caudillo, Mexico 1795–1853*. Westport, CT: Greenwood, 2000.

Fuente, Jesús M. de la. *Efemérides sanitarias de la Ciudad de Puebla*. Puebla: Talleres de Imprenta y Encuadernación de "El Escritorio," 1910.

Funes Monzote, Reinaldo. *Despertar del asociacionismo científico en Cuba 1876–1920*. Havana: Centro de Investigación y Desarrollo de la Cultura Cubana Juan Marinello, 2005.

Gaceta Médica de México. Mexico, 1864–72.

Gamboa-Ojeda, Ivanhoe A. "Raudon, cirujano poblano de 1810." *Cirugía y Cirujanos* 68, no. 4 (July–August 2000): 178–83.

García, Genaro, comp. *Correspondencia Secreta de los Principales Intervencionistas Mexicanos: La Intervención Francesa en México según el archivo del Gral. Bazaine*. 2 vols. Mexico: Editorial Porrúa, 1973.

García, Mónica. "Debating Diseases in Nineteenth-Century Colombia: Causes, Interests, and the Pasteurian Therapeutics." *Bulletin of the History of Medicine* 89, no. 2 (Summer 2015): 293–321.

– "Typhoid Fever in Nineteenth-Century Colombia: Between Medical Geography and Bacteriology." *Medical History* 58, no. 1 (January 2014): 27–45.

Gardeta Sabater, Pilar. "El Real Tribunal del Protomedicato en la Audiencia de Santa Fe durante la segunda mitad del siglo XVIII: un acercamiento al estudio de las transferencias de esta institución Española." *Dynamis: Acta Hispanica ad Medicinae Scientiarumque Historiam Illustrandam* 12 (1992): 209–24.

Gazette Hebdomadaire de Médecine et Chirurgie: Bulletin de l'enseignement médical. Paris, 1862–70.

Gelfand, Toby. "The History of the Medical Profession." In *Companion Encyclopedia of the History of Medicine*, ed. W.F. Bynum and Roy Porter, 1:1119–50. London: Routledge, Bynum Dictionary, 1993.

– *Professionalizing Modern Medicine: Paris Surgeons and Medical Science and Institutions in the 18th Century.* Westport, CT: Greenwood, 1980.

Graue Wiechers, Enrique, Rolando Neri Vela, Leonardo Zeebaert, and Carlos Núñez Mendoza. *XXV Aniversario: Instituto de Oftalmología Fundación Conde de Valenciana.* Mexico: Instituto de Oftalmología Fundación Conde de Valenciana. Institución de Asistencia Privada, 2001.

Gutiérrez Sedano, José Luis, Gral. *Historia del Servicio de Sanidad Militar en México.* 3 vols. Mexico: Secretaría de la Defensa Nacional, 1997.

Hau, Michael. *The Cult of Health and Beauty in Germany: A Social History, 1890–1930.* Chicago: University of Chicago Press, 2003.

Headrick, Daniel R. *The Tools of Empire: Technology and European Imperialism in the Nineteenth Century.* New York: Oxford University Press, 1981.

Heller, Robert. "*Officiers de Santé*: The Second-Class Doctors of Nineteenth-Century France." *Medical History* 22 (1978): 25–43.

Hermoso, Jesús. *Manual de geografía y estadística de la República Mexicana* (1857). 2nd ed. Mexico: Institutio de Investigaciones Dr José María Luis Mora, 1991.

Hernández Franyuti, Regina, comp. *La Ciudad de México en la Primera Mitad del Siglo XIX.* 2 vols. 2nd ed. Mexico: Instituto de Investigaciones Dr José María Luis Mora, 1998.

Hernández Sáenz, Luz María. *Learning to Heal: The Medical Profession in Colonial Mexico 1767–1831.* New York, Peter C. Lang, 1997.

– "'Pues no haviendolo aquí…' Médicos extranjeros residentes en México, 1750–1850." In *Migrantes y comerciantes en la Nueva España: Origen y formación de las oligarquías mexicanas*, coord. Luz Marina Morales, 33–52. Puebla: Benemérita Universidad Autónoma de Puebla, 2002.

– "Seamen, Surgeons and Empire: The Impact of Spanish Medical Naval Reform on New Spain in the Eighteenth Century." *Northern Mariner/ Le Marin du Nord* 10, no. 1 (January 2000): 21–36.

Hernández Torres, Alicia. "El sitio de Cuautla y las epidemias de 1813–1814." In *Ensayos sobre la historia de las epidemias en México*, ed. Enrique Florescano and Elsa Malvido, Colección Salud y Seguridad Social, Serie Historia, 2:551–64. Mexico: Instituto Mexicano del Seguro Social, 1992.

Herr, Richard. *The Eighteenth-Century Revolution in Spain.* New Jersey: Princeton University Press, 1958.

Higea: Periódico de la Salud, April–August 1833. Mexico DF: Ignacio Cumplido, 1833.

Hoffmann-Axthelm, Walter. *History of Dentistry*. Translated by H.M. Kehler. Chicago: Quintessence Publishing, 1981.

Howard, David. *The Royal Indian Hospital of Mexico City*. Special Studies no. 20. Center for Latin American Studies. Tempe: Arizona State University, 1980.

Huerta Jaramillo, Ana María Dolores. *Los boticarios poblanos 1536–1825*. Puebla: Benemérita Universidad Autónoma de Puebla, 2008.

Icaza, J.R., and Miguel Cordero. "Extracto del Acta de su Fundación." *Actas de Sesiones de la Academia Nacional de Medicina*, I (December 1864–October 1879): 1–4.

Instrucción para el gobierno económico político de las provincias. Decree of 23 June 1813. Cádiz, 1813.

Izquierdo, José Joaquín. *Montaña y los orígenes del movimiento social y científico de México*. Mexico: Ediciones Ciencia, 1955.

– *Raudón cirujano poblano de 1810: Aspectos de la cirugía mexicana de principios del siglo XIX en torno de una vida*. Mexico DF: Ediciones Ciencia, 1949.

Jacyna, L.S. "Au Lit des Malades: A.S. Chomel's Clinic at the Charité, 1828–9." *Medical History* 33 (1989): 420–49.

Jaffary, Nora E. *Reproduction and Its Discontents in Mexico: Childbirth and Contraception from 1750 to 1905*. Chapel Hill: University of North Carolina Press, 2016.

Jamain, Alexander. *Nouveau traité élémentaire d'anatomie descriptive et de préparations anatomiques*. Paris, 1853.

Jiménez, Miguel Francisco. "Abscesos del hígado: Lecciones de Clínica médica del Dr Miguel F. Jiménez." *La Unión Médica de México* 1 (1856–8): 49, 137, 158, 163, 179, 307, 328.

– "Resumen." *Gaceta Médica de México* 2 (1866): 385–7.

– "Sesión de clausura del Año Social 1866." *Gaceta Médica de México* 2 (1866): 385–7.

Jourdanet, Denis. "Comunicado sobre la respiración en las alturas." *Gaceta Médica de México* 1 (1864–5): 183–5.

– "Consideraciones sobre el tifo." *Gaceta Médica de México* 1 (1864–5): 191–7.

– *Du Mexique au point de vue de son influence sur la vie de l'homme*. Paris, 1861.

– *Le Mexique et l'Amerique tropicale: climats, hygiene et maladies*. Paris, 1864.

Jourdanet, Denis, Angel Iglesias, and José María Reyes. "Profilaxia de la fiebre amarilla." *Gaceta Médica de México* 1 (1864–5): 369–76.

Journal de chimie médicale de pharmacie et toxicologie 4 (1828).

Journal de chimie médicale de pharmacie et toxicology. 2nd ser., 3 (1837).

Jouve Martín, José R. *The Black Doctors of Colonial Lima: Science, Race, and Writing in Colonial and Early Republican Peru.* Montreal and Kingston: McGill-Queen's University Press, 2014.

Knaut, Andrew L. "Yellow Fever and the Late Colonial Public Health Response in the Port of Veracruz." *Hispanic American Historical Review* 77, no. 4 (1997): 619–44.

La Berge, Ann F. "A.J.B. Parent-Duchatelet: Hygienist of Paris, 1821–1836." *Clio Médica* 12, no. 4 (1977): 279–301.

– *Mission and Method: The Early Nineteenth-Century French Public Health Movement.* New York: Cambridge University Press, 1992.

– "The Paris Health Council, 1802–1848." *Bulletin of the History of Medicine* 49, no. 3 (Fall 1975): 339–52.

La Berge, Ann F., and Caroline Hannaway. "Paris Medicine: Perspectives Past and Present." *Clio Médica/The Wellcome Series in the History of Medicine* 50, no. 1 (1999): 1–69.

Ladd, Doris. *The Mexican Nobility at Independence 1780–1826.* Austin: Institute of Latin American Studies, University of Texas, 1976.

Lallemand, François. *Des pertes seminales involuntaires.* Paris, 1838.

Lanning, John T. *El Real Protomedicato: La reglamentación de la profesión médica en el Imperio español.* Edited by John Jay TePaske. Translated by Miriam de los Ángeles Díaz Córdoba and José Luis Soberanes Fernández. Mexico: Facultad de Medicina, Instituto de Investigaciones Jurídicas, Universidad Nacional Autónoma de México, 1997.

– *The Royal Protomedicato: The Regulation of the Medical Professions in the Spanish Empire.* Edited by John Jay TePaske. Durham, NC: Duke University Press, 1985.

La Revolución francesa y su interpretación médica en México. Mexico: Academia Nacional de Medicina, 1989.

Larrey, M. le Baron. *Commission Scientific du Mexique: Programme d'instructions sommaires sur la médecine.* Paris, 1864.

La Unión Médica de México: Organo de la Academia de Medicina. 1856–8.

Leavitt, Judith Walzer. "Medicine in Context: A Review Essay of the History of Medicine." *American Historical Review* 95, no. 5 (December 1990): 1471–84.

Lecaillon, Jean François. *La champagne du Mexique: Récits de soldats 1862–67*. Paris: Bernard Giovanangeli Éditeur, 2006.

León, Nicolás de. *Apuntes para la historia de la medicina en Michoacán.* Mexico, 1886.

– *Historia de la Medicina en Michoacán.* 2nd ed. Morelia: Gobierno del Edo. de Michoacán de Ocampo y Universidad Michoacana de San Nicolás de Hidalgo, 1984.

– *La obstetricia en México.* Mexico, 1910.

Léonard, Jacques. *La France médicale, médicins et malades au XIXe siecle.* Paris: Gallimard/Julliard, 1978.

L'Estaffette. Mexico, 1866.

Leyes de Reforma: Gobiernos de Ignacio Comonfort y Benito Juárez, 1856–1863. Mexico DF: Empresas Editoriales SA, 1955.

Ley sobre la policia general del Imperio. Mexico, 1865.

Liceaga, Casimiro. "Reseña histórica del Establecimiento de ciencias medicas." *Periódico de la Academia de Medicina* 3 (1838): 430–40.

Liceaga, Eduardo. *Mis recuerdos de otros tiempos.* Mexico DF: Talleres Gráficos, 1949.

Lista de los profesores de Medicina, Cirujia, Farmacia y Flebotomia. Mexico, 1835.

López, Gregorio. *El tesoro de medicinas de Gregorio López, 1542–96.* Madrid: Ediciones Cultura Hispánica del Instituto de Cooperación Iberoamericana, 1982.

Ludmerer, Kenneth. *Learning to Heal: The Development of American Medical Education.* New York: Basic Books, 1985.

MacLeod, Roy, and Milton Lewis, eds. *Disease, Medicine and Empire: Perspectives on Western Medicine and the Experience of European Expansion.* London: Routledge, 1988.

Maillefert, Eugenio. *Directorio del comercio del Imperio Mexicano, 1867.* Facs. ed. Mexico: Instituto Dr José María Luis Mora, 1992.

Malvido, Elsa, and Sonia Flores. *Documentos de Valentín Gómez Farías y Antonio Serrano.* Archivalía Medica no. 1 Nueva época. Mexico: Universidad Nacional Autónoma de México, Facultad de Medicina, Departamento de Historia y Filosofía de la Medicina, 1986.

Mark, Catherine, and José G. Rigau-Pérez. "The World's First Immunization Campaign: The Spanish Smallpox Vaccine Expedition, 1803–1813." *Bulletin of the History of Medicine* 83, no. 1 (Spring 2009): 63–94.

Martín, José R. Jouve. *The Black Doctors of Colonial Lima: Science, Race and Writing in Colonial and Early Republican Peru.* Montreal and Kingston: McGill-Queen's University Press, 2014.

Martinez Barbosa, Xóchitl. "Atención y regulación médica en los siglos
  XVI–XVII." In *Historia de la medicina en México,* ed. Carlos Viesca
  Treviño, 129–43. Mexico: Universidad Nacional Autónoma de México,
  Facultad de Medicina, Departamento de Historia y Filosofía de la
  Medicina, 2007.

– *El Hospital de San Andrés.* Mexico: Siglo XXI, 2005.

Martínez Barbosa, Xóchitl, and Jorge Zacarías Prieto. *Libro de Juntas de
  Profesores de la Escuela de Medicina 1851–1883.* Archivalía Médica
  no. 10, Nueva época. City: Universidad Nacional Autónoma de México,
  Facultad de Medicina, Departamento de Historia y Filosofía de la
  Medicina, 2014.

– *Rafael Lucio: Su trayectoria en la Escuela de Medicina.* Archivalia
  Médica no. 5. Mexico: Universidad Nacional Autónoma de México,
  Facultad de Medicina, Departamento de Historia y Filosofía de la
  Medicina, 2006.

Martínez Cortés, Fernando. *Carpio, Laennec y la Invención del estetoscopio.* Mexico: Facultad de Medicina, Universidad Nacional Autónoma de
  México, 1986.

– *De los miasmas y efluvios al descubrimiento de las bacterias patógenas:
  Los primeros cincuenta años del Consejo Superior de Salubridad.*
  Mexico: Consejo de Salubridad General, 1998.

– *El Dr Miguel Francisco Jiménez y la clínica moderna en México.*
  Mexico: Facultad de Medicina, Universidad Nacional Autónoma de
  México, 1986.

– "La clínica en México en la segunda mitad del siglo XIX: Antece-
  dentes." In *Historia de la Medicina en México*, coord. Carlos Viesca
  Treviño. Mexico, Universidad Nacional Autónoma de México, Facultad
  de Medicina, Departamento de Historia y Filosofía de la Medicina,
  2007.

Martínez Cortés, Fernando, and Xochitl Martínez Barbosa. *El Consejo
  Superior de Salubridad: Rector de la Salud Pública en México.* Mexico:
  Smithkline Beecham, 1997.

Martínez Cortés, Fernando, and José Napoleón Guzmán Ávila, coord.
  Ensayos sobre la Historia de la Medicina. Morelia: Instituto de
  Investigaciones Históricas, Universidad Michoacana de San Nicolás
  Hidalgo, 2003.

Martínez Larrarte, José Pedro, and Yusimi Reyes Pineda. "El Protomedicato: Los Inicios de la docencia médica superior en Cuba." *Revista
  Cubana de la Educación Media Superior* 14, no. 1 (2000): 83–5.

Mata, Pedro. *Tratado de medicina y cirugía legal.* Madrid, 1846.

Mateos, Juan A. *Historia parlamentaria de los congresos mexicanos.*
Mexico: Instituto de Investigaciones Legislativas LVI Legislatura,
Cámara de Diputados, 1997.

Maulitz, Russell C. "Channel Crossing: The Lure of French Pathology for
English Medical Students, 1816–36." *Bulletin of the History of
Medicine* 55 (1981): 475–96.

– *Morbid Appearances: The Anatomy of Pathology in the Early
Nineteenth Century.* New York: Cambridge University Press, 1987.

*Memoria de la Secretaría del Consejo Superior de Salubridad correspondi-
ente al año de 1842.* Manuscript. ASSA Fondo Salubridad Pública,
Sección Presidencia, Serie Secretaría, caja 2, exp. 60.

Memoria del Consejo Central de Salubridad, 17 de enero de 1867.
Mexico, 1867.

*Memoria del Ministro de Justicia e Instrucción Pública presentada a las
Cámaras del Congreso General por el Secretario del Ramo.* México,
1845.

*Memoria sobre la necesidad y utilidad de reunir el estudio de medicina de
la universidad, el de cirujia del hospital de naturales, y el de botanica del
jardin de palacio en un colegio de medicina y ciencias naturales.*
México, 1823.

Mendoza, Gumercindo, and Alfonso Herrera. "Cantáridas, insectos vesicantes indígenas." *Gaceta Médica de México* 2 (1866): 264–6.

– "El Yoloxóchitl." *Gaceta Médica de México* 2 (1866): 223–5.

Mendoza Cornejo, Alfredo. *Ciento setenta años de legislación en materia
de educación pública superior en Jalisco 1823–1993.* 2 vols.
Guadalajara, Jal.: Universidad de Guadalajara, Congreso del Estado de
Jalisco, 1993.

Meneses Morales, Ernesto. *Tendencias educativas oficiales en México
1821–1911.* Mexico: Centro de Estudios Educativos, Universidad
Iberoamericana, 1998.

Micheli Serra, Alfredo, de. "Médicos y cirujanos insurgentes." *Gaceta
Médica de México* 133, no. 5 (1997): 467–71.

Moll, Aristides Alcibiades. *Aesculapius in Latin America.* Philadelphia:
W.B. Saunders, 1944.

Mora, José María Luis. *Ensayos, Ideas y Retratos.* Biblioteca del
Estudiante Universitario, 2nd. ed. México: Universidad Nacional
Autónoma de México, 1964

– 1822, *Obras completas.* 8 vols. 2nd ed. Mexico: Instituto de
Investigaciones Dr José María Luis Mora, 1994.

Morales, Luz Marina, coord. *Migrantes y comerciantes en la Nueva España: Origen y formación de las oligarquías mexicanas*. Puebla: Benemérita Universidad Autónoma de Puebla, 2002.

Moody, Joseph N. *French Education since Napoleon*. Syracuse: Syracuse University Press, 1978.

Muñoz, José Miguel. *Memoria Histórica en la que se refieren el origen, progresos y estado de brillantez del hombre físico entre los estrangeros y el empirismo con que se ejerce entre nosotros por falta de colegios especiales donde se estudie teorica y prácticamente*. Mexico, 1823.

Muriel, Josefina. *Hospitales de la Nueva España*. 2nd ed. Mexico: Universidad Nacional Autónoma de México, Instituto de Investigaciones Históricas, 1991.

Murphy, Terence D. "The French Medical Profession's Perception of Its Social Function between 1776 and 1830." *Medical History* 23 (1979): 259–78.

"Necrología del Dr Carlos A. Ehrmann." *Gaceta Médica de México* 6 (1871): 184.

Neri Vela, Rolando. "La evolución de la oftalmología mexicana: Resumen histórico." In *XXV Aniversario Instituto de Oftalmología: Fundación Conde de la Valenciana*, ed. Enrique Graue Wiechers, 11–39. Mexico: Instituto de Oftalmología, Fundación Conde de la Valenciana, 2001.

– "La práctica de la oftalmología en México." In *Historia de la Medicina en México: Temas selectos*, ed. Carlos Viesca Treviño, 165–86. Mexico: Universidad Nacional Autónoma de México, Facultad de Medicina, Departamento de Historia y Filosofía de la Medicina, 2007.

Noticioso General. Mexico.

Numbers, Ronald. *The Education of the American Physician: Historical Essays*. Berkeley: University of California Press, 1980.

Ocaranza, Fernando. *Historia de la Medicina en México*. 2nd ed. Mexico: Consejo Nacional para la cultura y las Artes, 1995.

Oliver Sánchez, Lilia V. *Salud, desarrollo urbano y modernización en Guadalajara (1797–1908)*. Guadalajara: Universidad de Guadalajara, 2003.

Osborne, Michael A. *Nature, the Exotic and the Science of French Colonialism*. Bloomington, IN: Indiana University Press, 1994.

Oscoy, Susana, and Francisco Fernández del Castillo. *Efemérides de la Medicina Mexicana*. Mexico: Universidad Nacional Autónoma de México, Facultad de Medicina, Departamento de Historia y Filosofía de la Medicina, 1983.

Palluault, Florent. "Medical Students in England and France 1815–1858: A Comparative Study." PhD diss., University of Oxford, Trinity, 2003.

Palmer, R.R. *The Improvement of Humanity: Education and the French Revolution.* Princeton, NJ: Princeton University Press, 1985.

Palmer, Steven. *From Popular Medicine to Medical Populism: Doctors, Healers, and Public Power in Costa Rica, 1800–1940.* Durham, NC: Duke University, 2003.

Pani, Erika. *Para mexicanizar el Segundo Imperio: El imaginario político de los imperialistas.* Mexico: El Colegio de México y el Instituto de Investigaciones Dr José María Luis Mora, 2001.

Penyak, Lee M. "Obstetrics and the Emergence of Women in Mexico's Medical Establishment." *Americas* 60, no. 1 (2003): 59–85.

Periódico de la Academia de Medicina. 2nd ser., 1843.

Periódico de la Academia de Medicina de Mégico. 6 vols. 1836–43.

Periódico de la Academia de Medicina de México. 1852.

Periódico de la Sociedad Filoiátrica (manuscript). Mexico, 1840.

Periódico de la Sociedad Filoiátrica. Mexico, 1844.

Peterson, M. Jeanne. *The Medical Profession in Mid-Victorian London.* Berkeley: University of California Press, 1978.

Plan general de estudios de la República Mexicana (Baranda Plan). México, 1843.

Plan Provisional para los estudios de los colegios, 1834. Published in *Telégrafo: Periódico Oficial del Gobierno de los Estados-Unidos Mexicanos,* 13 November 1834, 6:74.

Prieto, Guillermo. *Memorias de mis tiempos.* Mexico: Editores Mexicanos Unidos, 2002.

Proal, Maurice, and Pierre Martin Charpenel. *Los Barcelonnettes en México,* Prólogo de Jean Meyer. Mexico DF: Editorial Clío, Libros y Videos, S.A. de C.V. 1998.

Pruna Goodgall, Pedro M. *Ciencia y científicos en Cuba colonial: La Real Academia de Ciencias de la Habana 1861–1898.* Havana: Sociedad Económica de Amigos del País, Editorial Academia, 2001.

Pyenson, Lewis. *Civilizing Mission: Exact Sciences and French Overseas Expansion 1830–1940.* Baltimore: Johns Hopkins University Press, 1993.

Quiroz Zamora, Mario. *Historia de México.* Mexico: Pearson Educación, Mexico, 1997.

Ramsey, Mathew. *Professional and Popular Medicine in France, 1770–1830.* Cambridge: Cambridge University Press, 1988.

Rawlings, Helen. *The Spanish Inquisition.* Oxford: Blackwell Publishing, 2006.

Recuil de Mémoires de Médecine de chirurgie et de pharmacie militaires.
Paris, 1863–70.

Reglamento de Enseñanza y policia médicas. Mexico, 1842.

Revista Médica. Mexico, 1851.

Reyes, José María. "Enseñanza clínica," *Periódico de la Sociedad
Filoiátrica* (1844): 97–100, 172–5.

Richard, Achille. *Elements d'histoire naturelle.* Paris, 1831.

Risse, Guenter B. *Hospital Life in Enlightenment Scotland: Care and
Teaching at the Royal Infirmary of Edingurgh.* Cambridge: Cambridge
University Press, 1986.

Rodríguez, María Eugenia. "La Academia Nacional de Medicina de
México 1836–1912." *Gaceta Médica de México* 149 (2013): 569–75.

– *La Escuela Nacional de Medicina 1833–1910.* Mexico: Universidad
Nacional Autónoma de México, Facultad de Medicina, Departamento
de Historia y Filosofía de la Medicina, 2008.

Rodríguez, María Eugenia, and Jorge Zacarías Prieto. *El Hospital de
Maternidad e Infancia, 1865–1905. Caridad, moralidad e instrucción.*
Mexico: Universidad Nacional Autónoma de México, Facultad de
Medicina. Departamento de Histtoria y Filosofía de la Medicina, 2012.

Rodríguez O., Jaime E. "Down from Colonialism: Mexico's Nineteenth-
Century Crisis." Distinguished Faculty Lecture. Irvine, University of
California, 28 May 1980.

Rodríguez Pérez, and Jorge Zacarías Prieto. *El Hospital de Maternidad
e Infancia en la ciudad de M[exico, 1865–1905: Caridad, moralidad
e instrucción.* Mexico: Universidad Nacional Autónoma de México.
Facultad de Medicina. Departamento de Historia y Filosofía de la
Medicina, 2012.

Rodríguez-Sala, María Luisa. *Los cirujanos privados en la Nueva España
y México. Segunda Parte: 1770–1838.* Mexico: Universidad Nacional
Autónoma de México, Instituto de Investigaciones Sociales, Academia
Mexicana de Cirugía, Patronato del Hospital de Jesús, 2012.

Rosenberg, Charles E. *The Care of Strangers: The Rise of America's
Hospital System.* Baltimore: Johns Hopkins University Press, 1995.

– *The Cholera Years: The United States in 1832, 1849 and 1866.* Chicago:
University of Chicago Press, 2009.

Saldaña, Juan José. "Los Historiadores de la Ciencia y Michoacán: Nicolás
León y Enrique Beltrán." *Tzintzun: Revista de Estudios Históricos* 24
(July–December 1996): 58–72.

Sánchez Díaz, Gerardo, "Las contribuciones michoacanas a la medicina y
la salud pública en el siglo XIX." In *Ensayos sobre la Historia de la*

Medicina, ed. Fernando Martínez Cortés and José Napoleón Guzmán
   Avila, 123–56. Morelia: Instituto de Investigaciones Históricas,
   Universidad Michoacana de San Nicolás de Hidalgo, 2003.

Sanfilippo, B., and Sonia Flores. *Manuel Carpio y el inicio de la medicina
   moderna en México*. Mexico: Departamento de Historia y Filosofía
   de la Medicina, Facultad de Medicina, Universidad Nacional Autónoma
   de México, 1991.

Sarfatti Larson, Magali. *The Rise of Professionalism: A Sociological
   Analysis*. Berkeley: University of California Press, 1977.

Schepers, R.M.J. "Towards Unity and Autonomy: The Belgian Medical
   Profession in the Nineteenth Century." *Medical History* 38 (1994):
   237–54.

Shyrock, Richard. *Medicine and Society in America 1600–1860*. New
   York: Cornell University Press, 1960.

Sims, Harold. *The Expulsion of the Spaniards from Mexico, 1827–1828*.
   Pittsburgh: University of Pittsburgh Press, 1990.

Smith, Michael. M. *The "Real Expedición Marítima de la Vacuna" in New
   Spain and Guatemala*. Philadelphia: American Philosophical Society, 1974.

Sobrino, Julián. "Contestación al Sr Andrade." *Periódico de la Academia
   de Medicina de Mégico* 4 (1839): 86, 158–60.

Somolinos Palencia, Juan. *La Revolución francesa y su interpretación
   médica en México*. Mexico: Academia de Medicina de México, 1989.

Soriano, Manuel S. "Academia de Medicina de Mexico: Libro de
   Acuerdos, 1864–1892" (manuscript). Mexico, 1892.

– "Discurso biográfico del señor Don Lino Ramírez." *Gaceta Médica de
   México* 4 (1869): 87–96.

Sowell, David. "Contending Medical Ideologies and State Formation: The
   Nineteenth-Century Origins of Medical Pluralism in Contemporary
   Colombia." *Bulletin of the History of Medicine* 77, no. 4 (2003):
   900–26.

– *Medicine on the Periphery: Public Health in the Yucatan, Mexico,
   1870–1960*. Lanham, MD: Lexington Books, 2015.

Staples, Anne. *Recuento de una batalla inconclusa: La educación mexicana de Iturbide a Juárez*. Mexico: El Colegio de México, 2005.

Strathern, Paul. *Napoleon in Egypt*. New York: Bantam Books, 2008.

*Suplemento a las Constituciones de la Nacional y Pontificia Universidad
   de Mégico*. Mexico, 1839.

Sussman, George D. "Enlightened Health Reform, Professional Medicine
   and Traditional Society: The Cantonal Physicians of the Bas-Rhin,
   1810–1870." *Bulletin of the History of Medicine* 51 (1977): 565–84.

– "The Glut of Doctors in Mid-Nineteenth-Century France." *Comparative Studies in Society and History* 19, no. 3 (July 1977): 287–304.

Tanck de Estrada, Dorothy, "La Colonia." In *Historia de las profesiones en México,* ed. Francisco Arce Gurza et al., 5–68. Mexico: El Colegio de México, 1982.

– *La educación ilustrada, 1786–1836: Educación Primaria en la ciudad de México.* Mexico D F: El Colegio de México, 2005.

Thomson, Guy P.C. *Puebla de los Angeles: Industry and Society in a Mexican City 1700–1850.* Boulder, C O: Westview, 1989.

Tucker Thompson, Angela. *Las otras guerras de México Epidemias, enfermedades y salud pública en Guanajuato, México, 1810–1867.* Guanajuato: Ediciones La Rana, 1995.

Tzintzun: Revista de Estudios Históricos. Biannual publication. Morelia: Instituto de Estudios Históricos de la Universidad Michoacana de San Nicolás de Hidalgo.

Valle, Rafael Heliodoro. *La Cirugía Mexicana en el siglo XIX.* Mexico: Tipografía S A G, 1942.

Vázquez, Josefina Zoraida, Dorothy Tanck de Estrada, Anne Staples, and Francisco Arce Gurza. *Ensayos sobre Historia de la Educación en México.* 2nd ed. Mexico, El Colegio de México, 1996.

Velasco Ceballos, Rómulo. *El Hospital Juárez, Antes Hospital de San Pablo, Caridad y Asistencia Pública en México.* Mexico, 1934.

– *La Cirugía Mexicana en el siglo XVIII.* Mexico: Archivo Histórico de la Secretaría de Salubridad y Asistencia, 1946.

Vess, David M., *Medical Revolution in France, 1789–1796.* Gainsville: University Presses of Florida, 1975.

Viesca Treviño, Carlos, ed., *Historia de la Medicina en México: Temas selectos.* Mexico: Universidad Nacional Autónoma de México, Facultad de Medicina, Departamento de Historia y Filosofía de la Medicina, 2007.

Villar, Pedro, del. *Pedro del Villar, profesor de cirujía médica, consultor agregado al cuerpo de sanidad militar, tiene el honor de esponer al Excelentísimo Presidente de los Estados-Unidos Mexicanos las consideraciones que apoyan el proyecto de reforma que presenta para el establecimiento Nacional de Cirujia fundado en el estinguido Hospital de Naturales, á fin de que en uso de sus facultades se sirva aprobarlo, por seder en honor del Supremo Gobierno, en favor de los adelantos de la profesion y alibio de la humanidad México.* Mexico, 1829.

W.M.M. "Phrenology in Mexico." *Phrenological Journal and Magazine of Moral Science* 20 (1847): 459, https://books.google.ca/books?id=rrLQs3

oGyKUC&pg=PA459&lpg=PA459&dq=W.M.M.+phrenology+in+mexi
co&source=bl&ots=X7Kx5YMfpL&sig=loJZpO8Qjykg7t_q5Xn_K5V
SUrc&hl=en&sa=X&ved=oahUKEwi_3Z7ogtDVAhUj5YMKHSAiDUU
Q6AEIKDAA#v=onepage&q=W.M.M.%20phrenology%20in%20
mexico&f=false.

Waddington, Keir. "Mayhem and Medical Students: Image, Conduct, and
   Control in the Victorian and Edwardian London Teaching Hospital."
   Social History of Medicine 15, no. 1 (2002): 45–64.

Walker, David W. *Kinship, Business, and Politics: The Martínez del Río
   Family in Mexico, 1824–1867.* Austin: University of Texas Press, 1986.

Warner, John Harley. *Against the Spirit of System: The French Impulse in
   the Nineteenth Century American Medicine.* Princeton, NJ: Princeton
   University Press, 1998.

– "Remembering Paris: Memory and the American Disciples of French
   Medicine in the Nineteenth Century." *Bulletin of the History of
   Medicine* 65 (1991): 301–25.

Warren, Adam. *Medicine and Politics in Colonial Peru: Population Growth
   and the Bourbon Reforms.* Pittsburgh, PA: University of Pittsburgh
   Press, 2010.

Wasserman, Mark. *Everyday Life and Politics in Nineteenth Century
   México: Men, Women, and War.* Albuquerque: University of New
   Mexico Press, 2000.

Weber, Hermann. "Notes on the Climate of the Swiss Alps, and on Some
   of Their Health Resorts and Spas." *Dublin Quarterly of Medical Science*
   37 (February and May 1864): 15–43.

Weiner, Dora B. "Public Health under Napoleon: The Conseil de Salubrité
   de Paris 1802–1815." *Clío Médica* 4 (1974): 271–84.

Weisz, George. "Constructing the Medical Élite in France: The Creation
   of the Royal Academy of Medicine 1814–1820." *Medical History* 30
   (1986): 419–43.

– "The Medical Elite in France in the Early Nineteenth Century."
   Minerva: A Review of Science, Learning and Policy 25, nos 1–2 (Spring–
   Summer 1987): 150–70.

– *The Medical Mandarins: The French Academy of Medicine in the
   Nineteenth and Early Twentieth Centuries.* New York: Oxford
   University Press, 1995.

– "The Politics of Medical Professionalization in France 1845–1848."
   Journal of Social History 12, no. 1 (Autumn 1978): 2–30.

Zacarías Prieto, Jorge, Xóchitl Martínez Barbosa, and María de Jesús
   Ángel Rodríguez. *Los Recintos de la Escuela de Medicina de México,*

1833–1854. Mexico: Universidad Nacional Autónoma de México, Facultad de Medicina, Departamento de Historia y Filosofía de la Medicina, 2010.

Zavala Batle, Abraham. "El Protomedicato en el Perú." *Acta Médica Peruana* 27, no. 2 (2010): 151–7. http://sisbib.unmsm.edu.pe/BVRevistas/acta_medica/2010_n2/pdf/a13v27n2.pdf.

Zedillo, Lorena, ed. *Antiguo Hospital de San Pedro, albergue de la memoria/The Old Hospital of St Peter, Haven of Memory*. Puebla: Museo Poblano de Arte Virreinal, 1999.

Zedillo Castillo, Antonio. *Historia de un hospital: El Hospital Real de Naturales*. Mexico: Instituto Nacional del Seguro Social, 1984.

Index